Historical Romances of John Buchan

A Lost Lady of old Years

-

Witch Wood

-

Sir Quixote of the Moors

British Library Cataloguing-in-Publication Data
A catalogue record for this book is available from the
British Library

John Buchan

John Buchan, first Baron Tweedsmuir of Elsfield, was born in Perth, Scotland in 1875. In his youth, his father immersed him in the history, legends and myths of Scotland, and he was an avid reader, stating some years later that John Bunyan's *The Pilgrim's Progress* was a "constant companion" to him. Buchan's education was uneven, but at the age of seventeen he obtained a scholarship to study classics at Glasgow University, where he began to write poetry. His first work, *The Essays and Apothegms of Francis Lord Bacon*, was published in 1894, and a year later he enrolled at Oxford University to study law.

In 1900, Buchan moved to London, and two years later accepted a civil service post in South Africa. In the years leading up to World War I, he worked at a publishers, and also wrote *Prester John* (1910) – which later became a school reader, translated into many languages – as well as a number of biographies. In 1915, Buchan become a war correspondent for *The Times*, and published his most well-known book, the thriller *The Thirty-Nine Steps.* After the war he became a director of the news agency Reuters.

Over the course of his life, Buchan would eventually publish some one hundred books, forty or so of which were novels, mostly wartime thrillers. In the latter part of his life he worked in politics, serving as Conservative MP for the Scottish universities and Lord High Commissioner of the Church of Scotland (1933-34). In 1935, Buchan moved to Canada, where he became the thirty-fifth Governor General of Canada. He died in 1940, aged 64.

CONTENTS

A Lost Lady of Old Years

Book I

Chapter I. The Birkenshaws of that Ilk and their Fortunes.. Page 17

Chapter II. How Mr.Francis Birkenshaw Departed His Native City.. Page 28

Chapter III. Forth and Tweed Chapter

IV. A Journey in Late Summer........................ Page 43

Chapter IV. A Journey in Late Summer.......... Page 56

Chapter V. The Portrait of a Lady.................. Page 70

Chapter VI. On the Edinburgh Highway....... Page 84

Chapter VII. Of a Lady on a Grey Horse........ Page 99

Book II

Chapter VIII. The Journey to the North......... Page 119

Chapter IX. My Lord of Lovat....................... Page 133

Chapter X. Waste Places................................ Page 156

Chapter XI. The Prince's Cabinet of War....... Page 171

Chapter XII. After Culloden.......................... Page 188

Chapter XIII. Crabbed Age and Youth........... Page 200

Chapter XIV. How Mr. Francis Came to the Low Country Once More...................................... Page 216

Book III

Chapter XV. The House of Broughton........... Page 231

Chapter XVI. A Council of Honour.............. Page 243

Chapter XVII. The Journey to the South....... Page 254

Chapter XVIII. Of an Interview in an Unlikely Place... Page 268

Chapter XIX. The Last of the Secretary.......... Page 283

Chapter XX. The Death of the Lord Lovat..... Page 295

Chapter XXI. The Temptation of Mr. Francis.. Page 305

Chapter XXII. A Long Leave-taking.............. Page 314

Chapter XXIII. In the Nature of a Postscript.. Page 318

Witch Wood

PROLOGUE.. Page 323

I. THE COMING OF THE MINISTER....... Page 331

II. THE ROAD TO CALIDON..................... Page 355

III. GUESTS IN CALIDON TOWER........... Page 373

IV. THE FAITHFUL SERVANT.................. Page 393

V. THE BLACK WOOD BY DAY................ Page 417

VI. THE BLACK WOOD BY NIGHT.......... Page 435

VII. THE FIRST BLAST................................ Page 453

VIII. THE SECOND BLAST......................... Page 472

IX. BEFORE LAMMAS.................................. Page 490

X. WHAT THE MOON SAW....................... Page 507

XI. THE MINISTER GIRDS UP HIS LOINS.. Page 524

XII. THE MAN WITH THE SQUINT......... Page 545

XIII. WHITE MAGIC.................................... Page 563

XIV. THE COUNTERBLAST....................... Page 587

XV. HALLOWMASS.. Page 604

XVI. THE WITCH HUNT............................ Page 625

XVII. WOODILEE AND CALIDON............ Page 655

XVIII. THE PLAGUE...................................... Page 676

XIX. THE SACRIFICE.................................... Page 702

XX. THE JUDGMENT.................................... Page 717

XXI. THE GOING OF THE MINISTER...... Page 745

EPILOGUE .... Page 762

Sir Quixote of the Moors

Preface.. Page 769

1. On The High Moors................................ Page 771

2. I Fare Badly Indoors................................ Page 782

3. I Fare Badly Abroad................................. Page 796

4. Of My Coming To Lindean.................... Page 804

5. I Pledge My Word.................................. Page 814

6. Idle Days... .. Page 829

7. A Daughter Of Herodias......................... Page 838

8. How I Set The Signal.............................. Page 846

9. I Commune With Myself........................ Page 859

10. Of My Departure.................................. Page 867

A Lost Lady of Old Years:

A Romance

By

John Buchan

TO DUNCAN GRANT WARRAND

My Dear Duncan:

To you, the well-read historian, there is little need to say that every event in this tale is not recorded for gospel. It is the story of the bleak side of the Forty-five, of goodness without wisdom, of wisdom first cousin to vice, of those who, like a certain Lord, had no virtue but an undeniable greatness. You will ask my authority for Francis's mission to Lovat,—or the singular conduct of Mr. John Murray. You will inquire how the final execution came six months too soon, and you will ransack Broughton's Journal in vain to find my veracious narrative of the doings of his beautiful wife. Such little matters are the chronicler's licence. But some excuse is needed for the introduction of your kinsman, the lord President, and the ragged picture of so choice a character. My apology must be that my canvas is no place for honest men, and the Laird of Culloden would have been discredited by his company. But, such as it is, I dedicate to you this chronicle of moorland wars, for the sake of an "auld Highland story" which neither of us would wish to see forgotten. J. B.

BOOK ONE

CHAPTER I.

The Birkenshaws of That Ilk and Their Fortunes.

When Gideon Birkenshaw—of Birkenshaw Tower in the Forest and the lands of Markit beneath the brow of remote Cheviot—was summoned by death to his account, he left all to his eldest son and turned the other penniless upon the world. Robert, the heir, stepped unthinking into the dead man's shoes, and set himself to the family task of amassing gear. He was a man already grim and aging at thirty, with the stoop of an inquisitor and deep eyes to search out the intents of the heart. Of old the house had been insignificant raiders, adding field to field and herd to herd by a method which it seemed scarce fair to call plunder, so staidly was it pursued. No minstrel sang their deeds, no tale of them was told at nightfall in the village, but in all decency and hardness they went like oxen to their resting-places. They cared naught for politics, but every now and again the stock bred a religious enthusiast. A Birkenshaw had served with the Lords of the Congregation, and another had spoken his testimony in the face of the Grassmarket and a thousand people, and swung off valiantly into eternity. The watchword of all was decency and order, and as peace settled upon the land they had left off their old huntings and harryings and fallen to money-making with the heartiest good-will. And they prospered deservedly. While the old poor Lamberts, Horsebrocks, and Burnets, whose names were in a hundred songs and tales, who had fought with quixotic gallantry forever on the losing side, and spent their substance as gaily as they had won it, sank into poverty and decline, the crabbed root of the Birkenshaws budded and put forth shoots. With anxious eyes and prayerful lips they held on their wonted path, delighting in the minutes of bargaining and religious observance, yet full of pride of house and brave with the stubborn valour of the unimaginative.

It was indeed their pride of race, their inherited spirit, and their greater wealth which alone marked them off from the burly farmers of the countryside. To see them at kirk or market, their clothes were as coarse, their talk as rude, and their companions the same as their neighbours of the sheep-farms. But all knew and owned the distinction. Somewhere in the heavy brow and chin of a Birkenshaw there lurked passion and that ferocity which can always awe the born retainer. The flashes were scarce, but they were long remembered. When a son of the house broke the jaw of Chasehope for venturing to sell him a useless collie bitch, the countryside agreed that the man but got his deserts for seeking to overreach a Birkenshaw beyond the unwritten rules of dealing. And darker stories were told—of men maimed and slain in change-houses, even it was whispered at the door of the House of God, for chancing in their folly upon the family madness.

They married women like themselves, hard, prudent, and close-lipped; seeking often far and wide for such a wife and never varying from their choice. Such marriages were seldom fruitful but never barren; one or two sons or daughters were always left to hand on the name and the inheritance. No man had yet been found of sufficient courage to mate with a daughter of the house, and so it fell out that those gaunt women, strong and tall as the men, stayed in the Birkenshaw Tower till their brothers' marriage, and then flitted to the lonely dwelling of Markit, where there always waited some brother or uncle in need of a housekeeper. Such an order in life brought its reward. There were no weaklings to spoil the family credit, and like a stripped unlovely pine the stock survived, abiding solitary on its hill-top and revelling in storms.

But in their lives they paid assiduous court to a certain kind of virtue. In the old riding days the house had robbed and harried, as it were, under protest; and now, being fallen on settled times, they cultivated honesty with the greatest diligence. A Birkenshaw's word was as good as his oath, and his oath as his bond, and woe befall the man who doubted one or the other. The milk of human kindness was confined with them to family channels and embittered with the grudging which comes of obedience to the letter. By the canon of the Word of God they were men of a singular uprightness, but it was a righteousness which took the colour of the family traits. They set diligence, honour, and a freedom from gross vices on the one hand, and passion, relentless severity, and little love for their neighbours on the other, and, finding the result to be a species of pride, labelled it an excellence. Withal their penuriousness made their lives frugal and their toils gave them health, so that, a race of strong men, they ran their imperious course, feared in their faults and hated in their virtues.

The pastimes of their class were little thought of. It was long since one of the name had been seen with the deer-hounds or playing a salmon in the floods of Tweed. Long days of riding over their broad lands were varied with noisy mornings in the clatter of a market-place or evenings filled with the sleep of well-fed lassitude. But when they came among their fellows it was with something of a presence,—the air of masters who cared little for the quibblings of superiority but were ready if occasion came to prove it by deed. Hence came the owercomes of "A Birkenshaw's glower," and "'Gang out o' my gate,' quo' auld Birkenshaw," with which the conversation of the valley was garnished to repletion.

In such manner did life pass by in the grey stone dwelling which crowned the Yarrow braes, with Yarrow crooning in the nooks below. It was but yesterday I passed the place, which no lapse of years can change. The vale of long green hills which falls eastward from the lochs is treeless and desert for miles, with a wan stream sweeping 'neath barren hill-shoulders and the grey-green bent lending melancholy to all. But of a sudden it changes to a defile; the hills huddle together till the waters can scarce find passage; and a forest of wildwood chokes the gorge. Brown heather and green hazels crest every scarred rock and fringe the foot of Birkenshaw Tower, which looks steeply down on its woodland valley. Soft meadowgrass is shaded by a tangle of ashes, and in every dell the burn's trickle slips through a wild flower-garden; while in broad pools and shining stretches Yarrow goes singing her ageless song for evermore.

Of the two sons born to Gideon Birkenshaw in the house on the hill, the elder was even as his father, a man of few words and hard deeds, ungenial, honest, and with all his qualities grounded on that rock of devilment which lay deep in the temper of his house. His person was such as his nature, and it was not hard to see in the spare and sinewy figure of the son the immature presentment of the father. But the younger, Francis, was like a changeling in the place. From his birth he had none of the ways of the rest; his very form was like a caricature of the family traits, and whatever was their strength was in him perverted to weakness. He had the Birkenshaw high cheek bones, the fleshy chin and the sunken eyes, but all were set carelessly together, as if by nature in a moment of sport. He had his father's long limbs and broad back, but in him the former were feeble and knoitering, the latter bent in an aimless stoop. In character the parody was the more exaggerated. Shrewdness became a debased cunning which did not halt at a fraud; energy, mere restlessness; and persistence, stupidity. Also the mastery over the bodily appetites which marked the kin was wholly absent in him, and early in life he took to brandy-drinking and tavern-loafing. Every fold has its black sheep and every house its weakling, but to the proud family whence he sprung Francis was something more than a ne'er-do-weel. He was a lasting disgrace, always at the doors, staring in their faces at kirk and market. It is the curse of such a kin that a man who shows somewhat weaker than the rest goes straight to the devil without a chance of redemption, and the house of Birkenshaw with drawn lips and averted eyes suffered the prodigal to go his way.

But in the trivial Mr. Francis there remained some shreds and rags of quality unperceived by his kinsfolk. He alone in the whole history of his race possessed some tincture of the humanities, picked up in a ragged way but worthy of some note. He had something of a poetic soul and saw wonders in hill and water which were not for the busy men of affairs who rode their horses over the countryside solely that they might reach an end. He was humane in little matters and no dumb creature suffered ill-usage at his hands. Even in his vices he preserved some tatters of kindliness and *bonhomie* which endeared him to the folk with whom he consorted. In a dim, confused way he strove to guide his shambling life in the way of mercy, and in his stumbling made helpless efforts to rise.

It was clear to all that such a state of matters could not long continue, and the mind of the countryside waited for a crisis. It arrived at length and in the expected way. The blacksmith of Birkenshaw was one Reuben Gowanlock, a drunken ill-conditioned fellow, with a set hatred of the family in the Tower and a marvellous power of quarrelling. His daughter Marion, a handsome girl of twenty, fell much in the way of Mr. Francis in his village sojournings, and an intimacy sprang up between them which endured all through the spring and summer of a year. No record exists of its nature, but it is certain that the couple took long walks in the sunset vale, during which Francis would charm her ears with his flowery rhapsodical talk and her vanity with his presence. In the winter a child was born, and in the eyes of all, the laird's son stood confessed as the father. The blacksmith cursed deep and swore vengeance; poor Marion dared not show herself abroad; and things looked black enough for both. But worse was still to follow, for the place was startled one morn by the news that Francis had married the girl in all honour and good faith. Here was food for gossip and speculation, and it was the common verdict that the man had made such reparation in terror of Reuben's menaces. Yet it is certain that nothing was less in Francis's mind. Whatever grave lack he had, there was no stint in his share of the family courage. His motive for the deed was an indistinct sense of honour, a certain ill-defined compassionateness of heart, which he scarcely realised and would not have sought to defend.

For the twain the end came sharp and cruel. There was long speech in the place of the interview between Francis and his father, and stray fragments of what passed were spread abroad. The wretched creature with his farcical handsomeness and strength stood shivering before the terrible old man, who represented the essence of a long line which knew no mercy. Every inch of his face was browned and wrinkled with sun and wind; his eye glanced steely as an October sun; and his figure was alive with vigour and wrath. He had been absent on a visit to Markit when the events occurred and all was over ere he returned. So in riding-boots and greatcoat he sat at the table's end with a hunting crop before him. He heard the village explanation of his son's folly and he was not slow to believe it. His sentences came out with a dry rasp and with an ominous accompaniment of lowering brows. "I will not speak of the crime against God's law as written in His book, for that is a matter between you and your saul." Indeed, it was said that others of the Birkenshaws had erred in like manner, and in any case it was not a sin which involved any surcease of pride. "But of one thing I will speak," he went on, "and that is of your offence against the bluid of the man that begat ye and the house that gives ye your name. Ye have mairrit a tinkler lass, you, ye splaittering body, because ye were feared at her faither's mauvering. By God, there was never yet ane o' your race wi' sic a taid's hert."

The wretched son made no attempt at a defence which he would have scarcely told to himself. He shuffled with ineffectual feeling, a prey to sentiment and inward tears.

"But 'my son' did I say?" the other went on. "Na, na, ye are nae son o' mine. Gang to the midden ye've been pikin' on and let a cleanly honest house be quit o' ye. Gang off, the pair o' ye, and breed up bairns to rin for porters and serve in byres. By the Lord Almichty I disown ye, and I wis nae mair than to see ye in the kennel ye've made for yoursel'. Gang out o' my sicht, ye thing o' strae."

Francis went out of the room with an indistinct pain of heart, for he was no more than sober from his morning cups. Yet the grating tones had scarcely ceased, the door was scarcely closed, ere the old man laid his head on his hands and suffered in dry-eyed misery the pangs of pride wounded through affection.

Of the exact movements of Mr. Francis after that hour there remains no adequate record. He could not bide in the house, nor did his remnants of pride suffer him to remain in the village. With such small belongings as were his he took himself and his wife to Edinburgh and set up dwelling in a dingy room in the Monk's Vennel. How he lived no man could tell, but it seems likely that when all his gear had gone for brandy this scion of a reputable house did odd jobs for whoever was willing to hire him, from copying a bill to carrying a bundle. One thing is certain, that his course, whatever it was, soon drew to an end. His body was never strong, and his impressionable and capricious temper of mind was not far removed from craziness. Poverty and dram-drinking so wrought upon him that soon he was little better than an enfeebled idiot, sitting melancholy on tavern benches and feeding the fire of life on crude spirits. Two more children—daughters—were born to him, and some five years after his departure from home, Mr. Francis Birkenshaw had become a mere wreck of his former wreckage, a parody of a parody. Six months later a fever took him, and kindly Death stepped in with his snuffer and turned the guttering candle into blackness.

Hitherto we have not spoken of Mistress Marion Birkenshaw who adorned the dim house in the Monk's Vennel. Her beauty, at first considerable, had grown with the years to heaviness, and nought remained but singular black eyes. Her nature was not extraordinary, but rejoiced in the niceties of gossip and the refinements of housekeeping. Her early behaviour was the sudden blossoming of romance in an orderly mind, and with the advancing months she returned to the placid level of the common. Had she married decently and dwelled in her native village she would have been a matron without reproach, a mistress of gossip and old-wives' tales, glorying in little hospitalities and petty hatreds, an incarnation of the respectable. As it was, she ruled the household with a bustling hand, and found neighbours in a desert of strangers. The clack of her tongue sounded all day about the doors, or was sunk in the afternoon to a contented sing-song when Mistress Gilfillan dropped in to sew with her and tell her woes. Even in so hard a place she attained to some measure of happiness, and speedily ordered sprawling children and feckless husband with a pride in the very toil which would have cheered one's heart. Loud-tongued, noisy, coarse as sackcloth, a wallower in the juicily sentimental, she yet had something of the spirit of a general, and marshalled her ragged forces in decent array.

On the death of Mr. Francis her action took a characteristic path. For, meeting Robert, now master of the broad lands of Birkenshaw, in the High Street, one chill February morn, she forthwith detailed to him his brother's debts, and with the abandon of her class glided from becoming tears into the necessary question of maintenance. The Laird's feelings at the moment would be hard to tell. The thought that one of his house should have sunk so low that his widow had to beg her bread, stung him like a lash. He lost for the moment his habitual reserve. With a mumbled "Tak' it, wumman, tak' it; there'll be mair to follow," he thrust some gold into her hand; and thenceforth came quarterly payments from Birkenshaw with a bare word of communication. Marion took them gladly, for she had no other choice, and on such means she reared her children to grown age.

One incident in her character remains which is eloquent in its strangeness. From the day of her departure she held no communication with her folk at the smithy, manifesting no interest in their doings and shunning even the mention of their names. Deep in her soul was a well of sentiment. She had mated with a Birkenshaw and some peace-offering was due to the fetich of the family pride. A sense of an honour paid to her hung ever on her conscience; it made her look with respect on her own children as something higher than herself; and it forced her to the severance of natural ties. It is doubtful, indeed, whether they were ever tightly knit, for the drunken father had little kindness for any. But, such as they were, they were gladly renounced, and with something not far from heroism this foolish woman took loneliness for her portion, a solitude brightened with the halo of a great connection.

CHAPTER II.

How Mr. Francis Birkenshaw Departed His Native City.

The child Francis grew up to manhood with something of precipitancy, for in that house life was not suited for a lengthy play-day. At five he had been as ugly as sin in face, though well-grown and straight in body. His father's hard features and ruddy skin were joined to Marion's sloe-black eyes and hair, and such a conjunction is not fair in childhood. So peculiarly sinister an appearance would have made him the butt of his coevals, had he not possessed a hot temper and an uncommonly hard fist. From his sixth year battles were of daily occurrence, and it was rarely that the week-end found him with his face unmarked. But inch by inch, wound by wound, he fought his way to fame, till the mere sight of his black countenance was more than enough to hush the wrangling of the others and incline their ears to his words.

But with those days we have little to do, and it is at the maturity of eighteen that we would take up the tale of his life. His sisters, Jean and Lisbeth, were now grown to high-coloured, loud-spoken girls, who shared their mother's likings and their mother's comeliness. The Birkenshaw payments made comfort possible, and the house was conducted in a pleasant stir, with gossips sitting at all hours and the sharp tones of the housewife guarding its cleanliness and order. The two lasses were the blacksmith's true grandchildren, and in no way different from a thousand such maids in the city. They loved to dress in their best of a Sabbath and walk in decent procession to the Cross Kirk, where the ministrations of Mr. Linklater were sugared with the attentions of the young apprentices. They were notable cooks and wrought all day to their mother's bidding with a cheery bustle. In a word, they were of their mother's pattern,—honest, fresh-coloured, hearty, and friendly to all.

Had it not been for their brother's presence, the household in the Monk's Vennel might have been an abode of prosperous peace. But Francis was a puzzle to most folk and a grief to his mother such as her foolish loose-lived husband had never been. The years brought him height and strength and a handsome face. It would have been hard to find in all the town a nobler figure of a man, when anger did not distort the features. From some unknown forebear he derived an air of uncommon masterfulness, and a carriage which might have vied with that of the greatest buck of the day, my Lord Craigforth himself. His temper was like his body, fierce, and strong, and hot as a red fire, so that no man could anger him with safety. In happier conditions he might have followed the paths of virtue, for there seemed nothing ignoble in that brow and eye. But in the kitchen of his home, among the clatter of neighbour tongues and women's gossip, in the presence of his mother and sisters and the rotund housewives who called them friends, he was wofully out of place.

In his childhood he had cared little for the thing, for the street was his home at most hours; but as he grew to age the whole life oppressed him with deep disgust. To him alone had fallen a share of the Birkenshaw temper, and he revolted from this unctuous existence. For his kin he had fits of tenderness, but at his age no feeling is so weak as domestic love. The result was not hard to foresee. With such share as he had of the family income he took to his own pleasures, and the house saw him not save at meal-time and the late night.

Who shall tell of the glorious Edinburgh of that age in all its colour and splendour and dirt? The years of last century were still young, the second George was but new on the throne, and in the northern city life flowed freely and hotly in a muddy, turbulent stream. The drums of war were still in men's memories, and soldiers from the Castle still thronged the street. In the narrow alleys which wound like snakes among the high, dark houses there lurked filth and disease which have long since gone from the land. Ragged Highland lairds and broken gillies, fine periwigged gentlemen, ministers many with their sombre black, fair ladies and country wives, honest shepherds in homespun from the South, half the gentry of the land, as well as the staid merchant or the wandering southerner, were jostled on the narrow causeway by French agents and priests in hiding, or fell a prey at dark corners to the lurking cut-purse. Roaring east winds disturbed the trials in the Parliament House, where half a dozen learned judges administered the law, ere hurrying back to dinner and their unfinished treatises on Taste and the Sublime. And the same wind caught at the throats of half-starved loyalists shivering in entries, and praying and plotting for that day when the King should come back to his own. Every now and again the streets were in an uproar over some straggling news of a fresh landing, and the good citizens listened to the bugle on the Castle rock with a feeling of confirmed security. It was the day of riot and bright colour, of fine dresses and rags, of honest poverty and the blackguard shuffling in the same kennel,—a day when no man knew his own mind or his neighbours', and the King's peace was more brittle than the King desired.

But above all it was the hey-day of taverns, great houses of festivity where beside leaping fires a motley crew dined and grew drunk in all good fellowship. The age must be thick with alarums and perils of war to produce the fine flower of tavern-life. It is when a man's mind is hot with wild news or the expectation of its reception that he leaves his ingle and seeks the steaming hearth and the talk of neighbours. And who can tell of the possibilities which lie in such an evening, of a door flung open and a stranger coming full of unheard-of tales? The inn-lounger is as surely a glutton for the romantic as the adventurer upon the sea.

To such homes of the soul went Francis with more zeal than discretion. There, and not in the female atmosphere of the Monk's Vennel, he found the things in which his heart delighted. The talk of men in its freedom and brutality was his delight, and in the motley concourse of folk he had matter for a living interest. A strain of inherited vice made the darker side of it soon cease to appall him, and in time he passed from the place of a spectator to that of a partaker in many carousals, a sworn friend to half the riff-raff in the city, the ally of loose women and causeway sots.

Yet in this spring-tide of wild oats there was none of the sower's zest. After all, he was very much of an amateur in vice, restrained from excess by many bonds of memory, convention, and human kindliness. His course was the recoil from the paths of fireside virtue, the outcome of something uncommon and heroical in a nature run to seed. At moments a sense of the folly of it all oppressed him, but the fatal rhetoric of a boy's thoughts put the graver reflection to flight. He would regain his self-respect by fancying himself a man of the world, living with a hand close on the springs of life, one who in all folly was something beyond his allies. And in consequence he sank but rarely into brutish drunkenness,—a sin (for the confusion of all doctrines of heredity) which had little hold upon him,—and even from such lapses recovered himself with a certain alertness of spirit. Yet this was but the immaturity of his character, a thing to pass away with years, and in a little Francis might have looked to grow to a blackguard of some quality.

To his mother his life was a source of uncomprehending grief. Her efforts of kindness were now repelled and now met half-way with an inconsistency which confounded all her notions. When her son staggered home in the small hours, or when Mistress Leithen of the Candle Row retailed strange stories of his evil-doing, the unhappy woman was, if anything, less pained than mystified. Maternal affection, which for the glorifying of poor humanity, is strongest in the coarsely sentimental, bade her sorrow, when all the rest of her nature bade her only wonder. So with a patience and a denseness too deep for words, she persisted in her tenderness, bore his lordly humours, and revolted his soul with a thousand nauseous vulgarities, since to the rake the only intolerable coarseness is the respectably plebeian.

Now it chanced that Fate took it upon her to order events for the saving of Francis' soul. About his eighteenth year he had entered a writer's office in the city, for no other cause than to give himself some name whereby to describe his life. An odd strain of worldly prudence kept him from neglecting his duties to dismissal point, and in a sort of careful idleness he copied deeds, visited ground for seisin, and collected rents in and out of the town. He had no ill-will to the work, provided it did not bear too hardly upon his time. But meanwhile in the burgh of Dysart, which sits perched on the steep shore of Fife, there lived a Mr. Gregor Shillinglaw, who as the one lawyer in the place had a good livelihood and a busy life. He was growing old, and in the natural course bethought him of a successor. His head clerk, John Henryson, was able and willing for the place, but Mr. Shillinglaw belonged to a school of men who have less respect for long services than for family ties. Once on a time a Birkenshaw had married a distant cousin of his, and the two names had a kinship in his memory. So it fell out that, being in Edinburgh at the office of Trumbull and Gleed, who were Francis's masters, he saw the lad, heard his name, and was affected with a sudden kindness.

He asked after his business merits. Good, admirable, said Mr. Trumbull, with a smile. And his character? Oh, well, some folk are young and fresh in blood, and the same rule does not hold for all, said the lawyer, amazed at his own heresy, but bound in honour to say nothing to the discredit of his house or servants. Mr. Shillinglaw heard and was satisfied; the hint of gentlemanly vices only increased his friendliness for the young man; so before the week was out Francis received an offer to go to Dysart to a place which with care might bring him to an old age of opulence and respect.

To Dysart Francis went with a mixture of feelings. He had never lived elsewhere than in Edinburgh, and he was glad to make trial of a new habitat on the very edge of the sea. More, he had many deeds to his name in Edinburgh which would scarce bear the inevitable scrutiny which the days must bring. His credit, too, was low, and his debts great; so with a light heart and much hope he betook himself to the dark rooms in the little wind-worn town, where a man's lips are always salt with the air from the sea, and a roaring East sweeps in the narrow lanes.

The ancient town is now a very little place, unsightly with coal and dingy with stagnant traffic. But in the days of Mr. Shillinglaw it was a bustling port, where skippers from Amsterdam came with strong waters and cheeses and Lord knows what, and carried away beer and tallow, hides and sea-coal. It boasted of a town-house where the noisy burgesses met, and elegant piazzas where foreign merchants walked and chaffered. In the rock-hewn harbour lay at all times twoscore and more of schooners, and the high red-tiled houses looked down upon an eternal stir of shipping and unlading. It was a goodly place to live, for health came with the clean sea-wind and wealth with every tide.

Of Francis's doings in this place there is scant account save for the brilliant episode which marked his departure. It seems that at first he wrought well under Mr. Shillinglaw's guidance, and the two would drink their claret of a night in all amity. But untoward events soon thickened in the younger's path, and, aided by his uncertain temper, he began anew his downward course. From the time when he first saw Nell Durward his doom was assured, and thereafter his master might grieve or storm, but Francis remained untouched. Nell was the provost's daughter, tall and comely, with bright cheeks and saucy black eyes which captured his roving thoughts. Thenceforth he was her slave, running at her every beck and nod, till her father, with some inkling of how matters stood, resolved to put an end to his daughter's coquetry, and plainly told the eager lover that Nell was already betrothed to a Baillie of the town, one Gow by name, and would shortly be his wife.

Francis flung himself out of the house, and from that hour till after the celebration of the wedding drank more deeply than he had ever done before, and bade Mr. Shillinglaw and his business go to the devil whence they had come. For three weeks he was the bye-word of the town; then, when all was over, he returned to his right mind and relapsed into decency with some apology for his absence.

But Fate had still further tricks to play on him. It chanced that a yearly dinner was held in the Bunch of Grapes in memory of some former benefactor of the town, and thereafter dancing went on till morning in the roomy upper chamber, where faded silk hangings and a frowning portrait proclaimed antiquity. Hither went Francis in a sober mood, and after the meal drank his toddy with the fathers of the burgh as befitted a grave notary. But after he had his fill of their company and had grown hot with the fumes of spirits, he mounted the stair, and sitting by the fiddlers surveyed the gay scene. Suddenly to the assembly there entered Baillie Gow, with the aforetime Nell Durward blushing on his arm. The devil of boastfulness, born of early and deep potation, drove the man in the direction of his rival. He gaped before him, and then with many abusive words delivered him a moral homily. The blood of Francis, hot at the best, was roused to madness by the man's conduct and the thought of his own unrewarded love. "Let go his arm, my dear," he said quietly to the girl, and struck the portly baillie clean on the jaw so that he dropped like a felled ox.

Now Mr. Gow was a great man in the town, and at the sight a party, with the landlord, one Derrick, at their head, made to lay hands on his assailant. But Francis was strong and young, and with a bench he cleared a space around him and fought his way to the door. His head was in a muddle, and his one thought was to reach the street. But at the stair-top the landlord confronted him, and with a cudgel struck him smartly on the face. The blow roused madness to action. With a sudden crazy resolution, Francis drew his knife and stabbed the man in the side, and then breaking through the crowd on the steps reached the open and ran straight for the distant woods.

The remainder of the incident goes with still greater spirit. For three days Francis lay hid among the brackens with the terror of murder on his soul. But none came to seek him, and with the hours his confidence grew, till he summoned his courage and sallied out at the darkening of the fourth day. With infinite labour he avoided observation, and entered the narrow wynds. Now came his chief toil. He must learn of the landlord's fate to ease his mind and determine his plans. So in much trepidation he betook himself to the only haven he could think of, the house of one Berritch, a man of reputed wealth but no reputation, a former ally of his own in tavern-drinking, and esteemed a trafficker in the contraband.

Thither he crept, and won immediate admittance. He heard with relief that his enemy was all but recovered, that the wound had been a mere scratch, and that his name was free at least from such a stain. But otherwise, Mr. Berritch admonished him, things looked black indeed. Mr. Shillinglaw had repudiated him, and the respectability of the place had made their faces flint against him. It was currently believed that he had returned to the purlieus of Edinburgh.

In such a state of affairs Francis was ripe for an offer, and Mr. Berritch did not fail him. He himself would undertake to bring him to France in one of his boats, and set him down where there was chance and room for likely young lads unburdened with a conscience. He could not remain in Dysart, and the city was but a halting-place on the road to beggary. That night a lugger would sail from the Wemyss Rocks in which he was welcome to a passage.

The conclusion of the episode was yet more varied; for when all had won to the starting-place, word was brought that the Burnt island gaugers had got tidings about Mr. Berritch and his occupation, which would lead them that night to pay a visit to his dwelling. The unfortunate man bowed to fate in a transport of cursing, and set his face to the boat and the sea; but in the nick of time he had mind of valuable monies left in the house, which he would little like to see in the hands of the law. He was at his wits' end, when Francis, with the uneasy generosity of one in debt, offered to go to fetch them. Accordingly he set out and made his way through the dark and filthy east streets of Dysart, not without some qualms of anxiety. But at the High Street corner he met a man in an advanced stage of drunkenness, stumbling over ash-buckets and suffering from the narrowness of the path. A glance convinced him that it was none other than Baillie Gow, returning from some borough dinner, and flown with wine and talk. A plan grew in Francis's mind which made him shake with mirth. Slipping his arm through the Baillie's, he led him to Mr. Berritch's house and set him in Mr. Berritch's chair, with Mr. Berritch's wig on his head and a tumbler of rum at his elbow. Then he secured the gold, and slipped outside the window to wait the result. His patience was little tried, for soon there came the tramp of men down the street, a knocking at the door, a forced entrance, and a swoop upon their prisoner. He heard them read the paper of identification, and give a one-voiced consent to every detail. Then with aching sides and smarting eyes he watched them lift the innocent upon their shoulders; and when their tread died away he betook himself to the cutter in huge delight at his own boyish humour.

With this bravado begins the history of the doings of Mr. Francis Birkenshaw, which he did in the years of our Lord seventeen hundred and forty-five and seventeen hundred and forty-six in the reign of George the Second, King of England. In such a fine fervour of conceit and daring he launched out upon his course. The events of the past weeks seemed like an ancient tale from which he was separated by years of maturity. In a night he had outgrown any vain schemes for a reputable life of good-citizenship. Now he was free to go whither he pleased, and carve his fortune in the manner best suiting him without restraint of prejudice. As the vessel rode on the waters and the wind sang in the sheets, his heart was strengthened with pleasing self-praise, not without a hint of mirth at the comedy of life.

But for all great designs money was needful, and Mr. Berritch himself was the first to mention it. Now the secret of the Birkenshaw payments had always been kept hid from him, and he thought that the family substance came from some fortune of his father's. There must be some portion remaining to him, he thought, and on this he set his hope. So it was settled that the lugger should lie well into the Lothian coast during the day, and in the evening he should be put ashore to seek his own. Then once again they would set sail for their longer voyage.

The plan was carried out to the letter, and at eight the next night Francis was knocking at the door of his mother's house. From within came the noise of tongues and women's laughter, and the cheerful clatter of dishes which marks the close of a meal. His mother opened to him, wiping her mouth with her apron in a way she had, and smirking over her shoulder. At the sight of him she started, and he entered unbidden. The place bore all the marks of comfort, and in the firelight he saw two women of the neighbourhood, old gossips of his sisters and mother. His entrance hushed their talk, and sidelong looks and a half-giggle succeeded. Somehow the sight roused his gorge unspeakably. He, with his mind intent upon high adventure, with the smell of the salt and the fierce talk of men still in his memory, loathed this glosing prosperity, these well-fed women, and the whole pettiness of life. He took his mother aside and demanded the money which was his share. She, good soul, did not tell him the truth, but wrapping herself up in her rags of pride, went to a drawer and gave him a meagre bag of gold. It was the latest payment, and its loss meant straitened living for months. But he knew nothing of this, thought it but his share, and grumbled at its smallness. With the irony which riots in life, at that moment he was pluming himself upon superiority to such narrow souls, when all the while pride in one was making a sacrifice of which he knew nothing. His remnants of filial love made him take a kindly farewell of his mother; and then, with nose in the air and a weathercock of a brain, he shook off the dust of the domestic, and went out to the open world.

With the doorway of his former home, he passed from vice frowned upon and barely loved to vice gilded and set upon a pedestal. A sense of high exhilaration grew upon him. He would follow his own desires, with the aid of a strong hand and a courageous heart. In his then frame of mind the only baseness seemed to lie in settling upon his lees in the warm air of the reputable. A hard conscience and a ready hand were a man's truest honour, and with this facile catchword he went whistling into a new life.

But at the moment something from the past came to greet him. As he passed a tavern door a girl with the face and attire of the outcast hailed him boisterously and made to link her arm with his. He knew her well for one of his aforetime comrades. Her face was pinched, and the night wind was blowing through her thin frock. But from Francis she got no kindness. His heart at the time was too steeled on his own path for old regrets. With a curse he struck her harshly with his open hand, and watched her stagger back to the causeway. The blow comforted his soul. It was the seal upon his new course, the rubicon which at length he had crossed; and when he came to Musselburgh sands and the lugger, it was with an increased resolution in his fool's heart.

CHAPTER III.

Forth and Tweed.

The wind was already shaking in the sails when he clambered aboard, and the windlass groaned with the lifting anchor. Mr. Berritch cried a cheery greeting from the bow, as Francis, heavy with sleep, tumbled down below to bed. The moon was up, the night airs were fine, and in a little the lugger was heading by the south end of Inchkeith for the swell of the North Ocean.

At dawn Francis was up and sniffing the salt air over the bulwarks. A landsman born, he had little acquaintance with the going down to the sea in ships, and the easy movement and the brisk purpose of the lugger delighted his heart. He was still in the first heat of adventure; the white planking, the cordage, and the tarry smell were all earnests of something new; and with the vanishing smoke and spires he beheld the end of a life crimped and hampered. He felt extraordinary vigour of body and a certain haphazard quality of mind which added breadth to his freedom. But at the last sight of the Pentlands' back, sentiment woke for one brief moment ere she shook her wings and fled.

He turned from his meditation to find Mr. Berritch at his elbow with a smile and a good-morning. Seen in the first light his face had an ugly look about the eyes and ponderous jaw, a shadow in the lines of his mouth.

With him came another, whose face Francis had not seen before,—a lean youth with bleak eyes, a hanging chin, and a smirk always on the verge of his lips.

"Ye came well off frae your venture, Francie," said Mr. Berritch. "I have to present to ye Mr. Peter Stark, a young gentleman out o' Dumbarton, bound on the same errand to France as yoursel'. Starkie, this is Mr. Birkenshaw I telled ye o'."

The two bowed awkwardly, and the elder man went off and left them. Francis got little comfort from the sight of the gawky boy before him. If this were a type of the gentleman-adventurer, then it would have suited better with his tastes to have chosen another trade. As for Mr. Stark, he assumed an air of wonderful shrewdness, which raw youth at all times believes to be the mark of the man of affairs.

"What's garred ye take the road, Mr. Birkenshaw?" said he, with the drawling accent of the West.

The other looked him up and down with rudeness and leisure, scanning every detail of his rustic clothes, his ill-tied hair, and the piteous aping of the fine gentleman in his carriage. This was no better than the tavern sots in Edinburgh with whom he had brawled a year before.

"What if I do not care to make my business public on every shipboard, sir?" he said with chill insolence.

"Do you think I should go about making proclamation of my past?"

The boy looked aggrieved and taken aback. "But between men of honour," he said sullenly.

Francis laughed the laugh of the man to whom all old burdens are now but the merest names. "Honour!" he said, with a sense of diplomacy in the assumption of a part, "honour is not a luxury for you or me, my friend. We're running atween the jaws o' government warships, and whatever we may have done it's unlikely that there'll be much talk o' fair trial for suspects. Every man is his neighbour's enemy till he has put his breast before him to the bullet. Then there may be friendship. But what talk is this of honour, sir, atween two chance acquaintances?" And he stood, darkly suspicious, in a fervour of self-admiration.

The other bent low in respect for this new revelation of spirit. He felt a tingle of shame for his petty villainies in the presence of one whose crimes might yet be called high-treason. By a mere chance Francis had fallen upon the part best suited to take his comrade's fancy. Henceforth he might act as he pleased and yet loom heroic to the reverent eyes of Mr. Stark. The frank homage pleased him, and he felt a morsel of liking for this uncouth westlander. So leaning over the rail, they spoke of their joint fortunes.

With the freshets of the wider seas Francis rose in spirits. His mind, in the Edinburgh and Dysart days, had always been panoramic, raking the future with its spy-glass and finding solace in visions. He had never entered a brawl or a debauch without some glimpse of himself in the act of cutting a fine figure to cheer his fancy. For the mere approval of gossip he had cared little, but much for the verdict of a certain select imaginary coterie who kept house in his brain. Now his part was the adventurer, and he sought to play it to his satisfaction.

"They say that France is weel-filled wi' Scots," said Mr. Stark. "I hae near twae hunner guineas I took frae my faither, and I'm the lad to mak' mair." And he stuck his hat more jauntily, and whistled the stave of a song.

"Guineas for auld men," said Francis. "For me, I have little thought on gear, if I but get free hand and fair play. Lasses and gear fall soon to the high hand. For myself, I am for the King's court, the rightful King's, as a gentleman should. Ye'll be a Whig since ye come from the Westlands, Mr. Stark?"

"Whig did you say? Na, na! I was a Whig yince when Kate Mallison was yin, and I gaed to the Kirk to watch her. But noo I'll sing *Jamie come hame* wi' any braw lad that's to my mind." And the boy grimaced and swaggered with fine abandonment.

Something in the attitude struck the finical Francis with disgust. This Dumbarton apprentice had not the figure or speech of a King's man. He was on the point of giving him back some rude gibe, when a thought of his new part smote upon him. He checked his tongue and held a diplomatic peace. To the true master no tool was too feeble for use, so he set to to flatter Mr. Stark.

It may be guessed that the task prospered, for soon the face of the one beamed with conscious worth. Then the voice of Mr. Berritch broke roughly in upon the colloquy.

"Heh, Starkie, come and gie's a lift wi' this wecht."

The boy looked queerly at his companion and ambled off to obey. He came back with face flushed from stooping, only to find in Francis a mood of stony disdain.

For a little he looked out to sea and bit his lips. Then he said in accents of apology: "He askit little to tak' me ower, so I maun needs help him in his bit jobs."

"I have nothing to do with your affairs," said his immovable comrade, "but I would be sweered to fetch and carry for any man. And what talk is this o' money? Does he charge hire like an Alloa ferryman?"

To the bargaining mind of the other such a tone seemed uncalled for. "Ye wadna expect him to dae't for love? I couldna dae't mysel'."

"Then, by God, Mr. Stark, ye have most of the lessons of gentility to learn."

At this moment of time the voice of Mr. Berritch was again audible. He came aft the vessel with his brow shining from toil. Now, on the high seas, he was a different man from the secret gentleman of Dysart. His tones were boisterous and full of authority, his eye commanding, and his figure trimmer. More, his jaw looked uglier, and his narrow, unkindly eyes a full half more disconcerting.

"Starkie, my lad," he shouted, "ye maun come and gie's a hand. And you, Mr. Birkenshaw, gang to the bows and help Tam Guthrie wi' the ropes. I'm terrible short-handed this voyage, and I canna hae idlers."

The hectoring note roused contradiction in Francis's blood. He bore no dear affection for Mr. Berritch, and he had no mind to serve him. He scarcely even felt the debt of obligation, for had he not already risked his liberty for the captain's gold?

"Ye would not have me work like a tarry sailor, Mr. Berritch?" said he.

"E'en so," said the bold ship's captain. "I would have ye work like a tarry sailor when ye're on my lugger." And he looked the young man up and down with insolent eye.

Francis became for the moment magnanimous. "If ye were to ask it as a favour, I would be the first to oblige ye, but ..."

The other cut him short, frowning.

"Weel, weel, sir, if ye're mindit to play the fine gentleman ye can dae it and be damned to ye. But ye'll pay me twenty guineas down for your passage, when I micht hae been content wi' ten if ye had shown decent civility."

Francis grew dusky with sudden wrath.

"I thought I had paid ye for my passage already," said he, hoarsely. "Besides, I had a thought that there was a talk o' friendship in the matter."

Mr. Berritch laughed long and loud. "Is't like," he said, "when ye winna dae a bit obleegement when I ask ye? Na, na, my man, ye'll gie me the twenty afore ye steer frae thae boards, and seein' that ye're payin' for it a' ye can take your leisure like a gentleman."

It would be hard to tell the full irritation of his hearer's mind. To be blocked and duped thus early in his career of adventure by a knavery more complete than his own, was bitter as wormwood. A certain trust in the generous and the friendly had remained to him even in his renunciation of virtue, and now its loss seemed more vexatious than consisted with his new view of the world.

He was in a maze of self-distrust and wounded sentiment, to which, as the minutes passed, was joined the more wholesome passion of anger.

For one brief second he was tempted to a curious course. He had almost paid the money demanded, posed as the wounded friend, and continued in this lofty character. But the feeling passed, and his vexation sealed his resolve to send Mr. Berritch and his crew to the devil rather than yield.

"What's he taking from you?" he asked Starkie, who stood watching the result with the interest of malice.

"He's daein' it for ten," was the answer.

"Then this is my word to you, Mr. Berritch," and Francis drew himself up with bravado. "Ye offered to take me over for friendliness, and, though we fall out over the matter of friendship, I hold ye to your bargain. You land me in France hale and safe, or I'll ken the reason why," and he tapped his sword-handle with rising pride.

"And this is my word to you, Mr. Birkenshaw," said the captain, his face aflame with rage. He had flung down the rope-end, and stood with arms on hips and blazing eyes. "I hae three men here wi' me, ilka ane a match for you, and I mysel' could soon gar ye pit up your bit swirdie. But I'm a man o' peace, and I likena violence. If ye dinna pay me your farin' here and now, I land ye in Berwick afore night, whaur I ken o' some who will hae meikle to say to ye aboot your misdeeds."

The man's whole carriage had changed from the bluff bravado he had once affected to an air of cunning and respectable malice. Francis felt the hopelessness of his case, and his thoughts grew hotter. He drew his blade and was in the act of rushing upon his foe, when that worthy whistled shrilly, and at the sign the three ship hands, truculent fellows all, came running to his side. Francis glanced toward Starkie and there read the folly of his action. If the Westlander had but joined him he would have forthwith attacked the quarto with some good-will. But his comrade clearly had no love for the sight of steel, for with a very white face and shaking legs he was striving to act the mediator.

The captain regarded his opponent grimly and calmly. As the anger ebbed from Francis' brain his reason returned and he regarded his folly with some little shame. But sufficient remained to make him obdurate. "Take me to Berwick if it please ye," he cried, "but ye'll never see the glint o' my money."

"To Berwick ye'll gang," was the sour answer, "and I wis ye may like it." And without more words he went about his business.

Francis went over to the gunwale and looked out to sea. The September day was ending in a drizzle of mist and small rain. He could not see the shore, save as a dim outline; but he guessed that they must be well down the Berwick coast, seeing that they had rounded the Bass in the early morning. The threat of Mr. Berritch had no special terrors for him, his misdeeds were out of the region of actual crime, and in any case Berwick was too far away for punishment. But, unless he liked to face a ship's crew and captain with the bare sword, he would be carried ignominiously into harbour, and find himself stranded purposeless once more in his own land. And yet he would never pay the money, he reflected, as he became cognisant of his own root of pride. He had sudden yearnings towards virtue, produced by his sudden disgust at villainy in another. But above all the bitterness rose highest that he should be thus frustrated in the first glamour of his hopes.

The gallant Mr. Stark came up with consolations—not without timidity. His respect for his companion had grown hugely in the last minutes, and he was disposed himself to assume something of a haughty bearing. But he got no word from the sullen figure at the bulwarks, till he had exhausted his vocabulary of condolence.

"Mr. Birkenshaw," said he, "I hae a word to say to ye anent your ways o' getting to France. I haena your experience, but I can see wi' my ain een that this road is no the safest. If ye were to land at Berwick, it's no abune ninety mile across the country to the west. Ye could walk it in three days, and there ye'd find a boat to set ye ower for something less than this man's twenty guineas."

Francis flamed up in wrath. "And ye would have me carried ashore like a greeting child! No, by God, though I have to sweem for it, that man and his folk will never lay their tarry hands on me," and he stared fiercely into the mist.

But as he looked and meditated some fragments of a plan began to grow up in his brain. It would be little to his disadvantage to cross the land and embark from the west. It would save him the intolerable humiliation of a voyage in Mr. Berritch's company and another scene of wrangling at the end. Moreover, it would save him money, and somewhere in Francis, now that he was cast on himself, there lurked a trace of the old Birkenshaw providence. Again, it would keep up his reputation in the eyes of Starkie and his own self-respect; both weighty considerations for a vain man. But the matter of the landing still stuck in his throat and had all but driven him to the paths of virtue.

Then Mr. Stark spoke out with resolution.

"It maitters little to me what way I gang, and I thocht o' offering ye my company. Twae men are aye better than yin, and I ken the Westlands." The boy spoke with a fine air of the heroical which took the other's fancy. The offer screwed Francis's decision to the point of some crazy piece of bravado, and none the less stirred some hidden generosity.

"I have taken a great liking to ye, Mr. Stark," he replied with condescension, "and I own I'll be glad o' your company. But there's one thing I must tell you if ye would come with me. If when we come to Berwick they offer to put hands on me and set me in their bit boat, there and then I gang overboard and sweem ashore. Are you fit for the ploy, Mr. Stark?"

"Sweem," cried the other, joyfully, seeing in this a chance of bravery without peril. "I was bred aside the sea, and I've leeved in the water since I was a bairn."

It might have been five in the afternoon, but in the misty weather it was hard to guess the time. They were coasting near the land, for the light breeze was clear behind them, and the water lay deep under the shadow of the craggy shore. Through the haze they could discern the red face of the cliffs, thatched with green and founded on a chaos of boulders. Even there they heard the lip of water on the beach above the ceaseless hiss of rain. Gulls hung uneasily about their track, and through the damp air came the cry of sandpipers, thin and far. It was mournful weather, and the heart of the soaked and angry Francis suffered momentary desolation.

But he was recalled to action by the harsh voice of Mr. Berritch behind him. "Well, my lad," said the captain, "are ye in a better frame o' mind? Yonder's Berwick and mouth o' Tweed, and yonder ye gang if ye dinna dae my bidding. So if we are to continue our way thegether, I'll trouble you for your guineas, Mr. Birkenshaw."

Francis looked over the gunwale to the low shore, not three hundred yards off. A glimpse of house and wall to the left showed where the town began. To hesitate would be to end all his bravado in smoke, so he glanced with meaning at the excited Starkie and spoke up with creditable boldness,—

"I told ye before, I'm thinking, Mr. Berritch, that you would get no guineas of mine, and I'm no used to go back on my word."

"Then we'll hae the boat," said the captain. "Geordie, get the boat oot."

"And I have something more to say to ye, ye thief o' a Fife packman. Ye've matched me this time with your promises and smirks, but I'll win my ways without ye and pay ye for a' this and mair some day. So I'll bid ye good-day, Mr. Berritch, till our next meeting."

And with this tearful defiance he was over the bulwarks, followed by the dauntless Stark, leaving the grim Mr. Berritch someway between irritation and laughter. Two heads dipped on the misty waters, and a little after two mortals were wringing their clothes on the sanded beach.

CHAPTER IV.

A Journey in Late Summer.

The cold of the water dispersed Francis' high sentiments. He shook himself ruefully, and looked back at the dim outline of the ship. The journey had fairly tired him, and it vexed him to see Starkie, the better swimmer, as active as ever. But by the time he had wrung his clothes and shaken the salt from his hair his spirits had returned, and with the other at his heel he clambered up the bank of red earth and made for the nearest houses.

The darkening was already on the fall, and the roofs of the town shone faint over a field of corn. The plashing Mr. Francis had no care to find a road, but held straight through the crops with a fine disregard of ownership. At the end they came to a low stone dyke, and beyond it a muddy road of the same unfriendly colour of soil. Thence the cobbles began and a line of little houses, stretching steeply down to what seemed a wide grey flood. For a second Francis' heart quickened with interest. This was the great river of Tweed, from whose banks came his family and his name. The sight momentarily enlivened for him the listless scene and the clammy weather.

Both were hungry and cold, and there was little cause to be finical in the matter of lodging; for to both these young adventurers thriftiness was something of a noble quality, and they sought to husband their present resources. So they went boldly to the first door in the line of houses and sought admittance.

A woman came, a tall, harsh-featured woman of forty and more, with her arms bare and her coats kilted. She stared at the intruders with incivility, and waited their question.

"Can you give us a bed for the night, mistress? We are two seafaring men who came ashore the day and are ettlin' to travel up the water to our hames. We're unco wet and famished, and will pay ye for all that ye may gie us."

"Whatna vessel came ye aff?" said the woman, with suspicion in her eye.

"The 'Kern' o' Leith," said Francis, readily.

"And whaur may your hames be?"

"In Yarrow at the Tinnies' Burnfoot," seizing upon the only place of which he had heard the names.

"The Tinnies' Burn," said the woman, meditatively. "There were Scotts in it in my time, but I heard they had flitted. Ye'll be some o' the new folk. Come in, and I'll see what I can dae for ye!"

And she led the ready pair into the kitchen.

The place was high and wide, with cobwebbed, smoke-grimed rafters and a searching odour of comfort. But soon the heat drew the salt fumes from the wet garments, and the place smelt like a ship's cabin. The woman sniffed and bustled angrily. Then with some brusqueness she bade them get up to the garret and put on her husband's breeks, for she would have no sailor-folk making her kitchen like the harbour-end.

Dry clothes and the plain warm meal which followed restored the two to their natural cheerfulness. They sat by the fire and fell to speaking in low tones about their way overland to the West. It was an ill-timed action, for the housewife's suspicious ears caught names which she liked ill, and the whispering made her uneasy. She came over to the ingle and with arms squared broke in on the talk.

"What garred ye come ashore sae ill set-up, lads? I've seen mony sailor-men, but nane sae puirly fitted as yoursels."

"We're juist ashore for a wee," said Francis. "We got the chance o' winnin' hame and we took it. Twae days will bring us to Yarrow, twae days back, and by that time the 'Kern' 'ill be lying loadin' in the harbour. It wasna an errand to tak ony plenishing wi' us."

The woman laughed sardonically. "What bit o' the harbour did ye lie in?" said she.

Francis was at a loss, and cast about warily for an answer.

"I've never been here but the yince," said he, "so I canna just tell ye richt. But we cam maybe a hundred yairds up the river and syne cast anchor by the richt wall."

Again the woman laughed. "And how did ye win up the river? Did ye a' get oot and shove the boat wi' your shouthers?"

"Are you daft, wife?" said the dumbfoundered Mr. Stark.

"No, my lad," said she; "but ye're the daft anes to come to me wi' a story like that. The river the noo is no three feet deep a' ower wi' sands and the shift o' the tide-bar. Ye're nae sailors. I warrant ye dinna ken a boom frae a cuddie's tail, and yet ye come here wi' your talk o' sailors. Na, I'll tell ye what ye are. Ye're Hielandmen or French, I'll no say which, but ye're ower here on nae guid errand. Ye cam frae a ship; but it was in a boat under the Tranen rocks. Oot o' my house ye gang, and ye may bless the Lord I dinna rin ye to the Provost."

The woman stood frowning above them, so clearly mistress of the situation that the hearts of the two wanderers sank. The soul of Mr. Stark, already raised high with vague belief in his comrade's dark and terrible designs, was genuinely alarmed by this shrewd reading of purpose. He looked to see Francis falter and stammer, and when he saw his face still calm and inscrutable, his voice yet unshaken, he bowed in spirit before a master.

As for Francis, he followed the broad path of denial.

"Hielandman or French," he cried with a laugh. "Is't like, think ye, when I haena a plack to spare I should take up my heid wi' beggars' politics? Na, na, a Whig am I and my faither afore me. I wadna stir my thoomb for a' the Charlies that ever whistled. Gin this were a change-house, mistress, and a bowl o' yill were on the board afore me, ye wad see me drink damnation to a' Pretenders, and health to King Geordie."

His words were so violent and so honestly given that the woman looked momentarily satisfied. "I've maybe mista'en ye," she said; "but at ony rate, whatever ye are, ye're shameless leears."

"Maybe we are, gudewife," said Francis, with ingratiating candour; "but for us wandering men we never ken when we are wi' freends. The truth o' the maitter is that we cast oot wi' the Captain, and have e'en ta'en the road to the West whaur we'll find another ship. Ye'll forgie us the lee, mistress?"

"Ye look like honest men," said the woman, slowly and hesitatingly. "You at ony rate," and she turned to Francis. "Ye've far ower long and sarious a face to be a blagyird."

* * * * *

In the morning they were up betimes, and ready for the road. The shadow of Mr. Berritch still hung over both, and a dim mist of suspicion was in the atmosphere of the dwelling. The final affront came at parting. Francis, with conscious honesty, offered payment for the night's lodging. The woman haggled and raised the price till she had all but angered him; then, with a hearty slap on the back, she bade him begone and live like an honest man. "D' ye think," said she, "I wad tak payment frae twae forwandered callants? Gang your ways, man, and try gin ye can be as honest as ye're bonny." And her laugh rang in his ears as he went down the street.

At first, the glory of the morning set his spirits high. They were already on the western outskirts of the town, where the grey sea-beat tenements dwindle to outlying cottages which stare abruptly over meadowland and river. The September haze was rising in furling battalions before the wind, and the salt ocean air strove with the serener fragrance of shorn hay-fields. There was something extraordinarily fresh and blithe in the wide landscape falling to the eye under the blue, and the bitter crispness of morn. Insensibly their limbs moved faster, they flung back their shoulders, and with open mouth and head erect drank in the life-giving air.

But as they plodded on, Francis soon fell into the clutches of memory, and his reflections pleased him little. The whole thought of the day before was full of irritation. On the threshold of high-handed adventure he had met with a closed door, and had been driven to a poverty-stricken compromise. Hitherto in dark moments of self-revelation he had buoyed himself with a flattering picture of a keen brain and a dauntless will. Now, both seemed to have failed grievously; he had been tricked and laughed at by a peddling sailor. Even the rhetorical parting did not comfort him. Seen in the cold light of day it seemed crude and boyish. He could have torn his tongue out with rage when he thought on the grinning Mr. Berritch and the gaping crew.

But more than this folly, he regretted his lapse from his first resolution. The fine renunciation of virtue which he had performed two nights before on the doorstep of his home was rapidly being made of no avail. He had been betrayed into compromise, into honesty. The words of the woman at Berwick still rang in his ears. She had clearly taken him for some truant apprentice, some temporary recreant from the respectable. The thought was gall and wormwood. He, the master, the scorner of the domestic, the Ulysses and Autolycus to be! And—alas for human consistency!—there was still another trouble of a vastly different kind. In one matter he was ashamed of deception. He had worn the badge of whiggery in the eyes of Mr. Stark, and though the need for the step had been apparent, he could not divest his mind of some faint scruples, the relics of an earlier ideal of gentility.

The result of such meditations was to drive the meditator into a fine bad temper, which he proceeded to vent on the ill-fated Starkie. This gentleman had spoken little, being filled with thoughts of his own. Somewhere in his curious nature was a strain of sentiment, which revelled in cheap emotions and the commonplaces of memory. The charms of Kate Mallison still held her fugitive lover, and as he travelled he lingered pleasantly over her face and figure, and formed his mouth to words of endearment. The virulence of his companion did not disturb him. For this he had made up his mind long ago. After all, if one seeks a great man as a friend, one must be prepared to bear with his humours. And when Francis, roused by memories of his fall into virtue, talked shrilly of desperate plans, Starkie inclined a deaf, yet willing ear, and went on with his fancies.

But by and by with the hours, another feeling grew upon the elder's mind. The road ran among low birches with a sombre regiment of pines flanking it on the right. Through the spaces gleamed the blue sky, pale with the light haze of September, and on the left among reeds and willows twined and crooned the great streams of Tweed. Francis was diverted against himself, and, ere ever he knew, the old glamour of the countryside had fallen upon him. He, too, it was his proud reflection, was a son of this land, born of a family whose name was old as the hills and waters. The ancient nameless charm which slumbered with the green hillsides, flashed in the streams, and hung over the bare mosses, stole unbeknown into his soul, and the stout Francis was led captive by the poetry of the common world.

The mood lasted till near evening, when they slept at a little public somewhere by Leader-foot. In the morn they were early awake, for those days of delay in their own land were irksome to both. Now they were in a stranger country, where hills came down to the water's edge, and the distance showed lines of blue mountain. The weather was still the placid and soothing warmth of a late summer with roads running white and dry before them, and the quiet broken only by the sounds of leisured, rustic toil. For the nonce the bustling fervour died in Francis' breast, and he took his way through the gracious valley in a pleasant torpor of spirit.

But by midday, all this was driven to the winds by the conduct of Mr. Stark. This gentleman, awakened from his sentiments of yesterday, fell to the purposeless chatter in which he specially excelled. Thence, finding his companion irresponsive, he glided naturally to the plotting of mischief. He had some desire to vindicate his name of adventurer in the eyes of his saturnine friend. So he cast about him for a fitting object.

Now ill luck sent him an opportunity at once too facile and too mean, for, when the pair stopped at a wayside cottage for water, he adroitly contrived to filch a cut of dried beef from the wooden dresser. In glee he showed it to Francis as they halted at midday a mile beyond. He expected approval, or at the least tolerance; but his reception sorely discomfited him, for to Francis, the thing appeared so aimlessly childish, so petty, that his gorge rose at the sight. It was the act of a knavish boy, and the whole soul of this man of affairs was stirred to anger. If there was any flicker of honesty in the feeling it was sternly suppressed, but to the disgust he gave full rein.

"What for did ye do that?" he asked fiercely.

"Oh, juist to keep my hand in, belike," said the Westlander.

"Ye damnable bairn," cried Francis, "d' ye call this a man's work, robbing auld wives of their meat, when ye have no need of it? I'll learn ye better. Come back with me, see, this minute, and if ye dinna pay her what she asks, you and me will quit company. D' ye think I will have ye running at my heels like a thieving collie?"

The elder man had too menacing a brow and angry tone for the feeble Mr. Stark to resist. He followed him grumbling, and suffered to be led like a sheep within the cottage. The place was bare and poor; the woman, thin and white as a bone, and long fallen in the vale of years.

"My friend happened to lift something o' yours, mistress, and we e'en came to pay ye for it," and Francis regarded the strange place with some pity.

"Were ye starvin', lads?" she asked in a piping voice, "for if sae ye may keep the meat and welcome. But it wad hae been mair faisable to speir."

But, try they their best, she would take no payment, and they had to leave in despair. The thing put both into an ill humour. Starkie nursed a grievance, and Francis had much the same temper as the Christian who laments the failure of judgment upon the wicked. They spoke no words, but stalked silently on different sides of the road, with averted eyes and tragic bearing.

But continued surliness was little in Starkie's way. At the end of half an hour he was jocose and making farcical overtures to friendship. When he found his efforts repulsed, he comforted himself with a song, and when in a little they came to a village and a public, turned gladly to the relief of drink. Now, whether it was that the landlord's whisky had extraordinary qualities or that Starkie drank a wondrous amount, it is certain that ere he had gone far it became clear that he was grossly drunk.

Thence the course of the two became troubled and uncertain. Starkie drew up to the other in maudlin amity. Francis had drunk little and his gloomy temper still held him. He had never loved drunkenness, and at the moment his thoughts dwelt on the failure of his plans. So he sent Mr. Stark to the devil with no mincing words. With drunken gravity Starkie retorted, and then with more drunken heroism squared himself to fight. The patience of Francis fairly gave way. Gripping his assailant by the collar and breeches he tossed him easily to the roadside.

"Lie there, ye drunken swine," he cried, "and I'm glad I'm quit o' ye."

So, pursued by thickly-uttered reproaches, he hastened forward alone.

* * * * *

With the next dawn Francis found himself on the confines of great hills, where the river, now shrunk to a stream, foamed in a narrowed vale. The weather had changed with the night to cloud and cold, and the even drizzle of a Scots mist obscured the sun. The slopes gloomed black and wet, every burn was red with flood, and the sparse trees dripped in dreary silence. The place was singularly dispiriting, for nought met the eye but the mire underfoot and the murky folds of mist.

Early in the day he stopped a passing shepherd and asked him his whereabouts. He was told with great wealth of detail which further befogged his mind. Then on a sudden impulse he asked where lay Yarrow and the Birkenshaw Tower. "D' ye see that hill ower the water?"

was the answer. "That's the Grey Drannock, and the far side o' 't looks straucht down on the Yarrow water." This then was the confines of his own land, these were haply his forefathers' hills; a sudden pride went through his heart, but the next moment he was looking drearily on his lamentable fortunes.

He was sick of himself, disgusted with his ill-success, and half inclined to rue his parting with Mr. Stark. Where were his fine resolutions? All vanishing into air under the blast of his spasmodic virtues. As he looked back on the events of the past days he was driven by his present sourness especially to loathe his glimpses of decency. The dismal weather helped to harden him. After all, he reflected, the world is a battle-ground, where he wins who is least saddled with the baggage of virtue. Man preys upon man; I may expect no mercy from others; and none shall others get from me. So it was with fierce purpose and acrid temper that Francis travelled through the clammy weather. It had been Starkie, he thought with irritation, and not himself that had the true spirit; and he cursed the hour when he had left the little Westlander in the ditch.

By the evening it cleared and the sun set stormily over monstrous blue hills. He had passed through the town of Peebles in the early afternoon, and now followed the wide western road up the green pastoral dale of the upper Tweed. The dusk was drawing on as he left the river and took the path which ran to Ayr by Lanark and Clyde. Just at the darkening the lights of a little village beckoned him,—a line of white houses and a cluster of rowans by a burnside. His legs were growing weary, and he had not yet supped; so he turned to the inn to bide the night.

CHAPTER V.

The Portrait of a Lady.

In such rough and casual fashion Francis came to his Destiny. But to him there was little sign of aught momentous. The inn-kitchen was half-filled with men talking boisterously, while the landlord's deep tones gave directions to the serving-girl. The noise of soft south-country talk came pleasantly on his ears after the clip-clap of the Fife, and a wholesome smell of food and drink comforted his senses.

He sat by himself in a corner, for he was in the mood to shun publicity. Supper was brought him, and then he lit a pipe and stretched his legs to the fire, since already the evenings grew chilly. In this lethargic comfort his follies ceased to trouble him, and he tasted the delights of wearied ease.

But as the hour grew late the room cleared, and Francis awoke to interest in his surroundings. He asked the landlord what the place might be.

He was told, "Brochtoun."

The name stuck in his memory. Broughton—he had heard it somewhere, linked with some name which had slipped his recollection. He asked who owned the land.

"Murray," was the answer, "Murray o' Brochtoun, kin to them o' Stanhope. A graceless lot, aye plottin' and conspirin' wi' them that's better no named. Even now him and his leddy wife are awa to the North, trokin' wi' the wild Jaicobites and French." The landlord's politics were clear and vehement.

At the word Francis sat up in earnest. Murray of Broughton was already a noted name in the land, the catchword of the whole tribe of needy loyalists, reputed to be the confidant and companion of the Prince himself. And in every Edinburgh tavern he had heard the toast of the beautiful Mrs. Murray given with drunken leers and unedifying tales. If all stories were true, she was a lady of uncommon parts and spirit and not too nice a conscience. This, then, was the home of the Murrays on which he, the out-at-elbows adventurer, had stumbled. As he thought of himself he felt a singular antipathy to this tribe of aristocrats,—doubtless filled with pride of race and the fantastic notions of honour from which he had parted for ever.

The thought had scarce left him when a man who had been sitting at the door came up and touched his sleeve from behind. He turned to find a face familiar to him,—a little man with ferret eyes and bushy eyebrows, poverty staring from the rents in his coat. He knew him for a chance acquaintance in that lowest deep of city life to which he had made some few excursions.

"D' ye no mind me?" said the man, eagerly.

"I've seen ye before," said Francis, ungraciously.

"Dod Craik," said the man, "I'm Dod Craik. Ye mind Dod Craik. I've seen ye at the *Pirliewow* and *M'Gowks* and the *Three Herrins*, and, d' ye no mind, ye aince betted me twa crouns I couldna find my way across the street ae nicht when I was blind-fou. Ay, and I stottit the hale length o' that lang vennel and fell under a baillie's coach and was ta'en aff to jail." And the wretched creature laughed with the humour of it.

"Well, supposing I mind you, Mr. Craik," said the unbending Francis, "I'll trouble ye to tell me what ye want. If it's siller, ye'll get none from me, for I'm as toom as a kirk plate."

"It's no siller," cried the man. "Na, na, from a' I hear ye're just a venturer like mysel'. But it's a thing wi' siller in 't, and I thocht ye micht like to hae a finger in the job."

The notion pleased, and Francis held out a relenting hand to the little man. "If that's your talk, Mr. Craik, then I am with you."

"Then maybe ye could step ootside wi' me for the maitter o' a few meenutes," said the other, and the two went forth into the street.

The man led Francis out of the light of the houses into the gloom of the birk-lined road. "I kenned aye ye were a man o' speerit and withoot prejudices, Mr. Birkenshaw," he began.

"Let my spirit and prejudices alone," said Francis, shortly.

"And wi' nae scruples how ye cam by money if aince ye but had it."

"Man, will ye come to the point?" said Francis, who was in doubt whether to be pleased or angry at this narration of attributes.

"Weel, it's this. The Hoose o' Brochtoun is standin' toom or as guid as toom, save for a servant or twae. It's kenned that Murray is in league wi' rebels and has the keepin' o' their gold. It's beyond credibeelity that he can hae ta'en it to the North wi' him, so it maun be left here. Now I propose that you and me as guid subjects find a road intil the hoose and lay our hands on thae ill-gotten gains. I've lang had this ploy in my heid, and I had trysted wi' anither man for the nicht, but he's failed me. The short and lang o' the maitter is that the job's ower big for ae man, so when I got a glisk o' ye, I made up my mind to gie ye the chance." He waited nervously for the answer.

Francis flushed for the moment. "D' ye ken what ye ask me to do, Mr. Craik?" said he. "It's a job that some folk would call house-breaking and stouthrief."

"Na," said the other, "it's no that. It's the lawfu' consequence o' poleetical principles. Think ye, if the sodgers in Embro had word o' siccan a thing they wadna be the first to tak it? If ye believe me, Mr. Birkenshaw, it's a naational necessity."

"But what do ye ken of my principles?" asked Francis. "Who telled ye I wasna as hot a Jacobite as Murray himself?"

The man looked shrewdly at his neighbour to detect his purpose. Then he laughed incredulously. "Gae awa wi' ye and your havers. Ye were aye ower fond o' a saft seat and a bieldy corner."

For a little Francis stood in a sorry hesitation, in two minds whether to join forces with this house-breaker or there and then to give him the soundest of thrashings. His parting with Starkie still rankled in his mind. He called up the designs which he had formed for himself, his abhorrence of trivial virtue, his deification of the unscrupulous. This was a chance both to better his means and restore his confidence. This would be the rubicon over which there was no returning to the dreary paths of the respectable. His course was clear, and yet with a vanishing pride he could have beaten this little city blackguard who called him companion.

So he told Mr. Craik of his compliance, and was rewarded with a sigh of relief. "Man, I kenned ye wad dae 't, and noo we're shure o' success. Come down the road till I tell ye the ways o' 't. I've been hereabouts for days till I ken ilka turn o' the place. The Hoose looks north ower a dean o' trees and a' to the south is the whinny back o' a hill. There's naether windy nor door kept lockit the noo on that gairden side, for at a' hoors there's a steer o' men comin' and leavin'." And with a crowd of such directions he led him into the shade.

It was clear that Murray's folk had small liking for their laird. There in the inn sat Whiggery triumphant, smiled upon by a Calvinist landlord and a score of staunch Presbyterian followers. Further down the water the Cause found many adherents, but there, on the very confines of the West, there was something dour and covenanting in the air, and the fervours of the master and his lady awoke no spirit among the men of Broughton. Had two such characters as Mr. Craik and Francis been seen in an Athole or Badenoch inn they would have been jealously spied upon; but there they were suffered to go their ways, and in a corner of the inn over their glasses they brought the project to completion.

An hour later the two men were climbing the brae which rose from the green haughs of the burn to the upland valley where stood the house. Francis had the same free stride as ever, but Mr. Craik hastened over the brighter patches of moonlight and stole gladly to the shadows. To himself Francis seemed something less worthy than before. The mist of daring and escapade, with which he fancied his course to be shrouded, had begun to disappear under the cold north wind of Mr.

Craik's company. He had set out on the ploy for money and self-satisfaction; but soon he wished that he had come alone, for his disgust rose at the sight of the ferret-faced thing which led him.

Soon they were on the bare hill-face and looking down upon the back windows of the dwelling. To the left there was light in the lower windows, where probably dwelt the few domestics, but otherwise the whole of the great wall was black with darkness. Mr. Craik chuckled joyfully and led the way across the garden fence and down an alley of flowers. At the edge of the lawn he stopped and held a whispered consultation.

"That windy forenent us is never barred; the lock's broke, for I was up last nicht to find oot. Now if ye gang in there ye come to a passage which takes ye to the maister's ain room. It's no the first door but the second on the left-hand side, and there he keeps his siller and valuables. It's aye lockit, but I've trystit wi' a servant lass to leave the key in the door. Aince ye won there, ye wad lock the thing on the inside and search the place at your leesure. Syne ye wad come back to me and I wad help ye oot. The reason why twae man's needit is that the windy canna open frae within, and if there werena ane oot bye to lift it, there wad be nae mainner o' escape. Now, whilk is to gang and whilk is to bide?" and he took a coin from his pocket to toss.

"Ye'd better let me try it," said Francis. "I'm bigger and stronger, and maybe I've a better eye for a hidy-hole." Already he was beginning to loathe the business, and chose this part of it as the less discreditable. It was better to have his hand at the work than to wait outside like a child.

"Man, ye've speerit," said the other, admiringly and not without gratitude. Fear had already begun to wrestle with his avarice.

So Francis raised the window, which fitted like a portcullis into a socket above. His companion held it open till his long legs had struggled through. He found himself in a narrow corridor, pitchy dark, save for the glimmer from the window. A musty smell, as of an old and little-used house, hung all about it, and his groping feet detected an uneven floor. An utter silence prevailed, in which as from a great distance he heard the click of the shut window.

He felt out with his hand along the left wall. One door he passed, of stout ribbed oak securely fastened. Then the place widened, and he seemed to be in a hall with some kind of matting upon the floor. Here his feet went noiselessly, and some faint degree of light obtained from a window far in front. Then his hand came on the space of a second door, and he stopped to test it. This was clearly the place where the key was to be found, as Mr. Craik had directed.

But this was no less closely bolted than the last, and the key-hole was empty. He put his shoulders to the panel and shook it. He heard only the rasp of a great lock in its place, but the door did not give an inch. Again he tried, and this time the wood work cracked. But the noise warned him, echoing in that still place with double power, and he desisted.

Nothing remained but to try elsewhere, so he groped further down the hall. Again he touched a handle, and this time with better success; for to his amazement he found the door ajar, and pushing it open entered a wide room. He turned to look for a key, but found none; this, too, was not the place appointed; but since he had found an entrance he resolved to go further. The place was black with night. A dim haze of light seemed to hang at the end, which doubtless came from a shuttered window. As he groped his way he stumbled on furniture which felt rich and softly draped to the touch. A faint odour of food, too, lurked in the air, as if the room had been used for dining.

This was not the goal which he had sought, but even here something might be found. So Francis was in the act of beginning a hasty scrutiny when a sound brought him to a stop. A footstep was crossing the hall and making for the room. A pioneer ray of light gleamed below the door. He was in a quandary, uncertain whither to turn; he could not flee by the door, and no other way was apparent. To hide behind some curtain or cabinet was possible, and he was about to creep hastily to the back when a hand was laid on the latch. Some instinct prompted him to sink quietly into a chair and wait the issue.

The light of a lamp flooded the room, showing its noble size and costly furnishing. Francis sat silent in his chair, curious of the result, and busily searching his brains for some plausible tale. The light-bearer saw at the table-end a long man, his face dark with the sun, dressed decently yet with marks of travel, and bearing somewhere in his dress and demeanour the stamp of a townsman, who sat waiting on the newcomer's question with eyes half apologetic and half bold.

As for Francis himself he saw a vision which left him dumb. He had expected the sight of a servant or at most some gentleman of the cause using the house as a lodging. But to his wonder, at the doorway stood a woman holding a lamp above her and looking full from its canopy of light into the half-darkness. In the dimness she seemed tall and full of grace, standing alert and stately with a great air of queenship. Her gown was of soft white satin, falling in shining folds to her feet, and showing the tender curves of arm and bosom. Above, at the throat and wrists, her skin was white as milk, and the hair rose in dark masses on her head, framing her wonderful face,—pale with the delicate paleness so far above roses. Something in her eye, in the haughty carriage of the little head, in the life and grace which lay in every curve and motion, took suddenly from Francis the power of thought. He looked in silent amazement at this goddess from the void.

He had waited for surprise, anger, even fear; but to his wonder he found only recognition. She looked on him as if she had come there for no other purpose than to seek him. A kindly condescension, the large condescension of one born to rule and be obeyed, was in her demeanour.

"Ah, you are here," she said. "I thought you had not come. You are my Lord Manorwater's servant?"

For an instant Francis' wits wandered at the suddenness of the question. Then his readiness returned, and with some shrewdness he grasped the state of matters. He rose hurriedly to his feet and bowed with skill. "I have that honour, my lady," said he; and he reflected that his sober dress would suit the character.

As he stood a tumult of thoughts rushed through his brain. This was the famous lady whom he had so often heard of, she who was the Cause, the Prince, and the King to so many loyal gentlemen. His eyes gloried in her beauty, for somewhere in his hard nature there was an ecstatic joy in mere loveliness. But the bodily perfection was but a drop in the cup of his astonishment. She had clearly been receiving guests in this old house, and guests of quality, for the rich white gown was like a state dress, and jewels flashed at her neck and fingers. A swift and violent longing seized him to be one of her company, to see her before him, to be called her friend. In her delicate grace she seemed the type of all he had renounced for ever—nay, not renounced, for in his turbid boyhood he had had no glimpse of it. To this wandering and lawless man for one second the elegancies of life were filled with charm, and he sighed after the unattainable. Then his mood changed to one of fierce revulsion. This was a lady of rank and wealth, doubtless with a crazy pride of place and honour, condescending gravely to him as to one far beneath; and he, he was the careless, the indomitable, who would yet laugh in the face of the whole orderly world.

But such sentimental reflections were soon succeeded by thoughts more practical. He had run his head into a difficult place, and might yet escape by this lucky chance which called him a servant of Lord Manorwater's. But there was little time to lose, lest the real lackey should come to confront him. His ready brain was already busy with plans when the lady spoke again.

"Your master will have told you your errand. This is the letter which I desire you to carry and put into the hands of Mr. Murray of Broughton at his lodging in the Northgate of Edinburgh. Your master told me you have travelled the same road before to the same place."

Francis said "Ay."

"Then I have but one word for you. Take the hills from here and keep off the high-road, above all near the inn of Leidburn. For I have heard to-night that a body of rebel soldiers is lying there. When you come to my husband, he will give you his directions, whether to go with him and the royal army or to return here. But in any case I can trust the diligence and loyalty of one of my Lord Manorwater's men." And she smiled on him graciously.

"And they brought you in here and left you in darkness," she said, as if in self-reproach. "It is a hard thing to live in such troubled times. And perhaps you have not supped?"

Francis protested that he had already had food, in mortal fear lest she should delay him with refreshment.

"I will let you out myself," she said, and lifting the lamp she led the way from the room, her soft skirts trailing and the light flickering in her dusky hair. Francis followed in a fervour of delight. The sudden vista of a great plan had driven all sentiment from his mind. Now at last he might get free of petty ill-doing, and exercise his wits on matters of greater import. He carried a letter which meant money from any officer of Government; he scented plot and intrigue all richly flavoured with peril. He felt himself no more the casual amateur, but the established adventurer, meddling with the great affairs of nations. The thought restored him to his perverted self-respect.

She opened the hall-door and let him pass into the front garden with a word of good-speed. As he departed he turned for a moment, and his sentiment flickered to life, for as she stood, a radiant figure of light in the arch of the door, his mind reverted to this great loveliness.

But a second later such thoughts had fled, and, with no care for the patient Mr. Craik waiting silently by the back window, Francis took his path for the highway and the Leidburn inn.

CHAPTER VI.

On the Edinburgh Highway.

The moon was up, whitening the long highway to the north, as Francis sped gaily on. It was still early night; lengthy hours were to come before the dawn; and Leidburn inn was no more than a dozen miles. But the exhilaration of escape, of new hope, drove him with eager legs, and he watched the trees fall away and the barer hills draw together with pride in his fleet strength.

At the watershed the moors stretched dim and yellow on either hand in a melancholy desolation. A curlew piped on the bent, and then all was still as the grave but for the clack of his shoes on the hill-gravel. He fell out of his run and took to the stride with which he had been wont to stalk through the back-vennels of the city. The soft odours of moorland weather hung about the place as over a shrine. The luminous sky above had scarcely a hint of dark, but shone like an ocean starred with windy isles in some twilight of the gods.

His first resolution had grown and made itself clear in every part. He pictured gleefully the incidents of his course. The soldiers found, he called for their Captain and delivered his letter. The tide of war was turned, he was honoured with reward, and a life of bold intrigue awaited him. Exultantly he pictured his fate,—how the world would talk of him with fear, how his name would be on all men's lips and his terror in every heart. Then haply Mr. Francis Birkenshaw would set his heel on the neck of his oppressors.

But his importunate common-sense drew him sharply back from his flights. It meant but a guinea for his pocket and a glass of wine for his thirst, for he could only pose as a lackey if he wished for credence. Yet even in this there was promise. It needed but his wits and his habitual bold presence to push his fortune far. Here, in his own land, lay his field. Far better to seize a spoke of Fate's wheel as she twirled it here than hunt the jade in nations oversea.

The way led him through a bogland meadow and up again to the skirts of a hill. In a little he was among trees, whence came the chilly echo of running water and a gleam of light from some sequestered dwelling. Already a wider vale seemed to open and high, dark hill-shapes rose on the left. The road was wide and even, for by it men chiefly travelled to Carlisle and the South. Even as he sped a rumble of wheels came to his ear, and he was in the roadside heather watching a four-horse carriage go by. The horses seemed weary with forcing, and within the coach by the moonlight he had a glimpse of anxious faces. Lord Smitwood, or the great Lady Blaecastle, or the famous Mrs. Maxwell, he thought, on their way to put their sundry houses in order against an evil day. Clearly wars and rumours of war were thickening in the North, and he was soon to have a hand in the game.

And with this he fell back on thoughts of Broughton and the lady of the Jacotot lace and dusky hair. Something in her image as it flashed on his memory roused keen exaltation. He would trick this proud woman and all her kind, crush them, use them for his purpose. Each feature, as he reflected on it, roused his hatred. She was fair; well, beauty for the joy of the strong. Men said she was clever; well, he would match her with counter-wits and gain the victory. Three hours before, and he had never seen her; now she filled his whole fancy with her hateful beauty. He thought of her freely, grossly, as he had trained himself to think of women. But somewhere in the man there was a string of fine sentiment which jarred at the incongruous. The exquisite freshness of her beauty forbade her a place in a gallery of harlots, and to his disgust he found himself forced to regard her with decency.

The thing stuck in his memory and began to vex him. Vigorously he questioned himself if he were not falling back to his boyish virtue. Re-assured by the hot and lustful spirit within him, he searched for some catchword or badge of his resolve. So all the latter part of the way he hummed rags of ill-reputed ditties, and now and then in the near neighbourhood of a cottage made the night hideous with a tune. For he was now at the verge of settled country, where King George held a tight rein, and no loyalist gentry would be at hand with a bullet from the wayside. So leisurely had been his course that the autumn dawn was already breaking ere he rounded the hill and came out on the level Leidburn moss. The place was desert,—acres of peat with the film of morn still raw on the heather, and the black reaches of a lazy stream. But through the midst ran the fresh-coloured highway, and there, half a mile distant, rose the white walls of the inn. Even as he walked the thin air of dawn brought him the noise of hens' cackling and the first stir of life. Beyond all there stretched a great wide country of meadow and woodland to the horizon of the morning, the smoke of a city and the broad curve of the sea.

The scene was so airy and clear that Francis fell into a rich good-humour with himself, and drew near to the inn with pleasant confidence. He had expected to find some traces of military, some neighing from the stable or bustle of servants, but to his wonder the house was silent. The kitchen door stood open, and through it he passed with the appearance of a lackey's haste.

"Landlord," he cried, in a voice of importance, and a heavy man came down a trap-stair from a garret. Francis's manner assumed the ease of politeness and good-fellowship mingled. "I have word with the Captain," he said, "and I maun see him before I hae my breakfast. But quick, man, get something ready for me."

"The Captain!" the landlord cried with disgust, "and whatna Captain, my lad? I've had eneuch o' captains in thae fower walls this last week to mak hell ower thrang for the deil himsel'. But they're a' cleared noo, gone yestreen the last o' them to fecht the Hielandmen. God,

I wish them luck. They'll find a Hieland cateran's dirkie a wee bit less pleasin' in their wames than my guid bannocks."

Here was news of vexation. "But where have they gone, and can I no meet up wi' them?" he asked.

"It's easy to tell that," said the sarcastic host. "They're just in Embro and nae further. Cope has landed some way doun the Firth, and a' King George's lads are drawing to that airt. They say the Chevalier and his Hielanders gang oot the day to meet them. Weary fa' them for spoilin' an honest man's trade! Fechtin' tae wi' oot breeks and wi' nae skeel in pouther and leid! God!" And the man laughed deep and silent.

"The Chevalier?" Francis stammered.

"Ay, the Chevalier," said the man. "Whaur hae ye been wanderin' a' thae days that ye havena heard o' him? Chairlie's king o' the castle the day, though he may be doun wi' a broken croun the morn."

"I have been long in the South," said Francis, hastily, "and forbye, I am given to doing my ain business and no heeding the clash of the country."

"Weel, weel, maybe sae. But if I were your maister, my lad, I wad pick ane mair gleg at the uptak than yoursel'." And the landlord went off, rolling with his heavy gait, to fetch the stranger breakfast.

Francis sat down to reflect on this state of matters with some philosophy. It meant a longer journey for himself ere he disposed of his business, and a greater risk of frustration. He thought for a moment of playing the faithful messenger after all, and casting his services at the Secretary's feet. But the thought was scarce serious, for with it came the unpleasant consideration that his position would still be a lackey's, and that he would be likely to have difficulties if he ever came within range of Lord Manorwater or the Secretary's wife. Soon he was reconciled even to the twenty odd miles which still awaited him, for the holding of Edinburgh and the landing of the English general meant a crisis of war, when news would be bought and sold at a higher price. But he must be wary and quick, or any wandering loyalist might trick him. So he cried to the landlord to hurry the meal, and stretched his already wearied legs in a chair.

"Are ye for Embro?" asked the landlord.

"Even so," said Francis, guilelessly, "since ye say the Captain is there."

"Ye'll hae a gey wark finding him, my lad," said the other. "Captains will be as thick as fleas in Embro the noo, and the maist o' them withoot the breeks. If ye're wise ye'll look for the man ye're seekin' mair east the country on the road to join the ithers. What did ye say was his name?"

"I wasna told any name," said Francis, feeling himself on the edge of a hazard. "A' I got was 'The Captain at Leidburn inn'."

The landlord laughed. "They keep ye muckle in the dark on your side tae. I had thocht that that wark was left for the Hielandmen."

"What side do ye incline to yoursel'?" asked Francis.

"Nae side," said the man, shortly. "I treat a' the warld as my customers, whether they wear the breeks or no. But my faither was ane o' the Cameronian kind, and I'm half persuaded that way mysel'."

But at this moment a rattle at the door proclaimed another visitor. Francis turned anxious eyes, for might not this be some servant of the Murrays or Manorwaters? But the sight of the newcomer re-assured him, for there in all the dust of travel and abandon of weariness stood the deserted Starkie.

He had not prospered in these last days, for his clothing was much soiled and his face was lean with exertion. He fell back at the sight of his aforetime comrade, as if doubtful of his reception. But Francis was in the humour in which to hail his arrival with delight. Yesterday he had repented his loss, and now he was in a mood to atone for it. He greeted him with a cry of pleasure, and drew the hesitating Westlander to the fire.

"We've forgathered again," said he, "and now we'll be the better friends. In these stirring times, Mr. Stark, there's no room for ill nature."

"And I'm glad to see ye, Mr. Birkenshaw, for I have missed ye sair. God, I'll ne'er forget that weary wander ower the Tweed hills. I've been a' airts but the right yin since I saw ye."

Both ate their breakfast ravenously, while mutual questioning filled the pauses. As they talked, the anomaly of their course came forcibly before each mind, and each asked the reason of this unexpected meeting-place.

"What brought ye to this part, Starkie? This is no road to Clyde and the West."

"Oh, I've nae doubt it was the same reason as yoursel'. When I came by the top o' Tweed the hale land was turned upside doun wi' rumours o' war, and ilka plooman gettin' his musket and sword. They telled me Embro was gotten by the Prince, and that a' the brave lads were rinnin' to his flag. So, thinks I, I may as weel try my luck in my ain land as in the abroad. Forbye, I'll pay out my faither, for gin he heard o' siccan daeings he wad gang out o' his mind. He bides ower near the Hieland Line to love the Hielandmen. But if ye've nae objections, I wad like to hear what brocht you yersel' this gate."

"Wheesht, Starkie," said Francis, looking darkly at the landlord, "I've a ploy on hand to make both our fortunes." And he watched the host till he had betaken himself to the far back of the kitchen. Then he leaned forward and tapped his companion on the arm. "Starkie, man, I have a letter."

The Westlander's eyes brightened. "That's guid, and whae is it frae?"

"From the Secretary's wife to the Secretary's self."

The announcement was made in stage tones and received with proper awe. "Mr. Birkenshaw, ye're great," said Starkie, and Francis's vanity was appeased. It had been somewhat wounded by the independent tone which his companion had seen fit to assume since their severance.

Then in brief words he proceeded to unfold his plans. He would make straight for the east shore of the Firth, and meet the Government leaders. The near crisis of the war would heighten his value and gain him favour. He had heard enough of the Prince's men to have little faith in them; time would soon work their ruin; and then would come reward for the loyal adherent. Starkie listened and approved, so both in their ignorance saw a roseate horizon to their boyish policy.

But the businesslike Westland mind had one addendum. The letter might be of the highest consequence; again it might be a trifle, which would merely expose the bearer to contempt. It would be well to inquire into its contents.

Francis pondered, hesitated, and then blankly refused. Something, he knew not what, held him from opening it. He scouted the idea of honour,—that was flung far behind,—but a sense of fitness even in the details of roguery was strong upon him. He had still some memory of the hands from which he had got the letter, and his sentiment had not utterly flown. The feeling might permit high, audacious treachery, but not so mean and small a piece of bad faith. He was on the verge of the humour in which two days before he had flung his companion into the ditch.

In his luckless way Starkie ministered to the growing repulsion. The thought of the future delighted him, and he hastened to sketch its details. Alike in his childishness and his flashes of shrewdness he was repugnant to the maturer Francis. His view of the conduct of affairs was so plainly ingenuous that it filled the other with despair, and his idea of happiness was the craziest mixture of the respectable and sillily wicked. Francis, still in the heat of a great plan, with his brain yet fired from the deeds of the night before, had no tolerance for such a huckstering paradise.

From ill temper the two were rapidly drifting to a quarrel. These last days had found Starkie some independence, and he was scarcely disposed to bear with his comrade's megrims. He assumed a tone of consequence, and replied to Francis's gibes with flat rustic retorts. The landlord came up betimes and tried in vain to mediate. Francis had the grace to hold his peace, but not so the other. He sank from vituperation to complaint, and was on the verge of confiding all grievances to the open ears of the host.

Meanwhile the hours were passing, and a hot blaze of sun in the windows warned Francis that he must soon be stirring. For a second he was tempted to leave his companion then and there, but he curbed his irritation with the bridle of policy and reflected on his probable usefulness. He was in the act of conciliating him by timely concession,—by falling in with the tune of his hopes and throwing him crumbs of flattery, when a noise of hooves and wheels sounded without on the road and then stopped short at the inn-door.

Both men sprang to their feet, while the landlord hurried to clear the table. A woman's voice was heard as if giving orders, and then a step on the threshold, and the door was opened. The blinking eyes of Mr. Stark saw a lady, tall and fair, in a travelling cloak of dark velvet, with a postilion at her back. But Francis's breath stopped in his throat, for he knew the face of the woman he was playing false to.

"Landlord," she cried in her clear high voice, "the right horse has gone lame, and I must be in Edinburgh in an hour. Quick, get me a fresh beast, and have the other looked to." Then, as she haughtily cast her eyes around the place, she caught sight of the gaping Starkie and Lord Manorwater's trusted servant. For a second her face looked bewilderment; then a quick gleam of comprehension entered, and her cheeks grew hot with anger.

"So," said she, "I have found you at last, you cur. You thought to trick me with your tales and profession. Doubtless you are now on your way to your own master with your news. Perhaps it will please you to know that it is valueless, since the Prince's army has taken the field. It was well that I warned you against this place, else I might have missed this proof of your fidelity. Truly my Lord Manorwater is happy in his servants."

Plainly she still took him for a lackey, and the thought added gall to his discomfiture. To be defeated in bold treachery was bad, but to stand condemned as a lying menial was bitter to a man's pride. For a second he tried to brazen it, but his overpowering vexation made him quail before her eyes.

But now the landlord spoke out in his harsh, obstinate voice,—

"You will get nae horse frae my stable, my leddy. I am a King's man, and will see you and your Prince in hell ere I stir a fit to help. Ye maun e'en gang further and try your luck, mistress."

"Do you refuse?" she cried. "Then, by Heaven, I will take it myself, and lash you round your own yard. I will burn the place over your head ere the week is out, and then you may have leisure to repent your incivility."

The fierce rhetoric of her tone cowed the recalcitrant host, but he had no time for a second thought. "Robin," she turned to her man, "you will get the horse while I wait here and talk to these gentlemen. But, see, give me your whip. I shall have need of it."

The fellow went, and she turned again to the three astounded spectators.

"Stop! What the—" cried the landlord, but she checked him with uplifted arm. "I have no ill-will to you," she said, "and would prevent you from doing yourself a hurt. I am the wife of the Secretary Murray, and you will find me hard to gainsay. So I beg you to keep out of my quarrel."

Then she turned once more to the pair with her intolerable scorn.

"And you are men," she cried, "made in the likeness of those who are fighting at this hour for their honour and King, while you cower in an alehouse and lay plots for women. But, bah! I waste words on you. Angry words are for men, but a whip for servants. You pair of dumb dogs, you will get a dog's punishment." And she struck Francis full in the face with her lash.

At the first crack of the whip, Starkie with the instinct of his kind made for the door, and had the fortune to escape. He had no stomach to encounter this avenging Amazon with her terrible beauty and cruel words. But Francis stood immovable, his mind crushed and writhing, his cheeks flaming with disgrace. This bright creature before him, with queenly air and her high tone of command, had tumbled his palace of cards about his ears. He felt with acid bitterness the full ignominy, the childish, servile shame of his position. The charm of her young beauty drove him frantic; her whole mien, as of a world unknown to him and eternally beyond his reach, mocked him to despair. For a moment he was the blacksmith's grandson, with the thought to rush forward, wrest the whip from her hands, and discomfit this proud woman with his superior strength. But some tincture of the Birkenshaw blood held him back. In that instant he knew the feebleness of his renunciation of virtue. Some power not himself forbade the extremes of disgrace,—some bequest from more gallant forbears, some lingering wisp of honour. He stood with bowed head, not daring to meet her arrogant eyes, careless of the lash which curled round his cheek and scarred his brow. Marvellous the power of that slender arm! He felt the blood trickle over his eyes and half blind him, but he scarce had a thought of pain.

Then she flung down the whip on the floor.

"Go," she cried, "I am done with you. You may think twice before you try the like again."

He moved dumbly to the door, and as he passed lifted his eyes suddenly to her face. Dimly he saw that her gaze was fixed on his bleeding forehead, and in her look he seemed to see a gleam of pity and at her mouth a quiver of regret. Then with crazy speed he ran blindly to the open moor.

CHAPTER VII.

Of a Lady on a Grey Horse.

The sun was far up in the sky and the world lay bathed in the clear light of noon. The long rough expanse of bog lay flat before him with its links of moss-pools and great hags of peat. But he ran as on open ground, leaping the water, springing from tussock to tussock of heather, with his cheeks aflame and his teeth set in his lips. He drove all thoughts from his mind; the bitterness of shame weighed upon him like a mount of lead; when he looked back at times and saw the inn still in view, the sight maddened him to greater speed. So keen was his discomfiture that he scarcely felt weariness, though he had been travelling for a day and a night, with no sleep. When at last he came to the limit of the desert and emerged on fields of turf he ran the faster, till a ridge of hill hid the hateful place from his sight, and he sank on the ground.

In a little he sat up, for though utterly tired, his whirling brain did not suffer him to rest. Now, when the scene of his disgrace was no more before his eyes, he strove to take the edge from his mental discomfort. Drearily he conjured back every detail, and for a little it seemed as if his shame would be driven out by the more bearable passion of anger. But the attempt failed lamentably. He had wholly lost his old sentiment of bravado; he saw his flimsy schemes wither before the bright avenging presence and himself a mere knavish servant in her eyes. In his misery the sight of her obstructed all his vision. At one moment he hated her with deadly vehemence; at the next he would have undergone all humiliation for a sight of her face. The inflated romance which had first driven him out on his travels was centred for the time on this one woman, and with it there followed the bitterness of despair.

Then he feebly clutched at his wits and set himself to review his position. It was black, black, without a tincture of hope. He had failed in his treachery, and something within him made him dimly conscious that this form of roguery was somehow or other shut to him henceforth. The rôle of the high-handed adventurer could not be his; even in a simple matter how dismally he had failed. And yet he could scarcely regret it, for at the moment the part had lost its charm. He must follow his first intentions and sail abroad, but with what altered hopes and spirit! For at that hour Mr. Francis Birkenshaw in his youth and strength felt that already he was verging on the dull confines of age. But with it all the thought of that foreign journey was unpleasing. He had ruined his life in his own land, but yet he was loth to leave it, for the vague sentiment which was working in his heart was all associated with this barren country and the impending wars. He had the sudden thought that his services might still be worth their price in either army, but again he found no comfort. King George's forces, alien in race and unglorified by any fantastic purpose, did not attract him; the other side was a dream, a chimæra, and moreover his breach of faith had cut him off from it for ever. An acceptable recruit he would appear, when Murray of Broughton was a leader!

So with hopeless purpose he set out over the well-tilled country for the shores of the Firth. This new ferment would make Edinburgh as safe for him as a foreign city, and it was an easier task to sail from the Firth than from a western port. He tried hard to recover his attitude of scorn for fate and firm self-confidence. But it was little use. No casuistry could persuade him to see his folly in a brighter light; he had lost his grip on the world, and now was driven about like a leaf where aforetime he had purposed to hew a path.

It was well on in the afternoon ere he struck a track, for he had taken his course at right angles to the main highway and found himself mazed in a country of sheepwalks. Thence the road ran down into a broad lowland vale, set with clumps of wood and smoking houses, with a gleam of water afar among low meadows. Autumn was tinging leaf and stalk, and her blue haze rimmed the farthest trees and the line of abrupt hills. But the golden afternoon had no soothing effect upon him; he saw all things in the light of his own grey future, and plodded on with bent head and weary footstep. The effects of his toil, too, were beginning to come over him, and he found himself at times dizzy and all but fainting. The few people he met—farmers with carts, packmen, and a half-dozen country lasses—looked curiously at the tall, dishevelled man with his weather-stained clothing.

He stopped no one to ask the way, for the road ran clear to the city, and at its high places gave a prospect of roofs and steeples against the silver of the Forth. But sleep overcame him before nightfall, and he had to content himself with a lodging in the nearest village.

This he found to be a straggling place with one great inn in the middle, and a little church in a wood of birches at the end. His limbs were so weary that he would fain have gone straight to the inn and found supper and a soft bed; but he reflected that he must husband his money and find humbler quarters in some shed of hay. But first he had need of meat, so to the inn-kitchen he went and ordered a modest meal, which he ate ravenously. The room was full of men, taling hastily in a rich haze of tobacco-smoke, and the stranger's entrance passed unnoticed. But Francis, weary as he was, could not keep from catching scraps of their conversation. In all a note of fear seemed dominant. Words—"the Hielandmen," "Chairlie," and a throng of ill-pronounced Gaelic names—occurred again and again till he was perforce roused to interest. Some great event must have happened since the morning, for the taking of Edinburgh was news already old. He touched the nearest speaker on the arm, and with his best politeness asked the cause of the uproar.

"Whaur d' ye come frae?" said the man, with the Lowland trick of answering with a new question.

"I'm frae the South," said Francis, "a wearty traivel I have had. But I've heard no word of anything, so I beg ye to tell me."

"Weel, it's just this. The lad they ca' the Prince has lickit Johnnie Cope and the redcoats the day at Prestonpans, and the hale land is like to be fou o' skirlin' Hielandmen."

Here was news. Francis' eye brightened, and he was for asking more. But the man had had enough of speaking to an ignorant stranger, and once more he was in the heat of debate, the subject apparently being an abstruse calculation of the time it would take this new power to give the land to the Pope.

"Sune," said a grave old man, "sune we'll see the fair eedifeece o' the Kirk coupit, and the whure o' Babylon, as ye micht say, uphaudin' her heid amang the ruins."

"Sune," said a Laodicean, "we'll see something mair serious, a wheen men wi' red heids and naething on but sarks routin' ilka decent man out o' house and hame."

Thereupon some eyes began to turn to Francis as the last comer and a probable centre of suspicion. His clothing marked him for higher quality than a countryman, and something ragged and desolate in his whole appearance might argue the Jacobite.

"What side are ye on, mannie?" one asked him.

"None. I am for my own hand," said Francis, truly, as he thought of his ill-fated incursion into high politics; and with brief good-night he rose to go.

The night had fallen with a great air of dew and freshness, and without in the village street the smoke smelled pleasantly in the nostrils, and the noise of the stream rose loud in the silence. From afar, as from the city, came an echo of a great stir, drums beating, maybe from the Castle, or the pipers playing briskly over the victory. The sense of his desolation, his folly, the ruin of his hopes, smote heavily on Francis in this starry quiet. And with it all his weariness was so deep that it all but drowned the other; and finding a shed at the village-end he lay down on a pillow of hay and was soon asleep.

He was wakened about nine in the morning by a heavy hand pulling at his coat. He stared sleepily and saw a man in the act of yoking a cart-horse, and another pulling his pillow from below his head. They were ready to abuse him for a gangrel, but something in his appearance as he rose stopped their tongues, and they gruffly assented as he gave them good-morning and went out to the open. Half a mile further on the road he bathed head and shoulders in a passing stream, and then, with some degree of freshness, set his face to the six mile road to the town. Again the day had risen fair, and all the way, beneath the ancient trees or through fields of old pasture, was fragrant with autumn scents. The electric air quickened him against his will, and he strode briskly along the curving highway till it dipped over a shoulder of hill to the city's edge.

That the place was in a ferment was clear from the din heard even at that distance,—the intermittent notes of bugles, the drone of pipes from different quarters, and at intervals the rattle of a drum. Francis found no guard set; doubtless in the great panic of the one party and the first jubilation of the other precautions had not yet entered men's minds. The cluster of little hamlets which lay around the city's extremities seemed quiet and desert; doubtless all and sundry were even now adding their share to the main confusion. But when once he had entered the streets there was a different tale to tell. Never before had he seen the Highland dress on any number of men, and now the sight of bright tartans and fierce dark faces, as with a great air of triumph Macdonalds and Camerons hastened along the causeway, affected him with wonder and delight. The honest burgesses wore woful countenances, as they saw trade gone and gains lessened. The graver and more religious deplored the abomination at street corners in muffled tones for fear of the passing victors; while the younger sort, to whom the whole was a fine stage play, talked excitedly of the deeds of yesterday, the tales which rumour had already magnified. Francis heard names occur in the snatches of talk, names of Grants, Thrieplands, and Ogilvies, linked with stories of daring. The ferment was too high to admit of formalities, and each man joined the first group of strangers and bore his part in the frightened gossip. In this way he heard the tale of the fleeing band of dragoons racing for the Castle with a single Highlandman at their heels, of the gate shut in his face and his defiant dirk stuck in the oaken panels. Confused tales of rank Hanoverian cowardice, the superhuman daring of the Prince's men, were diversified with wild speculating on the ultimate course of things. The Prince was already on his way to the capital, and in twelve hours the world would be turned topsy-turvy.

In all the stir Francis found himself in the position of a melancholy alien. He had no share in this triumph, no share even in the consolation of defeat. In all this babble of great deeds and brave men he must remain untouched, for had he not failed lamentably alike in loyalty and knavery? He was a mere popinjay, a broken reed, and to his unquiet sight there lurked a sneer in every passer's eye as if they divined his worthlessness. The man grew acutely miserable. This was his own city, his home; somewhere in this place his mother and sisters dwelled; the streets were sprinkled with his aforetime comrades. And he loathed them all: at the mere thought of his boyhood with its dreams of future bravado and its puerile vices, he sickened with disgust. Indeed this honest gentleman was fast approaching that attitude towards life which ends in its renouncement.

He drifted aimlessly to the end of the town where the streets were thronged to meet the coming army. The Camerons, who had marched straight from the battle, were there to meet them, and a host of great ladies and little lords with the Jacobite favours on their breasts and knots of white ribbon at bridle and sword-hilt. Even as he stood staring with lacklustre eyes at the sight, there rose through the lower gate the brisk music of the pipes and the tread of many men. No music has so dominant a note, and yet few are so adaptable. In the hour of death it rises and falls like the wail of a forlorn wind, at a feast it has the drunken gaiety of a Bacchante, and in the lost battle from it there comes the final coronach of vain endeavour. But in triumph it is supreme, a ringing call to action, a pæan over the vanquished, the chant of the heroic. Now with its note went the tramp of feet and the clatter of horses' hooves, and then up the narrow street came the dusty, war-stained conquerors. A cry of welcome went up from God-fearing citizen and ragged Jacobite alike, for in that moment creeds and practice were forgotten in the common homage to bravery.

But Francis had no eyes for the lines of brown-faced men or the stained and ragged tartans. Among the bright crowd which greeted them were many whom he knew from old days, wits and gentlemen of the town, ladies of fashion, names linked with many tales. In some eyes shone the mere pleasure in a gallant show, some were wild with enthusiasm, some in a caustic humour. My Lord Craigforth kept up running comments with Mrs. Cranstoun of Gair, and the young and witty Miss Menteith chattered to Lady Manorwater with a vivacity too sharp for enthusiasm. Young gentlemen with French elegance in their dress flicked the dust from their cravats, and smiled with gracious condescension to popular feeling. But others—rosy old lairds from the South and the dark retinue of Highland gentlemen—wore a different air. As the tune of "The King shall enjoy his own again"—a catch long hummed in secret—rose clear and loud in the open street, their feelings rose beyond control, and with tears running down their cheeks those honest enthusiasts joined their prayers for the true King.

But with Lady Manorwater rode another, whom Francis' eyes followed till she was lost in the thickening crowd. She sat her grey horse and gazed on the advancing troops with eyes so honestly earnest, shining with such clear delight, that the throng on the causeway whispered her name with something like affection. Her bridle and trappings were decked with knots of white ribbon, and on her heart was pinned a cockade of white roses. The face above the dark velvet riding-cloak seemed pale with weariness,—or was it excitement?—and her hand visibly trembled on the rein. The mark of her lash was still on Francis' cheek, but the sting on his soul smarted a thousand-fold worse. Had she been gay and lively, he would have hated her like death, this woman who had mocked him. But her white face and the glory in her eyes affected him with a sentiment too elusive for words,—a compound of pity and a hopeless emulation of a rare virtue.

He turned from the show down a little alley, and ran as if from the avenger. Soon he came to more empty streets which the people had deserted for the sight of the entering army. He felt himself starving, so at a very little tavern he ordered a meal. But the food choked him, and he left the dish almost untasted. He had no mind to think out a future course, for, at the present, emotion had broken down the last battlements of sober reason. Soon the street grew full again, and he had to bear the scrutiny of many eyes. He had no design in his walking; all he sought was to crush the hot pain of discomfiture which gnawed his heart. Once the coolest and most fearless, he grew as nervous as a woman. He fancied his life lay open like a book to every chance passer; and he detected scorn in idly curious eyes. Sometimes he passed a face he knew, but he waited for no recognition. His whole past life was so hateful to his thoughts that he shunned anything that might recall it. In his wanderings he passed by old haunts of his own, yea, under the very windows of his mother's house. But old memories had no place in his mind; the dissolution of a scheme of life had crushed out the circumstances of his past. He had room merely for a bitter thought on the farce of this return to his native town; and then his mind was back once more in the dulness of regret.

Toward evening the stir died down, and save for the sight of armed men and the excited talk of street-corners, he felt himself back in the Edinburgh of his youth. His misery only grew the more intolerable, but it seemed to shape to a purpose. He might yet redeem all and play a manful part in life. He had tried the rôle of the adventurer and failed; there yet remained the more difficult path of honour. The portrait of the lady which filled his mind seemed not wholly adamant. He had a dim remembrance of a gleam of pity at the inn, and the white light of enthusiasm at the pageant of the morning. He thought upon his first meeting at the House of Broughton, and her graciousness, which then had roused his bitterness, seemed now his one hope of salvation. Before his pride had been his manliest attribute; now he realised clearly and mournfully that the time had come to humble himself to virtue. It was a grievous thought to the arrogant nature, but as he wandered through the streets in the late afternoon he was compelled inexorably to submit. And as a purpose shaped itself his humility grew deeper, till it brought him to unconditional surrender.

In the High Street he asked of a Highlander the way to the lodging of Murray of Broughton. The man told him, adding that the Secretary was with the Prince at the Palace of Holyrood. The news gave him hope, and in the September dusk he found the house-door with its watchful sentinel. Even now Francis' appearance was not discreditable: his clothes were good though sore worn, and he had just the figure that a poor loyalist would bear whose intentions were better than his fortunes. So the guard suffered him to pass, and the serving-man led him down a dark passage to a hall of some size and elegance. He was told that the Secretary's wife did much of her husband's work, often meeting the throng of visitors who crowded at all hours to the house. Now he was taken for one of those, and the servant opened a door and let him enter.

He found himself in a long dining-room wainscotted in brown oak, and lit by a blazing fire on the hearth. Two candles burned faintly on a table, where sat a lady poring over a great map. She started at his entrance, and then lifting a candle came forward to scan his face. Meantime he was in a pitiable state of fear. He who had once been cool and self-possessed beyond the ordinary, now felt his knees sinking beneath him. Keenly and cruelly he felt the measure of his degradation, and the last rag of pride fell from the skeleton of his hopes.

She glanced at his face and stepped back. Wrath entered her eyes, to be straightway replaced by sheer perplexity. She looked again at the haggard figure before her, waiting for some word to explain his presence. But his tongue was tied, his speech halted and stammered, and he could only look with entreating eyes.

"And what is your errand, sir?" she asked. "Has Lord Manorwater discharged you? I have not yet had time to tell him of your villainy, but doubtless he has found it out elsewhere."

The words, with the sting of a lackey's reproach, were the needed stimulant to Francis' brain.

"I am no servant," he said, and then hurriedly and brokenly he stammered a word of confession.

The lady drew back with angry eyes.

"And you dare to come to me and tell me this!" she cried. "I had thought it was but greed and a servant's temptation, and now you cut off your own apology and confess yourself doubly a liar. Do you think to get anything for this penitence? Do you think that the Prince has open arms for all the rabble of the earth? Or do you wish to frighten a woman?" And she laid her hand on a pistol, and stood erect and angry like a tragedy queen.

"I seek nothing," said Francis, with a groan. "God knows I am not worth your thought."

"You value yourself well, Mr. What's-your-name. If I had known you as I know you now, no lash of mine would have touched you. A whipping is for a servant's fault, which may yet be forgiven. But for such as yours ... And you are made in the likeness of a proper man," and a note of wonder joined with her contempt.

The wretched Francis stood with bowed head beneath this tempest of scorn. The words fell on dulled ears. His own shame was too heavy on his mind to allow of a poignant feeling. He felt like some ineffectual knocker at a barred door, some vanquished invader trying to scale a hostile parapet. By his own folly he had fallen to a place for ever apart from this proud woman's ken. He could but cry for pity like a child.

Then she cut short reproaches and looked at him keenly. Perhaps something in his face or his hopeless eyes struck a chord of pity. "What may be your name?" she asked, "if you say you are no servant."

He told her shortly, though the words burned his lips.

"Birkenshaw," she cried. "Of the Yarrow Birkenshaws?" And then she fell to musing, looking up at him ever and again with curious eyes. "I have heard the name. Maybe even it is kin to my own. I have heard the name as that of a great and honourable house. And you have lived to defile it!" And for a little she was silent.

"I would to God," she spoke again, "that you had been Lord Manorwater's lackey."

The man said nothing. Deep hidden in his nature was a pride of race and name, the stronger for its secrecy. Now he saw it dragged forth and used as the touchstone for his misdeeds. It was the sharpest weapon in the whole armoury of reproach. For one second he wished himself back in his old temper of mind. Why had he thus debased his manhood to the frigid and finicking virtue of a woman? Not till he looked again at the face of his inquisitor did he find justification for his course.

Again she spoke, but in an altered voice, and Francis seemed to read a hint of mercy.

"No," she said, "I was wrong. I am glad you are no lackey. Had you been but a lying servant there had been no room for repentance. But you come of honest folk, you have honest blood in your veins. Gentlemen are none so common that one should be lost in the making." And she twined her fingers, deep in meditation, looking to the fire with a face from which all anger had departed.

Francis' clouded soul cleared at this dawn of hope. He watched the pale woman with the marvellous eyes and hair, and a sudden wild exaltation shook him. Sufficient, more than sufficient for him to do the bidding of this great lady who had drawn him from the depths.

"Take me," he cried. "I am weak and foolish. I have no more sense than a bairn, and I have done the Devil's work with an empty head. But I swear that this is by and done with."

"You have made ill work of it in the past, Mr. Birkenshaw," said the lady. "Will you serve the Prince well, think you, if you have been false to me?"

"I can say nought," said Francis, "but I beseech you to give me trial." And then with a touch of old bravado he added, "I am a man who has seen much and can turn my hands and head to many purposes. I will prove myself worth the trusting."

The lady frowned and tapped with her fingers on the table, looking over his head to the wall beyond. "You have much to learn," she said gently. "Do you think it is any merit in your services which would make me take you for the Prince?" Then, as if to herself, "It is raw stuff, but it would be a Christian act to help in the shaping of it to honesty."

Then with a sudden impulse she walked straight up to him and looked in his eyes. "Lay your hand on mine," she said, "and swear. It is the old oath of my house, maybe, too, of your own. Swear to be true to your word, your God, and your King, to flee from no foe and hurt no friend. Swear by the eagle's path, the dew, and the King's soul."

"I swear," he said, his hand shaking like a leaf as it touched her slender wrist.

"Now you had better leave me," she said. "Maybe I have done wrong. I am but a weak woman, and the heart should be steeled for the high business which presses on the land. Yet you have sworn, and I have given you my trust. If you will come to-morrow morning you will learn my bidding."

BOOK TWO

CHAPTER VIII.

The Journey to the North.

In the autumn dusk Mr. Francis Birkenshaw rode down a path of mountain gravel into the glen of a little stream. Behind him were the flat meadows of his own country, with coiling waters and towns smoking in woody hollows. The sea lined the horizon with a gleam as of steel; and, fretted faintly against hillside and sky, all but vanishing into the evening haze, rose the spires and turrets of the city he had left. From the prosperous cornfields five miles back the way had risen slowly to the crest of a ridge, whence it turned sharply down to a cavernous mountain vale, which seemed to lead sheer into the heart of a gloomy land. All about were acres of dark hills, ribbed, curved, and channelled by myriad water-courses, forcing sharp peaks into the sunset or falling back in dismal lines to the east and north. Down the affronting cleft a storm was coming, and even as he looked it burst upon him, and he was cloaked in mist and rain.

He had ridden hard from Edinburgh since the early morn with the speed of a zealous messenger. On the day before, when he had gone to the Murrays' lodging, he had been tried with many questions, and then trusted with a message which even he, all untrained in the arts of war, knew to be of high import. His courage had all but failed him; he had stammered modest excuses; and then, heartened by bright eyes and brave words, accepted his commission with diffident if resolute purpose. With a smile and a face in his memory he had ridden out on the morning of this day into the new world for him but two nights old. Never before had he felt such lightness of heart. The September sunrise had been a masque of purple and gold, the clear air a divine ether. Once more he had found a standing-ground from which to view the world; he could look frankly in each passer's eyes; and behind all was a woman's face in the gallery of his heart to comfort his travelling.

The thought of the complexity and peril of his mission was scarcely present. That was still in the far future. Meantime there was the fervour of hope recovered, a fervour still stung at intervals by flickers of old pride, and stronger still the half-pharisaic feeling which springs from a dawning virtue. He had no thoughts; the tumult of his feelings left no space for the clearer emotions. But the sense of wild adventure was strong upon him. He was venturing on an errand of war into a land as little known to him as the steppes of Tartary. And the eternal memory of the lady freshened his fancy till youth returned once more to the broken man who had two days before been at the feet of fate. So with blithe heart he crossed the Firth by the Alloa ferry, where sea breeze and land breeze strive with the widening river, and took his path for the wall of mystic northern hills.

But now, as a darker country closed in on him, the strangeness began to weigh on his spirits. He was lowland bred, and, with all his boasted experience, a traveller within but narrow limits. Moors he knew, the soft comely deserts which line Yarrow and Tweed and break ever into green vales and a land of meadows. But this was something new,—this everlasting bleak land, where God's hand seemed to have placed no order. The stormy afternoon made the sight wilder, and all around him birds cried so constantly and so shrilly that the wilderness seemed to have taken to itself a voice. But soon his natural ardour rose triumphant to the influence of weather. All was but part of this new course, instinct with fierce adventure, a list for the conquest of haughty hearts. As the cold of evening grew, and heavy shadows fell on his path, he exulted in the mystery of his errand. He saw the long hillsides on either hand, grey with banks of rock and rough with birken tangles, down which at times came the cry of a fox or the cruel scream of a hawk. Little lochs were passed, framed in the ebony of black bogs or edged with dolorous rushes. All was strange, uncanny; and as he looked keenly for the light which should tell him of his journey's end and relief from the craggy path, he felt the joy of the crusader, the wanderer on a reputable errand.

But somewhere on the high hills a storm had gathered, and hurrying from mist-filled tarns choked the strait glens with sleet. It caught the traveller full in the face, and in a trice had him soaked to the bone. This was all that was needed to give the final exhilaration to his spirits. Gaily he urged his horse, wrapping his cloak about his shoulders and lowering his head to bide the brunt. It stung his face to fire, and sent the blood coursing through every vein. The man gloried in his strength. He cried defiance to all powers of weather, and thought lovingly on himself in this rôle of doughty knight-errant. Then through the sheer-falling water a light gleamed, all rayed like a star through the sleety veil; the way grew smoother; and Francis was aware of his lodging for the night.

Ere he had dismounted and stretched his legs, a throng of all ages and descriptions with lights of many sizes gathered about him. The place was small and the door narrow, and in contrast with the sharp out-of-doors the air smelled hot and close. Dazed like an owl, he stumbled down two steps into a wide low room, where some dozen men sat drinking round the fire or eating supper at a table. A fire of peat burned in the middle and the air was thick with a blue smoke, which gusts from a broken window were ever blowing aside. The inmates were all in Highland dress, save one man who was still at supper,—a florid and stout gentleman of middle age in knee-breeches and a dark-blue coat. Room was made for Francis on the settle by his side, and a meal placed before him.

With keen appetite he fell to his supper, looking often and curiously at his companions. The place reeked of food and drink and generous living. In a corner stood a great anker of whisky with a spigot, whence the

Highlanders replenished their glasses. A barrel of sugar with a small spade in it was by its side, and on the peats the water boiled for toddy. It was a good lodging for men who were fresh from wild, cold journeying, for such had no mind to mark the filth which was everywhere, the slatternly look of the maids, the exceeding dirtiness of the company. The Highlanders were all tall men, with gaunt dark faces and ragged tartans. One of them, smaller in stature, wore the trews instead of the kilt and seemed a thought more decent and presentable. They talked rapidly among themselves in Gaelic, and ever and again one would raise a catch, while the whole motley crew would join in. It was with some relief that Francis turned from watching them to the comfortable figure at his side. He caught the man's eye, and they gravely gave each other good-evening. Clearly he was a person of consequence, for his dress was good, and his rosy face had the tight lips and clean chin of the man used to give orders and be obeyed.

"It's a coarse day for a journey, sir," said he. "Ye'll be going south to Edinburgh?"

"Even so," said Francis, "and I hope to have the pleasure of your convoy on the road to-morrow." This personage had the look of a Whig, and there was no need to enlighten him.

"I am at your service," said the elder man, with a twinkling eye. Francis caught the twinkle and put a stricter bridle upon his tongue.

"I hear," said he again, "that there are stirring times in Edinburgh. We country folk in the north hear nocht of a thing till it's bye."

Francis saw the guile and checked the natural desire of the well informed to make a present of his knowledge to every inquirer. "I've heard something like it," he said, "but we'll not be long in hearing the truth. How long do you call in from here to the town?"

The other's rosy cheeks grew rosier with suppressed amusement. "That was the very question I was on the point of asking you myself," he said. "But go on with your supper, sir, and do not let me hinder a hungry man."

Francis ate with sidelong glances at his companion, who had lit a short pipe and smoked vigorously. Once and again he met his eyes, and both smiled. Truly this game of hide and seek was becoming amusing. Then he fell to studying the image of the man's looks as pictured in memory. Some hint of a likeness struck him; these lineaments, that figure, were known to him. Carefully he traced the web of his recollections, but could find no thread. Doubtless he had seen him in the old Edinburgh days, but where? when? He had all but finished his meal when a sudden lift of his comrade's arm, a motion to set right his cravat, furnished the key to the mystery. He had mind of days in the Parliament House, when he, the lawyer's clerk, took notes and papers to the great lawyers. Softly he whistled to himself, blinking with amazement.

The Lord President! So far, so good; he had the advantage of his companion; doubtless the famous Mr. Duncan Forbes had no wish to be recognised in this Highland tavern.

"It's a wild night," said Francis. "Had ye a hard day's riding?"

"Dub and mire," said the other. "Ye're splashed yourself, so ye ken the state of the roads."

"I think I had a glisk of ye five mile back at the bridge-end," hazarded the bold Francis.

"Maybe so. I had a mettle beast, and took the road well."

"Ay," said Francis, meditatively, "it's a lang dreary road to Culloden," and he looked innocently at his neighbour.

The man raised his eyebrows a trifle and bowed. "It appears," he said, "that my name and designation are better kenned in the land than I had thought. Ye have the advantage of me, Mr. ——"

"Robertson," said the other. "Mr. George Robertson, merchant in the Pleasaunce of Edinburgh, returning from transacting some business in the north."

Francis had overshot himself, and the man smiled. "I am at your service, Mr. Robertson of the Pleasaunce. Your name and trade do credit to your honesty and your own pretty fancy," and with a sly glance he knocked the ashes from his pipe.

The ground was dangerous, and Francis sheered away. Moreover, the rest of the company were fast approaching the state of maudlin good-fellowship which follows the pugnacious. The smell of hot drink was grateful in his nostrils after the bitter wind, and he was in a cheerful mood at the discomfiture of his neighbour. He filled a great jug with the piping spirits, and drank deeply to some chance toast. The stuff was raw but fiery, and it sensibly quickened his vivacity. Memories came back of old tavern nights in his boyhood. The smell of the place, the uproarious company fostered the impression, and for a little rough hilarity seemed the extreme of joy. The man's mind was elated by the day's ride, and still more by the sudden rebound from black despair. His animal boisterousness, always at hand in his nature, was beginning to assert itself under the influence of keen air and this northern whisky. He filled Mr. Forbes's glass till the rosy gentleman cried a truce, and toasted him with clinking bowls. Then he grew friendly with the others at the table. The little man in the trews made the first overtures to friendship by coming over to the pair, bowing with profound if drunken gravity, and asking them for their commands. Francis received him as a brother, and ere he knew, found himself singing riotously among the ragged Highlanders. Toasts in Gaelic were drunk with such generous frequency that Mr. Francis Birkenshaw, who had not been drunk above three times in his previous life, who had only that morn been a very storehouse of high sentiments, who was even now pluming himself on a diplomatist's wisdom, became gloriously drunk.

It is the nemesis of a vagrant youth that when at a later time the keynote is struck of some one of these youthful follies the maturer nature instinctively responds. The mere flavour of good-fellowship had brought him to a condition of which he would have been heartily ashamed even in his earliest lawlessness. Once more he was the vicious boy; his tongue was loosed, and he drew from the rich storehouse of his former experience. Soon the wild talk of the company had been raised to a pitch of indecent blasphemy which before it had wholly failed to attain; and the Highlanders, imperfect as was their English, looked with awe and reverence on this young spirit whose speech was even as the common sewer. Gaelic and English alternating filled the place with a din like Bedlam, while ever and anon some loyalist sentiment gave a chance for maudlin tears.

In a sudden spasm of such feeling the company waxed political. "Drink, gentlemen," cried Francis, "to the only King, the only Prince, and the only Cause. Drink good luck to all honest fellows who take their sword in their hand and their plaid on their back when their master bids them. May the dirty Germans be sent packing and our ain lad sit in St. James'."

All rose with wild cries and breaking glass, and a shrill Gaelic song, wild as a gled's scream, rasped through the place. All save one,—the sober Mr. Forbes, who sat smiling and self-possessed in his chimney-corner.

Then arose Long John of the Dow Glen with his broken speech. "There iss a man, a fat Southron of a man, who will not trink to the goot causs. By Heaven, he will get something mair in hiss guts than fusky, if he toes not." Robin Mactavish and Hamish the Black added like comments. The little man with the trews was too far gone to speak, but he waved a threatening glass.

Francis had still the wits to refrain from shouting the dissenter's name. But he called on him to drink to the King, or he, Mr. Francis Birkenshaw, would know the reason.

"I will drink a toast, Mr. Robertson (or is it Mr. Birkenshaw?)," said the man, and he rose slowly to his feet. "Gentlemen all," he cried, "I drink—to all good intentions."

The words sounded satisfactory and a great shout was the reply, as each man interpreted the toast into the tongue of his own sentiments.

But Francis was little content. "Ye're a Whig," he cried, "a smooth-spoken whigamore, unfit for the company of honest gentlemen." And he turned on him with the abuse of the stable-yard.

For a second the two were left alone, for a debate had arisen between Robin the Piper and him of the Dow Glen, which distracted the others. The elder man looked at his drunken opponent with angry and pitiful eyes.

"Your speech, sir," he said, "is most filthy and shameful. You belong to the wrong side, and I am glad of it, for it would be a disgrace for the right party to have you. But you have women in your cause whose memory should bridle your tongue. I know naught of you or your business, but it little becomes a man to thus forget himself, when he is of the same persuasion as so many honest ladies."

"You have spoken the word, sir," said Francis. "And now I propose that you join me in drinking to the best and bonniest. Gentlemen," he cried, "I give you the toast of the bonny Mrs. Murray."

The whole tipsy company caught at the name and drank deep to the health of the famous lady, some calling her by her strange Gaelic name, which meant "the dew of April." In the wildest glens of the north the story was told of her beauty, and she was as often on loyal lips as the Prince himself. So with all the good-will in the world the tipsy crew cried her name, while Mr. Forbes sat gloomily and angrily silent.

* * * * *

Francis awoke the next morning with a burning head and a heart from which all gaiety had gone. He dressed with woe-begone leisure and came into the kitchen rubbing weary eyes. The place was quiet utterly; about the door hens were clucking, a great hum of the farm-yard was in the air, and through the open entrance he saw the high steep shoulder of a hill. The company of the night before had gone early; in some haste he looked about for the Lord President, but he too had departed. He went out of doors and smelt the fresh air of morn. The rain had gone, and the whole narrow vale was bright with sun and swollen water. But the sky warned him that he had slept late, so he cried for the hostess. She came wiping her hands, a miracle of dirty unkemptness. Where had the others gone, he asked. "Ach, their own ways. She kent nocht of the folk that cam to her publick. She was only a poor woman, fightin' to keep body and saul together in evil days. All had left early, even the old man that was sae prawly drest." Francis plied her with irritable questions on the way he had taken. But the woman was trusty; Whig or Jacobite were nought to her, she would tell nothing of her guests; and to aid her pious resolution she discovered opportunely that she knew no more English than the barest smattering.

So he must needs take things as he found them, breakfast on eggs, pay a modest lawing, and ride off in a violent ill-humour. The memory of the night's doings still rankled in his heart. He had forfeited all claim to that character which he had fairly thought he had attained to. He had slipped back to the worst days of his youth, and got drunk in the company of filthy barbarians. The figure of the Lord President added bitterness to his reflections. The man of the world, the true man of affairs, had despised him as a lecherous boy. He pictured his own tipsy abandonment, his talk, his maudlin jests, all watched with the keen eye of the greatest man in the country. The shame of the thing made him cry out and curse his fortune.

But the gall of the matter was his toasting of his mistress. In his sober hours the very speaking of her name in such a company and such a place seemed the sheerest blasphemy. And the circumstances of the toast, the drunken laughter, the foul talk, the brazen defiance of all decency, made the crime more heinous. In a common alehouse he had insulted, grossly insulted, the name of her who had given him a reason to live. He reviewed every scene in his drama where she had entered,—the midnight raid on the House of Broughton, the tragic farce at the inn, the sight of the lady on the grey horse in the street of Edinburgh, and finally that strange meeting in her own house where he had seen the full nakedness of his own soul. The memory of her face nigh drove him frantic. He was riding on her errand, and, lo! he had betrayed her cause at the very outset.

But with the progress of the day his mind grew quieter. The more poignant shame died down, leaving only a regret. The weather was clear and bright, autumn without storm and heaviness. The road rose slowly from the straiter glens to a high table-land, where shallow vales marked the extreme upland waters of young rivers. A wide country lay bare to the view, all alike rough with wood and heather; while in the distance a circle of dark mountains made a barrier as of some great amphitheatre. The place had a soothing effect upon his spirits. Something in the moorland peace, the quiet of these endless fields of heather where deer couched and wild birds nested, brought ease and some sanity of mind. To the man who knew only the city wynds or the shrill-sounding beaches of Fife, this untilled land had an exquisite and elemental freshness, as of the primeval world.

At a turn in the road he saw a rider before him not a quarter of a mile ahead. He drew back and stared. Something in the figure and carriage were familiar. The man was riding in a hurry, for he used his whip frequently and with vigour. Then recollection came to Francis, and in spite of his gloom he had almost laughed. This was indeed the Lord President Forbes on his way to his house of Culloden, doubtless on some sudden business of state. The man's composure was almost restored. Clearly the great statesman feared him; he had been at the pains to deceive him and rise early to outwit him. Strange are the crannies of our nature; for it is a fact that the sight lessened Francis' self-loathing and the bitterness of Mr. Forbes' reproof. After all, he was still of some consequence in the world, and though his heart was repentant it was remorse without pain.

CHAPTER IX.

My Lord of Lovat.

That night he lay at a wretched cottage by the wayside where the hill-air came through the gaps in the heather roof and made the sleeper shiver on his couch of grass. The land was now a mere chaos of black mountains, and the road, which at first had borne some likeness to a highway, was now sunk to an ill-marked scar through the moss. It made heavy riding, and through the next day our traveller felt more weary than he cared to own. Had not the sun been bright and the weather dry, he might have missed the track utterly, for the bogs which lay among the hills were hard to wrestle through. At evening he was fain to stop at a hut which lay on the side of a long hill called Corryarrick, up which the road went in corkscrew fashion for half a score of miles. The man of the place gave him some kind of oaten porridge and a raw whisky which burned his palate, and told him many details of his way. This, it appeared, was still the country of the Athole Stewarts, but over the affronting hills began the lands of Stratherick and the domain of the Frasers. The fellow had little good to say of them; nay, by his account they were a clan of gruesome savages hated of God and their neighbours. So it was with some foreboding that Francis at the next dawning set his horse's face to the ascent.

All that day he rode in a bleak land, where wild tracts of moss with shining lochs scattered athwart them were frowned on by murky hills. And, to make the road worse, the place was scarred with horrific ravines running to the westward, at whose bottom foamed impetuous rivers. At the best they were spanned by rough bridges of tree trunks and heather, but more than once there was nothing for it but to make the steep descent and breast the waters. The day was still cloudless, but what with many wettings and the hardships of the path Francis fell into a dismal frame of mind. No human dwelling relieved the inhospitable waste, his store of provisions failed, and, to crown all, his horse fell lame at the crossing of a burn and had to be led heavily through the hags.

In the late afternoon three men arose as if from the bowels of the earth, and laid hands on horse and man. As it chanced, this was the best thing that could have happened, for they were men of Lovat's own clan in Stratherick, filthy, thieving rascals, but loyal to their lord. So it fell out that when they had plied Francis with unintelligible Gaelic, one, more learned than the rest, asked his name and business in a travesty of English. He replied that he sought the house of Macshimei at Castle Dounie, for so he had been told to speak of the head of the clan. The bare word was enough for the men, who straightway became friendly and set to relieve his wants. They dressed his horse's knee with a concoction of herbs, bandaging it after a fashion of their own, and led Francis to a cluster of cabins on the edge of a long loch. Here they gave him meat,—roast moor-fowl and eggs and a more palatable kind of bread, with a glass of excellent brandy. And in the morning one undertook to guide him past the narrows of the loch and set him well on his way to his destination.

When in the afternoon he crossed the river which formed the outlet of the lake, he found himself on the confines of a pleasant country. Set like an oasis among the stormy deserts lay meadows and haughlands and a fringe of woods, while beyond gleamed a quiet stretch of sea. The place was green and habitable, and on Francis's wearied eyes it fell like a glimpse of an Arcady. He could scarce believe his senses, for this looked more like the Lothians or the cornlands of Fife. But the high brown towers of the castle rising from the seaward slope and the bald scarp of Lovat on a cape in the Firth told of a chieftain's dwelling. The sky was darkening towards evening as he rode to the great pile, and his heart almost misgave him. He was on a nicely diplomatic errand, one, too, not without its peril. The man who dwelled there was one of the most famous names in the land, ill-reputed for lawlessness and treachery, notorious for a wit too subtle for prosaic earth. Who was he, a raw, unlettered vagrant, to meet such an one face to face and teach him his business? He was tired to death, too, with his moorland journey, and his brain was half clouded with sleep.

There was no guard at the gate,—nothing save two unkempt serving-men quarrelling over a jug of ale. They asked his business with a high gravity and led him into a damp courtyard where children squalled and serving-women chattered. The informality of such a place restored Francis to self-confidence, and he followed his guides with an assured step. A noise of rackety mirth fell on his ear, and he was ushered into the great dining-hall of the castle, where some fifty and more men sat at meat. The air was thick with the fumes of wine and hot dishes, bare-footed gillies ran hither and thither, and it took no extraordinarily acute eye or nostril to perceive that the place was exceeding dirty. At the lower end of the great table a crowd of ragged and dishevelled men quarrelled and scrambled for bones and offal. Thence there seemed to rise degrees of respectability from the common herd who supped on sheep-heads and whisky to the more honoured, the lesser gentry of the clan, who had good beef and mutton and plenty of claret. At the very top sat the lord himself with his more distinguished friends, Frasers of Gortuleg, Phopachy, and Byerfield, eating French dishes and drinking many choice wines. One of the ragged servants went to the chief's ear and whispered as he had been bidden, "Mr. Francis Birkenshaw with a message from Mr. Murray of Broughton;" and straightway room was made for the traveller at the honourable end of the table.

The cooking was of the finest, and Francis appeased his hunger with great satisfaction. No notice of him was taken by his neighbours to left and right, but each listened to his lord's pleasantries with the anxious care of the retainer. From the great man himself Francis could not keep his eyes, and in the pauses of the meal he found himself narrowly watching the mighty figure lolling in his carven arm-chair. Already beyond the confines of old age, an ungainly form with legs swollen with the gout and a huge rolling paunch, he lay in his seat like a mere drunken glutton. But when the eye passed from his body to the ponderous face and head, the mind drew his nature in different colours. The brow was broad and wrinkled with a thousand lines, hanging heavy over his eyes and fringed with great grey eyebrows. The thick fleshy nose, the coarse lips, the flaccid grey cheeks, were all cast in lines of massive strength, and the jaw below the cunning mouth was hard as if cut in stone. But the most notable point in the man was the pair of little eyes, still keen as a ferret's, and cruel in their resolute blue. He ate ravenously, and drank scandalously of every wine, keeping all the while a fire of compliments and jocularities, coarse as the gutter, at which the obedient assembly roared.

By and by, and not for a good hour, the feast came to an end, and the old lord was lifted from his seat by two servants. "Gentlemen," he cried, "there will be supper here in a matter of two hours, beefsteaks and claret for all that wish them. See that no man goes empty out of this house of Dounie. For mysel', ye see that the infirmities of age creep over me, and the thrang o' many cares compels me to quit ye. Guid e'en to ye, friends, guid fare and a safe returning." And he hobbled away, leaning heavily on his bearers.

After his departure the table was turned into a scene of riot, all shouting in Gaelic, drinking strange toasts and quarrelling at times in pairs and threes. Francis felt sadly out of place in a company where he was known to none and heard nothing but a strange language. So when a gillie touched his sleeve and bade him follow, for "ta great Macshimei wad speak with him," he rose gladly and left the reeking hall. The man led him into another room furnished with some approach to comfort, where rugs of deerskin covered the nakedness of the stone floor; thence into a passage which led to a narrow stone stair; and finally stopped at the entrance to a little turret-room. With an air of deep secrecy he tapped twice, and then with a flourish opened the door and showed Francis in, crying the announcement, "To speak with ta Lord Lovat."

The place was little and bright, with a cheerful fire and a long couch of skins. So thick were the walls, so narrow the space, that Francis felt himself secluded from the world. The chief lay stretched out with his feet to the blaze, a little black table with wine at his elbow. He looked up sharply at the entrance, and then stared once more into the fire as Francis came forward and stood before him. After a little he raised his head. "Young man," he said, "I pray you sit down. See to your ain comfort. Ye are admitted to a private and secret audience with a man who is not accessible to all. I trust ye have the sense to value your preevilege."

Francis bowed in some confusion. The look of arrogant strength in this strange old man crushed his spirits. He sorely distrusted his own wits in contest with this rock of iron.

"Ye will have a letter from the secretary?"

"Indeed, no," said Francis, "for the matter is somewhat too long for a letter. It is a thing for a discussion, my lord, and not for a scrawl on paper."

The old man looked grimly at the speaker. "And who are you in God's name," he rasped out, "that is thocht worthy to come and treat wi' me?—me, the first lord in the Hielands, the friend o' princes."

"My name is Francis Birkenshaw, at your service," said the other, conscious that those shrewd eyes were scanning every line in his face, every thread in his garments.

Once more his catechist plied him. "Are ye gentrice?" he asked.

At this some heat came into Francis' blood, and he answered warmly, "I am even as yourself, my lord. My descent is none so regular, but I have the name and blood of a gentleman."

Lovat frowned crossly, for the scandals of his family were common talk. "Ye have a ready tongue in your head, sir, but ye are somewhat lacking in respect. So ye are one of Murray's packmen?"

He waited for an answer, but Francis held his peace. "Ay," he went on, "a deeficult, dangerous job. Murray's a shilpit body, a keen man for his ain guid, but without muckle penetration. But his wife—weel, d' ye ken his wife?"

"I have the honour of her acquaintance," said Francis, stiffly.

"Have ye indeed?" said Lovat, smiling. "A fine woman, then, I can tell ye, sir. A bonny bitch! A speerity licht sort o' body!" and he looked from below his eyebrows to see the effect of his words.

"If you will pardon me, sir," said Francis, "I fail to see your point. You are talking of the character of those with whom I have nothing to do. Be assured I did not ride over your wet hills to indulge in moral disquisitions."

The man laughed long to himself. "So that's your talk," he said, "and you're no one o' Murray's fighting-cocks? Weel, the better for my business. Help yoursel' to some wine, Mr. Birkenshaw, for it's drouthy work talking."

Further he bade Francis draw his chair nearer the fire and stir the logs to a blaze. Then silence reigned in the room while the elder man stared into the glow with a face which even in the dim light seemed to his companion to be working with some emotion.

"It's a queer warld," he said at length, "and for the auld, a cruel one. Be sure, Mr. Birkenshaw, that it is a painful thing to feel the life sinking in your members and to mind again and again o' the days when ye were young and bauld. *Ebeu fugaces anni labuntur.* Weel, weel, it's the destiny of all."

He lay back on his couch so mighty a wreck of a man that Francis's pity was stirred. He was himself of just such a spirit, and he could forecast in imagination the bitter ebbing of vital force. He nodded gravely to each sentence. Then the old lord spoke again with a sharper tone.

"Ay, but that is no the worst of an auld man's lot. Ye see me here, me that has been the peer o' the best in the land, forced to keep the company o' a wheen wild caterans, and all the while the country asteer wi' war. I am auld and puir and weak, and so I maun sit still in this lonely stane tower and hear o' great events through the clash o' packmen. Once," and his voice rose high and querulous, "once I was the great Lord Lovat, and every man was cap in hand as I came down the High Street o' Edinburgh. Mair, far mair,—I hae carried the King himsel', God bless him, in my arms through the gardens o' Kensington, and my word was maybe no the least noted at Almack's and the Cocoa Tree. There have been days, sir, when I walked in St. James' Park, and many a braw lady cast eyes on the chief o' the Frasers and many great lords were proud to cleek my arm. And now I maun dwine away my life in the midst o' cauld hills and heathery mosses. I have no complaint against a merciful God, but is it not a sair dispensation? But were this all, I would say ne'er a word. But in my day I have had the feelings, ay, and maybe done the work, o' a statesman and a patriot. I have sat at the council-board with Hamilton and Queensberry, I have been the trusted adviser of Buccleuch and Tweeddale and Aberdeen, and not once or twice, but a score o' times did Maccallum Mhor himself call me his friend. Can I sit still then and see the land divided against itself, one king on the throne and another in the heather, and the wisest heads in braid Scotland at desperation wi' loyalty and religion pulling one way and common prudence the ither? Ay, and I maun sit and see and groan in my inmost heart, and all the while be sae clogged wi' this perishin' body that I canna move."

Lovat spoke fiercely and quickly, and Francis was impressed by the note of lofty resolution. He was dimly conscious of the grandiloquence, but the titanic strength of the recumbent figure made it seem only fitting.

"And then," the old man continued, "there is a different side to the whole matter. Now in this, the hinner end o' my days, I am quit o' all personal ambition, but I canna help that natural pride which the chief must feel in his own people. All the great northern clans are taking sides, Macdonalds, Camerons, and Stewarts for the Prince, Macleods and Macintyres against him. And whatever way it falls out they will aye have taken their part in the battle and won great glory. Is it like," he said simply, "that I could endure that the Frasers should lie quiet like auld wives or young bairns? You will pardon my enthusiasm for a poor rude, ignorant people, but they have followed me and my fathers and love my house dearly. Nay, sir, you who ken but the folk of the towns and the south country can have little notion of these poor folks' loyalty. I am called the thirty-eighth of my name and for every lord of Lovat they have spilled their blood like water. But now in the evil days, when their lands are narrowed, and men who ken nothing but how to fight must set themselves to tillage, you can believe that their heart is cast down. They look to me to help them, and I have nothing to give them, so the poor folk must quit their bits o' sheilings and the kindly glens where their fathers have dwelt since first a Frisel set foot in Scotland, and gang east and west and south to ither lands and stranger peoples. And there they make what shift they can to live, but their hearts are aye sair for the heathery hills and the auld glens and waters. I am no a man easily moved to tears, but the thought of my poor folk makes me greet like a bairn."

The melancholy voice, the sorrowful words, and the great figure, which, seen in the dim light, had lost all coarseness and was almost majestic, thrilled Francis in spite of himself. He had come with a distrust of this man, with a mind well stored with tales of his extraordinary character, and in consequence he had brought to the meeting a heart triply bound against all emotions. But this air of lingering pity was overcoming him. This fusion of the complaint of an exiled Aristides with the lament of a chief over the past glories of his clan was affecting in the extreme.

Then the other changed his tone utterly. Raising himself from his couch, he looked over to Francis with a keen face of interrogation. "I ken naught of your politics, Mr. Birkenshaw, though from your errand I might make a guess. But I assume that ye are an honest, open-minded man, and I will do ye the honour to speak plainly. I live out o' the warld, but I have een in my head to see. We will leave the question of politics aside, if you please, for the moment. It may be that I am for the present king, it may be for him that's ower the water. But, at any rate, the blood o' my fathers in my veins still cries out to strike a blow for a Stuart, and I canna see the Cause misguided without a pang. And what is it that I see? A brave young lad wi' nae experience o' war and little knowledge o' men, and a' around him a cleckin' o' wild Highland chiefs who fecht for their ain hand and nothing besides. And them that micht be advisers, what are they? A wheen bairnly boys, wi' guid coats on their backs and fine names, very ready wi' their bit swords, but poor silly sheep in the day of battle. Take my word, Mr. Birkenshaw, there are only two heads in the hale concern. There's the Athole Murray, Lord George. I bear nae guid will to him, but at least he is a man and a soldier. And there's Murray o' Brochtoun. Weel, the less said o' him the better. I have come across him in mony a ploy, and the heart o' him is as rotten as peat. But he is a man o' pairts, his hand is in the making o' every plan, and abune a' he has his bonny wife to help him. It's kenned that she has a' her lovers at her back, and that means half the gentry o' the land."

The old man leaned forward and scanned Francis' face. It was his aim to find out how far this messenger was sent by a petticoat, and to set him against his mistress. He had chosen his words with exquisite cunning, and he awaited the effect. Nor was he disappointed. The young man's face, to his huge irritation, flushed deeply, and he seemed suddenly bereft of words. His reason told him that such confusion was unwarrantable; it was no news to him that Mrs. Murray, the admired of all, had a train of gallants at her bidding. But the fact had never appeared to him so real; he had felt, he knew not why, that in this woman he had a private interest; his goddess seemed tarnished by a hint of common worship. Lord Lovat's plan had been well calculated, but he had just missed by a hair a proper estimate of his companion's character. Instead of the irritation with the world and despair which such news would have roused in the common man of sentiment, in Francis it merely awakened a deeper humility, a keener feeling of his own insignificance, a more hopeless devotion. The thought that his sentiment was shared by many showed the vast distance which separated her high virtue from his folly. Somehow the shaft had not only missed its mark, but performed the very work which its sender dreaded.

"I have spoken to you as friend to friend, Mr. Francis Birkenshaw," said Lovat. "Ye see my unhappy position. An alien to those in authority, prevented by my weakness from vigorous action, I must decide one way or another for the clan. Ye see the responsibility and the hardship."

Francis muttered assent, but his wits were busy with another question,—whither all this talk was tending. He had his clear mission to win this lord to the Prince's cause, but the problem had now a different aspect. With much trepidation he waited on the issue of affairs.

But Lovat had little disposition to give a ready answer. "Have ye any news for my ear?" he asked. "I have heard of the victory at Preston Pans, but I would like to ken if any mair lords have risen, if England is yet ripe, and if the army has gotten an increase."

Francis could say nothing but that Lord Lovat appeared as well informed as himself.

"Tut, tut, but this is a difficult business," said the old man, and he stared once more into the fire. "See here, sir, you see the wretched way I am placed. God knows I hold my country's welfare next to my own soul. I am ower auld to care a straw about which king has his backside on the throne; all I seek is that the land prosper. But it seems to me that the scales are about level. James would make a good king, and there's nae doubt but he has the richt on his side. Geordie makes a tolerable show, and if Chairlie is no strong enough to ding Geordie down, why, there Geordie will sit. If I thocht that there was a fair chance, I would set a' my people off the morn to fecht for the Stuarts. If I was clearly persuaded that there was none, they would join the ither side with all despatch, that the rising might be the sooner quelled and peace restored. I am ower auld to take the field mysel', and it's for my poor feckless folk I maun consult. But the devil of it is that I canna make up my mind one way or anither. I live ower far out o' the warld, and I've ower little news. My friends among the Jacobites are wi' the Prince, my friends on the ither side, like the Lord President, are a' in Edinburgh and like to be there for mony a day. Truth, I kenna where to turn," and he looked to the other with an air of great perplexity.

"On one matter I can ease your mind," said Francis. "I overtook the Lord President on the road, and as he was some three hours before me, he will be at his house of Culloden ere now."

Lovat shot one sharp glance at the speaker. "Say ye sae," said he. "Weel, I'm glad of it. But I fear ye maun be wrong, for Duncan in a time like this would come first to Castle Dounie. It was aye his way wi' his auld friends."

At the words and look which accompanied them, Francis had some suspicion that the presence of the Lord President in the north was well enough known to his interlocutor. He declared bluntly that he knew the face and had made no mistake.

"Weel, weel, we'll let the matter be," said Lovat. "If ye're richt, sae muckle the better for me. But how can I make up my mind when I get such word as this?" and he reached his hand to a packet of papers. "Here is a memorandum from Culloden's self with great news o' King George's forces and the peaceable and law-abiding spirit of the citizens of Edinburgh and the folk of the south. 'My dear lord,' he says, 'I do assure you that the thing will be nipped in the bud, so I counsel you to take no rash steps.' So says Mr. Duncan; but what says Lochiel? 'All the land is with us; forbye there are ten thousand French to be landed immediately, while in England every house of distinction is all for us and our Prince.' God, Mr. Birkenshaw, if ye had brought news to settle this kittle point, ye would have been an acceptable messenger."

Francis was in a quandary from which he saw no outlet. This man was clearly playing high for his own hand, but he had cloaked it cunningly under a pretence of love of clan and country. So he spoke guardedly. "You make the question difficult, my lord; but if the odds are so even, if whatever way you turn a like peril attends you, is there no sentiment to turn the scales?"

Lovat nodded wisely. "There ye are right," he said. "I have a sentiment for the old house, which is ever tugging against my prudence. When I heard the news o' Preston Pans I was daft. I cast my hat on the ground and drank damnation to the White Horse o' Hanover, and this very day I had seven hundred men drilled on the green, a' wi' their white cockades and springs o' yew in their bonnets. Were I no a discreet and weel-principled man, the clan would ere now have been marching over Corryarrick."

Francis spoke with rising irritation. "You see that I can advise you nothing, my lord. My opinion on the enterprise is my own, but I am here with a clear message. Are you willing to take the step and trust your fortunes and your clan's to God and the Prince, or will I take back the answer that my Lord Lovat is old and timid and prefers to bide at hame?"

"Na, you will do no siccan thing. I was but talking the matter over in a' its bearings, for my mind was made up lang syne. I am faun in years, but my spirit is not quenched, and it will never be said that the chief o' the Frasers was feared to take a chance. But I am no young hot-head to rin at the sound of a trumpet, and my habit of due consideration is strong in all things. Just rax me that pen, Mr. Birkenshaw, and I will write the Secretary the word ye want."

The old lord mended a quill and wrote diligently for some minutes, while Francis watched the great mask-like face with a mixture of admiration and distrust. He dimly guessed at the purpose of the whole talk, and this sudden decision did not increase his faith. By and by the writer finished and looked up with a twinkling eye. "Ye're a trusted servant of the Cause, Mr. Birkenshaw, so ye'll be preevileged to hear a bit o' my epistle. Am I to add any kind messages about yoursel'? Ye will see that I have omitted no one of the flowers o' sentiment which ye so admire." And he read:—

"I solemnly protest, dear sir, that it was the greatest grief of my life that my indisposition and severe sickness kept me from going south to my dear brave prince, and never parting with him while I was able to stand, but venture my old bones with pleasure in his service and before his eyes, while I had the last breath within me. But I send my eldest son, the hopes of my family and the darling of my life, a youth about nineteen years old, who was just going abroad to finish his education, after having learned with applause what is taught in our Scots universities, and was graduate Master of Arts. But instead of sending him abroad to complete his education, I have sent him to venture the last drop of his blood in the glorious prince's service; and as he is extremely beloved, and the darling of the clan, all the gentlemen of my name (which, I thank God, are numerous and look well and are always believed to be as stout as their neighbours) are gone with him.

"What do ye think o' that effort in your own line, sir?"

"I am not sure that I take your meaning," said Francis. "You cannot go yourself, but you will send the clan under your son?"

"That is my meaning," said Lovat, "and what do you think of it?"

"Why, that it is most honourable and generous," said Francis, in incredulous tones.

The old lord looked at him for a little, then pursed up his mouth and smiled. "Honour and generosity," he said, "are qualities o' my house, and we'll let that subject alane. But I look to reap the reward o' my action, sir. This is no wild clanjamphray sent down from the hills, but a great and weel-disciplined clan wi' my own son at its head. If the rising ends in naething, then there's my poor folk at the mercy o' their enemies, when they were sent out maybe against their will by their chief, who a' the while was weel disposed to both governments. If, again, the Prince gets his desires, there is honour and glory for man and master. I put both possibilities before you as a man o' some sense and experience, and I trust that if the first case come about before ye get the length o' the Prince's army, this letter whilk I have written will never get further than your pocket. And, further, that supposing you have delivered it, you will do your best to see it destroyed."

Francis stared in downright amazement. This was an extreme of brazen audacity which he had not reckoned with. The man's eyes were peering into his, and every line of that strange face spoke of daring and wit. "But," he stammered, "the clan will be out, and that will involve you without any scrawl of writing."

"Precisely," said Lovat, "the clan will be out, but perhaps it may be in spite o' their loyal chief, who sits at hame lamenting their defection and the woful ingratitude of children." His eyes were filled with sardonic mirth as he watched the changing face of his companion.

But Francis was already roused to keen suspicion, and he found at once voice and a cool bearing.

"Your methods are simple, my lord, and do credit to your politic mind. I will not say that they are dishonourable, for I have no reason to judge you. You have talked to me of your forethought for your people, which does you credit, and if this were the only motive your policy might be blameless. But I have heard talk of a dukedom for the lord of Lovat if all turned out well."

"Ay, and what of that?" asked the old man, with great calmness.

"Why, this," said Francis, "that if a man have recourse to tricks for the sake of others, he is pardoned, but if for his own advantage, he gets a more doubtful name."

"Meaning?" said the other.

"Meaning," said Francis, "that men use the ugly word treachery."

"Your knowledge of affairs is excellent, Mr. Birkenshaw, and what do ye say yoursel' in the matter?"

"Why," said Francis, "if you press me, I will say that I have heard that there were such virtues as honour and loyalty in the world."

The speaker was astonished at the issue of his words. The old man's face grew white with rage, and he half raised himself in his seat. Then he fell back with a cry as the pain twinged, and lay scowling at Francis, mumbling strange oaths. "You talk to me o' honour," he cried, "me, a very provost in the virtue, who for threescore years have lived wi' gentlemen o' the highest repute. And a whippit bitch o' Edinburgh lad comes here and preaches in my lug about honour! Honour," and he laughed shrilly, "as if honour werena mair than the punctiliousness o' a wheen conceited bairns."

Then as his anger passed, his face softened and he looked quizzically at Francis. "Ye are doubtless a mirror o' all the virtues yoursel', Mr. Birkenshaw, since ye talk about them sae weel. But I thought I heard word o' a daft lad in the publick o' Clachamharstan, no three days syne, whose tongue wagged to a different tune. The description I got o' him wasna unlike yoursel'."

Francis grew hotly uncomfortable as the memory of his folly came back to him, but it roused his anger and obstinacy. He was no more to be laughed out of his purpose than terrified by a dotard's threats. So he looked squarely at his tormentor with no sign of irritation.

Then Lovat changed his tone and spoke kindly. "Ye are a sensible man, Mr. Birkenshaw, and gifted wi' some subtlety o' mind. I will do ye an honour I am little used to do to folk, and explain my exact views on this matter. It is possible that I may desire safety for my folk and honour for myself both with the highest intentions. I may have thoughts of the great old glory of my name and seek to see it bright once more in these latter days. I may have a great and patriotic policy of my own which I seek to work out through the clatter and fechtin' o' Whig and Jacobite. I may feel my own power, and ken that through me and me alone a better time can come for this auld land. I may believe all this and mair, Mr. Birkenshaw; and who is to blame me if I use what means I can summon? I have heard the word that the end justifees the means; and I can tell ye, sir, there are things better than honour, and these are knowledge o' the times and a great love for an oppressed people."

The words were spoken in a low, soft voice and with an accent of deep pathos. The effect was nicely calculated, but once more it missed by a hair. Francis was touched in his emotions, but surprise at the recent scheme of bold impudence was still strong upon him. Earlier in the night the old lord had moved him almost to tears, but somehow this boastful romantic stuff left him untouched.

"I will bring this letter to the Secretary Murray," said he, "whatever be the upshot. On no other conditions can I take it from your hands."

Lovat sighed deeply, sealed the missive, and gave it to the other. "I maun e'en be content," he said, "and I trust that God will prosper the richt."

Then his whole demeanour changed, and he lay back and laughed long and heartily. "Sic a warld!" he cried. "Here's a young man thinks me a traitor when he serves Murray o' Brochtoun, who could give lessons to the Deil. Well-a-day, Mr. Birkenshaw, get ye gone and be damned to ye for a sour pernickety law-lander. Keep this meeting weel in mind, for be sure it's the first and last time ye ever will forgather wi' a man o' intellect. But, dear, dear, Simon, ye're back at your auld boasting ways, whilk is a bad example to the young man. Tak a glass o' wine, Mr. Birkenshaw, and one o' my men will show ye where ye are to sleep. But stop, man, ye winna get through the Fraser country in sic a time without a bit word from me. This will pass you," and he gave him one of the many rings from his fingers. "Take it and keep it in memory of auld Simon Fraser, who some way or ither took a fancy to ye. But I doubt, sir, ye've mista'en your trade. Ye should hae been a minister and a prop o' the Kirk."

And with the queer cackling laughter of age still in his ears, Francis left the room.

CHAPTER X.

Waste Places.

The next morning before the crowd of guests were well awake, Francis had left the haughlands which lined the Firth and ridden once more into the land of storms. The image of the old lord was still vivid in his memory. Every word in their conversation, every look of that strange face, was clear in his mind, and he rehearsed the tale a dozen times in the first hour of his journey. Plainly he had been of sufficient consequence to be worth conciliating. This in itself gave him pleasure; but to temper it he had the other thought that Lovat in some way had heard of his conduct at the inn and had thought his character a fit mark for cajolery. The air of powerful cunning, of sinister wit, which the great lord seemed to bear, had left in his mind a sense of his own futility. This man had been pleased to play with him as a cat with a mouse, to talk him fairly and treat him well; but the same man, had he so willed, could have crushed him like a child. For a little he tried to fathom his own political feeling, but could find no more than a personal sentiment. The enterprise had no charms for him; he had as little care for the Prince's success as for the Prince's person; and he saw with cruel exactness the quixoty of the whole business. But he had no mind to see any man play false to a cause with which he had linked himself; and he swore that Lovat would find himself bound to his promise. If he could reach Edinburgh before the army left for the South, it would be possible to give Murray the letter and so bind the clan to follow the Prince's standard whether the wind blew fair or foul. If he were too late, some reverse might happen which should send the Frasers and their chief to the arms of the Government. Clearly the best policy was speed.

Yet in his feelings to Lovat much kindliness was mixed with awe. That huge and intricate face had humour and rich nature in its crannies. He remembered the infinite changes of his speech, his heroical sentiments, his coarseness, his essays in the pathetic. The whole attitude of the man awakened a kindred sentiment in his own heart. He liked his great vigour, his rhodomontade, his palpable and masterful strength. This was the man whom a month ago he would have worshipped as the perfection of the loftily unscrupulous. Now though he was somewhat estranged from such an admiration and there was something repellant in what would once have been wholly attractive, yet enough survived to make the figure pleasing to his memory. He had a mind to help the cause which he had espoused, but if the interests did not clash, he was a partisan of Lovat's. The great lord's ring glistened on his finger, a garnet cut with a cluster of berries, and as he looked at it he felt for its giver almost the affection of a clansman.

When he crossed the river at the neck of the loch and entered the steep glens of Stratherick, he found his purpose of speed hindered. The road, which had hitherto been like a rough carriage-track, was now suddenly transformed into a bridle-path among rocks and heather, sometimes obscured in bog, as often winding steeply along a hillside where a stumble might mean death. The morning had been cloudy, and now a wind from the south-east brought up great banks of wrack and obscured hill and valley. Francis had no desire to follow the devious track he had come by, for he had been told of a better path leading into the upper Spey valley and thence into the Athole country and the head-waters of the Garry. He had planned to stay the night at the house of a cousin of Lovat's among the wilds at the head of Nairn, but the place was difficult to come at and needed clear weather. At the first sign of storm his spirits dropped, for craggy heights when cloaked in rain-clouds had still a dreary effect upon his soul. Now, as he looked, he saw the whole land grow wilder and bleaker. The glen up which the bridle-path mounted opened on a flat space of moorland, whence ran the waters of another stream on a new watershed. Down this burn lay his path, but to find it was a hard matter, when there were few marks of a track and the traveller was supposed to be guided by hill-tops invisible. Just at the edge of the moss the first drizzle of rain began, and Francis looked blankly into a wall of grey vapour, rising sheer from the plashy heath and merging in the lowering sky. The air was bitter cold, and he was ill-provided for a winter journey, seeing that he had ridden from the city at short notice. The man was hardy and bold, but mere hardihood is not enough to find the track in an unknown moorish country. So, bewildered and all but afraid, he set himself to grope his way across the desert.

Then came an hour of incontinent misery. He no sooner found the road than he lost it. The rain wet him to the skin, the wind buffeted his face till he was half-dazed, and ever and again he would find his horse floundering in a hag and panting miserably. The moor was seamed with craggy water-courses, and once astray from the track he could not tell what awful ravines lurked below the white shroud. The mere constant looking-for of danger became a bodily discomfort. His eyes were strained and aching, and his head seemed to swim with his incessant vigilance.

At last the flat ground ceased and he felt dimly that he was descending a slope. He could hear a loud rushing as of a multitude of streams, but the mist hid all from view. Sometimes the noise grew louder, sometimes it seemed to die away, and only the slipping of the horse on the sodden ground saluted his ears. He was cold, wet, and hungry, and now he began to be eerily afraid. This could be no path; he must be astray in this chaos of fierce hills, where precipice and loch barred the traveller's way. By a resolute closing of his thoughts he kept his head, and gave all his care to holding up his horse. Meantime that strange din of waters was never silent: now and then he seemed almost on the edge of a great stream; but nothing appeared save the white wall and the wet earth beneath.

Then the expected mischance came, and with fatal suddenness. Gradually it became clear that his horse was slipping, and that the ground beneath was an abrupt green slope where no beast could find footing. He pulled it up by the head, but the time for restraint was over. The poor creature with terror in its eyes and its nose between its forelegs was sprawling down the hill ever nearer to the awful roar of cataracts. Francis after a second's wild alarm flung himself from its back and fell on the slippery descent. The horse, eased of its burden, made one desperate effort to stop, but the struggle only quickened its speed. With a neigh of terror it went over some abrupt brink into some gulf of waters. The sound of the fall was drowned in the greater noise, and Francis was scarcely aware of it till he himself, clutching wildly at the spongy soil, shot over the verge into a spray-filled chasm.

He felt a great wash of waters over his head, and then with choking heart he came to the surface in the midst of a whirling, seething pool. He made feeble strokes for the shore, but all his efforts achieved was to carry him into the main line of the current. He felt himself being whirled downward, and then with a sickening thud he was driven against a rock. His left foot caught in a cranny. Down, far down, under the stream his head sank. He had no power to move his leg till by a merciful chance it slipped, and he was able once more to come to the top and ease his bursting heart. He felt his strength ebbing, and made futile clutches at every tuft of heather and jutting stone. But his hands had no power, and they all slipped from his grasp like the cords which a man in a nightmare lays hold on to drag himself from an abyss. It had soon been all over for this world with Mr. Francis Birkenshaw, if the storms of the last winter had not blown a rough pine-tree right athwart the torrent. The swollen waters lipped against its side, and he found himself washed close under the rugged bole. With despairing strength he gripped it and struggled till his head and breast lay over it. Then it was but a matter of time, and slowly inch by inch he worked his way to the bank and fell exhausted in a covert of bracken.

He lay for half an hour with the water forming pools at his side and feet. Then he shivered and half-roused himself to ease his breath. The thought of his horse struck him; it had long since gone to death among the misty waters. He crawled to his feet and essayed to walk, and then for the first time he felt his feebleness. His left ankle was broken, a mere trailing encumbrance with a hot fire burning in the splintered bone. His faculty of thought began to return to him, and he weighed brokenly the difficulties of his position. Speed was his aim; ere now he should have been near the house of Lovat's cousin; and instead he was lying in a nameless ravine with his horse lost and his body maimed and shaken. He felt hazily that he was very ill, and at the helplessness of it all he leaned his head on a bank of heath and sobbed wearily.

Then he set his teeth and began to drag himself from the place. A deer-track seemed to lead upwards, and thither he crawled. At the top of the chasm he saw a hill-slope to the right and a glen in front which seemed to promise easier walking. He tried hard to think out his whereabouts, for it might be that this stream flowed back to the Ness waters and in following it he would be returning upon his tracks. But his mind refused its duty, and he could get nothing but a blank confusion. He had no hope now of fulfilling his mission and scarcely any desire; all he sought was to reach a human dwelling and have rest from his agony. His body was the seat of pain of which his bruised ankle was the smallest part. It was so bitterly cold that even in his anguish he felt the hostility of the weather. For the grey mist was drawing closer, and the land was growing mossier and rougher. Slowly, laboriously he limped through the waste, sinking up to the knee in bog-pools, or falling heavily on banks of stone. He was so scourged by rain that his clothes seemed no cover to his nakedness; he felt bleached and scourged as a whitening bone among the rocks.

Hitherto he had kept a tight curb upon his wandering wits. But as exhaustion grew upon him and the flickerings of hope died away, wild fancies arose, and he was hag-ridden by memory. He began to forget the disappointment of his errand,—how Mrs. Murray would call him faithless and believe him returned to his old paths, when all the while the Badenoch winds were blowing over his bones. He lost all immediate recollection, and in the stress of his physical want was back once more in the old Edinburgh days, busy picturing the gross plenty of the life. Now he was wearied, wet, and famishing, and as if to point the contrast there rose a vision of reeking suppers, of rich, greasy taverns, and blowsy serving-girls. His high sentiment of the past week was a thousand years away, and he revelled in the very unctuous vulgarity and dirt. There, at any rate, had been human warmth and comfort; and in that endless moorland his thoughts were lowered to the naked facts of life.

The mist hung more loosely, and it was possible to see some yards in front, though the sight was blinded by a solid sheet of rain. Rocks and dwarf trees raised their heads like islands, and a chance bog-pool seemed so vast that he crazily fancied he had come to the sea-coast. The path was growing easier, and a flat valley-bottom seemed to be taking the place of the precipitous glen. A trail of fog looked for a moment like smoke, and he hailed it as a sign of human dwelling; but as the mirage grew commoner even the comfort of delusion failed him, and a horror of great darkness grew upon his soul. His wits were growing clearer—intolerably clear. He saw the whole wretched panorama of his misfortunes, and the blank ending which stared in his face. His mind was still in the bondage of old memories, and the revulsion sickened and drove him crazy. He stopped and leaned on a crag to give himself breath, and as in a flash the memory of Mrs. Murray and all her high world passed over him with disgust unutterable.

"Curse her!" he cried. "Am I to be damned in hell for a woman's face?" He poured forth a torrent of hideous abuse to the bleak weather. But for that proud jade with her face and hair he would have been content to seek common pleasures and the luxury of the unscrupulous. She seemed to mock him out of the fog, mock him with her beauty and her arrogant eyes. Passion made him half a maniac. He leaped forward with a drawn sword, but it fell from his nerveless hand and slashed his knees. "May she grow old and poor and withered, may she be a thing of the streets, may her pride be crushed in the gutter, may she see her friends killed before her eyes, and may she be damned immortally at the end!" And then his maledictions died away in a moan of weakness.

And now the cold seemed to have gone from the air, and his body grew hot with fever. Night was already beginning to turn the white wall of mist to black, and with the darkness came a surcease of storm. In still, dripping weather he stumbled onward down the valley. Flushes of heat passed over his face. Somewhere in his head a great wheel was revolving, and he forgot the pain of his foot in telling the number of its circles. One, two, three, he counted, six, ten, one hundred, and then he wandered into immensity. Something seemed to block his path, on which he hurled his weight despairingly. He felt himself borne back, and then the soft contact of the dripping earth, and the grip of a man's hand. Then the darkness deepened into unconsciousness.

* * * * *

A sudden flash of light pierced his brain, and he seemed to be staring glassily through his eyes. He saw light—a fire, and the outline of a dwelling. Men seemed crowded all about him, choking him, pushing him for room, and laughing with idiot laughter. One held a point of light in his hand, which seemed the gold of a ring. Hazily he was conscious that this was his ring, which Lord Lovat had given him, and even in his utter ruin of body he felt the aching of the finger from which it had been roughly pulled. He cried for it like a child, and then the whole concourse seemed to leap upon him and stifle the life from his heart.

* * * * *

The days passed into weeks and months while Francis lay helpless and raving. Once he awoke and found himself on a bed of brackens in a low-roofed, smoke-filled hut. Snow blocked the window, and he saw that it was the winter-time. But the thick odour of the peat-reek choked him, and he sank again into that terrible deep slumber which lies on the boundary of death. Meantime the people of the cottage went in and out on their work, nursing cheerfully the stranger who lay by the wall. They had found him in the last stage of weakness on the hill, and would have doubtless left him to die but for the chance of plunder. And when they brought him to the light they saw the chief's ring on his finger, so in all honesty, accepting this as a mandate from their lord, they had set themselves simply and ungrudgingly to nurse him to life. They were wretchedly poor, and could give him only the coarsest nourishment. The household, five in all, consisted of the father, Neil Mor na Cromag (Great Neil of the Shepherd's Crook, as the words mean), who was a herd of Lovat's on the farthest south-east hills of his territory. There were his wife and two sons, Rory, who played the pipes ravishingly, and Black John, who was his father's helper, both tall, well-grown men, who flourished on the rough fare and toilsome life. Then there was a girl just growing to womanhood, whose name Francis never heard, for all spoke of her as M'eudail or Caileag Beg, when they were well-pleased, or harsher names, Oinseach—witless or shameless—when they were angry. But for the most part they were good-humoured, for the Lovat men were génial, cunning, and abundantly humourous, very little like the short, dark Campbells or the fiery Stewarts. There was a cow in a shed not five feet from his couch, and three goats fed on the hill. Thence they got milk, and at times a kid to roast. Also Neil Mor would get a sheep for himself now and then at the gatherings of the herds, when he tossed the caber a yard further than any other, and he would sometimes take deer on the mountains and trout and salmon in the river. At times he even went down to the corn country, and bought bolls of fine meal, which all relished gladly after the tiresome diet of flesh and herbs. But they prospered all of them on the fare, and grew ruddy, full-blooded, and straight of limb. All day the men-folk were out on the hills, while the women cooked meals or carded wool in the firelight. Then at night Rory would get out his pipes and play springs which set the feet trembling, or sad wild strains of the men of old and the great kings of the North and the days that are gone. Sometimes, too, he played a lilt of the fairies who dwell in the green-wood and the crooks of glens, and the listeners would hush their breath and look to the barring of the door.

In the height of his illness the people of the cottage had given Francis up for dead, and walked with stealthy step and spoke softly as befitting those with death in the house. The winter was mild, but some blasts of snow came from Monadliadh, and made the women heap on peats and wood and choke the room with smoke. All this was little good for the sick man who lay wrestling with fever. They had dressed his ankle and put it in the way of healing; but the more dangerous ailment was so little known to them that they came near to killing him altogether, for they used to bathe his brow with cold well-water, and allow him to toss the coverings from his body. But for his extreme strength he would have died in the first week. As it was, the fever burned him to a shadow and then fled, and he was left with just sufficient life to struggle through. For two days his life trembled; then his eager vitality triumphed, and slowly he began to mend.

The people had little English, and they were so far from the chief's dwelling that they heard nothing of what happened. Francis in his ravings had often mentioned Lovat's name, and they heard with nods of recognition, arguing that this was some trusted friend of the great lord's. When dawning consciousness brought him power of speech, the whole miserable and futile tale of his misfortunes was clear in his memory, and he realised how bitterly he had failed. He strove to find out the turn of events from his hosts, but one and all they were ignorant. They knew dimly of a certain Tearlach, who was said to be a Stewart and a king, and they had heard that all the Rannoch and Athole men and the western clans had taken the field with him. But it was as nothing to them, for the old kings of Scots had no place in their mythology, which embraced so many other kings, and no straggler of Tearlach's had ever strayed to their door. But they told him of other things, all the simple talk of their narrow world; and strangely enough, these men who had rescued him with designs of plunder now cheered his recovery as if he had been their own blood-brother. Rory would play him soft, low tunes on the pipes, and John would tell of the days of herding and hunting; and every one waited on him with grave, silent courtesy.

But on the girl fell the chief share of his entertainment. She was little compared with her tall brothers, but wonderfully slim and active, with eyes like sloes, hair blown over brow, and a crooning voice. In the early days of his recovery, while he still lay on his back, she would give him food and bend over him with strange Gaelic caresses in the frankness of innocent pity. She was never more than half-dressed, for indoors her breast and shoulders were always bare, and outside a plaid was all their covering. Then as he grew stronger and the early spring came, he would lean on her as he hobbled out of doors, and sit by her side on the green bank above the stream or in the midst of birches on the hill. As colour came back to his cheeks and some of his old vigour to his frame, it may be that the simple child fell in love with the tall stranger. Be this as it may, no thought on the matter ever crossed his mind. He endured her pitying caresses and the warm touch of her skin without a tremor. He had never been the prey of such emotions, and now he was something less than before. The fever had purged him of much of his old fervour, and raised, as it were, a bar between this new man and his old life. The one thing which survived strong and vivid from the wreck of memory was the image of the lady who had sent him on this errand, and even in the thought of this goddess his former boyish sentiment had departed. It was a grave, old-featured man who looked down the glen of an afternoon and prayed for the return of full strength and tried to redd the tangle of his affairs.

Then at last it befell that one evening Neil Mor returned from a lambing-visit to the Nairnside with news. Tearlach had come again, this time from the South, with a great tail of dhuinewassels and Sassenach lords, and a following of Macdonalds and the like. Also the folk said that the Southron forces were waiting for him in the North and that a great battle would be fought ere the moon was old. Francis puzzled over this word, and by dint of counting the weeks of his own illness, guessed at the truth. Some great misfortune had overtaken the Prince in the South, and he had returned hither to make his stand. His services might still be wanted. The whole news was so vague that he might yet have the chance to fulfil his errand. So with new hope he set about brushing his garments and preparing for the way.

CHAPTER XI.

The Prince's Cabinet of War.

Black John set him some miles on his way, leading him down glen and up corry till he brought him out on the strath of Nairn. The day was warm for a northern spring, and the guide grew exceeding cheerful and hymned the joys of war. "There will be braw battles," he cried, "for all the craws will be fleeing north, and they are the birds that ken." Sometimes they met a lonely shepherd, and then John would stop for a parley in Gaelic and leave Francis to find the path for a mile or so alone. But when once they sighted the broad river valley, he left him with shrill farewells. "If seed o' mine meet seed o' yours," he said, "brothers they sall be," and he spat in his hand and clasped his parting guest's.

And now it was clearly the seat of war, for the tracks in the vale were rough with ruts and all the meadowland was trampled. There were few houses in the land—now and then a turf sheiling on the brae-face and once the grey wall of a castle; but the place was Lowland and habitable contrasted with the wild country he had dwelled in. He had already walked far, and soon his head began to swim with faintness. It was a long toil for a man so lately sick, and it was with many pauses and long, helpless reclinings on the wayside heather that he made the journey. He had a desperate fear of falling ill a second time,—a thing bitter to dream of now on the very seat of war. And yet his hopes hung on the frail thread of his strength, so with circumspect and elderly care he nursed his body, choosing dry places to lie on, drinking but moderately from the hillburns, and sipping the whisky which he had carried out with him from the morning.

One man only he met in all that green, silent vale. This was a pedlar with a pack, a man seemingly half-witted, but to Francis' delight able to speak Scots easily. When he met him he was swinging on, with a vacant eye on the hill-tops, singing some nonsensical catch. He was about to pass without noticing his presence, but Francis stopped him short and asked him the way. Clearly there could be no danger in getting news of the land from a crazy packman.

"Saw ye any soldiers," said Francis, "as ye came up the water?"

The man with difficulty cut short his star-gazing and looked at the questioner.

"Sodgers ay, sodgers mony," said he, and he went on with his singing,—

"If ye hae plenty and winna gie, Besouthen, Besouthen! The deil will get ye when ye dee, And awa' by southron toun!"

Francis weariness made him cross. "Where saw ye them?" he asked.

"There were some at the Nairn and mae at Iverness and mony mae at the Spey-side," said the man. "There'll be war, bluidy war, and mony deid at Beltane."

"Then where is the Prince's army?"

"Whatna Prince?" said the man, dreamily.

For answer Francis took him by the collar and shook him soundly.

"Give me a plain answer, you fool. Ye may be daft, but ye are none so daft as that."

The man looked at him quizzically. "See here, my freend," he said, "if ye are an honest man like me and nae moss-trooper, but traivellin' for your ain eedification, when ye meet a man in thae camsteery times ye'll let on that ye're no quite wise. It's the safest way. As for the Prince, as ye ca' him, he's in Inverness; but Cumberland's at Nairn, and they say that Chairlie will march out to Culloden the nicht to be ready for him."

"And Culloden," said Francis, "where is it?"

"Ten mile doun the haughs when ye win by the hills and come to the land muir. And guid day to ye, freend." The man went off, and as if anxious to keep his hand in, fell back on his old melody. Francis heard the words quavering down the road,—

"My shoon are made o' the red-coo's hide, Besouthen, Besouthen! My feet are cauld, I canna bide, And awa' by southron toun!"

Those last ten miles were not far from the limits of his endurance, but with teeth set fast in his lips and his knees knoitering he accomplished them. A great wide plain running straight to the sea-line lay before him; so vast it was that it looked like the beginning of a shoreless ocean. Woods seemed to rise on the far right, and to the left the dim points of spires, while many scores of miles away over Firth and haughland rose blue ridges of mountain. Not half a mile off a bald, square house stood in the waste, and all around was rough with heather and ridges of moor.

But what chiefly caught his eye was the stir around the house, a great armament of men already in camp, and straggling lines still coming from the North. It was already almost sunset, and fires were being lit in the hollows of the moss, and rough tents stretched on their poles. Troops of horse seemed to move about like pawns on a board, and even at the distance he could hear distinct words of command. And yet it was not the sight of a great army entrenched, but rather of a gathering of reiving bands, already in the act of moving. The chimneys of the house smoked as if it were well inhabited, and the sight of men hurrying in and out proclaimed it the Prince's quarters.

The first sentry he met was a wild man of the Camerons, who had scarce a word of English, and showed much desire to dispute the passage. As it was, he marched by his side with drawn claymore, till he handed him to a more civil clansman with many warnings. Francis found himself led through a line of bivouacs to what seemed to be the limits of a garden. There he trod the relics of a lawn, all trampled into ruts, with the bushes torn to ribbons and field-pieces lying blackly in the twilight. At the house door two sentries in kilts stood negligently, while a dozen ragged wretches quarrelled before the threshold. From within came a great riot as of many men speaking at once, mingled with shrill wailing from some miserable women who cowered in the shadow. Even in the mysterious half-light of the spring dusk the place and people seemed tattered, dishevelled, and ill-ordered. This was no camp of a conquering force; rather the hopeless last standing-ground of desperate men. Every face was pinched like his own, and their clothing was sadly worn. The hollow eyes had the look of famine, and weariness blinked in their unheeding looks.

He was led through the hall up a narrow oak staircase to a room above the chief door of the house. Here he had to give an account of his errand; before "business with the Prince" had been sufficient pass-word. But now he must declare himself the bearer of a letter, news of moment to the Cause. He had no thought of the nature of his reception. He had his duty to do, to give the letter; this fact alone in his weakness was clear to his brain. He was months late; events to change an era might have come to pass while he lay helpless; after all, it was but an empty errand to fulfil the letter of his mission; and then—ah, then he might wander to the ends of the earth and leave the struggle. An overwhelming desire for rest and sleep was upon him, and he faced the ordeal of the council-room with scarcely a thought.

Five men sat up and down the room, one at a table busily writing, another in a great arm-chair by the fire, and the three others taking off their boots at the hearth. The soldier—one of Cluny's Macphersons—walked to the man in the chair with a rough salute and told him Francis' errand. Then he closed the door, and the messenger advanced heavily to the company.

He in the chair was a slim young man dressed in the somewhat tarnished splendour of stained tartans, dusty lace, and dull gold braiding. His hair was powdered badly in patches, and his whole air was of unrest and weariness. Dark hollows lay below his eyes, and his cheek-bones stood out so sharply that he seemed to be smiling. Something of grace, of delicate breeding and long-descended pride, lay in his mien, but he was so huddled with lassitude that one could not judge him. He looked up drearily as Francis entered, and then with the forced grace of kingship asked him his business.

"I am the bearer of a letter from the Lord Lovat to your Highness," said Francis, and he laid it humbly in his hand.

At the word all looked more curiously, and the man at the table jumped to his feet. He was a big, handsome man with a large, well-formed face and little twinkling eyes. Here in this land of want he seemed the one thing prosperous, for there was something lawyer-like and diplomatic in his smooth forehead and mobile, twitching lips. He stood watching his master with eager eyes as he broke the seal.

At the first look the Prince cried out and flung the letter to the other. "Why, man, it is dated from October. The thing is months old, and you come with it here! What has delayed you, in Heaven's name, or do you think this is a fitting time to play a fool's pranks on desperate men?"

Francis heard him only as if far away. His weariness had come over him as he stood, and a sea of angry men seemed to be rising on all sides. He staggered, and caught at the table to save himself.

"Tut, the man is ill," cried the Prince, with ready sympathy, and he poured out a glass of wine from a bottle at his elbow and handed it to Francis. "It's ill speaking with a fainting man."

Meantime the Secretary had read the letter carefully through with his face puckered in smiles. "So," he said, "this is Lovat's confession of faith! Little he thinks that it has just reached us, or I'll warrant the Frasers would be anywhere but in the field;" and he passed it to a tall man in tartans who had risen from the hearth.

"But I am waiting on your answer," said the Prince. "How comes it that you are so far behind the day?"

The tall man read the letter and threw it on the table. "It's a thing of no value," he said; "ye may burn it whenever ye like. But tell me, sir, [this to Francis] how ye came to keep the thing back?"

Francis' ears were humming again, and he looked helplessly from one to the other. "I fell ill," he said aimlessly; "I fell ill somewhere in the hills and am just now recovered."

"A likely story!" cried the tall man, but the Prince bade him hold his peace. "The man's condition speaks for itself, my lord," he said; "he has the look of one walking in delirium."

"But who in God's name are ye?" cried the Secretary. "I have never seen ye in my life, and kenned nothing of your errand to the Lord Lovat."

Francis put a strong grip on his wits and answered him. "It was at the bidding of Mrs. Murray of Broughton that I went that road."

"Oh, ho," said the man, whistling softly, "and that was one of Meg's ploys. Well, well, she kens her own mind as well as most," and he fell to turning up a small book of memoranda. "Here it is," he cried, "written with her own hand. 'Mr. Francis Birkenshaw sent to a great Gentleman in the North, September 29. M. M.' Well, Mr. Francis Birkenshaw, ye have made a bonny hash of the business."

Now Francis heard the rest scarcely at all, but the mention of Mrs. Murray pierced clearly to his dazed wits. Who was this smooth, sleek man to talk of her thus? His hands itched to get at his throat.

But the Prince saved him by breaking in. "Let the poor fellow alone, Mr. Murray; it's no time for recrimination. God knows we're all in the devil's own mess, and there's not one to mend another."

In a moment Francis' wits were awake and he was staring hard at the Secretary. This, then, was her husband. He had pictured a strong, silent man, wise in council and great in battle, one stern, proud, irreconcilable. And this was the real thing, this man who looked almost elderly, who had the air of a cunning lawyer rather than a great captain! He had been ready to hate or worship Murray of Broughton, to resent bitterly his unattainable power or to follow him with the hopeless loyalty that bound him to his wife. Instead he found a man he could all but despise, and his heart rejoiced. If he were unworthy of the lady's glance, still more was this thing that called her wife.

"We will put off Mr. Birkenshaw's story to a happier time," said the Secretary. "Meantime it may rejoice him to hear that the clan of Fraser has been in the field for months. No ill, trust me, sir, has been done by your misfortune, save that our deep affection for the Lord Lovat had had some time to wait for confirmation." And he folded the letter and placed it in his pocket.

Then the men turned to other matters and fell a-talking. Francis still stood gazing at the coals and leaning on the table, uncertain of his purpose and too weary to care. He heard much talk of the mad surprise-party which Lord George was to lead that very night, and he noted that this Athole man was the only one of the Council who had the air of brisk, soldierly bravado. He talked boldly of success, and stirred the others to some hope. The Secretary still sat quiet at the table, drumming with his fingers, and the Prince had risen and was walking uneasily about the room. Months of hazard had left their mark on him, for his eye had no brightness and his step halted; he looked like one on the eve of a great crisis, so much depressed by the overwhelming chance that even the uttermost defeat would set him at peace with himself. One thing burned into Francis' memory. Charles came near the window and looked out to the wild camping-scene. Then he turned drearily to the fireplace. "My lords," he said, "we are a little people and a poor. It is the war of the stag against the hunters." And, leaning his head on the wall, he burst into tears in his foreign fashion, while the grave lords around him looked on wonderingly.

Then he raised his head, and seeing the drooping Francis, was recalled to his business. Calling a sentry he bade him send for Golis Macbean. "You will be better for a long sleep, Mr. Birkenshaw," he said, "and on the morrow you will be fresher for the difficult job before us. I will give you in charge of one of my own body-servants, who will see to your quarters." Then, turning to the Secretary, "And what are your plans, Mr. Murray?" he asked. "Will you stay here or go back to Inverness? I should recommend the latter, for this will scarcely be a safe place for a sick man."

"I will go back to Inverness," said the Secretary, dolefully. "My legs are no fit to carry me two yards. These humours of the body affect me painfully, and though I grieve to part from your Highness' side, yet I am more in the nature of an encumbrance than an aid."

Francis looked at him and saw that for all his air of health, the man was indeed sick, for his face flushed and paled irregularly, and when he rose his legs tottered below him. But the sight of him wakened a remembrance in his mind, and he turned to him doubtfully.

"It's a small thing that I have to ask, but I promised my Lord Lovat that the letter would be destroyed when the clan came out. I have to beg you to lay it on the fire and so set me free of my promise."

"What a daft-like request!" said the Secretary, laughing. "It shall be done of course, for it is not the custom of the honest side to keep incriminating scrawls. Set your mind at ease, Mr. Birkenshaw, I will see it done."

Then he hobbled from the room with many apologies. A minute after a huge man entered and bowed at the Prince's hand. "Take this gentleman, Golis," said the Prince, "and see that he has some refreshment and as comfortable quarters as may be. It will be a poor recompense for his misfortunes."

Francis followed the big man through the house into a small out-building where a fire burned with beds stretched round it. Here he was given some food, coarse and scanty, and with the remnants of the whisky-flask he washed down his supper. His attendant clearly had little English, for he sat and watched him stolidly through the meal. Outside a small rain was beginning to fall, and beat through the broken window. The place was full of the sighing of wind, and as he lay down before the sputtering fire, Francis felt that he was indeed in a land forlorn, waiting the last extremity of a dying cause.

* * * * *

He slept the dreamless sleep of exhaustion till near midnight, when he was awakened by a noise of men and horses,—the return of the fruitless night-expedition. When he woke again it was early morning, and Golis was shaking him. He felt almost vigorous; the weakness of the night before had gone, and though his limbs ached he was no longer the feeble wanderer on the verge of faintness. Golis brought him food, and when asked of the events of the night shook his head dolefully. "It was no good," he said, "for the road was as black as hell and they made ower muckle noise. Some they were wantin' to go on, but Lord George he wad not agree, and the Prince, Got bless him, is very thrawn. It will have been a bad night's work for all." And he relapsed into taciturnity.

Half in a dream Francis heard the drums and the skirl of the pipes, and found himself looking over the level moor to where it grew black with Cumberland's troops. He saw the new addition of Frasers and Macdonalds, he watched the marching of the clan-regiments to position with the far-away interest of a spectator at a show. One thing he saw clearly, that the Loyalists were utterly outnumbered, and in their ragged, starved look he saw the premonition of death. Once Charles passed him and greeted him with a smile. "You will be still too weak for this work, Mr. Birkenshaw, so you had better stay behind with me and my attendants." Then as the forenoon wore on and the enemy grew so near that he could see the outline of their features and the details of their dress, they opened a cannonade on the Highland army, which was answered as best they could. It was the signal for the fight, and as the Prince rode down the ranks with brave words on his lips, the men answered with that cheering which only the desperate raise,—the fierce cry of hopeless bravado.

From his position in the rear he saw the whole battle at his feet. A wild blast of snow came down from the northeast sheer in the face of the Highland lines. In the teeth of the storm the long ranks of the hopeless pulled bonnet over brow, set their teeth, and went forth into the mist. It was no ordered charge, for the Macintoshes had broken away without word of command, and the Athole men, the Camerons, the Frasers, and the Macleans followed in a tempestuous rush. As if from far off came the noise of the meeting, and then through the hail there came a glimpse of a wild mêlée, of heaped ranks of the dead, and a deadly phalanx of foes. But there at least was the shock and fury of fight. On the left wing all was different. The Macdonalds stood rigid, like pawns on a board, their ranks ploughed up by the enemy's musketry, too proud to fight in their ignoble position,—men with the face of death hewing at the heath with their swords in an impotent fury. In the murky weather and the loud din of war Francis could not see the close of that bitter drama. Though the Duke of Perth implored them to follow him, declaring that thenceforth he would call himself Macdonald, though their own chieftain Keppoch besought them with tears not to shame his name, the stubborn irreconcilables stood still, waiting upon death. As the whole Highland lines were broken, and clan after clan fled to the South, the Macdonalds too gave way. Not so their chief. "My God, the children of my race have forsaken me!" said he, and with pistol and sword he rushed to his doom among the advancing lines.

In a very little it was all over. The host seemed to recoil upon its rear-guards, and in a trice Francis was swept wildly back by a rabble of dying and wounded. He was separated from the Prince and Golis, enclosed fast in a haggard troop who with wild eyes and wilder lamentations staggered over the heather. Their faces dripped with blood and sweat; many were gashed to the open bone, and every now and then one sank on the ground to be trodden under by the panic-stricken. Behind was a broad pavement of carnage, up and down which rode the English horse, slaying the hale and giving the last stroke to the dying. The air sickened with the hot, fresh smell of blood, and as they fled Francis' old sickness came back on him and he well-nigh fainted. At last the rout grew thinner as it widened out on the extremity of the moor, and with a sob of fatigue he sank in a hollow among the rushes.

He lay for a little choking with the new excitement, listening to the thunderous trampling of hooves which seemed to assault the heavens. These moments were his salvation, for the van of cavalry passed by after the others and left the moor open to the right for escape. In a little he got to his feet and looked out. The air was still dim with snow and powder, but he saw scattered troops riding up and down, and the dull red blotch on the heath where the fight had been hottest. He had no plan of flight save to regain the hills he had left, haply to find Lord Lovat and share his fortunes. But when he tried to walk he found his legs bending under him, and he was dismally conscious that at this pace he would fall an easy victim to any wandering trooper.

At that moment a horseman appeared on the right, galloping hard toward him, an English orderly on a good mount, looking spick and clean even from the dust of battle. Francis, haggard and silent, crouched in the heather; it was his one chance for life, and he was desperate. The man came nearer, riding easily, with a pleased smile on his face as of a bloodless conqueror. Suddenly a wild man rose from the earth and gripped him by the leg. A pistol cracked into the air, and a bullet splashed in a bog-pool; the next instant the elegant young gentleman was rolling in mud, and Francis was trying wearily to mount the frightened beast. Lying like a sack on its back, he suffered it to bear him whither it pleased; then slowly and painfully he clambered upright in the saddle and found rein and stirrup. The horse went back on its haunches, and Francis stared round the blurred landscape, seeking direction. He found it in the sight of old Culloden house rising bare on the right, and thither he turned. At the wall of the courtyard he found a party of dragoons set round a huge man who alone and wounded to the death still kept a fierce front to his assailants. A dozen lay dead around him; his head was gashed on either side, his breast bled freely from bayonet stabs, and he could scarcely stand with a broken thigh-bone. Francis recognised Golis, his friend of the morning, and with a cry to him to bear up, he urged his horse towards him. After all, death must come, thought he, and this seemed a fitting place and time. But Fortune would have none of such aimless heroism. A stray bullet grazed his horse's flank and set that already maddened beast off in a wild fury to the South. Francis could only cling feebly, careless whither he went and praying vainly for some rest from this awful toil.

Of a sudden he found himself in the thick of a party riding pell-mell from the moor to the hills. A man looked up and recognised him.

"Who are ye for?" said Francis, dismally.

"For the Prince," said the man.

"And where is he?" asked Francis.

The man pointed to a little body somewhat in front, with a man in soiled fine clothes in the middle, hurried along on a weary horse led by a barefoot Highlander.

"There goes your master," said the man, "and this is the end of an auld sang."

CHAPTER XII.

After Culloden.

By midday the line of fugitives was in the thick of the dark hills, with Francis sitting dumb on his horse and puzzling his poor wits with vain projects. A council had been held at the Nairnside when they crossed the Ford of Falie. Thence the remains of the troops were sent to Ruthven in Badenoch, while the Prince with some dozen of a suite set out for the West. Francis went with him, caring little where he went so long as the way took him far from the accursed field. By chance he had heard the name of Fraser and Lovat linked with their destination. The words were centres round which to gather his wandering wits. Drearily he felt that as his mission had been to Lovat, so he must see it through to the end. The Cause was lost; why, then, he must perish with the Cause, and as he had drawn the old lord into the affair, he must get to his side in the disastrous climax.

But his horse was wearied and wounded, and its rider was foolish with sickness. So at the house of Faroline he began to lag behind the party, and two miles further had given up the vain effort. In the sleet of midday he managed still to follow their tracks, but when the weather cleared in the early afternoon he saw them many miles ahead in the extremity of the glen. The sky changed to an April blue, and with the warmth and freshness his exhaustion grew less burdensome. He stopped and bathed in a roadside tarn till the mire of battle was washed off, and then with more spirit he crossed the nick of the pass and came out on a wide, boggy moor with the great square house of Gortuleg set in the middle, and a few wretched sheilings jumbled into a clachan by the highway. There was no man in sight; clearly the Prince's party had but halted for a moment and gone on. The moss-pools were shining blue, and a great crying of birds enlivened the stillness, while through the midst gleamed the links of a slow stream.

The great house was in disorder, for the door stood wide to the wall and from within came the shrill cry of women. The news had already reached them, and there was mourning for a lost cause and ruined fortunes. The hall was empty and littered with a confusion of cloaks and riding-gear, with half-cooked food placed at random. A little girl stood weeping by the stair-foot, and at the sight of Francis ran screaming down a passage. The place was like a house seen in a bad dream, where all things are upside down and no human being appears. But Francis was beyond ceremony. He knew the place for a dwelling of the Frasers, and here he could not fail to have news of the chief. So he climbed the stairs heavily, only to find a worse confusion above, and some dozen ragged serving-girls who fled like rats at his approach. He opened the door of a room which was empty and stripped of all furniture. Again and again he tried, but all alike were tenantless. Then at a little room in the far corridor he found the door locked and heard the sound as of some one moving within. Angry with his aimless search, he put his shoulder to the wood and drove the hasp back. As the door flew open a little chamber was revealed with a dying fire on the hearth and an old man sitting hunched up in a chair. The figure turned a quick eye to the intruder, and Francis saw with joy that it was Lovat himself.

"Come in, sir," said the old man. "Come in, and God speed ye if your errand be fair." And he turned a face of such dumb misery, such baffled wrath at war with the feebleness of age, that Francis took two steps forward and then came to a standstill. He knew that he was not recognised, and, all unknown, was the spectator of the tragedy of a career.

"Come in, man, I say," piped the old voice. "If ye are a freend, what news bring ye o' the last dispensation?" And he turned his ambiguous eyes upon the newcomer to give a further shade of doubt to his ambiguous words.

But something caught his notice in Francis' face and awakened recollection. He pulled himself up in his chair and glared at the other. "Is't you?" he cried, "you, the man that played the hell wi' my fortunes and set me out on a daft venture! Come awa in, Mr. Birkenshaw, for 'faith ye're a welcome guest. Ye're the man of honour to be sure, and ye've come to gloat ower the issue of your wark. Ay," he cried shrilly, "it was your accursed tongue and your damnable clash that has been the ruin o' an auld man and a loyal people. Ye'd best see your job to the end. There's no a man in this house, nothing but greetin' women. If ye have sic an animosity to the name o' Lovat, here's an auld life wad thank ye for a speedy quittance. I kenna if ye're still for the Prince, since you gentry have a trick of keeping your honour and your pouches on the bieldy side o' the wall; but if so be ye are, here's auld Simon Fraser who wad drink damnation to the Prince for leading him sic a road. Simon's a renegade, do ye hear? He renounces the Stuarts and a' their warks. So do to him as ye think fit. Or if ye are for King George, ye see before ye a man who sent his folk to the forefront o' the battle, one who canna look for mercy and doesna seek it." And he held out his great hands and craned his neck as if for a blow.

The sight and the words sickened Francis. The trivial inflation of the talk, the luring cajolery of the eyes, were hateful to one who had just ridden from the naked terrors of war. Remorse for his share in this man's fate slipped from him like a garment; he felt relieved, but he had also the bitterness that here had gone his last friend in the North. Had he found the Lovat of his former interview he had been ready to follow him to the death; now the last mooring had been cast from the bark of his unsteady fortunes.

He turned to go, wearily, dismally, while the old lord yelled obscene reproaches through the open door. "Gang back to the jade that sent ye," he cried; "gang back to the weemen, man. Ye're ower empty and nice for the warld o' men." Then he did a queer thing, for with infinite difficulty he struggled to the window, and there watched

Francis pick his way through the moss, till he was swallowed up in the smoky clachan.

Meantime that unfortunate gentleman was in a sad temper. He had seen the degeneration of enthusiasm; he had been a witness to the palpable decay of a man's spirit. The sight of the great cumbrous body, leering, twisting in an agony of fear, made him despair of life. When he came to the village he found some makeshift for an inn in a two-roomed thatched cot, where a dirty red-haired man sold raw whisky and pointed out straw-beds to forlorn travellers. Francis had great arrears of sleep to overtake, his head rang, and his limbs ached from weakness. He ate what meal they could give him, and then asked for a place to sleep undisturbed. The landlord nodded, and led him to a garret between the ceiling and the thatch, where on a bed of bracken and heather those might sleep who desired rest and a hiding-place. The temper of the man was fast sinking to a dogged carelessness. In a few hours these hills would be scoured, and King George's men would be knocking at this very door. Let them come, let them take him; after all, a tow on the Carlisle walls would be a brave ending to an inglorious and hopeless life.

The afternoon was hot after the storm and drew to a quiet evening. Without on the moor broken men passed at odd times, now sitting on a worn horse, now leading their mount, or haply merely stumbling on foot. They were the rearguard of the fugitive, for in an hour after there came a lonely party of horse, picking their way with many complaints. This in turn was the van of the pursuit, and from Culloden field to the West there would soon stretch a line of redcoats, and there would be no passage beyond the Stratherick hills.

Francis slept on till the garret-loft was dark and stars twinkled through the thatch. Then there came a rattling of the ladder which disturbed his dreams. Half-dazed, he saw the landlord's red head thrust up, and the landlord's dirty fingers beckoning him down. From his wanderings he had learned the need of quick action, so he scrambled to his feet and followed, rubbing sleep from his eyes with weary knuckles. The red-haired man wore an air of secrecy, and he noted that the one door was closely bolted. Had the man not been clearly of the honest party, it would have savoured of betrayal. But when he entered the room he saw the reason of the thing. An old fleshy man lay groaning on a sedan-chair which had been set near the fire. "It's the chief himsel'," said the innkeeper, urging Francis forward and retreating nervously to the back. "It's the great Lord Lovat."

The door closed with a clang, and the pair were left together. Francis with drowsy brain looked hard at the unwieldly presence before him. Then Lovat checked his groanings, recognised him, and cried out in the kindliest tones.

"Ye'll excuse my ill-tongue in the morning, Mr. Francis. I was the deil's ain plaything wi' the gout. Ach, the unholy gripes, they play hell-fire wi' a man's speerit and mainners. Forget an auld man's clavers. I have come the night at sair bodily discomfort to make it up wi' ye. And oh, sir, is this not an awful thing that has happened?"

Francis drew his breath short and sat down. Culloden was still too raw in his memory to speak of it lightly. "I have an explanation to make to you, my lord. I was a poor carrier of your letter. I had not gone twenty miles in this vile country when I met with an accident which laid me on my back for months in a hillside cottage among your own clansmen. I have to thank your ring for the hospitality. It's not a week since I recovered, and it was only yesterday that I gave the Prince your letter. The clan had been long out, the thing was so much waste paper, the Secretary said; but though the time was bye I had to complete my errand."

He stopped, appalled by the change on the old man's face. He scrambled from his chair, seized Francis' hand, and mumbled it like a child. "Ye havena given the letter, my dear laddie! Blithe news, bonny news. There's life in the auld dowg yet, gentlemen." And then, as he dimly heard the last words, his mirth ceased. He flung the hand from him, lay back like a snarling dog, and gloomed from beneath shaggy brows. "Just yestreen, nae further back than yestreen," he moaned, "and I was a safe man. A merciful God stretches the doited creature on a sick bed, and the thing defeats the purposes of the Almighty by rinnin' to the Prince, like a leevin' corp, and giein' him my bit letter. And now there's a rope round

Simon's craig as sure as if King Geordie's self had tied it. Oh that a Fraser had stuck a dirk intil ye afore ye did the evil! What for in God's name was I sae daft as to gie ye the ring? Ye micht have fund fine clean caller burial in the Stratherick heather, and nae man been the wiser or the waur. Eh, hech, the auld man and the puir people!" and he sighed with maudlin pity.

Francis saw the position at a glance. The clan had been sent out while the chief thought that the Prince already had his letter. As the unhappy cause grew hopeless they had not been recalled, doubtless because Lovat saw himself already involved beyond escape. Now, in the final desolation, on him as one of the greatest rebel lords the punishment must fall heavy. And the bitterness of it all was that but for this scrawl of a letter he might yet be safe. He himself had not taken the field; he might represent his clan's action as flat rebellion, the disobedience of a son.

"The letter seems to stick in your throat," said Francis. "I had mind of your desire and asked the Secretary Murray to destroy it before me."

"And you saw it done?" cried Lovat. "Say ye saw the damned thing in twenty pieces and I'll gie ye a' I hae in the warld."

"The Secretary was ill and on the road for Inverness, so I dared not press him. He swore he would destroy it with his own hands, for it was not the custom of the honest party to do otherwise."

"But did ye no see him dae it?" screamed the old man.

"I confess I did not," said the other.

"Then it's a' up. Murray o' Brochtoun has the letter. Had it been any ither man it would have mattered little. The Prince, Lord George, Lochiel, Keppoch, they're a' men o' honour, but the Murray—my God, the thing has faun intil the richt hands. Murray! His heart is as black as bog-water; he's an easy, canty man, what ye ca' a pleasant fellow, but I would sooner lippen to the traitor Judas than just this canny Murray."

The man buried his face in his hands and rocked himself in his chair.

Francis was in lamentable despair. In his heart he could not contradict Lovat's words, for he still had mind of the Secretary's eye, and he cursed his own inertness at the moment of parting. He had been culpably remiss, for he had played into a traitor's hands; and though the victim was no stranger to treachery, it was treachery of the open, braggadocio kind, and no cowardly fear of his skin. But as he looked at the figure before him repulsion began to choke his remorse. This ungainly man with white hair all dishevelled and a mottled, rubicund face who alternated between the foulest abuse and a beggar's flattery—it was hard to rise into heroics in such a cause. For a moment Francis clapped his hands to his head and looked into sheer vacancy. His wits wandered, he seemed to be leading a crazy, phantasmal life. Without was the black darkness of endless moors and hideous, ragged hills, men were seeking him as a fugitive, his whole course was that of a derelict without aim or hope; and within the sordid room was this phrasing chieftain, weeping senselessly or leering with the ugliness of age. He was astray on the very backbone of creation, tethered to a madman's company. The thought roused a ghastly humour, and sitting on the table he laughed shrilly till even Lovat stopped his moaning—the laughter of wits half-unhinged and a fainting body.

"See here, my lord," he cried, "we are two men in misfortune. I have done you an ill turn, though I never intended it. But this is your own country. It cannot be hard to find faithful servants to carry you to the wilder hills, where you can bide till the blast blows by, and laugh at Murray and all his kind."

"Dinna talk," said Lovat, solemnly. "The finger of God is upon me. I was intemperate in my youth, I loved wine and women, and now in my declining years I am carried whither I will not. I canna put foot to the ground on a carriage-road, and is it like I could gang on the stanes o' Corryarrick? Forbye I must traivel wi' mony little elegancies and necessaries for the toilet and the stamach. I am no rude barbarian, sir, to be ready to flee at a moment's notice. I am an auld man wi' an uncommon experience o' the warld and its ways, and some pretensions to fashion. Is it no a peetiful thing that I must tak to the muirs like a bog-blitter?"

He had raised his head and twisted his extraordinary face into an expression of grave sorrow.

"I do not presume to advise your course," said Francis. "I only say that whatever you may choose I am willing to share its danger."

Lovat looked him up and down gravely.

"There's some sense in that thick heid o' yours, Mr. Birkenshaw. But what will ye serve? Ye will be but another mouth to feed."

"Also another sword in extremity," said Francis, dryly. He felt himself bound to stand by this strange man, in whose ill-fortune he had had some hand. It was his one remaining duty, and irksome though it was he had braced his mind to it. But this reception of his generosity damped him sorely.

The thing so set his teeth on edge that he resolved with obstinacy to see the game to the end.

"Do you accept me, my lord?" he said humbly.

But Lovat had seen fit to change his mood. He adopted a gushing, patriarchical kindness and welcomed him with effusion. "I accept you," he cried. "Ye are my one true freend, my one support, the son of my old age. May the Lord in Heaven reward ye for standing by an auld man in the day of his affliction. I can give ye nocht in return but my blessing." And there and then he pronounced solemn beatitudes on the confused Francis with the air of a desert saint.

At the door his natural manners returned. "Keep the door wide open, ye gander," he yelled. "Can a camel win through the eye of a needle or an auld gross man through a key-hole?"

CHAPTER XIII.

Crabbed Age and Youth.

In two hours Francis found himself at the tail of a little troop of men heading across the hills to the North. There were four stout bearers, for Lovat could move only in a litter, three strong fellows who carried food, and one special servant of the chief,—these were all the House of Gortuleg could muster. The night was moonless, but the men picked their way with surprising rapidity over the break-neck land. At first they seemed to traverse an interminable ascent, up which the bearers struggled with short breath. Then at a ridge they dipped all but sheer into a woody valley, where thickets of birch and ash made a tanglewood around a brawling river. In a little they lighted on the shore of a loch at a place where a cottage was built and a boat lay beached. The thing was rough and tarry, but four strong arms sent it quickly across the moonlit water. Then began another dreary climb, this time up a rocky cleft in the hills, where fine hill-gravel made the feet slip and an incessant dust troubled the eye. Once more they were on the high moors, crossing one shoulder of hill, skirting another great barrier ridge, till Francis—East-country bred—felt a whiff of salt in the air and knew the near presence of the sea. His legs ached with travel, he had been hurried since midnight up dale and over mountain at a speed which he could only marvel at. These tall men, even with the burden of a litter, could cover their hills like a good horse on a level road. For himself he was all but broken down; only the thought of the sneering Lovat kept him from yielding to exhaustion.

Just before dawn they came to the last ridge and looked down on a green strath with a firth lying pale in the midst of it. The place looked faint and far-away in the haze of night, save that in the foreground an angry glow told of burning dwellings. The men stopped and looked over the edge with scowling faces and harsh Gaelic oaths. Lovat himself awoke from his broken sleep and made shift to look down on the valley. Instantly his brows grew dark, and he cried shrilly for Francis. "Look there," he cried, "that is my braw house, my ain Castle Dounie, loweing like a pharos on a rock." His tone was half-jocular, but in a moment his rage mastered him. "God, my lads," he cried, "if I had just my fingers on your thrapples, I'd thraw them fine and send your gutsy sauls to the deil that begat them." He clenched his thick hands and remained staring at the sight. But soon rage gave place to deep self-pity, and in a little he was moaning on his back for the hours he had once dwelled in it, and calling on his fathers to pity their miserable son.

With the open daylight they shifted their course to the wilder parts, and marched with frequent pauses in the deep recesses of the hills. Lovat slept, snoring loudly under the midday heat. Francis drank of every well to ease his thirst, and followed the strange procession with no sense of purpose or hope. No one there save the chief himself, had any English, and even though they had spoken his own tongue, it is like that he would have had small disposition to talk. The man had lost all interest in his life; cold, sickness, and war for months had so wrought upon him that he had grown a new creature from the fantastic Mr. Birkenshaw of the Edinburgh taverns, even from the punctilious gentleman of the journey to the North. Again and again through the dreary day he asked himself the cause of this mournful position. Whence had flown his hopes; what had befallen that far-reaching scheme of high ambition which he had once planned to follow? Yet in the severing of each strand one remained firm. Had he looked to the bottom of that dogged instinct to share Lovat's fortunes he would have found the lingering sentiment which inspired his whole errand. His mission had been to Lovat, a lady's lips had joined their names in one command, and by Lovat's side he would see the end of the play.

As he stumbled along, when his thoughts rose from his immediate bodily weakness, they rested with disgust on the sleeping figure in the litter. To Francis—thin, blackavised, in the main free from gross excess—this cumbrous load of elderly flesh was indescribably repellant. He could not resist a dim affection, for the old lord had that tolerant humour, that sudden warmth of kindliness, which is no unfailing sign of charity of heart. The first interview had produced on his mind an impression of an extraordinary intellect and an abundant knowledge of life. Somewhere in his heart pity lurked,—pity for the ruin of it all, the frustration of deep-laid plans, and the misfortunes of one already feeble with age. When he did not look at the litter he was prepared to serve this fallen chieftain to the last, but one sight of the heavy face and his nice senses revolted. Times had changed with one who had revelled once in the raw vulgarities of the Pleasaunce that now he could not abide a slovenly, unheroic old man. Nor is the explanation hard; for he had met this man when still in the first heat of sentiment, he had grouped him in his mind with the choicer figures of memory, and now he resented the degradation with the fierceness of one whose sacred places are profaned.

At midday they stopped for food, and a rough feast was spread on the grass from the stores they carried. It was good, even rare, of its kind, for the indomitable gourmand had left Gortuleg with excellent provision for meat and drink. It seemed a strange thing to be drinking rich French wines on the short heather under a blazing sun, when the limbs were aching, and to Francis, at least, an hour's sleep would have been more than all the vintage in the world. Lovat's eyes brightened at the display; he fell back to his old humour, and was for quizzing Francis. But the poor boy turned on him so dull an eye that he forbore, and had recourse instead to crazy affection, which was harder still to bear. Once more the poles of his chair were raised, and the troop climbed slowly the skirts of a great, mossy hill, where the feet sank at every step and savage water-courses barred the road. Then they came to a greener country,—an upland valley between precipitous hill-walls, level for many yards on either side the stream, and sweet with hawthorn-blossom. Here stood a sheiling, a heather-roofed place of some pretensions, and the shepherd came running out and talked darkly with the chair-bearers. Lovat asked him some questions in Gaelic, and his face cleared at the replies. "The road is open yet," he cried to Francis. "He says that no one has come this way for a month save two packmen from Dingwall, and that he saw no sign of any man when he went round the hill this morning. We'll jink the lads yet, Mr. Birkenshaw, for the Fraser is on his ain rock, as the auld proverb says."

The shepherd accompanied them to the Glenhead, while the old lord plied him with questions on his work, his kin, and his profits. "Is the lambing to be guid this year?" he asked, and the man replied in good Lowland Scots, for he was from the south of Perth, and had another tongue than the Gaelic. Then he wandered into a string of tales about the shepherd's south-country kinsmen, and though the thing was the purest fancy the intention was kindly and the result good, for the lonely man's eyes brightened and he drank in the stories with greedy ear. Francis walked on the other side of the chair, and as he watched the shepherd's placid face, the strength and ease of his great stride, and his open front to the world, he felt a sudden envy. The hills were full of the crying of sheep; it was the time of the shepherd's harvest, the birth-time of the flocks, when a man is on his feet from dawn to sunset, striving against the weather for the life of his charge. This man spent his quiet days here in this fragrant solitude, face to face with nature and death and life, an intimate of the elements, an heir of deep mountain calm. And here was he, a poor straw on the whirlpool of events, playing a desperate game with little spirit. At other times he would have consoled himself with the thought that after all he played for high stakes in a high region where success, if won, was more worthy than in a little field. But now every vestige of self-esteem had been driven forth; his eyes looked blankly upon naked facts, and he knew himself for the puppet of Fortune.

The way had grown more perilous as the stream grew smaller, and soon they were walled between sheer sides of rock, while water brawled far down in scooped troughs of slate-grey stone. The road seemed to end again and again, but always there was some passage around some shoulder of hill, some byway among tanglewood which the shepherd showed them. At length they came out on the shore of a dark lake, which ran from the shadow of frowning hills to an open ridge of moor, whence the eye could discern a wide sunset country falling to the sea. By the loch shore was a cottage, empty save for a boat which lay across the floor. The men launched it and pulled to an island near the further shore, a place some hundred yards either way and planted with wind-blown firs. Here all had been made ready for a prolonged concealment. The low hut was scarcely distinguishable from the banks of heather, and the smoke of a fire was so sheltered by trees that no one from the shore could see a sign of habitation. Once inside, the place seemed extraordinarily large and well-equipped. There were barrels of meal in one end, and dried venison hams hung from the roof. A little old man greeted them, casting himself before the chief's litter and mumbling blessings. Lovat cut him short with a word, and surlily bade his bearers lift him to a chair. The sight of this final rest, which was like cold water to the wearied Francis, vexed him with the thought of his great stone halls now the shelter of others.

Throughout the evening the place was scarce habitable for his venomous tongue. There are some men—great souls—whom no trouble can crush; there are some—little souls—who are prostrate at its advent. Lovat, a mixture of both, laughed at misfortunes, but his ridicule was filled with irritation and chiefly affected his friends. He stormed at every servant in impetuous Gaelic, for his voice had lost none of its strength, and had found with old age a harsh, penetrating note which rasped on the ears. He had out the French wine from the baggage, and drank it greedily without the common civility of passing the bottle. Francis noticed nothing, for he slept in snatches since ever he had come to the hut. But Lovat needed someone to torment in such frolicsome moods, and he preferred one nearer his own quality than his clansmen. So he woke him effectually from his slumbers, and poured into his unwilling ears much low gossip about great folk, many tales of his own wrongs, and much other scandal without point or foundation. Francis listened, patiently polite. He had volunteered to share this man's exile, and whatever the provocation, he swore to do it with a good grace. The filth wearied him, for had he not once been a connoisseur in the unbecoming, but he gave exact attention with a fixed smile, till Lovat returned to an easy humour.

* * * * *

A week passed in the place, and Francis would have called it years. He could go abroad as he pleased, but the country was the most desolate conceivable, a plain of broken moor flanked by abrupt treeless hills. It was a type of that cold land to which the greater royalists were already fleeing, and round which Cumberland's lines were slowly drawing. But as yet no redcoat came to the lake shore, and Francis was left, with illimitable moors abroad and a querulous old man indoors, to pass his laggard days. The weather was broken by cold and wet, and the few bright days that intervened found a soaked and blackened country and brimming rivers. Once he shot a deer, which caused a violent outburst on the old lord's part, inasmuch as the animal was out of its proper season. The fare, too, in the cottage dwindled to poverty. The finer viands were soon consumed by the chief's improvidence, and the party were reduced in three days to oatmeal brose, tough venison steaks, and plain water from the loch. This last was the prime grievance, for by an oversight little spirits had been brought, and though the Lovat men searched the country round, none were to be had for love or money. Lovat groaned deeply over his tasteless dishes, and observing that Francis ate with equanimity, heaped on him the most childish insults.

"Does that mind ye o' the day when your mother fed ye, Mr. Francis?" he would say. "Parritch is halesome fare, an excellent diet for the lower classes in this land, as doubtless ye ken by experience, sir." Then, failing to irritate him by such clumsy means, he inevitably fell back on the subject of the Secretary and the Secretary's wife, and when the poor boy with burning cheeks marched out of doors he was pursued by the chuckle of elderly malice.

Yet with it all these days had the strange effect of strengthening the tie between the ill-matched pair. The helplessness of the one in spite of his bravado appealed to the good nature of the other. The more Lovat stormed and fumed, the harder was Francis' life and consequently the easier was his conscience, for then and only then he felt the satisfaction of the man who is struggling to accomplish the wholly unpleasant. Every hint of comfort vexed his soul, for he felt bitterly that he had marred everything he had laid his hand to, and that while wiser and better men were in peril of their lives, it was a disgrace that he should be in safety. So much for his humility, but the novel virtue in his nature had not rid itself of his awkward pride. It was a torture for him to be mocked at before the servants; had they understood English well, it is probable that he would have finally revolted. A dozen times a day he found himself pulling savagely across the loch with an odious, leering face dancing in his memory. The old lord knew nothing of his family history, and but the barest scraps of his life; but by shrewd inconsequence he stumbled upon the truth not once but many times, and Francis had a hard fight of it to keep from rage. Once he was betrayed into reprisals. Lovat was on his unfailing topic of women,—a topic in this case not localised but airily, generally treated by a master mind.

"What's become o' your wife a' this time, Mr. Birkenshaw?" he asked.

Now this was a subject on which Francis was open to no assault, so he had a less strict guard on his tongue, since there was no anger at heart to preach carefulness.

"What's become o' yours, my lord?" he said, in unthinking, rude repartee.

In a moment he remembered the notorious scandals of the Lovat household, and repented his words. His companion became a volcano of emotions. Screaming out curses he lay back in his seat with a purple face and eyes red and starting. His men rushed to help him, but he waved them back and bade them leave him alone with this Lowland swine. Then for an hour he made Francis' ears tingle with abuse, ending it all with a sudden flight to the pathetic. Sobbing like a child, he deplored the ingratitude of youth. "Me that micht be your father, Francie, an auld man that surely deserves the consideration due to a loving parent. But ye're of a piece with the rest. Auld Simon is the butt of one and all, and every midden-cock craws ower the Fraser's downfa'."

Then came a near approach to apoplexy, and Francis loosed his cravat amid maudlin upbraidings.

Two days later Francis went out to the hill to shoot hares. It was the breeding season, but necessity compelled, since the table must be replenished. He stayed out till the late afternoon, and as he came down to the loch he saw to his amazement the boat leave the island with several men on board. Horses were waiting for them at the shore, and they rode off to the deeps of the moor. Twenty minutes later he arrived breathless at the edge and pulled himself over. A dozen vague notions ran in his head: was this some treachery, an attack upon their solitude, or was it a lonely conclave of the army's remnants? When the keel touched the reeds he leaped on shore and ran hard for the hut.

In a corner of the place the servants were talking eagerly in whispers. Lovat was as usual huddled by the fire, but something in his look struck Francis as strange. His forehead was puckered into large knots, and the veins on his face and neck stood out with extraordinary prominence. He spoke to himself, and his lips were twitching with what might be anger or delight. Francis laid his hand on his shoulder ere ever he looked round, and the great face turned slowly from its meditations. "Sit down, Mr. Birkenshaw," he said, and he spoke with a precise accent very different from the freedom of his usual talk, "sit ye down, for I have much to say to ye.

"I have had a visit from some of our north-country gentlemen," he said, "who are sojourning just now in these parts."

Francis nodded in silence.

"I need give no names, but Lochiel and Clanranald were of the number, and there were others who are no less well-kenned."

He took snuff gravely, and, for the first time, tendered his box. It marked the admission of the younger man to a great intimacy.

"We talked of the late unhappy events, and we had some words of a plan. I need have no secrets from you, Mr. Birkenshaw, for I can trust you. I proposed to defend these mountains with a body of men till we were granted fair terms of war. They jumped at the thought one and all, but when I looked at them I saw their unfitness. Brave, honest gentlemen, sir, but with no brains—no sae muckle as a spoonfu'—in one o' their skulls. So I told them I despaired of it, and they rounded on me and called me a turncoat." All this he said with a certain mournful amusement, as of one above all base suspicion.

"A wheen men o' strae, sir, I tell ye," he went on. "Had I been a younger man I might have thought fit to move them to my purpose and guide their efforts; but I am auld, and I can but sit and look helpless on. They upbraided me, as if I were safe and they the ones in peril.

My God, sir, it's hell to me to bide here, to see my whole castle of ambition in the stour, and to thole these moorland vapours. And I foresee worse to come. When the redcoats warm to their work and the hunt gets hotter, it'll no be a decent cot-house for Simon Fraser, but wet bogs and heathery hillsides. But I make no complaint. It is the common heritage of unfortunate Loyalists. What I have to say concerns ye more closely. The Secretary Murray was one of those who came here to-day."

"Murray," cried Francis; "then he is recovered?"

"Recovered! Oh, in a fashion. The body still looks dwining, but that was aye a common thing with Master John when his plans went ill. He is in a lamenting, Lord-forgie-me kind o' mood, and no the brisk crouse lad ye'll probably have mind of. But there's one thing that may interest you. He spoke sagaciously to me of the folly of the hale business, and to try him I affected surprise, declared I was wholly innocent, that the Government had no grip on me, that I would welcome the sight of a redcoat, and that I was out here on the muirs for my health. He got as thrawn as Satan. 'Ye're muckle mistaken, Simon,' says he. 'The law has terrible long fingers, and can lay its hand even on you.' It was easy seen what he meant, and ye ken now the way the wind blaws."

"But the man may not be taken. There's every chance that he may win to France, where he'll be free from any temptation to hurt you. The man's young, and as likely to escape as any."

"So, so," said Lovat, drily. "That is true enough if Mr. Murray o' Broughton were willing to let Providence take His ain way with him. But what think ye o' our gentleman going to meet the pursuit and give himself up to justice?"

"And turn a traitor?" said Francis, in amazement.

"Ay, just that," said the old lord, "and become one o' the fingers on the hand o' the Law that he's aye craikin' about. For our gentleman's game will be like this. Barisdale, Clanranald, and the others gang north and west. Mr. Murray gangs south under pretence of finding shelter in the Appin country. But at the first chance he is south of the Forth, in his ain house of Brochtoun, where the Government finds him, a melancholy man, lamenting his pitiful follies. What can they do wi' such a penitent but take him into favour, and in the course of private conversation it comes out that he had a bit scrawl that incriminates a great Highland lord whom they have long been seeking. So Mr. Murray gets a free pardon, and this Highland lord, if they lay hands on him, will even get his heid chappit off;" and he laughed wildly.

Francis' face was hot with dismay. "Forgive me, my lord," he cried, "if I have been the cause of your peril."

"Nay, Francis, I dinna blame ye. Indeed it is me that has to ask your pardon, for I have been an ill companion on these traivels. But now I can at least die with a clean hand and a proud heart. It shall never be said that a Fraser, though feeble and stricken in years, was feared o' the hale black gang o' them. *In utrumque paratus*," he quoted with inimitable gusto, "*seu versare dolis, seu certæ occumbere morti*."

Francis went to bed, but not to sleep. The image of the savage, heroic old man, his hypocrisy discarded, fronting death with equanimity, was burned on his mind. A fierce anger against Murray possessed him, and as he thought of what one proud woman would think of such conduct, and all the misery which awaited her, he groaned in bitterness of spirit. But his wits were clearer, now he had a plainer duty before him, something which an active man might effect without presumption. Above all, now was his task more closely connected with her who had been his task-mistress. Henceforth he wrought for her direct, palpable good.

In the grey misty morning Lovat was wakened by the young man standing at his bedside.

"I have come to make my farewells, my lord, for it is time for me to be off."

"Are you like the rest then, Francis, and leave the sinking ship?"

"You know well enough to the contrary, my lord. I go to seek the Secretary."

"Good lad," said Lovat, "but how will you find him? I ken nothing of his road save that he went south by Appin."

"Then I will go to Appin, and maybe I will get word of him there."

"And then, when ye get him?..."

"Why, then," said Francis, "Mr. Murray and I will have words, and a certain bit of paper will find its way to my pocket, or I will ken the reason why."

"It's a great plan, Francis," cried the old man, "and God speed your hand. Shake the tod weel, once for me and once for yoursel' and once for his leddy wife. If I never see ye again in this world, I'll see ye in ..."

But the place was empty, and Francis was gone.

CHAPTER XIV.

How Mr. Francis Came to the Lowlands Once More.

At this point the industrious narrator passes from a sober tale into the realms of wild romance. Nor can he help himself. For take a wild young lad, or rather a serious man still in his youth, whose mind has been strung high by vain enthusiasms, who is spurred by a desperate hope. Conceive such an one to have climbed with difficulty the first steps of the ladder of virtue, to have curbed his mad fervours, to have bowed before the eternal commonplaces of love and duty, to have found himself in a difficult and unmanly place, and now at last to have a faint chance of great deeds. Suppose him strong in body—for the week in Lovat's hut had restored him—give him a plain task, a sword at his side, not a word of Gaelic, the mistiest notion of the hill-country, and burning cause for speed—and you will find that he will run into many stone walls ere he pass the Highland line.

With Lovat's directions he came to the Linnhe coast and met no mishap. The way had been a terrible toil over a birk-clad moorland and bare scarps of slaty hill. Finding some poor fishermen on the beach, he slept the night in their hut, giving them a piece of Lovat's money in payment for the oatcake and dried fish which they put before him. The men were honest and considered the payment ample, for they took him aboard the lugger and set down the loch to one of the long water-arms which run into the east. He repeated the name *Appin*, at which they nodded to the beach; and when he found himself ashore he comprehended their gestures, recalled the old lord's directions, and realised that this was indeed Appin. That night he slept on the moor in a ditch among heather, and at daybreak was on his way in a pleasing land of green valleys, where the smell of salt hung over bent and tussock. By the afternoon he had come to the house which he had been bidden to seek, the house of John Roy Stewart, called sometimes John Howglass and sometimes John of the Hairy Legs. The man was kin to the Fraser, and—what was far above pedigree—had some little English. When Francis had eaten his fill and slept heavily for some hours, he put the question to his host.

"Murray?" cried the man, "Murray never came here, though he sent a man to beg from me while he was hiding by the Leven Loch. That was a week syne. Murray darena show his face in Appin, for ten years back he had a kind o' bicker wi' Ardshiel, and it's kenned that the Drummonds canna thole him. Faith, it would be a back-cast of the Lord's hand that sent Murray to Appin, and Sim maun be failing in mind or he would have had the sense to ken that."

"It was Murray's own word," said Francis.

"And Sim believed him! Dinna tell me that! Na, na, your gentleman will be skelping lang ere this ower Balwhidder braes, and he'll soon be casting his coat in his ain house of Brochtoun. That's to say, if ye read him richt, but I confess I had a juster opinion of the man."

"If he's gone south, then south I must go," said Francis.

His host propounded to him a choice of roads: He might go south by the Campbells' country, take a chance of a ferry over the lochs, and come to the right shore of the Clyde above Dumbarton. Thence lay a level ride to Broughton in a quiet land among Whiggish countrymen. Or he might go straight through the wilds of Awe to the young streams of Forth and enter the Lowlands by Lennox or Lanark. Francis chose the first, and so all the next day he strode through the green country of Appin in a land channelled with bright streams and ever filled with the noise and scents of the sea. Few of the people had been out; but it was a miracle that he passed unchallenged, for the place was watched jealously by its neighbours of Lorn, seeing that of old Campbell had been at war with Stewart. At night he came to a herd's dwelling on a lonely hill, where his path turned inland. The man gladly kept him the night on the mention of John Howglass, but again it was a monotonous feast of silence, where he sat and smiled into the eyes of a friendly tangled giant.

The weather still kept calm and blue as he struck the next morning into the remoter deserts. Twenty miles straight by the south-east wind, John Roy had said, and he would come to the sea. But Francis had little hillcraft, and it may be that the twenty became forty ere he looked down on a dark sea-loch, sleeping between strait mountain walls. All day he had met not a soul, save that an hour before midday he had seen two figures on the skyline of a hill at the head of the glen in which he patiently stumbled. They, too, seemed to have caught sight of him, for instantly the place became void. This was the one warning he got that he was in a country of war; but he was puffed up by the ease with which he had won thus far, and forgot the thing the minute after.

Ere he came to the shore he learned the moral of the figures on the hill-top. As he slipped heavily from rock to rock down one of the shallow corries which dropped on the sea, a bullet suddenly sang by his ear and bored into a bank of sand. He had the sense to lie prone in the stream and pray that the shot might have been intended for other game than himself. But the noise of feet on the stones spoiled his hopes; he was too footsore to run; so he surrendered helplessly to three ragged men who leaped on him from above. One who had some words of English asked, "What ta devils he was crossing ta Cruart Vhan so hot-foot;" but Francis' reply sounded deeps of language unknown to him, and all that was left was to hurry the unhappy captive along the hill-face, till his arms seemed torn from their sockets with rough handling.

How long and how far he went he soon lost the power to guess. His shoes were filled with small sharp stones which galled him severely. He struggled to prevail upon his guides to slacken pace, but their only reply was deep, convulsive laughter. At last their path was barred by a deep glen down which a salmon stream roared to the Firth. At its foot was a rude fisherman's hut,—a few stakes and boulders with a simple roof of turf,—which seemed to be the goal of the violent journey. At the door stood a very great personage, dressed in plain Lowland garb, save for a magnificent scarlet hat which surmounted a very well-kept periwig. The three men greeted him with the most abject reverence, and pushing Francis forward left him to explain the posture of affairs.

"And who may you be, sir?" said the great man, tapping a snuff-box and looking with disfavour at the three dirty Highlanders.

"I have yet to know by whose orders I am held prisoner," said Francis, "and who it is that has the right to ask me."

"Hoity, toity," said the man, "heard ye ever the like? Are ye aware, sir, that this is the Campbell country, and that I am the Duke's own cousin? Do ye ken, sir, that the Campbells, serving as they do the lawful king, have a warrant to search these hills for any members of the disaffected clans or Lowland rebels who may be lurking there? And ye question my right!"

"I ask your pardon, my lord," said Francis, with diplomacy. "I am glad indeed to find allies in a good work. I am at present in pursuit of a notorious Jacobite, one John Murray of Broughton, who is known to have come from Appin southward through this very country; and if you can enable me to lay hands on him I will be everlastingly your lordship's debtor."

The man was vastly flattered by the tone—still more by the tide.

"Then it is my part to ask your pardon for the unseemly conduct of my poor people, Mr. ——"

"Birkenshaw," said Francis, speaking the truth at random.

"And if it turns out to be as you say, and I doubt not it will, I will aid you with all my heart. Meantime I must beg your company to sup on such poor fare as is here provided. My uncle of Inverforth will be here in three hours' time, and he will explain matters to you more fully."

"Three hours' grace," thought Francis, for before Inverforth he must stand unmasked, seeing that he had no tale to meet the ear of one who had been at Culloden and was famed as the bitterest foe of the Prince's in the land. Before three hours' time he must give this gaudy gentleman the slip, and with the help of Providence put the loch between himself and his pursuers. He had noticed a boat on the beach; if he could but reach it, he was safe. Once over the water and he was not far from the confines of settled country, if he minded John Roy's words aright.

They supped daintily on fresh-caught salmon, hill mutton, and some bottles of foreign wine which the man fetched from a store in the hut. The Campbell talked volubly on a score of subjects, as if glad to find one less barbarous than the hill-men to listen to his elegant talk. Francis humoured him as far as he was able, and bandied the names of great folk to his own admiration. Three several scandals linked with the name of Lord Craigforth did he invent on the spur of the moment, and tell to the greedy ears of his companion. He had to listen in turn to many weary recitals of slights and successes, of days in Edinburgh and London where it seemed that Mr. Campbell had played a great part, and a minute account of the interminable Campbell pedigree. Meantime he feigned exceeding interest and a growing fuddledom. His cheeks flushed and he rubbed his eyes, blinking. Then he complained of the heat, and the effect of wine on one who had been so long without it, paying a compliment to the strong head of the other. He wound up with a request for a second's walk in the open. "I am somewhat confused with my long journey and the strength of the Bordeaux. Three turns on the heather will set me right, so I beg of you to excuse me."

Mr. Campbell, himself approaching hilarity, was graciously pleased, and in a second Francis was on the moor and out of sight of the gillies. The loch lay purple-black, for the night was moonless, but a line of pale light marked where the stream entered and the boat lay moored. A minute, and he was there, feeling for the chain and the stone to which it was fastened. To his chagrin the thing was padlocked, and passed through a stout ring of iron in the boat's stern. He searched for a weak spot but found none, nor could he move the great stone which did duty for an anchor. Despair seized him, and he tore at the thing like a madman. The ring creaked, then as the tugging grew fiercer the stern planks shivered, till at last the wood gave and he found himself sprawling with the chain in his hand and a ragged end of timber encircling the ring. The noise was loud enough to be heard across the loch, so in a fright he scrambled into the boat and put out the oars.

He could hear men come crying from the hut as he shot into the blackness. If this were the only boat, he was safe enough; but he dare not risk the nearest point of the far shore, but drew down the water as he guessed its direction. The mountains rose wall-like in inscrutable night, towering into the blacker arch of the high heavens. He scarce could see the tips of his oars, scarcely the murky water beneath; he felt like one entering into a fantastic land without law or limit; and yet he was no more weary, but extraordinarily light and active. Then he heard in his wake the clear splash of oars; the gillies must have found another boat and be giving chase. He was hailed in strident Gaelic by some angry man, and then the world was quiet save for the monotonous sound of rowing. Francis grew perfectly cheerful. Often on the Fife coast had he played at this game—on an angry firth and not on a placid, land-locked sea. He could tell that the boat behind was not gaining, for though there seemed to be two men at the oars, it must be heavier and coble-shaped, whereas his was an elegant pleasure-boat.

But as the minutes passed and the chase continued he began to cast about for a refuge. If he turned into the shore, they would follow; and now, as his arms grew sore, he could not hope to put such a distance between them and himself as would suffer him to land unnoticed. His wits failed him, and he could think of nothing. Wild schemes of upsetting his boat and swimming ashore flitted across his mind, but a remembrance of the width of the loch as seen by daylight warned him to prudence. Even in darkness his pursuers could track him easily by the sound, so he could not hope to baffle them by any ruse of turning. Suddenly, to his delight, a chance arose for his salvation. The outline of a ship all blurred with night leaped up on his left, apparently not more than twenty yards away. Here was a case for neck or nothing. With a moment's thought he kicked off his shoes, tossed the oars into the water, and dived overboard, and a minute later was clambering up the bowsprit of the vessel.

He ran down from the bows to the deck-house, picking his way amid a multitude of ropes and bales. The door was shut, but a light came through the foot, so without parleying he opened. A man sat alone at a table, working out some figures and sweating with the toil.

"Francis Birkenshaw!" he cried in amazement, as he saw his visitor.

Francis stared; then "Andra Gordiestoun" he stammered, in open-mouthed surprise.

"So ye've taken to this trade," said the captain, sourly. "I suppose ye will be for him they ca' the Chevalier."

"Indeed I am," said Francis.

"I micht have jaloused it. Ye were a blagyird in the auld toun o' Dysart, and it's no like ye'd be convertit on the Hieland hills."

"There's a boatful o' men behind me," said Francis. "Are you minded to give me up?"

"To be sure I am," said the man. "I am a decent supporter o' the King—God bless him,—and I'll hae nae rinaway Jaicobites on my vessel."

At the moment there came a great crying from the bows, as the pursuers came up with the deserted boat and the moored ship. The men hailed the captain in their scanty English, and Francis sat down despairingly to await the issue. The conversation—heard in snatches—was of a kind to cheer and surprise him. For the captain argued, first, that no man had come aboard; secondly, that if one had, it was no business of theirs;

and, thirdly, that they might be damned for a set of dirty Highland beggars, and, if they stayed longer, he would rouse his men and send them and their boat to a better place. Which last point—and the gestures and tone which accompanied its deliverance—was found so convincing that the party retired in haste.

"You're better than your word, Andra," said Francis, on his return.

"Say nae mair about it," said he. "And look ye here, Mr. Birkenshaw, ye may be a michty scoondrel, as I have nae doot ye are, ye may be fresh frae cuttin' the throat o' Maccallummore himsel'; but ye come frae my ain toun, and I have drunk mony glesses wi' ye at the Harbour-walk, so I'll see ye through wi' this bit business, if it does na interfere wi' mine."

"If you can put me in by the Renfrew shore you will do me a great obligement."

"And it so happens that that is my very road," said the captain, "so the Lord has lookit after ye better than ye could guide yoursel'."

As Francis lay down in a ship's berth he could hear the anchor lifting, and soon they were dropping down the loch with a fair breeze behind. When he awoke late in the morning, they had already left the loch and were making their course by the south end of an island in what seemed a broad sea, lined on one side with craggy hills and on the other by far-stretching lines of level country. For the whole of a long day they made slow progress up the Firth, tacking against a difficult wind, while Francis looked idly from the bows, busy with his own reflections. The skipper was always by his side, leaving him only to make short inroads below or to yell orders to his men. To his amazement Francis found that he was no more the godless Andra Gordiestoun of the old days, but an enthusiast in religion on the watch for a proselyte. True, his language was violent as ever, and he seemed little less drunken; but his talk was always of theological mysteries, and unctuous texts fell easily from his lips. He preached Francis a vehement sermon on the error of his ways, adjured him to flee from a wrath to come, painted this wrath in awful colours, and dwelt zealously on the joys of the redeemed. Francis heard him out with impatient grace. He himself had been the arena of so severe a struggle, good and evil had fought such a duel in his breast, that he was willing to lend an ear to anyone who could teach him the way of life. But these phrases, this fluent rhetoric, seemed paltry to one whose soul was scarred with the grim reality. He was in the actual throes of a vain endeavour; little to him these commonplaces of the throng. And yet this man, sent with such words out of his own tattered past, was a sting and a remembrance of years mis-spent.

"I will pray for ye, Francie," said the man, on parting, "that ye may yet be reclaimed. It's a puir warld withoot hopes o' a better."

"I say 'Amen' to that," said Francis, and he stepped ashore on Lowland earth.

BOOK THREE

CHAPTER XV.

The House of Broughton.

By the afternoon of the next day Francis had put many broad Lanark and Renfrew cornfields between himself and the sea, and had come to the upmost streams of Clyde, where the land begins to fall away towards pleasant Tweeddale. He had bought a horse with some of his Highland gold, since his business demanded speed, and ridden through the quiet Whig clachans with none to gainsay him. Only at the change-house of Roberton did he stop to wet his dry lips with ale. The landlord was an honest, sunburnt countryman, so Francis ventured a question.

"What like is Tweeddale now when the steer is over? Are there still Murrays to vex it?"

The man looked suspicion for a second and quietly stroked his right cheek. By luck Francis knew the current Jacobite sign and responded.

"I ken but ae thing o' the state o' affairs in Brochtoun," said the man, "The Leddy was bidin' there hersel', but yestreen yin came bye on a blae horse and syne yin on a broun, and I think the last was awfu' like the shape o' the Laird. Hae ye ony word yoursel'?"

"None save that soon there's like to be a flittin' from Brochtoun House."

"Across the water belike?" said the man.

"Maybe scarcely so far," said Francis.

"But he'll ne'er be ta'en. Brochtoun's a dour bit, but the lave o' Tweeddale is leal and no Whiggish ava'."

"I have nought to tell you," said Francis, "but if you do not hear within a week that Mr. John Murray went up the Edinboro' road wi' a company o' dragoons to keep him cheery, then thank God for saving a poor gentleman from himself." And he rode on, leaving the man a prey of vague suspicions.

The flush of early summer was on hill and wildwood as he rode from the green moor-road into the shadowy vale. To one sick of rock and heather and the sour unkindly odours of moss and torrent, the place seemed goodly beyond dreams. It was mid-afternoon, and in the mellow glow all was softened, touched with enchantment and old romance. The glen was asleep; scarcely a murmur of water reached his ears; the white stone cottages by the meadow-edge, the grey walls of the Place among the trees, the faint lines of far-away mountains,—all were part of an ancient primordial peace o' the world. And the air of the place bewitched him till he lost all settled thoughts. Before he had been puzzling sore over the knots in his destiny and striving to form a clear plan of conduct. Now he was in a fairyland of sentiment, where a woman's face shone ever from the still and golden skies.

He came on the Edinburgh highway above the bridge of the burn, some hundreds of yards from the road to the Place. His heart began to beat painfully at the thought of the near meeting. The whirligig of time had been playing pranks since that morning a year before when he had ridden down Edinburgh streets to the North. And what had been the end of his mission? Dust and ashes! He had no news but the worst, news of treachery, of suffering and black fortune. Was she likely to find pleasure in his presence for all his high-flown dreams of service? And at the thought Francis brought his horse to a walk and braced himself for the inevitable.

Suddenly, at a turn of the bridge, he came full before the eyes of a party of three who were riding leisurely up towards the great avenue. They turned round at the sound of steps, and his heart stood still, while he felt the blood palpitate about his forehead. For the meeting he longed for and dreaded had come. The lady rode between two tall, harsh-looking gentlemen, one a grey-headed man with a soldier's bearing, the other younger, but with the same grim, narrow features. A far-away resemblance in the eyes made him hastily set them down as distant kinsmen.

At the sight of him the lady's eye grew wide with wonder, and she involuntarily drew rein. Then she nodded to her companions.

"Wait for me, Henry," she said, "I have a moment's business with this gentleman," and she turned and cantered to the bridge-end.

"You have returned, Mr. Birkenshaw," said she. "Have you any news for me?"

For a little Francis could only look. Her face was so pale and thin, her eyes so impenetrably sad, that he was lost in pity. Then, "I took your message to the Lord Lovat," he said lamely, "but was prevented from returning by a sore sickness. I saw the Prince on the eve of Culloden, and was by his side in the battle. I followed him to Gortuleg, and there, finding the Lord Lovat, I conceived it to be my duty to attach myself to his cause. Now I am come from him on a matter which closely concerns yourself."

"You have done well," she said. "I heard that you had reached Lovat from other sources, and when no further news came of you, I had thought you were dead. I am glad to see you safe. But I cannot wait longer lest I make my friends impatient. You have done my errand loyally, and I thank you from my heart. I would offer you the hospitality of my house were it not old and half-dismantled; but the village-inn will receive you for the night. I will lay no more toilsome missions on you.

Farewell, Mr. Birkenshaw." And ere he could say a word she had ridden up to the others.

Francis' heart sank to the ground. This was the dismissal, the end of his long service. For this he had endured sickness and weariness, cold mosses and the cruel hills. She had used him only as a servant, when he had thought he was a friend. His humiliation was bitter, his disappointment so utter as to benumb his mind. In a state of dreary bemazement he turned his horse's head to the village.

But he had told her of private news, and she had not waited to listen. What woman, least of all what woman of her eager temper, could have acted thus? And then her talk of the inn—and with this, light broke in upon his brain. She had feared suspicion on the part of the two sour-looking cavaliers. She had to all intents bidden him go to the inn and await her further commands. Clearly she would find ways and means to visit him. The thought was so wholly comforting that he fell into a state of unreasoning joy. She seemed solitary and friendless; then he, and he alone, would right her wrongs. This pale-cheeked lady was not the glorious beauty he had left, but she was something finer, subtler, more enchanting, pure gold refined in the furnace of sorrow.

The landlord of the inn was changed, the stout old Whig being dead, and a zealous Murray's man reigning in his stead. He eyed Francis with undisguised annoyance, clearly suspecting the designs of a stranger so near a noted harbour of the outlawed. Nor did Francis improve matters by his cunning questions to find out the man's leanings. The host adopted a robustious Whig tone, and professed a violent love for Hanover and all its appurtenances. This compelled the other to a like avowal of loyalty, and soon the two stood in a posture of mutual suspicion. Then the main purpose of his errand began to stir in Francis's heart, and he asked cautiously about the Laird's whereabouts, if haply he were yet lurking in the place. The man affected secrecy and drew him aside.

"Ye ken the tap house in the clachan," he said. "Weel, that's John Bertram's, and at its backside is a bit gairrden. There abune the tattie beds is a kind o' hole in the solid rock, whaur Murray has been hiding thae twae days."

The news fired Francis to action. Could he but get speech of Murray all might yet be well, false faith might be prevented, and the honour of a great family saved. He learned his directions from the man, and made his way up the fields to the garden back. With some pains he pierced the thick thorn hedge and found himself in a lone strip of ground, half planted with greens and half the bare rock of the hill. By dint of much searching he found a hole of some dimensions, and bearing marks of recent use. But now it was empty, utterly. When he came out he saw through the dusk a face at an open window in the cottage watching him closely. He ran down to the garden foot, but ere he reached it the window was shut and closely barred; and though he knocked hard at the back door he could get no admittance.

In some irritation he made his way back to the inn, where he found the landlord waiting with a clouded face.

"Why the Devil did you send me on such a goose-chase, sir?" Francis asked fiercely. "Where is Murray?"

"Let that be," said the man, sullenly. "Look ye here, sir. This is a letter sent to you this moment from a certain lady. Now, before ye get a sicht o' 't, ye will tell me plainly your way of thinking, for I will see ye damned afore I will have this lady come to any hurt."

The man stood so fully revealed by his words that Francis felt the need of caution no longer. "Why, man," he cried, "I am honest to the backbone. I have just come from the North with news for my Lady. I was by the Prince's side at Culloden, and am not a week from my Lord Lovat's company."

The landlord looked relieved, and gave him the note without further scruple. It proved to be a mere line to arrange an hour of meeting. Nine of the evening was the time she fixed, when with her servant she would seek Mr. Birkenshaw's presence. Francis read it and dropped it into the fire.

"Perhaps you will tell me now where the Laird lies," said he.

"Till this morning he was in that hole I telled ye o', and I kenna why he left it. He micht hae lain there canty for months. This countryside was ill-inclined to him, but there's no a man wad cheep a word o' where he was hidin'. But this morning he gaed off to Powmood to his guid-brither's, and I sair misdoot if he'll find it as quiet a biggin'. The mail gaed bye the day wi' twae-three lads that hadna the look o' Moffat dealers. I wis I kent if they gaed bye Powmood."

Francis groaned in spirit. This was the confirmation of his worst fears. Even now the man might be in the Government's hands with all his weight of secret knowledge. His first thought was to fly to Polmood and strive by main force to arrest calamity. But the thought of his own frailty deterred him, and, moreover, it was near the hour appointed for the meeting with Mrs. Murray. Even as he waited the clock struck the half-hour; so he went upstairs to spend the thirty minutes in snatching supper.

He had finished his meal and sat watching the firelight strive with the last fading glow of day on the wainscotted walls. He felt very melancholy, what with the ruin of a great cause and the futility of his little plans. Of what worth was he after all save to follow a greater's lead? He had not it in him to originate or to command. Something of his boyish sickness for cutting a fine figure in life came back to him at the moment, and added a pang to his regrets. And bitterer than all was the thought of his mistress's sorrows, of the long loneliness and shame which lay like a pall athwart her future.

Then when he had lost all cognisance of the present and was deep in dismal fancies, the door opened and two women entered. One was a maid, a little, rosy-faced countrywoman, and the other was the lady of his dreams. She advanced to greet him with both hands held out after her impulsive fashion, and before he knew he had taken them and led her to a seat. She wore a heavy dark cloak, and when at length she laid it aside, there were no bright robes beneath, only a sombre gown which made her white face paler. Her manner, too, had changed utterly. Of old she had looked at him with the calm, sovereign air of a mistress, now there was hesitation, diffidence, the tremulousness of grief.

"You understood me, Mr. Birkenshaw. I was vexed to turn from you so hastily, but my cousins of Romanno are ever suspicious. And now I can thank you for doing my work so well. In this lamentable confusion, when the best blood has been spilled like water, it is a pleasure to see a kenned face. And you will have heard, sir, I am desolate now, and have no one to look to save such honest gentlemen as serve me out of good will," and she smiled a little ghost of a smile.

Francis' blood was painfully stirred. He could not bear to see her sitting there so changed from her high estate. A great tumult of compassion arose in his soul.

"And now for your news," she said, "for I believe you have something to tell me in private. My maid is a sharer of all my secrets."

Here was a quandary for the unhappy man. How could he tell this pale heroic woman of her husband's perfidy? It seemed cruel beyond thought, and his heart failed him.

"It had to do with your husband," he stammered; "but if—"

He got no further, for at the word "husband" he saw she knew all. She covered her face with her hands and her bosom heaved with her sobbing. "Oh, it is true," she cried. "I am near crazy. I have fought—Oh my God!—I have fought to prevent it, but I could not. I knew his heart, but he denied it when I asked him, and put me off with smooth phrases till it was too late. And now he has gone to Polmood, and I am left to curse my woman's weakness. And he was the King's friend, the first man in Scotland to stand by the Prince, and the wisest head in his councils." She rocked herself to and fro in an impotence of agony.

Suddenly she rose to her feet and had flung herself beside him with her hands on his arm. "Oh, save me from myself," she cried. "I shall go mad, I have been alone for so long and my mind is sick with care. Oh, help me, help, do not go away. The Saints sent you here to-day, and I have been alone so long, and I have no friends but you." And she ended in stormy tears.

Francis was at his wit's end with sorrow and perplexity. To see his proud mistress humbled pierced him to the heart. He raised her and with the help of the maid reduced her to something like calm. All the while there was an undercurrent of crazy delight. Now at last she had summoned him to her aid, he need fear no rival in her service any more; and at the thought he felt the ragged ends of his life gather to a centre. Here lay his duty and task; his toil was but beginning.

At that moment through the window came the noise of a carriage driving rapidly along the highway to the North. It had the sound of a great equipage, and Francis instinctively drew back to the shadow of the curtain. Then came the sound of a stopping at the inn-door. The three in the room looked at each other in fear; even Mrs. Murray's eyes lost their vacancy. Francis peeped through the curtain's edge, but all he could see was a splash of light in the mid-road from the carriage lamps and the open inn-door. There was the sound of a man alighting, then of some talking with the landlord, in which the remaining inmates seemed to join. Then the man re-entered, the door was closed, and the echo of wheels died in the village street.

Francis rushed from the room with a foreboding of tragedy. He met the landlord at the stair-head with a face somewhat whiter than his own. There was no need of question; the man's look was eloquent of all.

"It's twae captains frae the Castle," he faltered, "and Murray o' Brochtoun is sitting atween them."

CHAPTER XVI.

A Council of Honour.

When Francis came to the house on the next forenoon he found it silent as a mausoleum. The smokeless chimney, the wide avenue beginning to show traces of lack of gardening, the great mass of untrimmed blossom on wall and border, and the sealed, dusty windows seemed to tell of a masterless home. Curlews screamed over the flower-garden, and in one spot where the heather had encroached on a clipped lawn two melancholy peacocks strutted in the confusion.

The solemn maid opened the door to him and took him to the self-same room where he had sat that night a year before and waited on the lady with the lamp. The same air of lost splendour which had afflicted him without, oppressed him within,—the deep rich wainscotting, the carved shelves of books, the emblazoned mantelpiece, all with a subtle atmosphere of neglect and disuse. The carpet still bore the mark of a man's mud-stained boot: here doubtless the Secretary Murray had bidden farewell to his house and his honour.

Then Mrs. Murray came to greet him, and led him to a summer-room looking out upon the hill and the western valley. She was no more the distracted woman of yesterday, but composed and pale, with heroism at her lips and eyes weary of life. Francis trembled at the sight of her, for this face argued some quixotic resolve and he anticipated troublous days. Night had worked changes in his temper. He had lost his first tumultuous anger and grief; the fervours of his spirit had abated and left his soul cold and exceeding bleak. He wavered nothing from his purpose, but he would have welcomed gladly yesterday's high sentiment. What though it were but vain elation, it had at least made the world roseate for an hour. Now he was a wiser, stronger man, but one with teeth set and his back to the wall, fighting against inclination, prudence, and his own unregenerate heart.

But this new mood of his lady's matched his own, and relieved him of one difficulty. For with all his compassion he had a horror of tears, a shrinking from the pathetic; and the spectacle of a weak woman looking to him alone for aid could in certain moods arouse only repugnance. But now all dealings between the two were passionless and kindly. This tall lady was again the mistress, and he waited to do her bidding. He asked her purposes.

"There can be but one way," said she. "He will go to London, and there I must follow him. I cannot hope to mend matters, for I am poor and have little purchase, but I may see him and try. I have no hope, Mr. Birkenshaw, but it is better to press on in some sort of endeavour than eat out my heart here in despair."

"But where can you bide in London?" asked Francis. It was his duty to look after the plain fact in the wrapping of the romantic.

"I do not know," she said, "unless with my cousin Lady Manorwater, who is of my religion, and if all else fails will take me with her over-seas."

"But how will you make the journey?" he asked.

"Why, how would I make it but alone, with my own horses and the one servant who is left me?" she said, with a faint attempt at vivacity.

"But who is to see to your lodging on the road and guide you safe through an unsettled country?" he asked again.

"Ah, I cannot tell. I must use my mother wit—and there is all the need in the world for hurry;" and she twisted her hands with a sad gesture of impotence.

"And above all, my lady, is it likely that you will convince your husband in a hurried sight of him, if you failed before his arrest when you had leisure and safety?"

"I can but try," she said simply. Then, "Oh, Mr. Birkenshaw, the thing is less a journey of hope than of despair. I well know that I have left nothing undone, and that may be a solace in the dark years that remain to me."

She spoke so sadly that Francis was moved, and the old sentiment began to rise in his heart.

"I owe a duty to—a great Highland lord," he said, "which I must sometime fulfil. If you go to the South I go also. Our journeys have the same purpose and may well lie together, and perhaps I may help you in some of the difficulties of the road."

At his words, her face shone for a moment with gratitude, then it suddenly paled. "I will only be a drag, and my company will be the least safe in the world for you. I am already deep in your debt, and I cannot accept this service."

"But if the lord be the Lord Lovat," said Francis, "if I have sworn to him that I would keep the Secretary from any such step though I followed him to the Tower, will this not change your decision?"

"But you said yourself that the errand was idle. How will you get a sight of him; and even if you see him how will you bring him to a better mind?"

"I can but trust to chance to show me a way," said he, speaking thoughts which had been with him on his road from the Highland glens. "I do not value my life at overmuch, and for a desperate man there are many paths. But if the mischief is not done and he still lie unconfessed in the Tower, there is some hope; for a road may be found out of that place even for Mr. Murray of

Broughton." Yet while he spoke he felt the futility of such a scheme—these two folk in a moorland house half a thousand miles from the capital, plotting a great state crime.

But to the lady it seemed a way out of all perplexities. "We can do as Lady Nithsdaill did, as Anne Carew and Sir John Haltwhistle, and many others. Oh what a thing is a bold man's mind! With you to help me I have hope, and I thank you from my heart, for it is most noble and generous to risk your life in my desperate cause. I cannot thank you, but God knows I shall ever remember." And as cheek and brow flushed with the emotion of the feelings, Francis for a moment sat lord and king in a crazy palace of cloud.

"We must not delay," said she, "for they will let no grass grow under their feet now they have got him. I have already made preparations for the journey, and I cannot see how two people should not travel quicker than a body of horse. There is my maid Anne who will follow me to the end of the world, and I will take a serving-man to see to the horses. You will find me the road, Mr. Francis?"

Francis felt anew the desperation of his quest, but he had not the heart to throw obstacles in the way. This heroic lady might bid him steal the crown-jewels, were her mind to be set at ease by such a deed.

"I accept the charge, my lady. God grant we meet with a happy fortune!"

"Nay, but I will have no 'my ladies' or 'Mrs. Murrays' or 'madames,'" she cried. "Do you not see that the quest is ours, and we cannot enter upon it with a hedge of formalities between us? You have shown yourself a gallant gentleman, sir, and we set out on this journey as sister and brother. You will be Francis to me, and let me be Margaret, and then we shall be the better friends." She spoke simply, but a blush rose to her cheek, and she played with the tassel of her chair.

Francis bowed, himself in turn violently out of composure. It was a wise rule for both; but the sudden change in his position, the dizzy companionship of a dream, threw him out of his bearings.

He rose and went to a window which looked over a courtyard to a long wooded valley. There was now no bustle in the place, no moving of horses, nor running of serving-men. Only in a corner stood a great travelling-coach, which a single groom had washed and made ready, and was passing a brush over the panels.

Mrs. Murray had come over to his side, and looked on at the picture. He could not forbear to glance at her as she stood by his shoulder, so tall that her hair was but little below his cheek; and he noticed that her eye had filled as she gazed.

"What is the fellow doing?" he asked.

"He is doing my commands," she said. "Can you not see his work? He is painting out the arms of Murray from the panel, that no roadside passer may know them and witness the tragedy of an old house."

He looked, and sure enough the man had all but obliterated any colour from the level black wood.

"It was a handsome coat as one might see in all the land," she said softly, as if speaking to herself. "First and fourth there was the old coat of Murray, three silver mullets on an azure chief with a black hunting-horn below on a silver field; second, it bore three silver fraises for the kinship to the house of Fraser, and third, the three gold cushions of the vanished house of Romanno. Did you know the motto and crest of Mr. Secretary Murray, Francis? There it is; Robin is almost at it, and soon it will be no more. A dove with an olive branch, and *Pacis nuntia* for a device! Now I wonder what old raider chose that foolish text to set below his arms. I had never heard that the Murrays carried peace to all men in their hearts, save—Ah, God help me!—that traitor's peace that one of the house is now seeking! A dove with an olive branch. Ay, it is suitable irony, and I praise the wit and foresight of the old cynic who first wrote it. At any rate it is all done with now, and I go out to the world without blazon or history. Heigho, I feel quit of a load, and yet I am melancholy to-day over the end of so long a story."

Then Francis took his leave and went down to the village, where he found the landlord and held long consultation; for much of Mrs. Murray's own possessions were to be left in his charge against that seizure of the house which must soon follow. But the main point was the line of journey, and here he found a ready informant. For in the old days of the '15 this man had travelled far into the Midlands of England, and since then had gone many times to the South with droves of cattle. He drew up an itinerary as far as his knowledge permitted, and gave it into Francis' keeping, adding many prudent hints about lodging by the way and the least frequented paths. The honest fellow had much ado to speak clearly, for grief at the melancholy fortunes of his mistress choked his voice and confused his judgment "We hae a' our troubles in thae times," he cried, "but to see the sair end fa' on our puir feckless leddy is eneuch to wring tears frae a heidstane. The men are to bide canty at hame, but the women must up and awa' to weir their herts on a desperate ploy. Lord, siccan days!"

When he returned to the house on some small errand it was already drawing toward evening. He found Margaret in the same west-looking room, fingering for the last time her treasures. "I must carry little," she said in answer to his look, "for a burdenless rider gangs easily, as the folk say, so I am taking a last look at certain old things for which I have a sort of affection. Men sit loose in those matters, but we women are cumbered about with a host of memories, and must always have our trinkets." She placed some jewels in their case, and shutting it went towards a spinet which stood by the window. "I used to play old tunes on it," she said, "for the amusement of my father when he tired of idleness in his latter days. It's a long farewell to my spinet as to all else, but I must play one last air before I shut it. Have you any favourite catch, Francis?"

Francis shook his head, for in truth he had little music in his soul save of the large rough-and-ready order.

"Then I will play you an old tune of the Cause, which loyal ladies have sung for many years and will doubtless sing for years to come, seeing that there is little hope of their dreams being fulfilled. It is called 'Lady Keith's Lament,' and the music was made by the King's own piper, who was a Macrimmon of the Macleods. It goes haltingly to a spinet, but you shall hear it." And she played a wild melody, singing to it some such words as these:—

"A' are gane, the gude, the kindly,
Low in the moss and far on the sea,
Men o' the North, men o' the muirlands,
Brave to battle and laith to flee.
I was aince a lady o' pride,
High my hame abune the heather;
Now my silken gown I tine,
I maun fare in wind and weather.

"Kin and kith in weary battle
By stranger waters across the faem

Fell, and dying had mind o' sweet Argos,
The man of auld and the hills of hame.
The ship is rocking by the pier,
The hour draws nigh when we maun pairt.
Then fare thee weel, my loved, my dear,
Bide I canna, though breaks my hert."

"They are rude, simple verses," she said, "but to me they are extraordinarily touching. There are some other lines which tell of a brighter hope." And with some enthusiasm in her voice she sang:—

"But though I now maun wander dowie,
And drap the tear on cheek sae pale,
Yet shall our dule be turned to joy,
For God maun let the richt prevail.
My father was a gude lord's son,
My mither was an earl's daughter;
And I'll be Lady Keith again
The day the King comes ower the water."

As she finished, she sat for a long time motionless, looking out of the western windows. As for Francis, he fell into a like mood, and neither spoke for long. The sight of this woman, young, unfortunate, bright with a long-descended, subtle beauty, sitting there singing a sad old ballad on that last day of calm before the stormy morrow, moved him more than he could tell. Something in the haunting notes of her voice, the sunset light on her hair, or the long line of golden hill-land which gleamed from the window, seemed to him an epitome of all the fervours and sorrows of life. He sat musing till Margaret rose and shut the spinet.

"It is time to have done with old songs, Francis. Henceforth it is grimmer work for you and me."

CHAPTER XVII.

A Journey to the South.

From Broughton to Moffat is a short day's journey even for an old travelling coach, but the way is rough and grass-grown up the narrow glen of Tweed to the high moors and the precipitous source of the Annan. Thence in a long day through pleasant Annandale you may come to the Bridge of Esk and pass on to Carlisle walls. The two days were days of sunny, windless weather, and the clear air of the hill-tops put an edge upon the travellers' spirits. Margaret seemed to forget her troubles, and after the way of woman, was interested in each passing face. As for Francis he had a heavier burden, but even he accepted the inevitable. He served the lady in a somewhat clumsy fashion, for he had no notion of the civilities of a fine society; but as the hours passed the two grew very excellent companions, while some spice of humour enlivened their sombre talk. For take any two clear and honest souls and set them in such a position; you will find them at first constrained and foolish, but as time goes on they will know each other for the human being that he or she may be, and look sanely into the future.

Carlisle was in an extraordinary stir, what with things political and the yearly summer fair. Daily batches of prisoners came South to these walls, and soon many brave hearts sighed out their life from a tow on the

Gallows-hill. Farmers from the hills were everywhere in the streets, drovers and wide-eyed shepherds thronged the ports; and each inn was filled with brown-faced bedlamites who made the night hideous with their din. In a little inn near the south gate, Francis found lodging; this much he had settled at Broughton, for the place was quiet, and the landlord no ill friend to the lost cause. There he left Margaret and her two servants, and went out to the streets in the late evening to ponder over the tangle of his affairs.

Money must soon be thought of, for his funds were already running low. He had no knowledge of the lady's wealth, but though she had been amply rich he would have died sooner than let her pay a single crown. When she came to Lady Manorwater's house his task would be ended; meantime she was his charge, the journey was by his advice, and he alone would see to the lawing. It was an old-faced, grim-looking man who stalked through the rabble of drovers in the noisy, darkening street.

Suddenly he brushed against a man who stared full in his eyes. It was the face of an elderly grizzled gentleman, clad in stout, simple country clothes, with a long jowl and deep eyebrows. Something in the air demanded recognition, and Francis involuntarily stopped. The man did likewise, and for a second the two blocked the causeway. Then like a flash came a happy intuition to Francis' brain. "May I have a word with you, sir?" he asked.

The stranger nodded and led the way across the street to a little public, where he climbed a stair to a room above the causeway. The place was still yellow with sunset, and in a mirror on the wall Francis saw his own reflection. He almost cried aloud, for save for the twenty or thirty years' difference in age his was almost a double of his companion's face. His chance thought was now certainty.

"And now, sir, what is your business with me?" said the elder man.

"Why, my business is simple," said Francis. "I have come to claim kinship, sir. You, I think, are my uncle Robert?"

"So," said the man solemnly, "I jaloused as much the first glisk I got of ye. Ye will be Francie's son. Ye favour him, save that ye're sae muckle wiser-lookin' as ye seem less drunken. God, man, ye have the Birkenshaw glower maist uncannily in your een. Ye are the leevin' image o' my father. And what is it ye seek wi' me, nevoy Francis? Abune a', what brings ye to Carlisle toun in thae days o' war?"

"Listen to me," said the other, "and I will tell ye a bit story." And briefly he told of the last year, of his wanderings and his toils, and now of his final charge. The man heard him out with a grim face.

"Ye are like your kind, Francie, you and your trokings wi' outlawed Jaicobites. There was never a Birkenshaw afore took up wi' sic a bairnly cause."

"I have heard bits o' the family history," said Francis, "but I never heard that it was the wont of our folk to leave a man when his back was at the wall or to refuse a woman aid."

"Ye may put it that way if ye like," said the man, "but ye canna deny that it's unprofitable."

"Then I leave that branch of the family's work to you, my dear uncle. I am content if I can keep a coat on my back. Has Markit paid well these last years?"

"Off and on," grumbled the other. "The land's ower unsettled for peaceable folk to dae guid business."

"Because I am about to ask the loan of a hundred guineas," said Francis, boldly.

"A hundred guineas," cried Mr. Robert Birkenshaw. "A hundred golden guineas! The man's mad! Heard ye ever the like o' sic a speiring! A hundred guineas, quotha! Mair like a hundred pence!"

"But you will give it me?" said Francis, "seeing that a journey cannot be decently finished without gold."

"But what's the need o' the journey, man? Gang back to Dysart to Gregor Shillinglaw and clerk awa' among the writer lads like an honest man."

"You know fine you would never have me do that," said Francis. "Is our auld house fallen so low as to neglect a plain duty for lack of gear?"

Mr. Robert Birkenshaw presented a lamentable sight, his face red with emotion and twitching between love of his gold and the impulses of an honest heart. "What can I dae?" he cried miserably. "I'm no mean and I wad uphaud the family honour, but I'm dooms puir though folk ca' me rich." Then with a splutter he took out a bag of gold from a flap-pocket and flung it on the table. "Damn ye, Francie, tak' it," he cried. "Tak' it and use it weel. I've nae bairns, and whae's to lend to the family if it's no mysel'? Ye say ye are serving a leddy. Sit ye doon, and we'll drink to her if she's bonny. What's her name?"

At the mention of it the old pagan cried aloud in glee: "I aince saw her, and she was as bonny as Queen Mary. Francie, lad, it's a guid errand ye're on, and I'll risk anither hundred if ye need it." And so the lady's health was drunk and Francis sat on at the wine till late, hearing old fragments of family tales. So when at last he sought the inn, it was with some affection for his fellows and a more kindly outlook on life.

It would be hard to follow that hurried journey after the style of an itinerary, for it was monotonous and without interest save the casual variation of weather. Among the Westmoreland hills the drought broke in a chain of storms which set every hill-water roaring and made the fords hard for a carriage to pass. It was weary work both for Francis without on his horse, opposed to the buffeting of rain, and for Margaret and her maid within, who had no outlook but the dull streaks of water against the panes and a perpetual line of rough hill-land. Sometimes it cleared towards evening, and then the lady would dismount and walk down the yellowing mountain track where the pools glowed in links of pure fire. In these hours she became cheerful, but in the long black showers she was sad and absent-minded, dwelling always on the past and its melancholy change. As for Francis, he was so old a wayfarer that he endured all weathers with equanimity. Only, when soaked to the skin and with no sight but blank hills, he would begin to think on the futility of his errand and torment his brain with projects of vain endeavour.

But with the Lowlands came July days when the sun was hot in the sky and the roads white underfoot. It was now that Margaret recovered her spirits and found humour in every halting-place and something pleasant to her curiosity in the vivid life of the road. Her cheeks got a touch of colour, till she no longer formed such a sharp contrast to the gipsy Francis. Yet the life had still all the hardships of a journey, for the roads were broken in many places with recent passage of armies, the inns were filled with an air of suspicion, and piteous sights were always at hand to remind of war. This was in the North, but as they drew to the Midlands they found a lush and settled country which seemed terribly unfriendly to fugitives from a mourning land. For the first time they felt their presence among a people of alien sentiments and blood, a peaceable folk who dwelt among orderly hedgerows and neat, garden-like fields. And with the thought the bright and bitter past grew more irrevocable, and both alike were plagued with hapless memories.

For Francis each day meant much careful forethought and not seldom high-handed intrusion. As it chanced, many of the inns were filled with the stream of travellers between North and South, and to get comfort he had to assume a high air of dignity and show a bluff self-confidence he did not feel. Fortunately his purse was heavy, and in this easy land he found money a passport to more things than in the flinty North. But his mind was in a perpetual worry, for to haggle about the little things of life had never been his task before, and he found it irksome. His consolation lay in Margaret's entire immunity from such trivial cares; if her life must be sorrowful and vain, it would at least be free from the grossness of worry.

The road was uneventful though it was the morning after a war, and one incident alone is worthy of record. In a little town on the Warwick borders they halted for a night, and after dusk Francis went out as his custom was to sober his thoughts with the night air. A year ago he had been a boy; now he felt himself an aging broken man, driven in curb along a stony path of virtue, a man passionate yet austere, with a cold, scrupulous heart and a head the prey of every vagrom fancy. A man with great capacities, truly, but scarcely a man to live pleasantly, at ease with himself and the world.

Round the gate of the inn-yard there was the usual idle throng. As he jostled his way through, one turned sharply round, recognition shining in his eyes. He put his hand on Francis' shoulder and followed him to the street. "Mr. Birkenshaw, my dear man," he cried, "do I trust my ain een? What brings ye here o' a' places on earth? I have had hell's luck since I left you at Leidburn, but you look stout and flourishing."

When Francis recognised in the tattered lad the great Starkie, his former friend, his first feeling was of rage, fierce and unthinking. What right had this tatterdemalion, this ghost from the past, to come here and remind him of his folly, when he loathed it with his whole heart and soul? It was a pitiable figure, unshaven, haggard, with blear eyes and a shambling walk,—a thing all but over the verge of beggary. And this had once claimed him as companion and now called him friend!

"Ye're the lad for me, Mr. Birkenshaw. Ye've the master mind. I see ye've your braw leddy here that flyted on ye at Leidburn. Ye wad sune mak' it up wi' her, for ye were a lad wi' weemen?" And he wandered into obscenity.

Francis took him by the collar and held him firm. "See here, Mr. Stark, if ye mention the lady's name again I will fling ye over the brig as I once flung ye into a ditch. You and me quitted partnership lang syne. If it's money ye want I will help ye to the best of my power, but let there be no talk of friendship."

The boy whimpered. "What's ta'en ye at an auld freend?" he cried.

"We have taken different roads, you and me," said Francis.

"Ye may set yoursel' abune me if ye please. I am puir and ye are rich, but I never took anither man's wife to traivel the high-roads wi' me."

Francis' fingers itched for his ears. "I am not a patient man, as ye know, Mr. Stark."

"Patient or no, what do I care? But there's ae thing I can see wi' my een, and that is that there's some o' His Majesty's sodgers wad be glad to ken that ye were here and this leddy wi' ye." He shrieked out his words while cunning twinkled in his little eyes.

"If ye say a word more, sir, or if ye dare but try what ye threaten, by God I'll send ye to your Master or ever ye can cheep. Do ye think I'm to be trifled wi' that ye try my hand here?" And he spoke so fiercely and with such angry eyes that the wretched Starkie seemed to shrivel up into apology.

"God, Francie!" he cried, "gie me siller and let me off, for I'm starving."

Francis thrust some coins into his dirty palm and watched him turn with scarcely a word of thanks and shuffle back to the inn. He was angry with himself, angry and ashamed. He almost pitied the wretch, and yet he loathed him and feared him and all the black past which he stood for. All his little self-composure was sent broadcast on the winds. He knew himself for the ragged, inconstant fool that he was, with but a thought dividing his veneer of virtue from the stark blackguardism of the vagrant. It was a stormy-souled man who tossed that night upon his bed, and rose in the morning with something greyer and bleaker in his determination.

As they passed out into the street a hollow-faced boy, still half-tipsy from the night's debauch, cried good morning and a pleasant journey.

"Who is that man?" asked Margaret, carelessly.

"He was one of my former friends," said Francis, and rode forward.

* * * * *

As they came near the city where the roads from the North converged into one great highway, their journey was hindered with the constant passing of military. Once more they were in the air of war, for a prisoner would pass, or a forlorn and anxious band of his kinsfolk, or a great northern lord or lady—all on their way to the great centre of fate. Francis felt no fear of recognition, for his part, though played in the thick of affairs, had been secret from the multitude. Once only, when a lady whom he knew for Miss Cranstoun of Gair, looked curiously at the tall, brown, sombre cavalier, did he turn away his face in doubt. But for the most part he held his head carelessly amid the throng of wayfarers.

The last night's halting-place was in a little town on the edge of Hertfordshire, a place among green meadows and rushy waters. At its one inn they found no one but a groom rubbing down a horse in the courtyard, and from the look of beast and man it seemed as if some person of importance were using the hostel. In the one dining-room when both sat down to supper a man was looking out of the window and drumming on the pane. He turned round at their entrance, and in a second Francis had in his mind the Highland inn and the carousing by the fire; for in the stranger he saw the rosy face and heavy figure of Forbes of Culloden, the Lord President.

He felt he was recognised, he felt too that this man was well aware who was the lady who sat down with him. As it chanced Margaret, who had seen the great lawyer scores of times, saw in him only a chance stranger; the dusk was gathering, she was tired with the day's toil, and she had no memory for faces. Forbes bowed to her curtly and without a word withdrew.

Francis ate his meal in a fever of anxiety. This man held both in his hands, and on the one former occasion of meeting he had insulted him, using as a weapon the name of this very lady. He knew of the popular report which made the Lord President's name a synonym for kindliness; but would he forgive so arch an offender, would he believe in the honesty of one who had so recently played a very different part? As soon as he could he left the room on some pretext to go in search of him.

He found him on the threshold, smoking with great deliberation and watching the glow of sunset over the fields. "So we meet again, Mr. Birkenshaw?" he observed drily.

"It is on that point I have come to speak, my lord," said Francis. "You favour the other side in politics, but folk say that you are not a man that loves extremes. You see our wretched position, and I would ask your forbearance."

"Ye are a Jacobite renegade," said the other, "and ye ask me to let ye be. That I can understand. But what for does this lady go with you? Are ye up to some new devilry, Mr. Birkenshaw? For if ye are, lad, and would drag the bonniest woman in the land into the same bog, then by God I will make you pay for it with every bone in your body." And his honest old eyes twinkled with wrath.

Then Francis with a shamefast air had to set to and tell him the history of the whole business, leaving out only such parts as concerned Lovat and the Prince. The old man stopped him once and again, bidding him say no more about this or that matter, as it might be best for him to hear least. To the whole tale of Murray of Broughton he listened eagerly, murmuring under his breath. Then he took Francis' hand, and stared hard into his eyes till he was fain to shut them against that steely glitter.

"I believe ye to be a true man, Mr. Birkenshaw, and I ask your pardon. But this is a most lamentable tale ye have to tell me. Lord, man, I am driven crazy wi' the cruelties that are being perpetrated in the North on the puir people. I have run to and fro atween Stair and Tweeddale and got satisfaction nowhere. Aye, I have even licked the boots o' Cumberland, that haggis of a man, and suffered his clownish insults. I have been fleein' here and there night and day on the business of that fule Cromarty, and now I come up here to try once more and wring water out of a stane. Heard ye o' the death o' the two lords, Balmerino and Kilmarnock? God, there was a tale for history! And now there may be a third, if a' ye say is true, seeing that my Lord Lovat is taken."

"Taken!" cried Francis; "when, how?"

"I kenna," said the other, shortly. "But a day syne a coach passed me and a great guard o' dragoons. I asked at the captain whae was his prisoner and he bade me look inside; and there, grinning like a wull-cat, was the auld wizened face o' the Fraser."

CHAPTER XVIII.

Of an Interview in an Unlikely Place.

Lady Manorwater greeted her cousin with a dignified kindliness. She was a pale woman of middle age, with the faded blue eyes and yellow hair of one type of Scotswoman. Fervently devout, as was the habit of her house, she carried her devotion beyond the other Catholic ladies of her time, and seemed ever posturing as a colourless saint. She thought of politics and her kinsfolk only as things far away; for her the living reality of life was found in the little chapel where at frequent hours she would retire to a dim world of candles and paternosters. Her two sons were boys in their early teens; and these with the servants made up the whole household in Great Marlow Street. A perpetual air of peril hung over the house, for men came there on short visits by day and night whose names had been proclaimed at law, and under the cloak of her pious and unworldly name treason had flourished and many a secret conclave had met undisturbed. She welcomed her cousin with kindness, for she had ever been fond of the beautiful girl; more, it pleased her that she should flee to her of all her kin at this hour of danger. It seemed like a recognition of that sanctity she believed to be hers.

Towards Francis she wore the stiffness which she used to all mankind. He was beyond the circle of her thoughts, unrelated by blood and alien in creed. The place was in no disorder; the life was as full of punctiliousness as in a great house in times of peace. At first it irritated Francis, for he who had come on solemn business had no inclination for a farce of comfort. But soon he was glad, for it distracted Margaret's thoughts and restored her to some portion of the elegancies of life. For her there was no going in and out and sharing in the gaieties of town. London was bitterly hostile to her cause; the streets were full of a mob shouting coarse party cries; and every day almost there was some fresh death for the populace to gape at. So the women abode indoors, while Francis wandered fiercely about the city.

As soon as he might, he sought out the lodging of the Lord President in the Haymarket. Forbes sat before a pile of papers, in a fine reek of tobacco smoke, while two harassed clerks scribbled in a corner. At the sight of the visitor he opened the door to a smaller sitting-room and bade him follow.

"Well, Mr. Birkenshaw, how have ye been employing your time hereaways?" he asked.

"As best I could," said Francis. "This much I know, that Murray lies in the Tower with his honour still untarnished. Traitor or no, his treachery has not yet been put to proof."

"True enough," said Forbes. "His examination begins next week. Have ye any work on hand ye may desire my help in?"

"It is my wish to get speech of the Secretary."

Forbes hummed a little. "It is unconstitutional," he said, "but it might be managed, though I see not what it will serve. Ye will be bearing him messages from his wife and kin?"

"I will be striving to bring him to a better mind," said Francis. "You know what I mean, my lord."

"Pardon me, sir, I ken nothing but what I choose to ken. Besides, when so much is thrust down my throat there is no need for idle guesses;" and he looked up with a twinkle of intelligence which served the other's purpose.

There was silence for a little, while street cries floated up and a catch of a song which the Lord President whistled. "I know the desperation of my plans," said Francis; "but then it is no time for little makeshifts."

"If ye kenned the circumstances o' the time better, sir, ye might think them a little more desperate. Here are you, a lad without penetration, with no knowledge of the world, and ye are for visiting a noted prisoner of state and 'bringing him to a better mind;'" and the old man laughed sarcastically.

"I fight for my own hand," said Francis, gloomily; "I can at least harm no man but myself."

Forbes looked at him shrewdly for a second, and then drew his chair closer with a serious face.

"Would ye wonder greatly if I were to give ye some hint of the way the wind blows, Mr. Francis? Would it amaze ye to hear that those in power are none so keen about this affair of the Secretary? His intention is ower plain to mistake, and I can tell ye, sir, there are many on our side forbye myself that do not like it. The rising is utterly broken, and two great lords have already paid the penalty with their heads. It is a civilised people making war within itself, and the best statesmen have no craving for a glut of blood. Now mark ye what happens. The thing appears to be near a natural end. Scores of the common folk have swung for it, and there is hope that the worst is over. Then here comes the arch-plotter and gives himself up of his own free-will. Any bairn can make the inference. Mr. Murray has something to tell, and there is but one person in our hands that such a tale can affect. This person, as it chances, is of great fame and far stricken in years. Ye follow my words, Mr. Birkenshaw?"

Francis nodded, seeing a gleam of light.

"It is true that all the bloodhounds of the courts and the common ruck of the nation are never tired of butchery; but I speak of the great and wise who have the real ordering of the land, and alone think truly of its welfare. Do you not perceive that this has some bearing on your case, sir?"

"Then I may hope—" began Francis, eagerly.

"Softly, sir," said the Lord President. "I have nothing to do with what you hope. As an officer of law it is my business to see that you hope nothing. I was declaring a point of pure theory. Supposing, sir, supposing, I say, that the King's government woke up to-morrow and found Mr. Murray no longer a resident in a certain place, the best and most powerful would be the least sorry."

"But the thing you speak of is near impossible."

"Not so," said the other. "It would be possible—again I consider it in theory—for a powerful minister even to use some influence to see that the chance of the aforesaid gentleman's departure at least was there. The guard might be selected with some discretion on that particular night, Mr. Francis."

Francis was looking steadfastly at the floor, in a profound study.

"I think I have followed, my lord," he said, looking up. "I cannot tell you my gratitude."

"There is a further matter to mention," said Forbes. "I presume that in such a supposed event a certain gentleman would fall into the hands of the law," and he looked with meaning.

"It seems the only way," said Francis.

"Then, of course, you have understood that the full rigour of the law's vengeance would fall on such an one. Whatever the Government might think in its private heart, it must show a severe front to the world. The lad that sought to fill Mr. Secretary's place would swing from a tow ere the week was out."

"I have considered it, my lord," said Francis, though with a whitening face.

"Yet, supposing the lad to have a great spirit, he would deem his neck's safety a small thing compared with the honour of his friends?"

"Doubtless he would," said Francis, between closed teeth.

At this the Lord President rose and gathered his papers together. "I have to tell ye, sir," he said gravely, "that I honour ye for a very gallant gentleman." Then, as he conducted him to the door of his lodging, he spoke quietly in his ear, "I would recommend the third night from this if any one thought of putting the supposititious theory into practice."

Hitherto a certain gentleman has come but little into our tale; now he must enter for an hour ere taking a long farewell. Times had changed with John Murray of Broughton, and it was a careworn, peevish man who sat in his prison chamber looking forth at the evening sky from a barred slit in the massive stone. He still wore the stained clothes he had travelled in, and what with the bare furnishing and the high, shadowy vaulting the scene and the man looked dismally comfortless. Most of his time he spent in pacing the length of his chamber, with knitted brow and lips that muttered ceaselessly. The toil had soon worn him thin; he had lost his old florid colour; and what with his past privations and his present disquietude, it was a mere shade of his old self that sat moodily in the dusk of the evening.

Suddenly the door was opened by a turnkey and a visitor was ushered in. The warder left without locking the door, and the stranger advanced to his side. He had risen and stood inquiringly regarding a tall man, dressed plainly, and with a great horseman's jacket turned up about his ears. Not till he had advanced some paces to the light did he see clearly, and then he went forward to greet him with outstretched hands. For it was a mark of the Secretary that no name or face which he once heard or saw was ever forgotten.

"God bless you, Mr. Birkenshaw, and I am blithe to get a sight of an old face. I am dying in these walls for some token that my friends have not forgotten me. But how comes it that you are admitted? for they keep me here as close as a mad tyke. I trust you have run into no grave personal risk on account of my worthless self?"

"It matters little how I came in, sir, and be assured I am running no risk. I have come to have some talk with you on a little private matter. But I would inquire after your health. How do you bear the mournful events of these latter days?" Francis spoke shortly but not uncivilly, for indeed the man's old rank and present discomfort impelled him to some politeness.

"Alas for a poor people!" cried the Secretary, sinking back in his chair. "It is the way of all great causes, when brave hearts perish and senseless force crushes out loyalty and honour. You saw the saddest day in Scotland's history, unless there have been more awful crimes since I last saw the open sky." He spoke in the style of Lovat, but to Francis, knowing the man only too shrewdly, the words seemed void of meaning.

"Many honest fellows have been swinging on Hairibee," said he, "and two great lords have met their doom on the Tower hill."

The Secretary shut his lips to hide the quivering. "Even so," he said, "death is the end of all our desires. Did you bring any message from our friends in the North?"

"None," said Francis, "for my errand was but a matter of personal satisfaction. I came to ask if you fulfilled my request before the unhappy day at Culloden?" And he looked hard at the other.

"Why, yes," said Murray, simply. "The letters have long perished. But what makes you so eager to ken?"

"The Lord Lovat is now in his enemies' hands," said Francis, "and, as there is like to be much brought against him, I wished to have no sad reflections that remissness of mine had brought him to his undoing. I do not hint anything of blame to you in the matter, but if perchance the thing had been mislaid, it would be a formidable article in the charge."

Murray ignored the slur and fastened on the mere statement, but it was clear that the words moved him.

"Lovat is taken, you say?" he cried. "God, that is the end of the Cause with a vengeance, for they have gotten the greatest intellect in all Scotland or France. Have they brought him here?"

"It is some days since," said Francis.

"But what can they prove against him?" he asked excitedly. "He wasna out with the rest no more than Traquair and the Macleods. They're safe enough in their hidy-holes, and wherefore no Lovat? Ye say they will have much matter to bring against him, but it beats me to tell where they'll get a boddle's worth. I tell ye, sir, it will be a glorious acquittal." And he looked on Francis with keen, sagacious little eyes.

To his hearer every word was offensive, so clearly did it argue a black purpose. No doubt the man acted his part cunningly, but there was a trip in his tongue, a falter in his readiness which belied him. Francis stared on him with gathering brows.

"And how is it with yourself, Mr. Murray? Are you too to have a glorious acquittal, or are ye deep in the black books of the Government, like the honest gentlemen who are gone?"

The Secretary shook his head and passed his hand over his eyes.

"My days are numbered," he said, "numbered like the rest. I cannot look for mercy, for I have been at my master's side in all his calamities, and my name is near as well kenned as his own. Think you they will let me go now they have got me?" and even in his fright his breast seemed to swell with importance. "I could have wished to die in my own land by the side of the brave Keppoch at Culloden or among the heather hills; but I have screwed my courage to the cauld death which awaits me. After all, it is but a short and easy passage to a better world."

Francis sat in silence, his eyes scanning him up and down so intently that the voice quavered in the last words.

"It is of this chiefly that I came to speak," he said. "Your friends in the North, me among the rest, and many others whom it would not be well to name, have considered that you, as the Prince's best friend, would be a sore loss to the Cause. So by perilous ways we have contrived a means whereby you may escape and get safely over the water."

Murray lifted his head, and looked with wild eyes upon the speaker.

"It's a device of little subtilty, and it has been used before with some success. You and I are much of a height. You have only to change clothes with me, wrap this same riding-cloak about your ears, and take your leave. I have purposely made the clothing somewhat kenspeckle, that the men may notice it and pay less heed to the face. The warders are picked men, and more than one are in the secret. At the last gate you will meet one of our own countrymen, an Argyle Campbell, who will give you the word, 'To which passage?' You have but to answer, 'To the Fords of Tyne,' and he will follow you beyond the bounds, and see you safely to the door of your wife's lodging. There all is ready for flight this very evening, and ere morn you may be on the high seas. But you must hasten, Mr. Murray, for the hours pass."

But the Secretary's face showed no joyful surprise, no eagerness, only discomfort, timidity, and doubt. He rose stammering from his chair.

"I am grateful, Mr. Birkenshaw, grateful to you and all the good friends. Be sure I am grateful;" and he walked hastily up and down. "But, my lad, it canna be. You purpose to stay in my place. Do ye not see that it means that your life will be forfeit, that you alone will be left to bear the wrath of a tricked government? I may be soured and ill-grained, but God knows I have not come to such a depth as to allow such a cruel sacrifice. A young life," he repeated. "It canna be."

"But I am willing," cried Francis. "Think what the thing involves. I am a landless, kinless man, and no one will mourn my end. Nay, it would be a matter of highest satisfaction to myself that I could die so well. But you have a wife, you are a member of a great house, above all, you are one of the few props of a feeble cause." Even as he spoke the words disgusted him. He saw treachery written so plainly on this man's face that he would have been glad to catch him by the neck and drive him out perforce. Something of his feelings must have been apparent, for Murray asked suddenly,—

"Had Meg anything to do with this errand? It would be like one of her daft games."

"Surely your wife has a hand in the matter," said Francis, "seeing that even now she is waiting to carry you with her to France."

"I might have guessed it," he said. "But what sort of scheme is it? How could you think it so easy to win aboard when the sea-shore is watched by the King's dragoons like the Tower courtyard? It is mere madness, Mr. Birkenshaw; I canna consent."

Now in these last words the true reason of all lay apparent. He had some plan on hand which would bring him certain safety, and he had no mind to change this security for the difficult chance of a midnight flight. He was so stripped to the framework of his nature that Francis could all but read his thoughts in his eye, and at the sight the young man's blood ran hot with rage.

Then of his own accord Murray brought the farce to its close. He sat down squarely in his chair, and looked guilelessly at the other. "You have my best thanks, but the thing is beyond my power. I cannot hold my safety, nay, even the safety of a great cause, dearer than my honour, and if I consented to your plan my conscience would never give me another moment's peace. I am no coward, sir, to fear death, and in waiting here I but await the doom of many of my own kinsmen and kindest friends."

He stopped abruptly, for Francis stood over him, a fury of hate. "My God, sir," he cried, "if you value your soul, stop this canting talk. I will tell you why you will not leave this place. You have some Judas secret to tell to our enemies which you hope may save your own coward neck and give you back your possessions. That is the hell's trick you would play, and may the Lord in heaven have pity on you, you lying dog, for I will have none."

For a second the Secretary's life hung in the balance. The "Birkenshaw glower," once famed over Tweeddale, burned deep in the eyes of this young avenging fury. His fingers twitched at his sword's handle. The thought of slaying this man and so putting an end to all the difficulty, had occurred to him once and again, and had always been put from him. Now it rose uppermost in his mind. The thought of a woman's tears drove him frantic, and Francis for one instant was on the verge of murder, while Murray lay back gasping in his chair.

But the white, weak, unwholesome face deterred him. The man seemed worn with toils, seemed spiritless, friendless, and feeble. He could not draw upon him any more than upon a woman. With a cry of despair he turned upon his heel and left the room.

At the last gate the Campbell hailed him. "To what passage?" he asked.

"To the Fords—" said Francis, mechanically, while the man made as if to join him. Then, recollecting himself, "No, no, Heaven knows where," he cried almost with tears, and hastened out into the darkness.

* * * * *

As Margaret sat watching by the window in a pitiful state of anxiety, Francis came roughly into the room. She ran swiftly forward and laid a hand on his arm, for such little tendernesses had been common in her ways of late.

"Why, you are back!" she cried, "and I had never thought to see you again;" and with all her striving she could not keep a ring of exultation from her words.

"It is all up, my dear lady," said Francis, hoarsely. "I was a useless messenger. The Secretary has scruples about leaving his present quarters, and I was unable to persuade him bye them." And with a foolish smile he laid his horseman's cloak on the table.

Margaret stood looking with sad, drooped eyes. "Nevertheless you have done your most, Francis."

But he was not listening. He had set himself down before the table, and had leaned his head on both hands. "Oh," he cried, "I have no gift of success. Whatever I take up miscarries. I am but a poor sort of fushonless creature, meant to be guided by stronger men. All that I do ends in moonshine. I can see no light in the whole black pit of this life."

"Nay, Francis," said she, "surely there is some comfort, for though you could not save others, you have brought yourself back unharmed."

It was a silly woman's argument, but he, lifting his eyes carelessly at the words, saw something in the lady's face which made him redden and stare hard out of the window.

CHAPTER XIX.

The Last of the Secretary.

Amid a crowd of notables and fashionables, where the wits of the coffee-houses rubbed elbows with the beaus of the Mall, Francis pressed to hear the last scene in the drama which had been played athwart his own life. The Lord President had gained him admission, and so this morning he stood in the great hushed Westminster chamber, watching the lords in their robes, the frowning bench of judges, and at the bar the huddled figure of the old lord with his two piercing eyes still mocking at the world.

It was a farce even to his layman's eye,—a cruel, fantastic farce, with death waiting to pull down the curtain. Lovat had no aid but his own tongue, and for days he had toiled, cross-questioning witnesses on the other side, putting the necessary inquiries to his own supporters, till his face had grown ashen grey and he had swooned at the bar. His four counsel were of the most ineffectual cast, and would have turned the whole affair into an ugly mimicry by catching at points of form but for the old man's restraining voice. At first he did his work well, even jocularly, but as his weariness grew greater his questions lost all their pith and he relapsed into dignity and silence. The bearing of the old traitor struck Francis with admiration,—at once deferential and free, defiant and courteous. He had his compliments for the Lords, his tags of quotation, his excellent sentiments;

but the certainty of death seemed to give a nobility to what had seemed before a silly farrago.

But as Francis listened and waited, the finishing touch was added to the picture; for into the witness-box came a shamefast figure, the very one he had held at his mercy in that Tower chamber, and to which he had shown a way of life it would have none of. Every eye in the assembly turned to these square feet of wood where the witness stood meekly, looking with conciliating eyes to the benches of Lords and nervously fingering his cravat. Every face was eager with curiosity, some dark with ill-concealed disgust, while among the few friends of the prisoner there were twitching lips and hands hard at side.

Lovat had sunk in a stupor of weakness, and had not noticed the new arrival. Murray answered questions glibly and precisely in a tone of utmost cheerfulness. Then the clerk read the statement wherein he, John Murray, umquhile of Broughton, with the deepest penitence for past errors, with promise of amends and hope of his Majesty's infinite clemency, told to his gracious captors the full tale of the late lamentable events, more especially the part played by Simon Fraser, called the Lord Lovat, certain documents being adduced in clear proof of such statements. As the soft voice of the witness and then the hard clerk-like tones fell on his ear the old lord roused himself to interest. The shaggy head grew erect, and the eyes played with the unhappy man as he shifted his balance from one foot to the other and sought in all that place for a friendly glance. Ere the thing was finished he had hazarded a look at the man he had ruined and then drawn back in terror. He could not face the silent mockery of those eyes, the eyes of the wisest head in Scotland. Much they had seen, those eyes, at home and abroad, at the King's court and in the wild Stratherick. And now, with no fear of man, they looked through the one who had lent the chief hand to his overthrow.

The Lord High Steward asked if he would question the witness.

Lovat bowed politely. "Nay, my lord," he said, "I think Mr. Murray and I already understand each other;" and the smile on his lips was caught by the rest till Francis found himself all but laughing at the singular comedy.

The clerk rose according to custom, to read the portion of the defence which had been set in writing against Murray's charges. It was excellent rhetoric, stinging words under which the unfortunate gentleman cowered in some misery.

"Murray, the most abandoned of mankind," ran the paper, "who hath sought like another Catiline to patch up a broken fortune upon the ruin and distress of his native country; stealing into France to enter upon engagements upon, your Lordships may believe, the most sacred oaths of fidelity, and now appearing at your

Lordships' bar to betray these very secrets, which he confessed he had drawn from the person he called his lord, his prince and master, under the greatest confidence." So the clerk read, while the assembly grinned, and Lovat smacked his lips at his own invective.

Francis had no heart for more, but as he turned to push his way back, he caught a glimpse of the Lord President in the crowd. He also seemed about to leave, and the two met in the great corridor.

"This is the work of your friends," said Francis, wildly.

"It is the wark of my friends, and I am bitter ashamed. The fules! To set an auld man on a pinnacle to mock at till he gets him an appearance of virtue he never could have worn elsewhere. I have been Sim Fraser's neist neighbour all my days, and though I could not help but like the man, I kenned him ower weel to trust him with a boddle. But I think shame to see him worried like a rabbit in a dyke, and him wi' his grey hairs. Be sure, Mr. Birkenshaw, the Fraser will come out of the game with the maist credit."

"I want a further favour, my lord," said Francis, "and it is that I be allowed to visit Lord Lovat before his end. There are some matters that I would like to talk over, and certain passages between us want redding up."

Forbes knit his brows. "It canna be till the trial's ower," he said. "They keep him ower close. But after—it is possible. Maybe you might win to him the last night."

Francis thanked him and hurried out to the cheerful life of the street. The place was full of cries and the rattle of vehicles, the shouts of chairmen, and the hum of voices. It was a fresh, breathing world, and above was the infinite unchangeable blue of sky. For a second the cobwebs of miserable intrigue were cleared from his brain. He saw the littleness of man's schemes, the ease of death, the cataclysm of hopes and fears, as in a sharp moment of time. But again he was back at his sad memories. Here in this alien place the last blow was being struck at a cause he had stood for. Tush! It was little he cared about the Cause, it was the people he had served and loved, the old memories and sentiments of the few against the many, which were being swallowed up in this callous present.

For days he wandered fiercely in the streets, picking up fragments of news and cursing his powerlessness. He heard of the verdict, and then of the sentence of death received with a cheerful composure, even with a joke. At the hearing his old admiration revived for the indomitable man who could wait on the last enemy with a gibe. He counted the hours till the day of meeting. This, after all, was the fortunate warrior, who could go out of life with a twitch of his cloak and a word of scorn to his tormentors. The grossness, the cunning, the malice were all forgotten; he remembered only Lovat of the many generous sentiments, the great chief of Fraser, and the wisest brain in the North.

In the chill of the last Wednesday evening he was admitted at the gate of the Tower and led to the prisoner's chamber. As they went down the passage there were sounds of riotous mirth coming from the melancholy place. The warder looked hopelessly bewildered. "This is the way those wild Scots prepare for death," he cried. "I have had twenty-three honest gentlemen in my hands before they took their last walk, and all spent their last evening in meditation and prayer." When the door was opened the room seemed filled with tobacco reek and the fumes of punch. Through the smoke Francis saw some few of Lovat's near kin, making as merry as if it were an alehouse in Inverness. General Williamson, the Lieutenant-colonel of the Tower, sat opposite the prisoner, apparently in some discomfort. The old lord himself was reading from a paper, with a pair of enormous spectacles stuck on his nose and a handkerchief in his hand. A fire burned in the grate, but the prisoner's blood seemed chilly, for he wore enormous hose turned up over his knees and a pair of buckled slippers. His face had lost its pallor and shone with the heat and the wine.

"I am touched," cried he, looking at the paper. "Here's this body—Paynter they call him, a noble-hearted fellow for certain—writes to Mr. Secretary Pelham, and I hear he has petitioned his Majesty likewise. And what do ye think the purport is? He wants the honour of being beheaded in the Lord Lovat's stead. See the creature fair fleeches and begs! 'I pray you, sir, intercede with the King that the Lord Lovat may be pardoned.' These are his words." And he took off his spectacles, wiped them carefully, and then surveyed the company. "I thank God that there are still good men in the world. 'Greater love than this hath no man, that a man lay down his life for a friend.' What think ye o' that, gentlemen?"

The Lieutenant said something about the man's being crazed.

"And indeed I am of your opinion," said Lovat. "Clearly the creature must be daft. For see what he calls me—'a vile traitor, an ungrateful wretch.' Weel, weel, I doubt the poor gentleman is weary of living in this wicked world."

Then, catching sight of Francis, "Eh, here's a welcome face!" he cried, "my ancient friend Francie come to bid the auld man guid e'en. Here's a seat by my side, lad," and he pointed to a chair near the fireplace. "Now, sir, this is a merry meeting, and, as we cannot reasonably drink to many mair, we will even drink to it as it stands." And the Frasers filled up their glasses with due solemnity.

"Ye did weel, sir," he said, speaking in Francis' ear. "I have heard from Duncan Forbes of your efforts, and be sure I do not forget them. But, lad, I couldna jouk my fate, and I must e'en submit. I thought I got a glisk o' ye in the Hall some days syne. Did ye hear my defence that I had the clerk set to read? Was it no bonny, and was it no dine to see yon scunnering creature, Murray, shift about as I told the world what I kenned of him?"

Then he fell into a long strain of moralising after his fashion, but the near approach of death gave a flavour to his words which exalted them almost to wisdom. "See, Mr. Birkenshaw," he said simply, "ye are a young man and may take a word of counsel. I have maybe made a hash of my life, for I was ower wild and headstrong, and maybe ower given to the sins of the flesh. But after all I have had my sport out o' life. I have had my fingers in every pie that's been making, and, faith, I have created some sort of a steer in the world. And that would ever be my counsel to young blood—to gang forrit, set the world in a bleeze if ye can, and if ye get your hair singit as I've got mine, ye need never care for the sake o' the graund spectacle."

He took out his watch and considered. "Twelve hours more in this middenstead of a world," he said, speaking loud to all. "Now mind ye, Shamus Fraser," and he turned to one of his friends, "ye hear the last injunctions of your chief. Ye will have my body buried in the kirk of Kirkhill, for there lie all the generations of Lovat, and I've put a note in my will by which I leave bountith to all the pipers frae John o' Groats to Edinburgh to play before my body. Lord, it will be a braw music, and I wish I could be there to hear it. But it's like that the Government will not allow it," he said sadly. "King Geordie is no sae mensefu' as King Jamie, and he has nae sense o' humour." He looked at the embers for a little and then turned round more cheerfully. "At any rate all the old women in my own country will cry the coronach, and it will be a wonderful crying, for I am the greatest chief in all the Highlands. And I will never see the heather hills more, nor the rigs o' Corryarrick;" and for a second his mocking face relaxed into plain sorrow.

"I drink a good journey to you, Mac Shimei," and a tall Fraser rose with a trembling glass.

"Amen," said Lovat, tossing off a cup, and then emptying his pipe ashes on the hearth. "See, gentlemen, the end of human life is like this snuff o' tobacco. A moment we are bleezing finely, and then we go out and nothing is left but grey ashes." And he sighed and sat for a little with his head on his breast.

He turned to the Lieutenant and asked to see his little daughter. "Where's the wee bairn that used to come in and play hunt-the-gowk wi' me? She'll no be in bed yet, and I would like to bid farewell to her. She was a fine little lass."

"I fear, my lord, you cannot see her," said the man, huskily. "She has done nothing but weep for two days since ever she heard of your fate. She is a little traitor at heart, for she abuses the King and his judges most roundly. I heard her only yesterday designing an escape for you from prison such as was given to the Apostles at Philippi. She will miss her play-fellow most bitterly."

"Will she indeed?" said the old lord. "God bless the dear child, and make her eternally happy, for she is a good, kind-hearted lass."

Shortly after this he desired that all should leave him save Francis and the Lieutenant. When they were alone he asked the latter to fetch Mr. Baker, the chaplain of the Sardinian ambassador, to give him the last comforts of the Church. "But I had thought you a Presbyterian, my lord," said the Lieutenant. "You passed for such through most of your career."

"Policy often makes havoc wi' a man's creed," said Lovat, smiling wickedly, "but I have ever abode in the faith of the only true Kirk. I adhere to the rock on which Christ built his gospel. I ground my faith upon St. Peter and the succession of pastors from him down to the present, and I reject and renounce all sects and communities that are rejected by the Kirk. That is my confession of faith, and if you think it of sufficient importance to the world, sir, I will put it down in writing."

"I did not know you were a theologian," said the other, in some wonder.

"The world little kens what I am," said Lovat, and it was hard to tell whether the whole thing was jest or earnest. "Some day mayhap the world will do me justice, and the little children of the clan will be proud to think of their chief. But I've been like the Almighty, hiding my ways in the sea and my paths in the great waters, and it will take a wise man and a cunning to find them out. Francis, you have seen much of me, and I might have looked to you for a proper understanding of me, if ye hadna been so thick in the heid and dour in your ain conceit."

"I have one question, my lord," said Francis. "I have bungled the trust you laid on me, but I have striven to keep my word. Do you absolve me from any blame in your death? It would let me lie down with an easier heart."

"Absolve ye, lad? Freely; and mair, I have to thank ye kindly. I bid ye good-bye, for there'll be little time the morn. Gang back to your ain land, lad, and take my blessing with ye. And now I must ask ye to leave me to myself for a little, that I may prepare for the putting away of mortality."

"But, my lord," cried the Lieutenant, "I have heard that there are differences even within your creed. The Sardinian chaplain has the name of a rank Jesuit. Are you too of that persuasion?"

"A Jesuit?" said Lovat, with a twinkling eye and a gesture of doubt. "Faith, no, when I think upon it, I am a Jansenist. But anything in the shape o' a priest will serve my turn. Good-night to ye, gentlemen." And with this last piece of mystification he bade them farewell.

CHAPTER XX.

The Death of the Lord Lovat.

The morning was mist and rain with a wind blowing from the east up the packed streets. It was like a fête-day in the town with people in Sunday clothes hastening Tower-wards. When Francis came down to the dining-room, a maid was scrubbing the hearth, the windows were open, and in the raw early chill there came a babble as of a city in expectation. He had slept scarcely a wink, being full of thought and a kind of bitter excitement. He knew the whole evil of Lovat's life, but this sounding fate seemed to elevate him into the heroic. For Francis the world at the moment held but one event and one man, and at the thought rage, compassion, and regret made a medley of his feelings.

Margaret came down wrapped up in a thick cloak against the rawness of the morning. She wore the heavy veil she had thought needful for the open streets, and all her garments were of the sombrest black.

"I could not go dressed otherwise," she said. "I could not put on a fine gown to witness the death of a friend. My cousin tells me to stay at home, for I shall only break my heart to no purpose; but when so few of his countrywomen will be near, I should think shame to be absent."

Tales of Lovat's deeds and last dying confession had been printed in flying sheets, and were hawked up and down the causeways. The crush was already setting eastward, and one man was telling to another his version of this great affair. The name of this terrible outlawed monster had been long in the people's ears, and now they were to have a sight of him in all the pomp and contumely of a traitor's death. From the hanging windows crowds of fine ladies had dared the morning air to look down upon the throng; some even had risen early and in their coaches sought a stand upon Tower hill.

The cheerful holiday crowd brought tears to Margaret's eyes, as Francis with his great shoulders clove a way through, his dark, uncommon face bringing him a certain respect.

"We are strangers in a strange place," she said sadly. "What do these folk care for our broken King and people? And yet they say he had many well-wishers in this place."

At Temple Bar the shrivelled heads of the Lords Balmerino and Kilmarnock grimaced at the crowd. At the sight Margaret clung closer to his arm. The rousing tale of Balmerino's conduct on the scaffold had stirred even the most Whiggish blood, and she looked at the poor dumb mouth, her face blanched with excitement, as in the old days when she had sat on horseback watching the entrance of the Camerons.

"But he was young and strong," she cried, "and he might well face death courageously. But my Lord Lovat is old and feeble, and he cannot stand squarely against his foes." Then with a catching of the breath she would have stopped. "Oh, it is horrible! And this is the issue of great expectations!"

The whole hill was black with folk, and on stands were many more of the better sort, all agape for the spectacle. The two halted yards off at the verge of the dense throng, where some carriages stood waiting. Afar like a toy building stood the scaffold with its bare timbers and the black-draped block and the guarded alley leading thither from the Tower gate. The thought of this one man alone or all but alone in this vast hostile sea of faces stirred Francis wildly, and he could scarcely bide still. The same thought was in Margaret's mind, for she looked with piteous eyes at the thick wall of men. "Oh, that we could get near him," she cried, "that he might have kind faces to look upon at the end!"

As Francis looked round he saw in a coach among the others the Lord President. At once he made his way to his side. "May I beg you, my lord," he cried, "to watch over this lady and take her home when all is over? I would fain get near Lovat to-day."

Forbes glanced at the slim, beautiful figure which he knew so well. "With all my heart, Mr. Birkenshaw," he said, while he held out a hand to Margaret. "The lady will see the last of our poor friend as well here as elsewhere. I wish you God-speed on your errand."

"I shall win to him, though the crowd were ten times greater. It is better to leave you than to stay." And in a second he was lost in the thick of men.

For many minutes he struggled as only the desperate can, elbowing fiercely, being struck again and again, gripping his opponents and half-suffocating them, till he had forced his way past. Now and then he would come to a knuckle of rising ground whence he saw the scaffold, and always he noted gladly that it was empty. Weaker men were fainting all about him, but his supple vigour had its effect, and soon he was half-way through, and then only a quarter of the space was left. He was breathless, hatless, his coat torn in many places, and his face sorely scratched. Then, as he saw the wooden planks almost within reach, he heard a great sigh of expectation go through the multitude, and the tramp of men above the other din told him that Lovat was coming.

As he stood panting in the dense throng below, Lovat stood above him and cast a curious glance round the assembly. It happened on Francis, and his eager eyes told their tale. "I pray you, sir," he asked the Sergeant, "to allow this young gentleman to come up beside me. He is a dear friend, and has but newly arrived." The Sergeant, willing to pleasure the old man, gave an order, the crowd was opened by soldiers, and Francis found the way clear for him to ascend the platform. In a moment he was by Lovat's side, a new spectator of the last act in the play.

Around—apparently for miles—was a dim circle of faces, and a hum rose from them, silent though they were, like the breathing of a great wild beast. Now and again a woman's or a boy's scream would break the air, only to be hushed again in the pitiless mass. It was as if one stood on a pinnacle, watched by a million hungry eyes which bit into the soul. Lovat cowered for a second, for no feeling is more awful for a moment than to be one against a host; then his spirit came back to him, and he turned to Francis, smiling.

"The last time I stood before men under the sky was at my ain Castle Dounie," he said, "when I heartened my folk to die for the Prince. I am like to need all the heartening myself now." Then a twinge took him, and he all but fell into Francis' arms, while his clansman, Shamus Fraser, ran forward to help him. Supported thus, he limped across the platform, making a strange clatter in the quiet.

Suddenly in the midst of the crowd something horrible happened; for the scaffolding of a stand gave way, and the erection with its inmates fell on the packed array of heads. In a moment there was a wild panic, to which soldiers fought their way with difficulty. For a little it seemed as if a great catastrophe impended, for several men were taken up dead and mangled, and the crowd was all but hysterical. Then slowly the tumult subsided, the dead were borne out, and eyes turned again to the scaffold.

Lovat had watched the scene with delight. "There's some o' them killed," he whispered breathlessly. "Weel, weel, so be it. The mair mischief the better sport." Francis looked at him in amazement. A second ago he had been ready to venerate this man as a hero; now, behold, it was the old Lovat back again, a very malicious, jeering hero, laughing cruelly in the article of death.

"The sport's bye," he said, as expectant silence reigned again, "and now it's my turn to divert my friends. It's as weel, Francis, that it's an easy job, demanding small exertion on my part, for I am a done auld man."

His whole humour seemed to change, as if he felt that men expected something high and heroical in his final bearing. He gave one last glance at the crowd. "God save us," he cried, "why should there be such a bustle about taking off an auld grey head that canna get up two steps without two men to support it? Francie, your airm, my son!"

He limped up to the block, nodded cheerfully to the executioner, and begged to see the axe. "It might be sharper," he said, "but it hasna far to gang, and will maybe do." Then taking his gold-headed cane, he cried to a young lad who stood weeping behind him, "Alistair, my dear lad, take my staff and keep it weel for my sake.

Ye've been a kind callant, and I wish I had a better gift." The poor boy took it, crying very bitterly, and turned away his face.

Then taking off his coat and cravat with Francis' aid, he laid them down carefully, bidding the executioner keep them if he cared. Beside the block stood his coffin, and stooping down he read the inscription.

"*Simon Dominus Fraser de Lovat*," he read, "*decollat ætat. suæ 80.*"

[* Lord Fraser of Lovat— Beheaded for High Treason, at the Age of Eighty.]

For some seconds he continued gazing, and then turned away with a sigh.

"Happily my fame does not rest on this short line, Francis," he said. "But, indeed, what am I thinking of?" and he declaimed:—

*"'Nam genus et proavos, et quæ non fecimus ipsi, Vix ea nostra voco.'"**

[* As for things done by our ancestors and other people than ourselves, I say we can have no credit for them. —Ovid, *Metamorphoses*, XIII, 140.]

He turned to Shamus Fraser, and taking both hands bade him farewell. "My dear Shamus," he cried, "I am going to heaven, but you must continue to crawl a little longer in this evil world." And then he spoke to him shortly of his dying bequests, and his messages to his kinsfolk. The man was white and speechless, his dark face working with suppressed tears.

Meantime Francis was in no better plight. He had been with this man in fair and foul, he knew his innumerable vices, his treachery, his selfishness, and yet in this last moment he could look on him only as a heroic gentleman. On this scaffold in the midst of the waiting crowd he lived again the days in the hot weather, the fury of the lost battle, and the whole tale of his undoing; and always for a centre was the figure of this man with whom all his toils had been shared. It was a quivering hand that took Lovat's wrinkled palm, and his lips were drawn to a thin line.

"And you, Francie," said the old lord, "what shall I say to you? You have been more than a son to me, and, O lad, I wish you had been Master o' Lovat, and we two would have set a different face upon the business. You have the blessing of an auld man, my dear lad, and may you live long and die happy and be kindly treated as you have been kind to me."

And then with great deliberation he turned to the block, and looking over the throng uttered the wellworn line, the last in the mouth of the hopeless,—

"Dulce et decorum est pro patria mori."

[*It is sweet and seemly to die for one's country. — Horace, *Odes*, III.2.13.]

The next moment he had kneeled down, and ere Francis could look clearly the axe had fallen, and the head lay in the basket.

As, with brain in a ferment and eyes hot with unshed tears, he staggered from the platform, he heard in the hushed silence the voice of the headsman crying, "This is the head of a traitor!"

* * * * *

With head lowered like a mad animal, Francis pushed his way through the choking streets. Some turned to stare at him, but his speed was so great that he left no time for more than a glance. A great impulse was on him to run to the ends of the earth till the madness of his physical strength and burning heart should be quelled. He comprehended the joys of battle; he would have gloried in that hour to stand with his back to the wall against a multitude. One insulted citizen gripped him by the arm as if to demand some apology for jostling; but before he knew the man was sitting in the gutter and Francis was many yards down the street. And all the while there was the cold of rain about him and a wind which blew grateful on his forehead. He was going out into the cold earth, kinless, purposeless; yet a man who had once lived and dared.

When he came to his lodging, he found Margaret sunk motionless in a chair in her outdoor clothes, her eyes fixed vacantly on the leaping fire. She rose quickly with burning cheeks at his entrance.

"Oh, tell me all! I saw nothing save the horrid deed. How did my lord bear himself to the end?"

Then Francis told her the whole tale, marvelling the while at his excitement. His voice rose high ere he had done, and with unconscious art he pictured the old lion in the midst of the crowd dying with a brave word on his lips. He told of the last greetings and the message to his kinsfolk. And all the while Margaret stood twining her hands, tears shining in her eyes.

"It was great, it was the death of a hero. Oh, God send we all show as brave a face to death. My heart has been bursting with rage all day, Francis, and yet I am half crazy with joy. We have not failed, though the Cause is lost and the Prince an exile, for we have shown a poor-spirited people how gentlemen may die. I shall pray ever for the soul of the Lord Lovat and the true men who have fallen. *Dona æternam quietem, Domine*," and as the soft Latin fell from her lips, her wearied nerves failed her, and she fled sobbing like a child.

CHAPTER XXI.

The Temptation of Mr. Francis.

That night there was little sleep for Francis. The figures and deeds of the day formed a long procession through his brain. He felt again in all their acuteness the emotions which had branded his soul. The truth is that the man was tired to death, what with physical labour and the more wearing toil of spirit. He was no more the sober, passionless man who had carried the message to Lovat in the North, but a tempest-tossed, sorely-battered creature who had been strung to a pitch of high excitement, and was now sinking to a dull recoil.

But when he got some quiet from such vain dreaming, he set himself to shape out the future. It stretched grey and level before him, featureless, even now irrevocable. There was but one thing for him to do. For the last year he had been striving desperately to virtue. Now he must return to the writer's office and his old evil reputation. He must go back to Dysart and settle there as the sober man of law, and try to work out for himself a position of respect. There must be no more quixotry, no thought of mad capers in wars over sea. He must shape out his salvation in the place he had been called to, and settle to a life of loneliness cut off for ever from the past.

The thought was bleak, but he never wavered, for the man had true steel and fire in his soul, and had the daring to face an age of melancholy and routine, and he too in years but at the threshold of life. There seemed even something grimly humourous in it all. That he who had been a firebrand, all but an outlaw, should go back to the common task, was an irony for the gods to laugh at.

But this outlook of his own was but a little matter; there remained the graver question of the woman whose path fate had joined with his. He had seen how day by day her eyes sought his with a growing confusion; even in his blindness he had felt that this lady had come to regard all things as less than a word of his mouth. He stood to her as a hero, girt with the purple and fine gold of her fancy; he was the embodied Cause for which she had striven; and now at the turning of the ways there must come a day of reckoning. Her love was his for the accepting,—she the great lady, with that delicate beauty and that marvellous spirit; and for a second his heart beat exultantly. But the thought was banished, scarcely even with regret. For this man had outgrown temptation, and now this subtlest of all failed to touch him. He had but to join his life with hers, to go abroad and push his fortunes aided by her abundant wealth; it was a dazzling career which gleamed in the avenues of the future. Yet the renunciation cost him little, for with all his fire his nature was cold to the commoner human affections. He was returning to the vulgarity of home; and always in his mind would remain the image of the woman he had once toiled for. But to be with her always, to bring her into the glare of common day and the pettiness of household life,—he had no heart for such degradation. In his soul he knew that each was better apart, living for the other's memory, fighting the hard battle with the other's name on the lips. But for aught else he was cold and careless; for his nature was capable of all the heroical virtues, but unfit for the little moralities. He was ever in revolt from the domestic, the eternal wanderer in the ways of the world. He had no care for ease or settled delights, he must be ever up and following the old hopeless, goalless path, even though it led through grey and dreary years.

Lady Manorwater alone came to breakfast the next morning. He had always been a little in fear of this austere virginal woman who carried devotion writ on her face. She had an air of the monastic which seemed strange to the prosaic Francis. But now she talked gravely and kindlily.

"It is now time for my cousin Margaret to make up her mind, Mr. Birkenshaw. I have tried to induce her to bide with me, but she cannot bear the thought of this land longer and declares she must go abroad. She is of my religion, but I have never tried to influence her plans. But she declares for a convent now. She would devote her life to God after the many sorrows she has faced in this world; and I have not tried to persuade her otherwise, for it would give her the days of rest which only He can give to the weary."

"Where would she go?" he asked.

"I have already thought of that. I once knew the Abbess well at the little convent of St. Thérèse by Arras. For my sake she would gladly receive the poor lass and tend her like a mother. It will vex me sorely to part with Margaret, but I cannot grudge her to God. And she will be happy if they can be happy who dwell in quiet and purity."

"And I too must be going," said Francis.

"And where?" said Lady Manorwater.

"I go North again, back to my own people."

"But why?" she said. "You are young and stirring. Is there not a better field for you than that sad and bloodstained land? A word, and I can get you service abroad, and then you would find a chance for a man's work."

"It cannot be," said Francis, resolutely. "I thank your ladyship, but I have some faults to amend and some restitution to make before I can be at peace with myself. Forbye I am but a pedestrian nature after all, and cannot easily get old things out of my mind. I must bide in my own land, for I cannot flee from myself, and to go to the foreign wars would be to try to forget a sore heart in the hurry of battle."

Later in the forenoon a servant brought him word that her mistress wished to speak with him. He found her in the library, where above the fireplace the three lions' heads of Manorwater were cut deep in the oak. She was standing by the window, and her face seemed pale above her dark gown.

"Good morning, Francis," she said. "I was so weary with yesterday that I was late of rising this morning. Our work is over now, my friend, so we can take a rest."

"I have heard of your plans," he said. "Your cousin has told me that you go to France to a convent. And I too am about to go, so it is time for good-byes."

She bit her lips at the words, and her voice had a quaver. "These months have tired me so that I longed for quiet to think and remember. Now that my work is done and all that I have lived for made hopeless, you cannot wonder that I wish for peace."

Francis listened with bowed head. "You can do no wrong, Margaret," he said.

"And you?" she said suddenly; "what will you do?"

"I go back to where I came from."

"Oh, never," she cried. "It cannot be, it is too hideous and cruel. You might hew your way to fortune wherever you pleased. There is always need of a strong man all over the earth, and you are strong and sure."

He did not speak, but the words were bitter to him,—the very quintessence of gall in his parting.

Then she turned round till she looked full in his eyes.

"You cannot mean it?" she said. "Ah, mercy! we have shared too many hopes together, we cannot part thus and go each our way into the bleak unknown. I was never fit for a life of piety, and you are too strong for a narrow fate. Oh, take me, Francis, and let us go away together. I am too noble a woman for God, it is a sacrifice which the Blessed Virgin herself could not bear to look upon. I know that I am speaking of sin, but what matters sin if we both can share it? Why, we might yet change the woful fate of this land if we worked together."

In a deep-set mirror on the wall she caught a glimpse of her face.

"See, dear," she said, "I am near as tall as you," and she smiled tremulously. "We are a handsome pair, and we will yet make great men bow to us." And she laid her cheek on his shoulder.

"You are not angry with me?" she cried. "I know I am wicked, but I cannot help it. I cannot part from you, and what are old foolish ties to a woman's love? O my love, take me and let us face fortune hand in hand."

Francis held her wrists very gently and looked into the deeps of her marvellous eyes. His heart never wavered, but in his soul he felt a great tenderness towards this beautiful, loving woman.

"Nay, dear," he said, "you know better than I that this cannot be. Long ago you gave me a hand to raise me out of the mire, and I cannot have you be false to yourself. Be sure that I shall ever have you in my mind as the best and bravest woman God ever made. But we have each our own ways to take, and one cannot fight the battle better by beginning it with a foolish step. Marriage and love are for the peaceable settled folk, but you and I are not of their order. For good or ill we are on the open road of life, and we cannot turn back or aside."

Margaret covered her face with her hands when he let her go, and her bosom heaved with sobbing. Then she lay back in a deep chair with closed eyelids.

"I am so weary," she said, "and, oh, I am so foolish. You are right, Francis, and God forgive me for my weakness. But we cannot forget each other, and there in that foreign place my thoughts will always be of you and the lost days. It is near the time for farewells, dear. Kiss me, that I may have something to remember, for I am sure that no other woman's lips will ever touch you."

With bursting heart he leaned over her, and for an instant the long white arms were about his neck. Then she let him go, and he stumbled from the room, a mere plaything of emotions.

* * * * *

That evening the house was unwontedly gay, for some few Jacobite gentlemen had been bidden to supper, and the friends of the Manorwaters had come to bid good-byes before the journey into France. After the fashion of the broken party they allowed no sign of melancholy to appear, and the scene was as gay as if the time had been happy alike for all. Francis was in no mood for any meeting with others, but he could not in grace refuse to appear. In a little he was glad, for it comforted him to see how the end of the drama was played with spirit. As he watched the brave sight he felt how little a thing is failure in act if the heart be unbroken.

But the vision of Margaret fairly surprised him. She had dressed herself in her gayest gown, putting on her old jewels which had lain untouched for months. Like a girl at the dawning of life she moved among the guests, cheerful, witty, incomparably fresh and lovely. Once again she was the *grande dame* who had guided the Prince's councils and the honest gentlemen who stood for his Cause. For a second, he felt an overpowering, jealous craving for this woman, a repugnance to the greyness of his lot. And then it passed, and he could look on her and be thankful for this final spirit. It was the last brave flickering of life before the ageless quiet of her destiny.

CHAPTER XXII.

A Long Leave-Taking.

The way lay over grassy ridges of hill and then at intervals among the bracken and gnarled boles of a great wood. The mist of the morning lay in all the far distances, and one might guess that behind the veil lay a wild and tangled land, that the slope did not stop a little beyond the edge of the haze but rose sheer into precipitous crags. It might have been Scotland, and as the coach rumbled down the highway Margaret when she looked to right and left saw a glimpse of a landscape now for ever lost to her.

To Francis, who rode as before at her side, the same sentiment kept recurring. It was the air and look of a northern glen, here in this soft English south country. He noted Margaret's abstraction.

"I am looking my last at a sight I love dearly," she said. "Oh, is not that cold, misty place like the kind country I have left? I can almost smell the heather and the old fragrance of the fir-wood at Broughton. You are happy, Francis, in your lot, for you will always be at home, and sleep at the end among kindly folk."

Slowly the land changed till by the afternoon they were on the seaward slopes and caught afar the long sweep of waters. In front rose the spires of the little fishing town whence they were to sail, and on the red roofs the evening light fell in a burning haze.

Amid the bustle of departure on the quay Margaret was left unnoticed. She stood apart, under the weather-worn sea-wall, looking wistfully to the maze of waters.

"There is a text from the Scriptures running in my head," she said. "Some one of the prophets wrote it. It is, 'Weep not for the dead neither bemoan her; but weep sore for her that goeth away, for she shall return no more nor see her native country.' My life is ended, Francis, for all my joy has perished."

"Nay, my dear lady," he said, with something rising in his throat, "you will have many happy days, and you will forget old sorrows. These last years have been but a little confusion of moorland wars, fought in the wind and rain by a poor people. You will soon cease to think of them and wonder at your present grief."

"Do you think so?" she said sadly. "I fear it will be very different with me. It is not the way of our exiles to forget easily. Nay, rather they fight all their battles with the old words in their heart, and at the last, why, as my song says, they 'fall, and dying have mind of sweet Argos.'"

Then she turned abruptly.

"How long will you take to be back in the North?"

"A matter of weeks," he said, "for it will be done on foot. I am a poor man once more, and shall sell my horse before I start."

"And what will you do then?"

"Seek a place in Mr. Shillinglaw's office and give my mind to my work."

"And after that?"

"Why, I shall grow old, like all men, and wander about the doors. Then death will come with a kindly face and I shall bid good-bye to the world—perchance to find a better."

She smiled as if at the moment she saw the whole comic littleness of life.

"Our ways are not so different. After the colours the sober grey, for you as well as for me, Francis."

Lady Manorwater was already aboard, and Margaret followed. The cables were slipped, and soon with a creaking of cordage and a flapping of canvas the vessel stood out from the quay. Slowly the faces grew less, till a mere blur of white marked where Margaret stood by the ship's side. A kerchief fluttered for a moment and he answered, and then only a speck remained in the circle of sea.

He stood at the far end of the quay, one foot on a broken stone, watching the sails melt into the evening. The salt fresh smell of the air was growing rawer with the advent of night; the once shimmering waters were sobbing below the piles; and afar to east and west a leaden dulness crept over the waves. But to the south there was still a track of light, and suddenly, clear and sharp, rose the vessel's outline against the rising dusk. In a second it was no more, and over the whole sky was rolled the curtain of evening.

But the man sat still till the last light had gone and the mist came up from the sea.

CHAPTER XXIII.

In the Nature of a Postscript.

The patient scribe who has chronicled this tale has employed his leisure in seeking for further news of the two who figure chiefly. Nor has his zeal been unrewarded. Among the Manorwater family-papers he had access to the letters of that Countess of Manorwater who when left a young widow married the Duke of Sanctamund, and cut something of a figure in the Regency days. Her ladyship was famous for her wit and her odd prettiness. She was of the school of Sensibility, and, it is recorded, made pilgrimages to the grave of Rousseau. She was famed too in polite circles in Paris in the early days after the Terror, and through her kinship to the De Noailles claimed all the virtues of the old régime. But in the midst of her gossipy epistles there is one little letter in which she tells her dear friend, Emily Norton, of a visit to Arras and an hour spent in the graveyard of the convent of St. Thérèse.

". . . Yesterday, ma chère, was a heavenly day, blue with white clouds sailing above, and all the place was green with the tender spring of this climate. I found the graveyard, which is hidden away among cloistral grey walls, but kept trim by the piety of the Sisters. After much searching I came on a little stone, much grown about with white roses, and on it the simple letter M, and the words, '*Pro sua patria.*' It was indeed the tomb of my unfortunate kinswoman. I confess, my dear Emily, that I could not look on it without a tear. Here in this green place lay my brave Margaret—*la Marguerite des Marguerites*—whose name as a little girl I used to worship. People say she went far from the paths of virtue, that she used her beauty and her talents unscrupulously for a foolish cause, but I cannot believe it. Here the memory of her gentleness and goodness is still fresh, and the old sisters have much to tell of *la belle Écossaise.* Well-a-day, we cannot judge; at any rate she has got peace; and I confess I wept to think that even in her death she remembered her own land and asked that the white Jacobite rose might be set above her grave.... I fear I can write no more at present. The emotions of the day have discomposed me, and I go to bed. In three days we return to England, and till then with eternal love believe me your ever-affectionate

"Victoria Manorwater."

On the other hand the writer has searched the excellent series of monographs on the Fife burghs for traces of Mr. Francis. There he was unsuccessful, but in a series of papers contributed by a former provost of Dysart to that most enterprising sheet, "The Fife Journal and Herald of the Kingdom," and composed from the town papers, he has found something of interest.

". . . In our list of talented townsmen of a former time, none should be more highly esteemed than Francis Birkenshaw, who succeeded John Henryson as Provost of the burgh. He was a writer, having succeeded to the business of Gregor Shillinglaw (for whom see last number). There were always queer stories in the town anent him, for he was a wild lad in his youth and disappeared unaccountably during the Rebellion, returning much graver and wiser, which gave colour to a belief that he had seen service with one or the other side. Nevertheless, he soon acquired a responsible position in the place, and as head of a flourishing business, was elected Provost in the year 1765. He introduced many reforms, particularly a system of town pumps where the burgesses could get clear water, their former source having been invaded by the sea. His portrait hangs in the Town-house, and shows a grey-haired, hard-faced man, with cold, unfriendly-looking eyes. This indeed seems to have been his character, for he rarely graced the social board, but lived unmarried and utterly by himself, finding all his interest in his work and the town-affairs. He died at the early age of fifty-two, leaving the business to his head-clerk, and his fortune—which was considerable—to the burgh."

THE END

Witch Wood

By

John Buchan

WITCH WOOD

PROLOGUE

Time, my grandfather used to say, stood still in that glen of his. But the truth of the saying did not survive his death, and the first daisies had scarcely withered on his grave before a new world was knocking at the gate. That was thirty years ago, and to-day the revolution is complete. The parish name has been changed; the white box of a kirk which served the glen for more than two centuries has been rebuilt in red suburban gothic; a main railway line now runs down the Aller, and the excellent summer service brings holiday-makers from a hundred miles distant: houses and shops have clustered under the Hill of Deer; there may be found a well-reputed boarding school for youth, two inns--both of them reformed--a garage, and a bank agent. The centre of importance has moved from the old village to the new town by the station, and even the old village is no more a clachan of thatched roofs straggling by a burnside. Some enemy of the human race has taught the burn to run straight like a sewer, and has spanned it with a concrete bridge, while the thatch of the houses has been replaced by slates of a metallic green. Only the ruins of the old kirkton have not been meddled with; these stand as I remember them, knee-deep in docks and nettles, defended by a crumbling dry-stone dyke against inquisitive cattle from Crossbasket.

The old folk are gone, too, and their very names are passing from the countryside. Long before my day the Hawkshaws had disappeared from Calidon, but there was a respectable Edinburgh burgess family who had come there in the seventeenth century; now these have given place to a rawer burgess graft from the West. The farmers are mostly new men, and even the peasant, who should be the enduring stock, has shifted his slow bones. I learned from the postman that in Woodilee to-day there was no Monfries, no Sprot, but one Pennecuik, and only two bearers of the names of Ritchie and Shillinglaw, which had once been plentiful as ragwort. In such a renovated world it was idle to hope to find surviving the tales which had perplexed my childhood. No one could tell me when or why the kirk by the Crossbasket march became a ruin, and its gravestones lay buried in weeds. Most did not even know that it had been a kirk.

I was not greatly surprised by this, for the kirk of Woodilee had not been used for the better part of three centuries; and even as a child I could not find many to tell me of its last minister. The thing had sunk from a tale to an "owercome," a form of words which every one knew but which few could interpret. It was Jess Blane, the grieve's daughter, who first stirred my curiosity. In a whirl of wrath at some of my doings she prayed that the fate of the minister of Woodilee might be mine--a fate which she expounded as to be "claught by the Deil and awa' wi'." A little scared, I carried the affair to my nurse, who was gravely scandalized, and denounced Jess as a "shamefu' tawpie, fyling the wean's mind wi' her black lees." "Dinna you be feared, dearie," she reassured me. "It wasna the Deil that cam' for the minister o' Woodilee. I've aye heard tell that he was a guid man and a kind man. It was the Fairies, hinny. And he leev'd happy wi' them and dee'd happy, and never drank out o' an empty cup." I took my information, I remember, to the clan of children who were my playmates, and they spread it among their households and came back with confirmation or contradiction. Some held for the Devil, some for the Fairies--a proof that tradition spoke with two voices. The Fairy school slightly outnumbered the others, and in a battle one April evening close to the ruined kirk we routed the diabolists and established our version as the canon. But save for that solitary fact--that the minister of Woodilee had gone off with the Fairies--the canon remained bare.

Years later I got the tale out of many books and places: a folio in the library of a Dutch college, the muniment-room of a Catholic family in Lancashire, notes in a copy of the second Latin edition of Wishart's Montrose, the diaries of a captain of Hebron's and of a London glove-maker, the exercise book of a seventeenth-century Welsh schoolgirl. I could piece the story together well enough, but at first I found it hard to fit it to the Woodilee that I knew-- that decorous landscape, prim, determinate, without a hint of mystery; the bare hilltops, bleak at seasons, but commonly of a friendly Pickwickian baldness, skirted with methodically-planned woods of selected conifers, and girdled with mathematical stone dykes; the even, ruled fields of the valley bottom; the studied moderation of the burns in a land meticulously drained; the dapper glass and stone and metal of the village. Two miles off, it was true, ran the noble untamed streams of Aller; beyond them the hills rose in dark fields to mid-sky, with the glen of the Rood making a sword-cut into their heart. But Woodilee itself--whither had fled the savour? Once, I knew from the books, the great wood of Melanudrigill had descended from the heights and flowed in black waves to the village brink. But I could not re-create the picture out of glistening asphalted highway, singing telegraph wires, spruce dwellings, model pastures, and manicured woodlands.

Then one evening from the Hill of Deer I saw with other eyes. There was a curious leaden sky, with a blue break about sunset, so that the shadows lay oddly. My first thought, as I looked at the familiar scene, was that, had I been a general in a campaign, I should have taken special note of Woodilee, for it was a point of vantage. It lay right in the pass between the Scottish midlands and the south--the pass of road and water--yes, and--shall I say?-- of spirit, for it was in the throat of the hills, on the march between the sown and the desert. I was looking east, and to my left and behind me the open downs, farmed to their last decimal of capacity, were the ancient land of Manann, the capital province of Pictdom. The colliery headgear on the horizon, the trivial moorish hilltops, the dambrod-pattern fields, could never tame wholly for me that land's romance, and on this evening I seemed to be gazing at a thing antique and wolfish, tricked out for the moment with a sheep's coat. . . . To my right rose the huddle of great hills which cradle all our rivers. To them time and weather bring little change, yet in that eerie light, which revealed in hard outline while it obscured in detail, they seemed too remote and awful to be the kindly giants with whose glens I daily conversed. . . . At my feet lay Woodilee, and a miracle had been wrought, for a gloom like the shadow of an eclipse seemed to have crept over the parish. I saw an illusion, which I knew to be such, but which my mind accepted, for it gave me the vision I had been seeking.

It was the Woodilee of three hundred years ago. And my mind, once given the cue, set out things not presented by the illuded eye. . . . There were no highways--only tracks, miry in the bogs and stony on the braes, which led to Edinburgh on one hand and to Carlisle on the other. I saw few houses, and these were brown as peat, but on the knowe of the old kirkton I saw the four grey walls of the kirk, and the manse beside it among elders and young ashes. Woodilee was not now a parish lying open to the eye of sun and wind. It was no more than a tiny jumble of crofts, bounded and pressed in upon by something vast and dark, which clothed the tops of all but the highest hills, muffled the ridges, choked the glens and overflowed almost to the edge of the waters--which lay on the landscape like a shaggy fur cast loosely down. My mouth shaped the word "Melanudrigill," and I knew that I saw Woodilee as no eye had seen it for three centuries, when, as its name tells, it still lay in the shadow of a remnant of the Wood of Caledon, that most ancient forest where once Merlin harped and Arthur mustered his men. . . .

An engine whistled in the valley, a signal-box sprang into light, and my vision passed. But as I picked my way down the hillside in the growing dusk I realized that all memory of the encircling forest had not gone from Woodilee in my childhood, though the name of Melanudrigill had been forgotten. I could hear old Jock Dodds, who had been keeper on Calidon for fifty years, telling tales for my delectation as he sat and smoked on the big stone beside the smithy. He would speak of his father, and his father's father, and the latter had been a great hero with his flintlock gun. "He would lie in the moss or three on the winter mornin's, and him an auld man, and get the wild swans and the grey geese when they cam' ower frae Clyde to Aller. Ay, and mony's the deer he would kill." And when I pointed out that there were no deer in the countryside, Jock shook his head and said that in his grandfather's day the Black Wood was not all destroyed. "There was a muckle lump on Windyways, and anither this side o' Reiverslaw." But if I asked for more about the Wood, Jock was vague. Some said it had been first set by the Romans, others by Auld Michael Scott himself. . . . "A grand hidy-hole for beasts and an unco bit for warlocks." . . . Its downfall had begun long ago in the Dear Years, and the last of it had been burnt for firewood in his father's day, in the winter of the Sixteen Drifty Days. . . .

I remembered, too, that there had been places still sacrosanct and feared. To Mary Cross, a shapeless stone in a field of bracken, no one would go in the spring or summer gloaming, but the girls decked it with wild flowers at high noon of Midsummer Day. There was a stretch of Woodilee burn, between the village and the now-drained Fennan Moss, where trout, it was believed, were never found. Above all, right in the heart of Reiverslaw's best field of turnips was a spring, which we children knew as Katie Thirsty, but which the old folk called the Minister's Well, and mentioned always with a shake of the head or a sigh, for it was there, they said, that the minister of Woodilee had left the earth for Fairyland.

CHAPTER I

THE COMING OF THE MINISTER

The Reverend David Sempill began his ministry in Woodilee on the fifteenth day of August in the year of grace sixteen hundred and forty-four. He was no stranger to the glen, for as a boy he had spent his holidays with his grandfather, who was the miller of Roodfoot. In that year when the horn of the Kirk was exalted the voice of a patron mattered less; Mr. Sempill had been, as they said, "popularly called," and so entered upon his office with the eager interest of the parish which had chosen him. A year before he had been licensed by the presbytery of Edinburgh; he was ordained in Woodilee in the present year on the last Sabbath of June, and "preached in" on the first Sabbath of August by the weighty voice of Mungo Muirhead, the minister of Kirk Aller. His plenishing--chiefly books--had come from Edinburgh on eight pack- horses, and, having escaped the perils of Carnwath Moss, was now set out in an upper chamber of the little damp manse, which stood between the kirk and Woodilee burn. A decent widow woman, Isobel Veitch by name, had been found to keep his house, and David himself, now that all was ready, had ridden over on his grey cob from his cousin's at Newbiggin and taken seisin of his new home. He had sung as he came in sight of Woodilee; he had prayed with bowed head as he crossed the manse threshold; but as he sat in the closet which he named his "study," and saw his precious books on the shelf, and the table before him on which great works would be written, and outside the half-glazed window the gooseberry bushes of the garden and the silver links of the burn, he had almost wept with pure gratitude and content.

His first hour he had spent exploring his property. The manse was little and squat, and gave lodging in its heather-thatched roof to more than one colony of bees. The front abutted on the kirkton road, save for a narrow strip of green edged with smooth white stones from the burn. The back looked on a garden, where stood a score of apple trees, the small wild fruit of which was scarcely worth the gathering. There was also a square of green for bleaching clothes, a gean tree, a plot of gillyflowers and monkshood, and another of precious herbs like clary, penny-royal, and marjoram. At one end of the manse stood a brewhouse and a granary or girnel, for the storing of the minister's stipend meal; at the other a stable for two beasts, a byre with three stalls, a hen-house of mud, and, in the angle of the dykes of the kirk loan, a midden among nettles.

Indoors the place was not commodious, and even on that warm August day a chill struck upward from the earthen floors. The low-ceiled lobby had no light but the open door. To the right of it was the living-room with a boarded ceiling, a wooden floor, and roughly plastered walls, where the minister's eight-day clock (by John Atchison, Leith, 1601) had now acclimatized itself. To the left lay Isobel's kitchen, with a door leading to the brewhouse, and Isobel's press-bed at the back of it, and a small dog-hole of a cellar. The upper story was reached by a wooden staircase as steep as a ladder, which opened direct into the minister's bedroom--an apartment of luxury, for it had a fireplace. One door led from it to the solitary guest-chamber; another to a tiny hearthless room, which was his study or closet, and which at the moment ranked in his mind as the most miraculous of his possessions.

David ranged around like a boy back from school, and indeed with his thick, sandy hair and ruddy countenance and slim, straight back he seemed scarcely to have outgrown the schoolboy. He spilt the browst in the brewhouse, and made a spectacle of himself with pease-meal in the girnel. Isobel watched him anxiously out of doors, where he sampled the fruit of the apple trees, and with various rejected specimens took shots at a starling in the glebe. Then, in response to his shouts, she brought him a basin of water and he washed off the dust of his morning ride. The August sun fell warm on the little yard; the sound of the burn in the glen, the clack of the kirkton smithy, the sheep far off on Windyways, the bees in the clove gillyflowers, all melted into the soothing hum of a moorland noontide. The minister smiled as he scrubbed his cheeks, and Isobel's little old puckered apple-hued face smiled back. "Ay, sir," she said, "our lines is fallen intil a goodly place and a pleasant habitation. The Lord be thankit." And as he cried a fervent amen and tossed the towel back to her, a stir at the front door betokened his first visitors.

These were no less than three in number, neighbouring ministers who had ridden over on their garrons to bid the young man welcome to Woodilee. Presently stable and byre were crowded with their beasts, and the three brethren had bestowed themselves on the rough bench which adjoined the bleaching-ground. They would have their dinner at the village ordinary--let not Mr. Sempill put himself about--they would never have come thus unannounced if they had thought that they would be pressed to a meal. But they allowed themselves to be persuaded by the hospitable clamour of Isobel, who saw in such a function on her first day at the manse a social aggrandizement. "Mr. Sempill would think black burnin' shame if the gentlemen didna break breid. . . ." There was walth o' provender in the house--this moment she had put a hen in the pot-- she had a brace of muir-fowl ready for brandering that had been sent from Chasehope that very morn. . . . The three smiled tolerantly and hopefully. "Ye've gotten a rare Abigail, Mr. Sempill. A woman o' mense and sense--the manse o' Woodilee will be well guidit."

The Reverend Mungo Muirhead had a vast shaven face set atop of a thick neck and a cumbrous body. He had a big thin-lipped mouth which shut tight like a lawyer's, a fleshy nose, and large grey eyes which at most times were ruminant as a cow's, but could on occasion kindle to shrewdness. His complexion was pale, and he was fast growing bald, so the impression at first sight was of a perfect mountain of countenance, a steep field of colourless skin. As minister of Kirk Aller he was the metropolitan of the company, and as became a townsman he wore decent black with bands, and boasted a hat. The Reverend Ebenezer Proudfoot, from the moorland village of Bold, was of a different cast. He wore the coarse grey homespun of the farmer, his head-covering was a blue bonnet, his shoes were thick brogues with leather ties, and he had donned a pair of ancient frieze leggings. A massive sinewy figure, there was in his narrow face and small blue eyes an air of rude power and fiery energy. The third, Mr. James Fordyce from the neighbouring parish of Cauldshaw, was slight and thin, and pale either from ill- health or from much study. He was dressed in worn blue, and even in the August sun kept his plaid round his shoulders. In his face a fine brow was marred by the contraction of his lean jaws and a mouth puckered constantly as if in doubt or pain, but redeemed by brown eyes, as soft and wistful as a girl's.

At the hour of noon they sat down to meat. Mr. Muirhead said a lengthy grace, which, since he sniffed the savour from the kitchen, he began appropriately with "Bountiful Jehovah." All the dishes were set out at once on the bare deal table--a bowl of barley kail, a boiled fowl, the two brandered grouse, and a platter of oatcakes. The merchant in the Pleasance of Edinburgh had given his son a better plenishing than fell to the usual lot of ministers, for there were pewter plates and a knife and a fork for each guest. The three stared at the splendour, and Mr. Proudfoot, as if to testify against luxury, preferred to pick the bones with his hands. The home-brewed ale was good, and all except Mr. Fordyce did full justice to it, so that the single tankard, passed from hand to hand, was often refilled by Isobel. "Man, Mr. David," cried Mr. Muirhead in high good-humour, "this is a great differ from the days of your predecessor. Worthy Mr. Macmichael had never muckle but bannocks to set before his friends. But you've made us a feast of fat things."

David inquired about his predecessor, whom he remembered dimly from his boyhood as a man even then very old, who ambled about the parish on a white shelty.

"He was a pious and diligent minister," said Mr. Muirhead, "but since ever I kenned him he was sore fallen in the vale of years. He would stick to the same 'ordinary' till he had thrashed it into stour. I've heard that he preached for a year and sax months on Exodus fifteen and twenty-seven, the twelve wells of water and three score and ten palm trees of Elim, a Sabbath to ilka well and ilka tree. I've a notion that he was never very strong in the intellectuals."

"He wrestled mightily in prayer," said Mr. Proudfoot, "and he was great at fencing the Tables. Ay, sirs, he was a trumpet for the pure Gospel blast."

"I doubt not he was a good man," said Mr. Fordyce, "and is now gone to his reward. But he was ower auld and feeble for a sinful countryside. I fear that the parish was but ill guided, and, as ye ken, there was whiles talk of a Presbytery visitation."

"I differ!" cried Mr. Muirhead. "I differ in toto. Woodilee has aye been famous for its godly elders. Has it not Ephraim Caird, who was a member of Assembly and had a hand in that precious work of grace done in the East Kirk of St. Giles's two years syne? Has it not Peter Pennecuik, who has a gift of supplication like Mr. Rutherford himself? Ay, and in the Bishops' War you'll mind how Amos Ritchie was staunch to uphold the Covenant with the auld matchlock that had been his gudesire's. There's no lack of true religion in Woodilee."

"There's no lack of carnal pride, Mr. Mungo. The folk of Woodilee are ready enough for any stramash in Kirk or State. But what of their perishing souls, I ask? Are they striving to get a grip of Christ, as a bird scrapes with its claws at a stone wall? And do they bring forth works meet for repentance?"

"There was no clash of cauld morality in worthy Mr. Macmichael," said Mr. Proudfoot sourly.

"Is there the spirit of God in the people? That's what I want to ken. There's ill stories in the countryside anent Woodilee. The Black Wood could tell some tales if the trees could talk."

Mr. Muirhead, having finished his meal and said a second grace, was picking his teeth in great good-humour.

"Hoot toots, Mr. James, you'll give our young brother a scunner of the place, to which it has pleased the Almighty to call him, before he has had a look at it himself. I'm not denying that the Wood is ower near Woodilee. It's a wanchancy thing for any parochine to have a muckle black forest flung around it like a maud [plaid]. And no doubt the Devil walks about like a roaring lion in Woodilee as in other bits. But there's men of God here to resist him. I tell you, sirs, there have been more delations to the Presbytery for the sin of witchcraft in Woodilee than in any other parish on the water of Aller."

"And what does that prove, Mr. Mungo?"

"That there's wealth of prayerful and eident [careful] folk to confound the Adversary. This is no season to despair of Kirk and Covenant, when this day they hold the crown of the causeway. You'll no have heard of the astonishing mercy vouchsafed to us in England? A post came to Kirk Aller yestreen, and it seems that some weeks syne there was a great battle beside the city of York, where our Scots wrought mightily, and our own Davie Leslie gave the King's horsemen their kail through the reek. What does that portend?"

"It portends," said Mr. Proudfoot, whom food did not mellow, "that our pure and reformed Kirk of Scotland is linked more than ever with sectaries and antinomians and those, like the bloody and deceitful Cromwell, that would defile the milk of the Word with the sour whey of their human inventions. What avails a triumphant Kirk if its doctrine be sullied?"

Mr. Muirhead laughed. "It portends nothing of the kind. The good work goes cannily on, and the noble task to which the Assembly of Divines at Westminster set itself is advanced by a long mile. Man, Eben, you folk at Bold live ower far from the world. It's the Kirk of Scotland that holds the balance to-day and can enforce its will on both King and sectaries. Two days back I had a letter from that gospel-loving nobleman, the Earl of Loudoun . . ."

Mr. Muirhead was mounted on his high horse. He lit his pipe and for the space of half an hour dealt comprehensively with politics, labouring to show the happy posture of affairs for what he called the "good cause." The Solemn League and Covenant bound all Scotland in a pact with the Lord, and presently all England would follow suit. There would be soon that comfortable sight which had been foretold by their godly fathers, a uniform Kirk and a pure Gospel established by law from London to the Orkneys, and a covenanted Sion to which all the peoples of the earth would go up. Mr. Muirhead was eloquent, for he repeated a peroration which he had once used in the General Assembly.

"I have heard," he concluded, "that in Woodilee there was a signing of the Covenant by every soul that could make a scart with a pen. That for your encouragement, Mr. David."

Mr. Fordyce shook his head. "How many appended their names out of fear or from mere carnal policy? Mankind will run like jukes after a leader. I much misdoubt if there is any spiritual health to be got from following a multitude under duress. I would have left the choice to every man's conscience."

"You're not sound," cried Mr. Muirhead. "You're shaky on the fundamentals, Mr. James. I will confound you out of the Word. When King Josiah made a solemn covenant, did he leave it to ilka man's fancy to sign or no? Nay, he caused all--all, I say--in Jerusalem and Benjamin to stand to it. See Second Chronicles thirty-four and thirty-two."

There was a touch of asperity in the one disputant and of recalcitrance in the other, so David for good-fellowship's sake suggested that he might show them the manse in its new guise. But at that moment Isobel appeared with word that Chasehope was at the door seeking speech with the minister of Kirk Aller. At her back appeared the fiery head of the visitor, who was that Ephraim Caird whom Mr. Muirhead had already praised as a pillar of the Covenant and who farmed the largest tack in the parish. He was a big fellow, red as a fox, with a white freckled face, no eyebrows, and greenish blue eyes, a man of over forty, whose muscular frame was now somewhat overlaid by flesh. His mouth was small and generally puckered together, a habit which gave him an air of thought and gravity. He had been an opponent of David Sempill before the call, but had acquiesced in the majority vote and had welcomed the new minister at the "preaching in" with a great show of goodwill. To- day he was apologetic and affable. He asked pardon for his intrusion--he would take neither bite nor sup--he had heard that the ministers were at the manse, and he begged a word with Mr. Muirhead on Presbytery matters which would save him a journey to Kirk Aller, when he was busy with the bog hay. So David took the other two to his closet and left Chasehope and Mr. Muirhead to their colloquy.

Mr. Proudfoot eyed with disapproval the books in the little dark chamber. He was content, he said, with the Bible and the Institutes of John Calvin and old Robert Rollock's commentary on the Prophet Daniel. He read the lettering on one volume, Sancti Clementi Opera, and on another, a work by a Dutch theologian, De Sancti Pauli Epistolis. The word "Saint" roused his ire. "Rags of Popery," he muttered, as he banged the books back on their shelves. "What for 'Saint' Paul and not 'Saint' Moses or 'Saint' Isaiah? It's a queer thing that Antichrist should set himself to miscall the godly Apostles of the New Testament and let the auld prophets alone. You're a young man, Mr. Sempill, and, as is natural in youth, with but a small experience of religion. Take the advice of an older man, and no clog yourself on the road to Heaven with ower much printit lear, when you can put the whole Word of God in your pouch."

But Mr. Fordyce looked at the shelves with greedy eyes. The moor- fowl at dinner had loosened a tooth, and now it came out in his hand and was wrapped carefully in his kerchief. "I have kept ilka tooth I have ever cast," he told the others, "and they will go into my coffin with me that my bodily parts may be together at the Resurrection." "Would you shorten the arm of the Lord?" Mr. Proudfoot had asked testily. "Can He no gather your remnants from the uttermost parts of the earth?" "True, true," the other had answered gently, "but it's just my fancy to keep all my dust in the one place." This ceremony over, he flung himself on the books like a hungry man on food. He opened them lovingly, read their titles, fingered them as if he could scarcely bear to part with them. "You're no half my age," he told the owner, "but you've twice as many books as there are in the Cauldshaw manse. You start well provided, Mr. David."

The theology he knew already and approved, but there were other works over which he shook a moralizing head. "You've a hantle of pagan writers, Mr. David. I would counsel a young minister to apply himself rather to the Hebrew than to the Greek, for though the Greek was the tongue of the New Testament, it was also the tongue of lascivious poets and mocking philosophers, whereas the Hebrew was consecrate wholly to God. . . . But you have the Hebrew too, I see. Losh, here's the lexicon of Bamburgius, of which I have read but have never seen. We must consult, Mr. David. I've a new theory of the Hebrew accents on which I would like your judgment."

As he ran over the list he suddenly cried aloud with pleasure, and then checked himself almost shamefacedly. "Preserve us, but here's Hieronymus Cardanus, and other astrologic works. Man, I've diverted myself whiles with the science of the stars, and can make a shape at calculating a nativity. I cannot see why the thing should not be turned to holy uses, as when the star guided the Wise Men of the East to Bethlehem. You and me must have long cracks some day. These books will be like the Pole Star to draw me to Woodilee, and I'm looking to see you soon at Cauldshaw. It's but a poor desert bit, but there have been precious occasions there and many an outpouring of grace. I'm sore troubled with the gravel, Mr. David, and the goodwife has had a flux in the legs this twelvemonth back, but the Lord has showed me singular favour, and my damps are lightened since a leech in Edinburgh prescribed a hyperion of bourtree and rue. . . . We're a childless household, for we had but the one bairn, and sax year syne the Lord gathered her to Himself."

Downstairs Mr. Muirhead had finished his talk, and the three ministers took their leave--they of Bold and Cauldshaw to jog the moorland miles to their homes, he of Kirk Aller to take his "four- hours" with Chasehope at Lucky Weir's in the clachan. Each of the three kissed David on the cheek and blessed him after his fashion. "May you live to be a pillar of the Kirk," said Mr. Muirhead. "Keep a Gospel walk," said Mr. Proudfoot, "on the narrow rigging of the truth." But Mr. Fordyce took the young man's hand, after saluting him, and held it with a kind of wistful affection. "I pray," he said, "that your windows may be ever open towards Jerusalem."

When his guests had gone David Sempill explored once more his little domain, like a child who counts his treasures. Then, as the afternoon mellowed into evening, the slopes of the Hill of Deer, red with flowering heather, drew him for a walk. He wanted a wide prospect, to see his parish in its setting of hill and glen, and recall the landmarks now blurred in his childhood's memory. His black coat and breeches were of Edinburgh make and too fine for moorland work, but he had stout country shoes and hose of ram's wool, the gift of his cousin's wife at Newbiggin, and he moved over the bent with the long stride of a shepherd. He crossed the burn of Mire, and saw below him the farm-town of Mirehope, with barley and nettles at strife in the infield, and the run-rigs of the outfield feathered with very green oats. Presently he was on the Hill of Deer, where the long stacks of peats were drying so well that every breath of air sent up from them a fine flurry of dust. The Mirehope cattle, wretched little black beasts, were grazing under the charge of a herd-boy, and the Mirehope sheep, their coats matted with tar till they looked like monstrous slugs, were picking up an uneasy livelihood among the heather bushes, leaving tufts of smelly wool behind them on the scraggy twigs which were still charred from the March moorburn. He reached the low summit, and flung himself down on a patch of thymy turf between the whinstone screes, with his face to the valley.

His holiday mood still held. The visit of his ministerial brethren had not dashed him, for he saw their prosiness through a golden haze. Mr. Muirhead was a stout warder on the walls of Sion, Mr. Proudfoot a guardian of the purity of the Temple, and Mr. Fordyce beyond question a saint, with his haggard face and his wistful eyes. It was Mr. Fordyce who stuck in his memory. A lovable saint, with his cast teeth saved up to make easy the business of a bodily resurrection, his love of the stars, his pathetic bookishness. David was full of the zest of his calling, but for himself he was ready to circumscribe its duties. Not for him to uphold the Kirk against its ill-wishers in the State; in that cause he would do battle when the need arose, but not till then. He left to others the task of keeping the canon of truth pure from alloy: he accepted the Kirk's doctrine loyally, but let others do the dogmatizing. The work for which he longed was to save and comfort human souls.

Seen on that hilltop the minister of Woodilee was a different figure from that beheld by his colleagues in the dim light of the manse. His active form, his colour, his tumbled hair, spoke of the boy, but his face was not boyish. In its young contours there were already thought and resolution and spiritual fineness, and there was a steady ardour in the eyes. If his chin was the fighter's, his mouth was the comforter's. Five years before he had been set on a scholar's life. At the college he had been a noted Grecian, and in Robert Bryson's bookshop at the Sign of the Prophet Jonah in the West Bow his verses, Latin and English, had been praised by the learned.

When religion called him it was as a challenge not to renounce but to perfect his past. A happy preoccupation with his dream made him blind to the harshness and jealousies which beset the Kirk, and he saw only its shining mission. The beauty which was to be found in letters seemed in very truth a part of that profounder beauty which embraced all earth and Heaven in the revelation of God. He had not ceased to be the humanist in becoming the evangelist. Some had looked askance at him as too full of carnal learning for the sacred office, some as too cheerful for a shepherd of souls in a perishing world. But his critics as yet were few, for David carried with him a light and warmth which it was hard for the sourest to resist. "He is a gracious youth," an old minister had said at his ordination. "May the Lord deal tenderly with him!"

David's eyes from his perch on the hilltop rested first on the kirkton of Woodilee. He saw the manse among its trees, and the church with its thatched roof--the roof had been lead till Morton the Regent stripped it and melted it down for bullets. He saw the little beehive cottages in the clachan with the taller gable-end of Lucky Weir's ale-house. He saw the adjoining farm-towns--the Mains, Chasehope, Nether Windyways, Crossbasket, the two Fennans, each with its patches of crops lifted well above the bogs of the glen. He saw the mill of Woodilee at present idle by the burn, and hay being cut on the side of Windyways hill, and what looked like the clipping of the miller's sheep. In the bright evening the scene was all of peace and pastoral, and David's heart kindled. There dwelled his people, the little flock whom God had appointed him to feed. His heart yearned over them, and in a sudden glow of tenderness he felt that this sunset prospect of his parish was a new and more solemn ordination.

It was long before he lifted his eyes beyond the glen to the great encircling amphitheatre of the hills. At first he gazed at them in an abstraction, till childish memories came back to him and he began to name the summits to himself one by one. There was the bald top of the Lammerlaw, and the peak of the Green Dod, and far beyond the long line of the great Herstane Craig, which in that childhood had been the synonym for untravelled mystery. He saw the green cleft in the hills where the Aller came down from its distant wells, and the darker glen of the Rood where bent was exchanged for rock and heather. He saw the very patches of meadow by Roodside which he had made his boyish playground. Such a hilltop prospect he had never before known, for a child lives in a magnified world, and finds immensity in short vistas. One thing struck hard on his mind. Never before had he realized the extent of the forest ground. He remembered travelling to Roodfoot through trees, and all up the water of Rood there had been a drift of scrub. But it was the meadows and the open spaces that had been his kingdom, and his recollection was of a bare sunny land where whaup and peewit cried and the burns fell headlong from windy moors. But now, as he gazed, he realized that the countryside was mainly forest.

Everywhere, muffling the lower glen of the Woodilee burn and the immediate vale of the Aller, and climbing far up the hillside, was the gloom of trees. In the Rood glen there was darkness only at the foot, for higher up the woods thinned into scrub of oak and hazel, with the knees of the uplands showing through it. The sight powerfully impressed his fancy. Woodilee was a mere clearing in a forest. This was the Silva Caledonis of which old writers spoke, the wood which once covered all the land and in whose glades King Arthur had dwelt. He remembered doggerel Latin of Merlin the Bard and strange sayings of True Thomas--old wives' tales which concerned this sanctuary. He had grown up beside it and had not known of it, and now he had come back to a revelation. Silva Caledonis! Up the Rood water lay the house of Calidon. Were the names perhaps the same?

The young man's fancy was quick to kindle, and he looked with new eyes at the great cup of green, broken only at one spot by Aller side with the flash of water. At first in the soft evening light it had worn a gracious and homely air, even the darkness of the pines seemed luminous, and the feathery top of a patch of birches was like the smoke of household fires. . . . But as the sun sank behind the Rood hills a change seemed to come over the scene. The shade became gloom, a hostile, impenetrable darkness. The birches were still like smoke, but a turbid smoke from some unhallowed altar. The distant shallows of Aller caught a ray of the dying sun and turned to blood. . . . The minister shivered and then laughed at himself for his folly.

The evening deepened in the hollows, though the hilltops were still faintly bright. The great wood seemed now to be a moving thing, a flood which lapped and surged and might at any moment overflow the sandspit which was Woodilee. Again the minister laughed at himself, but without conviction. It must be an eerie life under the shadow of that ancient formless thing. Woodilee could not be quite as other parishes, or its folk like other folk. The Wood, this hoary Wood of Caledon, must dominate their thoughts and form their characters. . . . Had not some one called it the Black Wood?--Yes, they had spoken of it that afternoon. Mr. Muirhead had admitted that it must be queer to live so near it, and Mr. Fordyce had shaken his head solemnly and hinted at tales that would be told if the trees could speak. . . . Did the Devil use the place as a stronghold and seduce the foolish into its shadows? Could it be said of a lost soul, Itur in antiquam silvam?

David was less superstitious than most men, but he had too ready a fancy and a mind too well stored with learning to be easy at the thought. Already he felt that he had found an antagonist. Was Woodilee to prove a frontier-post for God's servant against the horrid mysteries of heathendom? . . . He gave a sudden start, for a voice had sounded behind him.

The voice was singing--a charm against bogles which he remembered himself using as a child:

"Weary, Ovie, gang awa', Haste ye furth o' house an' ha', Ower the muir and doun the burn, Wearie, Ovie, ne'er return."

A grotesque figure emerged from the dusk. It was a tall fellow, who seemed to have been broken in the middle, for he walked almost doubled up. His face, seen in the half-light, was that of a man of thirty or so, with a full black beard and red protuberant lips. His clothes were ruinous, an old leather jerkin which gaped at every seam, ragged small-clothes of frieze, and for hosen a wrapping of dirty clouts. There were no shoes on his feet, and his unwashed face was dark as a berry. In his hand he had a long ash pole, and on his head a blue cowl so tight that it was almost a skull-cap.

David recognized the figure for Daft Gibbie, the village natural, who had greeted him with mewing and shouting at his ordination. In the clachan street he had seemed an ordinary deformed idiot--what was known locally as an "object"--but up on this twilight hilltop he was like an uncouth revenant from an older world. The minister instinctively gripped his staff tighter, but Gibbie's intention was of the friendliest.

"A braw guid e'en to ye, Mr. Sempill, sir. I saw ye tak' the hill and I bode to follow, for I was wantin' to bid ye welcome to Woodilee. Man, ye gang up the brae-face like a maukin [a hare]. Ower fast, I says to mysel', ower fast for a man o' God, for what saith the Word, 'He that believeth shall not make haste!'"

The creature spoke in a voice of great beauty and softness--the voice rather of a woman than of a man. And as he spoke he bowed, and patted the minister's arm, and peered into his face with bright wild eyes. Then he clutched David and forced him round till again he was looking over the Wood.

"The Hill o' Deer's a grand bit for a prospect, sir, for is it no like the Hill o' Pisgah from which ye can spy the Promised Land? Ye can lift up your eyes to the hills, and ye can feast them on the bonny haughs o' the Aller, or on the douce wee clachan o' Woodilee, wi' the cots sittin' as canty round the kirk as kittlins round an auld cat."

"I was looking at the Wood," said David.

The man laughed shrilly. "And a braw sicht it is in the gloamin' frae the Hill o' Deer. For ye can see the size o' the muckle spider's wab, but doun in the glen ye're that clamjamphried wi' michty trees that your heid spins like a peery and your e'en are dozened. It's a unco thing the Wud, Mr. Sempill, sir?"

"Do you know your ways in it, Gibbie?"

"Me! I daurna enter it. I keep the road, for I'm feared o' yon dark howes." Then he laughed again, and put his mouth close to the minister's ear. "Not but what I'll tak' the Wud at the proper season. Tak' the Wud, Mr. Sempill, like other folk in Woodilee."

He peered in the minister's face to see if he were understood. Satisfied that he was not, he laughed again.

"Tak' Gibbie's advice, sir, and no gang near the Wud. It's nae place for men o' God, like yoursel', sir, and puir Gibbie."

"Do they call it the Black Wood?"

Gibbie spat. "Incomin' bodies, nae doot," he said in contempt. "But it's just the Wud wi' nae 'black' aboot it. But ken ye the name that auld folk gie'd it?" He became confidential again. "They ca'd it Melanudrigill," he whispered.

David repeated the word. His mind had been running on heathen learning, and he wondered if the name were Greek.

"That might mean the 'place of dark waters,'" he said.

"Na, na. Ye're wrong there, Mr. Sempill. There's nae dark waters in Melanudrigill. There's the seven burns that rin south, but they're a' as clear as Aller. But dinna speak that name to ither folk, Mr. Sempill, and dinna let on that Gibbie telled ye. It's a wanchancy name. Ye can cry it in a safe bit like the Hill o' Deer, but if ye was to breathe it in the Wud unco things micht happen. I daurna speak my ain name among the trees."

"Your name is Gibbie. Gibbie what?"

The man's face seemed to narrow in fear and then to expand in confidence. "I can tell it to a minister o' the Word. It's Gilbert Niven. Ken ye where I got that name? In the Wud, sir. Ken ye wha gie'd it me? The Guid Folk. Ye'll no let on that I telled ye."

The night was now fallen, and David turned for home, after one last look at the pit of blackness beneath him. The idiot hobbled beside him, covering the ground at a pace which tried even his young legs, and as he went he babbled.

"Tak' Gibbie's advice and keep far frae the Wud, Mr. Sempill, and if ye're for Roodfoot or Calidon haud by the guid road. I've heard tell that in the auld days, when there was monks at the kirkton, they bode to gang out every year wi' bells and candles and bless the road to keep it free o' bogles. But they never ventured into the Wud, honest men. I'll no say but what a minister is mair powerfu' than a monk, but an eident body will run nae risks. Keep to fine caller bits like this Hill o' Deer, and if ye want to traivel, gang west by Chasehope or east by Kirk Aller. There's nocht for a man o' God in the Wud."

"Are there none of my folk there?"

For a second Gibbie stopped as if thunderstruck. "Your folk!" he cried. "In the Wud!" Then he perceived David's meaning. "Na, na. There's nae dwallin' there.

Nether Fennan is no far off and Reiverslaw is a bowshot from the trees, but to bide in the Wud!-- Na, na, a man would be sair left to himsel' ere he ventured that! There's nae hoose biggit [built] by human hand that wadna be clawed doun by bogles afore the wa' rase a span frae the grund."

At the outfield of Mirehope Gibbie fled abruptly, chanting like a night bird.

CHAPTER II

THE ROAD TO CALIDON

The minister sat at his supper of porridge and buttermilk when Isobel broke in on him, her apple-hued face solemn and tearful.

"There's ill news frae up the water, Mr. Sempill. It's Marion Simpson, her that's wife to Richie Smail, the herd o' the Greenshiel. Marion, puir body, has been ill wi' a wastin' the past twalmonth, and now it seems she's near her release. Johnnie Dow, the packman, is ben the house, and he has brocht word that Richie is fair dementit, and that the wife is no like to last the nicht, and would the minister come up to the Greenshiel. They've nae bairns, the Lord be thankit; but Richie and Marion have aye been fell fond o' ither, and Richie's an auld exercised Christian and has been many times spoken o' for the eldership. I doot ye'll hae to tak' the road, sir."

It was his first call to pastoral duty, and, though he had hoped to be at his books by candle-light, David responded gladly. He put his legs into boots, saddled his grey cob, flung his plaid round his shoulders, and in ten minutes was ready to start. Isobel watched him like a mother.

"I'll hae a cup o' burned yill [ale] waitin' for ye to fend off the cauld--no but what it's a fine lown [mild] nicht. Ye ken the road, sir? Up by Mirehope and round by the back o' the Hill."

"There's a quicker way by Roodfoot, and on this errand there's no time to lose."

"But that's through the Wud," Isobel gasped. "It's no me that would go through the Wud in the dark, nor naebody in Woodilee. But a minister is different, nae doot."

"The road is plain?" he asked.

"Aye, it's plain eneuch. There's naething wrong wi' the road. But it's an eerie bit when the sun's no shinin'. But gang your ways, sir, for a man o' God is no like common folk. Ye'll get a mune to licht ye back."

David rode out of the kirkton, and past the saughs and elders which marked the farm of Crossbasket, till the path dipped into the glen of the Woodilee burn and the trees began. Before he knew he was among them, old gnarled firs standing sparsely among bracken. They were thin along the roadside, but on the hill to his right and down in the burn's hollow they made a cloud of darkness. The August night still had a faint reflected light, and the track, much ribbed by tree roots, showed white before him. The burn, small with the summer drought, made a far-away tinkling, the sweet scents of pine and fern were about him, the dense boskage where it met the sky had in the dark a sharp marmoreal outline. The world was fragrant and quiet; if this be the Black Wood, thought David, I have been in less happy places.

But suddenly at a turn of the hill the trees closed in. It was almost as if he had stripped and dived into a stagnant pool. The road now seemed to have no purpose of its own, but ran on sufferance, slinking furtively as the Wood gave it leave, with many meaningless twists, as if unseen hands had warded it off. His horse, which had gone easily enough so far, now needed his heel in its side and many an application of his staff. It shied at nothing visible, jibbed, reared, breathing all the while as if its wind were touched. Something cold seemed to have descended on David's spirits, which, as soon as he was aware of it, he tried to exorcise by whistling a bar or two, and then by speaking aloud. He recited a psalm, but his voice, for usual notably full and mellow, seemed not to carry a yard. It was forced back on him by the trees. He tried to shout, with no better effect. There came an echo which surprised him, till he perceived that it was an owl. Others answered, and the place was filled with their eldritch cries. One flapped across the road not a yard from him, and in a second his beast was on its haunches.

He was now beyond the throat of the glen, and the Woodilee burn had left him, going its own way into the deeps of Fennan Moss, where the wood was thin. The road plucked up courage, and for a little ran broad and straight through a covert of birches. Then the pines closed down again, this time with more insistence, so that the path was a mere ladder among gnarled roots. Here there were moths about--a queer thing, David thought--white glimmering creatures that brushed his face and made his horse half crazy. He had ridden at a slow jog, but the beast's neck and flanks were damp with sweat. Presently he had to dismount and lead it, testing every step with his foot, for there seemed to be ugly scaurs breaking away on his left. The owls kept up a continuous calling, and there was another bird with a note like a rusty saw. He tried to whistle, to shout, to laugh, but his voice seemed to come out of folds of cloth. He thought it was his plaid, but the plaid was about his chest and shoulders and far from his mouth. . . . And then, at one step the Wood ceased and he was among meadows.

He knew the place, for after the darkness of the trees the land, though the moon had not risen, seemed almost light. There in front was the vale down which Aller flowed, and on the right was his own familiar glen of Rood. Now he could laugh at his oppression--now that he was among the pleasant fields where he had played as a boy. . . . Why had he forgotten about the Black Wood, for it had no part in his memories? True, he had come always to Roodfoot by the other road behind the Hill of Deer, but there were the dark pines not a mile off--he must have adventured many times within their fringes. He thought that it was because a child is shielded by innocence from ugliness. . . . And yet, even then, he had had many nightmares and fled from many bogles. But not from the Wood. . . . No doubt it was the growing corruption of a man's heart.

The mill at Roodfoot stood gaunt and tenantless, passing swiftly into decay. He could see that the mill-wheel had gone, and its supports stood up like broken teeth; the lade was choked with rushes; the line of a hill showed through the broken rigging. He had known of this, but none the less the sight gave him a pang, for David was a jealous conserver of his past. . . . But as the path turned up the glen beside the brawling Rood, he had a sudden uplifting of spirit. This could not change, this secret valley, whose every corner he had quartered, whose every nook was the home of a delightful memory. He felt again the old ardour, when, released from Edinburgh, he had first revisited his haunts, tearful with excited joy. The Wood was on him again, but a different wood, his own wood. The hazels snuggled close to the roadside, and the feathery birches and rowans made a canopy, not a shadow. The oaks were ancient friends, the alders old playmates. His horse had recovered its sanity, and David rode through the dew-drenched night in a happy rapture of remembrance.

He was riding up Rood--that had always been the thing he had hoped to do. He had never been even so far as Calidon before, for a boy's day's march is short. But he had promised himself that some day when he was a man he would have a horse, and ride to the utmost springs--to Roodhope-foot, to the crinkle in Moss Fell where Rood was born. . . . "Up the water" had always been like a spell in his ear. He remembered lying in bed at night and hearing a clamour at the mill door: it was men from up the water, drovers from Moffat, herds from the back of beyond, once a party of soldiers from the south. And up the water lay Calidon, that ancient castle. The Hawkshaws were a name in a dozen ballads, and the tales of them in every old wife's mouth. Once they had captained all the glens of Rood and Aller in raids to the Border, and when Musgrave and Salkeld had led a return foray, it was the Hawkshaws that smote them mightily in the passes. He had never seen one of the race; the men were always at the wars or at the King's court; but they had filled his dreams. One fancy especially was of a little girl-- a figure with gold hair like King Malcolm's daughter in the "Red Etin of Ireland" tale--whom he rescued from some dire peril, winning the thanks of her tall mail-clad kin. In that dream he too had been mail-clad, and he laughed at the remembrance. It was a far cry from that to the sedate minister of Woodilee.

As he turned up the road to the Greenshiel he remembered with compunction his errand. He had been amusing himself with vain memories when he was on the way to comfort a bed of death. Both horse and rider were in a sober mood when they reached the sheiling, the horse from much stumbling in peat-bogs, and the man from reflections on his unworthiness.

Rushlights burned in the single room, and the door and the one window stood open. It was a miserable hut of unmortared stones from the hill, the gaps stuffed with earth and turf, and the roof of heather thatch. One glance showed him that he was too late. A man sat on a stool by the dead peat-fire with his head in his hands. A woman was moving beside the box bed and unfolding a piece of coarse linen. The shepherd of the Greenshiel might be an old exercised Christian, but there were things in that place which had no warrant from the Bible. A platter full of coarse salt lay at the foot of the bed, and at the top crossed twigs of ash.

The woman--she was a neighbouring shepherd's wife--stilled her keening at the sound of David's feet.

"It's himsel'," she cried. "Richie, it's the minister. Wae's me, sir, but ye're ower late to speed puir Mirren. An hour syne she gaed to her reward--just slipped awa' in a fit o' hoastin' [coughing]. I've strauchten'd the corp and am gettin' the deid claes ready--Mirren was aye prood o' hers, and keepit them fine and caller wi' gall and rosmry. Come forrit, sir, and tak' a look on her that's gane. There was nae deid-thraws wi' Mirren, and she's lyin' as peacefu' as a bairn. Her face is sair faun in, but I mind when it was the bonniest face in a' Rood water."

The dead woman lay with cheeks like wax, a coin on each eye, so that for the moment her face had the look of a skull. Disease had sculptured it to an extreme fineness, and the nose, the jaw, and the lines of the forehead seemed chiselled out of ivory. David had rarely looked on death, and the sight gave him a sense first of repulsion and then of an intolerable pathos. He scarcely heard the clatter of the shepherd's wife.

"She's been deein' this mony a day, and now she's gane joyfully to meet her Lord. Eh, but she was blithe to gang in the hinner end. There was a time when she was sweir to leave Richie. 'Elspet,' she says to me, 'what will that puir man o' mine dae his lee lane?' and I aye says to her, 'Mirren, my wumman, the Lord's a grand provider, and Richie will haud fast by Him. Are not twa sparrows,' I says--"

David went over to the husband on the creepie by the fireside, and laid his hand on his shoulder. The man sat hunched in a stupor of misery.

"Richie," he said, "if I'm too late to pray with Marion, I can pray with you."

He prayed, as he always prayed, not in a mosaic of Scripture texts, but in simple words; and as he spoke he felt the man's shoulder under his hand shake as with a sob. He prayed with a sincere emotion, for he had been riding through a living, coloured world, and now felt like an icy blast the chill and pallor of death. Also he felt the pity of this lifelong companionship broken, and the old man left solitary. When he had finished, Richie lifted his face from his hands, and into his eyes, which had been blank as a wall, came the wholesome dimness of tears.

"I'm no repinin'," he said. "The Lord gave and the Lord has taken away, and I bless His name. What saith the Apostle--Mirren has gane to be with Christ, whilk is far better. There was mony a time when the meal-ark was toom [empty], and the wind and weet cam' in through the baulks, and the peats wadna kindle, and we were baith hungry and cauld. But Mirren's bye wi' a' that, for she's bielded in the everlasting arms, and she's suppin' rich at the Lord's ain table. But eh, sir, I could wish it had been His will to hae ta'en me wi' her. I'm an auld man, and there's nae weans [children], and for the rest o' my days I'll be like a beast in an unco loan [strange lane]. God send they binna mony."

"The purposes of the Lord are true and altogether righteous. If He spares you, Richie, it's because He has still work for you to do on this earth."

"I kenna what it can be. My fit's beginnin' to lag on the hill, and ony way I'm guid for nocht but sheep. Lambin's and clippin's and spainin's [weanings] is ower puir a wark for the Lord to fash wi'."

"Whatever you put your hand to is the work of the Lord, if you keep His fear before you."

"Maybe, sir." The man rose from his stool and revealed a huge gaunt frame, much bowed at the shoulders. He peered in the rushlight at the minister's face.

"Ye're a young callant to be a minister. I was strong on your side, sir, when ye got the call, for your preachin' was like a rushin' michty wind. I mind I repeated the heids o' your sermon to Mirren. . . . Ye've done me guid, sir--I think it's maybe the young voice o' ye. Ye wad get the word from Johnnie Dow. Man, it was kind to mak' siccan haste. I wish--I wish ye had seen Mirren in life. . . . Pit up anither petition afore ye gang--for a blessin' on this stricken house and on an auld man who has his title sure in Christ, but has an unco rebellious heart."

It seemed to David as he turned from the door, where the shepherd stood with uplifted arm, that a benediction had been given, but not by him.

The moon had risen and the glen lay in a yellow light, with the high hills between Rood and Aller shrunk to mild ridges. The stream caught the glow, and its shallows were like silver chased in amber. The young man's heart was full with the scene which he had left. Death was very near to men, jostling them at every corner, whispering in their ear at kirk and market, creeping between them and their firesides. Soon the shepherd of the Greenshiel would lie beside his wife; in a little, too, his own stout limbs would be a heap of dust. How small and frail seemed the life in that cottage, as contrasted with the rich pulsing world of the woods and hills and their serene continuance. But it was they that were the shadows in God's sight. The immortal thing was the broken human heart that could say in its frailty that its Redeemer liveth. "Thou, Lord," he repeated to himself, "in the beginning hast laid the foundations of the earth, and the heavens are the work of Thy hands. They shall perish, but Thou shalt endure; they all shall wax old as doth a garment, and as a vesture shalt Thou change them, and they shall be changed: but Thou art the same, and Thy years shall not fail."

But as the road twined among the birches David's mood became insensibly more pagan. He could not resist the joy of the young life that ran in his members, and which seemed to be quickened by the glen of his childhood. Death was the portion of all, but youth was still far from death. . . . The dimness and delicacy of the landscape, the lines of hill melting into a haze under the moon, went to his head like wine. It was a world transfigured and spell- laden. On his left the dark blotch which was Melanudrigill lay like a spider over the hillsides and the mouths of the glens, but all in front and to his right was kindly and golden. He had come back to his own country, and it held out its arms to him. "Salve, O venusta Sirmio," he cried, and an owl answered.

The glen road was reached, but he did not turn towards Roodfoot. He had now no dread of the wood of Melanudrigill, but he had a notion to stand beside Rood water, where it flowed in a ferny meadow which had been his favourite fishing-ground. So he pushed beyond the path into a maze of bracken and presently was at the stream's edge.

And then, as he guided his horse past a thicket of alders, he came full upon a little party of riders who had halted there.

There were three of them--troopers, they seemed, with buff caps and doublets and heavy cavalry swords, and besides their own scraggy horses there was a led beast. The three men were consulting when David stumbled on them, and at the sight of him they had sprung apart and laid hands on their swords. But a second glance had reassured them.

"Good e'en to you, friend," said he who appeared to be the leader. "You travel late."

It was not an encounter which David would have sought, for wandering soldiery had a bad name in the land. Something of this may have been in the other's mind, for his next words were an explanation.

"You see three old soldiers of Leven's," he said, "on the way north after the late crowning mercy vouchsafed to us against the malignants. We be Angus men, and have the general's leave to visit our homes. If you belong hereaways you can maybe help us with the road. Ken you a place of the name of Calidon?"

To their eyes David must have seemed a young farmer or a bonnet- laird late on the road from some errand of roystering or sweethearting.

"I lived here as a boy," he said, "and I'm but now returned. Yet I think I could put you on your way to Calidon. The moon's high."

"It's a braw moon," said the second trooper, "and it lighted us fine down Aller, but the brawest moon will not discover you a dwelling in a muckle wood, if you kenna the road to it."

The three had moved out from the shade of the alders and were now clear under the sky. Troopers, common troopers and shabby at that, riding weary, ill-conditioned beasts. The nag which the third led was a mere rickle of bones. And yet to David's eye there was that about them which belied their apparent rank. They had spoken in the country way, but their tones were not those of countrymen. They had not the air of a gaunt Jock or a round-faced Tam from the plough-tail. All three were slim, and the hands which grasped the bridles were notably fine. They held themselves straight like courtiers, and in their voices lurked a note as of men accustomed to command. The leader was a dark man, with a weary thin face and great circles round his eyes; the second a tall fellow, with a tanned skin, a cast in his left eye, and a restless dare-devil look; the third, who seemed to be their groom, had so far not spoken, and had stood at the back with the led horse, but David had a glimpse above his ragged doublet of a neat small moustache and a delicate chin. "Leven has good blood in his ranks," he thought, "for these three never came out of a but-and-ben." Moreover, the ordinary trooper on his way home would not make Calidon a house of call.

He led them up to the glen road, intending to give them directions about their way, but there he found that his memory had betrayed him. He knew exactly in which nook of hill lay Calidon, but for the life of him he could not remember how the track ran to it.

"I'll have to be your guide, sirs," he told them. "I can take you to Calidon, but I cannot tell you how to get there."

"We're beholden to you, sir, but it's a sore burden on your good- nature. Does your own road lie in that airt?"

The young man laughed. "The night is fine and I'm in no haste to be in bed. I'll have you at Calidon door in half an hour."

Presently he led them off the road across a patch of heather, forded Rood at a shallow, and entered a wood of birches. The going was bad, and the groom with the led horse had the worst of it. The troopers were humane men, for they seemed to have a curious care of their servant. It was "Canny now, James--there's bog on the left," or "Take tent of that howe;" and once or twice, when there was a difficult passage, one or the other would seize the bridle of the led horse till the groom had passed. David saw from the man's face that he was grey with fatigue.

"Get you on my beast," he said, "and I'll hold the bridle. I can find my way better on foot. And do you others each take a led horse. The road we're travelling is none so wide, and we'll make better speed that way."

The troopers docilely did as they were bidden, and the weary groom was hoisted on David's grey gelding. The change seemed to ease him, and he lost his air of heavy preoccupation and let his eyes wander. The birch wood gave place to a bare hillside, where even the grey slipped among the screes and the four horses behind sprawled and slithered. They crossed a burn, surmounted another ridge, and entered a thick wood of oak, which David knew cloaked the environs of Calidon and which made dark travelling even in the strong moonlight. Great boulders were hidden in the moss, withered boughs hung low over the path, and now and then would come a patch of scrub so dense that it had to be laboriously circumvented. The groom on the grey was murmuring to himself, and to David's amazement it was Latin. "Ibant obscuri sola sub nocte per umbram," were the words he spoke.

David capped them.

"Perque domos Ditis vacuas et inania regna, Quale per incertam lunam . . ."

The man on the horse laughed, and David, looking up, had his first proper sight of his face. It was a long face, very pale, unshaven and dirty, but it was no face of a groom. The thin aquiline nose, the broad finely arched brow, were in themselves impressive, but the dominant feature was the eyes. They seemed to be grey--ardent, commanding, and yet brooding. David was so absorbed by this sudden vision that he tripped over a stone and almost pulled the horse down.

"I did not look," said the rider, in a voice low-pitched and musical, "I did not look to find a scholar in these hills."

"Nor did I know," said David, "that Virgil was the common reading of Leven's men."

They had reached a field of wild pasture studded with little thorns, in the middle of which stood a great stone dovecot. A burn falling in a deep ravine made a moat on one side of the tower of Calidon, which now rose white like marble in the moon. They crossed the ravine, not without trouble, and joined the main road from the glen, which ended in a high-arched gate round which clustered half a dozen huts.

At the sound of their arrival men ran out of the huts, and one seized the bridle of the leader. David and the groom had now fallen back, and it was the dark man who did the talking. These were strange troopers, for they sat their horses like princes, so that the hand laid on the bridle was promptly dropped.

"We would speak with the laird of Calidon," the dark man said. "Stay, carry this ring to him. He will know what it means." It seemed curious to David that the signet given to the man was furnished by the groom.

In five minutes the servant returned. "The laird waits on ye, sirs. I'll tak' the beasts, and your mails, if ye've ony. Through the muckle yett an it please ye."

David turned to go. "I've brought you to Calidon," he said, "and now I'll take my leave."

"No, no," cried the dark man. "You'll come in and drink a cup after the noble convoy you've given us. Nicholas Hawkshaw will be blithe to welcome you."

David would have refused, for the hour was already late and he was many miles from Woodilee, had not the groom laid his hand on his arm. "Come," he said. "I would see my friend, the student of Virgil, in another light than the moon," and to his amazement the young man found that it was a request which he could not deny. There was a compelling power in that quiet face, and he was strangely loth to part from it.

The four dismounted, the three troopers staggering with stiff bones. The dark man's limp did not change after the first steps, and David saw that he was crippled in the left leg. They passed through the gate into a courtyard, beyond which rose the square massif of the tower. In the low doorway a candle wavered, under a stone which bore the hawk in lure which was the badge of the house.

The three men bowed low to the candle, and David saw that it was held by a young girl.

CHAPTER III

GUESTS IN CALIDON TOWER

"Will you enter, sirs?" said the girl. She was clad in some dark homespun stuff with a bright-coloured screen thrown over her head and shoulders. She held the light well in front of her, so that David could not see her face. He would fain have taken his leave, for it seemed strange to be entering Calidon thus late at e'en in the company of strangers, but the hand of the groom on his arm restrained him. "You will drink a stirrup-cup, friend. The night is yet young and the moon is high."

A steep stairway ran upward a yard or two from the doorway. Calidon was still a Border keep, where the ground-floor had once been used for byres and stables, and the inhabitants had dwelt in the upper stories. The girl moved ahead of them. "Will you be pleased to follow me, sirs? My uncle awaits you above."

They found themselves in a huge chamber which filled the width of the tower, and, but for a passage and a further staircase, its length. A dozen candles, which seemed to have been lit in haste, showed that it was raftered with dark oak beams, and that the walls were naked stone where they were not covered with a coarse arras. The floor, of a great age, was bare wood blackened with time and use, and covered with a motley of sheepskins and deerskins. Two long oak tables and a great oak bench made the chief furniture, but there were a multitude of stools of the same heavy ancient make, and by a big open fireplace two ancient chairs of stamped Spanish leather. A handful of peats smouldered on the hearth, and the thin blue smoke curled upward to add grime to an immense coat of arms carved in stone and surmounted by a forest of deer horns and a trophy of targes and spears.

David, accustomed only to the low-ceiled rooms of the Edinburgh closes, stared in amazement at the size of the place and felt abashed. The Hawkshaws had made too great a sound in his boyhood's world for him to enter their dwelling without a certain tremor of the blood. So absorbed was he in his surroundings that it was with a start that he saw the master of the house.

A man limped forward, gathered the leader of the party in his arms and kissed him on both cheeks.

"Will," he said, "Will, my old comrade! It's a kind wind that has blown you to Calidon this night. I havena clapped eyes on you these six year."

The host was a man about middle life, with the shoulders of a bull and a massive shaggy head now in considerable disorder from the fact that a night-cap had just been removed from it. His clothes were of a comfortable undress, for the tags of his doublet and the points of his breeches were undone, and over all he wore an old plaid dressing-gown. He had been reading, for a pipe of tobacco marked his place in a folio, and David noted that it was Philemon Holland's version of the Cyropædia. His eyes were blue and frosty, his cheeks ruddy, his beard an iron grey, and his voice as gusty as a hill wind. He limped heavily as he moved.

"Man, Will," he cried, "it's a whipping up of cripples when you and me forgather. The Germany wars have made lameters of the both of us. And who are the lads you've brought with you?"

"Just like myself, Nick, poor soldiers of Leven's, on our way home to Angus."

"Angus is it this time?" The host winked and then laughed boisterously.

"Angus it is, but their names and designations can wait till we have broken our fast. 'Faith, we've as wolfish a hunger as ever you and me tholed in Thuringia. And I've brought in an honest man that guided us through your bogs and well deserves bite and sup."

Nicholas Hawkshaw peered for a moment at David. "I cannot say I'm acquaint with the gentleman, but I've been that long away I've grown out of knowledge of my own countryside. But ye shallna lack for meat and drink, for when I got your token I bade Edom stir himself and make ready. There's a good browst of yill, and plenty of French cordial and my father's Canary sack. And there's a mutton ham, and the best part of a pie--I wouldna say just what's intil the pie, but at any rate there's blackcocks and snipes and leverets, for I had the shooting of them. Oh, and there's whatever more Edom can find in the house of Calidon. Here's back your ring, Will. When I read the cognizance I had a notion that I was about to entertain greater folk--"

"Than your auld friend Will Rollo and two poor troopers of Leven's. And yet we're maybe angels unawares." He took the ring and handed it to the groom, who with David stood a little back from the others, while Nicholas Hawkshaw's eyes widened in a momentary surprise.

An ancient serving-man and a barefoot maid brought in the materials for supper, and the two troopers fell on the viands like famished crows. The groom ate little and drank less; though he was the slightest in build of the three travellers, he seemed the most hardened to the business. The lame man, who was called Will Rollo, was presently satisfied, and deep in reminiscences with his host, but the other required greater sustenance for his long wiry body, and soon reduced the pie to a fragment. He pressed morsels upon the groom--a wing of grouse, a giblet of hare--but the latter smiled and waved the food away. A friendly service, Leven's, David thought, where a servant was thus tenderly considered.

"Yon were the brave days, when you and me served as ensigns of Meldrum's in the Corpus Evangelicorum. And yon was the lad to follow, for there never was the marrow of the great Gustavus for putting smeddum into troops that had as many tongues and creeds as the Tower of Babel. But you and me were ower late on the scene. We never saw Breitenfeld--just the calamitous day of Lutzen, and the blacker day of Nordlingen, where Bernhard led us like sheep to the slaughter. That was the end of campaigning for you, Will. I mind leaving you on the ground for dead and kissing your cheek, the while I was near my own end with a musketoon ball in my ribs. Then I heard you were still in life and back in Scotland, but I was off with auld Wrangel to Pomerania, and had to keep my mind on my own affairs."

So the talk went on, memories of leaguers and forced marches and pitched battles, punctuated with the names of Leslies and Hamiltons and Kerrs and Lumsdens and a hundred Scots mercenaries.--"I got my quietus a year syne serving with Torstensson and his Swedes--a pitiable small affair in Saxonia, where I had the misfortune to meet a round shot on the ricochet which cracked my shin-bone and has set me hirpling for the rest of my days. My Colonel was Sandy Leslie, a brother of Leslie of Balquhain, him that stuck Wallenstein at Eger, but a man of honester disposition and a good Protestant. He bade me go home, for I would never again be worth a soldier's hire, and faith! when the chirurgeon had finished with my leg I was of the same opinion.--So home you find me, Will, roosting in the cauld rickle of stones that was my forbears', while rumours of war blow like an east wind up the glens. I'm waiting for your news. I hear word that Davie Leslie . . ."

"Our news can wait, Nick. We've a gentleman here to whose ears this babble of war must sound outlandish." It seemed to David that some secret intelligence passed between the two, and that a foot of one was pressed heavily on the other's toes.

"I am a man of peace," David said, for the talk had stirred his fancy, "but I too have word of a glorious victory in England won by the Covenant armies. If you have come straight from the south you can maybe tell me more."

"There was a victory beyond doubt," said the tall man with the squint, "and that is why we of Leven's are permitted to go home. We have gotten our pay, whilk is an uncommon happening for the poor soldier in this land."

"I have heard," said David, "that the ranks of the Army of the Covenant fought for higher matters than filthy lucre."

"For what, belike?"

"For the purity of their faith and the Crown honours of Christ."

The other whistled gently through his teeth.

"No doubt. No doubt. There's a braw sough of the Gospel in Leven's ranks. But we must consider the loaves and fishes, good sir, as well as the preaching of the Word. Man canna live by bread alone, but he assuredly canna live without it, and to fill his belly he wants more than preaching. Lucre's none so filthy if it be honestly earned, and goes to keep a roof over the wife and bairns. I have served in many lands with a kennin' o' queer folk, and, believe me, sir, the first thing a soldier thinks of is just his pay."

"But he cannot fight unless he has a cause to fight for."

"He'll make a very good shape at it if he has been learned his business by a heavy-handed sergeant. I have seen the riddlings of Europe stick fast as rocks before Wallenstein's horse, because they had been taught their trade and feared death less than their Colonel's tongue. And I have seen the flower of gentrice, proud as Lucifer and gallant as lions, and every one with a noble word on his lips, break like rotten twigs at the first musket volley. It's discipline that's the last word in war."

"But if the discipline be there, will not a conviction of the right of his cause make a better soldier?"

"You have spoken a true word, and there's a man in England this day that knows it. That is what Cromwell has done. He has built up a body of horse that stand like an iron wall and move like a river in spate. They have the discipline of Gustavus's Swedes, and the fires of Hell in their hearts. I tell you, there is nothing in this land that can stand against them."

"I have no love for sectaries," said David. "But cannot our Scots do likewise, with the Covenant to nerve them?"

The other shrugged his shoulders.

"The Covenant's but sour kail to the soldier. Davie Leslie has hammered his men into a wise-like army, because he learned his trade from Gustavus. But think you our bannock-fed foot-sentinels care a doit for the black gowns at Westminster? A man will fight for his King and for his country, and for liberty to worship God in his own way. But, unless he has a crack in his head, he will not fight for a fine point of Church government."

David was becoming ill at ease. He felt that it was his duty to testify, or otherwise he would be guilty of the sin of Meroz, the sin of apathy when his faith was challenged. But he was far from clear as to the exact nature of his faith. There was no blasphemy in questioning whether the Covenant were truly in the hearts of the people. Had not the minister of Cauldshaw that very afternoon expressed the same doubt?

Nicholas Hawkshaw was peering at him intently.

"I should ken you, friend, for they tell me you belong to this countryside. And your face sticks in my memory, but I canna put a name to it."

"They call me David Sempill. I am the new-ordained minister of Woodilee."

Nicholas cried out. "Auld Wat o' the Roodfoot's grandson. I heard of your coming, sir, and indeed I'm your chief heritor. I'll nave your hand on that. Man, I kenned your gudesire well, and many a pouchful of groats I had from him when I was a laddie. You're back among kenned folk, Mr. Sempill, and I wish you a long life in Woodilee."

The troopers did not seem to share their host's geniality. Quick glances passed between them, and the tall man shifted his seat so that he came between David and the groom. This latter had taken no part in the conversation, indeed he had not spoken a word, but after his meal was finished had sat with his head on his breast as if sunk in meditation. Now he raised his eyes to David, and it was he who spoke.

"I am not less loyal to the Kirk of Scotland than you, Mr. Sempill. You are a placed minister, and I am a humble elder of that Kirk."

"In what parish?" David asked eagerly.

"In my native parish benorth of Forth."

The man's dress and station were forgotten by David when he looked at his face. Now that he saw clearly in the candle-light, it was not the face of a common groom. Every feature spoke of race, the firm mouth of command, the brooding grey eyes of thought. The voice was sweet and musical, and the man's whole air had a gentle but imperious courtesy.

The movement of the tall trooper, while it had separated David from the groom, had brought the latter full into the view of Nicholas Hawkshaw. Then a strange thing happened. The host, after a long stare, during which amazement and recognition woke in his eyes, half rose from his seat and seemed on the verge of speaking. His gaze was fixed on the groom, and David read in it something at once deferential and exulting. Then the toe of the lame man's boot came down on his shin, and the lame man's hand was laid on his arm. The lame man, too, said something in a tongue which David could not understand. Nicholas subsided in his chair, but his face remained both puzzled and excited.

The groom spoke again.

"You are a scholar, and you are young, and you are full of the ardour of your calling. This parish is fortunate in its minister, and I would that all Scotland were as happily served. What is it that you and I seek alike? A pure doctrine and a liberated Kirk? Is there no more?"

"I seek above all things to bring men and women to God's mercy- seat."

"And I say Amen. That is more than any disputation about the forms of Presbytery. But you seek also, or I am mightily mistook in you, the freedom and well-being of this land of ours--that our Israel may have peace and prosperity in her borders."

"If the first be won, all the rest will be added unto us."

"Doubtless. But only if the first be truly won--if the Kirk attend to the work of salvation and does not expend her toil in barren fields. Her sovereign must be King Jesus. Take heed that instead it be not King Covenant."

The words recalled to David Mr. Fordyce's doubts, which had been so scornfully repelled by the ministers of Kirk Aller and Bold.

"Does it lie in the mouth of a minister or an elder of the Kirk to cavil at the Kirk's doings?" he asked, but without conviction in his tone.

The other smiled. "You give due loyalty, as the Scripture enjoins, to the King, Mr. Sempill?"

"I am faithful to his Majesty so long as his Majesty is faithful to law and religion."

"Even so. It is my own creed. The King must respect the limits of his prerogative--it is the condition on which he rules in a free land. My loyalty to the Kirk is in the same case. I am loyal when she fulfils those duties which God has laid upon her--that duty, above all, of bringing mortal men to God. If she forget those duties, and meddle arrogantly with civil matters that do not concern her, then I take leave to oppose her, as in a like case I would oppose his Majesty. For by such perversities both King and Kirk become tyrants, and tyranny is not to be endured by men who are called into the liberty of Christ."

"Or by Scots," added the tall trooper.

"I have no clearness on the point," said David after a pause. "I have not thought deeply on these matters, for I am but new to the ministry, and my youth was filled with profane study."

"Nevertheless, such study is a good foundation for a wise theology. I judge that you are a ripe Latinist--maybe also a Grecian. You have read your Aristotle? You are familiar with the history of the ancient world, which illumines all later ages? I would point my arguments from that armoury."

"I cannot grant that the doings of ancient heathendom give any rule for a Christian state."

"But, sir, the business of government is always the same. We have our Lord's warning that there are the things of Cæsar and the things of God. The Roman was the great master of the arts of government, and he did not seek throughout his empire to make a single religion. He was content to give it the peace of his law, and let each people go its own way in matters of worship. It was in that tolerant world which he created that our Christian faith found its opportunity."

"Doubtless God so moved the Roman mind for His own purpose. But I join issue on your application. The Church of Christ is now in being, and the faith of Christ is the foundation of a Christian state. Civil law is an offence against God unless it be also Christian."

The young man smiled. "I do not deny it. This realm of ours is professedly a Christian realm--I would it were more truly so. But that does not exempt it from obedience to those laws of government without which no realm, Christian or pagan, may endure. If a man is so ill a smith that he cannot shoe my horse, I will be none the better served because he is a good Christian. If a land be ill governed, the disaster will be not the less great because the governors are men of God. If his Majesty--to take a pertinent example--override the law to the people's detriment, that tyranny will be not the less grievous because his Majesty believes in his heart that he is performing a duty towards the Almighty. Honest intention will not cure faulty practice, and the fool is the fool whether he be unbeliever or professor."

David shook his head. "Where does your argument tend? I fear to schism."

"Not so. I am an orthodox son of the Kirk, a loyal servant of his Majesty, and a passionate Scot. Here, my friend, is my simple confession. There is but one master in the land, and its name is Law--which is in itself a creation of a free people under the inspiration of the Almighty. That law may be changed by the people's will, but till it be so changed it is to be revered and obeyed. It has ordained the King's prerogative, the rights of the subject, and the rights and duties of the Kirk. The state is like the body, whose health is only to be maintained by a just proportion among its members. If a man's belly be his god, his limbs will suffer; if he use only his legs, his arms will dwindle. If, therefore, the King should intrude upon the subject's rights, or the subject whittle at the King's prerogative, or the Kirk set herself above the Crown, there will be a sick state and an ailing people."

Nicholas Hawkshaw had been listening intently with a puzzled air, his eyes fixed on the groom's face, but the two troopers seemed ill at ease.

"Man, James," said the tall man, "you've mistook your calling. You should have been a regent in the college of St. Andrews, and hammered sense into the thick heads of the bejaunts."

Rollo, the lame man, shifted his seat and seemed inclined to turn the conversation.

"Patience, Mark," said the groom. "It's not often a poor soldier of Leven's gets a chance of a crack with a like-minded friend. For I'm certain that Mr. Sempill is very near my way of thinking."

"I do not quarrel with your premises," said David, "but I'm not clear about the conclusion."

"It's writ large in this land to-day. There are those that would make the King a puppet and put all authority in parliaments, and there are those who would make the Kirk like Calvin's at Geneva, a ruler over both civil and religious matters. I say that both ways lie madness and grief. If you upset the just proportion of the law you will gain not liberty but confusion. You are a scholar, Mr. Sempill, and have read the histories of Thucydides? Let me counsel you to read them again and consider the moral."

"What side are you on?" David asked abruptly.

"I am on the side of the free people of Scotland. And you by your vows are on the same side, for your concern is to feed the flock of God which is among us. Think you, sir, if you depress the balance against the King, that thereby you will win more for the people? Nay, nay, what is lost to the prerogative will go, not to the people, but to those who prey on them. You will have that anarchy which gives his chance to the spoiler, and out of anarchy will come some day a man of violence who will tyrannically make order again. It is the way of the world, my friend."

"Are you for the Covenant?"

At the question the others started. "Enough of politics," cried Rollo. "These are no matters to debate among weary folk." But the groom raised his hand, and they were silent.

"I am for the Covenant. Six years back I drew sword for it, and I did not sheathe that sword till we had established the liberties of this land. That was indeed a Covenant of Grace."

"There is another and a later. What say you of that?"

"I say of that other that it is a Covenant of Works in which I have no part, nor any true lover of the Kirk. It is a stepping of the Kirk beyond the bounds prescribed by the law of God and the law of man, and it will mean a weakening of the Kirk in its proper duties. And that I need not tell you, as a minister of Christ, will be the starvation and oppression of Christ's simple folk. Quicquid delirant reges, plectuntur Achivi. Is it not more pleasing to God that His ministers should comfort the sick and the widow and the fatherless, and guide souls to Heaven, than that they should scrabble for civil pre-eminence?"

Into David's mind came two visions--that of the complacent ministers of Kirk Aller and Bold as they had discoursed at meat, and that of the old herd at the Greenshiel, sitting by his dead wife. The pictures belonged to different worlds, and at the moment he felt that these worlds were eternally apart. He had the disquieting thought that the one had only the husks of faith, and the other the grain. Dimly he heard the voice of the groom. "I will give you a text, Mr. Sempill. 'The vineyard of the Lord of hosts is the house of Israel, and the men of Judah His pleasant plant; and He looked for judgment, but behold oppression; for righteousness, but behold a cry.'"

He scarcely realized that the others had sprung to their feet, and it was only when Nicholas Hawkshaw exclaimed that he turned his head.

A girl stood before them, the girl who had opened the door, but whose face he had scarcely seen at the time in the poor light.

"Katrine, my dear, you've been long of coming." It was Nicholas who spoke. "I thought you had slipped off to your bed. This is my sister's child, sirs, who keeps me company in this auld barrack-- Robert Yester's daughter, him that fell with Monro in the year 'thirty-four. You see three gentlemen-troopers of Leven's, my dear, and Mr. Sempill, the new minister of Woodilee."

The girl was dressed in a gown of blue velvet, the skirts of which were drawn back in front to show an embroidered petticoat of stiff yellow satin. It was cut low at the neck and shoulders, and round the top ran a broad edging of fine lace. Her dark hair was caught up in a knot behind, but allowed to fall in curls on each side of her face. That face, to David's startled eyes, was like none that he had ever seen before, certainly like none of the Edinburgh burgher girls whom he had observed in their finery on the Saturday causeway. It was small and delicately featured, the cheeks flushed with youth and health, the eyes dark, brilliant, and mirthful. At another time he would have been shocked at her dress, for the fashion of a low bodice had not spread much beyond the Court, but now he did not take note of what she wore. He was gazing moonstruck upon a revelation.

She smiled on him--she smiled on them all. She curtsied lightly to her uncle, to Rollo, and to the dark man. But she did not curtsy to the minister. For suddenly, as she looked at the groom, her composure deserted her. Her mouth moved as if she would have spoken, and then she checked herself, for David saw that the groom had put his finger to his lips. Instead she curtsied almost to the ground, a reverence far more deep than she had accorded to the others, and when he gave her his hand she bent her head as if her impulse was to kiss it.

All this David saw with a confused vision. He had scarcely spoken ten words in his life to a woman outside his own kin, and this bright apparition loosened his knees with nervousness. He stammered his farewells. He had already outstayed the bounds of decency, and he had a long ride home--he wished his friends a safe conclusion to their journey--in the course of his pastoral visitations he would have the chance of coming again to Calidon. "'Deed, sir, and you'll make sure of that," said the hospitable Nicholas. "There's aye a bite and a sup at Calidon for the minister of Woodilee."

He bowed to the girl, and she looked at him for the first time, a quizzical appraising look, and gave him a fleeting smile. Five minutes later he was on his horse and fording Rood.

He took the long road by the back of the Hill of Deer, riding in bright moonshine up the benty slopes and past the hazel thickets. His mind was in a noble confusion, for on this, his first day in his parish, experiences had thronged on him too thick and fast. Out of the welter two faces stood clear, the groom's and the girl's. . . . He remembered the talk, and his conscience pricked him. Had he been faithful to his vows? Had he been guilty of the sin of Meroz? Had he listened to railing accusations and been silent? . . . He did not know--in truth he did not care--for the sum of his recollection was not of an argument but of a person. The face of the young man had been more than his words, for it had been the face of a comrade, and an intimate friendliness had looked out of his eyes. He longed to see him again, to be with him, to follow him, to serve him--

but he did not know his name, and they would doubtless never meet again. David was very young, and could have wept at the thought.

And the girl . . . ? The sight of her had been the coping-stone to a night of marvels. She was not like the groom--he had been glad to flee from her company, for she had no part in his world. But a marvel beyond doubt! The recollection of her made him a poet, and as he picked his way over the hill he was quoting to himself the lines in Homer where the old men of Troy see Helen approaching, and wonder at her beauty. . . . [Greek text]--how did it go? "Small wonder that the Trojans and the mailed Greeks should endure pain through many years for such a woman. In face she is strangely like to some immortal."

And then he felt compunction, for he remembered the worn face of the dead woman at the Greenshiel.

CHAPTER IV

THE FAITHFUL SERVANT

For two days the minister of Woodilee was a man unbalanced and distraught. He sat at his books without concentration, and he wandered on the hills without delight, while Isobel's face puckered in dismay as she removed his scarcely tasted meals. It was hot thundery weather, with storms that never broke in rain grumbling among the glens, and to this she set down his indisposition to eat. But David's trouble was not of the body. He had thought himself the mailed servant of God, single in purpose, armed securely against the world, and lo! in a single night he had been the sport of profane fancies and had rejoiced in vanities.

The girl he scarcely thought of--she had scared rather than enthralled him. But the Wood of Melanudrigill lay heavy on his conscience. Where was his Christian fortitude if a black forest at night could set him shivering like a lost child? David had all his life kept a tight hand on his courage; if he dreaded a thing, that was good reason why he should go out of his road to face it. His instinct was to return alone to Melanudrigill in the dark, penetrate its deepest recesses, and give the lie to its enchantments. . . . But a notion which he could not combat restrained him. That was what the Wood wanted, to draw him back to it through curiosity or fear. If he yielded to his impulse he would be acknowledging its power. It was the part of a minister of God to deny at the outset that the place was more than a common wilderness of rock and tree, to curb his fancies as things too vain for a grown man's idlest thought.

On this point he fixed his resolution and found some comfort. But the memory of Calidon and the troopers and the groom's words remained to trouble him. Had he not borne himself in their company as a Laodicean, assenting when he should have testified? . . . He went over every detail of the talk, for it stuck firmly in his mind. They had decried the Solemn League and Covenant in the name of the Kirk, and he had not denounced them. . . . And yet they had spoken as Christian men and loyal sons of that Kirk. . . . What meant, too, the groom's disquisition on law and government? David found the argument hard to gainsay--it presented a doctrine of the state which commended itself to his reason. Yet it was in flat contradiction of the declared view of that Kirk which he was sworn to serve, and what then became of his ordination vows? . . . But was it contrary to the teaching of the Word and the spirit of his faith? He searched his mind on this point and found that he had no clearness.

His duty, it seemed, was to go to some father-in-God, like the minister of Kirk Aller, and lay his doubts before him. But he found that course impossible. The pale fleshy face of Mr. Muirhead rose before him, as light-giving as a peat-stack; he heard his complacent tones, saw the bland conceit in his ruminant eyes. Nor would he fare better with the militancy of his brother of Bold, who classed all mankind as Amalekites, save the chosen few who wore his own phylacteries. Mr. Fordyce might give him comfort, and he was on the point many times of saddling his horse and riding to the manse of Cauldshaw. . . . But each time he found it impossible, and when he asked himself the cause he was amazed at the answer. Loyalty forbade him--loyalty to the young man, habited as a groom, who had spoken both as counsellor and comrade. That was the enduring spell of that strange night. David as a youth in Edinburgh had had few familiar friends, and none that could be called intimate. For the first time he had met one from whom had gone forth an influence that melted his heart. He recalled with a kind of aching affection the gentle, commanding courtesy, the winning smile, the masterful and yet wistful grey eyes. "I wonder," he thought, "if I was not meant to be a soldier. For I could follow yon man most joyfully to the cannon's mouth."

On the third day peace returned to him, when he buried Marion of the Greenshiel. The parish coffin was not used, as was the custom for poor folk, since the farmer of Reiverslaw, Richie's master, paid the cost of a private one, and himself attended the "chesting" the night before. On the day David walked the seven miles to the cottage, where Richie had set out a poor entertainment of ale and oatcakes for the mourners. It was not the fashion for the minister to pray at the house or at the grave, as savouring of Popish prayers for the dead, nor was it the custom for a widower to attend the funeral; but David took his own way, and prayed with the husband, the wailing women, and the half-dozen shepherds who had assembled for the last rites. The light coffin was carried by four young men, and David walked with them all the way to Woodilee. The farmer of Reiverslaw joined them at a turn of the road--his name was Andrew Shillinglaw, a morose, dark man not over-well spoken of in the parish--and he and the minister finished the journey side by side. The bellman, Nehemiah Robb, who was also the gravedigger and the beadle, met them at the entrance to the kirkton, and with him a crowd of villagers. Preceded by the jangling of Robb's bell, the procession reached the shallow grave, the women remaining at the kirkyard gate. The coffin was lowered, the earth shovelled down, and the thing in five minutes was over. There was no "dredgy" [funeral feast] at the poor house of the Greenshiel to draw the mourners back upon the seven moorland miles. The men adjourned to Lucky Weir's, the kirk bell was restored to its tree, a woman or two sobbed, and the last of Marion Smail was a thin stream of figures vanishing in the haze of evening, one repeating to the other in funereal voices that "puir Mirren had got weel awa'."

Yet the occasion, austere and bare as poverty could make it, woke in David a mood of tenderness and peace. The lowering clouds had gone from the sky, all morning it had rained, and the afternoon had had a soft autumn freshness. He had prayed with Richie, but his prayers had been also for himself, and as he walked behind the coffin on the path by the back of the Hill of Deer his petition seemed to have been answered. He had an assurance of his vocation. The crowd at the kirkyard, those toil-worn folk whose immortal souls had been given into his charge, moved him to a strange exultation. He saw his duty cleared from all doubts, and there must have been that in his face which told of his thoughts, for men greeted him and then passed on, as if unwilling to break in on his preoccupation. Only Reiverslaw, who was on his way to Lucky Weir's, whence he would depart drunk in the small hours, was obtuse in his perceptions. He took the minister's hand and shook it as he would a drover's at a fair, seemed anxious to speak, found no words, and left with a grunted farewell.

It was a fine, long-drawn-out back-end, the best that had been known for twenty years. All September the sun shone like June, and it was well into October before the morning frosts began, and the third week of November before the snow came. The little crops-- chiefly grey oats and barley, with an occasional rig of peas and flax--were well ripened and quickly reaped. The nettie-wives were busy all day in the fields, and the barefoot children made the leading in of the harvest a holiday, with straw whistles in their mouths and fantastic straw badges on their clothing. Then came the threshing with jointed flails, and the winnowing on barn roofs when the first east winds blew. There were no gleaners in the empty stubbles, for it was held a pious duty to leave something behind for the fowls of the air. Presently the scanty fruits of the earth were under cover, the bog hay in dwarfish ricks, the unthreshed oats and bear in the barns, the grain in the girnels, and soon the wheel of the Woodilee mill was clacking merrily to grind the winter's meal. In that parish the burden of the laird lay light. Nicholas Hawkshaw asked no more than his modest rental in kind, and did not exact his due in labour, but for a week the road by the back of the Hill of Deer saw a procession of horses carrying the "kain" meal to the Calidon granary. As the minister watched the sight one day, Ephraim Caird, the Chasehope tenant, stood beside him, looking gloomily at his own beasts returning. "That's the way our puir crops are guided," he said. "As the auld folk used to say, 'Ane part to saw, ane part to gnaw, and ane to pay the laird witha'.'" His eyes showed that he had no love for Calidon.

Hallowmass that year was a cheerful season. The elders shook their heads at the Hallowe'en junketings, and the severe Chasehope was strong in his condemnation. But on the night of Hallowe'en, as David walked in the bright moonlight and saw the lights in the cottages and heard laughter and a jigging of fiddles, he did not find it in his heart to condemn the ancient fashions. Nor apparently did Chasehope himself, for David was much mistaken if it was not Ephraim's great shoulders and fiery head that he saw among the cabbage-stalks in Nance Kello's garden. He had been to Hallowe'en frolics himself in past days when he stayed with his cousin at Newbiggin, but it seemed to him that here in Woodilee there was something oppressed and furtive in the merriment. There was a secrecy about each lit dwelling, and no sign of young lads and lasses laughing on the roads. He noticed, too, that for the next few days many of the people had a look of profound weariness-- pale faces, tired eyes, stealthy glances--as if behind the apparent decorum there had been revels that exhausted soul and body.

With the reaping of the harvest the ill-conditioned cattle were brought from the hills to the stubbles, and soon turned both outfield and infield into a miry wilderness. David, whose knowledge of farming was derived chiefly from the Georgics, had yet an eye in his head and a store of common sense, and he puzzled at the methods. The land at its best was ill-drained, and the trampling of beasts made a thousand hollows which would be puddles at the first rains and would further sour the rank soil. But when he spoke on the matter to the farmer of Mirehope, he was answered scornfully that that had been the "auld way of the land," and that those who were proud in their own conceit and had tried new-fangled methods--he had heard word of such in the West country--could not get two bolls from an acre where he had four. "And Mirehope's but wersh [sour] land, sir, and not to be named wi' the Clyde howms."

When the November snows came all live stock was gathered into the farm-towns. The cattle were penned in yards with thatched shelters, and soon turned them into seas of mud. The milking cows were in the byre; the sheep in paddocks near-by: the draught-oxen and the horses in miserable stables of mud and heather. It was the beginning of the winter hibernation, and the chief work of the farms was the feeding of the stock on their scanty winter rations. The hay--coarse bog grasses with little nutriment in them--went mainly to the sheep; horses and cattle had for fodder straw and messes of boiled chaff; while Crummie in the byre was sometimes regaled with the débris of the kailyard and the oddments left from the family meals. Winter each year was both for beast and man a struggle with famine, and each was rationed like the people of a besieged city. But if food was scarce at the best, Woodilee did not want for fuel. It had been a good year for peats, for they had ripened well on the hills, and the open autumn had made them easy to carry. Each cottage had its ample peat-stack, and when harvest was over there had been also a great gathering of windfalls from the woods, so that by every door stood a pile of kindlings.

Melanudrigill in the bright October days had lost its menace for David. He had no occasion to visit it by night, but more than once he rode through it by day on his pastoral visitations to Fennan or the Rood valley, and once in a flaming sunset he returned that way from Kirk Aller. The bracken was golden in decay, and the yellowing birches, the russet thorns, and the occasional scarlet of rowans made the sombre place almost cheerful. In his walks on the hill the great forest below him seemed to have grown thin and open, no longer a vast enveloping cloak, but a kindly covering for the ribs of earth. Some potency had gone from it with the summer, as if the tides of a fierce life had sunk back into the ground again. He had seen deer in the glades, and they looked innocent things. . . . But he noticed as curious that none of the villagers in their quest for wood penetrated far into it, and that on its fringes they only gathered the windfalls. Up at the back of the Hill of Deer and in the Rood glen men were busy all day cutting birch and hazel billets, but no axe was laid to any tree in the Black Wood.

A week before Yule came the great snow. It began with a thin cold fog which muffled every fold of the hills. "Rouk's [fog] snaw's wraith," said the parish, and saw to its fuel-stacks and looked gloomily at its shivering beasts. The thick weather lasted for three days and three nights, weather so cold that it was pain to draw breath, and old folk at night in their box beds could not get warmth, and the Woodilee burn was frozen hard even in the linns. It was noted as a bad omen that deer from Melanudrigill were seen in the kirkton, and that at dawn when the Mirehope shepherd went out to his sheep he found half-frozen blue hares crouching among the flocks. On the fourth morning the snow began, and fell for three days in heavy flakes, so that it lay feet deep on the roads and fields. Then the wind rose and for six furious hours a blizzard raged, so that the day was like night, and few dared stir from their doors. David, setting out to visit Amos Ritchie's wife, who was sick of a congestion, took two hours over a quarter of mile of road, wandering through many kitchen middens, and had to postpone his return till the wind abated in the evening, while Isobel in the manse was demented with anxiety. The consequence was that the snow was swept bare from the knowes, but piled into twelve-foot drifts in the hollows. It was an ill time for the sheep in the paddocks, which were often one giant drift, where the presence of the flock could only be detected by the yellowish steaming snow. Chasehope lost a score of ewes, Mirehope half as many, and Nether Fennan, where the drifts were deep, the best part of his flock. To David it seemed that the farmers' ways were a tempting of Providence. Had the sheep been left on the hill they would have crowded in the snow to the bare places; here in the confined paddocks they were caught in a trap. Moreover, on the hill in open winter weather there was a better living to be picked up than that afforded by the narrow rations of sour bog hay. But when he spoke thus his hearers plainly thought him mad. Sheep would never face a winter on the hills--besides, the present practice was the "auld way."

The snow lay till the New Year was a week old, and when the thaw came and the roads ran in icy streams, David took to his bed for two days in utter exhaustion. All through the storm he had been on his legs, for there were sick folk and old folk in Woodilee who would perish miserably if left alone. The farm-towns could look after themselves, but in the scattered cottages of the kirkton there was no one to take command, and neighbourliness languished when each household was preoccupied with its own cares. Peter Pennecuik, a ruling elder, whose gift of prayer had been commended by Mr. Muirhead, had lost a tup and had his byre roof crushed in by the drift, so he became a fatalist, holding that the Lord had prepared a visitation which it would be impiety to resist, and sat lugubriously by his fireside. David's fingers itched for his ears. From Amos Ritchie the blacksmith he got better assistance. Amos was a shaggy, black-bearded man of thirty-five, a great fiddler and a mighty putter of the stone, whose godliness might have been suspect but for his behaviour in the Bishops' War. His wife was at death's door all through the storm, but he nevertheless constituted himself the minister's first lieutenant, and wrought valiantly in the work of relief. There were old women too chilled and frail to kindle their fires in the morning and melt snow for water; there were households so ill provided that they existed largely on borrowed food; there were cots where the weather had broken roof or wall. Isobel in the manse kitchen was a busy woman, and her girdle was never off the fire. David had looked forward to the winter snows as a season of peace, when he could sit indoors with his books; instead he found himself on his feet for fourteen hours out of the twenty-four, his hands and face chapped like a ploughman's, and so weary at night that he fell off his chair with sleep while Isobel fetched his supper.

Yet it was the storm which was David's true ordination to his duties, for it brought him close to his people, not in high sacramental things like death, but in their daily wrestling for life. He might visit their houses and catechize their families, but these were formal occasions, with all on their best behaviour, whereas in the intimate business of charity he saw them as they were.

The new minister was young and he was ardent, and his duties were still an adventure. His Sabbath sermons were diligently meditated. For his morning lecture he took the book of the prophet Amos, which, as the work of a herdsman, seemed fitting for a country parish. His two weekly discourses dealt laboriously with the fourfold state of man--his early state of innocence, his condition after the Fall, his state under grace, his condition in eternity. That winter David did not get beyond the state of innocence, and in discoursing on it he exhausted his ingenuity in piecing texts together from the Scriptures, and in such illustrations as he believed would awaken his hearers' minds. Profane learning openly used would have been resented, but he contrived to bring in much that did not belong to the divinity schools, and he escaped criticism, it may be, because his Kirk Session did not understand him. His elders were noted theologians, and what was strange to them, if it was weightily phrased, they took for theological profundity.

At ten o'clock each Sabbath morning Robb the beadle tinkled the first bell; at the second the congregation moved into the kirk, and Peter Pennecuik, who acted as precentor, led the opening psalm, reading each line before it was sung. When Robb jerked the third bell, David entered the pulpit and began with prayer. At one o'clock the people dispersed, those who came from a distance to Lucky Weir's ale-house; and at two fell the second service, which concluded at four with the coming of the dark. The kirk, with its earthen floor, was cold as a charnel-house, and the dimness of the light tried even

David's young eyes. The people sat shivering on their little stools, each with the frozen decorum and strained attention which was their Sabbath ritual. To the minister it seemed often as if he were speaking to sheeted tombstones, he felt as if his hearers were at an infinite distance from him, and only on rare occasions, when some shining text of Scripture moved his soul and he spoke simply and with emotion, did he feel any contact with his flock.

But his sermons were approved. Peter Pennecuik gave it as his verdict that he was a "deep" preacher and sound in the fundamentals. Others, remembering the thrill that sometimes came into his voice, called him an "affectionate" preacher, and credited him with "unction." But there were many that longed for stronger fare, something more marrowy and awful, pictures of the hell of torment which awaited those who were not of the Elect. He had the "sough," no doubt, but it was a gentle west wind, and not the stern Euroclydon which should call sinners to repentance. Their minister was a man of God, but he was young; years might add weight to him and give him the thunders of Sinai.

To David the Sabbath services were the least of his duties. He had come to Woodilee with his heart full of the mighty books which he would write in the solitude of his upper chamber. The chief was that work on the prophet Isaiah which should be for all time a repository of sacred learning, so that Sempill on Isaiah would be quoted reverently, like Luther on the Galatians or Calvin on the Romans. In the autumn evenings he had sketched the lines of his masterpiece, and before the great snow he had embarked on its prolegomena. But the storm made a breach in his studies. He felt himself called to more urgent duties, for he was a pastor of souls before he was a scholar. His visitations and catechizings among his flock were his chief care, and he began to win a name for diligence. On nights when even a shepherd would have kept the ingle side, David would arrive at a moorland cottage, and many a time Isobel had to welcome in the small hours a dripping or frozen master, thaw him by her kitchen fire, and feed him with hot ale and bannocks, while he recounted his adventures. He was strong and buoyant, and he loved the life, which seemed to him to have the discipline of a soldier. His face high-coloured by weather, his cheerful eyes, and his boyish voice and laugh were soon popular in the length of the parish. "He is a couthy lad," said the old wives, "and for a man o' God he's terrible like a plain body."

Also he took charge of the children. In Woodilee there was no school or schoolmaster. There were three hundred communicants, but it was doubtful if more than a dozen could read a sentence or write their names. In the Kirk Session itself there were only three. So David started a school, which met thrice a week of a morning in the manse kitchen. He sent to Edinburgh for horn-books, and with them and his big Bible taught his class their rudiments. These were the pleasantest hours of the day for master and children, and weekly the gathering grew till there was not a child in the kirkton or in the farm-towns of Mirehope and Chasehope that would have missed them. When they arrived, blue with cold and often breakfastless, Isobel would give each a bowl of broth, and while the lesson proceeded she would mend their ragged garments. Indeed more than one child emerged new clad, for the minister's second-best cloak and an old pair of breeches were cut up by Isobel--expostulating but not ill-pleased--for tattered little mortals.

David was more than a private almoner. He and his Session had the Poor Box to administer, the sole public means of relieving the parish's needs. Woodilee was better off than many places, in that it possessed a mortification of a thousand pounds Scots, bequeathed fifty years earlier by a certain Grizel Hawkshaw for the comfort of the poor. Also there was the weekly collection at the kirk services, where placks and doits and bodles, and a variety of debased coins, clinked in the plate at the kirk door, and there were the fines levied by the Session on evil-doers. In the winter the task of almoner was easier, for there were few beggars on the roads, and those that crossed the hills came as a rule only to die, when the single expense was the use of the parish coffin. Yet the administration of the scanty funds was a difficult business, and it led to David's first controversies with his Session. Each elder had his own favourites among the poor, and Chasehope and Mirehope and Nether Fennan wrangled over every grant. The minister, still new to the place, for the most part held his peace, but now and then, in cases which he knew of, he asserted his authority. There was a woman, none too well reputed, who lived at Chasehope-foot, with a buxom black-eyed daughter, and whose house, though lamentably dirty and ill guided, seemed to lack nothing. When he opposed Chasehope's demand that she should receive a benefaction as a lone widow, he had a revelation of Chasehope's temper. The white face crimsoned, and the greenish eyes looked for a moment as ugly as a snarling dog's. "Worthy Mr. Macmichael . . ." he began, but David cut him short. "These moneys are for the relief of the helpless poor," he said, "and they are scant enough at the best. I should think shame to waste a bodle except on a pitiful necessity. To him or her that hath shall not be given, while I am the minister of this parish." Chasehope said nothing, and presently he mastered his annoyance, but the farmer of Mirehope--Alexander Sprot was his name--muttered something in an undertone to his neighbour, and there was tension in the air till the laugh of the Woodilee miller broke it. This man, one Spotswood, reckoned the richest in the parish and the closest, had a jolly laugh which belied his reputation. "Mr. Sempill's in the right, Chasehope," he cried. "Jean o' the Chasehope-fit can manage fine wi' what her gudeman left her. We daurna be lovish wi' ither folks' siller." "I am overruled," said Chasehope, and spoke no more.

Little news came in those days to Woodilee. In the open weather before the storm the pack-horses of the carriers came as usual from Edinburgh, and the drovers on the road to England brought word of the doings in the capital. Johnnie Dow, the packman, went his rounds till the snow stopped him, but in January, when the weather cleared, he broke his leg in the Tarrit Moss, and for six weeks disappeared from the sight of men. But Johnnie at his best brought only the clash of the farm-towns and the news of Kirk Aller, and in the dead of the winter there was no chance of a post, so that David was buried as deep as if he had been in an isle of the Hebrides. It was only at Presbytery meetings that he heard tidings of the outer world, and these, passed through the minds of his excited brethren, were all of monstrous portents.

The Presbytery meetings in Kirk Aller were at first to David a welcome break in his quiet life. The one in November lasted two days, and he, as the youngest member, opened the exercises and discoursed with acceptance on a Scripture passage. The business was dull, being for the most part remits from the kirk sessions of contumacious heritors and local scandals and repairs to churches. The sederunt over, the brethren adjourned to the Cross Keys Inn and dined off better fare than they were accustomed to in their manses. It was then that Mr. Muirhead in awful whispers told of news he had had by special post from Edinburgh. Malignancy had raised its head again, this time in their own covenanted land. Montrose, the recusant, had made his way north when he was least expected, and was now leading a host of wild Irish to the slaughter of the godly. There had been battles fought, some said near Perth, others as far off as Aberdeen, and the victory had not been to the righteous.

Hideous tales were told of these Irish, led by a left-handed Macdonald--savage as Amalekites, blind zealots of Rome, burning and slaughtering, and sparing neither sex nor age. The trouble, no doubt, would be short-lived, for Leven's men were marching from England, but it betokened some backsliding in God's people. The Presbytery held a special meeting for prayer, when in lengthy supplications the Almighty was besought to explain whether the sin for which this disaster was the punishment lay with Parliament or Assembly, army or people.

To David the tale was staggering. Montrose was to him only a name, the name of a great noble who had at first served the cause of Christ and then betrayed it. This Judas had not yet gone to his account, was still permitted to trouble Israel, and now he had crowned his misdeeds by leading savages against his own kindly Scots. Like all his nation he had a horror of the Irish, whose barbarity had become a legend, and of Rome, whom he conceived as an unsleeping Antichrist, given a lease of the world by God till the cup of her abomination was full. The news shook him out of his political supineness, and for the moment made him as ardent a Covenanter as Mr. Muirhead himself. Then came the storm, when his head was filled with other concerns, and it was not till February that the Presbytery met again. This time the rumours were still darker. That very morning Mr. Muirhead had had a post which spoke of Montrose ravaging the lands of that light of the Gospel, Argyll-- of his fleeing north, and, at the moment when his doom seemed assured, turning on the shore of a Highland sea-loch and scattering the Covenant army. It was the hour of peril, and the nation must humble itself before the Lord. A national fast had been decreed by Parliament, and it was resolved to set apart a day in each parish when some stout defender of the faith should call the people to examination and repentance. Mr. Proudfoot of Bold was one of the chosen vessels, and it was agreed that he should take the sermon on the fast-day in Woodilee in the first week of March.

But David was now in a different mood from that of November. He repressed with horror an unregenerate admiration for this Montrose, who, it seemed, was still young, and with a handful of caterans had laid an iron hand on the north. He might be a fine soldier, but he was beyond doubt a son of Belial. The trouble with David was the state of his own parish, compared with which the sorrows of Argyll seemed dim and far away.

January, after the snows melted, had been mild and open, with the burns running full and red, and the hills one vast plashing bog. With Candlemas came a black frost, which lasted the whole of February and the first half of March. The worst of the winter stringency was now approaching. The cattle in the yards and the sheep in the paddocks had become woefully lean, the meal in the girnels was running low, and everybody in the parish, except one or two of the farmers, had grown thin and pale-faced. Sickness was rife, and in one week the kirkyard saw six burials. . . . It was the season of births, too, as well as of deaths, and the howdie [midwife] was never off the road.

Strange stories came to his ears. One-half of the births were out of lawful wedlock . . . and most of the children were still-born. A young man is slow to awake to such a condition, and it was only the miserable business of the stool of repentance which opened his eyes. Haggard girls occupied the stool and did penance for their sin, but in only one case did the male paramour appear. . . . He found his Session in a strange mood, for instead of being eager to enforce the law of the Kirk, they seemed to desire to hush up the scandals, as if the thing was an epidemic visitation which might spoil their own repute. He interrogated them and got dull replies; he lost his temper, and they were silent. Where were the men who had betrayed these wretched girls? He repeated the question and found only sullen faces. One Sabbath he abandoned his ordinary routine and preached on the abominations of the heathen with a passion new to his hearers. His discourse was appreciated, and he was congratulated on it by Ephraim Caird; but there was no result, no confession, such as he had hoped for, from stricken sinners, no cracking of the wall of blank obstinate silence. . . . The thing was never out of his mind by day or night. What was betokened by so many infants born dead? He felt himself surrounded by a mystery of iniquity.

One night he spoke of it to Isobel, very shamefacedly, for it seemed an awful topic for a woman, however old. But Isobel was no more communicative than the rest. Even her honest eyes became shy and secretive. "Dinna you fash yoursel', sir," she said. "The Deil's thrang in this parochine, and ye canna expect to get the upper hand o' him in sax months. But ye'll be even wi' him yet, Mr. Sempill, wi' your graund Gospel preachin'." And then she added that on which he pondered many times in the night watches. "There will aye be trouble at this time o' year so long as the folk tak' the Wud at Beltane."

The fast-day came, and Mr. Proudfoot preached a marrowy sermon. His subject was the everlasting fires of Hell, which awaited those who set their hand against a covenanted Kirk, and he exhausted himself in a minute description of the misery of an eternity of torment. "They shall be crowded," he said, "like bricks in a fiery furnace. O what a bed is there! No feathers, but fire; no friends, but furies; no ease, but fetters; no daylight, but darkness; no clock to pass away the time, but endless eternity; fire eternal that ever burns and never dies." He excelled in his conclusion. "Oh, my friends," he cried, "I have given you but a short touch of the torments of Hell. Think of a barn or some other great place filled up topfull with grains of corn; and think of a bird coming every thousand years and fetching away one of those grains of corn. In time there might be an end of all and the barn might be emptied, but the torments of Hell have no end. Ten thousand times ten millions of years doth not at all shorten the miseries of the damned."

There was a hush like death in the crowded kirk. A woman screamed in hysterics and was carried out, and many sobbed. At the close the elders thronged around Mr. Proudfoot and thanked him for a discourse so seasonable and inspired. But David spoke no word, for his heart had sickened. What meant these thunders against public sin when those who rejoiced in them were ready to condone a flagrant private iniquity? For a moment he felt that Montrose the apostate, doing evil with clean steel and shot, was less repugnant to God than his own Kirk Session.

The frost declined in mid-March, there was a fortnight of weeping thaw and a week of bitter east winds, and then in a single night came a south wind and spring blew up the glens.

Isobel chased the minister from his books.

"Awa' to the hill like a man, and rax [stretch] your legs. Ye've had a sair winter, and your face is like a dish-clout. Awa' and snowk up the caller air."

David went out to the moors, and on the summit of the Hill of Deer had a prospect of the countryside, the contours sharp in the clear April light, and colour stealing back after the grey of winter. The Wood of Melanudrigill seemed to have crowded together again, and to have regained its darkness, but there was as yet no mystery in its shadows. The hill itself was yellow like old velvet, but green was mantling beside the brimming streams. The birches were still only a pale vapour, but there were buds on the saughs and the hazels. Remnants of old drifts lay behind the dykes, and on the Lammerlaw there was a great field of snow, but the breeze blew soft and the crying of curlews and plovers told of the spring. Up on Windyways and at the back of Reiverslaw the heather was burning, and spirals of blue smoke rose to the pale skies.

The sight was a revelation to a man to whom spring had come hitherto in the narrow streets of Edinburgh. He had a fancy that life was beating furiously under the brown earth, and that he was in the presence of a miracle. His youth, long frosted by winter, seemed to return to him and his whole being to thaw. Almost shamefacedly he acknowledged an uplift of spirit. The smoke from the moorburn was like the smoke of sacrifice on ancient altars-- innocent sacrifice from kindly altars.

That night in his study he found that he could not bring his mind to his commentary on the prophet Isaiah. His thoughts ranged on other things, and he would fain have opened his Virgil. But, since these evening hours were dedicate to theology, he compromised with Clement of Alexandria, and read again the passage where that father of the Church becomes a poet and strives to mingle the classic and the Christian.--"This is the Mountain beloved of God, not a place of tragedies like Cithæron, but consecrate to the dramas of truth, a mount of temperance shaded with the groves of purity. And there revel on it not the Mænads, sisters of Semele the thunderstruck, initiate in the impure feast of flesh, but God's daughters, fair Lambs who celebrate the holy rites of the Word, chanting soberly in chorus."

In these days his sermons changed. He no longer hammered subtle chains of doctrine, but forsook his "ordinary," and preached to the hearts of the people. Woodilee was in turn mystified, impressed, and disquieted. One bright afternoon he discoursed on thankfulness and the praise due to God. "Praise Him," he cried, "if you have no more, for this good day and sunshine to the lambs."

"Heard ye ever the like?" said Mirehope at the kirk door. "What concern has Jehovah wi' our lambin'?"

"He's an affectionate preacher," said Chasehope, "but he's no Boanerges, like Proudfoot o' Bold."

The other agreed, and though the tone of the two men was regretful, their eyes were content, as if they had no wish for a Boanerges in Woodilee.

CHAPTER V

THE BLACK WOOD BY DAY

On the 22nd day of April the minister went for a walk on the Hill of Deer. He had heard news from Isobel which had awakened his numbed memory. All the long dark winter Woodilee had been severed from the world, and David had also lived in the cage and had had no thoughts beyond the parish. Calidon and its people were as little in his mind as if they had been on another planet. But as spring loosened the bonds word of the neighbourhood's doings was coming in.

"Johnnie Dow's ben the house," Isobel had said as he sat at meat. "He's come down the water frae Calidon, and it seems there's unco changes there. The laird is awa' to the wars again. . . . Na, Johnnie didna ken what airt he had ridden. He gaed off ae mornin' wi' his man Tam Purves, baith o' them on muckle horses, and that's the last heard o' them. It seems that the laird's gude-sister, Mistress Saintserf frae Embro, cam' oot a fortnight syne to tak' chairge o' Calidon and the young lassie--there's a lassie bides there, ye maun ken, sir, though nane o' the Woodilee folk ever cast een on her--and the puir body was like to be smoored [smothered] in the Carnwath Moss. Johnnie says she's an auld wumman, as straucht as a wand and wi' an unco ill tongue in her heid. She fleyed Johnnie awa' frae the door when he was for daffin' wi' the serving lasses."

It was of Calidon that David thought as he took the hill. Nicholas Hawkshaw, lame as he was, had gone back to the wars. What wars? Remembering the talk of that autumn night he feared that it could not be a campaign of which a minister of the Kirk would approve. Was it possible that he had gone to join Montrose in his evil work? And the troopers and the groom? Were they with Leven again under the Covenant's banner, or were they perilling their souls with the malignants? The latter most likely, and to his surprise he felt no desire to reprobate them. Spring was loosening other bonds than those of winter.

It was a bright warm day, which might have been borrowed from June, and the bursting leaves were stirred by a wandering west wind. David sat for a little on the crest of the hill, gazing at the high summits, which, in the April light, were clear in every nook and yet infinitely distant. The great Herstane Craig had old snowdrifts still in its ravines, and he had the fancy that it was really built of marble which shone in places through the brown husk. The Green Dod did not now belie its name; above the screes and heather of its flanks rose a cone of dazzling greenness. The upper Aller glen was filled with pure sunshine, the very quintessence of light, and the sword-cut of the Rood was for once free from gloom. There was no gold in the landscape, for the shallows, even when they caught the sun, were silver, the bent was flushing into the palest green, the skies above were an infinity of colourless light. And yet the riot of spring was there. David felt it in his bones and in his heart.

The herd of Reiverslaw was busy with his late lambs. The man, Prentice by name, was a sour fellow whom an accident in childhood had deprived of a leg. In spite of his misfortune he could move about on a single crutch at a good pace, and had a voice and a tongue which the parish feared. He was a noted professor, with an uncanny gift of prayer, and his by-names in Woodilee were "Hirplin' Rab" and the "One Leggit Prophet." But to-day even Prentice seemed mellowed by the spring. He gave David a friendly good-day. "The voice o' the turtle is heard on the yirth," he announced, and as he hobbled over a patch of old moorburn, sending up clouds of grey dust, Prentice too became a figure of pastoral.

David had rarely felt a more benignant mood. The grimness of winter had gone clean out of his mind, and he had entered on a large and gracious world. He walked slowly like an epicure, drinking in the quintessential air of the hills, marking the strong blue swirl of the burns, the fresh green of the mosses, the buds on the hawthorns, the flash of the water-ouzels in the spray of the little falls. Curlews and peewits filled the moor with their crying, and as he began to descend into the Rood glen a lark--the first he had heard--rose to heaven with a flood of song.

His eyes had been so engaged with the foreground that he had not looked towards Melanudrigill. Now he saw it, dark and massy, the only opaque thing in a translucent world. But there was nothing oppressive in its shadows, for oppression could not exist in a scene so full of air and light and song. For a moment he had a mind to go boldly into its coverts by way of Reiverslaw and make for the lower course of the Woodilee burn. But the sight of the wild wood in the Rood glen detained him. It was a day not for the pines, but for the hazels and birches, where in open glades a man would have always a view of the hills and the sky. So he slanted to his right through the open coppice, meaning to reach the valley floor near the foot of the path which led to the Greenshiel.

The coppice was thicker than he had imagined. This was no hillside scrub, but a forest, a greenwood, with its own glades and hollows, its own miniature glens and streams. He was in the midst of small birds who made a cheerful twittering from the greening boughs, cushats too were busy, and the thickets were full of friendly beasts. He saw the russet back of a deer as it broke cover, and the tawny streak of a hill-fox, and there was a perpetual scurrying of rabbits. Above all there was a glory of primroses. The pale blossoms starred the glades and the sides of the dells, clung to tree-roots, and climbed into crannies of the grey whinstone rock. So thick they were, that their paleness became golden, the first strong colour he had seen that day. David was young and his heart was light, so he gathered a great clump of blooms for his manse table, and set a bouquet in his coat and another in his bonnet. These latter would have to go before he reached the highway, or the parish would think that its minister had gone daft. But here in the secret greenwood he could forget decorum and bedeck himself like a child.

Presently he had forgotten the route he had planned. He found himself in a shallow glade which ran to the left and away from the Greenshiel, and down which leaped a burn so entrancing in its madcap grace that he could not choose but follow it. Memory returned to him; this must be the burn which descended near the mill at Roodfoot; he knew well its lower course, for he had often guddled trout in its pools, but he had never explored its upper waters. Now he felt the excitement of a discoverer. . . . The ravine narrowed to a cleft where the stream fell in a white spout into a cauldron. David made the passage by slithering down the adjacent rocks and emerged wet to the knees. He was as amused as a boy playing truant from school, and when he found a water-ouzel's nest in the notch of a tree-root he felt that he had profit of his truancy. There came a more level stretch, which was a glory of primroses and wood-anemones, then another linn, and then a cup of turf rimmed with hazels, where the water twined in placid shallows. . . . He looked up and saw on the opposite bank a regiment of dark pines.

He had come to the edge of Melanudrigill. The trees rose like a cloud above him, and after the open coppice of birch and hazel he seemed to be looking into deep water where things were seen darkly as through a dull glass. There were glades which ran into shadows, and fantastic rocks, and mounds of dead bracken which looked like tombs. Yet the place fascinated him. It, too, was under the spell of Spring, and he wondered how Spring walked in its recesses. He leapt the stream and scrambled up the bank with an odd feeling of expectation. He was called to adventure on this day of days.

The place was not dark, but dim and very green. The ancient pines grew more sparsely than he had imagined, and beneath them were masses of sprouting ferns--primroses too, and violets, which he had not found among the hazels. A scent of rooty dampness was about, of fresh-turned earth, and welling fountains. In every tree-root wood-sorrel clustered. But there were no small birds, only large things like cushats and hawks, which made a movement in the high branches. A little farther and he was in a glade, far more of a glade than the clearings in the hazels, for it was sharply defined by the walls of shade.

He stood and gazed, stuck silent by its beauty. Here in truth was a dancing-floor for wood nymphs, a playground for the Good Folk. It seemed strange that the place should be untenanted. . . . There was a rustling in the covert, and his heart beat. He was no longer the adventurous boy, but a young man with a fancy fed by knowledge. He felt that the glade was aware and not empty. Light feet had lately brushed its sward. . . . There was a rustling again, and a gleam of colour. He stood poised like a runner, his blood throbbing in a sudden rapture.

There was the gleam again and the rustle. He thought that at the far end of the glade behind the red bracken he saw a figure. In two steps he was certain. A green gown fluttered, and at his third step broke cover. He saw the form of a girl--nymph, fairy, or mortal, he knew not which. He was no more the minister of Woodilee, but eternal wandering youth, and he gave chase.

The green gown wavered for a moment between two gnarled pines and then was lost in the dead fern. He saw it again in the cleft of a tiny rivulet which came down from a pile of rocks, but he missed it as he scrambled up the steep. It seemed that the gown played tricks with him and led him on, for, as he checked at fault, he had a glimpse of it lower down, where an aisle in the trees gave a view of the bald top of a mountain. David was young and active, but the gown was swifter than he, for as he went down the slope in great leaps it vanished into the dusk of the pines. He had it again, lost it, found it suddenly high above him--always a glimmer of green with but a hint of a girl's form behind it. . . . David became wary. Nymph or human, it should not beat him at this sport of hide-and-seek. There was a line of low cliffs above, up which it could not go unless it took wings. David kept the lower ground, determined that he would drive that which he followed towards the cliff line. He succeeded, for after twice trying to break away, the gown fluttered into a tiny ravine, with thick scrub on both sides and the rock wall at the top. As David panted upward he saw in a mossy place below the crags a breathless girl trying to master her tumbling tresses.

He stopped short in a deep embarrassment. He had been pursuing a fairy, and had found a mortal--a mortal who looked down on him with a flushed face and angry eyes. He was furiously hot, and the pace and his amazement bereft him of speech. It was she who spoke first.

"What does the minister of Woodilee in the Wood--and bedecked with primroses?"

The voice was familiar, and as he brushed the sweat from his eyes the face too awoke recollection. She was far cooler than he, but her cheeks were flushed, and he had seen before those dark mirthful eyes. Mirthful they were, for her anger seemed to have gone, and she was looking down on him with a shy amusement. She had recognized him too, and had spoken his name. . . . He had it. It was the girl who had curtsied to Nicholas Hawkshaw's guests in the candle-light at Calidon. His abashment was increased.

"Madam," he stammered, "Madam, I thought you were a fairy."

She laughed out loud with the abandonment of childhood. "A fairy! And, pray, sir, is it part of the duties of a gospel minister to pursue fairies in the woods?"

"I am shamed," he cried. "You do well to upbraid me. But on this spring day I had forgot my sacred calling and dreamed I was a boy once more."

"I do not upbraid you. Indeed I am glad that a minister can still be a boy. But folks do not come here, and I thought the wood my own, so when I saw you stumbling among the fern I had a notion to play a trick on you, and frighten you, as I have frightened intruders before. I thought you would run away. But you were too bold for me, and now you have discovered my secret. This wood is my playground, where I can pick flowers and sing ballads and be happy with birds and beasts. . . . You were a man before you were a minister. What is your name?"

"They call me David Sempill. I lived as a child at the Mill of the Roodfoot."

"Then you have seisin of this land. You too have played in the Wood?"

"Nay, madam, the Wood is strange to me. I have but ridden through it, and till to-day I have had some dread of it. This Melanudrigill is ill reputed."

"Old wives' havers! It is a blessed and innocent place. But I do not like that name--Melanudrigill. There is dark magic there. Call it the Wood, and you will love it as I do. . . . See, I am coming down. Make room, please, and then I will take you to Paradise. You do not know Paradise? It is the shrine of this grove, and none but me can find the road."

This was not the stately lady in the gown of yellow satin and blue velvet who had abashed him that night in Calidon tower. It was a slim laughing girl in green who presently stood beside him, her feet in stout country shoes, her hair bound only by a silk fillet and still unruly from the chase. He suddenly lost his embarrassment. His reason told him that this was Katrine Yester of Calidon, a daughter of a proud and contumacious house that was looked askance at by the godly, a woman, a beauty--commodities of which he knew nothing. But his reason was blinded, and he saw only a girl on a spring holiday.

She led him down the hill, and as she went she chattered gaily, like a solitary child who has found a comrade.

"I saw you before you saw me, and I hoped you would follow when I ran away. I liked you that night at Calidon. They told me that ministers were all sour-faced and old, but you looked kind. And you are merry, too, I think--not sad, like most people in Scotland."

"You have not been long in this land?" he asked.

"Since June of last year. This is my first Scottish spring, and it is different from France and England. In those lands summer comes with a rush on winter's heels, but here there is a long preparation, and flowers steal very softly back to the world. I have lived mostly in France since my father died."

"That is why your speech is so strange to my ears."

"And yours to mine," she retorted. "But Aunt Grizel is teaching me to be a good Scotswoman. I am made to spin till my arms are weary, and to make horrid brews of herbs, and to cook your strange dishes. 'Kaatrine, ye daft quean, what for maun ye fill the hoose wi' floorish and nesty green busses? D'ye think we're nowt and the auld tower o' Calidon a byre?' That is Aunt Grizel. But she is like a good dog and barks but does not bite, though the serving- maids walk in terror. I play with her at the cartes, and she tells me tales, but not such good ones as Uncle Nick's. Heigho! I wish the wars were over and he were home again. . . . Now, sir, what do you think of this? It is the gate of Paradise."

She had led him into a part of the wood where the pines ceased and a green cleft was lined with bursting hazels and rowans and the tassels of birch. The place was rather hill than woodland, for the turf was as fine as on a mountain-side, and in the centre a bubbling spring sent out a rivulet, which twined among the flowers till it dropped in a long cascade to a lower shelf. Primroses, violets, and anemones made it as bright as a garden.

"I call this Paradise," she said, "because it is hard for mortals to find. You would not guess it was here till you stumbled on it."

"It's away from the pines," he said.

She nodded her head. "I love the dark trees well enough, and on a day like this I am happy among them. But they are moody things, and when there is no sun and the wind blows they make me sad. Here I am gay in any weather, for it is a kindly place. Confess, sir, that I have chosen well."

"You have chosen well. It is what the poet wrote of--Deus nobis hæc otia fecit."

"La, la! That is Latin, and I am not learned. But I can quote my own poets." And in a voice like a bird's she trilled a stanza of which David comprehended no more than that it was a song of Spring, and that it was Flora the goddess herself who sang it.

"O fontaine Bellerie, Belle fontaine chérie De nos Nymphes, quand ton eau Les cache au creux de ta source, Fuyantes le Satyreau Qui les pourchasse à la course Jusqu'au bord de ton ruisseau, Tu es la Nymphe éternelle De ma terre paternelle--"

Some strange and cataclysmic transformation was going on in David's mind. He realized that a film had cleared from his sight, and that he was looking with new eyes. This dancing creature had unlocked a door for him--whether for good or ill he knew not, and did not care. He wanted the world to stand still and the scene to remain fixed for ever--the spring glade and the dark-haired girl singing among the primroses. He had the courage now to call her by her name.

"You have a voice like a linnet, Mistress Katrine. Can you sing none of our country songs?"

"I am learning them from the serving-maids. I know 'The Ewebuchts' and 'The Yellow-hair'd Laddie' and--ah, this is the one for Paradise," and she sang:

"The King's young dochter was sitting in her window, Sewing at her silken seam; She lookt out o' a bow-window, And she saw the leaves growing green, My luve; And she saw the leaves growing green."

"But Jean, the goose-girl who taught it me, remembered just the one verse. I wish I was a poet to make others."

Above the well was one of those circles of green mounds which country people call fairy-rings. The girl seated herself in the centre and began to make posies of the flowers she had picked. David lay on the turf at her feet, watching the quick movement of her hands, his garlanded hat removed and the temperate sun warming his body. Never had he felt so bathed in happy peace.

The pixie seated above him spared time from her flowers to glance down at him, and found him regarding her with abstracted eyes. For he was trying to fit this bright creature into his scheme of things. Did the world of the two of them touch nowhere save in this woodland?

"Your uncle is the chief heritor in Woodilee parish," he said, "but you do not come to the kirk."

"I was there no longer back than last Sunday--" she said.

"Sabbath," he corrected.

"Sabbath, if you will have it so. Calidon is in Cauldshaw parish, and it was to Cauldshaw kirk we went. Four weary miles of jogging on a plough-horse, I riding pillion to Aunt Grizel. Before that the drifts were too deep to take the road. . . . I have heard many a sermon from Mr. Fordyce."

"He is a good man."

"He is a dull man. Such a preachment on dismal texts. 'Seventhly, my brethren, and in parenthesis--'" she mimicked. "But he is beyond doubt good, and Aunt Grizel says she has benefited from his words, and would fain repay him by healing his disorders. He has many bodily disorders, the poor man, and Aunt Grizel loves sermons much, but her simples more."

"You do not love sermons?"

She made a mouth.

"I do not think I follow them. You are learned theologians, you of Scotland, and I am still at the horn-book. But some day I will come to hear you, for YOUR sermons I think I might understand."

"I could not preach to you," he said.

"And wherefore, sir? Are your discourses only for wrinkled carls and old rudas wives? Is there no place in your kirk for a girl?"

"You are not of our people. The seed can be sown only in a field prepared."

"But that is heresy. Are not all souls alike?"

"True. But the voice of the preacher is heard only by open ears. I think you are too happy in your youth, mistress, for my solemnities."

"You do me injustice," she said, and her face was grave. "I am young, and I think I have a cheerful heart, for I can exult in a spring morning, and I cannot be very long sad. But I have had sorrows--a father slain in the wars, a mother dead of grieving, a bundling about among kinsfolk who were not all gracious. I have often had sore need of comfort, sir."

"You have found it--where?"

"In the resolve never to be a faintheart. That is my creed, though I fail often in the practice."

To an ear accustomed to a formal piety the confession seemed almost a blasphemy. He shook a disapproving head.

"That is but a cold pagan philosophy," he said.

"Yet I learned it from a sermon, and that little more than a year back."

"Where was it preached?"

"In England, and in no kirk, but at the King's Court."

"Was it by Mr. Henderson?"

"It was by a Presbyterian--but he was no minister. Listen, and I will tell you the story. In March of last year I was taken to Oxford by my lady Grevel, and was presented by her to the Queen, and her Majesty deigned to approve of me, so that I became a maid- of-honour, and was lodged beside her in Merton College. There all day long was a coming and going of great men. There I saw"--she counted on her fingers--"his grace of Hamilton--him I did not like-- and my lord of Nithsdale, and my lord of Aboyne, and my lord Ogilvy, and that very grave person Sir Edward Hyde, and my lord Digby, and the wise Mr. Endymion Porter. And all day long there were distracted counsels, and the King's servants plotting in side- chambers, and treason whispered, and nowhere a clear vision or a brave heart. Then there came among us a young man, who spoke simply. 'If the King's cause go down in England,' he said, 'it may be saved in Scotland.' When they asked him what he proposed, he said--'To raise the North for his Majesty.' When they asked him by what means, he said--'By my own resolution.' All doubted and many laughed, but that young man was not discouraged. 'The arm of the Lord is not shortened,' he said, 'and they who trust in Him will not be dismayed. . . .' That was the sermon he preached, and there was silence among the doubters. Then said Mr. Porter: 'There is a certain faith that moves mountains, and a certain spirit which may win against all odds. My voice is for the venture!' . . . And then the Queen, my mistress, kissed the young man, and the King made him his lieutenant-general. . . . I watched him ride out of the city two days later, attended by but one servant, on his mission to conquer Scotland, and I flung him a nosegay of early primroses. He caught it and set it in his breast, and he waved his hand to me as he passed through the north gate."

"Who was this hero?" David asked eagerly, for the tale had fired him.

The girl's face was flushed and her eyes glistened.

"That was a year ago," she went on. "To-day he has done his purpose. He has won Scotland for the King."

David gasped.

"Montrose the malignant!" he cried.

"He is as good a Presbyterian as you, sir," she replied gently. "Do not call him malignant. He made his way north through his enemies as if God had sent His angel to guide him. And he is born to lead men to triumph. Did you not feel the compulsion of his greatness?"

"I?" David stammered.

"They told me that you had spoken with him, and that he liked you well. Yon groom at Calidon was the Lord Marquis."

CHAPTER VI

THE BLACK WOOD BY NIGHT

Word came of a great revival in the parish of Bold. Men called it a "Work," and spoke of it in hushed voices, attributing it to the zeal and gifts of Mr. Ebenezer Proudfoot, the minister. For, after much preaching on fast-days in the shire, Mr. Ebenezer had fallen into a rapture and had seen visions, and spoken with strange voices. The terror of the unknown fell upon his people, fasting and prayer became the chief business of the parish, and the most careless were transformed into penitents. For a season there were no shortcomings in Bold; penny-bridals and fiddling and roystering at the change-houses were forgotten; even swearing and tippling were forsworn; the Sabbath was more strictly observed than by Israel in the Wilderness. To crown the Work, a great field- preaching was ordained, when thousands assembled on Bold Moor and the sacrament was dispensed among scenes of wild emotion. In Bold there was a lonely field of thistles, known as Guidman's Croft, which had been held to be dedicate to the Evil One. The oxen of all the parish were yoked, and in an hour or two it was ploughed up and sown with bear for the use of the poor, as at once a thankoffering and a renunciation.

People in Woodilee talked much of the Work in Bold, and the Session sighed for a like experience.

"Would but the wind blow frae that airt on our frostit lands!" was the aspiration of Peter Pennecuik. But David had no ears for these things, for he was engrossed with the conflict in his own soul.

Ever since that afternoon in Paradise he had walked like a man half asleep, his eyes turning inward. His first exhilaration had been succeeded by a black darkness of doubt. He had adventured into the Wood and found magic there, and the spell was tugging at his heartstrings. . . . Was the thing of Heaven or of Hell? . . . Sometimes, when he remembered the girl's innocence and ardour, he thought of her as an angel. Surely no sin could dwell in so bright a presence. . . . But he remembered, too, how lightly she had held the things of the Kirk, how indeed she was vowed to the world against which the Kirk made war. Was she not a daughter of Heth, a fair Moabitish woman, with no part in the commonwealth of Israel? Her beauty was of the flesh, her graces were not those of the redeemed. And always came the conviction that nevertheless she had stolen his heart. "Will I too be unregenerate?" he asked himself with terror.

The more he looked into his soul the more he was perplexed. He thought of the groom at Calidon, to whom had gone out from him a spark of such affection as no other had inspired. That face was little out of his memory, and he longed to look on it again as a lover longs for his mistress. . . . But the man was Montrose the recreant, who was even now troubling God's people, and who had been solemnly excommunicated by the very

Kirk he was vowed to serve. . . . And yet, recreant or no, the man believed in God and had covenanted himself with the Almighty. . . . What were God's purposes, and who were God's people? Where in all the round earth should he find a solution of his doubts?

The study, now warm in the pleasant spring gloamings, saw no longer the preparation of the great work on Isaiah. It had become a closet for prayer. David cast his perplexities on the Lord, and waited feverishly for a sign. But no sign came. A horde of texts about Canaanitish garments and idol worship crowded into his mind, but he refused their application. A young man's face, a girl's eyes and voice, made folly of such easy formulas. . . . Yet there were moments when in sheer torment of soul David was minded to embrace them--to renounce what had charmed him as the Devil's temptation, and steel his heart against its glamour.

One day he rode over to Cauldshaw to see Mr. Fordyce. He was in the mood for confession, but he found little encouragement. Mr. James was sick of a spring fever, and though he was on his feet he had been better in bed, for his teeth chattered and his hand trembled.

They spoke of the household at Calidon. "Mistress Saintserf has beyond doubt her interest in Christ," said the minister of Cauldshaw. "When I have gone to Calidon for the catechizing I have found her quick to apprehend the doctrines of the faith, and her life is in all respects an ensample, save that she is something of a libertine with her tongue. But the lassie--she's but a young thing, and has sojourned long in popish and prelatical lands. Yet I detect glimmerings of grace, Mr. David, and she has a heart that may well be attuned to God's work. My wife pines for the sight of her like a sick man for the morning. Maybe I fail in my duty towards her, for she is lamentably ignorant, but I cannot find it in me to be harsh to so gracious a bairn."

David returned with his purpose unfulfilled, but a certain comfort in his soul. He would rather have Mr. Fordyce's judgment than that of the Boanerges of Bold or the sleek minister of Kirk Aller. His doubts were not resolved, but the very uncertainty gave him ease. He was not yet called to renunciation, and having reached this conclusion, he could let the memory of Paradise sweep back into his mind in a delightful flood.

Yet youth cannot be happy in indecision. David longed for some duty which would absorb the strong life that was in him. Why, oh why was he not a soldier? He turned to his parish, and tried to engross himself in its cares. It may have been that his perception was sharpened by his own mental conflicts, but he seemed to detect a strangeness in Woodilee.

It had been a fine spring, with a dry seed-bed, and the sowing of crops and the lambing had passed off well. The lean cattle had staggered out of byres and closes to the young grass, and their ribs were now covered again.

Up on the hills lambs no longer tottered on weak legs. There was more food in the place, for there had been feasts of braxy mutton, and the hens were laying again, and there was milk in the cogies. The faces of the people had lost their winter strain; the girls had washed theirs, and fresh cheeks and bright eyes were to be seen on the roads. Woodilee had revived with the spring, but David as he went among the folk saw more than an increase in bodily well-being. . . . There was a queer undercurrent of excitement--or was it expectation?--and the thing was secret.

Every one did not share this. There seemed to be an inner circle in the parish which was linked together by some private bond. He began to guess at its membership by the eyes. Some looked him frankly in the face, and these were not always the best reputed. Amos Ritchie, the blacksmith, for instance--he was a profane swearer, and was sometimes overtaken in drink--and the farmer of Reiverslaw had, in addition to the latter failing, a violent temper, which made him feared and hated. Yet these two faced him like free men. But there were others, whose speech was often the most devout, who seemed to have shutters drawn over their eyes and to move stealthily on tiptoe.

Woodilee was amazingly well-conducted, and the Poor Box received the scantiest revenue in penalties. Apart from the lawless births in the winter, there were few apparent backslidings. David rarely met young lads and lasses at their hoydenish courtings in the gloamings.

Oaths were never heard, and if there was drunkenness it was done in secret. Not often was a Sabbath-breaker before the Session, and there were no fines for slack attendance at the kirk. But as David watched the people thronging to service on the Sabbath, the girls in their clean linen, walking barefoot and only putting on shoes at the kirkyard gate, the men in decent homespun and broad bonnets, the old wives in their white mutches--as he looked down from the pulpit on the shoulders bent with toil, the heavy features hardened to a stiff decorum, the eyes fixed dully on his face--he had the sense that he was looking on masks. The real life of Woodilee was shut to him. "Ye are my people," he told himself bitterly, "and I know ye not."

This was not true of all. He knew the children, and there were certain of the older men and women in the parish who had given him their friendship. Peter Pennecuik, his principal elder and session-clerk, he felt that he knew to the bottom--what little there was to know, for the man was a sanctimonious egotist. With Amos Ritchie and Reiverslaw, too, he could stand as man with man. . . . But with many of the others he fenced as with aliens; the farmers, for example, Chasehope and Mirehope and Nether Fennan, and Spotswood the miller, and various elderly herds and hinds, and the wives of them. Above all, he was no nearer the youth of the parish than when first he came. The slouching hobbledehoy lads, the girls, some comely and high-coloured, some waxen white--they were civil and decent, but impenetrable. There were moments when he found himself looking of a Sabbath at his sober respectable folk as a hostile body, who watched him furtively lest he should learn too much of them. . . . Woodilee had an ill name in the shire, Mr. Fordyce had told him the first day in the manse. For what? What was the life from which he was so resolutely barred--he, their minister, who should know every secret of their souls? What was behind those shuttered eyes? Was it fear? He thought that there might be fear in it, but that more than fear it was a wild and sinister expectation.

On the last day of April he noted that Isobel was ill at ease. "Ye'll be for a daunder, sir," she said after the midday meal. "See and be hame in gude time for your supper--I've a rale guid yowe-milk kebbuck [cheese] for ye, and a new bakin' o' cakes--and I'll hae the can'les lichtit in your chamber for you to get to your books."

He smiled at his housekeeper. "Why this carefulness?" he said.

She laughed uneasily. "Naething by ordinar. But this is the day they ca' the Rood-Mass and the morn is the Beltane, and it behoves a' decent bodies to be indoors at the darkenin' on Beltane's Eve. My faither was a bauld man, but he wadna have stirred a fit over his ain doorstep on the night o' Rood-Mass for a king's ransom. There's anither Beltane on the aucht day of May, and till that's by we maun walk eidently."

"Old wives' tales," he said.

"But they're nane auld wives' tales. They're the tales o' wise men and bauld men."

"I thought of walking in the Wood."

"Mercy on us!" she cried. "Ye'll no gang near the Wud. No on this day o' a' days. It's fou' o' bogles."

Her insistence vexed him, and he spoke to her sharply. The heavy preoccupation of his mind had put him out of patience with folly. "Woman," he cried, "what concern has a servant of God with these heathen fables? Think shame to repeat such folly."

But Isobel was not convinced. She retired in dudgeon to her kitchen, and watched his movements till he left the house as a mother watches a defiant child. "Ye'll be hame in guid time?" she begged.

"I will be home when I choose," he said, and to show his independence he put some cheese and bannocks in his pockets.

The afternoon was warm and bright, with a thin haze on the highest hills. Spring had now fairly come; the yews in the kirkyard were russet with young shoots, the blossom was breaking on the hawthorn, and hazel and oak and ash were in leaf. His spirit was too laden to be sensible of the sweet influences of sky and moorland as on the walk which had first taken him to Paradise. But there was in him what had been lacking before--

excitement, for he had tasted of magic and was in the constant expectation of finding it again. The land was not as it had once been, for it held somewhere enchantments--a girl's face and a girl's voice. From the summit of the Hill of Deer he looked towards Calidon hidden in the fold of the Rood hills. Was she there in the stone tower, or among the meadows whose green showed in the turn of the glen? Or was she in her old playground of the Wood?

He had resolved not to go near the place, so he set himself to walk in the opposite direction along the ridge of hill which made the northern wall of the Rood valley. As he strode over the short turf and scrambled through the patches of peat-bog his spirits rose. It was hard not to be light-hearted in that world of essential airs and fresh odours and nesting birds. Presently he was in view of Calidon tower, and then he was past it, and the Rood below him was creeping nearer to his level as its glen lifted towards its source. He strode along till he felt the sedentary humours leave his body and his limbs acquire the lightness which is the reward of the hill walker. He seemed, too, to gain a lightness of soul and a clearness of eye. In a world which God had made so fair and clean, there could be no sin in anything that was also fair and innocent.

The sun had set beyond Herstane Craig before he turned his steps. Now from the hilltops he had Melanudrigill before him, a distant shadow in the trough of the valley. Since that afternoon in Paradise awe of the

Wood had left him. He had been among its pines and had found Katrine there. He watched the cloud of trees, growing nearer at each step, as earlier that day he had watched the environs of Calidon. It was her haunt; haply she might now be there, singing in the scented twilight?

When he stood above Reiverslaw the dusk was purple about him, and the moon, almost at her full, was climbing the sky. He longed to see how Paradise looked in this elfin light, for he had a premonition that the girl might have lingered there late and that he would meet her. There was no duty to take him home--nothing but Isobel's silly fables. But in deference to Isobel he took the omens. He sent his staff twirling into the air. If it fell with the crook towards him, he would go home. The thing lighted in a heather bush with the crook at the far end. So he plunged downhill among the hazels, making for the glade which slanted eastward towards the deserted mill.

He found it, and it was very dark in that narrow place. There was no light to see the flowers by, and there was no colour in it, only a dim purple gloom and the white of the falling stream, for the moon was still too low in the heavens to reach it.

In time he came to the high bank where the pines began. He was looking for Paradise, but he could not find it. It was not among the pines, he remembered, but among the oaks and hazels, but he had gone to it through the pines, led by a flitting girl. . . . He found the point where he had entered the darker Wood, and resolved to try to retrace his former tracks.

The place was less murky than he had expected, for the moon was now well up the sky, so that every glade was a patch of white light. . . . This surely was the open space where he had first caught the glimmer of a green gown. . . . There were the rocks where she had stood at bay. . . . She had led him down the hill and then at a slant--but was it to right or left? Right, he thought, and plunged through a wilderness of fern. There had been briars, too, and this was surely the place where a vast uprooted trunk had forced them to make a detour.

Then he found a little stream which he fancied might be the outflow of the Paradise well. So he turned up hill again, and came into a jungle of scrub and boulder. There was in most places a dim light to move by, but a dim light in a broken wood is apt to confuse the mind. David had soon lost all sense of direction, save that of the upward and downward slopes. He did not know east or west, and he did not stop to think, for he was beginning to be mesmerized by the hour and the scene. Dew was in the air and an overpowering sweetness of fern and pine and mosses, and through the aisles of the high trees came a shimmer of palest gold, and in the open spaces the moon rode in the dusky blue heavens--not the mild moon of April, but a fiery conquering goddess, driving her chariot among trampled stars.

It was clear to him that he would not find Paradise except by happy chance, since he was utterly out of his bearings. But he was content to be lost, for the whole place was Paradise. Never before had he felt so strong a natural magic. This woodland, which he had once shunned, had become a holy place, lit with heavenly lights and hallowed by some primordial peace. He had forgotten about the girl, forgotten his scruples. In that hour he had acquired a mood at once serene and gay: he had the light-heartedness of a boy and the ease of a wise philosopher; his body seemed as light as air, and, though he had already walked some twenty miles, he felt as if he had just risen from his bed. But there was no exuberance in him, and he had not the impulse to sing which usually attended his seasons of high spirits. . . . The silence struck upon him as something at once miraculous and just. There was not a sound in the Wood--not the lightest whisper of wind, though there had been a breeze on the hilltops at sundown--not the cry of a single bird--not a rustle in the undergrowth. The place was dumb--not dead, but sleeping.

Suddenly he came into a broad glade over which the moonshine flowed like a tide. It was all of soft mossy green, without pebble or bush to break its carpet, and in the centre stood a thing like an altar.

At first he thought it was only a boulder dropped from the hill. But as he neared it he saw that it was human handiwork. Masons centuries ago had wrought on it, for it was roughly squared, and firmly founded on a pediment. Weather had battered it, and one corner of the top had been broken by some old storm, but it still stood foursquare to the seasons. One side was very clear in the moon, and on it David thought he could detect a half-obliterated legend. He knelt down, and though the lower part was obscured beyond hope, the upper letters stood out plain. I. O. M.--he read: "Jovi Optimo Maximo." This uncouth thing had once been an altar.

He tiptoed away from it with a sudden sense of awe. Others had known this wood--mailed Romans clanking up the long roads from the south, white-robed priests who had once sacrificed here to their dead gods. He was scholar enough to feel the magic of this sudden window opened into the past. But there was that in the discovery which disquieted as well as charmed him. The mysteries of the heathen had been here, and he felt the simplicity of the woodland violated and its peace ravished. Once there had been wild tongues in the air, and he almost seemed to hear their echo.

He hurried off into the dark undergrowth. . . . But now his mood had changed. He felt fatigue, his eyes were drowsy, and he thought of the anxious Isobel sitting up for him. He realized that this was the night of Rood-Mass--pagan and papistical folly, but his reason could not altogether curb his fancy. The old folk said-- folly, no doubt, but still--He had an overpowering desire to be safe in his bed at the manse. He would retrace his steps and strike the road from Reiverslaw. That would mean going west, and after a moment's puzzling he started to run in what he thought the right direction.

The Wood, or his own mind, had changed. The moonlight was no longer gracious and kind, but like the dead-fires which the old folk said burned in the kirkyard. Confusion on the old folk, for their tales were making him a bairn again! . . . But what now broke the stillness? for it seemed as if there were veritably tongues in the air--not honest things like birds and winds, but tongues. The place was still silent so far as earthly sounds went--he realized that, when he stopped to listen--but nevertheless he had an impression of movement everywhere, of rustling--yes, and of tongues.

Fortune was against him, for he reached a glade and saw that it was the one which he had left and which he thought he had avoided. . . . There was a change in it, for the altar in the centre was draped. At first he thought it only a freak of moonlight, till he forced himself to go nearer. Then he saw that it was a coarse white linen cloth, such as was used in the kirk at the seasons of sacrament.

The discovery affected him with a spasm of blind terror. All the tales of the Wood, all the shrinking he had once felt for it, rushed back on his mind. For the moment he was an infant again, lost and fluttering, assailed by the shapeless phantoms of the dark. He fled from the place as if from something accursed.

Uphill he ran, for he felt that safety was in the hills and that soon he might come to the clear spaces of the heather. But a wall of crag forced him back, and he ran as he thought westward towards the oaks and hazels, for there he deemed he would be free of the magic of the pines. He did not run wildly, but softly and furtively, keeping to the moss and the darker places, and avoiding any crackling of twigs, for he felt as if the Wood were full of watchers. At the back of his head was a stinging sense of shame-- that he, a grown man and a minister of God, should be in such a pit of terror. But his instinct was stronger than his reason. He felt his heart crowding into his throat, and his legs so weak and uncontrollable that they seemed to be separate from his body. The boughs of the undergrowth whipped his face, and he knew that his cheeks were wet with blood, though he felt no pain.

The trees thinned and he saw light ahead--surely it was the glen which marked the division between pine and hazel. He quickened his speed, and the curtain of his fear lifted ever so little. He heard sounds now--was it the wind which he had left on the hilltops? There was a piping note in it, something high and clear and shrill--and yet the Wood had been so airless that his body was damp with sweat. Now he was very near air and sanctuary.

His heart seemed to stop, and his legs wavered so that he sunk on his knees. For he was looking again on the accursed glade.

It was no longer empty. The draped altar was hidden by figures-- human or infernal--moving round it in a slow dance. Beyond this circle sat another who played on some instrument. The moss stilled the noise of movement, and the only sound was the high, mad piping.

A film cleared from his eyes, and something lost came back to him-- manhood, conscience, courage. Awe still held him, but it was being overmastered by a human repulsion and anger. For as he watched the dance he saw that the figures were indeed human, men and women both--the women half-naked, but the men with strange headpieces like animals. What he had taken for demons from the Pit were masked mortals--one with the snout of a pig, one with a goat's horns, and the piper a gaping black hound. . . . As they passed, the altar was for a moment uncovered, and he saw that food and drink were set on it for some infernal sacrament.

The dance was slow and curiously arranged, for each woman was held close from behind by her partner. And they danced widdershins, against the sun. To one accustomed to the open movement of country jigs and reels the thing seemed the uttermost evil--the grinning masks, the white tranced female faces, the obscene postures, above all that witch-music as horrid as a moan of terror.

David, a great anger gathering in his heart, was on his feet now, and as he rose the piping changed. Its slow measure became a crazy lilt, quick and furious. The piper was capering; the dancers, still going widdershins, swung round and leaped forward, flinging their limbs as in some demented reel. . . . There were old women there, for he saw grey hair flying. And now came human cries to add to the din of the pipe--a crying and a sighing wrung out of maddened bodies.

To David it seemed a vision of the lost in Hell. The fury of an Israelitish prophet came upon him. He strode into the glade. Devils or no, he would put an end to this convention of the damned.

"In the name of God," he cried, "I forbid you. If you are mortal, I summon you to repent--if you are demons, I command you to return to him that sent you."

He had a great voice, but in that company there were no ears to hear. The pipe screeched and the dance went on.

Then the minister of Woodilee also went mad. A passion such as he had never known stiffened every nerve and sinew. He flung himself into the throng, into that reek of unclean bestial pelts and sweating bodies. He reached the altar, seized the cloth on it, and swept it and its contents to the ground. Then he broke out of the circle and made for the capering piper, who seemed to him the chief of the orgiasts.

In his flight through the wood David had lost his staff, and had as weapon but his two hands. "Aroynt you, Sathanas," he cried, snatched the pipe from the dog-faced figure, and shivered it on his masked head.

With the pause in the music the dance stopped suddenly, and in an instant the whole flock were on him like a weasel pack. He saw long-nailed claws stretched towards his face, he saw blank eyes suddenly fire into a lust of hate. But he had a second's start of them, and that second he gave to the piper. The man--for the thing was clearly human--had dealt a mighty buffet at his assailant's face, which missed it, and struck the point of the shoulder. David was whirled round, but, being young and nimble, he slipped in under the other's guard, and had his hands on the hound-mask. The man was very powerful, but the minister's knee was in his groin, and he toppled over, while David tore the covering of wood and skin from his head. It crumpled under his violent clutch like a wasps' nest, and he had a glimpse of red hair and a mottled face.

A glimpse and no more. For by this time the press was on him and fingers were at his throat, choking out his senses.

CHAPTER VII

THE FIRST BLAST

Late in the forenoon of the next day David awoke in his own bed in the manse of Woodilee. He awoke to a multitude of small aches and one great one, for his forehead was banded with pain. The room was as bright with sunshine as the little window would permit, but it seemed to him a dusk shot by curious colours, with Isobel's head bobbing in it like a fish. Presently the face became clear and he saw it very near to him--a scared white face with red-rimmed eyes. Her voice penetrated the confused noises in his ears.

"The Lord be thankit, sir, the Lord be praised, Mr. David, ye're comin' oot o' your dwam. Here's a fine het drink for ye. Get it doun like a man and syne ye'll maybe sleep. There's nae banes broke, and I've dressed your face wi' a sure salve. Dinna disturb the clouts, sir. Your skin's ower clean to beal [fester], and ye'll mend quick if ye let the clouts bide a wee."

Her arm raised his aching head, and he swallowed the gruel. It made him drowsy, and soon he was asleep again, a healthy natural sleep, so that when he awoke in the evening he was in comparative ease and his headache had gone. Gingerly he felt his body. There were bruises on his legs, and one huge one on his right thigh. His cheeks under the bandages felt raw and scarred, and there was a tenderness about his throat and the muscles of his neck, as if angry hands had throttled him. But apart from his stiffness he seemed to have suffered no great bodily hurt, and the effects of the slight concussion had passed.

With this assurance his mind came out of its torpor, and he found himself in a misery of disquiet. The events of the night before returned to him only too clearly. He remembered his exaltation in the Wood--the glade, the altar. He recalled with abasement his panic and his flight. The glade again, the piping, the obscene dance--and at that memory he had almost staggered from his bed. He felt again the blind horror and wrath which had hurled him into the infernal throng.

Isobel's anxious face appeared in the doorway.

"Ye've had a graund sleep, sir. And now ye'll be for a bite o' meat?"

"I have slept well, and I am well enough in body. Sit you down, Isobel Veitch, for I have much to say to you. How came I home last night?"

The woman sat down on the edge of a chair, and even in the twilight her nervousness was manifest.

"It wasna last nicht. It was aboot the hour o' three this mornin', and sic a nicht as I had waitin' on ye! Oh, sir, what garred ye no hearken to me and gang to the Wud on Rood-Mass?"

"How do you know I was in the Wood?"

She did not answer.

"Tell me," he said, "how I came home."

"I was ryngin' the hoose like a lost yowe, but I didna daur gang outbye. At twal hours I took a look up the road, and again when the knock was chappin' twa. Syne I dozed off in my chair, till the knock waukened me. That was at three hours, and as I waukened I heard steps outbye. I keekit oot o' the windy, but there was naebody on the road, just the yellow mune. I prayed to the Lord to strengthen me, and by-and-by I ventured out, but I fand naething. Syne I took a thocht to try the back yaird, and my hert gied a stound, for there was yoursel', Mr. David, lyin' like a cauld corp aneath the aipple tree. Blithe I was to find the breath still in ye, but I had a sair job gettin' ye to your bed, sir, for ye're a weary wecht for an auld wumman. The sun was up or I got your wounds washed and salved, and syne I sat by the bed prayin' to the Lord that ye suld wauken in your richt mind, for I saw fine that the wounds o' your body would heal, but I feared that the wits micht have clean gane frae ye. And now I am abundantly answered, for ye're speakin' like yoursel', and your een's as I mind them, and the blood's back intil your cheeks. The Lord be thankit!"

But there was no jubilation in Isobel's voice. Her fingers twined confusedly, and her eyes wandered.

"Do you know what befell me?" he asked.

"Eh, sirs, how suld I ken?"

"But what do you think? You find me in the small hours lying senseless at your door, with my face scarred and my body bruised. What do you think I had suffered?"

"I think ye were clawed by bogles, whilk a'body kens are gi'en a free dispensation on Rood-Mass E'en."

"Woman, what is this talk of bogles from lips that have confessed Christ? I was assaulted by the Devil, but his emissaries were flesh and blood. I tell you it was women's nails that tore my face, and men's hands that clutched my throat. I walked in the Wood, for what has a minister of God to fear from trees and darkness? And as I walked I found in an open place a heathen altar, and that altar was covered with a linen cloth, as if for a sacrament. I was afraid--I confess it with shame--but the Lord used my fear for His own purpose, and led me back in my flight to that very altar. And there I saw what may God in His mercy forbid that I should see again--a dance of devils to the Devil's piping. In my wrath I rushed among them, and tore the mask from the Devil's head, and then they overbore me and I lost my senses. When I wrestled with them I wrestled with flesh and blood--perishing men and women rapt in a lust of evil."

He stopped, and Isobel's eyes did not meet his. "Keep us a'!" she moaned.

"These men and women were, I firmly believe, my own parishioners."

"It canna be," the old woman croaked. "Ye werena yoursel', Mr. David, sir. . . . Ye were clean fey wi' the blackness o' the Wud and the mune and the wanchancy hour. Ye saw ferlies [marvels], but they werena flesh and bluid, sir. . . ."

"I saw the bodies of men and women in Woodilee who have sold their souls to damnation. Isobel Veitch, as your master and your minister, I charge you, as you will answer before the Judgment Seat, what know you of the accursed thing in this parish?"

"Me!" she cried. "Me! I ken nocht. Me and my man aye keepit clear o' the Wud."

"Which is to say that there were others in Woodilee who did not. Answer me, woman, as you hope for salvation. The sin of witchcraft is rampant here, and I will not rest till I have rooted it out. Who are those in Woodilee who keep tryst with the Devil?"

"How suld I ken? Oh, sir, I pray ye to speir nae mair questions. Woodilee has aye been kenned for a queer bit, lappit in the muckle Wud, but the guilty aye come by an ill end. There's been mair witches howkit out o' Woodilee and brunt than in ony ither parochine on the Water o' Aller. Trust to your graund Gospel preachin', Mr. David, to wyse folk a better gait, for if ye start speirin' about the Wud ye'll stir up a byke that will sting ye sair. As my faither used to say, him that spits against the wind spits in his ain face. Trust to conviction o' sin bringin' evildoers to repentance, as honest Mr. Macmichael did afore ye."

"Did Mr. Macmichael know of this wickedness?"

"I canna tell. Nae doot he had a glimmerin'. But he was a quiet body wha keepit to the roads and his ain fireside, and wasna like yoursel', aye ryngin' the country like a moss-trooper. . . . Be content, sir, to let sleepin' tykes lie till ye can catch them rauvagin'. Ye've a congregation o' douce eident folk, and I'se warrant ye'll lead them intil the straucht and narrow way. Maybe the warst's no as ill as ye think. Maybe it's just a sma' backslidin' in them that's pilgrims to Sion. They're weel kenned to be sound in doctrine, and there was mair signed the Covenant--"

"Peace," he cried. "This is rank blasphemy, and a horrid hypocrisy. What care I for lip service when there are professors who are living a lie? Who is there I can trust? The man who is loudest in his profession may be exulting in secret and dreadful evil. He whom I think a saint may be the chief of sinners. Are there no true servants of Christ in Woodilee?"

"Plenty," said Isobel.

"But who are they? I had thought Richie Smail at the Greenshiel a saint, but am I wrong?"

"Na, na. Ye're safe wi' Richie."

"And yourself, Isobel?"

Colour came into her strained face. "I'm but a broken vessel, but neither my man nor me had ever trokin's wi' the Enemy."

"But there are those to your knowledge who have? I demand from you their names."

She pursed her lips. "Oh, sir, I ken nocht. What suld a widow- woman, thrang a' the day in your service, ken o' the doings in Woodilee?"

"Nevertheless you know something. You have heard rumours. Speak, I command you."

Her face was drawn with fright, but her mouth was obstinate. "Wha am I to bring a railin' accusation against onybody, when I have nae certainty of knowledge?"

"You are afraid. In God's name, what do you fear? There is but the one fear, and that is the vengeance of the Almighty, and your silence puts you in jeopardy of His wrath."

Nevertheless there was no change in the woman's face. David saw that her recalcitrance could not be broken.

"Then listen to me, Isobel Veitch. I have had my eyes opened, and I will not rest till I have rooted this evil thing from Woodilee. I will search out and denounce every malefactor, though he were in my own Kirk Session. I will bring against them the terror of God and the arm of the human law. I will lay bare the evil mysteries of the Wood, though I have to hew down every tree with my own hand. In the strength of the Lord I will thresh this parish as corn is threshed, till I have separated the grain from the chaff and given the chaff to the burning. Make you your market for that, Isobel Veitch, and mind that he that is not for me is against me, and that in the day of God's wrath the slack hand and the silent tongue will not be forgiven."

The woman shivered and put a hand to her eyes.

"Will ye hae your bite o' meat, sir?" she quavered.

"I will not break bread till God has given me clearness," he said sternly; and Isobel, who was in the habit of spinning out her talks with her master till she was driven out, slipped from the room like a discharged prisoner who fears that the Court may change its mind.

David rose next morning after a sleepless night, battered in body, but with some peace of mind, and indeed a comfort which he scarcely dared to confess to himself. He had now a straight course before him. There was an evil thing in the place against which he had declared war, an omnipresent evil, for he did not know who were the guilty. The thing was like the Wood itself, an amorphous shadow clouding the daylight. Gone were the divided counsels, the scruples of conscience. What mattered his doubts about the policy of the Kirk at large when here before his eyes was a conflict of God and Belial? . . . For the first time, too, he could let his mind dwell without scruples upon the girl in the greenwood. The little glen that separated the pines from the oaks and the hazels had become for him the frontier between darkness and light--on the one side the innocency of the world which God had made, on the other the unclean haunts of devilry. . . . And yet he had first met Katrine among the pines. To his horror of the works of darkness was added a bitter sense of sacrilege--that obscene revelry should tread the very turf that her feet had trod.

That afternoon he set out for Chasehope. The matter should be without delay laid before his chief elder, and the monstrous suspicion which lurked at the back of his mind dispelled. He was aware that his face was a spectacle, but it should not be hidden, for it was part of his testimony. But at Chasehope there was no

Ephraim Caird. The slatternly wife who met him, old before her time, with a clan of ragged children at her heels, was profuse in regrets. She dusted a settle for him, and offered new milk and a taste of her cheese, but all the time with an obvious discomfort. To think that Ephraim should be away when the minister came up the hill! . . . He had had to ride off that morn to Kirk Aller upon a matter of a bull that Johnnie Davidson had brought from Carlisle-- an English bull to improve the breed--and he would not be home till the darkening. The woman was voluble and hearty, but it seemed to David that she protested too much. . . . Was her husband all the while between the blankets in the press-bed?

On his way back, at the turn of the road from the kirkton, he encountered Daft Gibbie. The idiot had throughout the winter been a satellite of the minister, and had had many a meal in the manse kitchen. When they met it was "Eh, my bonny Mr. Sempill," or "my precious Mr. David," and then an outpouring of grotesque but complimentary texts. But now the first news he had of Gibbie was a small stone that whizzed past his ear, and when he turned he saw a threatening figure with a face twisted into a demoniac hate. A second stone followed, very wide of the mark, and when David threatened pursuit, the idiot shuffled off, shouting filth over his shoulder. A woman came out of a cottage, and said something to Gibbie which caused him to hold his peace and disappear into a kailyard. . . . But the woman did not look towards the minister, but hurried in again and closed the door. Was the whole parish, thought David, banded in a tacit conspiracy? Was this poor idiot one of the misbegotten things of the Wood?

The next Sabbath, which was the fifth of May, the kirk of Woodilee showed a full congregation. That day, save for infants in arms, there were few absentees. Never had the place been more hushed and expectant. David preached from the text, "Enter into the rock, and hide thee in the dust for fear of the Lord," and he delivered his soul with a freedom hitherto lacking in his carefully prepared discourses. Not the Boanerges of Bold could have outdone the fiery vigour with which he described how Israel went astray after forbidden gods and how the wrath of the Almighty smote her with death and exile. But when he came to the application, which should have been as a nail fastened in a sure place, he faltered. The faces below him, set, composed, awful in their decency, seemed like a stone wall against which he must beat with feeble hands.

"I have the sure knowledge," he said, "that there are altars set up to Baal in this very parish, and that this little Israel of ours has its own groves where it worships the gods of the heathen--ay, the very devils from the Pit. Be assured that I will riddle out this evil mystery and drag it into the light of day, and on the priests of Baal in Woodilee, be they libertines or professors, I will call down the terrors of the Most High. I summon now in this place all poor deluded sinners to confession and repentance, for in the strength of the Lord I will go forward, and woe be to those that harden their hearts."

But his words seemed to be driven back upon him by the steely silence. He saw his elders--the heavy white face of Chasehope, the long sanctimonious jowl of Peter Pennecuik, the impish mouth of Spotswood the miller now composed in an alien gravity, the dark sullenness of Mirehope--they relished his vigour, but their eyes were hard as stones. And the folk behind them, men and women, old and young, were attentively apathetic. There was none of the crying and weeping and the spasms of conviction which had attended the fast-day service of the minister of Bold. Were they a congregation of innocents to whom his summons had no application? Or were they so thirled to their evil-doing that his appeals were no more than an idle wind?

His Session congratulated him on his discourse.

"Ye had a gale on your spirit this day, Mr. Sempill," said Chasehope. "Yon was a fine waft o' the Word ye gie'd us, and it's to be hoped that it will be blessed to many."

As David looked at the pale cheeks and the red hair of the man he had a sudden assurance. It was a mild day, but Ephraim Caird wore a strip of flannel as if he were nursing a cold. And was there not a discoloration of the skin around his fleshy jaw and a dark bruise below his left ear?

Next day David sought out Amos Ritchie, the smith. He learned that the man was on a job at Nether Windyways, and he watched for him on the hill-road as he returned in the evening. The big loose-limbed figure of Amos, striding down the twilit slopes with his bag of tools slung on his shoulder, was a pleasant sight to eyes that hungered for a friend. For with the smith David had advanced far in friendliness since their partnership in the winter snowstorm. The man was of a high spirit and a complete honesty, and his professions were well behind his practice. Rough of tongue and apt in a quarrel, he had a warmth of heart that did not fail even those he despised. He was no purveyor of edifying speech, but the milk of human kindness ran strong in him. It was a saying in the village that there was "mair comfort in an aith from Amos than a prayer from Peter Pennecuik."

But on this occasion the smith's straightforward friendliness seemed to have deserted him. When David appeared before him he looked as if he would fain have avoided the meeting. His eyes were troubled, and he increased the pace of his walk when the minister fell into step beside him.

"How's the wife?" David asked.

"Fine, sir. Her kist's stronger, and I'm hopin' the simmer will pit colour intil her cheek." But as he spoke his eyes were on a distant hill.

"I want a word with you, Amos. You and I are, I believe, true friends, and I can speak to you as to a brother. I have become aware of a horrid evil in this parish. There is that in the Wood which tempts men and women to abominations. With these eyes of mine I saw it on Beltane's Eve."

There was no answer.

"You were in the kirk yesterday, Amos, and you heard my sermon. The decision is on Woodilee to choose whom they will serve. You are my friend, and, apart from certain backslidings, a man of a Christian walk and conversation. I summon you to my aid, and conjure you by Christ who died for you, to tell me what you know of this great sin and who are the sinners."

Amos came to a standstill. He laid down his tools, and looked the minister in the face.

"Let it alane, sir. I rede ye, let it alane."

"In the name of God, what folly is this?" David cried. "Are you, too, my own familiar friend, entangled in this wickedness?"

The man's face crimsoned.

"Deil a haet! Na, na, I never could abide thae trokin's wi' the Wud. But oh, Mr. Sempill, ye're but a callant, and ye kenna the wecht o' the principalities and poo'ers that are against ye. Hae patience, sir, and gang cannily. Trust in the Word, whilk it is your duty to preach, to bring conviction o' sin in the Lord's ain gude time, for if ye're ettlin' [intending] to use the arm o' flesh it will fail ye."

It was the counsel which Isobel had given, and David's heart sank. What was it in Woodilee which made honest men silent and craven in the face of proved iniquity?

"Man, Amos," he cried, "I never thought to get a coward's counsel from you. Am I to reckon you among my enemies, and among God's enemies? I tell you I see my duty as clear before me as the Hill of Deer. I must unveil this wickedness and blast its practisers into penitence or I fail in my first duty as the minister of this parish. And from you, my friend, I get only silence and contumacy, and what is worse, the advice of a Laodicean. Alas! that you who have fought stoutly in your country's battles should be such a poor soldier in God's battles."

There was no answer. The two had resumed their walk, and the smith strode at a pace which was almost a run, his eyes steadily averted from his companion.

"This is my last word to you, Amos," said David, as they reached the turn where the loan ran to the manse. "Wednesday--the day after the morn--is the second Beltane, and I fear that that night there will be further evil in the Wood. I will go there and outface the Devil, but the flesh is weak, and I am one against many, and I would fain have a friend. Will you not bear me company?"

The smith stopped again. "Deil hae me if I gang near the Wud! Na, na, I'll no pit my heid intil ony sic wull-cat's hole. And, Mr. Sempill, be you guidit by an aulder man and bide at hame."

"You are afraid?"

"Ay. I'm feared--but mair for you than for mysel'."

"You're like the men of Israel that failed Gideon at the waterside," David cried angrily as he turned away.

The next two days were spent by the minister in a strange restlessness. He walked each afternoon some violent miles on the hilltops, but for the rest he stayed in the manse, principally in his study. Isobel believed him to be at prayer, and indeed he prayed long and fervently, but he was also busied about other things. Among his belongings was a small-sword, for he had won some skill of fence in Edinburgh, and this he had out and saw to its point and edge. Also he read much in books which were not divinity, for he felt himself a soldier, and would brace his spirit with martial tales. With Isobel he exchanged no word save commonplaces, and the old woman, who had the air of a scolded child, showed no desire to talk. His meals were set before him in silence, and silently the table was cleared. Amos Ritchie came to the manse on some small repairing job, and he too seemed to be anxious to get his work done and leave. David saw him arrive as he set out for a walk, and when he returned the shoulders of the smith were disappearing past the stable end.

Wednesday evening came, an evening of mellow light and a quiet sunset, and after his early supper David retired to his study to prepare himself for his task. He had already written out an account of what he had seen in the Wood and of what he proposed to do, and this he signed and directed under cover to Mr. Fordyce at Cauldshaw. Whatever mischance befell him, he had left a record. He had also written a letter to his father, setting forth what, in the event of his death, was to be the destination of his worldly goods. Then on his knees he remained for a while in prayer.

The clock struck nine, and he arose to begin his journey, strapping the sword to his middle, and taking also a great stick which the shepherd of the Greenshiel had made for him. The moon would rise late, and there was ample time.

But he found that the door of his study would not open. It had no lock, and had hung on a light hasp, but now it seemed to have bolts and bars. It was a massive thing of oak, and when he shook it it did not yield.

He shouted for Isobel, but there was no reply. Then he assaulted it furiously with knees and feet and shoulder, but it did not give. There was no hope from the window, which was a small square through which a child could not have crept.

Further attacks on the door followed, and futile shouting. By the time the late light had faded from the little window David had acknowledged the fact that he was imprisoned, and his first fury had ebbed from sheer bodily fatigue. But the clock had struck one before he attempted to make a bed on the floor, with for pillow a bag of chaff which Isobel had placed there for a winter footstool, and the dawn was in the eastern sky before he slept.

He was awakened by Isobel in the doorway.

"Peety on us," she wailed, "that sic a thing suld hae come to this hoose! Hae ye spent the nicht in this cauld chamber and no in your bed? The wyte's [blame] on me, for I got Amos Ritchie yestereen to put a bar on the door, for there's walth of guid books here and I wad like to steek the place when ye're awa' to the hills and me maybe in the kitchen. I maun hae steekit it to see if it wad wark, no kennin' ye were in inside. And syne I gaed doun to my gude- brither's to speir after his bairn, and I was late in getting back, and, thinks I, the minister will be in his bed and I'll awa' to mine. Puir man, ye'll be as stiff as a wand, and ye'll maybe hae got your death o' cauld. . . . See and I'll get ye a het drink, and your parritch's on the boil. . . . Wae's me that I didn' tak' a thocht . . ."

"Silence, woman, and do not cumber your soul with lies." David's white face as he strode from the room did more than his words to cut short Isobel's laments.

CHAPTER VIII

THE SECOND BLAST

On the following Sabbath the minister's text was, "When the light within you is darkness, how great is that darkness!" This time there was no faltering in the application. The congregation, men and women, were arraigned at the bar as sinners by deed or by connivance, and he had an audience hushed not in the ordinary Sabbath decorum, but in a fearful apprehension. Every moment he seemed to be about to name the sinner, and if he did not single out persons he made it blindingly clear that it was not for lack of knowledge. Never had he preached with greater freedom, never had passion so trembled in each sentence. Words seemed to be given him, stinging, unforgettable words that must flay the souls of the guilty. "Blinded self-deceivers," he cried, "you think you can tamper with devilry and yet keep your interest in Christ. You are set up with covenants, public and private, but I tell you that your covenant is with Death and Hell. The man who believes he is elected into salvation, and thinks that thereby he has liberty to transgress and that his transgressions will be forgiven him, has sinned against the Holy Ghost--that sin for which there is no forgiveness." He declared that till there was a general confession and repentance there would be no Communion in the parish of Woodilee, for those who sat down at the Lord's Table would be eating and drinking damnation to themselves. . . . But at the end he broke down. With tears in his eyes and a sob in his voice he besought a people whom he loved to abase themselves before the Mercy Seat. "You poor folk," he cried, "with your little dark day of life, with your few years of toil and cold and hunger before the grave, what have you if you have not Christ?" He was moved with an ecstasy of pity, and told them, like the Apostle, that if he could but save their souls, he was willing that his own should be cast away.

Not the oldest remembered such a sermon in the kirk of Woodilee, and the fame of it was soon to go abroad in the countryside. The place emptied in a strange silence, as if the congregation went on tiptoe, and men and women did not look at each other till they were outside the kirkyard gates. The elders did not await the minister in the session-house, and as David walked the hundred yards to the manse he saw what looked like the back of Peter Pennecuik, crouching behind a turf dyke to avoid a meeting.

These were days of loneliness and misery for the minister of Woodilee. He saw himself solitary among enemies, for even those whom he thought his friends had failed him. It was clear that Amos Ritchie had conspired with Isobel to imprison him in his study on the eve of the second Beltane, and though their motive was doubtless affection it but emphasized the hopelessness of his task. He had to bring conviction of sin into a parish where even the innocent were ready to cumber his arm. These honest creatures feared for him--what? Anger would choke him at the thought of such contempt for his sacred mission, and then awe would take its place, awe at the immensity of the evil with which he fought. "Principalities and powers," Amos had said--yes, the Powers of the Air and the Principalities of Darkness. He had no doubt that the Devil and his myrmidons were present in the Wood in bodily form, mingling with the worshippers, and that the tongues which he had heard were in very truth mutterings of the lost. There were times when ordinary human fear loosened his knees, and he longed to flee from the parish as from a place accursed. But his courage would return, and his faith, for he knew that the armies of Heaven were on his side, and wrath would cast out fear, wrath and horror at the seducers of his flock. Nevertheless in these days his nerves were frayed, he lay awake of nights listening anxiously for noises without, and he would awake suddenly in the sweat of a nameless terror.

But his chief burden was that he did not know how to shape his course. The pulpit rang with his denunciations, but there was no response; no stricken Nicodemus came to him by night. On the roads and at the house-doors people avoided his eyes. There were no more stones from Daft Gibbie--indeed Gibbie had resumed his fawning friendliness--but none waited to speak a word with him. Isobel had recovered her cheerfulness, and sought to atone for past misconduct by an assiduous attention to his comforts, but Amos Ritchie shunned him. And the children, too, who had been his chief allies. Perhaps their parents had warned them, for a group would scatter when he came near, and once when, coming up behind him, he laid a kindly hand on a boy's head, the child burst into tears and fled. What was the 'fama' of the minister which had been put about in Woodilee?

The worst of it was that he could contrive no plan of campaign. Evidence which was overwhelming to his own mind would not convince the Presbytery or the Sheriff. He could not bring a reasoned charge against any man or woman in the parish. As the days passed he began to sort out his flock in his mind as the guilty and the abettors. Some were innocent enough, save for the sin of apathy; but others he could believe to have shared in the midnight debauches--heavy-browed, sensual youths, women with shifty eyes, girls high-coloured and over-blown, whose sidelong glances seemed to hint at secrets, old wives, too, whose wild laughter he heard at cottage doors. But of one, his first certainty was giving way to doubt. Ephraim Caird's white face had got a wholesome tan from the summer sun, and he alone in the parish seemed to seek out the minister. He gave him a cheerful greeting when they met, spoke wisely of parish matters, had a word of humble commendation for the Sabbath discourses. "It's gaun to be a braw year for the aits," he said, "gin the weather hauds, and the lambs are the best I've yet seen on Chasehope hill. Let us hope, sir, that the guid seed ye've sown will come to as bountiful a hairst." The words were so simply spoken that they seemed no hypocrisy.

A plan of campaign! On that David could get no clearness, and the anxiety was with him at bed and board. He shrank from confessing himself to his brother-ministers, for what could they do to help him? Kirk Aller would pooh-pooh the whole thing, since Woodilee had been so forward in signing the Covenant. Bold would no doubt believe, but his remedy would be only a stiffer draught of doctrine. Even Mr. Fordyce at Cauldshaw seemed a broken reed, for Mr. Fordyce was an ailing saint, and this task was for the church militant. No, he must fight his battles alone, and trust to God to send him allies. He wanted men of violence, who would fight not with words but with deeds, Israelitish prophets who with their own hands cut down groves and uprooted altars and hewed Agag in pieces. And where would he find them in a countryside where the good were timid as sheep and their pastors like loud voices in a fog?

June was a month of hot suns and clear skies, when the hills were bone-dry and the deepest flowe-moss could be safely passed. It was weather for the high tops, and one afternoon David, walking off his restlessness on the Rood uplands, stumbled unexpectedly on a friend. For at the head of the glen where the drove-road crosses from Clyde to Aller, he fell in with the farmer of Reiverslaw leading his horse up a steep patch of screes.

This man, Andrew Shillinglaw, was something of a mystery both to parish and minister. He was a long lean fellow of some forty years, black-haired, black-bearded, whose sullen face was redeemed by a humorous mouth, so that the impression was of a genial ferocity. He was reputed the most skilful farmer in the place, and some held him a rival in worldly wealth to the miller, but beyond the fact that he had in Reiverslaw the best of the hill farms, there was no clue to his prosperity. He had the only good riding- horse in Woodilee, and was a notable figure on the roads, for he travelled the country like a packman. For weeks on end he would be away from home, and he was heard of in Galloway and the west and as far south as the Border, so that speculation about his doings became a favourite pastime among his neighbours. He neither sold nor bought in the parish, and he kept his own counsel, but his profession was clear enough had there been eyes to see. For he was dealer and middleman as well as farmer, and in a day when stock and produce scarcely moved beyond parish bounds, he sold and bought in outlying markets. In a district of home-keepers he was the sole traveller.

Few liked him, for there was always an undertone of satire in his speech. But all feared him, for his temper was on a hair-trigger. Drink made him quarrelsome, and the spence at Lucky Weir's had seen some ugly business, since with him blow followed fast on word. Three years before he had buried his wife, there were no children, and he lived at Reiverslaw with an aged cousin for housekeeper, who was half blind and wholly deaf. His attendance at the kirk was far from exemplary; in winter there were the drifts and the full bogs to detain him, and in summer he was as often as not on his travels. The Session, who did not love him, had talked of citing him to appear before them, but in the end they seemed to shrink from belling so formidable a cat.

At the head of the little pass, which in that country is called a "slack," he halted and let David approach him.

"A guid day to ye, sir," he cried. "We'll let Bess get her wind, for it's a lang gait frae Crawfordjohn. I rade ower yestereen to see the sma' Cumberland sheep that the Lowther herds are trying on yon hills. I hae nae great broo o' them. They'll maybe dae on yon green braes where the bite is short, but they're nae use for a heather country. . . . Sit ye doun, sir. What brings ye sae far ower the tops? Ye werena ettlin' to gie me a ca' in at Reiverslaw?"

David gladly stretched himself on the bent beside him. The man seemed willing to talk, and of late he had had little speech with his fellows.

"I came here for the caller air," he said, "and to drive ill humours from body and mind. There are whiles when I cannot draw breath in Woodilee."

"Ay," said the man. "Ay! Just so." He pursed his lips and looked at the minister under half-shut eyes.

"Were you born in this parish?" David asked.

"Na, na. Far frae that. I'm but an incomer, though I've had the tack o' Reiverslaw for a dizzen years. My father, honest man, was frae the Glenkens, and my mither cam' frae the Cairn side. I was born at a bit they ca' Dunscore, but I was a stirrin' lad in my young days and I've traivelled the feck o' the Lawlands, frae the Forth to the Solway. But now I've got my hinderlands doun in Woodilee, and it's like I'll lay my banes here."

The man spoke in a different voice from the people of the place, and to David he seemed as one detached from the countryside, sharing neither its interests nor affections. As he looked at him, sprawling in the heather bush with one foot on his horse's bridle, he had a sense of something assured and resolute and not unfriendly.

"Ye're an incomer like mysel', sir," Reiverslaw said after a pause. "What think ye o' Woodilee?"

"I think that the Devil has chosen this miserable parish for his own."

"Ay. . . . Well, I wadna say ye were wrang. I jaloused [guessed] frae your last discourse that ye were perplexed wi' the Enemy. And they tell me that ye've stirred up an unco byke against ye."

"Are you one of them?" David asked.

"No me. If there's fechtin' to be done, I'm on your side. I aye likit a bauld man, and it's a question, sir, if ye ken yoursel' how bauld ye are when ye offer to drive the Deil frae Woodilee."

David had got to his feet, for these were the first words of sympathy he had had.

"Andrew Shillinglaw, I command you to tell me if you have kept yourself clean from this mystery of evil which scourges the parish."

The man still sprawled on the ground, and the face he turned to the minister was twisted in a grim humour.

"Ay. I'll swear ony aith ye like. I'll no deny my backslidin's, and, as ye may ken, my walk and conversation's no to boast o'. But as sure as God made me, I wad burn off my richt hand in the fire afore I wad file mysel' wi' the Babylonish abominations o' the Wud. I whiles drink a stoup ower muckle, and I whiles gie a waur straik than I ettle when my bluid's het, but these are honest stumblin's whilk I hope the Lord will forgie. But for yon--" and he spat viciously.

"Then, if you are yourself clean from this evil, tell me what you know of it, and who are its chief professors."

"That's easy speirin' [asking], but ill to answer. How suld I ken the covens that rampage in the Wud? I bide cheek by jowl wi' the muckle black thing, and often I wish it was a field o' strae in a dry back-end so that I could set fire to it and see it burn frae Reiverslaw to Windyways, and frae Woodilee to the Aller side. But I've never entered the place in mirk or licht, for my wark's wi' sheep, and the honest beasts will no gang near it."

"But you must have heard . . ."

"I've heard nocht. I have maybe guessed, but it's no like I wad hear a cheep. I never gang near the clachan except to kirk or to Lucky Weir's, and the Woodilee folk are pawky bodies even when they're fou, and ony way I'm nae clatter-vengeance to be clypin' wi' auld wives at the roadside. But I've my ain notion o' what's gaun on, and I can tell ye, sir, it's gaun on in mony anither godly parochine in this kingdom o' Scotland, and it's been gaun on for hundreds o' years, long afore John Knox dang doun the Pape. But it's gotten a braw new tack in these days o' reformed and covenantit kirks. What do your Presbytries and Assemblies or your godly ministers ken o' the things that are done in the mirk? . . . What do they ken o' the corps in the kirkyairds buried o' their ain wull wi' their faces downwards? . . . They set up what they ca' their discipline, and they lowse the terrors o' Hell on sma' fauts like an aith, or profane talk on the Sabbath, or giein' the kirk the go-by, and they hale to the cutty-stool ilka lass that's ower kind to her joe. And what's the upshot? They drive the folk to their auld ways and turn them intil hypocrites as weel as sinners."

"Hush, man!" said the scandalized David. "That is impious talk."

"It's true a' the same, though it's maybe no for a minister's lugs. The Kirk is set against witchcraft, and every wee while a daft auld wife is brunt. But, God help us, that's but the froth on the pat. Na, na, Mr. Sempill. If you're lookin' to get to grips wi' the Adversary, it's no the feckless camsteery lad ye maun seek that likes a randan, or the bit lassie that's ower fond to wait for the Kirk's blessin', or the grannie that swears she rade to France on a kail-runt. It's the dacent body that sits and granes aneath the pu'pit, and the fosy professor that wags his pow and deplores the wickedness o' the land.--Yon's the true warlocks. There's saunts in Scotland, the Lord kens and I ken mysel', but there's some that hae the name o' saunts that wad make the Deil spew."

Reiverslaw had risen, and in his face was such a flame of fierce honesty that David's heart kindled. He had found an ally.

"Give me names," he cried. "I will denounce the sinner, though he were one of my own elders."

"I speak nae names. I have nae proof. But ye've seen yoursel'. They tell me ye broke in on the coven at their wark."

"I had but a glisk of them, before they beat the senses out of me. But I intend to go back to the Wood, and this time I shall not fail."

"Ay. Ye've a stout heart, Mr. Sempill."

"But I must have help. Out of the mouths of witnesses I must establish the truth, and the innocent in Woodilee are very fearful. I have nowhere to look but to you. Will you come with me when I return to the Wood?"

"I'll no say that, for there's maybe better ways o' guidin' it. But this I will say--I'll stand by ye; for may the Deil flee awa' wi' me or I see a guid man beat. There's my hand on't. . . . And now I maun be takin' the road again. Come na near the Reiverslaw, sir, for that would set the bodies talkin'. If ye want word wi' me, tell Richie Smail at the Greenshiel."

The knowledge that he had found a friend lightened David's heavy preoccupation of mind. Athanasius now was not alone against the world, and his path was not towards martyrdom but to victory. He walked with a more assured step and turned a bolder face to the furtive hostility of the parish. When he met Amos Ritchie he looked on him not in reproach but in defiance. His sermons were now less appeals than challenges, as of one whose course was proclaimed and whose loins were girded.

To his consternation he found that he now sat very loose in his devotion to the Kirk. The profession of religion was not the same thing as godliness, and he was coming to doubt whether the insistence upon minute conformities of outward conduct and the hair-splitting doctrines were not devices of Satan to entangle souls.

The phrases of piety, unctuously delivered, made him shudder as at a blasphemy. The fact that his only supporter was one looked askance at by strict professors confirmed his shrinking. Had not Christ set the publican and the sinner above the Pharisee?

One consequence of his new mood was that his thoughts turned again to the girl in Paradise. In his season of desolation he had not dared to think of her; she belonged to a world of light, and had no part in his perplexities. To let her image fill his memory seemed sacrilege, when that memory held so many foul shadows. But as the skies cleared for him her figure appeared again in the sunlight and he did not banish it, for it was she who was the extreme opposite of the horror of the Wood--she and her bright domain of oaks and hazels. He would go again to Paradise for his soul's comfort.

He chose a day when he was certain she would be there. There was a week of fiery weather--moist heat and heavy skies and flying thunderstorms, and after it came a spell of long bright days, when the sunshine had a dry tonic in it, and the afternoons were mellow and golden. On one such afternoon he crossed the Hill of Deer and entered the glen which divided the pines from the hazels.

Midsummer had changed the place. The burn-side turf was all thyme and eyebright and milkwort, with the stars of the grass of Parnassus in the wet places. The water was clear and small, and the cascades fell in a tinkling silver. He had no doubts as to his road now.

Paradise was among the hazels, but one could find it only by descending the glen to where the pines of the Wood began and then turning to the right towards the Greenshiel.

Presently the pines in a sombre regiment rose on the steep to the left. He looked at the beginning of the Wood with an awe which had now no fear in it. The place was hateful, but it could not daunt him. It was the battleground to which he was called. . . . On the edge of the trees was a great mass of dark foxgloves, the colour of blood, and they seemed to make a blood-trail from the sunlight into the gloom.

He turned up the right bank, and through hazel copses and glades, breast-high with bracken, he made his way as if by instinct. He found the shallow cup lined with birches and the blossoming rowans, and as he brushed through the covert he saw the girl sitting on the greensward by the well.

Motionless he watched her for a little, while his heart played strange pranks. She had a basket beside her full of flowers, and she was reading in a book. . . . She laid down the book, and shook her curls and dabbled her fingers in the water. She sang as she dabbled, low and clear in snatches, a song which he was to remember to his dying day:

"There's comfort for the comfortless, And honey for the bee, And there's nane for me but you, my love, And there's nane for you but me."

She crooned the verse twice, broke off to watch a ring-ouzel, and then sang again:

"It's love for love that I have got, And love for love again, So turn your high horse heid about And we will ride for hame, my love, And we will ride for hame."

He would fain have lingered and watched her, but he felt like an eavesdropper on her privacy. So "Mistress Katrine!" he cried softly, and "Mistress Katrine" a second time.

She sprang to the alert like a bird. Her face, when she saw him, showed no welcome.

"I give you good-day, sir," she said. "Have you maybe lost your road?"

"I am seeking Paradise," he replied.

"It is the quest of all mortals, they tell me. But the ministers say it is not to be found on earth."

"I was seeking the earthly one to which you yourself first led me."

"You entered then by my invitation, but I do not think I bade you come again."

"Then I beg for admission, mistress, for indeed I have sore need of Paradise."

She looked at him curiously. "You look older--and sadder. I have not been to your kirk, but they tell me that you are scorching the souls of your folk with your terrors."

"Would to God I could scorch them into salvation! . . . I have been in dire straits, Mistress Katrine. For I came again to find Paradise and I found it not, but stumbled into Hell."

The girl looked at him with compassionate eyes.

"You may sit down in Paradise," she said. "I permit you. And I will give you some of my wild strawberries. Tell me what has troubled you."

He told her of the doings of Beltane Eve, stumblingly, with many omissions. He told her of his strife with his parishioners, of his loneliness, of the mission to which he was vowed. "I am resolved," he said, "that though I go on alone I will not fail in courage. Your Montrose's comfort is mine--that the arm of the Lord is not shortened."

The girl brooded.

"Did you come here to find me?"

"I had a conviction that you would be in Paradise. This is no tale for a maid's ear, but I came here to warn you, mistress. The long glen that runs down to the Rood Mill is a frontier-line, which if you pass you are in the land of darkness. I found you first among the pines, and I beseech you go not again among them, though it were at high noon, for yon Wood is accursed."

She nodded. "I felt it too. When spring was passing I felt a gloom come over me as I walked there, and one day a terror seized me and I ran and ran till I was among the hazels. I cannot bear even to be in sight of the dark trees. You say that there is witchcraft there." She lowered her voice and her eyes were solemn. "What is this witchcraft?"

"I cannot tell, save that it is the nethermost works of darkness, and that it has seduced the hearts of my unhappy people. . . . God help me, but I have seen with my eyes what I cannot forget. . . . There is no smooth ministry for me, for now I am a soldier of Christ and must be fighting till I have got the victory."

"And you are alone?"

"I have one who will stand by me." And he told her of Reiverslaw.

"Nay, you have another," she cried. "You have me for a friend, and you have this greenwood for a sanctuary. If I cannot fight by your side, you will know that I am here and that I am wishing you well. See, I make you free of Paradise. It is yours now, as well as mine." She held out her hand.

He took off his hat.

"You were singing," he said, "and your song was true, for here's 'comfort for the comfortless.' You have put steel into my bones, Mistress Katrine. If I can come here and speak with you at times, it will be like the water beside the gate of Bethlehem to King David. . . . I will know when you are here without your sending me word."

"Then there is witchcraft in the greenwood," she said, smiling gravely, "for I, too, knew that you were coming to-day before you came."

CHAPTER IX

BEFORE LAMMAS

One day in July David saddled his horse and rode to Kirk Aller for a Presbytery meeting. He found a bewildered brotherhood. The usual "exercises" were omitted, there was no prelection on a set doctrinal theme for the benefit of the younger ministers, the sittings in the kirk were occupied mainly with prayers for a humbled Sion and a distracted country, and the dinner thereafter in the Cross Keys was not notable for good fellowship. But it was a crowded gathering, and among the lay members in the kirk was Ephraim Caird.

At the meal Mr. Mungo Muirhead, primed with letters from Edinburgh, gave ill news of the war in the North. Montrose the recusant continued to win battles, and was even now marching southward with his savage Irishry to strike at the citadel. "What for does Davie Leslie no hasten," he cried, "and what profits it to have a covenanted State and a purified Kirk if a mailed Amalekite can hunt our sodgers from Dan to Beersheba? I tell you, sirs, this war which has hitherto been fought among Hieland glens will soon be at our ain doorcheeks, and our puir folk will be called to testify, not with voice and word and the scart of a pen, but with sufferings and revilings and bloody murderings. Forth and Aller may yet run red, and the hand of death be on the Lowdon fields. Are we prepared, I ask, and I ask it yet again?

Whatna gifts will we bring to the altar in the coming day of sacrifice?"

His fears had given dignity to the minister of Kirk Aller. The man was a fighter, for his mouth shut tight, and there was a spark of fire in his heavy eyes. Nor was Mr. Proudfoot of Bold less ready for the fray. He had got himself a pair of great boots, and looked a very Ironside as he expanded his big chest and groaned assent to his leader's warning.

"Let us see that there is no Canaanitish thing in our midst," Mr. Proudfoot cried, "for the purge of the Lord is nigh. And let Israel dwell in unity, for a house divided shall not stand. These are the twin counsels for this day of wrath, a pure cause and a brotherly people. These, I say, are the dams with which to stem the tide of the heathen's rage."

"And that's a word in season for you, Mr. Sempill," said Mr. Muirhead. "I hear ye've set the haill parish of Woodilee by the lugs with wanton accusations. You'll admit none to the Table, says you, till there is public confession of some unkenned iniquity. I applaud zeal in a young minister, but it seems you've fair got your leg ower the trams, and the serious folk of Woodilee are troubled to ken what ye mean. Have a care, Mr. Sempill, lest this zeal of yours be but human impatience. This is no time to sow confusion among God's people."

The minister of Kirk Aller had lost his air of rough good-humour. It was a hard face and an inquisitorial eye that he bent on David.

"I take my stand on the first of Mr. Proudfoot's counsels," said the latter. "If the day of trial is coming, our cause must be pure, and there must be no Canaanitish thing in our midst. When I am clear about the sins of Woodilee, the Presbytery will have further news of me."

The young man's speech was too assured to please Mr. Muirhead. He drew down his eyebrows till they formed a straight line bisecting his huge expanse of face.

"Have a care, have a care, I counsel you," he said crossly. "I can tell you that there's many an auld exercised professor in Woodilee that's sore concerned about your doings."

Mr. Proudfoot added his reproof. "When I mind on the precious work I witnessed in that very parish in the month of March, I will not believe that the Devil has got the master hand. Examine yourself, I rede you, Mr. Sempill, and see if the beam be not in your own eye."

David rode away from Kirk Aller in the company of Mr. Fordyce of Cauldshaw, but they had not ridden a mile before there was a clatter of hoofs behind them, and the minister of Bold joined himself to their company. His beast was fractious, having had an unaccustomed feed of oats in the Cross Keys stable, and Mr. Proudfoot, since he was an awkward horseman, had to spend much of his energy in keeping it to the road. But what time he could spare from his task he devoted to catechizing David, and for the three miles during which their course lay together his tongue never stopped.

"There's an ill 'fama' of you gone abroad, Mr. Sempill, and it is my duty as your elder in the Lord's service to satisfy myself thereanent. It is reported that you pervert the doctrine of election into grace, maintaining that this blessed estate may be forfeit by a failure in good works, as if the filthy rags of man's righteousness were mair than the bite of a flea in face of the eternal purposes of God."

"I say that a man who believes that his redemption through Christ gives him a licence to sin is more doubly damned than if he had never had a glimpse of grace."

"But ye maun distinguish. The point is far finer than that, sir. I will construe your words, for there is an interpretation of them which is rank heresy."

The task of construing and distinguishing did not fare well, for every few minutes the teeth of Mr. Proudfoot were shaken in his head by his horse's vagaries. He had just reached a point of inordinate subtlety, when the track to Bold branched off, and his animal, recognizing at last the road home, darted down it at a rough gallop. The last seen of the minister of Bold was a massive figure swaying like a ship in a gale, and still, if one might trust the echoes the wind brought back, distinguishing and construing.

Even Mr. Fordyce's grave face smiled as he watched the fleeing Boanerges.

"He is a wilful man, and he has a wilful beast. But what is this rumour in the countryside, Mr. David? I fear that you are finding Woodilee a dour rig to plough."

"What do they say in Cauldshaw?"

"I have been little about of late, for these last weeks I've been sore troubled with my bowels. I'm like the Psalmist--the Lord trieth my reins in the night watches--and I've never made out my visit to you to have a read of Cardanus. But I cannot but hear orra bits of news from the next parish, and the speak in the countryside is that you have uncovered the nakedness of Woodilee and preach siccan sermons that the een of the folk turn inward in their heads. What's the truth of it, Mr. David? My heart yearns over you as if you were my own mother's son."

"I have uncovered a great wickedness--but not yet all. I wait and watch, and when I have fuller knowledge I will know better how to act. You told me the first day we met that Woodilee had an ill reputation, and, sorrow on me! I have proved the justice of your words. And I greatly fear that it is the loudest professors that are deepest in the mire."

"Man, David, that is a grievous business. Is it the Wood?"

"It is the Wood, and the blackest kind of witchcraft. Some old devilry of the heathen has lingered in that place, and the soul of my miserable parish is thirled to it. You will not find in Scotland a doucer bit, for there are no public sins and shortcomings. Man, there's times when Woodilee seems as quiet and dead as a kirkyard. But there's a mad life in its members, and at certain seasons it finds vent. In the deeps of night and in the heart of the Wood there are things done of which it is shameful even to speak."

"What witness have you?"

"My own eyes. I stumbled upon one of their hellish Sabbaths."

"God be kind to us! I have heard tell of siccan things, and I have read of them in old books, but I never experienced them. I'm positive they're not in Cauldshaw, for the place is ower bare and bright and the wind blows ower clean on our braes. There's no cover for the abominations which must be done in darkness. But I have aye had a scunner of yon Wood. . . . It's a queer thing the heart of man, Mr. David, and there's that in my own that whiles terrifies me. The work of redemption is done in an instant, but the job of regeneration is a lifetime's; and the holiest saint on his death-bed is but a bag of rottenness compared to the purity to which he shall yet attain. And at times I'm tempted to think that our way and the Kirk's way is not God's way, for we're apt to treat the natural man as altogether corrupt, and put him under over- strict pains and penalties, whereas there's matter in him that might be shaped to the purposes of grace. If there's original sin, there's likewise original innocence. When I hear the lassie Katrine Yester singing about the door at Calidon, I have an assurance of God's goodness as sharp as I ever got in prayer. If you ban this innocent joy it will curdle and sour, and the end will be sin. If young life may not caper on a spring morn to the glory of God, it will dance in the mirk wood to the Devil's piping."

Mr. Fordyce stopped short with a rueful face. "That's for your own ear, Mr. David. If the bruit of what I have said came to the manse of Bold, Mr. Ebenezer would be for delating me to the Presbytery. But if it's not orthodox it's good sense."

"I doubt orthodoxy is no salve against sin," said David. "The devils, it is written, believe and tremble, and it's my surmise that the leader of the witches' coven in Woodilee could stand his ground with Bold himself on matters of doctrine."

"You have formidable foes."

"I have a whole parish, for even those who are free of guilt are too timid to lift a hand. Likewise I have my Kirk Session."

Mr. Fordyce exclaimed.

"And it looks like I will have the Presbytery. I'm in ill odour with Mr. Muirhead for dividing Israel, and to Mr. Proudfoot I smack of heresy."

"You've aye gotten me on your side," said Mr. Fordyce. "No that I'm much of a fighter, for my bowels melt and my speech sticks in my throat and I sit like a dumb ox, and syne mourn on my bed in the night watches that I have been found wanting. But my heart is with you, Mr. David, and what voice my infirmities permit me, and you'll be never out of my prayers. . . . Come to Cauldshaw whenever ye long for speech with a friend. I can aye give you sympathy if I canna give you counsel."

But when David three days later turned his horse in the direction of Cauldshaw, it was not to the manse he went, but to the tower of Calidon. For Katrine Yester had become for him the only light on his path. She personified the cause for which he fought, the fair world that stood in contrast to the obscene shades, and since their last meeting in Paradise she was no longer a flitting wood-nymph, but a woman of flesh and blood and heart. He longed to see her in the house where she dwelt and among her own people.

But there was no Katrine in Calidon that afternoon, for she had gone to the greenwood. It was a still day of July in which no cloud tempered the heat of the sun, but the great upper chamber in the tower was cool and dusky. He asked for Mistress Saintserf, and was received by that grim lady in state, for she kept him waiting while she donned a new toy and kerchief for the occasion. She spoke a Scots as broad as any shepherd's wife, but the sharp vowels of Edinburgh took the place of the softer Border tones. Large and gaunt and domineering, her high-nosed face and prim mouth were mellowed by an audacious humour. Katrine had clearly never spoken of him (at which he was glad), but she knew him by repute and by his connection with the miller of the Roodfoot. She entertained him with shortcake of her own baking and elder wine of her own brewing, and her tone mingled the deference of a good woman towards a spiritual guide and the freedom of an old woman towards a young man.

"That gilpie o' mine suld have been here, but she's awa' to the hill. As weel try to keep a young juke frae the water as Katrine frae stravaigin' the countryside. And her bred denty in France and England whaur there are nae hills! If she had a joe [sweetheart] I wad say nocht, but she has nae joe but the whaups."

He asked concerning Nicholas Hawkshaw.

"And that's speirin'!" she cried. "He's fechtin' and him a lameter, but whaur he's fechtin' and in what cause the Lord alone kens! Since he gaed off wi' Tam Purves three months syne sorrow a word has come frae him. He's maybe in England and maybe in France, and maybe ryngin' with Montrose, and I'll wager, wherever he is, him and his swird and Tam and his firelock are in the het o't. Ye'll no fetter a Hawkshaw, and they can nae mair bide in the ae place than a puddock on a brae, as my puir sister that was married on him kenned ower weel. And the same bluid's in Katrine, wha suld hae been a laddie, and a tinkler laddie, for it's no her that will mind her seam or watch the pot when the sun's shinin'. She's a fine lassie for a' that, but by ordinar' forgetfu'. I wish I saw her wed."

Of Woodilee she had many questions to ask.

"It's a' Hawkshaw land, but I never likit the folk. There's a wheen fosy bodies yonder, wha pray mair with their tongues than their hearts, and they're as keen at a niffer [bargain] as a Musselburgh wabster--aye wi' the puir face and the greetin' word when it comes to payin' siller. Auld Dobbie in Murchison's Close-- he's our doer [man of business], ye maun ken, as his father was afore him--he has had mony a sair tuilzie for our bits o' rents. Now that Nicholas is at the wars it's my shouther that has to carry the burden, and there's never a post frae Embro but brings me Dobbie's scribin'. Ye'll ken that the mailin' o' Crossbasket is to let, and whaur am I to get a guid tenant wi' the land in siccan a steer?"

David told her the news he had heard at Kirk Aller.

"Keep us a'!" she cried. "God send Nicholas binna wi' Montrose, or we'll hae him and Tam Purves here rauvagin' his ain lands, and if Argyll gets the upper hand they'll be glorifyin' God at the end o' a tow in the Grassmarket. Hech, sir, we're surely faun on the latter days when, it is written, confusion will be on the people. I'm for the Kirk, but they tell me Montrose is likewise for the Kirk as he conceives it, and between her twa well-wishers it's like our auld Sion will get uncoly mishandled. But I hae nae broo o' poalitics. My poalitics is just an auld wife's poalitics that wants to be left in peace by her fireside. . . . But ye say Montrose is mairchin' south? He'll be for England, and that means the road by Aller Water. I'll hae to kilt my coats and pit the tower o' Calidon in a state of defence against Nicholas or ony ither, for if I let the laird intil his ain house we'll hae to answer for't before the Privy Council."

It was plain that Mistress Saintserf was not ill-pleased with David, for she talked freely and would hardly let him go.

"Ye're ower young for the sacred callin'," she told him when at last he took his leave. "And ye're ower wise-like a man for a minister. Saunts suld hae weak stomachs, like our ain Mr. Fordyce; it gars them sit loose to earthly affections."

"I would put up with his affliction if I could get one-half of his goodness," said David.

"'Deed that's weel spoken. I'm sure o' Heaven if I can get haud o' the strings of Mr. James's cloak. Never heed an auld wife's clavers. Come back and prie our grosarts when they're ripe, and if ye see that lass o' mine on the hill tell her I'm waitin' for her wi' a besom."

On his way home David had no sight of Katrine, but the next afternoon he met her in Paradise. She came to him smiling and friendly as a boy.

"You have been to Calidon and seen Aunt Grizel. I congratulate you on your conquest, sir, for my aunt is now your devout partisan and you have won another friend in this countryside. But what is this news of the Lord Marquis?"

They whiled away the summer afternoon with talk, rambling sometimes through the oak glades, but always returning to the nook by the spring, while David kept a jealous eye on the declining sun. The girl must be well on her way to Calidon before the first dusk began. When he came again they did not talk of his troubles, nor even of Montrose, but of little things--her childhood in France, her kin, the tales of the glen, his own youth at Edinburgh College. For she was not an ally so much as a refuge. When he was with her he was conscious that the world was still large and sunlit, the oppression lifted from his spirit, he saw himself not only victor in the quarrel, but a messenger of God with a new gospel to perplexed mankind.

One evening, when he had seen the girl descend through the hazels to the Rood vale, and had turned back towards the shoulder of the Hill of Deer, he saw a man's figure slanting across the hill as if coming from Melanudrigill. It was Reiverslaw, but though their paths all but intersected the farmer did not stop to talk. He waved a hand in greeting. "Ye suld gie a look in at the Greenshiel," he shouted. "They tell me Richie Smail is in need of consolation."

David took the hint, passed word to Richie, and the next evening met Reiverslaw in the herd's cottage. "Tak' a look round the faulds, Richie," said the master. "Me and the minister has something to say to ither," and the two were left alone in the dim sheiling.

"I've been spyin' oot the land," said Reiverslaw, "like the lads that Joshua sent afore him into Canaan. I canna say I likit the job, but I've been through the Wud east and west, and I've found the bit whaur the coven meets aside the auld altar. I think I could find the road till't on the blackest nicht. And I've been speirin' judeeciously in Woodilee."

"But surely they did not answer?"

The dark face of the farmer had a crooked grin.

"Trust me, I was discreet. But I've a name for takin' a stoup ower muckle, and when the folk thocht I was fou, my lugs were as gleg as a maukin's. They're preparin' for another Sabbath, and it fa's on the Lammas Eve. On that nicht you and me maun tak' the Wud."

David shivered, and the man saw it.

"The flesh is weak," he said, "and I'm feelin' like that mysel'. But you an' me are no the anes to pit our hand to the plew-stilts and turn back. Mr. Sempill, are ye young enough to speel a tree?"

"I was a great climber as a laddie."

"Weel, ye'll hae to be a laddie aince again. And I'll tell ye mair. Ye'll hae to leave this place afore the Lammas-tide. Is there ony bit ye can bide at, not abune twenty miles frae Woodilee?"

"There is my cousin at Newbiggin."

"Weel, to Newbiggin ye gang, and your departure maun be public. Crack about it for days afore. Tell the auld wife at the manse and deave her wi' your preparations. For, if you're no oot o' the parish in guid time, ye'll be lockit in your chamber, as ye were on the second Beltane. And ye maun be in the Wud that nicht as a witness, for there's just us twasome, you and me, and we maun be witnesses that the Presbytery and the Sheriff and the Lords in Embro cannot deny."

"I see that. But have you found out nothing more in Woodilee?"

"I've gotten a hantle o' suspeecions. Man, ye'd wonder to see how chief me and Chasehope are these days. I've been ower to see his English bull, and I've ta'en his advice about sheep, and I've sell't him a score o' gimmers at a price that made me voamit. He thinks I'm a dacent, saft, through-ither body, wi' his wits sair fuddled by strong drink, and has nae back-thochts o' ane that's just clay in his hands. . . . Ay, and I've been payin' muckle attention to his hen-house. His wife, ye maun ken, is a notable hen-wife, and she has a red cock that there's no the like o' in the countryside. I took Rab Prentice up wi' me to Chasehope toun, and I bade Rab tak' special note o' the red cock."

"But I do not see the purpose . . ."

"Ye needna--yet. Ye'll be tell't in guid time. I'm thinkin' o' the process afore the Presbytery, and it's witnesses I'm seekin'. I hae twa honest men, my herds Richie Smail and Rab Prentice, but Richie's ower auld to tak' the Wud and Hirplin' Rab wad dee afore he would pit his neb inside it. So there's just you and me for the chief job, though the ither twa will hae their uses."

The imminence of the trial made David's heart sick, for he had now brooded for three months on the mysteries of the Wood, whereas at Beltane he had stumbled upon them in hot blood unwittingly. He was confident in his cause, but he believed most firmly that the Devil in person would be his antagonist, and the cool tones of Reiverslaw struck him with admiration and awe.

"Man, you speak as calm as if you were making ready for a clipping. Is it that you do not believe in the power of Satan?"

"I believe in God," said the man, "and I've seen ower muckle o' the world no to believe in the Deil. But I'll no be feared o' a Deil that misguides auld wives and tak's up wi' rotten peats like Chasehope, and though he comes in a brimstane lowe I'll hae a nick at him."

Then began for David a time of doubt and heart-searching. He could not share the robust confidence of Reiverslaw, for his memory of Beltane was too clear and he had lived too long under its shadows. His imagination, always quick and easily kindled, ran riot, and he saw the Wood as an abode of horrid mysteries, which spread into subtle ramifications of evil the more he pondered them. His secular learning was so much fuel to this fire. Courage did not fail him, but brightness died out of his world, and he knew himself condemned to tread a dark winepress alone.

It was the thought of Katrine that most disquieted him. The Wood, the whole parish, the very mission on which he was engaged, seemed to him one vast pollution, to be kept hidden for ever from youth and innocence. The girl must not be allowed to come within sight of the skirts of it. There could be no friendship between them, and it was his first duty to warn her.

So when they met in Paradise it was a shamefaced young man that stood before her, a young man with a white face who kept his eyes on the ground and spoke terrible things. Words came unreadily, but his broken speech was more moving than eloquence. He bade her keep to the clean precincts of Calidon and come not even near the greenwood. God's curse was on the parish, and in the judgment preparing innocent might share with guilty. As for himself, he was no friend for such as she.

"I am too heavily burdened," he stammered. "I must touch pitch, and my hands will be defiled. I will blight your youth with my dark duties. . . . I will never come again to this place, and I plead with you to come no more, for it is too near the Enemy's country. . . . Go now, I beg of you, and forget that you have ever seen me and called me friend. You will torture me if you bide. . . ."

There was more of the same sort, and then David stopped, confident that he had done his purpose, and that no proud girl would linger in the face of such a warning. He waited, very cold and lonely at heart, and he thought he heard her departing feet on the grass.

But when he raised his eyes she had not moved, and her face was smiling.

CHAPTER X

WHAT THE MOON SAW

There was great heat at the end of July--sultry, thunderous weather, when the hills drowsed under a haze and the sun's beams seemed to be the more torrid for the screen of vapour through which they fell. The heavens were banking up for the Lammas rains. But each evening the skies cleared, and the night was an amethyst dome sprinkled with stars.

David made a great to-do about his visit to Newbiggin. On the Monday morning he announced it to Isobel, and in an hour the word had gone through the village. His housekeeper seemed to receive the news with relief. "Blithe I am to hear it, sir. Folk suld whiles change their ground like bestial, and ye've been ower lang tethered to this parochine. Newbiggin will be a caller bit in this lown weather, and while ye're awa' I'll get your chamber cleaned and the stairs washed doun. Dinna haste to come back, for I'll no look for ye or Setterday."

He set off on the Tuesday after midday, and there were many eyes in Woodilee to mark his going. That night he duly slept at Newbiggin, but the next day, which was Lammas Eve, he left his cousin's house and rode up Clyde water into the farthest moors. It was a wide circuit, which brought him in the afternoon to the uplands which separate Rood from Annan. All day he had been out of sight of human dwelling, and the first he saw was in the dusk, when he descended upon the tower of Calidon by the glen of the Calidon burn. At Calidon he left his horse with the grieve, promising to return for it on the morrow, and, with one look at the lit windows of the tower, he set out on foot to ford the Rood. About nine o'clock in the mulberry gloaming he reached the cottage of the Greenshiel.

Three figures greeted him there. One was the herd of the outer hirsel, Richie Smail; another was Rab Prentice, the herd of the home hirsel, who sat on the turf deas at the cottage-end with his crutch beside him; the third was Reiverslaw himself, who was also seated, smoking a pipe of tobacco.

"Ye're in braw time, Mr. Sempill," said the last. "Did ye pass ony folk on the road?"

"I have seen no man since the morning, except the Calidon grieve half an hour syne."

"And that's just as weel. Richie, kindle the cruisie, for our job is better done indoors."

The feeble light in the hut revealed a curious assembly. The two shepherds had faces of portentous gravity, and their twitching mouths and restless eyes were proof of an extreme discomfort. Reiverslaw wore his usual frieze small-clothes and boot-hose, but he had no coat, though he had slung on his arm what might have been that garment. He flung this on the settle. "It's ower het to wear that muckle maud till the time comes. We maun get to business, Mr. Sempill, for you should be on the road afore the moon rises. We're here to get our plan strauchtit oot and there's jimp [scarcely] time. Rab Prentice, ye've been twice wi' me to Chasehope in the last se'en days. Ye mind the braw red cock the wife has gotten?"

"Fine," said the shepherd.

"There's no sic another fowl in the countryside?"

"That I'll engage."

"Therefore if I show ye the morn a pluckin' o' red feathers, ye'll jalouse it's the Chasehope cock?"

"Ay. But I'm no gaun intil the Wud . . . not even in braid daylicht."

"If I bid ye, ye'll gang, Rab Prentice, though I suld carry ye myself. . . . Now, secondly, as the ministers say. Do ye see this bottle? Smell it, a' three of ye. That's a smell ye never fand afore? It's what they call oil of hennyseed, and I got it frae a horse-doctor at Carlisle. I'll wager there's no anither phial o' the same between here and Embro. It's a smell ye'll no sune forget. Pit a dab on yer sleeves to remind ye o't. If the three o' us gangs to Chasehope the morn and finds Chasehope's breeks and Chasehope's sark stinkin' o' this oil, ye'll be able to swear to it, and to swear that I showed it you this verra nicht and that ye kenned the smell when ye fand it again."

The two men agreed, sniffing the drop on their sleeve.

"Thirdly," said Reiverslaw, "I'm gaun to turn mysel' intil a guisyard."

He picked up the thing he had been carrying, and revealed it as a cloak of deerskins which fitted like a loose jerkin. Over his head he drew a cap of skins with slits for his eyes, a roughly-shaped nozzle like a deer's, and on the top the horns of a goat.

"Save us a'!" Richie cried, as he saw his master stand up, his lean, active body surmounted by a beast's head. "Save us a', ye're no gaun to tamper wi' the accursed thing?"

"That's what I ettle, but the intention is guid, and it's by our intentions we'll be judged, as Mr. Sempill will tell ye. Look at me, ye daft auld fules, for there's naething to be feared o'. I'm for the Wud the nicht, and it's my purpose to bide in cover till the folk are half dementit, and syne, when their een are blind, to join them. I've a notion that there will be some wark wi' the red cock, and I'd like a feather or twa as a keepsake. And I've a sort of notion that my auld friend Chasehope will be there; so as a token o' friendship I'll pit saut on his tail--whilk means that if I get the chance I'll anoint his dowp wi' the hennyseed. Now, you twa, take tent and listen to me. Ye will swear that I telled ye what I have telled ye, and that ye saw me at the Greenshiel dressed up like a merry-andrew. The horns suld hae been a stag's, but I was feared o' hankin' them in the busses, so the puir auld Reiverslaw billy-goat had to dee."

He was a crazy sight with the goat's head on him, and a formidable sight without it, for as he stood in that dusk beside two men bent with labour, the one maimed and the other past the allotted span of human years, David had an impression of something desperate and fearless and light-hearted. The shepherds were clearly torn between loyalty and terror, and he himself, while firm enough in his resolve, had to keep his thoughts battened down to prevent his knees knocking. But Reiverslaw seemed to have no fears. He had set about the thing as cannily as if he were selling sheep at Lockerbie fair, and now, with a venture before him which not two other men in Scotland would have contemplated, he was notably the least embarrassed of the party.

"I saw three pyets [magpies] flee intil the Wud this morning," said Prentice, "and but ane cam' back. That's an unco freit [omen] for the beginnin' o't!"

"Haud your tongue, ye auld wife," said Reiverslaw. "Freits fa' to them that fear them, and I'm no gaun to fash my heid about twa jauds o' birds. . . ."

"I had a vision yestereen," Richie put in. "I saw the haill land o' Scotland like a field o' aits, white until the harvest, the haill land frae John o' Groats to Galloway, a' but the parish o' Woodilee, whilk was unplewed and rough wi' briars and thrissles. An' says I to mysel', 'Whatever place is yon?' and says a voice to me, 'That's what we ca' the Deil's Baulk in the gospel field o' Scotland.'"

"And a very true observe, for Deil's Baulk is just what the Wud is, and it's for us to pit a plew intill't and mak' a fire o' the wastry. Set bite and sup afore the minister, Richie."

The shepherd produced some oatcakes, of which David ate only a mouthful, for though he had had no food since morning, his throat was dry and his tongue like a stick. He drank, however, a pint of buttermilk.

"Kirn-milk for you?" the host asked of Reiverslaw. "I hae nae yill, but Rab has brocht a flask o' aquavitty ye gied him at the lambin'."

"I'll hae spring water. Nae strong drink for me, for this nicht I'm like Jonadab the son of Rechab. . . . Are ye ready, Mr. Sempill? Ye maun start first, for ye've a tree to speel. There's nae hurry for me till the Deil begins his pipin'."

"You are either strong in the faith, or of a very stout heart," said David admiringly.

"No as strong as I might be," was the answer. "Afore we part, wad it no be weel for you to pit up a prayer?"

The minister prayed--and it was as if he confessed alone to his God in his closet. He himself was strengthened by it, and the comfort of Richie and Rab was visibly enlarged. But Reiverslaw stood through the devotions in no very devout position, and from him came none of the responses which flowed from the others. Before the "Amen" he had his goat-cap on, and was peering at the rising moon. He made his staff sing as he whirled it.

David took his strange confederate's hand, and his own shook. Reiverslaw noted his trepidation.

"Fear nocht, sir. It'll gang ill wi' the wirriecow gin we meet him. But what brocht a man o' peace like you into this tuilzie?"

"Jealousy for the honour of my God. And you? For it is less your quarrel than mine."

The man grinned. "Write it down that Andra Shillinglaw couldna see an honest man beat, and that he didna like kail-worms."

David had many times gone over in his mind the route to the glade of the altar, and had compared notes with Reiverslaw that very night. The distance was less than three miles, and he had a couple of hours to reach the place and still be in position well before midnight. As on all the nights of the past week, the oppressive haze of the day had lifted, and the sky rose to an infinite height, thick studded with stars, for the moon was only new risen. David made his way to the dividing glen between the pines and the hazels in a miserable disquiet. He had lost the first fierce anger which had stiffened him for his frustrated expedition on the eve of the second Beltane, and his tacit ostracism all summer by the folk of Woodilee had engendered a profound self-distrust. Even the thought of Katrine Yester did not nerve him; she belonged to a world separated by impassable gulfs from that black necromancy which he warred against. Nor did the fact that he had an ally comfort him, for Reiverslaw, he greatly feared, fought in his own strength and not in that of the Lord, and in such a strife the arm of flesh could not avail them. As he stumbled through the dark undergrowth David's lips moved in anxious prayers.

He entered the pines, and, shaping his course by the low line of cliffs, came to the place where he had first met Katrine. Thus far he felt that he was not wholly outside the pale of kindly things. But after that he was in enemy country, and the moon was still too low to give him help. He wasted half an hour in the thickets, till by a strong effort of will he forced himself to take his bearings and remember Reiverslaw's instructions. He scrambled up hill again till he was in touch with the outcrop of rock, and then suddenly found himself looking down on the glade where stood the altar.

It was very dark, and the stone was only a ghostly blur. But the darkness was a blessing, for the place was not as he had seen it before, and the sight of it did not revive the terrors he had feared. It looked no more than a woodland glade, and the fact that a rabbit scurried from under his feet seemed a friendly omen. On the far side the trees grew thick, and he selected a gnarled Scots fir as his perch for the night. Its trunk, branchless for sixty feet, was too thick to climb, but he found a younger and slimmer tree, up which he could squirm and from its upper branches traverse to the other. He had not tried the game since he was a boy, and at first his legs and arms seemed too feeble; but the exercise warmed him, and after twice sliding back to the ground, he at last reached the umbrella-like spread of the crest. To gain the other tree proved more difficult than he had thought, and he was compelled to let his body swing and make a long stretch with his right arm. But the task was accomplished in the end, and he found himself on a platform of crooked fir boughs, hidden from everything but the stars, and with a view through the gaps of the branches to the glade below him.

He had now a clear sight of the sky. The moon was three-quarters up, and the whole of Melanudrigill, with its slopes and valleys, was washed in silver. He was in it and yet above it and outside it, like a man on a hillside looking into a cleft. He made his body comfortable in a crutch of the tree, and looked down on the stage beneath him. It was now lighting up, and the altar was whitened by a stray moonbeam. For the first time that night he felt his spirits returning. The oppression of the Wood was not realized on this outer shell of it, for here only winged things dwelt, and the unclean things of the dark had no wings.

In this happier mood his eyes sought the whereabouts of Calidon. It was hidden by a ridge, the ridge to the west where lay Paradise. The thought gave him an unreasoning pleasure. He was not cut off from the world of light, for, whatever befell on the earth beneath him, he had but to lift up his eyes and they rested on a happier country.

As the moon rose, the multitudinous little noises of a wood at night were hushed. There was a sleepy muttering of cushats to the south of him, and then, with a clatter which made him jump, the birds rose in a flock and flew across the valley. After that there was no sound until the music began.

There was no fixed moment for its beginning, for it seemed to steal insensibly into the air. And it was scarcely music, but rather a delicate babble of tongues which made a crooning like the low notes of a pipe. The sound was all beneath him near the ground, and gathering from different quarters to one centre. Suddenly, in the midst of it came a sharp liquid note, several times repeated, a note with authority in it like a trumpet, and yet ineffably faint and distant as if it were the echo of an echo. It did not flutter David's heart, for there was no threat in it, but it had a strange effect upon his mind. For it seemed familiar, and there was that in him which answered it. He felt a boy again, for in the call there was the happy riot and the far horizons of childhood, and the noise of hill winds and burns, and the scent of heather and thyme, and all the unforgotten things of memory.

The silver trumpet did not speak again, but the soft babble was creeping nearer, and suddenly just beneath him it broadened and deepened into the sound of pipes. He looked down and saw that the dance had begun. As before, the piper with his hound mask sat cross-legged beyond the altar, and the dancers revolved widdershins around him. . . .

To his amazement he found himself looking on not in terror, but in curiosity. It was a graver dance than that of Beltane, not the mad riot of the bursting life of spring, but the more sober march of summer and the hot suns bringing on the harvest. . . . Seen from above, the figures were only puppets, moving at the bidding of a lilt that rose and fell like a lost wind. The passion of wrath with which he had watched the former Sabbath had utterly gone from him. He felt a curious pity and friendliness, for there was innocence here, misguided innocence.

"Will this be the way God looks down upon the follies of the world?" he asked himself. What was it that Reiverslaw had said?-- If the Kirk confines human nature too strictly, it will break out in secret ways, for men and women are born into a terrestrial world, though they have hopes of Heaven. . . . That was blasphemy, and he knew it, but he did not shudder at it.

How long these gentle dances continued he did not know, for he was in a dream and under the spell of the piping. . . . Then suddenly there came a change. The dancing-floor became dark, and he saw that clouds were coming over the moon. A chill had crept into the air. Lights sprang up out of nowhere, and though the wind had begun to sigh through the trees, he noted that these lights did not flicker. . . . The music stopped, and the dancers crowded together around the altar.

The hound-faced leader stood above them with something in his hand. The mysterious light seemed to burn redly, and he saw that the thing was a bird--a cock which was as scarlet as blood. The altar top was bare, and something bright spurted into the hollow of the stone. From the watchers came a cry which chilled David's marrow, and he saw that they were on their knees.

The leader was speaking in a high shrill voice like a sleepwalker's, and David caught but the one word often repeated--Abiron. Every time it was uttered the man dabbled his finger in the blood on the altar and marked a forehead, and as each received the mark he or she fell prostrate on the ground. . . .

There was no innocence now in that spectacle of obscene abasement. Terror entered into David's soul, and his chief terror was that he had not been afraid before. He had come very near falling himself under the spell.

There followed what seemed to be a roll-call. The leader read names out of a book, and the prostrate figures answered. The names seemed like an idiot's muttering, not good Scots words, but uncouth gutturals. And always like an undercurrent came the word Abiron.

Then with an unholy cry the whole coven was on its feet. The pipes began again, and music other than pipes, which seemed to soak out of the ground and the adjacent coverts. Gone was every trace of gentleness and innocency. It was witch-music made by the Devil himself on the red-hot chanter-reeds of Hell, and the assembly capered as if their feet were on the lake of burning marl. The Israelitish prophet in David awoke, and he saw it all with clear eyes and horror-stricken soul.

If the Beltane dance had been hideous, this was the very heart of bestial lust. Round and round it swept, a fury and yet an ordered fury, in which madness and obscenity were mingled. He recognized the faces of women, old and young, who sat devoutly beneath him in kirk of a Sabbath. The men were all masked, but he knew that if he could tear off the beast coverings he would see features which were normally composed into a pious decency. Figure would clasp figure and then fling apart, but in each circuit he noted that the dancers kissed some part of the leader's body, nozzling him like dogs on the roadside.

Up in his tree-top the minister had now an undivided mind. He had the names of several of the females of the coven firm in his memory, and for the men he must trust to Reiverslaw. There were some of the dancers with goat-horns, but as the rout swung round it seemed to him that a new goat-mask had appeared, a taller, wilder figure, who was specially devout in his obeisance before Hound- face. Was it Reiverslaw with his aniseed?

The night had become very dark, and the only light in the glade came from the candles which burned in its hidden hollows. And then suddenly a colder wind blew, and like the burst of a dam came a deluge of rain. The Lammas floods had broken, stealing upon the world, as is their fashion, out of a fair sky.

It seemed to David--and he held it part of the infernal miracle-- that the torrent did not quench the lights. In a trice he himself was soaked to the skin, but the candles still burned, though the rain beat on the floor of the glade with a sound like a whip-lash. . . . But it ended the dance. The silver pipe sounded again, and as the wind rose higher and the falling water slanted under it to search out even the bield of the trees, he saw figures moving hurriedly off. The next time he looked down through the spears of rain--for the hidden moon still made a dim brightness in the world--the glade was empty. Above the noise of the storm he thought he heard the strange babble of tongues, but now it was departing to the far corners of the Wood.

He waited for a little and then tried to descend. But he found it harder to get down than to get up, for he could not find the branch by which he had swung himself from the lesser tree, and in the end had to drop a good twenty feet into the bracken, whence he rolled into the empty glade. . . . He scrambled to his feet and made haste to get out of it, but not before he had sniffed the odour of unclean pelts.--And yes--surely that was the stink of Reiverslaw's aniseed.

He had no difficulty about his homeward course. Most of the way he ran, but fear had completely left his heart. The rain in his face seemed to cleanse and invigorate him. He had looked upon great wickedness, but he had looked down on it, like the Almighty, from above, and it seemed a frail and pitiful thing--a canker to be rooted out, but a thing with no terror for a servant of God. The Devil was but a botcher after all. And then he remembered how the first notes of the music had melted him, and he felt humbled.

Reiverslaw had arrived at the Greenshiel before him. The place was filled with the reek of burning hides, and David saw that the goat- mask and cloak had been laid on the peats. His ally, a weird dripping figure, sat on a stool sipping the aqua vitæ which Rab Prentice had brought with him. He, who had started the night's venture with such notable sang-froid, was now in a sweat of fright.

"Be thankit ye're safe," he stuttered, while the spirits spilled over his beard. "I never thocht to see ye mair, for I never thocht to win out o' yon awesome place. My legs are a' gashed and scartit, for I cam' here through stane and briar like a dementit staig [young horse]. Oh, sir, siccan a sicht for mortal een!"

"Saw ye the Foul Thief?" asked the awed Prentice.

"I saw ane in his image, and I got a drap o' the red cock's bluid, and I loupit like the lave, but it wasna wi' their unholy glee. Sir, I was fair wud wi' terror--me that am no gien to fear muckle-- for I got a cauld grue in my banes and my een turned back in their sockets. I tell ye, I forgot the errand I had come on, I forgot my name and my honest upbringing, and I was like a wean forwandered among bogles. . . . I've burnt thae skins, and when I get name I'll burn every stitch o' cleading, for the reek o' the Pit is on it."

"Did you recognize many?" David asked.

"No me. I had nae een to see wi'. I spun round like a teetotum, and I wadna say but I let out skellochs wi' the best--may God forgie me!"

"But the oil--the aniseed?"

Reiverslaw held up something which David saw was an empty bottle.

"I didna fail ye there. For the ae man I kenned in the coven was him that piped. When I cam' near him I felt a stound o' black hate, and there's but the ae man on God's earth that can gar me scunner like yon. So when it was my turn to bow down afore him, he gat mair frae me than a kiss. Unless he burns his breeks this very nicht there'll be a queer savour aboot the toun o' Chasehope the morn."

CHAPTER XI

THE MINISTER GIRDS UP HIS LOINS

Next day David returned to the manse in time for the noontide meal. He was greeted by Isobel with a hospitable bustle, in which was apparent a certain relief. She had known of the Lammas festival; she guessed, no doubt, that David too was aware of it, and she evidently took his visit to Newbiggin as a sign that he had at last taken her prudent counsel. But from her master she got no response. When questioned as to the welfare of his kin at Newbiggin he answered in civil monosyllables, ate his dinner in silence, and thereafter secluded himself in his study.

That evening he walked to the Greenshiel, where Reiverslaw and Prentice met him. The former was in an excited state and had clearly been drinking--to the scandal of the two shepherds, who wore portentous faces. Richie Smail had the air of an honest man compelled to walk in abhorred paths; he had been reading his Bible before their arrival, and sat with a finger in the leaves, saying nothing, but now and then lifting puzzled eyes to his master. Prentice's hard jaw was set, and he swung his crutch as if it had been a pikestaff.

"We were at Chasehope by eleven hours this mornin'," Reiverslaw announced. "I took Richie and Rab, as I forewarned Ephraim, to have a look at his new tups. But I needna tell you there was nae word of Ephraim. The wife said he was awa' to Kirk Aller, but she was like a hen on a het girdle a' the time, and I think we wad hae found him if we had ripit the press-beds. If he was lurking there he maun hae gotten a sair fricht, for I spak' that loud ye could hae heard me on the tap o' Chasehope hill."

"Did you find what you sought?" David asked.

"I fand eneuch." He drew from a pocket a bunch of feathers. "I got these last nicht in the Wud. Doubtless there'll be mair in the same place, if they havena been soopit up. But there's nae red cock the day in the toun o' Chasehope. I admired the wife's hens and speired what had become o' the cock, and was telled that it was deid--chokit last nicht on a grosart. I ken the kind o' grosart that ended the puir beast."

"And the aniseed?"

Reiverslaw laughed tipsily.

"We were just in time, sir. The wife had a fire lowin' in the yaird. 'What's burnin', mistress?' says I. 'Just some auld clouts,' says she. 'There was a gangrel body sleepit ae nicht in the loft,' says she, 'and he left some duds ahint him, as fu' o' fleas as a cadger's bonnet. I'm haein' them brunt,' says she, 'for fear o' the weans.' Weel, me and Richie and Rab stood aside the fire, and it loupit as if an oil can had been skailed on it, and the reek that rase frae it was just the reek o' my wee bottle. Mair nor that, there was a queer smell ayont the hallin--Richie and Rab fand it as weel as me. What name wad ye gie it, Rab?"

"It was the stink o' the stuff ye showed us in this house last nicht," said Prentice solemnly.

"Sae muckle for that," said Reiverslaw. "We've proof that the lad in the dowg's cap was nae ither than him we ken o'. Na, na, I never let on to the wife. I was jokesome and daffin' wi' her, and made a great crack o' the tups, and praised a' I saw about the toun, and Rab and Richie were as wise as judges. I had a dram inside me, and was just my canty ordinar'. But my een and my nostrils werena idle, and I saw what I've telled ye. . . . My heid was in sic a thraw last nicht that I canna sweir wi' ony certainty to ither faces, though I hae my suspeecions about the weemen. But you, sir, sittin' aloft on the tree-tap, ye maun hae had a graund view, for there was licht eneuch to read prent."

"I recognized certain women, to whom I can swear on my oath. About some I dare not be positive, but there were five of whom I have no doubt. There were Jean Morison and her daughter Jess."

"The folk o' the Chasehope-fit," Reiverslaw cried. "Ay, they wad be there. They've aye been ill-regarded."

"And old Alison Geddie in the kirkton."

"A daft auld wife, that skellochs like a sea-maw!"

"And Eppie Lauder from Mirehope road-end."

Richie Smail groaned. "The widow of a tried Christian, Mr. Sempill. A dacenter body than Wattie Lauder never walked the roads. It's terrible to think o' the Deil's grip on the household o' faith."

"And Bessie Tod from the Mains."

"Peety on us, but I sat neist her at the March fast-day when Mr. Proudfoot preached, and she was granin' and greetin' like a bairn. Ye surely maun be in error, sir. Bessie was never verra strong in the heid, and she hasna the wits for the Deil's wark!"

"Nevertheless she was there. I am as certain of it as that I was myself in the tree-top. Of others I have suspicions, but of these five I have certainty."

Reiverslaw rubbed his great hands. "Our business gangs cannily forward. We've gotten the names o' six o' the coven and can guess at ithers. Man, we'll hae a riddlin' in Woodilee that will learn the folk no to be ill bairns. Ye'll be for namin' them frae the pu'pit, sir?"

"I must first bring the matter before the Presbytery. I will prepare my dittay, and bring it before Mr. Muirhead of Kirk Aller as the Presbytery's moderator, and I must be guided by him as to the next step. It is a matter for the courts of the Kirk and presently for the secular law."

Reiverslaw cried out. "What for maun ye gang near the Presbytery? If ye stir up yon byke ye'll hae commissioners of justiciary and prickers and the haill clamjamphrie, and in the lang end an auld kimmer or twa will suffer, and the big malefactors will gang scot free. Chasehope's ower near the lug o' the law to tak' ony scaith, and yon's the kail-worm I wad be at. Be guidit by me, Mr. Sempill, and keep the thing inside the pairish. As the auld saying gangs, bleach your warst hanks in your ain yaird, for I tell ye if the Kirk and the Law hae the redding o't it's little justice will be done. Name and upbraid and denounce a' and sindry, but dinna delate to the Presbytery. A man may like the kirk weel eneuch, and no be aye ridin' on the riggin' o't. . . . I'll tell ye my way o't. Now that we ken some o' the coven, the four o' us can keep our een open, and watch them as a dowg watches a ratton; and at their next Sabbath, as they ca' it, we'll be ready for them. I can get a wheen Moffat drovers that fear neither man nor deil, and aiblins some o' Laird Hawkshaw's folk frae Calidon, and we'll break in on their coven and tear the masks frae the men, and rub their nebs in their ain mire, and dook the lot in the Water o' Aller. I'll wager that's the way to get rid o' witchcraft frae the parochine, for we'll mak' it an unco painfu' business to tak' the Wud. A witch or a warlock is a fearsome thing to the mind o' man, but they're bye wi't gin we mak' them gowks and laughing-stocks."

The two shepherds stared at the speaker with upbraiding eyes, and David's face looked as if a blasphemy had been spoken.

"You would fight the Devil in your own carnal strength," he said sadly. "It's little you would make of it. You talk as if this wickedness of the Wood were but a natural human prank, when it is black sin that can only be combated by the spirit of God and such weapons as God has expressly ordained. Man, man, Reiverslaw, you've but a poor notion of the power of the Adversary. I tell you last night I was trembling like a weaned child before yon blast that blew out of Hell, and you yourself were no better when I found you here. I durstna have entered the Wood except as a soldier of the Lord."

Reiverslaw laughed.

"I was sair fleyed [frightened], I'll no deny, but I got a juster view o' things wi' the daylicht."

"It would appear that you got courage also from Lucky Weir."

"True. I had my mornin' and my meridian and an orra stoup or twa sinsyne. I'm a man that's aye been used wi' a guid allowance o' liquor. But the drink, if so be ye're no fou, whiles gi'es ye a great clearness, and I counsel ye, sir, to keep wide o' the law, whether it be of the Kirk or the State. It's a kittle thing, and him that invokes it is like to get the redder's straik [the peacemaker's blow]. It's like a horse that flings its heels when ye mount and dings out the rider's teeth. . . . But hae your ain way o't, and dinna blame me if it's a fashious way. There's me and Rab Prentice and Richie Smail waitin' to sweir to what's in our knowledge, and if there's mair speirin' to be done in the Wud, I'll no fail ye. But keep in mind, Mr. Sempill, that I'm a thrang body, and maun be drawin' my crocks and sellin' my hog-lambs afore the back-end, and it's like I'll hae to traivel to Dumfries, and maybe to Carlisle. Richie will aye hae word o' my doings, and if ye want me it wad be wise to tell Richie a week afore."

That night on his return David summoned Isobel to his presence. The housekeeper appeared with a more cheerful countenance than she had worn for weeks, but the minister's first words solemnized her.

"Isobel Veitch, I asked you a question after Beltane and you refused me an answer. I, your minister, besought your aid as a confessing Christian, and you denied it me. I told you that I would not rest until I had rooted the idolatry of the Wood from this parish. Since then I have not been idle, and I have found men who did not fail me. Three days back I rode to Newbiggin, as I told you, but I returned on Lammas Eve, and on Lammas Eve I was a witness a second time to the abominations of the heathen. Not only myself, but another with me, so that the thing is established out of the mouths of two witnesses, while Robert Prentice and Richard Smail can speak in part to confirm me. Now I have got my tale complete, and it is to the Presbytery that I shall tell it. Will you implement it with such knowledge as you possess, or do you continue stiff in your recusancy?"

The old woman's eyes opened like an owl's.

"Wha went with you--wha was sae left to himsel'?" she gasped.

"Andrew Shillinglaw in Reiverslaw. . . . One man and five women stand arraigned on our witness. I will speak their names, and I care not if you put it through the parish, for soon the names will be thundered from the pulpit. The man was Ephraim Caird."

"I'll no believe it," she cried. "Chasehope's aye been a polished shaft in Christ's kirk. . . . He's o' your ain Session. . . . He cam' here, ye mind, when ye first broke bread in this house. Ay, and he was here when ye were awa' at Newbiggin. I was seilin' the milk when I heard his voice at the door--cam' here wi' ane o' his wife's skim-milk kebbucks that she kens weel how to mak', for she's frae the Wastlands--spoke sae kind and neeborlike, and was speirin' after the health o' the gude man my maister. . . Tak' it back, sir, for ye maun be mistook. Ephraim's weel kenned for a fair Nathaniel."

There was no doubt about her honesty, for the mention of Chasehope had staggered her.

"Nevertheless he is a whited sepulchre, painted without, but inside full of bones and rottenness."

"Oh, sir, bethink ye afore ye mak' this fearsome accusation. Your een may have played ye fause. And wha in their senses wad lippen to Reiverslaw? A muckle, black-avised, grippy incomer that nae man kens the get o' . . . sweirs like a dragoon when the maut's abune the meat. Ye'll never gang to the Presbytery in siccan company wi' siccan a tale! And Hirplin' Rab is a thrawn deevil, though I'll no deny he hae a gift o' prayer--and Richie Smail is sair failed in body and mind since last back-end when Mirren dee'd."

"There are also five women," David went on. "There are Jean and Jess Morison from Chasehope-foot."

"Sae that's where ye get your ill-will at Chasehope--because he's ower kind to turn twa randies intil the road! I hae nothing to say for the Morisons. They come oot o' a dirty nest, and they may ride on a saugh ilka nicht to Norroway for a' I ken."

"There is Eppie Lauder at Mirehope."

"Tut, man, as dacent a body as ever boiled sowens. And her man, Wattie, that dee'd in Aprile o' the year thretty-nine, was weel thocht o' by a'body. Ye've come till a frem'd toun wi' Eppie."

"And Alison Geddie."

"A tongue like a bell-clapper, but ettles nae hairm."

"Likewise Bessie Tod of the Mains."

"She's weak in her mind, sir. Lang syne she had a bairn to a sodger and it dee'd, and she never got ower it. Ye'll no convince me that there's ony ill in Bessie forbye the want o' sense."

"I have evidence of ill. I accuse, I do not condemn. It is for others to do the judging."

Isobel's timidity, which had been notable during the Beltane interview, seemed now to have left her. There was a sincere emotion in her voice.

"I plead wi' ye, sir, to halt while yet there's time, and if needs be content yoursel' wi' private examination. It's verra weel for Andra Shillinglaw, that's but an incomer, and rakes the country gettin' as he gangs, like a cadger's powny. But you're the minister o' Woodilee, and the fair fame o' the parochine suld be as dear to you as your ain. If ye tak' the gait ye speak o', ye'll mak' it a hissing and a reproach in a' the water of Aller. It's a quiet bien bit, wi' douce folk weel agreed, and ye wad mak' it a desolation, and a' because some daft lads and a wheen hellicat lassies dance their twasomes in the Wud. It's no as if they did ill things like garrin' the kye rin dry and the weans dwine."

"Then you admit knowledge of the sin?"

"I admit nocht, for I ken nocht. Young folk will be young folk, peety though it be. . . . But for Chasehope and my auld gossip, Eppie Lauder, the man's gyte that wad chairge them wi' idolatry-- and you can tell that to your drucken Reiverslaw."

For the first time since he had known her Isobel flung out of the room in a temper.

Next day he sought out Chasehope, and found him alone on the hill. The man greeted him with effusion.

"The Lammas rains is weel-timed this year, Mr. Sempill, nae ragin' flood, but just eneuch to slocken the ground. I start cuttin' the bog hay the morn. I heard ye were at Newbiggin, sir, and I trust ye found your friends in guid health. A blaw on the hills yonder is fine for a body after the lown air o' Woodilee."

"I returned home on the Lammas Eve. I ask you, Ephraim Caird, as you will answer to your God, where were you in the mirk of that night?"

The heavy face, now brick-red with summer suns, did not change.

"Where suld I be but in my bed? I gaed till't early, for I had a lang day wi' the hog-lambs."

"You know that that is a lie. You were in the Wood, as you were in the Wood at Beltane, dancing away your miserable soul to the Devil's piping. With my own eyes I saw you."

The astonishment of Chasehope was admirably simulated.

"Are ye daft, sir? Are ye gane clean gyte? Ye're no weel, Mr. Sempill. Sit ye doun, and I'll fetch you some water in my bonnet. Ye've got a blaff o' the sun."

"I am not mad nor am I sick. I have preached throughout the summer at the sin, and the time has now come to get to grips with the sinner. This is your last chance, Ephraim Caird. Will you confess to me, who have been set in spiritual authority over you, or must confession be wrung from you by other means?"

It was a warning which David felt bound to give, but he was silent as to the rest of his purpose, for he had decided that the time had not yet come to show his hand. He looked sternly at Chasehope, and under his gaze the man's face seemed to whiten, and his odd greenish eyes to waver. But it might be in innocent amazement.

"I kenna what ye speak o'," he stammered. "What concern have I wi' the Wud? Ask the wife, and she'll tell you that I sleepit the Lammas nicht in my bed. But oh--the thing fair coups the crans! . . . and me an elder thae ten year! Ye're no weel, or ye're dementit, to speak sic words to a man like me. Awa' hame, sir, and humble yoursel' on your knees and pray that ye may be forgiven. . . . I may cry out in the words of the Psalmist, 'They opened their mouth wide against me, and said Aha, our eye hath seen it.'"

David's hand clenched on his staff. "Before God," he cried, "I will strike you down if you utter another blasphemous word. You neglect my warning? Then your punishment be on your own guilty head."

He turned and strode away. Once he looked back and saw Chasehope still staring, the very image of virtuous dismay.

There was no sermon in the kirk the next two Sabbaths. Robb the bellman had orders not to ring the bell, but few came to the kirkyard gate, for the rumour had spread that the minister would conduct no ordinances until he had taken counsel with the Presbytery. David waited, hoping for he knew not what--some thaw to melt this icy impenitence. At last, on the sixteenth day of August, he rode to Kirk Aller to visit Mr. Muirhead.

He found the Moderator in his parlour in the little stone manse, which stood below the kirk on the knowe at the west gate above the brig of Aller. The room had few books, but a mass of papers, for Mr. Muirhead was an active ecclesiastic and noted for his conduct of church business. Also, as if to meet the disturbed times in which he lived, a pair of spurred boots, still with the mud on them, stood beside the table, on it lay a brace of ancient pistols, and from the peg of the door hung a great horseman's cloak.

Mr. Muirhead bent a preoccupied brow on David as he entered, but his face was well content. There were open letters before him, and it seemed that he had just been the recipient of welcome news.

"Come awa' in, Mr. David," he cried. He saw his visitor's eye stray to the pistols. "Ay, I've got me to the auld weapons. I had them with me at the memorable assembly in Glasgow in '38, when we dang down the Bishops. . . . I have a crow to pyke with you, but first I have some braw tidings for your ear. At the last Presbytery we met under the shadow of calamity, but the Lord has mercifully turned again the captivity of Sion. Yon devil's spawn, Montrose--alas that he should take his name from a burgh of which worthy Mr. Saunders Linklater was so long the faithful minister!-- yon Montrose, I say, approaches the end of his tether. It has been a long tether, and he has ravened like a hungry hound, but he will soon be back on his haunches with the rope tightening at his thrapple. The Almighty has wysed him with a sure hand intil the snare that was prepared for him."

"Has he been defeated?" David asked.

"By this time there is good hope that he has been scattered to the four airts of Heaven. After his savageries in the north he marches south to rend the fair fields of Stirling and the Lennox, and summon the towns of Glasgow and Embro, whilk are the citadels of our faith. Like Jeshurun he has waxed fat and kicked, but his pride will have a fearful fall; for long ere he wins to Clyde the trap will be sprung. He is bye Perth, and at this moment, I trow, at the skirts of the Ochils. Before him lie Argyll and Baillie with horse and foot, which are to his heathen hirelings as four men to one. The faithful folk of Fife are marching cannily against his left flank, and mustering from the Glasgow airt against his right are the braw lads of the West, led by those well-disposed noblemen, the Earl of Eglinton, the Earl of Cassilis, and the Earl of Glencairn. More--all the gentry of Clydesdale are on the road, commanded by the Earl of Lanark, and him and his Hamiltons are waiting to soop up the remnants of that which Argyll will shatter. Isna that a bonny tale, Mr. Sempill? Isna that a joyful recalling of our bondage, even as streams of water in the south?"

David assented, but to his surprise his interest was faint. He had more pressing problems than the public captivity of Israel.

"And now for other matters," said Mr. Muirhead, setting his mouth again in severe lines. "I have word of grave mishandling at Woodilee. You have created a stramash in the doucest and most God- regarding parish in the presbytery of Aller. You are sinning away your mercies, sir."

"It is of that I came to speak," said David. "I have to submit to you, and through you to the Presbytery, proofs of a dreadful wickedness among professing Christians in that unhappy place. Will you be pleased to run your eye over these papers? You will see certain names subscribed as witnesses."

Mr. Muirhead began to read the depositions carelessly, as if he knew what to expect from them. Then his attention deepened, and he wrinkled his forehead.

"Hoots! What's this?" he cried. "Ye were in the Wood? Ye saw this and that? Mr. Sempill, ye're not exempt from the charge of tampering with unlawful things."

"I went there as God's servant."

"Nevertheless--" He read on, and his brows darkened. He finished, flung the bundle on the table, and looked at David with a troubled and uncertain eye.

"Here's a bonny browst o' yill! You charge your chief elder with the sin of witchcraft--a man of noted godliness, as I myself can testify--and you conjoin in the libel five women who are unknown to me. What is your evidence, I ask? Your ain een, at a time when you were in no condition to see clear, and forbye you were on the top of a tree, and it was in the mid of the night. You have no corroboration. But I pretermit the women, and come to Chasehope. You have cherished a suspicion of him since

Beltane, says you, when you were present in the Wood. And what, I ask, did you there at that season, Mr. Sempill? I opine that your ain conduct wants some explanation."

"That I can give," said David.

"You have further the evidence of the man Andrew Shillinglaw, and the plot you prepared against Chasehope. Man, I see nothing in your red cock's feathers or your hennyseed, as you call it. The well is tainted, so how can you look for pure water? Your Reiverslaw is notoriously a wine-bibber and a ruffler and a despiser of ordinances. What hinders that he should be also a leear? The cock's feathers may all the time have been in his pouch, and he may have played some prank at Chasehope with the stinkin' oil. You have the witness of the herds, says you, but it's easy enough to begowk two landward simpletons. Your case will not hold water, sir, before any competent court, and Reiverslaw, your principal abettor, stands suspect. As the old owercome has it, he suld bide still that has riven breeks."

Mr. Muirhead spoke with a weighty assurance, and as David looked at his shrewd coarse face he felt a sudden helplessness. It would be hard to convince a tribunal so prejudiced--in whose ears, perhaps, Chasehope had already spoken.

"My advice to you," the voice went on, "is to get you home and let the steer settle. There's nothing in these papers that calls for action by the Presbytery--just hearsay and idle 'fama', the visions of an excited young man and the lees of a drucken reprobate. No doubt you mean well, but I will homologate no course which fastens evil on a man whose righteousness has been abundantly proven. Have mind of the virtue of charity, sir, which thinketh no evil. I opine that you're ower ready to think evil. Bring before me wise- like evidence and I will be prompt to act, but not these havers."

So far he had spoken with a kind of rough good-humour, but now his voice became harsh.

"They tell me you have conducted no public worship these last two Sabbaths," he said fiercely.

"I will not lead my folk into deeper hypocrisy," said David. "I will not preach or pray in the kirk till I also denounce the sinners, and that I purpose to do on the next Lord's day."

"You will do no such thing," said Mr. Muirhead sternly. "I, your elder, and father in God, forbid you."

"I must follow my own conscience," said David. "I am as convinced of the abominations of the Wood and of the persons that partake in them as that I am sitting with you here in Kirk Aller this August morning."

"You would add contumacy to your folly," the other roared. "You would sow dissension in the Kirk when it is necessary to set a stout front against the Kirk's oppressors."

"That," said David firmly, "is mere carnal policy. In the name of God, whose purity is a flame of fire, would you let gross wickedness go unchecked because it may knock a splinter off the Kirk? I tell you it were better that the Kirk should be broken to dust and trampled underfoot than that it should be made a cloak for sin. I refuse to obey you, Mr. Muirhead. Next Sabbath I will make every wall in Woodilee dirl under my accusation."

The two men were on their feet, David white with wrath, and the face of the other mottled with a like passion. "You rebellious schismatic," the minister of Kirk Aller cried, when a knock at the door called both to a sense of the proprieties.

It was the minister's man, who entered with a letter held reverently with the tips of his fingers.

"A dispatch, sir, from Embro. Brocht this moment by a mounted messenger, wha wouldna stay for meat, but maun post off doun the water."

When the man retired, Mr. Muirhead, still standing and puffing heavily, broke the seal. He seemed to have trouble with the contents, for he moved his spectacles, took them off and rubbed them, and then re-read the missive. His eyes stared, his face paled, and then at the last perusal reddened again. He turned to David in a flame of temper.

"The Kirk must suffer for you and your like," he cried. "The Lord had prepared an abundant mercy, whilk has been denied us because of the hardness of our hearts. Wae's me, wae's me for the puir sheep that have sic faithless shepherds! The auld and the bauld and the leal-hearted must go down because of conceited halflings like you that are Achans in the camp."

"You speak in riddles, sir," said David, whose sudden anger had gone at the spectacle of this strange transformation.

"It's a riddle you'll read or you're a month older in letters of blood and fire. . . . Riddle, says you? The riddle is why the Almighty should give our covenanted Kirk sic a back-cast of His hand, and to that you maybe ken the answer. Our deliverance has most lamentably miscarried, and our bondage is waxed more grievous. Get out of my sight, for I must be about the Lord's business, and there will be no rest for Mungo Muirhead this many a day. You have defied me, but wait on and see if you can defy your Creator."

"You have had bad tidings?"

"Bad, says you? Ay, bad for God's people and God's Kirk, but they're maybe blithe tidings for a schismatic like yourself. You'll maybe get Left-handed Coll and his

Irishry to purge your parish and burn the honest folk with whilk you are unworthily blessed. Awa' to Montrose, man, for yon's the lad for you!"

"Montrose!"

"Ay, Montrose. Know that yesterday, at Kilsyth, yon whelp of Satan was permitted to lay low the Covenant's banner, and rout the godly. This word I have gotten is a scribe from Argyll, on his road to Berwick, written from a boat at the Queen's Ferry. This very day it's like that Antichrist will be hammering on the gates of Glasgow."

CHAPTER XII

THE MAN WITH THE SQUINT

The sermon which was to indict by name the sinners was not preached in the kirk of Woodilee the next Sabbath.

For the day after his return from Kirk Aller a post reached the manse from the Pleasance of Edinburgh which in an hour set David on his horse riding hard for the capital. There was plague in the city, and his father was sick of it. It was the plague in a new form, for death did not come quickly; the patient lay for days in a high fever, afflicted with violent headaches and shiverings, and a contraction of muscles and nerves, and then, in nine cases out of ten, passed into a rigor which meant death. There was no eruption on the bodies, and the physicians were at a loss in the matter of treatment. But it was scarcely less deadly than the older visitations, and the dead-bell rang hourly, and the dead-cart rumbled day and night on the cobbles.

David found the old man conscious, but very clear that he was near his end. The family doctor had bled him copiously, applied leeches to his head, and brought a horrid regiment of drugs and vomitories. The son pled with his father to receive them patiently. "God works by means," he told him, "as Christ cured the blind man with clay and spittle, and what remedy could be more rude than these?"

"Aye, but it was the Lord that laid them on, Davie," said the patient, "and no an auld wife like McGlashan." So he sent the physician packing, and engaged a new one, a certain young Crosbie from the Monk's Vennel, who had studied in France and had at least the merit of letting a sick man die in peace. Instead of smothering the patient under bedclothes, he kept him lightly covered, ordered the window to be open day and night, and let him drench his system with small ale. It is likely that under any treatment the old man would have died, for he was in his seventy- fourth year and had long been ailing, and the plague only speeded the decay of age. But under the new regimen his last days were less of a martyrdom. His head remained clear and he could speak with his son--chiefly of his mother and his childhood.

David lodged not in the city, but in the village of Liberton, and walked in daily to his father's bedside. He read the Scriptures to him and prayed with him, as his duty demanded, but he felt a certain shyness at inquiring into his father's state towards God. Nor was the old man communicative. "I've made my peace lang syne," he said, "and I read my title clear, so there's no need of death-bed wark for me." But he was full of anxiety for his son. "You've chosen a holy calling, Davie lad, and I'm blithe to think you've got a downsetting in our calf-country. Man, there were Sempills in the mill o' the Roodfoot since the days of Robert Bruce. But the ministry in these days is a kittle job, for the preachers are ower crouse, and the Kirk has got its heid ower high. . . . What's come o' this Montrose they crack about? . . . Keep you humble before the Lord, my son, for Heaven's yett is a laigh yett."

He died peacefully on the third day of September, and David had a busy week settling his affairs--the sale of the business and the household effects and the payment of bequests to servants and distant kin. Hour after hour he sat with the lawyers, for there was a considerable estate, and to his surprise he found himself with worldly endowments such as few ministers of the Kirk possessed. There was money at the goldsmith's, and in his lawyer's boxes deeds and sasines and bonds on heritable property, and there would be more to come. His doer, a little old snuffy attorney of the name of Macphail, grew sententious as the business drew to its close. "You've both the treasure on earth, Mr. David, and the treasure in Heaven, and it's a pleasing thought that they're alike well-guided. Anent the latter, moth cannot corrupt, saith the Word, nor thieves break through and steal, and anent the former a moth will no do muckle ill to a wheen teugh sheepskins, and it would be a clever thief that got inside Georgie Gight's strong-room in the Canongate, where your bonds are deposited. So you can keep an easy mind, Mr. David, while you wrastle for souls in Woodilee."

Those were strange days both for death in a bed and for conducting business, for the stricken city was the prey of wild fears. Scarcely a traveller entered her infected precincts, but rumour was as busy as the east wind in May. The battle of Kilsyth had worked a revolution in Scotland. Glasgow had surrendered and welcomed the conqueror, with enthusiasm for his person and largesse for his soldiers. The shires and the burghs were falling over each other in their haste to make submission. Edinburgh had been summoned, and a delegation of the town council had gone out beyond Corstorphine to capitulate to the young Master of Napier. The imprisoned Lords went free from the Tolbooth; David saw the sight-- pallid men shivering with prison ague; only the Castle still held for the Covenant. Word came that the King had made Montrose Captain-general of all Scotland, and that soon the victorious army would move towards the Border; already, on the haugh of Bothwell by Clyde side, Sir Archibald Primrose had read the royal commission to the troops. A summons had gone out for a Parliament to be held presently in Glasgow--"for settling religion and peace," said the proclamation, "and freeing the oppressed subjects of those insufferable burdens they have groaned under this time bygone."

The ministers who walked the Edinburgh causeway wore gloomy faces. David had a sight of Mr. Muirhead, who sternly inquired of him what he did in the city. "I have come to bury my father," he replied. "If he died in the hope and the promise," was the answer, "he has gotten a happy deliverance, for the vials of wrath are opened against this miserable land." It was a phrase repeated like a password by others of his ministerial brethren, and he replied with a becoming gravity, but he could not in his heart feel any great sorrow. For he remembered the face of the groom at Calidon, and he wondered how that face looked as a conqueror. Pride, he was assured, would not be in it. . . . News came that Montrose was at Cranstoun and moving by Gala Water to the Border. For a moment David had a crazy desire to follow him, to be in his presence, for he had a notion that if he could but have speech again with that young man the shadows and perplexities might lighten from his mind.

At last he set off homeward, and under the rowans at Carlops brig he read a printed paper which had been circulated in the Edinburgh streets--torn across and cast away by many, but by others cherished and pondered. It was a manifesto of Montrose from the camp at Bothwell, and it set out his purpose. In it were the very words used by the groom that night at Calidon. The nobles had destroyed "lawful authority and the liberty of the subject," the Kirk had coerced men into a blind obedience worse than Popery. He took up arms, he said, for pure religion, "the restoration of that which our first reformers had;" for the King, and the establishment of a central authority; for the plain people and the "vindication of our nation, from the base servitude of subjects." He confuted the timorous souls "who can commit nothing to God." He repudiated the charge of blood-guiltiness, for he had never "shed the blood of any but of such as were sent forth to shed our blood and to take our lives." And he concluded by pointing to the miracles that faith had wrought: "What is done in the land, it may sensibly seem to be the Lord's doing, in making a handful to overthrow multitudes." The words came to David with a remembered sound, like the echo of a speaking voice. Could this man be the bloody Amalekite of the Kirk's denouncing? On which side, he asked his perplexed soul, did the God of Israel fight, for this man's faith was not less confident than that of the minister of Kirk Aller?

Isobel received him with the reverential gloom which the Scots peasantry wear on an occasion of death.

"So it's a' bye, sir. We got the word from the Embro carrier, but I wasna looking for ye yet awhile, for we heard ye were like to be thrang wi' the lawyer bodies. . . . He just slippit awa', for how could an auld man stand out against yon wanchancy pestilence? It's a gait we maun a' gang, and he would be weel prepared Godward, and at ease in his mind about warldly things, for they tell me he was brawly set up wi' gear. And there's just yoursel' to heir it, Mr. David? . . . But shame fa' me to speak o' gear in this sorrowful dispensation, for a faither is a faither though he live ayont the three score and ten years whilk is our allotted span."

"He died as he lived, Isobel, a humble but confident Christian. I think he was pleased to know that I was settled in his forebears' countryside."

"He wad be that, honest man. Fine I mind o' your gudesire, and mony a nievefu' o' meal I gat from him when I was a bairn. But I'm concerned for yoursel', Mr. David, and fearfu' lest ye have got a smittal o' the pestilence. Ye're fine and ruddy, but there's maybe fever in your veins. Drink off this wersh brew, sir--it was my mither's way to caller the blood--just kirnmilk boiled wi' soorocks."

David asked concerning the parish.

"Woodilee!" Isobel cried. "If Embro's a stricken bit, it's nae waur than this parochine. For the last se'en days it's been naething but wars and rumours o' war. Ye'll hae heard o' how Montrose has guidit our auld Sion, and now we've Antichrist himsel' on our waterside. Ay, he's no twenty miles across the hills, campin' with his Edomites somewhere on Yarrow, as welcome as snaw in hairst. The lads and lasses are a' fleyed out o' the sheilin's, for the Yerl o' Douglas--weary fa' him!--and his proud horsemen are drovin' ower frae Clyde like craws in the back-end. We canna move man nor bestial, and folk winna ride the roads except in a pack, and they tell me that Amos Ritchie wi' his auld firelock was sent for to convoy the minister o' Bold to Kirk Aller. The weans daurna keek past the doorstane, and Johnnie Dow winna gang his rounds, and he's been lyin' fou at Lucky Weir's thae three days. There's nae wark done in a' Woodilee, nor like to be done--it's a dowg's life we've gotten, muckle ease and muckle hunger."

"But the place has suffered no harm?"

"No yet, forbye a wedder o' Richie Smail's that Douglas's dragoons brandered and ate yestreen at the Red Swire. But ony moment a vial may be opened.--What hinders Montrose to come rauvagin' this airt? for if it's meat and drink he's seeking for his sodgers, Woodilee is a bien bit aside yon bare Yarrow hills. Forbye Calidon's no that far, and they tell me that our auld hirplin' laird, wha suld rather be thinkin' o' his latter end, is high in the command o' the ungodly, and him and yon sweirin' Tam Purves will be rampin' like lions in their pride. Hech, sir, our kindly folk are in the het o' the furnace, in whilk they will either be brunt to an ass, or come out purified as fine gowd. . . . But what am I claverin' here for, when ye're wantin' your denner? It's little I hae for ye, for our meal ark is nigh toom, and there's no a kain hen left on the baulks."

That night David sat long in his study. It was now the sixteenth day of September, and the sultry weather, which had fostered the plague, was sharpening towards autumn. He had returned from his father's death-bed in something of the mood in which he had first entered the manse. The confusion in the State was to him only a far-off rumour; he was not greatly concerned whether Covenant or King was a-top, for he had no assurance as to which had the right on its side. But he longed for peace, that he might be about his proper business, for the charge of Woodilee lay heavy on his soul. The wickedness against which he had raged seemed now to him as pitiful as it was terrible, a cruel seduction of Satan's against which he must contend, not without pity for the seduced. Charity filled him, and with his new tenderness came hope. He could not fail in the struggle before him--God would not permit his little ones to be destroyed.

Had he not forgotten the minister in the crusader? His books caught his eye--he had touched them little during the summer. What had become of that great work, Sempill on Isaiah? He pulled out his manuscript notes and for a little was happy in their contemplation. . . . The day's ride had been long and the sun had been hot. His head nodded, then dropped on his arm, and he fell asleep.

He awoke to a sound below the window. The manse stood at the extreme southern end of the kirkton, beyond the kirk, a long bowshot from the nearest dwelling, which was Robb the bellman's. To the west of it lay the broomy slopes of the Hill of Deer, to the east the glen of the burn and Windyways hill, and to the south the rough meadows through which the road dipped to the Wood. It was a lonely spot, as Isobel often testified, and after nightfall no soul came near it; even a traveller on the highway did not pass within half a mile.

His study window opened on the garden, and the sound seemed to come from some one knocking gently on the back door. David, still confused with sleep, took his candle and descended the stairs. Isobel had heard nothing--for the muffled sound of her snores came from the press-bed behind the kitchen. . . . Again the soft knocking came, this time with a more insistent sound. In some trepidation David unbolted the door, telling himself that it might be a summons to attend a dying parishioner.

There was little moon and a thick autumn haze covered the ground. Rising out of it, like ships out of the water, were huge figures, and he saw that they were mounted men. One of them sat his horse and held the other beasts; one was on his feet and supported a third, who seemed very weary.

David raised his candle, and saw the figure of the standing man. The face was dark with sun, but darker under the eyes with fatigue; the dress, once rich and splendid, was both mired and torn; and one hand was wrapped in a blood-stained kerchief.

"Do I speak with the minister of Woodilee?" the man asked, and at the first word David knew him. That voice had been echoing all the year in his chamber of memory.

"I am the minister," was his reply. "In what can I serve my Lord Marquis?"

The face relaxed into a smile, which made it for the moment gay in spite of the heavy eyes.

"You have not forgotten me? Nor have I forgotten you, and therefore I come to you in sore need to beg a charity. I do not doubt but you are of the opposite faction, but I know also that you are a faithful minister of Christ, whose custom was to do good to His enemies. Will you give shelter to this wounded comrade of mine, and thereby save the life of one whom you consorted with a year back in Calidon?"

"But this is but a poor manse, my lord. Why do you come here when Calidon is so nigh?"

"Alas! Calidon is no port for me or mine in this storm. Know, sir, that this day my army has been beaten on the Yarrow haughs and utterly scattered. Before morning Leslie's troopers will be knocking at Calidon door. I myself am a fugitive, and there is no safety till I cross the Highland line. But this comrade of mine has a broken leg, besides other hurts, and it is impossible that he should ride farther. If he does, he will impede us and we shall be taken. But where can I leave him, for I am in an unfriendly country, and if he is captured it will be the gallows for an honest fellow? I bethought me that you were minister of this parish, and that your heart was not likely to be steeled to common humanity, and a manse is the one place that the pursuit will miss. Will you take him and let him lie hid till the hunt passes? After that he will fend for himself, for he is an old soldier of the German wars."

"He has done no evil . . . ?"

"None save what I have done myself. He has drawn the sword in a brave cause which this day has sorely miscarried. But, sir, it is not of politics I speak, but of charity. For the sake of Christ's mercy, I beseech you not to refuse."

"It is a heavy charge, my lord, but I cannot say you nay."

Montrose shifted the burden of the wounded man to David's arm. "Farewell, Mark," he whispered. "The good cause is down but not dead, old friend. You know where to get news of me." Then he kissed his cheek and gave his hand to David.

"May God bless and reward you, sir. I dare not linger. We will take the third horse with us, for it would be too kenspeckle in your stable. Think kindly of me, whatever my fate, as I think tenderly of you, and pray for a lonely man whose feet are set on a long road."

The next moment the riders had disappeared in the fog. David stood in a dream, for he would have given worlds to recall the speaker. His voice, the sight of his face, had brought back tenfold the longing to be with him which had haunted him after the Calidon meeting. The man had been a conqueror and was now a fugitive, but earthly fortunes had no meaning for such an one. Those calm eyes would look on triumph and disaster alike unperturbed.

He was roused by the wounded man going limp in his arms, and he saw that he had fainted. He carried him up the steep stairs--Isobel's snoring still making a chorus in the background--and laid him on the bedstead in the guest-room. The bed was not made up, and it was clear that he must wake Isobel. As the man's head drooped on the bolster David turned his candle on it. The face was grimed and blood-stained, but there was no mistaking the features: it was the tall trooper with the squint whom he had once guided to Calidon.

David sought the kitchen and hammered at the door of the press-bed. The snoring ceased, and presently a scared and muffled voice demanded what was the trouble.

"Get up, woman," David ordered. "There's a sick man here that has need of you."

Three minutes later Isobel appeared, shawled and nightcapped. "Keep us, Mr. David, is't yoursel' that's seeck?" she wailed. "I didna like the look o' ye the day and--"

He cut her short.

"A friend of mine has had a mischance. His leg is broken, and I think there is other trouble. Listen, Isobel. . . . The man is one of Montrose's soldiers, and Montrose's army has suffered defeat. If he is found here by the pursuing troops, he will die. He is my friend, and

I would save him. You and I must nurse him between us, and no word of his presence here must pass these doors."

"Mercy on us! A malignant!" the old woman exclaimed.

"And my friend," said David curtly. "If I think it consistent with Christian duty to save his life, so well may you. You and I have no quarrel with stricken men. I appeal to the kind heart that is in you and your regard for me, and I do not think I will appeal in vain."

"Your wull be done," said Isobel. "Whaur is the body? See and I'll get blankets and pillows, for the bed hasna been made up this sax months."

The sight of the figure on the bedstead, his quilted and brocaded coat, his light cuirass, his long untanned boots much scratched and frayed, his feathered hat beside him on the floor, caused Isobel to shrink.

"A rampin' Edomite," she said. "Look at the long hair and the murderin' sword, stained, nae doot, with the bluid of the saints. Your friend, says you, sir? Weel, he's been walkin' ither than Gospel roads, I can see brawly, and gin he hadna been amang the craws he wadna hae been shot. . . . But the puir chield's in a dwam! Haste ye, sir, and help me off wi' thae Babylonish garments, and that weskit o' airn--what for suld folk gang to the smith for cleading and no to a wabster? And stap his swird aneath the bed, for I'm feared to look on't."

The man half recovered consciousness as they stripped off his coat and cuirass, and when it came to the breeches he groaned aloud. So they left them on him and slit the boot on the broken leg. It was a clean break of the shin, and Isobel, who showed some skill in the business, set the leg, and bound it in firm splints made of the staves of an old cask. Then they searched for further damage, and found that he was suffering from little except an extreme fatigue. There was a pike wound in his shoulder, which Isobel bathed and bandaged, and a pistol-ball had been turned by the mail he wore and had left a bruised rib. By the time the grime and blood were washed from his face, he had got his senses sufficiently back to find his voice.

"You are the minister?" he asked. "I am crippled, as you see, sir-- an accursed fail-dyke on Minchmoor did it--and you'll not be wanting this kind of merchandise long on your hands. A drink and six hours' sleep will set me up, and I'll make shift to take the road. Let me bide here till the morn's night, and you'll be rid of me."

"You'll not be fit to move for a week. You can sleep here securely. You're in a friend's charge."

The sick man was an old soldier who took life as it came. After he had drunk a bowl of gruel laced with usquebagh, he turned on his side and fell asleep. David and Isobel went down to the kitchen and, with the candle between them, looked at each other with something like consternation.

"We must burn those clothes," said David.

"Na, na. I'll make a bundle o' them and hide them in the cupples. It's braw raiment, gin it were cleaned. But oh, sir, this is a bonny kettle of fish! Who wad hae thocht to see such wark in the manse of Woodilee?"

"It is a work of mercy."

"There's some wad call it by anither name. There's some wad say it was turnin' back from the gude fight, and a faintin' and a backslidin' on the road. I'd be feared to think what yon thrawn minister o' Bold wad call it, but it wadna be mercy. He'd be for savin' the puir lad as Jael the wife of Heber the Kenite saved Sisera."

"I will be party to no such wickedness, which would be an offence against human charity as well as against the law of Christ."

"Ay, charity. I'm blithe to hear ye speak the word, sir." Isobel's eyes had an inclination to twinkle.

"I must follow the guiding of my own conscience. But I would not constrain you. If the thing offends you, I will even now, before it is light, carry the man to the Greenshiel . . ."

"A bonny gait that wad be. The avenger of blood will be chappin' ony hour at Richie's door, and there's nae space at the Greenshiel to hide a mouse. Na, na, I'm no denyin' your duty, Mr. David. There never was woman yet, young or auld, that was ill-set to a sodger, forbye yon randy Jael, wha maun hae been an unco trial to her man. And the lad upbye seems a decent body, though he skellies [squints] sair wi' his left ee. I'se do your bidding, sir, and I hope it winna be accounted to me for sin."

"Can we keep him here without any one knowing of it?"

"Brawly. The folk o' Woodilee are sweir to come near the manse thae days. They're feared o' the glower they micht get from you."

"But if Leslie's troopers arrive and offer to search--?"

"I'll search them! I'se warrant I'd be doun on them with my ten fingers like a gled on poutry. Isobel Veitch will learn the godless loons to mak' free with the house o' a man o' God. And mind, sir, if onybody speirs, ye maun brazen like a packman. Bleeze awa' about the needcessity o' speed in the guid cause and send them on their ways to Clyde, and maybe ye'll be spared the sin o' actual leein'."

"If need be I will not shrink from the false word, which will be forgiven in the cause of mercy."

"Fine, sir." Isobel grinned appreciatively on him; for this confederacy seemed to have ended the estrangement between servant and master. "There's a man ahint the minister in you, whilk is mair than ye can say for the feck o' the Presbytery."

"And, meantime, I must be up and doing."

"Ye'll awa' to your bed and sleep out your sleep. What's the need o' hurry when the body's leg is still to set. As my auld mither used to say, naething suld be done in haste but grippin' a flea. . . . But I'll look out some of your auld garments, for our friend will hae to cast his braw coat and put on homespun or he wins forth o' Woodilee."

CHAPTER XIII

WHITE MAGIC

The man upstairs slept for a round of the clock, and then awoke and clamoured for food. Isobel reported that he was cured of his weakness, and that the pike wound in his shoulder was no more than a scratch. "Forbye his leg, he's as weel as you or me, and he has the hunger o' a cadger's powny. It was an awesome sicht to see him rivin' my bannocks. He's speirin' to see ye, for nae doubt he has muckle on his mind." The old woman was in the best of tempers, and her wizened face was puckered in a secret smile, for she and her master were now restored to friendship as partners in conspiracy.

David found his guest clad in one of his own bedgowns, the hue of health once more on his unshaven cheeks. His first request was for a razor and for shears, and when Isobel had shorn his hair, and he had got rid of a three days' beard, it was a head of a notable power and dignity that rested on the pillow. The high-boned, weather-beaten face, the aquiline nose, the long pointed chin were no common trooper's, and the lines about mouth and eyes were like the pages of a book wherein the most casual could read of ripe experience. The brown eyes were dancing and mirthful, and the cast in the left one did not so much mar the expression as make it fantastically bold and daring. Here was one who had lived in strange places and was not used to fear.

"It's a sore burden I've brought on you, Mr. Sempill," he cried, "and it's you that's the good Samaritan. It was my lord's notion that I should throw myself on your compassion, for it's a queer thing, I own, for a cavalier to be seeking a hiding-place in a manse, though Mark Kerr has had some unco ports in his day. I mind in Silesia--But there's no time for soldiers' tales. You'll be wanting me out of this as soon as I can put foot to ground, and it's blithe I'll be to humour you. My leg is setting brawly, says that auld wife who is my chirurgeon, and in less than a week I'll be fit to go hirpling on my road."

"That will be to walk into the fire," said David. "If Montrose's army is scattered throughout the hills, there will be such a hunt cried as will leave no sheiling unsearched."

"Just so. I'll not deny that this countryside is unhealthy for folk like me. You'll be well advised to bury or burn the clothes I had on last night, and if you can lend me a pair of grey breeks and an auld coat, I'll depart with a lighter mind."

"You'll be for the sea and the abroad?"

"No me. It's at the coast that they'll be seeking me, and a wise man that's in trouble will go where he's no expected. I think I'll just bide hereaways. Put me in a frieze jacket and I'll defy Davie Leslie himself to see Mark Kerr, the gentleman-cavalier of Mackay's, in the douce landward body that cracks of sheep and black nowt. You'll maybe have me in your congregation, Mr. Sempill. I'm thinking of taking a tack of Crossbasket."

David stared. "Are you mad?" he asked.

"Not so--only politic, as is the way of us soldiers of the Low Germany. One of my profession must think well into the future if he's to keep his craig unraxed. I've had some such escapado in mind ever since I travelled north a year syne, and I've had a word on the matter with Nicholas Hawkshaw, so when the glee'd [squinting] auld farmer body from Teviotside seeks the tack of Crossbasket, the lawyer folk in Edinburgh will be prepared for him. Nicholas was like me--he kenned fine that our triumph in the North was fairy gold that is braw dollars one day and the next a nieve- full of bracken."

"Where is the laird of Calidon?"

"By a merciful dispensation we left him sick at Linlithgow, and Nicholas, being an eident soul, had a boat trysted at the Borrowstounness, and by this time doubtless will be beating down the Forth on his way to a kinder country. He'll be put to the horn, like many another honest gentleman, and his braw estates may be roupit. Thank the Lord, I have nothing to lose, for I'm a younger son that heired little but a sword."

"A month ago," said David, "Montrose was lord of all Scotland. You tell me that everything has been lost in one battle, and that you and others were confident of its loss. Man, how did he succeed with such a rabble of the half-hearted behind him?"

"I wouldna just call it half-hearted. We won because James Graham is the greatest captain since Gustavus went to God at Lutzen, and because he has a spirit that burns like a pure flame. But he did not ken this land of Scotland as me and Nicholas kenned it. He had a year of miracles, for that happened which was clean beyond all sense and prevision, but miracles have an ugly trick of stopping just when they are sorest needed. . . . A year syne there were three men on Tayside--Montrose and Inchbrakie and me--and that was the King's army. By the mercy of Providence we fell in with Alasdair Macdonald on the Atholl braes, and got a kind of muster at our back. . . . There's no Hieland blood in you, Mr. Sempill? No? Well, it's a very good kind of blood in its way, but it's like the Hieland burns--either dry as the causeway or a roaring spate. It's grand in a battle, but mortal uncertain in a campaign, if you follow me--and that James should have held it in leash till he had routed Argyll and Baillie and Hurry, and brought the Kirk and Estates to their knees, is a proof of genius for war that Gustavus never bettered. But for conquering Scotland, and keeping the conquest fixed--na, na! Hielands will never hold down Lowlands for long, and that Lowland support we reckoned on was but a rotten willow wand. My lord deceived himself, and it was not for me to enlighten him, me that had witnessed so many portents. So we kept our own thoughts--Nicholas and me--and indeed we had half a hope that a faith which had already set the hills louping might perchance remove the muckle mountains. But I tell you, sir, when we marched for the Borders I had a presage of calamity on me as black as a thundercloud."

"But you had the army that won Kilsyth?"

"Not a third of it. Yonder on Bothwell haughs it melted away like a snow-wreath. Macdonald--he is Sir Alasdair now and a Captain- general, and proud of it as an auld gander--must march off with the feck of his Irishry to Argyll to settle some private scores with Clan Diarmaid. The Gordons took the dorts [sulks]--a plague on their thrawn heids--and Aboyne and his horse went off in a tirrivee. James looked for a Lowland rising, for, says he, the poor folk for whom I fight are weary of the tyranny of greedy lairds and presumptuous ministers. If so, they are ower weary to show it. What can be done with lads that grovel before a Kirk that claims the keys of Heaven and Hell? . . . If that sounds blasphemy, sir, you'll forgive a broken man that is unlocking his heart and cannot wale [pick] his words. . . . Forbye, the Irish were like a millstone round our necks, for what profit was it to plead that Munro used them in Ireland for an honest cause? To the Lowland herds and cotters they were murdering savages, and the man that had them on his side was condemned from the beginning. The sons of Zeruiah were too strong for us."

"Is it true that they fight barbarously?" David asked.

"So, so. I'll not deny that they're wild folk, but they havena your Kirk's taste for murder in cold blood. There were waur things done in Methven Wood than were done at Aberdeen, and it's like that Davie Leslie is now giving shorter shrift to the poor creatures than ever they gave to the Campbells in Lorne and Lochaber. . . . We'll let that be, for there was never an army that did not accuse its enemies of barbarity, and the mere bruit of it on our side was enough to keep the Lowlands behind steekit doors. There were some of the nobles that we counted on--my Lord Home, and my cousin Roxburghe, and the sly tod Traquair. James was in good heart at their promises, but I mistrusted the gentry, and I was most lamentably justified, for when we were on Teviotside, where were my lords but in Leslie's camp?--prisoners, they said--but willing refugees, as I kenned braw and well."

"And the battle?"

A spasm of pain passed over the other's face.

"It was not, properly speaking, a battle, but more in the nature of a surprise and a rout. We were encamped on Yarrow at the gate of the hills, for the coming of Davie Leslie had altered our plans, and we were about to march westward to the Douglas lands. We were deceived by false intelligence--it was Traquair's doing, for which some day he will get my steel in his wame--but I bitterly blame myself that an old soldier of the German wars was so readily outwitted and so remiss in the matter of outposts. . . . In the fog of the morning Davie was on us, and Douglas's plough-lads scattered like peesweeps. There were five hundred of O'Keen's Irish, and five score of Ogilvy's horse, and for three hours we held Davie's six thousand. These are odds that are just a wee bit beyond my liking, forbye that we had no meat in our bellies. Brawly they fought, the poor lads, fought as I never saw men fight in the big wars--but what would you have? . . . It's no tale for me to tell, though it will be in my mind till my last breath."

He sighed, and for a moment his face was worn and old.

"Well and on, sir," he continued. "The upshot is that the bravest of Scottish hearts is now, by God's grace, somewhere on the road to the Hielands, and the great venture is bye and done with, and here am I, a lameter, seeking sanctuary of a merciful opponent. If to shelter me does violence to your conscience, sir, say the word and I'll hirple off as soon as the night falls. You've given me bite and sup, like a good Christian, and suffered me to get my sleep, and you've no call to do more for a broken malignant."

"My conscience is at ease anent succouring the wounded and saving a man's life. And I have no clearness about this quarrel of Montrose and the Kirk, and would therefore give it the go-by. But I will exact the promise that, if you come off safe, you will fight no more in Scotland. In that much I am bound to serve my calling."

"You shall have the promise. Mark Kerr is for beating his sword into a ploughshare. What says the Word? 'His speech shall be of cattle'--though, now I come to think of it, that's from what you gentry call the Apocryphal books and think little of. . . . I'm one that has no great love for idleness on the broad of his back. Have you no a book to while away the hours? Anything but divinity-- I've lost conceit of divinity these last months when I've been doing battle with the divines."

David furnished his guest with reading which was approved, and then went forth into Woodilee. The village made holiday, and every wife was at her doorstep. A batch of troopers were drinking a tankard at Lucky Weir's, and saluted him as he passed. The people he met had an air of relief and good temper, and looked with a friendly eye on the minister, forgetting apparently the Lammas controversies and the shut kirk, for he was a representative of the winning cause.

Peter Pennecuik, sitting on a big stone outside the smithy, was the chief dispenser of tidings. His cheeks were swollen and his voice faltered with pride.

"What for do ye bide in your tent, Mr. Sempill, in this hour of our deliverance? They tell me that Mr. Ebenezer of Bold has mounted his beast and ridden wi' the horsemen to harry the ungodly's retreat. Ay, and baith Chasehope and Mirehope have ta'en the road, for the haill land is fou' o' the wreckage of the wicked, as the sands o' the Red Sea were strewed wi' the chariots o' Pharaoh. Our General Leslie is no ane to weaken in the guid cause, for there's word that his musketeers hae shot the Irish in rows on the Yarrow haughs, ilk ane aside his howkit grave, and there's orders that their women and bairns, whilk are now fleein' to the hills, are to be seized by such as meet wi' them, as daughters of Heth and spawn of Babylon, and be delivered up to instant judgment. Eh, sir, but the Lord has been exceeding gracious us-ward, and our griefs are maist marvellously avenged. . . . Nae doot ye'll be proclaimin' a solemn fast for praise and prayer."

David ate his dinner with a perturbed mind, for if the countryside was being scoured for fugitives on this scale, it was unlikely that the manse would remain long inviolate. But Isobel reassured him. "They wad never daur ripe the house, and for the lave I can speak them fair in the gate." In the afternoon he set out to walk to the Greenshiel, since the road would give him a far-away glimpse of Calidon. Autumn was already chilling the air, and the horizon was a smoky purple, the heather was faded, the bracken yellowing, the rowan trees plumed with scarlet, the corn in the valley already more gold than green. To David, in whose ear was still the gloating voice of Peter Pennecuik, the place seemed to smell of death.

At the Greenshiel he found death in bodily form. On the plot of turf outside the cottage half a dozen troopers stared from their saddles at something that lay on the ground. The men were mostly a little drunk, and had the air of a pack of terriers who have chased a cat and found it at bay--an air that was puzzled, angry, and irresolute. David strode towards them, and they gave place to him, somewhat shamefacedly. On the turf lay a wretched draggle-tailed woman, her clothes almost torn off her back, her hair in elf-locks, her bare feet raw and bloody. Her face was emaciated and of an extreme pallor, her shrunken breast heaved convulsively, and there was blood on her neck. Richie Smail was on his knees attempting to force some milk between her teeth. But her lips shut and unshut with her panting, and the milk was spilled. Then her mouth closed in that rigor from which there is no unloosing.

Richie lifted his head and saw the minister.

"She's bye wi't," he said. "Puir thing, puir thing! She ran in here like a hunted maukin." Then to the soldiers: "Ye had surely little to dae, lads, to mishandle a starvin' lassie."

There was no sign of compunction on the coarse faces of the troopers.

"An Irish b-bitch," one hiccoughed. "What's the steer for a bawbee joe?"

"Tam Porteous kittled her wi' his sword point," said another. "Just in the way o' daffin, ye ken. She let out a skelloch and ran like the wund." The man put his hands to his sides and guffawed at the memory of it.

He did not laugh long, for David was on him like a tempest. The fuddled troopers heard a denunciation which did something to sober them by chilling their marrow. As men, as soldiers, as Christians, he left them no rag to cover them. "You that fight in God's cause," he cried, "and are worse than brute beasts! Get back to your styes, you swine, and know that for every misdeed the Lord will exact punishment a thousandfold." He was carried out of himself in his wrath. "I see each one of you writhing on a coming field of battle, waiting to change the torments of the flesh for the eternal agonies of Hell. You are the brave ones--your big odds gave you a chance victory over one that for a year hunted you and your like round the compass--and you purge your manhood by murdering frail women."

It was not a discreet speech, and a sentence or two of it pierced through their befuddlement, but it sent them packing. They were too conscious of the power of a black gown in Leslie's army to dare to outface a minister. David marched homeward with his heart in a storm, to find an anxious Isobel.

"These are dreidfu' days," she moaned. "We were telled that Montrose's sodgers were sons of Belial, but if they were waur than yon Leslie's they maun be the black

Deil himsel'. Wae's me, bluid is rinnin' like water on Aller side. There's awfu' tales comin' doun from the muirs o' wild riders and deid lasses--ay, and deid bairns--a' the puir clamjamphry that followed the Irish. It canna be richt, sir, to meet ae blood-guiltiness wi' anither and a waur. And yon thrawn ettercap frae Bold ridin' wi' the sodgers and praisin' the Lord when anither waefu' creature perishes! And Chasehope, they tell me--black be his fa'--guidin' the sodgers to the landward buts-and-bens like a dowg after rattons! Catch yon lad frontin' an armed man, but he's like Jehu the son of Nimshi afore defenceless women."

David asked if any one had been near the manse.

"That's what fickles [puzzles] me. There's been naebody at the door, but there's been plenty snowkin' round. There's a gey guid watch keepit. And waur than that, there's sodgers in the clachan-- ten men and ane they ca' a sairgent at Lucky Weir's. I heard routin' as I gaed by the kirkton, and, judging by the aiths, there's sma' differ between them that fechts for Montrose and them that uphauds the Covenant."

Next day the uneasiness of both increased. The place was thronged with troopers, among them the men whom David had denounced at the Greenshiel. It is probable that his hasty words had been reported, for dark looks followed him as he passed the ale-house. Moreover, Isobel had news in the village that Leslie's main forces were even now moving towards Woodilee, and that the triumphant general himself would lodge in the village. Where would such lodging be found except in the manse? At any moment the guest-room and its contents might lie bare to hostile eyes.

By the afternoon David had come to a decision. The wounded man must at all costs be moved. But where? Calidon would be as public as the street, and besides he had heard that a picket had been stationed there in case its laird came looking for shelter. . . . The hills were too open and bare, Reiverslaw would be suspect--in any case its tenant babbled in his cups. . . . Then he had an inspiration. Why not Melanudrigill, for its repute would at ordinary times make it the perfect sanctuary? He would be a bold man, it was true, who sought a lair in its haunted recesses, but this Mark Kerr did not lack for stoutness of heart. He found him yawning and extracting indifferent entertainment from a folio of Thuanus.

Kerr only grinned when he heard of the danger.

"I might have guessed that the place would soon be hotching with Davie's troops. And maybe I'm to have Davie in bed aside me? Faith, I fear we wouldna agree, though I'll no deny that the man has a very respectable gift in war. . . . I must shift, you say, and indeed that is the truth of it, but hostelries are no that plenty in this countryside for one like me that's so highly thought of by his unfriends."

Melanudrigill was set before him, and he approved.

"The big wood. Tales of it have come down the water, but I've never paid much attention to clavering auld wives. . . . There's black witchcraft, you say--you've seen it yourself? I care not a doit. There's just the one kind of warlock that frichts me, and that's a file of Davie Leslie's men. Find me a bed in a hidy-hole and some means of getting bite and sup till I can fend for myself, and I'll sit snug in Melanudrigill though every witch coven in Scotland sat girning round me with the Deil playing the bagpipes."

David was clear that he must be moved that night, but he was far from clear as to how it was to be done. He did not dare to take any other into the secret, not even Reiverslaw or Amos Ritchie, for hatred of Montrose was universal among the Lowland country folk. He and Isobel might make shift to get him to the Wood, for Isobel was a muscular old woman, but there was much to do besides that--a bed to be found, food transported, some plan made for a daily visit. There was no help to be found in Woodilee.

And then he remembered Katrine Yester.

For a long time he would not admit the thought. He would not have the girl enter a place of such defilements. The notion sickened him and he put it angrily from him. . . . But he found that a new idea was growing in his mind. The Wood had been a nursery of evil, but might it not be purified and its sorceries annulled if it were used for an honest purpose? The thought of Mark Kerr, with his hard wholesome face and his mirthful eye, eating and sleeping in what had been consecrated to midnight infamies, seemed to strip from the place its malign aura. . . . To his surprise, when he thought of Mark in the wood, he found that he could think of Katrine there also, without a consciousness of sacrilege. The man was her uncle's comrade-in-arms--he was of the cause to which she herself was vowed--she was a woman and merciful--she was his only refuge. . . . Before the dusk fell he was on the road to Calidon.

He had expected to find a house garrisoned and dragooned, and had invented an errand of ministerial duty to explain his presence. He found instead a normal Calidon--the evening bustle about the gates, an open door, and Katrine herself taking the air in the pleasance beside the dovecot. She came towards him with bright inquiring eyes.

"You have soldiers here?" he asked breathlessly.

She nodded to a corner of the house, which had been the shell of the old peel tower.

"They are there--three of them--since last night. They arrived drunk--with two wretched women tied to their stirrups. . . . We were most courteous to them, and they were not courteous to us. So Jock Dodds wiled them into the place we call the Howlet's Nest and gave them usquebagh and strong ale till they dropped on the floor. They are prisoners and woke up an hour ago, but they may roar long and loud before a cheep is heard outside the Howlet's Nest, and the door is stout enough to defy an army."

"But Leslie himself will be here. Other soldiers will come, and how will you explain your prisoners?"

The girl laughed merrily. "Trust Aunt Grizel. Two lone women-- violent and drunken banditti--locking them up the only way--and then a spate of texts and a fine passage about soldiers of the good cause setting an ensample. I will wager my best hawk that Aunt Grizel will talk down General Leslie and every minister in his train. . . . The women are safe in the garret, less hurt than frightened. The poor things talk only the Erse, and there's none about the town to crack with them."

He told her of the midnight visit to the manse and the lame man left on his hands.

"You saw him?" she whispered. "You saw the Lord Marquis. How did he look? Was he very weary and sorrowful?"

"He was weary enough, but yon face does not show sorrow. There's an ardour in it that burns up all weakness. He would continue to hope manfully though his neck were on the block."

"Indeed that is true, and that is why I will not despair. When I heard the news of disaster I did not shed a single tear. . . . Whom did he leave behind?"

"The tall man--Mark Kerr is his name--who was in this house of yours a year back. Him that has a cast in his eye."

"But that is the Lord Marquis's most familiar friend," she cried. "The occasion must be desperate which parts them."

"The occasion grows more desperate," he said, and told her of the need for instant removal.

When he spoke of the Wood she showed no surprise.

"Where else so secret?" she said.

"Dare you go into it?" he asked. "For unless I have your help the business is like to prove too hard for me. I will confess that it sticks in my throat to stir one step myself into the gloom of the pines, when I ken what has been transacted there, and it sticks sorer to have you in that unholy place. But if this Kerr is to be saved, there's need of us both. The man will have to be fed, and that would be done more easily from Calidon than from the manse."

"Why, so it must be. I have been pining for some stirring task, and here it is to my hand. I will be your fellow-labourer, Mr. David, and we begin this very night. For a mercy there is a small moon. . . . No, Aunt Grizel shall not hear of it. I have the keys and can leave and enter the house as I choose. When the dusk comes and our guests in the Howlet's Nest are quiet from hoarseness, I will bid Jock Dodds carry certain plenishing to Paradise."

A little before midnight, when even the clamour of Lucky Weir's was still, three figures stole from the manse, after David by many reconnaissances had assured himself that the coast was clear. Montrose's erstwhile captain was dressed like a small farmer, in David's breeches and a coat that had once belonged to Isobel's goodman. He had a rude crutch, with which he managed to keep up a good pace, having learnt the art, he said, during an escape from a patrol of Wallenstein's, which for greater security had manacled the prisoners in pairs leg to leg. Isobel prospected the road before him like a faithful dog, while David steadied him with his arm. In such fashion they crossed the Hill of Deer, and in a darkness lit only by the stars came to the glade called Paradise. There they found awaiting them a glimmering girl, at the sight of whom Isobel's fears broke loose, for she prayed in words not sanctioned by any Kirk, and her prayer was for mercy from the Good Folk.

Kerr made an attempt at a bow. "Mistress Yester, it is not the first time I have come for succour to women of your house. They say I must take to the shaws like Robin Hood, but the wildwood will be a palace if you are among its visitors."

"Yester," Isobel muttered to herself. "The young leddy o' Calidon! Wha wad have thocht that the minister was acquaint there? Certes, she's the bonny ane," and she bobbed curtsies.

Katrine was the general. "These bundles are bedding and food. Up with them, sir, and I will guide Captain Kerr. I have also brought a covered lantern, which will light us through the pines better than your candle, Mr. David. La, this is a merry venture."

The sense of company, the presence of Katrine and the soldier, the nature of the errand, above all the preposterous figure of Isobel, whose terrors of the Wood were scarcely outweighed by her loyalty to her master and her curiosity about the girl, took from the occasion for David all sense of awe, and even endowed it with a spice of fun and holiday. The mood lasted till they had crossed the boundary glen and entered the pines; it endured even when, feeling their way along the foot of the low cliffs, they looked downward and saw by the lantern light an eerie white stone in a dim glade. The girl guided them to a dry hollow where an arch of rock made a kind of roof and where a yard off a spring bubbled among the stones. It was she, and not Isobel, who made a couch of branches and fir boughs on which she laid the deerskins and plaids she had brought. It was she, and not

David, who gathered dry sticks against the morning fire and saw that Kerr had flint and steel and tinder. It was she, too, who made a larder of a shelf in the rock, where she stored the food, and fixed certain hours of the day for further provisioning, and enjoined a variation of routes to prevent suspicion. It was she finally who presented Kerr with a pistol, shot, and powder--belonging, it is to be feared, to one of the imprisoned troopers--and who saw him to bed like a nurse with a child.

"I'm as snug here as a winter badger," said Kerr contentedly. "I lack nought but a pipe of tobacco, and that I must whistle for, seeing that I left my spleuchan at Philiphaugh. . . . Mistress, you've the knack of an old campaigner. You might have been at the wars."

"The men of my race have always been at the wars, and the women have always dreamed of them," she said, and on his forehead she kissed him good-night.

David Leslie came to Woodilee in the morning, but did not halt, pushing on to Lanark in the afternoon. His army was in less of a hurry, and three troop-captains made their beds in the manse, while the minister slept on his study floor. They were civil enough, cadets of small houses in Fife, who had had their training in arms abroad, and cared as little for the cause they fought for as any mercenary of Tilly's. Within two days the neighbourhood was clear of soldiery, save for the garrisons left as earth-stoppers at houses like Calidon, which might be the refuge of malignants.

For a week Mark Kerr lay in the recesses of Melanudrigill, and for David the days passed like a seraphic vision. Every night after the darkening he met Katrine in Paradise, and the two carried to the refugee his daily provender--eggs and milk, ale from the Calidon buttery, cakes which were Mistress Grizel's, cheese which was Isobel's. For David the spell of the Wood had gone. He looked on it now as a man does at his familiar bedroom when he wakes from a nightmare, unable to reconstruct the scene of his terrors. His crusading fury, too, had sensibly abated, for part of his wrath against witchcraft had been due to his own awe of the Wood and his disgust at such awe. Now the place was a shelter for a friend, and a meeting-ground with one he loved, and the cloud which had weighed on him since he first saw it from the Hill of Deer gave place to clear sky. Men might frequent Melanudrigill for hideous purposes, but the place itself was innocent, and he wondered with shame how he came ever to think that honest wood and water and stone could have intrinsic evil.

Nightly, in the light mists of the late September, when pine trees stood up out of vapour like mountains, and the smell of woodland ripeness was not yet tinged with decay, David and Katrine threaded the aisles and clambered among the long bracken, till a pinpoint of light showed from beside a rock and was presently revealed as Kerr's bivouac. They would sit late with him, listening to his tales and giving him the news of the glens, while owls hooted in the boughs and from the higher levels came the faint crying of curlews. There was much business to be done between Mark and Calidon--business of Nicholas Hawkshaw's, who had been duly put to the horn, and over whose goods, by the intrigues of Mistress Grizel, a friendly curator had been appointed, and business of his own anent the tack of Crossbasket--and Katrine carried daily messages by letter and by word of mouth. When his leg was healed there was a certain polish to be given to his appearance, and the ladies of Calidon were busy with their needles. When he left his lair at last it was just before dawn--on foot, with a blue coat instead of the hodden grey of Isobel's goodman, and four miles on the Edinburgh road Jock Dodds from Calidon waited with a horse for him.

David would fain have had the leg prove troublesome, that the time of hiding in the Wood might be prolonged, for that season passed for him with the speed of a too happy dream. To be with Katrine was at all times bliss, but to be her partner on these dark journeys and in these midnight conclaves was a rapture of happiness. If he had lost his awe of the Wood, he had lost also the sense that in letting his heart dwell on the girl he was falling away from duty. The standards of the Kirk meant the less to him since he was in declared controversy with its representatives, and a succourer by stealth of its enemies. His canons of conduct were dissolving, and in their confusion he was willing to surrender himself to more ancient instincts. The minister was being forgotten in the man and the lover.

The lover--though no word of love was spoken between the two. They were comrades only, truant children, boy and girl on a Saturday holiday. It was a close companionship, yet as unembarrassed as that of sister and brother. In her presence David caught her mood, and laughed with it, but when absent from her he was in a passion of worship. The slim green-gowned figure danced through his waking hours and haunted his dreams. He made no plans, forecast no future; he was in that happy first stage of love which is content to live with a horizon bounded by the next meeting.

In such a frame of mind he may have grown careless, for he did not see what Isobel saw. His housekeeper, brisk with the consciousness of a partnership with her master in things unlawful and perilous, and under the glamour of Katrine's gentrice and beauty, was as unquiet as a hen with a brood of young ducks on the pond's edge. She clucked and fussed, and waited for David's return in an anxious tempest. "There's queer ongaein's in this bit," she told him. "When I hearken in the sma' hours I hear feet trailin' as saft as a tod's [fox], and whiles a hoast [cough] or a gant [yawn] which never cam' frae a tod's mouth. And yestreen when ye set out, sir, there was something slipped atween the birks and the wa' and followed. I wish it mayna be your deid wraith." He pooh-poohed her fears, but on the last night, when he parted from Katrine in Paradise, and according to his custom watched her figure as, faint in the moonlight, it crossed a field of bracken above Rood, he saw something move parallel to her in the fern. On his way home, too, as he passed the kirkton road in the first light, there was a rustling among the elders, and a divot fell mysteriously from the turf dyke.

CHAPTER XIV

THE COUNTERBLAST

He dreamed that night that he was being spied upon, and next day-- with no more meetings with Katrine before him to fire his fancy-- his cold reason justified the fear. The conviction was presently confirmed by a discovery of Isobel's. Mark Kerr's cast clothes had been hidden at first in the gloom of the rafters in David's camceiled bedroom, but the coming of Leslie's troops compelled her to change this place of disposal to the stable, where, in the space between the wall and the thatch, she bestowed them, wrapped stoutly in sacking. She kept an eye on the bundle, and one morning it had disappeared. More, it had clearly been stolen and hurriedly opened, for the sacking and a tarry rope which bound it were found among the nettles beyond the kirkyard wall. Compromising goods indeed to come forth of a minister's house!

That same day Isobel returned from a visit to her cousin with a queer tale.

"Something's gotten out, sir. The wives in the kirkton are clatterin' like daws. 'What's this they tell me, gossip,' says one, 'about Babylonish garments found in the manse?' 'Faith, I kenna,' says I. 'They're nane o' my findin', but wi' roarin' sodgers quartered in ilka chamber ye'll no surprise me if some unco gear were left behind.'

'But it's nae honest gear o' Davie Leslie's lads,' she says, 'but the laced coats and plumit hats o' the malignants. And there's a report that ithers hae sleepit in the manse this past se'nnight than our ain Covenant sodgers.' 'Wha tell't ye that, my wumman,' I says, 'was a black leear, and a thief forbye. I'd like brawly to ken wha has been snowkin' round our doors and carryin' awa' leein' tales and maybe some o' our plenishin'. Tell me the names, and, man or wumman, I'll hae my fingers at their lugs.' It was Jean of the Chasehope-fit that spoke to me, and she got mair frae me than she expeckit. There wasna ane o' her auld misdaein's I didna fling in her teeth."

The name of the woman disquieted David, and he asked what she had answered.

"Her! She took my flytin' wi' downcast een, and that angered me sae that I had muckle ado to keep my hands frae her face. Syne she says, quietlike, 'Ye needna get in a steer, Isobel Veitch. If Mr. Sempill's an honest man, he'll get his chance to redd up the "fama".' "Fama", says she, whatever yon may mean--there's a reek o' Chasehope about the word. And she went on wi' her saft een and her mim mou'.--'There's waur nor that, Isobel wumman,' she says. 'Our minister, that's sae fierce against warlocks, has been walkin' a queer gait. There's them that hae seen him in the Wud, and wha do you think he met wi' there? It's no a name that I daur speak, but folk hae brunt for less than sic a randyvoo.' Ye may fancy, sir, what a stound I got, but I just spoke the kimmer civil, and speired for mair. She wasna laith to tell. 'There's them,' says she, 'that saw the green gown o' the Queen of Elfhame, and the mune shinin' through her hair, and saw her gie a kiss to the minister.' Ye never kissed the leddy, sir?"

"God forbid," cried David, startled as if at an impiety.

"I thocht ye werena just as far forrit as that. . . . Weel, that's the tale they've gotten, and may it stick in their thrapples! I'm no feared for their blethers about fairies, but we'll need some stench lees to get the sodger's claes blawn over. I wish I kenned wha was the thief. I'll threip that they were left by Leslie's folk and that ye kenned nocht about them."

"Por me," said David, "I shall tell the plain truth, save in the mentioning of names. I command you, Isobel, to do likewise. The man is by now out of danger, and a falsehood, which may be pardoned if it is to save another, is black sin if used by a coward to save himself."

Isobel looked at him uneasily. "There will be an awfu' speak in the parish, sir. Bethink ye, is it wise to gie sic a handle to them that wad bring ye doun? . . . But I see your mind is made up, and nae words o' mine will turn ye. We maun hope that the question will never be speired, and I daur ony man or wumman in the place to get sae far wi' ME as the speirin'."

During David's absence in Edinburgh Mr. Fordyce, by the command of the Presbytery, had preached in the afternoon in the Woodilee kirk-- to but scanty audiences, for the news of Montrose's advance had inclined the people to keep inside their doors. On the first Sabbath after his return, when there were still troops in the place, the pulpit had been occupied by one of Leslie's chaplains, a stalwart member of the Church militant, who hailed from the Mearns, and whose speech was consequently understood with difficulty in the Border parish. But on the next, when Mark Kerr had gone from his refuge in the Wood, David changed his mind, and himself filled the pulpit. At the news a great congregation assembled, for in that joyous day of delivery it was believed that the sins of the parish would be left on one side, and that the service, as in the other kirks in the land, would be one of thanksgiving and exultation. To the surprise of most of his hearers--and to the satisfaction of the suspicious--there was no word of the recent crowning mercies, save a perfunctory mention in the opening prayer.

David, as befitted one who had just buried his father, discoursed on death. He was in a mood which puzzled himself, for gentleness seemed to have come upon him and driven out his jealous wrath. He had seen the righteous die, the man who had begot him, the last near kin he possessed, and memories of childhood and something of the wistfulness of the child had flooded in on his soul. He had seen, too, the downfall of human pride, the descent of greatness to dust, and yet in that dust a more compelling greatness. Above all, his love for Katrine had mellowed and lit the world for him; it had revealed depths of joy and beauty which he had never known, but the beauty and joy were solemn things, and of a terrible fragility. He felt anew the dependence of all things upon God, and the need of walking humbly in His sight. So he preached not like an Old Testament prophet, confident in his cause and eager to gather the spoil, but as one who saw from a high mountain the littleness of life against the vast background of eternity. He spoke of the futility of mortal hopes, the fallibility of man, the certainty of death. In a passion of tenderness he pled for charity and holiness as the only candles to light the short dark day of life--candles which, lit by a heavenly hand, would some day wax into the bright everlasting day of the New Jerusalem.

There were those among his hearers who were moved by his words, but to most they were meaningless, and to many they were an offence. Peter Pennecuik was darkly critical. "The man is unsound as a peat," he declared. "Whaur's the iron o' doctrine and the fire o' judgment in sic a bairnly screed? There's an ill sough there, sirs--he's ower fond o' warks and the rags o' our ain righteousness. Worthy Mr. Proudfoot will be garrin' the stour fly the day denouncin' the Laodiceans that wad be lukewarm in cuttin' off the horns o' the wicked. Is there ony such godly zeal in our man? Whaur's the denunciation o' the sins o' Montrose and his covenant-breakers? It seems that he's mair convinced o' his ain sins."

"He has maybe cause," Chasehope observed dryly.

It had been David's intention to visit the manse of Kirk Aller and obtain the answer of the Presbytery's moderator to the charges he had formulated. This was a duty which could not be shirked, since he had put his hand to it, but at the moment the fire of battle had died in him, and he had no zest in the task. He found himself longing to take Isobel's view and believe that his senses had played him false, that the events of the Beltane and Lammas nights were no more than illusions. So he had delayed journeying to Kirk Aller, hoping that his mood would change, and that that which was now a cold duty would revive as a burning mission. . . . Suddenly a post brought him a summons from Mr. Muirhead to wait upon him without delay.

He rode down the riverside in a day of October glooms and shadows. Sometimes a wall of haze would drop from the hills so that the water ran wan as in the ballads, and the withering fern and blanching heath had the tints of December. Then a light wind would furl the shrouded sky into fantastic towers and battlements, through long corridors of which the blue heavens would shine like April at an infinite distance, and the bald mountain-tops, lit by sun-gleams, would be revealed. When he rode over the crook-backed bridge of Aller, past the burgh gallows, he saw that the doomster had been busy at his work. Three ragged scarecrows hung in chains, the flesh already gone from their limbs, and a covey of obscene birds rose at his approach. Stragglers of

Montrose, he guessed, and he wondered how many gallows-hills in Scotland showed the same grim harvest. The thought, and the fantastic October weather, deepened the gloom which all morning had been growing on him.

He found a new man in the minister's chair. The victory of his cause seemed to have expanded Mr. Muirhead's person, so that he loomed across the oaken table like a judge in his robes. Pride pursed his lips, and authority sat on his forehead. Gone were the airs of tolerant good-humour, the assumption of meekness, the homeliness which had a greeting and a joke for all. This man sat in the seats of the mighty and shared in the burden of government, and his brow was heavy with the weight of it. He met David with a cold, inquisitorial eye, and greeted him with a formal civility.

"I sent for you, Mr. Sempill," he said, "anent the charge which you have set out in these papers, and on which you have already conferred with me. There has been no meeting of Presbytery, owing to the disturbances in public affairs, but I have shown the papers to certain of my brethren and obtained their mind on them. I have likewise had the privilege of the counsel of the godly laird of Wariston, who, as you no doubt ken, is learned alike in the law of God and the law of man. I have therefore taken it upon myself to convey to you our decision, whilk you may take to be the decision of the courts of the Kirk, and that decision is that there is no substance in your case. You are upset on the relevancy, sir. There is nothing here," and he tapped the papers, "which would warrant me in occupying the time of folk who have many greater matters in hand."

"I did not ask for a judgment, but for an inquiry, and that I must continue to demand."

"Ay, but you must first show a prima facie case, and that you have failed to do. You have brought grievous charges against one noted servant of God, and sundry women, of whom it can at least be said that they bear a good repute. Your evidence--well, what is your evidence? You say that you yourself have seen this and heard that, but you are a tainted witness--a matter to which I shall presently revert. . . . You have the man Andrew Shillinglaw in Reiverslaw, who, in the bit of precognition with which you have furnished me, tells a daft tale of dressing himself up like a mountebank, visiting the wood of Melanudrigill, and sharing in certain unlawful doings. I ask you, sir, what credence can be given to such evidence? Imprimis, he was himself engaged in wrongdoing, and so is justly suspect. Item, he is a notorious wine-bibber, and when the maut is in, the wits are out. Whatna condition was he in to observe justly in the mirk of the night in the Black Wood, where by his own account he was capering like a puddock and was all the time in a grue of terror? He claims on that occasion to have laid a trap for the accused and to have informed two men of undoubted Christian conversation of his purpose, and he claims that on the next day the same witnesses at the toun of Chasehope were cognizant of the success of his trap. As I live by bread and by the hope of salvation, this is the daftest tale that ever came to my ears. A smell of burning duds, and a missing hen! The veriest cateran that ever reived in the Hielands would be assoilzied on such a plea. There is not evidence here to hang a messan dog. Away with you, man, and let's hear no more of what I can only judge to have been a drunken cantrip."

"I demand that Ephraim Caird be interrogated by the Presbytery and confronted with me and my witnesses."

"You must first prove a prima facie case, as I say, for otherwise honest men might lose time and siller in being set to answer malicious libels. That is the law of Scotland, sir, and it is the law of every Christian land, and you have lamentably failed in that prior duty."

"There is my own evidence--the evidence of an eyewitness. You may account for Reiverslaw, but you have still to account for me."

"Just so." A grim humour seemed to lurk at the corner of Mr. Muirhead's mouth. "We have to account for you, Mr. Sempill, and it seems that it will be a sore business. For I have here"--he tapped a paper--"another dittay in which you yourself are named. It is painful for me even to give ear to accusations against a brother on whose head my own hands have been laid in holy ordination. But I have my solemn duty to perform, and must consider the complaints of a kirk session against a minister as carefully and prayerfully as those of a minister against a kirk session."

The effect on David was of a sudden clearing of the air and a bracing of nerve. This was, then, to be no one-sided war, for his enemies had declared themselves, and met attack by counter-attack. He smiled at the portentous solemnity of Mr. Muirhead's face.

"I can guess one of the names appended to the charge," he said. "It is that of Chasehope."

Mr. Muirhead turned over the paper. "Ephraim Caird is there, and others no less weighty. There is Peter Pennecuik . . . and Alexander Sprot in Mirehope . . . and Thomas Spotswood in the mill of Woodilee. If godly elders are constrained to delate him who has been set over them in spiritual affairs, it's scarcely a thing to be met with a smirk and a grin."

"I am waiting to hear the charge."

"It is twofold. The complainants allege that you have had trokings with the Wood and the evil of the Wood--and indeed on your own confession we know that you have frequented it when decent folk were in their beds. There are witnesses to depone to following you to the edge of the thing, as you made your way stealthily at dead of night. On what errand, Mr. Sempill? And in what company?"

"That is what I would like fine to know," said David.

"You were seen to meet a woman. They were simple folk who saw you and not free from superstition, so they jumped to the conclusion that the woman was no mortal, but the Queen of the Fairies. That's as it may be. You and me are not bairns to believe in fays and bogles. But the fact that emerges is that you were in the Wood at night, not once but many times, and that you were seen in a woman's company. That is a fine report on a minister of God, and it will want some redding up, Mr. Sempill."

"My movements were wholly innocent, and can be simply explained," said David. But the charge maddened him, he blushed deep, and he had much ado to keep his tongue from stammering. He wrestled with a pagan desire to buffet Mr. Muirhead violently on his large authoritative face.

"But can you explain THIS?" the latter cried, for he was not unconscious of David's confusion. "There is a second charge, and its gravamen is the heavier, seeing that it alleges an offence both against the will of God and the governance of this land. On the 26th day of the month of September in this year of grace there was found in the appurtenances of the manse of Woodilee--to wit, in the baulks of the stable atween the thatch and the wall--a bundle of garments, including a laced coat such as is worn by malignants, and sundry other habiliments strange to the countryside, but well kenned in the array of caterans whereof Montrose was the late leader. It is argued, therefore, that shelter was given in the manse to a fugitive, and that a minister of the Kirk connived at the escape from justice of one of the Kirk's oppressors. What say you to that, sir?"

"I say that it is true."

David was not prepared for the consternation in the other's face. Mr. Muirhead sat erect in his chair, his head was poked forward from between his shoulders like that of a tortoise from its shell, colour surged over cheeks and forehead and his bald crown, and his voice, when he found utterance, was of an unnatural smallness. His careful speech broke down into country dialect.

"Ye admit it! God peety you, ye do not blench to admit this awful sin! Have ye no shame, man, that ye sit there snug and canty and confess to a treason against Christ and His Kirk?"

There was more in the man's face than anger and incredulous horror; there was pity, regret, a sense of an unspeakable sacrilege done to all that he held most dear. David saw that the minister of Kirk Aller, though he might have little love for himself, would have given much had this confession been unsaid--that he felt that shame had been cast upon his calling and even upon his own self-respect. So he answered gently:

"A wounded man came to my door. I fed him and nursed him, and he is now, I trust, in health and safety. I would do the same thing again for any distressed mortal."

Mr. Muirhead's eyes goggled.

"Have you no notion--have you no glimmering of what you have done? I speak patiently, for I'm driven to think you're not right in the mind. You have loosed on the world a malefactor, a slayer and despoiler of God's people."

"I have his word that he will not again take up arms in Scotland. He was a soldier of the great Gustavus."

"What's the word of a malignant to lippen to? Man, you're easy begowked. When the Lord's command anent our enemy is Smite and spare not, you, an ordained minister, connive at his escape. . . . Ay, and there's more to it. I have news that you molested Leslie's troops in their pursuit of a light woman that followed Montrose's camp, and that you took the name of the Lord in vain in interdicting them from their manifest duty. Have you not heard that at the brig of Linlithgow the wantons were drowned in scores by the command of the worthy General, whilk was a notable warning to sinners and an encouragement to God's people? Are there not Commissions of the Estates and of the Kirk appointed to judge the captured malefactors in Edinburgh and St. Andrews, and gallows set on every burgh knowe besouth of Forth? And you dare help to cheat the wuddy of one who was no doubt the blackest of them? There's no a presbytery in the land but has sent in a memorial to encourage those in authority in their righteous work. For shame, man! Even in your own parish you have Chasehope lending a hand and riding the hills like a moss- trooper--the very man you would delate for sin."

"I obey God's word and my own conscience. I can imagine no blacker sin than cruelty to the defenceless."

"God's word!" cried Mr. Muirhead. "You've been lamentably ill- instructed. What did Joshua to the people of Jericho, but utterly destroy them, both man and woman, young and old? What did Gideon to the kings Zeba and Zalmunna? What was the command of the Lord to Saul when he went out against Agag king of the Amalekites but to slay both man and woman, infant and suckling, and when Saul would have saved Agag, what said Samuel to him?--'Rebellion is as the sin of witchcraft and stubbornness is as iniquity and idolatry.' Your eyes are full of fatness if you canna see the Lord's will. And your conscience! You would set up your own fallible judgment against God's plain command and the resolved opinion of the haill Kirk."

"I am a minister of Christ first and of the Kirk second. If the Kirk forgets its Master's teaching, we part company."

"And what's that teaching, prithee?"

"To have mercy and not sacrifice."

The minister of Kirk Aller closed his eyes as if in pain.

"You're deep deep in the mire of your carnal conceits," he said. "I thought you were only wayward and mistaken, but I see you're firm on the rock of your impenitence. Troth, Mr. Ebenezer of Bold was in the right--you've heresy in you as well as recalcitrance. This is Presbytery business, sir--ay, and maybe matter for the General Assembly. I would be a faithless guardian of the sheepfold if I didna probe it to its bottom. This complaint must go forward.--Meantime, till the Presbytery has adjudged it, I forbid you to conduct the ordinances in the kirk of Woodilee. I will appoint some worthier person, lest the pure gospel milk on your lips be turned to poison."

"I refuse to obey you," said David, "for you have no power to command. I stand on my rights to continue my ministrations till such time as the lawful authority sets me aside. Meantime I require that my charge against Chasehope go to the Presbytery equally with his charge against me."

Mr. Muirhead was on his feet, with the famous glower on his face which had aforetime awed timid brethren. It did not awe David, who gave him back stare for stare with a resolution to which he was little accustomed. Indeed the vigorous youth of his antagonist and something in the set jaw made the elder man pause. He shuffled off as if to end the interview, and David strode from the house with unseeing eyes and a burning heart.

All the way home his head was filled with a confusion of angry thoughts. He saw himself caught in toils at once absurd and perilous. He could imagine the prejudice which his sheltering of the fugitive would raise against him; he saw his indictment of Chasehope nullified by this legend of his own visits to the Wood; above all, the bringing in of Katrine made him clench his hands with a sense of furious sacrilege. In that moment he seemed to himself like a child without friends battering at a wall as broad as the earth and as high as the heavens. . . . But the consequent feeling was not of hopelessness but of a tight-lipped rage. He longed to be in a world where blows could be struck swift and clean, and where hazards were tangible things like steel and powder. Not for the first time in his life he wished that he had been a soldier. He was striving against folly and ignorance, blind prejudice, false conventions, narrow covenants. How much better to be fighting with armed men!

Isobel met him at the manse door with a portentous face.

"There's a new man come to Crossbasket," she announced. "His plenishin' cam' up the water this mornin'--four horse-loads--and the drovers are bringin' his sheep and kye. I saw the body himsel' in the kirkton an hour syne. He's the rale down-the-water fairmer breed, verra weel set up and no that auld, and he wears a maud like a herd. But Mr. David, sir"--she lowered her voice--"guess ye wha he is? I couldna be mistook, and when he cried me guid day I saw brawly that he kenned me and kenned that I kenned him. He ca's himsel' Mark Riddel, but it's the glee'd sodger man that lay in our best bed."

CHAPTER XV

HALLOWMASS

Ill news travels fast, and by noon next day word of the complaint against their minister, of Mr. Muirhead's suspension of him from the pulpit, and of David's defiance was in the mouth of every parishioner in Woodilee. David was aware of curious eyes following him as he went about the place, and of a new constraint on the part of most of his Kirk Session. Peter Pennecuik fled his approach, and could be seen hobbling into the nearest kailyard, while Mirehope, when he met him, gave him greeting with averted face. But he noted, too, a certain sympathy in others. Women, who had formerly avoided him, had now a friendly word, especially the young ones, and Alison Geddie--whose name had appeared in his charge--was overheard, as he passed, to comment in her pea-hen voice to her gossip: "Peety for sae wise-like a lad, and him aye with the kind word and the open hand to puir folk."

Isobel, whose face was now always heavy with unspoken news, he kept at a distance, for in these days he was trying to make peace with his soul. By day and by night, on the hills and in his closet, he examined himself to find in his conscience cause of offence. He went over every step in his past course and could discover no other way than that he had followed. He could not see matter for blame in an act of common charity, though Old

Testament precedents might be quoted against it; nor could he blame himself for his war against the things of the Wood. If he read his duty more by the dispensation of Christ than of Moses, it was Christ whom he had been ordained to preach. . . . Of Katrine he scarcely suffered himself to think. She was a thing too fine and gracious to be touched with such doleful cares. Yet it was the thought of her which kept youth alive in him, and in his dreariest moments gave him a lift of the heart. When he looked down from the Hill of Deer on the dark shroud of Melanudrigill and beside it the shaws of birch and hazel which stretched towards Calidon, he saw his strife as a thing natural and predestined, and he himself as only a puppet in the grip of primordial powers. The thought gave him the confidence which springs from humility.

On the Sabbath he preached from a text in Ecclesiastes: "So I returned, and considered all the oppressions that are done under the sun: and behold the tears of such as were oppressed, and they had no comforter; and on the side of their oppressors there was power; but they had no comforter." His hearers looked no doubt for some topical word, but they did not find it; few realized the meaning of a discourse which David preached rather to himself than to others. It was a confession of faith, a plea for personal religion, and an anathema against shibboleths and formulas which did not dwell in the heart. So long as religion is a pawn in a game of politics--the argument ran--so long will there be oppressors and oppressed, with truth the perquisite of neither side, and therefore comfort to none. . . . The congregation was notably reduced, for the five elders and their families were absent. But there was one new figure who sat modestly in the back parts of the kirk. It was that of a man of middle age, dressed like the other farmers in homespun, but holding himself with a spruceness rare in a place where men and women were soon bowed in the shoulders by unremitting toil. His cheeks were shaven, so that he stood out from the others, since, besides the minister, only Chasehope was unbearded. His skin was as brown as a hazel-nut, and though the face was composed to a decent gravity, there was a vigour in the lines of it which spoke of a life not always grave. The man had a blue bonnet of a pattern common nearer the Border-- smaller than the ordinary type which came from the Westlands--and after the fashion of Cheviot and Liddesdale he had a checked plaid of the kind called shepherds' tartan. But in the cast in the left eye, shown by a sudden lifting of the face, he revealed his identity.

The stranger did not wait to speak to the minister, but David found Amos Ritchie at the kirkyard gate, and asked concerning him. "It's the new man that has ta'en the tack o' Crossbasket," was the answer. "He's frae the far Borders--Jeddart way, they tell me--and it's no easy to understand the wild hill tongue o' him. But he's a decent, weel-spoken body, and it seems he's a skilly fairmer and a graund judge o' sheep. He has stockit his mailin' weel, and has a full hirsel on Windyways. . . . Na, he's a single man and bauds to himsel', though he has a name for a guid neebor."

Amos accompanied the minister to the manse, and there was a shy friendliness in his air, as if he regretted the estrangement of the summer. He spoke only of weather and crops, but his manner suggested a desire to say something by way of encouragement. Only at the manse gate, however, did he find utterance. "If there's deep waters to be crossed, sir, I'll ride the ford wi' ye," he muttered as he turned away.

Presently it was apparent that a change had come over the parish. David's doings in the summer had puzzled and alarmed it; even those with a clear conscience had thought of him as a danger to their peace and good repute. But now that he was himself in dire trouble, and indicted before the Presbytery, there was a revulsion in his favour; his friendliness was remembered, his kindness in the winter storms, his good looks and his youth. He had his own party in the place, a party composed of strange elements. There were in it noted professors like Richie Smail and Rab Prentice; Isobel and her kin were hot on his side; Reiverslaw, of course, many of the frequenters of Lucky Weir's ale-house, and all who from poverty or misdeeds were a little blown upon. If the Pharisees and Scribes were against him, he had the publicans and sinners. Also he had the children. By some secret channel the word had gone round in the circles of childhood that their friend was in trouble, and in queer ways they showed their affection. The girls would bring him posies; bowls of wild rasps and blaeberries would be left at the manse; and often on the doorstep Isobel found an offering of guddled trout neatly strung on rushes. Daft Gibbie, too, had become a partisan. He would dog David's footsteps, and when spoken to would only reply with friendly pawings and incoherent gabble. He would swing his stick as if it were a flail. "Sned them, sir," he would cry, "sned them like thristles."

But the comfort of the atmosphere in which he now moved was marred for David by the conduct of Reiverslaw. That worthy had been absent in Nithsdale when Philiphaugh was fought, and did not return till the week after the battle. It would seem that the general loss of stock due to the disturbances had benefited his pocket; he had sold his hog-lambs to advantage, and had had a prosperous deal in black cattle with Leslie's quartermaster. By the middle of October the work on the hill farms was all but over for the year, and Reiverslaw was a leisured man. Whether the cause was the new access of wealth or the excitements of Lammas, he fell into evil courses. There was word of brawls in ale-houses as far apart as Lanark and Kirk Aller, and he would lie for days in Lucky Weir's, sleeping off potations, only to renew them in the morning. His language coarsened, his tongue grew more unbridled, his aptitude for quarrels increased till he became a nuisance in the village and a public scandal. "A bonny friend ye've gotten in Andra Shillinglaw," Isobel said bitterly. "For three days he has been as fou as the Baltic, and cursin' like a cornet o' horse." David made several attempts to reason with him, penetrating to the back parts of the alehouse, but got no reply but tipsy laughter and owlish admonitions. It looked ill for the credit of his principal witness.

The call of Calidon was always in his ears, but he did not yield to it. October brought a fortnight of drenching rains, and Katrine came no more to Paradise. He could not bring himself to seek her in her home, for he dared not compromise her. Already a nameless woman appeared in the tales against him, and he would have died sooner than let the woman's identity be revealed. From her he had had kindness and comradeship, but these things were not love, and how could he ask for love when every man's hand was against him and he could offer nothing but companionship in disrepute? . . . But loneliness weighed on him, and he longed to talk with two especially--the minister of Cauldshaw and the new tenant of Crossbasket. But when he rode one afternoon to Cauldshaw, it was not only the minister's self that drew him there, but the remembrance that the Calidon household were among his parishioners.

Mr. Fordyce was scarcely recovered of an autumn ague, and his little bookroom was as bleak and damp as a grave. He sat in a wooden armchair, propped up with pillows, nightcap on head, a coarse drugget dressing-gown round his shoulders, and two pairs of stockings on his thin shanks. His wife was sick a-bed, outside the rain dripped steadily, there was no fireplace in the chamber, and gloom muffled it like a shroud. Yet Mr. James was casting a horoscope, and mild and patient as ever.

"Tell me the whole story, Mr. David, for I've heard naught but rumour. They say you've fallen out sorely with Mr. Mungo at Kirk Aller."

David recounted the events of the past months, beginning with Lammastide in the Wood, and ending with his last visit to Mr. Muirhead, The other heard him out with many sighs and exclamations, and mused for a little when he had finished.

"You havena been over-gentle with the Moderator," he said. "Far be it from me, that am so imperfect, to impute error to a brother, but you canna deny that you took a high line with Mr. Mungo."

"I was within my rights in refusing to obey his suspension. He had no resolution of the Presbytery behind him."

"Maybe no. But was there no excess of vehemence, Mr. David, in defying one who is your elder? Would not the soft word have availed better? You seem to have spoken to him like a dominie to a school bairn."

"Oh, I do not deny that I was in a temper, but if I was angry it was surely with a righteous anger. Would you have me let that black business of the Wood be smothered just because Chasehope, with his sleek face and his cunning tongue, has imposed on the Presbytery? And for the charge against myself, would you, I ask you, have refused succour to any poor soul that came seeking it, though his sins were scarlet on him?"

"I'll not say. I'm a timid man by nature, and I'm so deeply concerned with my own state towards God that I'm apt to give other duties the go-by--the more shame to me! In the matter of the Wood I think you have done honestly and bravely, and I doubt I wouldna have had the courage to do likewise myself. The Lord be thankit that such a perplexity never came my way! . . . As for Montrose's man, what am I to say? Mr. Mungo will quote Scripture against you, and it's not for me to deny the plenary inspiration of the whole Word, though I whiles think the Kirk in Scotland founds a wee thing over much on the Old Testament and forgets the New. But I can see great trouble for you there, Mr. David, for the view of Kirk Aller will be the view of the Presbytery--and the view of the General Assembly, if the thing ever wins that far."

"But what would you yourself have done in like case? Would you have turned the suppliant from your doors?"

"I do not know. To be honest with you, I do not know. I am a weak vessel, and very fearful. But in such a case I should pray--ay, I should pray to be given strength--to do as you did, Mr. David."

The young man smiled. "I've got the comfort I wanted. I'm content to be judged by you, for you are nearer the Throne than the whole Presbytery of Aller and the Merse."

"No, no. Dinna say that. I'm the feeblest and poorest of God's servants, and at the moment I'm weakening on what I said, and doubting whether a man should not bow to lawful authority, and cultivate a humble spirit, as the first of the Christian graces. What for did our Lord found the Kirk if it wasna to be obeyed?"

"Bide where you were, Mr. James. What kind of a Presbyterian would you make yourself out? By your way we should be still under the bondage of Rome, because Rome was once the lawful authority. A bonny Covenanter, you! If the Kirk constrains conscience unduly, and makes a tyranny out of Christian freedom, then the Kirk is no more to be respected than the mass the old priests mumbled in Woodilee."

Mr. Fordyce smiled wanly. "I daresay you're in the right. But what a tangle for an honest man! You've taken the high road, Mr. David, and I must keep jogging along the low road, for there's but the two of them. A man must either jouk and let the jaw go bye, as the owercome says, or he must ride the whirlwind. I have been given the lown downsetting, where I can nourish my own soul and preach Christ to the best of my power, and let the great matters of Kirk and State pass me, as a man hears the blast when he sits by his fireside. It is for stronger spirits like you to set your face to the storm. Alack and alas, I'm no fierce Elijah to break down the temples of Baal, and I'm no John Knox to purge the commonwealth of Israel. If you go forward in God's name, my dear young man, you'll have a hard road to travel, but you'll have the everlasting arms to support you. . . . But oh, sir, see that you fight in the Lord's strength, and not in your own. Cultivate a meek and contrite spirit, for I suspect that there is a good leaven of the old Adam in your heart."

"That's a true word. There's an unregenerate heat of temper in me at which I often tremble."

"And you must keep your walk and conversation most pure and circumspect. Let there be no cause of reproach against you save what comes from following your duty." Mr. Fordyce hesitated a little. "There was word of another count in Mr. Mungo's complaint anent you. . . . Wasna there some tale of a woman?"

David laughed.

"The Queen of the Fairies, Mr. Muirhead says, though he does not believe in her. . . . I have a confession to make to you, Mr. James, which I would make to no other ear. I have met with a lady in the Wood, for indeed she was engaged with me in the same errand of mercy. I had met with her before that, and I count the days till I may meet with her again. It is one whom you know--Katrine Yester."

"Mistress Katrine!" Mr. Fordyce cried out. "The young lassie from Calidon. Mr. David, Mr. David, is this not a queer business for a minister of the Kirk? Forbye that she is of a house that is none too friendly to our calling--though far be it for me to deny her Christian graces--forbye that, I say, she is of the high gentrice. What kind of wife would she be for a poor Gospel preacher?"

"Oh, man, there's no question of wife. You make me blush to hear you. The lady would never think of me any more than an eagle would mate with a throstle. But a minister is a man like the lave [rest], and this one is most deeply in love, though he has not the thousandth part of a hope. There's no shame in an honest love, which was a blessing given to man by God's own self in Eden."

"It's a matter I ken little of," said Mr. Fordyce shyly. "Me and Annie have been that long wedded that we've forgot what our wooing was like. She wasna by-ordinar in looks, I mind, but she had a bonny voice, and she had mense and sense and a fine hand for making apple jeely. . . . Mistress Katrine! You fly high, David, but I wouldna say--I wouldna say. . . . Anyway you've a well-wisher in me. . . . But Katrine Yester!"

David left the minister of Cauldshaw ingeminating that name, and in a blink of fine weather set out on his way home. He was on foot and beyond Reiverslaw, where the road first runs out of the birks to the Hill of Deer, when he was overtaken by a horseman. The mount was no farmer's shelty or minister's garron, but a mettled chestnut mare, with marks of breed in head and paces, and he who rode her was the new tacksman of Crossbasket.

In that open bright place there could be no eavesdropper. The rider dismounted and flung his arms round the minister.

"I pay my debt," he cried, "by becoming your dutiful parishioner, your next-door neighbour, and your faithful hearer ilka Sabbath. . . . Danger, you say. Man, the darkest hidy-hole is just under the light, and the best sanctuary for a hunted man is where he is not expected. They're riping the ports for Mark Kerr, once captain of Mackay's and till late a brigadier under the King's Captain-general, but they'll no trouble about honest Mark Riddel, a plain farmer-body from Teviotside, that comes up Aller seeking a better tack and has mair knowledge of sheep than any herd on the hills. And Mark will pay his way with good white siller, and will be a kind neighbour at kirk and market. My Roxburghe kin are buried deep, but there's folk in Woodilee already that mind of my great- aunt that was married into Annandale, and my cousin once removed that was a herd in Megget. Trust an old soldier for making a fine palisado around him of credible lees. I run no risk save the new ones that I make for myself, and I'm in no mind for that, for a peaceful year or two will be good for my soul, till I see whatna way the cat jumps. Montrose must get him abroad, and if I'm to bide quiet let it be in my own countryside and not in a stinking foreign city. . . . But for yourself, Mr. David? From all I hear you've been making an ill bed to lie on."

They sat down in the roadside heather, and David brought up to date the tale which he had first told him in the deeps of the Wood. To unburden himself to this man was a greater comfort than his talk at Cauldshaw, for this was one accustomed to desperate straits and chances, and of a spirit more akin to his own. The soldier whistled and looked grave.

"Faith, you've stirred up the hornets, and it's not easy to see where you will get the sulphur to smoor them. There's much in common between you and my Lord Marquis. You see the ills of the land and make haste to redd them, but you have no great notion of what is possible."

"You would not have had me do otherwise?"

"No, no. I like your spirit fine, and beyond doubt you've taken the honest road. But we live in a pitiful world, where honesty is an ill-requited trade; and you've let yourself be forced into defence, whilk is an unpleasant position for a campaigner. . . . Count me on your side, but let me take my own gait. It winna do for you and me to appear to be chief [friendly] in public. I'll make haste to conciliate the mammon of unrighteousness--whilk I take to be Chasehope--so dinna wonder if you hear that the two of us are like brothers. But it's the Kirk I fear, your own sacred calling, Mr. David. One shilpit body in bands and a Geneva gown, the way things are guided now, is more powerful than a troop of horse, and less easy to get upsides with. . . . Still and on, I'm at hand across the glebe, and we'll no be beat for lack of good contriving. The night's the time, when we can step across and collogue at our ease."

To have the soldier at Crossbasket gave a lift to David's spirit. But at first he saw him rarely, for it was wise to let the man settle down in the place before appearing in his company, lest people should suspect a previous friendship. Mark Riddel appeared to be for ever on the move, and the minister met him oftenest on the Rood road--generally in the early darkness. It pleased him to think that his neighbour was visiting Calidon, for it seemed to bring Katrine nearer. But he made no effort to see the girl himself. With the fall of the leaf the season for Paradise had gone, and he could not seek her at home till he had unravelled the tangle of his own perplexities.

The chief of them was the approach of Hallowmass. He was determined not for one moment to forgo his charge against Chasehope and his coven, whatever the counter-charge against himself might be, and if necessary to go in person again to the Wood. But his chief ally, Reiverslaw, spent his days drinking soddenly in the clachan, and when he sought him out at the ale-house he got nothing but fuddled laughter. Then one morning he found him on the hill, and apparently in a better mind.

"My ran-dan is bye," said Reiverslaw sullenly. "Ye've cause to upbraid me, sir, and no words o' yours can be waur than what I gie mysel'. It's apt to take me that way at this time o' year, and I think black burnin' shame that I should be sae thirled to the fauts o' the flesh--drinking like a swine in a stye among folk that, when sober, I wadna touch wi' a graip's end. I'm no better than the beasts that perish. But I've fand out ae thing in these humblin' days. There'll be nae Wud at Hallowmass. The folk we ken o' dinna fancy the Wud aince the Lammas is bye, and it's the clachan itsel' that will see their next cantrips."

"But there is no place that could contain them--" David began.

"I ken, but they maybe follow some ither gait. I'll be in the kirkton that nicht--na, na, ye needna fear for me, I'll no gang near the hostler-wife--the verra thocht o' yill and usquebagh staws [sickens] me. But I'll be there, and you maun be in the manse, and we'll guide our gait according to what the nicht brings forth. I'll wager Chasehope will no be long out o' my sicht, and if he meddles wi' me he'll find me waur than the Deil's oxter. . . . Keep a watch on yoursel' that day, sir, for there's mony will wish ye out o' the clachan."

The last day of October came, and David rose to find that the rain had gone, and that over the drenched hills had dawned a morning as bright as April. He spent the forenoon in distracted study, striving to keep his mind on printed pages, but his restlessness was such that after dinner it sent him to the moors. He took his old road for the Rood tops, and by three o'clock had reached the pass from Clyde, where in July he had had his talk with Reiverslaw.

The earth was soaked with the October rains, and as the sun's power declined in the afternoon a mist began to creep out of the glens. Insensibly the horizon shortened, the bold summit of Herstane Craig became a blur and then was hidden in clouds, the light wind of the morning died away, and over the land crept a blind eerie stillness. David turned for home, and long before he had reached the crest above Reiverslaw the fog was down on him. It was still a gossamer covering through which it was possible to see a hundred yards ahead, but objects stood up in it in unfamiliar outlines--a sheepfold like a city wall, a scrag of rowan like a forest tree.

A monstrous figure appeared in the dimness, which presently revealed itself as a man on horseback. David saw that it was Mark on his chestnut.

"Well met," the man cried. "I'm pushing for home, for I'm getting the yowes to the infield, but I saw you before the mist dropped and I guessed I would find you here. There's a friend of yours up bye that would be blithe to see you--up the rig from the auld aik on the road to the Greenshiel." With no further word Mark touched his mare and went off at a canter.

The friend, thought David, would be Richie Smail, who might have some message to him from Reiverslaw. So he turned as directed past the root of oak towards the ridge of the hill. In twenty yards a figure loomed before him, a figure on a horse. He fancied it was Mark returning, till as he drew nearer he saw that it was no man that sat the black gelding and peered into the thick weather.

It flashed through his mind that Mark had sent him here on purpose. And then something came into his soul which he had never known before, a reckless boldness, a wild joy which caught at his heart. The girl was looking away from him, and did not turn her head till he was close on her and had spoken.

"Mistress Katrine," he cried breathlessly.

She looked down on him, her face rosy, her hair bedabbled with the mist jewels. She did not start at his approach. Was it possible that she was expecting him?

"What does the minister on the hill?" she asked.

"What does Mistress Katrine? It will be a thick night and you are still far from Calidon."

She was dressed all in green, with a kirtle which scarcely reached her ankles and left her foot in the stirrup clear. The feather from her green hat hung low over her curls. David had never seen a woman gloved and booted for the hunt, and in that hour and in that wild place the apparition was as strange and as beautiful as a dream.

"I took out the hawks this morning with Edie the falconer, for the mallards were flighting over from Clyde. Edie went back an hour ago with the birds, and I lingered to watch the mist creep up. Maybe I have lingered too long."

"That was good fortune for me," he said. "I have not dared to come seeking you, but now that we are met I will convoy you to Calidon. Presently the world will be like the inside of a feather bed."

She made no protest, when he laid his hand on her bridle to turn her horse, and as he stole a look at her he saw that she was smiling. That smile sent a tremor through him so that he forgot every care and duty. He and she were enclosed in a magical world-- together and alone as they had never been before. . . . He felt that he could bring her safely through raging rivers and across mountains of stone, that for her he could scale the air and plough the hills, that nothing was impossible which she commanded. They two could make of the world a song and a rapture. So deep was his transport that he scarcely heard her voice when she spoke.

"I have been hearing of your troubles, Mr. David. He whom we must call Mark Riddel has told me."

"I have no troubles," he cried. "Now that I see you the world is altogether good."

"Will you tell that to the Presbytery?" she asked, laughing.

"I will tell it to the broad earth--if you give me leave."

A momentary confusion came over her. She slightly checked her horse, and as the ground shelved the beast stumbled. The slip brought her in contact with David's shoulder, and before she knew his hand was laid on hers.

"Oh, my dear, my dear," he cried. "Katrine, I must say it . . . I am daft for love of you. . . . Since I first saw you down in the greenwood your two eyes have been sun and moon to me. Your face-- God forgive me--comes between me and the Word. There are times when I cannot pray for thinking of you. . . . It's nothing I ask of you, Katrine, but just leave to tell you. What was it your song said?--'There's nane for me but you, my love'--and oh! it's the gospel truth."

She did not reply, but her hand did not move under his. They were descending the hill towards Rood, and the fog had grown so thick that each to the other was only a shadow. Before it had enclosed them in a visible encirclement; now it seemed to have crept so near that it dislimned the outlines of horse and rider. He held her by touch rather than by sight, and this disembodiment seemed to give him courage.

"I seek nothing," he said, "but that you should know my love. I am perplexed with coming battles, but so long as you're in life there's nothing can daunt me. I would not have you smirched with the stour of them, but if you'll let me think of you and mind of you and whiles see you I'll be as strong as Samson. The papist cries on his saints, and you are the saint whose name is written on my heart."

Still she did not speak, and he cried out in alarm.

"Have I angered you? Forgive me--forgive me--but I had to speak. Not one other word more will I say till we are at Calidon door."

Her answer, when it came, was strange, for it was a song crooned very softly:

"It's love for love that I have got, And love for love again."

A great awe came over David and checked his breath--the awe of one who sees and yet does not believe, the answer to a hopeless prayer. His hand tightened on hers, but she slipped it away. "So turn," she sang:

"So turn your high horse heid about And we will ride for hame, my love, And we will ride for hame."

The hand which had moved from under his was laid on his head. Suddenly a face bent down towards him and a kiss as light as a bird's wing brushed his forehead. He caught her to him from the saddle.

CHAPTER XVI

THE WITCH HUNT

David awoke next morning to a world which had been suddenly re- created. That Katrine should return his love upheaved for him the foundations of the globe. Nothing could be the same again, in face of this tremendous fact; his troubles lifted like mist in the sun, for what ill could befall one whom Katrine loved? Even the incubus of sin in Woodilee seemed to lighten, for evil could not prevail with such a lady walking the earth. He felt that he had come anew into the land of the living, and every fibre of him sang praises.

His new fortitude was proof against even the news which Reiverslaw brought. That worthy arrived at the manse with a long face. The coven in Woodilee had held their Hallowmass rites, and to the best of his belief they had held them in the kirk. . . . He had lost sight of Chasehope early in the evening, and had gone to Mirehope on a false scent. . . . They had been watching the manse and knew that the minister was from home. . . . He had hastened up the road seeking David and had been overtaken by the fog, and when he got back to Woodilee the place had been under a blanket. Doubtless the Devil was protecting his own. . . . There had been no cruisies lit in the cottages, even of those who were known to be of the coven. But, as luck would have it, he had entered the kirkyard and had seen a speck of light in the kirk. The door was locked, but he was clear that there were folk inside. . . . He had roused Robb to get the key, but no key was to be found. He had gone for Amos Ritchie to break open the door, and though Amos had refused to stir, he had borrowed a mell and a crowbar; but when he reached the kirk, the place was quiet and dark again, and the keys were lying on Robb's doorstep.

The man was really shocked, for this was a superfluity of naughtiness for which he had not been prepared. To David, with a memory of his Kirk Session, the sacrilege was less of a surprise; if men and women could defy their Maker by sitting at the communion table and by taking in vain the Gospel words, they would not shrink from polluting God's house. But it proved the boldness and security of the evildoers. It was Chasehope of whom he chiefly thought, Chasehope, that darling of the Presbytery, the ally of the Kirk in hunting down malignants, the one in all the parish who flaunted most his piety. The man grew in stature as he contemplated him. Here was no feeble sinner, but a very provost in the craft, who turned all the uses of religion to his foul purposes. And at the thought David, fired by his new happiness, almost rejoiced; he was fighting not with human frailty, but against a resolute will to damnation.

That day he received a summons to attend on the following Monday upon a special meeting of Presbytery at Kirk Aller for a preliminary examination. The thing seemed to him now to have lost all terrors. He had no anger against his accusers, for were they not dull old men who knew nothing of the ravishing world that had been opened to him? He would be very meek with them, for he pitied them; if they chose to censure and degrade him he would bear it patiently. His extreme happiness made him feel more than ever in the hands of the Almighty and disposed to walk softly before Him. He had given many hostages to fortune, but he had won something which could never be taken away. Thankful and humble he felt, in love with life and with all humanity, and notably less bellicose. His path of duty was clear, but he would not court antagonisms. He owed much to the less fortunate, he who daily met Katrine in the greenwood or on the hill in the soft noons which make a false summer at autumn's end.

So on the Sabbath he preached a sermon which was long spoken of in Woodilee. He discoursed of charity--a topic not popular in the Kirk, and commonly left to such as Mr. Fordyce who were afflicted with ill-health. For a young minister, his face ruddy with the hill winds and his figure as well set up as a dragoon's, to expand on such a matter seemed a mere waste of precious time, when so many more marrowy subjects lay to his hand. Yet there was that in David's earnestness which impressed his audience almost as much as if his sermon had been on death and judgment. He had a new hearer. A man sat beneath the pulpit whose eyes never moved from the minister's face--a mere lath of a man, thin to emaciation, with a narrow head and a much-freckled face, a ragged beard, and eyes with red lights in them like a ferret's. David noticed that, as the kirk emptied, the others seemed to shun the newcomer's proximity. As he moved to the door, there was a drift away from him, like sheep from a collie.

That night Isobel gave him news of the stranger.

"The pricker has come," she announced in a solemn voice. "He arrived yestreen and is bidin' wi' Chasehope. Yon was him in the kirk the day, yon body wi' the fernietickles [freckles] and the bleary een. They ca' him Kincaid--John Kincaid, and he's frae Newbottle way--anither than a guid ane, if a' tales be true. Eh, sir, this is a shamefu' business, routin' out puir auld bodies and garrin' them gie daft answers, and syne delatin' them on what they ca' their confessions. There's naebody safe that hasna a power o' keepin' a calm sough and giein' back word for word. I wadna be feared mysel' o' ony Kincaid, but if you was to cross-speir me, Mr. David, wi' your searchin' een, I daresay ye could get me to own up to ony daftness ye liked to pit to me. I dinna aud wi' this prickin' o' witches, and I can find nae warrant for it in the Word. Belike it's some device that thae weary Embro lawyers hae howkit out o' their rotten herts."

As he rode to Kirk Aller next day David reflected much on Isobel's tale. Who could have brought a pricker to Woodilee--and lodged him with Chasehope? Was it the work of the Presbytery? Was it a plan to cover up the major sin by hunting out minor sinners? He knew of the pricker class as of the worst repute, knaves and quacks who stirred up popular superstition and were responsible often for hideous brutalities. Even the Law looked askance at them. He did not like to be absent from his parish when such a creature was let loose in it.

The examination of the Presbytery lasted for two days. He had gone lightly to face it, but he found it a formidable affair. Business began with long prayers and prelections delivered to his address. The Moderator constituted the court with the formality of a Lord of Session and the solemnity of a minister fencing the tables at the Communion season. He announced that the matter for examination would be limited to the charge of assisting the Kirk's enemies. The prior charge of witchcraft preferred by the minister of Woodilee against certain parishioners would be relegated to a later day, since the Privy Council on his motion had issued a commission to inquire into the machinations of the Devil in that parish, naming as its members himself, the minister of Bold, and the Laird of Killiequhair. This, thought David, explains the pricker. Mr. Muirhead added that he had moved in the matter at the request of a godly elder, known to all of them, Ephraim Caird in Chasehope.

The court was composed of the two score of ministers in the Presbytery, and only Mr. Fordyce was lacking, for he was once more stretched upon a bed of sickness. As it was only a preliminary examination there were no witnesses, since the object was to give the accused a chance of stating his case and so narrow the issue to be ultimately tried. The Moderator read aloud sworn statements, to which no names were appended, the names, as he explained, being reserved for the time when the complainants should appear in person. To David it was obvious that, though one of the statements was by a soldier of Leslie's, the others must come from members of his own flock. There was nothing new in the details--the finding of the cavalier's clothes in the manse outhouse, the interference with the troopers at the Greenshiel, and certain words spoken on that occasion; but what surprised him was the fact that the avowal which he had made to Mr. Muirhead was not set down. It was clear from the Moderator's manner that he proposed to forget that episode, and was willing that David should deny any and every charge in the libel. Indeed he seemed to encourage such a course. "The Court will be glad," he said, "if our young brother can blow away these most momentous charges. Everybody kens that among wars and rumours of war daft tales spring up, and that things are done in the confusion without ill intent, whilk are not defensible. It is the desire of all his brethren that Mr. Sempill shall go forth assoilzied of these charges, which are maybe to be explained by the carelessness of a domestic and the thoughtless words of a young man carried for a moment out of himself, and no doubt incorrectly reported."

But David did not take the hint. He avowed frankly that he had entertained a fugitive of Montrose at the manse, and had assisted him to escape. Asked for the name, he refused to give it. He also confessed that he had endeavoured too late to protect an Irishwoman at the

Greenshiel, and had spoken with candour his opinion of her persecutors.

"It is alleged," said a heavy man, the minister of Westerton, "that you promised these poor soldiers eternal torments, and them but doing their Christian duty, and that you mocked at them as inferior in valour to the reprobate Montrose."

"No doubt a false report, Mr. Archibald," said the Moderator. "It's like that the worthy sodgers had been looking at the wine when it was red and werena that clear in their understanding."

"I cannot charge my memory with what I said," David replied, "but it may well have been as set forth. That, at any rate, was what I had it in my mind to say."

A sigh of reprobation rose from the Court, and the Moderator shook his head. He honestly desired to give David a way of escape, not from any love he bore him, but for the credit of the Kirk. This, too, was the general feeling. As David looked over the ranks of his judges he saw stupidity, arrogance, confusion, writ on many faces, but on none malevolence. This Court would deal mildly with him, if he gave them the chance, for the sake of the repute of their common calling.

He laboured to be meek, but no answers, however soft, could disguise the fact that he and they looked upon things from standpoints eternally conflicting. It was suggested to him again and again that the stranger at the manse had been entertained by his housekeeper, an ignorant woman and therefore the less reprehensible, for had she not rolled up the clothes and hidden them in the byre, as the accused admitted? But David refused to shelter behind any misapprehension. He had admitted the man, what was done had been by his orders, and--this in reply to a question by the minister of Bold--what he had done he was prepared to do again. The close of the first day's sederunt found the charges proven in substance by the admission, indeed by the vehement proclamation, of the accused.

For David there was no share in the clerical supper at the Cross Keys. He lay at a smaller inn in the Northgate, a resort of drovers and packmen, and spent such time as remained before bed in walking by Aller side, under the little hill crowned with kirk and castle, watching the salmon leap as they passed the cauld. Next day, the facts having been ascertained by admission, the Presbytery debated on principles, David was summoned to justify his conduct, and--with a prayer that he might be given humility--complied. With every sentence he rode deeper into the disapprobation of his hearers. He claimed that the cause of the helpless, however guilty, was the cause of Christ. Should a starving enemy be turned from the door, even though it was an enemy of the Kirk's?

"Man, can ye no distinguish?" thundered the minister of Bold. "Have you no logic in your head?" And he quoted a dozen savage Scriptural precedents against him.

Was the Court, David asked, in a time of civil strife and war between brothers, clear that the precedent of Israel and the tribes of Canaan held? The men they fought against were professing Christians, indeed professed Presbyterians. Granted that they were in error, was it an error which could only be extirpated in blood?

It was an unlucky plea, for it brought forth a frenzied torrent of denials. The appeal of his opponents was not only to Scripture, but to the decisions of the Kirk. Was there not here, one cried, that rebellion which was as the sin of witchcraft? What became, cried another, of the deference which a young man was bound to show to the authority of his fathers in God? "Are we to be like Rehoboam, who hearkened to callow and inexperienced youth, and not to those elders who partook of the wisdom of his father Solomon?"

Presently David was silent. He remembered that meekness became him, and he had a sharp sense of the futility of argument. Respectfully he bowed his head to the blast, while a dozen of his brethren delivered extracts from their recent sermons. The Moderator confirmed the sense of the Court.

"Our young brother is lamentably estranged from Christ," he said in a voice which was charged with regret as well as with indignation. "He is like the Church of

Laodicea, of whom it was written, 'Because thou art lukewarm, and neither cold nor hot, I will spue thee out of my mouth.' I tell you, sir, he that is not with us is against us, and that in the day of the Lord's judgments there can be no halting between two opinions. It is the duty of the Kirk to follow His plain commandment and to rest not till the evil thing be utterly destroyed from our midst, even as Barak pursued after the chariots to Harosheth of the Gentiles, and all the host of Sisera fell upon the edge of the sword, and not a man was left. You are besotted in your error, and till you repent you have no part in the commonwealth of Israel, for you are like Lot and have taken up your dwelling in the Cities of the Plain and have pitched your tents towards Sodom, whereas the Kirk, like Abram, dwelleth in the plain of Mamre, which is in Hebron, and hath built there an altar to the Lord."

The Presbytery refrained from any judgment on the case, that being deferred till a later meeting, when, if necessary, evidence could be called; but in view of the fact that the minister of Woodilee had acknowledged his fault and exhibited contumacy thereanent, he was by a unanimous decision suspended from occupying the pulpit and dispensing the Sacrament in the parish, and from all other pastoral rights and duties. As the winter was close on hand, when evil roads lessened church attendance, it was agreed that spiritual needs would be met if Mr. Fordyce were enjoined to conduct public worship alternately in Woodilee and Cauldshaw.

David rode home in a frame of mind which was neither sad nor glad. He felt no shame at his suspension, but he recognized with a pang the breadth of the gulf which separated him from his brethren, and the ruin of those high hopes with which a year ago he had begun his ministry. He realized that he was but a poor ecclesiastic, for he could not feel that loyalty which others felt to a Kirk which was mainly the work of men's hands. "They have lamentably perverted reason and justice"--he remembered Montrose's words; and yet most of them were honest men and pious men, and maybe their good on a wide computation was greater than their ill. It was his unhappy portion to have encountered the ill. But if the Kirk cast him off he had Christ--"Other sheep I have which are not of this fold," was Christ's word--and he must follow with all humility the light that was given to him. When the main trial came on he would not relent in his denunciation of the Wood, and his loss would be well repaid if, like Samson, he could bring down with him the pillars of Gaza. . . . He consoled himself thus, but he knew in his heart that he had no need of consolation, for the thought of Katrine was there like a live coal.

He came to the manse in the gloaming, to find Isobel waiting for him in the road.

"Heaven save us a'!" she said, "but there's an awfu' thing come to Woodilee. They've prickit a witch, and it's nane ither than puir Bessie Todd o' the Mains. Guid kens what they did till her, but a' nicht the clachan rang wi' her skirlin'. The pricker fand the Deil's mark on her back, and stappit a preen [pin] intil it up to the heid and nae bluid came, and they burnt her feet wi' lichtit candles, and hung her by the thumbs frae the cupples till they garred her own to awesome deeds. I canna believe it, the puir doited body, but if the ae half is true she's far ben wi' the Adversary, and oh, sir, it's fearsome to think what wickedness can be hidden in the hert o' man. She said the Deil gie'd her a new name, whilk she wadna tell, and she owned that ilka Lord's Day, when she sat under ye on the pu'pit stair, she prayed to him--'Our Father, which wert in Heaven.' But whatever her faut, it canna be richt the way they guidit her, lickin' her wi' a bull's pizzle and burnin' the gums o' her till she yammers like a bitted powny. If she maun dee, let death come quick. For the Lord's sake, Mr. David, get her down to the Kirk Aller tolbooth, for the Shirra is kinder than yon red brock [badger] o' a pricker. The verra sicht o' his wild een sends a grue to my banes--and Chasehope standin' by him and speakin' saft and wicked, and smilin' like a cat wi' a mouse."

David's heart sickened with disgust. Chasehope had turned the tables on him; he had diverted suspicion from himself by sacrificing a half-witted woman. And yet this Bessie Todd had been a member of the coven--he had seen her grey locks flying in the Wood. Chasehope was presiding at the examination and torture; he would no doubt take good care that no word of the truth came out in her delirium. And Isobel, who had denied with violence his own charges against this very woman, seemed to believe her confession. She was revolted by the cruelty, but convinced of the sin. That would no doubt be the feeling of the parish, for who could disbelieve avowals which must send the avower to a shameful death?

"Where is the wretched woman?" he asked.

"They have her lockit up in Peter Pennecuik's girnel. . . . They've gotten a' they want, and they say that the Shirra has been sent for to carry her to the Kirk Aller steeple, whaur they confine the warlocks. . . . They're in the girnel now, and the feck o' Woodilee is waitin' at the door. Will you stop for a bite? . . ."

David waited only to stable his horse, and to buckle on the sword with which he had girt himself on the night of the second Beltane. He ran so fast towards the clachan that he was at Peter Pennecuik's house before Isobel, labouring in his wake, had turned the corner of the manse loan.

The night had fallen dark, but from inside the girnel came a flicker of light. David had once before seen a witch hunt--in Liberton, as a boy--and then there had been a furious and noisy crowd surging round the change-house where the accused was imprisoned. But the Woodilee mob was not like that. It was silent, almost furtive. The granary was a large building, for it had once been the barn of the Mains farm; it was built of unmasoned stone cemented with mud, and had a deep roof of thatch; through the chinks of both walls and roof came thin streams of light. The spectators did not press on the door, but stood in groups some paces back, as hushed as in the kirk of a Sabbath. The light was too dim for David to recognize faces, but he saw that one man stood at the door as keeper, and knew him for Reiverslaw.

He had been drinking, and greeted the minister hilariously.

"We've gotten ane o' the coven," he whispered thickly, "ane you saw yoursel' in the Wud."

"But Chasehope is among her accusers."

"I ken, but we'll get that kail-worm too, in the Lord's guid time. At ony rate, we're sure o' ane o' the deevils."

"You fool, this is a trick of Chasehope's to divert attention from the Wood. This miserable woman has only confessed bairnly faults, and on that he'll ride off scot free."

The truth penetrated slowly to Reiverslaw's foggy brain, but in the end he saw it.

"God's curse on him, but ye're maybe right. What are ye ettlin', sir? Gie me the word and I'll come in by and wring the truth out o' him wi' my hands at his gutsy thrapple."

"Bide where you are, and let none leave this place unless I bid you. I will see if I can get justice done."

But when Reiverslaw opened the heavy door to let him enter, the first glance told David that he had come too late. The great empty place had straw piled at one end, and on a barrel in the centre a flickering lantern. By it, on an upturned barrow, sat the pricker, a paper in his hand and an inkhorn slung round his neck, his face wearing a smirking satisfaction. He had once been a schoolmaster, and at this moment he looked the part again. Behind him, sitting on kegs or squatted on the floor, were a dozen men--Chasehope at his elbow, Mirehope, the miller, Peter Pennecuik, Nether Fennan--David saw only a few faces in the dim light. Daft Gibbie by some means or other had gained entrance, and had perched himself in a crevice of the wall, whence his long shoeless legs dangled over Chasehope's head.

On the straw behind the lantern lay the witch. Her grey hair had fallen round her naked shoulders, and that and a ragged petticoat seemed her only covering. Even in the mirk David could see the cruel consequences of torture. Her feet were black and swollen, and her hands, with dislocated thumbs, were splayed out on the straw as if they were no longer parts of her body. Her white face was hideously discoloured in patches, and her mouth was wide open, as if there were a tormenting fire within. She seemed delirious, for she gabbled and slavered uncouthly to herself, scarcely moving her lips. Every now and then her thin breast was shaken with a frenzied shivering.

At the sight something gave in David's head. He felt the blood rush above his eyebrows, and a choking at the back of his throat. Always a hater of cruelty, he had rarely seen its more monstrous forms, and the spectacle of this broken woman awoke in him a fury of remonstrance. He strode to the lantern and looked down on her, and then turned away, for he sickened. He saw the gimlet eyes of the pricker--red like a broody hen's--and behind him the sullen, secret face of Chasehope.

"What devil's prank have you been at?" he cried. "Answer me, Ephraim Caird. Who is this mountebank, and what have you done to this unhappy woman?"

"All has been done decently and in order," said Chasehope. "The Presbytery is resolved to free this parochine of the sin of witchcraft, and this worthy man, who has skill in siccan matters, has been sent to guide us. There is a commission issued frae the Privy Council, as ye may have heard, to try those that are accused, but the first needcessity is to find the witches and exhort them to confession. This woman, Elspeth Todd, is convict out o' her ain mouth, and we've gotten a memorial o' the ill deeds she owns to. Word has been dispatched to the Shirra, and the morn, nae doot, he'll send and shift her to Kirk Aller."

The man spoke smoothly and not discourteously, but David would have preferred oaths and shouting. He put a great restraint on his temper.

"How did you extort the confession? Answer me that. You have tortured her body and driven her demented, and suffering flesh and crazed wits will avow any foolishness."

"We followed the means sanctioned by ilka presbytery in this land. It's weel kenned that flesh sell't to the Deil is no like common flesh, and the evil spirit will no speak without some sort o' compulsion."

David snatched the paper from the pricker and held it to the lantern. It was written clearly in a schoolmaster's hand, and though oddly and elliptically worded, he made out the sum of it. As he read, there was silence in the place, except for the babbling of the woman and the mowing of Daft Gibbie from his perch.

It seemed to him a bedlamite chronicle. The accused confessed that she had been guilty of charming, and had cured a cow on the Mains by taking live trouts from its belly. She had "overlooked" a boy, Hobbie Simson, at Nether Fennan, and he had sickened and lain for three months on his back. She had made a clay figure of one of the ewe-milkers at Mirehope and stuck pins into it, and the girl had suffered from pains and dizziness all summer. She had shot cattle with elf-bolts, and had cursed a field on Windyways by driving round it a team of puddocks. The Devil had trysted with her on a rig of Mirehope's, and had given her a name which she would not reveal, and on the rig there had been ever since an intractable crop of thistles. Her master visited her in the likeness of a black cat, and she herself had often taken the same likeness, and had travelled the country at night sitting on the crupper of one of the Devil's mares. By means of the charm of the seven south- flowing streams and the nine rowan berries, she had kept her meal- ark full in the winter famine. She confessed to having ridden John Humbie, a ploughman of Chasehope's, night after night to a witch- gathering at Charlie's Moss, so that John was done with weariness the next day and unfit for work. The said John declared that he woke with the cry of "Up horsie" in his ear. At these gatherings she admitted to having baked and eaten the witch-cake--a food made of grey bear and a black toad's blood, and baked in the light of the moon, and at the eating had sung this spell:

"Some lass maun gang wi' a kilted sark; Some priest maun preach in a thackless kirk; Thread maun be spun for a dead man's sark; A' maun be done ere the sang o' the lark."

She admitted that she had taken the pains of childbirth from women-- but what women she would not say--and that then the child had been born dead, and had so become a "kain bairn" for the Devil. Last, and most damning, she had between her shoulders the Devil's secret mark.

Some sentences from the document David read aloud, and in his voice there was bitter scorn. He believed most devoutly in the menace of witchcraft and in a Devil who could take bodily form and divert the course of nature to seduce human souls, but this catalogue of sins seemed to him too childish for credence. It was what any woman crazed with pain might confess in the hope of winning respite. Most of the details he remembered from his boyhood as common talk; the witch-cake rhyme he had sung himself; the charm to fill Bessie's meal-ark during the winter he knew to be false, for she had nearly died of want, and he had fed her from the manse kitchen. . . . He had seen her in the Wood, and yet there was no mention of the Wood. Chasehope had been present at the torture, and doubtless his fell influence had kept her rhapsody away from the point of danger. The poor soul was guilty, but not of this childishness.

He looked at her as she lay, mindless, racked, dying perhaps, and an awful conviction entered his mind. She was a human sacrifice made by the coven to their master. . . . He had read of such things, he half-remembered tales of them. . . . Perhaps she was a willing victim--he had heard of such--coming forward with a perverted joy to confess her shame. The torture--that would be to stimulate her imagination. Isobel had always said she was weak in her mind. . . . She might have been chosen by lot in the kirk on Hallowmass-e'en. . . . Chasehope was not her inquisitor, but the dark priest who conducted the ritual.

His anger and disgust rose to a fury. He tore the paper into little pieces and flung them in the pricker's face.

"What doubly damned crime have you committed?" he cried. "You have tortured a wretched weak woman and taken down her ravings for truth. You have maybe killed her, murderer that you be! Your sins cry out to God, and yours above all, Ephraim Caird, whose hands I have myself seen dipped in the blackest witchcraft."

Chasehope's face was smiling blandly.

"I kenna what right ye have to meddle, sir," he said. "The paper ye've torn is but a copy. The memorial itsel' will be in safe hands this nicht. Wad ye set yoursel' up against the Presbytery and the law o' the land, you that have been suspended this day, as is weel kenned, frae your rights as minister o' this parish? Ye'd best gang hame to your bed, sir, and pray that ye may be delivered frae the sin o' presumption. This woman will bide the nicht in this place under lock and key, till the Shirra sends for her."

"She will go with me to the manse this night--and, please God, I will nurse her back into life."

There could be no question of the consternation of the audience--it almost equalled his own. Chasehope alone kept his composure; the others stared in horror and growing anger.

"That will no be permitted," came from the lowering Mirehope, and "A bonny minister," cried another, "to file his house wi' a dirty witch. He maun himsel' be ower great wi' the Deil." The pricker twisted and grinned, and his eyes watched approvingly the spasms of the woman on the straw.

David was carried out of himself, and before he was aware of it had drawn his sword.

"She goes to the manse. I will suffer no let or hindrance in this plain duty. Whoever opposes me will rue it."

"Wad ye deforce the session?" Mirehope shouted in a voice like a bull and got to his feet. From the idiot on his perch came an unexpected encouragement. "Fine, sir. Fine, my bonny Mr. David," cried Gibbie. "Stap your sword in his wame. I'll uphaud ye wi' my staff, for the puir kimmer was ill-guidit. I couldna sleep a wink a' nicht for her skellochs."

A voice broke in on the storm, and David saw that it was the new tenant of Crossbasket.

"Put up your blade, sir," he said. "There's no need for fighting among Christian folk. These honest men have been following the light vouchsafed to them, and if there's blame to be cast it's on this pricker chiel that comes from I know not where."

There was something in the quiet tones which fell like oil on yeasty water. David settled back his sword into its sheath, Mirehope sat down again on his keg, Chasehope turned his head to the speaker with the first sign of discomposure he had yet shown.

"Ye'll forgive me, neighbours," Mark continued, "since I'm but new come to the parish, but I've seen a hantle o' the world, and I would be wae to see honest men run their heids against a stone wall. The woman may be a' you say and waur, but it looks as if her handlin' had been ower sair, and I'm muckle mista'en if she'll no be a corp ere morning. Consider, friends.--This is no a court constituted by a Privy Council commission; it's nae mair than a private gathering o' well-wishers to the Kirk and the Law. In my time I've meddled ower much wi' the Law for my comfort, and I ken something about the jaud. The Law has no cognizance of a pricker or onything like him, and if well-meaning folk under his guiding compass the death of a man or woman that has not been duly tried and sentenced, the Law will uphaud it to be murder, just as muckle as if a caird had cut a throat at a dyke-side. I greatly fear ye've brought yourselves into its danger by this day's work."

Mark spoke with an air of anxious and friendly candour that called for no opposition. Indeed it was plain that more than one of his hearers had similar doubts of their own.

"The wife's weel eneuch," said Mirehope. "Ye'll no kill a tough auld greyhen like that wi' a raxed thumb or brunt taes."

"I hope you're richt, neighbour," said Mark. "But if she suld dee, what will ye say to the Shirra--and what to the Court o' Justiciar? Ye've taken doun frae her mouth a long screed o' crimes, but I'm of the minister's opinion, that they're what ony distrackit body wad admit that wasna verra strong in the intellectuals and fand her paiks [punishment] ower sair for her. Lord bless me, but they're maist o' them owercomes I heard at my grannie's knee. I counsel ye in all friendliness to let the minister do his best to keep her in life, or it sticks in my mind that Woodilee will mak' an ill showing when the King's judges redd up the business."

Chasehope angrily dissented, but he had few supporters. Most of the others wore an anxious air.

"I come to the matter of the pricker." Mark's homely wheedling tones were like those of a packman in an ale-house kitchen. "I ken nocht about him, but I canna say I like the looks o' him. I doubt if I was strapped up by the thumbs and had yon luntin' een glowering at me I wad speak wi' strange tongues mysel'. It's no that difficult for a pawky body to gar a weaker vessel obey his will. . . . Get up off that barry," he said sharply. "Stand ayont the licht till I have a look at ye."

The words came out like a crack of a whip-lash. The atmosphere of the place had suddenly changed, the woman's mutterings had ceased, and, as David stood back from the lantern, he saw that Mark had moved forward and was beside the pricker, a yard from him, with the light between them, and the faces of both in full view of the rest. The one shambled to his feet and set his hand to his head as if to avert a blow, while the other, his dark face like a thundercloud, stood menacingly over against him.

"Look at me," Mark cried. "Look me in the een, if there's that muckle smeddum in your breast."

The eyes of the pricker were like small dark points in his dead- white eyeballs.

"Ye're one Kincaid, but ye've gone by mony names. Ye've been a dominie and a stickit minister, a thief and a thief-taker, a spy and a witch-finder, and ye'd fain be a warlock if the Deil thocht your soul worth half a bodle. . . . Turn your een to the licht, and keep them there. . . . Answer me ere the Pit opens for ye. Was there ever a word in your mouth that wasna as false as hell? Say 'I am a liar, like my father the Devil afore me.'"

"I am a liar," the man croaked.

Mark stretched out one hand and passed it over the pricker's brow.

"What's aneath here?" he asked. "Honest banes? Na, na, rottenness like peat." To the horrified spectators he seemed to pass his hand backwards and forwards through the man's head, as if a knife had gone through a pat of butter.

"What's in your een?" he cried, leaning forward. "I see the fires of hell and the worm that dieth not. God! the bleeze o' them is keekin' through!"

For a moment it seemed to all that a ruddy glow of flame leaped to the roof, and Daft Gibbie in his agitation fell from his seat and rushed to the door. The idiot flung it open and screamed beyond Reiverslaw to the waiting crowd, "Come inbye, every soul o' ye. The pricker that tormented puir Bessie is getting his paiks, and Glee'd Mark is drawin' hell fire out o' him. Come inbye and see the bonny sicht."

Reiverslaw and a dozen others entered the granary; the door remained half open and the night wind swept up the dust and chaff of the floor and made the red light seem a monstrous wavering cloud that hung like an infernal aureole over the wretched man.

Mark had him by the shoulder. "And what's this?" he cried, tearing his shirt aside and showing his bare throat. "As I live by bread, it's a Deil's pap!" Certainly to the audience it seemed that above the breast grew a small black teat.

The creature was in an extremity of terror. Fear had so drained the blood from his eyeballs that the pupils seemed to burn with an uncanny brightness, even after the red had gone out of the light.

"There's nae bull's pizzle needit to make this wauf [feeble] body confess." Mark's iron grip was still on his shoulder. "If ony neighbour has ony misdeed in his mind, I'll warrant to wring it oot o' the pricker as glib as a bairn's schule-lesson. I'll mak' him own to the Black Mass in the kirk on Hallowe'en. . . . There's nane speaks? Weel, we'll leave the dott'rel to his ain conscience."

He relaxed his grip, and the man dropped gibbering and half- senseless on the floor.

"There's your bonny pricker," said Mark to Chasehope. "There's your chosen instrument for getting truth out o' auld wives. Do as you like wi' him, but I counsel ye to get him furth o' the parish if he be a friend o' yours, or the folk will hae him in the deepest hole in Woodilee burn."

Chasehope, white and stammering, found himself deserted by his allies, but he still showed fight.

"I protest," he cried. "I kenna what hellish tricks ye've played on a worthy man--"

"Just the same tricks as he played on the auld wife--a wee bit o' speirin'."

"It's no my blame," said Chasehope, changing his ground, "if I have leaned on a broken reed. The man was sent here by folk that vouched for his worth. And nevertheless, whatever the weakness o' the instrument, the Lord has wrocht through him to produce a confession--"

"Ay. Just so," said Mark dryly. "But what kind o' instrument is yon to procure the truth? Will ye get caller water out o' a foul pipe?"

"The Lord works--" Chasehope began, but Mark broke in on him. His dark mocking face, in which the squint of the left eye was now most noticeable and formidable, was thrust close to the other's.

"See here, my bonny man.--Ye can get ony mortal daftness out o' man or woman if ye first put fear on them. Ye've seen the auld wife and ye've seen the pricker. Do YOU come forrit forenent the licht. Ye're a buirdly chiel, and weel spoken o' for canniness. Ye can keep your thumbs unraxed and your hide unscorched for me, but by the God abune us I'll warrant that in ten minutes by the knock I'll hae ye confessin' fauts that will keep the haill parish waukrife till Yule. . . . Will ye thole the trial?"

The big man shrank back. "Na, na. I kenna what spell the Deil has gien ye, but ye'll no lay it on me."

"So muckle the better for yoursel'." Mark turned to the others. "Ye've a' seen, neighbours, that my spell, as he ca's it, was nae mair than just an honest speirin'. I'm loth to think that this clachan should suffer for what has been done this day, so the sooner we get the wife to bed and weel-tended the better for us a'."

"She shall go to the manse at once," said David. He had been examining the tortured woman, who had passed into unconsciousness, and it seemed to him that her heart beat very faintly.

"That will be wisest, no doubt," said Mark, but at this point Chasehope found support in his protest. Mirehope, Nether Fennan, and the miller exchanged anxious looks.

"Take her to Alison Geddie," they cried. "She has a toom [empty] bed, and it's near by."

"She will go to my own house," said David, "and be nursed by my own hand. I trust no man or woman of you after to-day's devilry."

The place had filled up, and it seemed to him that the better part of the parish were now onlookers. It was clear that a considerable number were on Chasehope's side, for the mention of the manse had wakened a curious disquiet in many faces. David solved the problem by dragging out from the back of the granary a wooden sledge used for drawing peats. He covered it with straw and laid the woman on it.

"Reiverslaw!" he cried. "You take the one end and I'll take the other."

The farmer advanced, and for a second it looked as if he might be prevented by force. He turned fierce eyes on the crowd. "Ay, sir. I'll dae your bidding. . . . And if ony man lifts his hand to prevent me, he'll get a sarkfu' o' broken banes."

The strange cortège moved out into the darkness, without opposition. It may have been the honest feeling of the majority that let it go; it may have been the truculent Reiverslaw, or David with his white face and the sword bobbing at his belt: but most likely it was the fact that Mark Riddel walked by the minister's side.

Bessie Todd died just before morning. Isobel received her old gossip with tears and lamentations, laid her in the best bed, washed and salved her wounds, and strove to revive her with cordials. But the trial had been too hard for a frail woman far down in the vale of years. David watched all night by her bedside, and though at the end she became conscious, her mind was hopelessly unhinged, and she babbled nonsense and scraps of childish rhymes. If he could not pray with her, he prayed beside her, pleading passionately for the departing soul.

As Isobel straightened the body and closed the eyes, she asked anxiously if there had been any space given for repentance.

David shook his head.

"Puir thing, she got the Devil's fee and bountith, and muckle guid it did her. Let's hope, sir, that afore her mind left her she had grace given her to renounce him and creep to the Mercy Seat. . . . We'll gar some folks in Woodilee look gash [ghastly] for this. There was a time, Mr. David, when I wad have held ye back, but my word now is Gang forrit, till ye rive this parish wi' the fear o' God, and sinners we ken o' will howl on their knees for as quiet a death-bed as Bessie's."

CHAPTER XVII

WOODILEE AND CALIDON

The pricker disappeared from the parish in the night. The dead woman was buried decently in the kirkyard, and her male kin attended the funeral as if there had never been a word against her fair fame. There was indeed a certain revulsion of feeling among plain people in Woodilee. Bessie had been liked; she was regretted and pitied; the downfall of the pricker seemed to invalidate her confession. But there was a party--Chasehope was the leader--who held that solemn things had been trifled with and that the minister had gone far to bring God's curse on the parish. He had laid his hand to his sword like a malignant, and had made light of an awful confession before the pricker had been discredited. Bessie might have been innocent of witchcraft, but in his plea for her he had shown a discreditable leniency towards the sin. Women might be old and frail, but if they were leagued with Satan it was enough to put them beyond the pale of Christian sympathy. The minister was patently rebellious and self-willed, a scorner of the yoke of Kirk and Word.

But the night's events caused a notable increase in one reputation. The new tenant of Crossbasket had shown himself an ill man to counter. He had the interests of the parish at heart and had given wise advice, and he had confounded the pricker with a terrible ease.

Clearly a man with power; nor was there reason to think that the power was not given him from on high. A hard man to gainsay, as even Chasehope had found. His friendliness had made him popular, and folk were slipping into neighbourly ways with him. Soon he would have been "Mark" to most, and "Glee'd Mark" behind his back. But from that night formality and decorum invested him; he was "Crossbasket" even to the children, and the humbler doffed their bonnets when he drew near.

He came to David one evening when the candle was lit in the study.

"What arts were yon," the minister asked, "that turned the pricker from a man into a jelly?"

Mark had sat himself in a deep armchair covered with black leather, which had been David's father's and had come to the manse from the Pleasance after the roup. He had crossed his legs and let his head lie back while he puffed his tobacco-pipe. He laughed as he answered:

"A simple divertisement, but good enough for such a caddis-worm. A pinch of Greek powder in the lantern, and for the rest a device I learned among the tinklers in Hungary when some of us gentleman- cavaliers had to take to the hills and forests for a season. But the body was easy game. The sight of my een was enough to melt his wits. . . . Chasehope's another kind of lad--there's metal there, though it's maybe of the Devil's forging. . . . But for the moment we've fairly houghed his shelty."

"You saw how distraught he was," Mark continued, "ay, and others beside him, when you offered to carry the wife to the manse. The reason wasna ill to seek. When she was being tortured to confession, Chasehope was beside her and mastered her with his een. . . . She was one of the coven, you tell me. But once in your hands he was feared she would tell things of more moment than the blethers they wrung out of her. . . . She didna speak? Ay, I thought she was ower far gone. It was maybe as well that the puir thing died, for after the handling she got there was small bodily comfort left for her."

"By her death her tormentors are guilty in God's sight of murder," said David.

"No doubt. And maybe also in the sight of the Law. That's why I say we have houghed Chasehope's mare for him. He canna ride off on a pretended zeal for witch-hunts, for this one has notably miscarried. This pricker business is looked askance at by those that ken best, and it's certain it has no countenance frae the Justiciar. They've killed the wife with it, and their pricker will not show face again in this countryside. What becomes, think you, of the braw commission of the Privy Council that Chasehope had the procuring of? The thing is begowked before it is begun. The ministers of Kirk Aller and Bold, and yon knock-kneed haverel, the laird of Killiequhair, will e'en hae to content themselves at home, and Chasehope, in place of hiding his sins behind his zeal for burning witches, is left with his repute a wee thing touched, like a bad egg. There's folk in the parish beginning to speir questions that never speired them before."

"I am convinced that the woman Bessie Todd was a human sacrifice, decided on by the coven, and maybe accepted of her free-will. I have heard that every now and then they must pay such a teind to Hell. . . . She was weak in the mind, remember."

"I had the same notion myself. No, I wasna there when the pricker was busy, but them that were tell me that he put the feck of the words intil her mouth. That would consort with what I've heard of the black business elsewhere. She was doomed to die, as surely as if she had stood in the doomster's cart. . . . But I have found out another thing. Our neighbour Chasehope is a King-Deil."

"What in Heaven's name is that?"

"You may well speir. He is the priest of the coven, but he is more, for he is a kind of Deil on his own account. That is why you saw them in the Wood bowing before him and nozzling him like dogs. There's been King-Deils before this in Scotland. Francie Stuart was one--him that was Earl of Bothwell in the days of James the Saxt, and he had a braw coven down by Dunbar and the Bass."

"And the man an elder of the Kirk!" David exclaimed. "The words of Scripture are never off his lips, and more than once he has reproved me for sin."

"That's the lad. There's a holy pleasure to be gotten out of hypocrisy. And yet--and yet! I'll wager that Chasehope has no doubt but that he is a redeemed soul, and will get an abundant entrance at the hinder end. That Kirk of yours has so cunningly twisted religion that a man can grow fat in his own sins and yet spend his time denouncing the faults of others, for he is elected into grace, as they call it, and has got some kind of a title to Heaven. I'm a plain body that canna see how God and the Devil can be served at the one time, but there's many a chiel makes a trade of it. They've gotten one creel that holds their treasure in Heaven, and one full of the lusts of the flesh, and though they ettle to coup the latter before the day of death, they are confident that it winna canker what's in the other creel. It's queer doctrine, and maybe I havena riddled it out right, for I'm loth to believe that an honest man could uphold it, though I've heard it often propounded with an unction that made my flesh creep."

"You speak not of the Christian doctrine of election, but of its perversion," said David solemnly.

"Weel, it's the perversion that has gotten the upper hand these days. The Kirk has made the yett of grace ower wide for sinful men, and all ither yetts ower narrow. It has banned innocence and so made a calling of hypocrisy, for human nature is human nature, and if you tell a man that ilka honest pleasure is a sin in God's sight, he finds a way to get the pleasure and yet keep the name for godliness. And mind you, the pleasures he enjoys with a doubtful conscience will no long be honest. There will be a drop of black ink in the spring water that makes it drumly, and ere he kens he'll be seeking a stronger brew. The upshot will be that folk who sit under you in the kirk will dance in the Wood on the auld heathen holy-days, and the man whose word gangs furthest with the Presbytery will be hugging lusts to his bosom that would make a common foot-sentinel spew. For they've all their sure title, as they call it--they're all elected into grace, so what for should they fash themselves?"

Mark's face was smiling, but his voice had a note in it which was not humour.

"You laugh," David cried, "but I'm nearer weeping."

"I laugh, but it's to prevent me cursing." The other's jaw had set and there was a smouldering fire in his eyes. "I tell you the Cities of the Plain were less an offence to Almighty God than this demented twist of John Calvin that blasts and rots a man's heart. For if it makes here and there a saint, it is like a dung-heap to hatch out sinners."

David was suspended from officiating in the kirk, but he was still a placed minister, and there was no embargo upon his utterances elsewhere. So while every alternate Sabbath Mr. Fordyce came over from Cauldshaw to occupy the pulpit, and in defiance of the Presbytery ate his dinner at the manse, on the others David preached in the kirk-yard. Twenty years later these sermons in the open air were remembered, when Mr. Fordyce, then far advanced in age, was driven from Cauldshaw to hold preachings in the Deer Syke. . . .

There was a novelty in the practice which brought many the first day; and on later Sabbaths the audience increased, for David had never delivered such discourses in the Woodilee pulpit. One famous sermon was on the peril of trifling with salvation. A soul was not saved by an easy miracle, but must mount hardly and painfully to eternal life; to accept grace lightly was to cast scorn upon the atonement of the Cross. But doctrine figured little, nor were there any of the forecasts of hell and judgment which were the common proof of an earnest minister. "He is a guid dowg," Richie Smail was reported to have said: "he wad wyse folk gently to Christ." Something of the joy in his own heart revealed itself in a peculiar tenderness; often there were wet eyes among his hearers, and the children, squatted on the grass or on the flat gravestones, forbore to whisper and fidget, and listened with a grave attention. His elders did not attend; indeed, with the exception of Peter Pennecuik, they forbore even to grace the orthodox ministrations of Mr. Fordyce. Chasehope and his friends walked the five moorland miles to Bold to sup on the strong fare of Mr. Ebenezer till such time--early in the New Year, it was believed--as the Presbytery pronounced final judgment on their minister.

Woodilee had split into two factions. There was the party of the Session, who held David to be a malignant, or at best a Laodicean, one who gave a doubtful sound of doctrine, a rebel, a despiser of authority, a preacher of a cold morality. To this side belonged many of undoubted piety, who had been shocked by his defiance and gave ready ear to whispered scandal. Of David's party were respected professors like Richie Smail and Rab Prentice, several godly women, a decent hind or two, and a tail which was neither godly nor respected. Among his supporters were some whom he suspected of dealings with the Wood, and in general he had with him all that was least esteemed in the parish. To have Reiverslaw--who was again drinking hard--as his prophet, and Daft Gibbie as his fugleman, did not enhance the credit of his cause. Between the Jews and the Samaritans there were no dealings. Isobel, now a hot partisan, had quarrelled on this score with her nearest and dearest, and, encountering Jean of Chasehope-foot in the clachan, and being goaded by her tongue, fell on her tooth and nail and chased her into Peter Pennecuik's kailyard. Amos Ritchie, too, had declared his colours, and woe be to the man who, in his presence, spoke ill of the minister. He was no longer employed by the farmers around the kirkton, so the smithy fire was mostly unlit, while the smith did odd jobs at Reiverslaw and Calidon. Only the new tenant of Crossbasket mixed amicably with all. On the road he had the same greeting for Chasehope as for the minister, and he would drink a stoup at Lucky Weir's with Amos or Mirehope, Reiverslaw or the miller, in all good-fellowship. But this popularity rested more perhaps on fear than on affection. Dark whisperings began to spread. "What ken we o' Crossbasket?" said one. "Nae doot he's frae Teviotside, but whaur was he afore that? He never learned that glower on Jed Water." "He's a pawky carle," said another, "and ye canna get far ben wi' him. There's mair in his heid than the Word ever learned him. I wadna wonder some fine day to see him gang off in a fuff and a lowe. Ye say he has the speech o' a guid Christian? Weel-a-weel, a soo may whistle, though it has an ill mouth for it."

By late November winter should have closed in upon the glen with an iron hand. The first frosts should have stripped the trees, and the first snows lain at the dyke-back. But that year it seemed as if the seasons had gone widdershins. November was bright and calm, and the harvest, delayed by October rains, was soon gathered. Oats and bear, flax and rye--the little crops were housed within a week, and since the snows tarried, it was the middle of December before the cattle were in the byres and yards, and the sheep brought down to the infields. The countryside presented a strange spectacle. Heather lingered in bloom, and the leaves were on the ashes and hazels till long after Hallowmass. When they did fall there were no frosts to crumble them, and they lay in great drifts in the woods and by the roadside, and children dived and scrambled among them. There were swallows still in the thatch in November, and Amos

Ritchie, when he went out to the moss to intercept the travelling skeins of wild geese, found that the curlews and plovers had not yet flitted to the seashore and that there were no wildfowl to be seen in all the blue heavens. Morning after morning the sun rose clear as in June, the nights were mild and starlit, herbs which should have been snug below the earth sprouted prematurely, the hedgehog and the badger had forgotten to go to sleep, and only the short hours of light showed that it was midwinter. Reiverslaw, always a scorner of precedents, kept his sheep on the hills, where the pasture was as rich as in summer-time.

But the old and the wise frowned and shook their heads. One said it was such a year as '71, of which his grandsire had told, when winter did not begin till February, and did not end till June. Another recalled "saxteen fifteen, named the Lown Year, when there was nae frost, and a blight o' worms and cawterpillars and hairy objects fell on the land." And every wife in the parish, when at Christmas the grass was still rank and high, and hips and haws still hung on the bushes, quoted dolefully the saw that "a green Yule makes a fat kirkyard."

But if there was a presage of calamity in it for the thoughtful, it was weather of a rare beauty for those who had the heart to enjoy it. There was no sickness in the parish and as yet no hunger, so David's pastoral duties were light. He was on the uplands most of the day, and now his feet took him away from the Hill of Deer and the north ridge of Rood and across the glen to the hills between Calidon and Aller, for there he could meet Katrine with no fear of interfering parishioners. The garrison had been withdrawn from Calidon, since Nicholas was known to be out of the country and Mistress Saintserf was regarded as well affected, but David did not go there. So long as the short afternoons were crystal under a canopy of blue, and the sun set behind Herstane Craig in gold and crimson, the place for lovers was the hill, for there the world was narrowed to themselves.

But the minister's conscience smote him at last, and on New Year's morning he presented himself at Calidon door. By arrangement Katrine was not there, and from her aunt he got the tempestuous welcome which custom ordained as appropriate to the season.

"Sit ye down, sir, and prie our shortcake and October. Yours is the first stranger foot that has crossed this threshold, and it's surely propitious that it should be a minister's. Our ain Mr. James is lyin' again, for this lown weather doesna 'gree wi' him, though it's hard to say what 'grees wi' him, for the creature's body is sair failed. . . . It's mony a day since we cast een on ye here, Mr. David, and siccan days as they've been for me and mine."

She descanted on the troubles of the autumn, her success in saving Calidon from being sequestered--"Peter Dobbie, him that's our doer, is far ben wi' Wariston, ye maun ken, and worthy Mr. Rintoul in the West Kirk said a word in the right lug"--on the difficulty in getting funds to Nicholas Hawkshaw at Utrecht, on the garrisoning of Calidon--"They punished our yill, but they fashed us little, for they were sair hadden down by Katrine." But she said nothing of Mark, though in the end she had been made privy to that business, and she did not hint at the trouble in Woodilee which was the talk of the country. Behind all her garrulity lurked a certain embarrassment, and it did not make David's task the easier.

At last he took his courage in both hands.

"I came here this morn for a purpose," he said, and with halting voice and a fiery face he made his confession. The old woman regarded him with eyes that strove to express amazement and failed; it was clear that she had had her suspicions.

But her words when she spoke were those of one who had been startled out of all propriety.

"Heard ye ever the like?" she cried. "Man, d'ye ken of whom ye speak? Katrine is a leddy born--there's nae aulder or prouder stock in the land--and ye're the oy [grandson] o' the miller o' the Roodfoot, and ye seek to make her your marrow [mate]. We ken that the warld is coupit upside-down these days, but this fair cowes a'. Guid faith, ye're no blate."

David held his peace, for he had no answer. He felt in the pith of his bones his immense audacity.

"How would the lassie set wi' a manse, think ye?" she continued. "She's been brocht up amang papists and prelatists, and though she's had mony a swatch o' the Gospel frae honest Mr. James, she's no muckle wiser than a babe. Forbye, she's a daft quean that wad never mak' a 'sponsible minister's wife. Think ye that the King's court and dancin' and glee-singin' and ridin' on a horse is a guid preparation for a moorland parish and a fower-room house? How will ane that's been used to velvet and pearlins tak' wi' linsey-wolsey and drugget?"

"That is for Katrine to decide," he said humbly. "I have heard that true love can glorify a cot-house."

"Havers!" she cried. "There's a decency in a' things, and ye canna mate a blood-horse wi' a cadger's powny. Wedlock, as I weel ken, is nae business o' kissin' and rhymin', but a sober contrack, and if twa folks are gaun to live cantily thegither, they maun see that mair than their hearts are weel agreed. There maun be a chance--there's nae certainty in this perishin' world--o' a bien doun- settin', and a sufficiency o' gear, and a life that will be guid for baith. What say ye to that? A minister's wife! Guidsakes, the Session wad think her a randy, for she'd lauch at their solemnities, and your brither ministers, wha are maistly cotters' sons, wad be fleyed by her gentrice, and the folk wad be as feared o' her as a chuckie o' a pyet. Ye're a man o' sense, Mr. David. Ye canna deny that the thing is past a' reason."

"Oh, mistress," said the unhappy David. "There's truth in what you say--I cannot gainsay it. But I plead that true hearts may break down every obstacle, and Katrine's and mine are as true to each other as the dial to the sun. There was a time when you were young yourself, mistress--you mind that then there was no rule for lovers but their love."

"I mind weel," she said more gently, "but it's for auld folk to be eident and save the young frae folly. . . . I'll no deny that I would be blithe to see Katrine provided for. She's a fine lassie, but forbye mysel' she has nae near kin to mind her, now that Nicholas is put to the horn and hidin' amang the Hollanders. Fine I wad like to see her in safe hands. . . . But what can ye offer, Mr. David? It's no as if ye were on firm ground yoursel'. They tell me ye've cast out wi' your Session and are bickerin' wi' the Presbytery, and ony day may be turned out o' Woodilee and maybe excommunicat by the Kirk. That's a braw prospect for a wife. Wad ye have Katrine tak' a creel on her back, like a tinkler quean, her that has in her the bluid o' the Black Douglas and the auld kings o' Scots? Ye've made a bonny hash o' things, for ane that's ettlin' to be a bridegroom."

"I am set about with perplexities, and the hands of many are against me. But I have Katrine on my side--and I was in hopes that I might have you, mistress."

"I'm no against ye," she said, and there was kindness in her eye. "Never think that. I've heard the clash o' the country and I've riddled it out, and by my way o't ye've taken the richt road. I ken nocht about the Wud, but I ken something o' the tods and foumarts o' Woodilee, and for the business o' glee'd Mark Kerr it's no a Hawkshaw or a Yester or a Saintserf would cast a stone at ye. But it's solemn truth that ye've gotten on the wrang side o' the Kirk, and the Kirk is your calling, Mr. David. . . . Ye maun ken that I've had mony a crack wi' our Mr. James anent ye, and if it's the pure Gospel word I'm seekin' it's to him I'll gang and no to Kirk Aller. I'll tell ye what he said. 'Mr. David,' says he, 'has his plew on the wrang rig. He wad hae made a grand sodger, and if he had been a papist he wad hae made a guid monk. He has the makings o' a saint and he has the makings o' a warrior, but a manse is no the place for him. For,' says Mr. James, 'he canna, like me, withdraw himsel' into his closet--he is ower hale o' body and het in spirit for that--and he canna walk doucely as the Kirk ordains. For if he sees wrang he maun set it richt, though the Kirk tells him to bide still, and he'll no put his conscience in the keeping o' ony Presbytery. He's ower staunch a Presbyterian,' says he, 'for the Kirk of Scotland as at present guidit, whilk is a kind o' Papery wi' fifty Papes instead o' ane.'"

"Maybe that's the truth," said David.

"Ay, it's the truth, and I'm blithe to hear ye acknowledge it. . . . But we'll hae the lassie in, for this crack concerns her maist. The cunnin' limmer, to keep sae mum and begowk her auld auntie!"

When Katrine appeared, her cheeks a little flushed and her eye bright, she was greeted by Mistress Grizel with surprising gentleness.

"What's this I hear o' ye, lassie? Ye've gotten a joe and never telled me! . . . Na, na, my lamb, dinna be feared that I'll flyte on ye. It's a road we maun a' travel, and nae doubt wedlock is a holy and blessed state and a hantle better than spinsterhood, for a woman maun either be guidit by a husband or be subject to a' and sindry. But it's a serious step, and wants carefu' and prayerfu' thocht. I've had a word wi' Davie--for I tak' the liberty to ca' him Davie as if he were my ain son--and as in duty bound I've set forth the difficulties. I say naething against ye as a man, Davie. Ye're wise-like and weel-spoken, and ye've gentle ways, if ye hae na gentle bluid. But I say muckle against ye as a minister, and I canna picture Katrine as the leddy o' a manse. Forbye, there's the solemn fact that ye've made Woodilee ower het a bit to bide in, and what ye've done there ye'll dae in ony ither parochine in the land. . . . Sae hearken to me, sir. Ye've mista'en your trade, like mony anither honest lad, but the faut can be mended. Ye're young eneuch to start in a better."

Katrine had moved to David's side and laid her hand on his shoulder. "Aunt Grizel would have you forsake the Kirk for the world," she laughed.

"But I am solemnly vowed to God's service," he said.

"Nae doot," said Mistress Grizel. "But a man serves his Maker as weel in buckskin as in a Geneva gown--better, if a' tales be true. This is the counsel of ane that wishes ye weel, you and that denty lass at your elbuck. Mak' your peace wi' the Kirk--submit yoursel' to the Presbytery--ye need gie up nane o' your views, but submit yoursel' to the lawfu' authority. Tell them that ye'll be guidit in your public doings by them that has been set ower ye. . . . Troth, they'll no be sweir to mak' a brig for ye, for they dinna want a scandal in the Kirk. They'll censure ye lichtly for a thochtless callant, and the thing will drap. By that course ye'll dae nae violence to your conscience--ye'll just be humblin' yoursel' before your elders in the Lord, as we're commanded."

"But what of the witchcraft in Woodilee?" he asked.

"Let it gang by the board. It's no you or ten like you will clean out that dirty nest. Leave it to the Almighty, whose judgments are slow and siccar [sure]."

"You would have me sit silent in Woodilee in the midst of that iniquity?"

"Na, na. I would have ye get out o' Woodilee as fast as a bird when the thack's burnin'. We've Mr. James's opinion, whilk ye canna controvert, that ye were never meant for a minister. I'se warrant it will be made easy for ye--the Presbytery will no object, and Calidon's the chief heritor, and I'll get a word spoken to Mr. Rintoul. Ye'll leave wi' a guid name, at peace wi' God and man, and there's a' braid Scotland for ye to find a habitation. . . . Peter Dobbie tells me that your father, honest man, made a hantle o' siller and that ye've heired the haill o't. Gang down the water to the auld Yester lands, and buy a bit estate and set up Katrine in her forebears' countryside. Ye're young and yauld and there's muckle guid work to be done in Scotland by ane that lives in the fear o' God, be he laird or minister."

David turned to Katrine, but her face was impassive. From her he would get no guidance. Like her aunt, she awaited his answer.

For a moment he wavered. On one side he saw peace, comfort, a new life with his beloved in a new place, the cutting of a tangle which constricted his youth; on the other--a thankless fight, where victory was wellnigh impossible, a sordid struggle which would darken the sunlight for both and taint all the springs of joy. He dropped his head on his breast and suffered for an instant the anguish of indecision. Then he spoke, and his eyes were on Katrine.

"I cannot. I would be going back upon my vows--I would be false to my faith--I would deserve to be cried out upon as a coward--I would be making terms with the Devil."

"Thank God!" said the girl, and her arms were round his neck.

The old woman stared at him, coughed dryly, and then very deliberately took her seat in the big armchair which had been Nicholas Hawkshaw's. The two stood before her like prisoners brought to judgment.

"Ye'll tak' that puir lassie and expose her to the ill-will o' the Kirk and the countryside.--Ye'll set her up as a mark for clash and scandal.--Ye'll condemn her to a wearifu' battalation that can have but the one end, for those that are against ye are mair than those that are for ye. A man may fecht stoutly his lee lane, but he is sair trauchled by a wife."

"I will reply," Katrine cried. "I am a Yester. What cognizance does Yester bear, Aunt Grizel?"

"Azure a chevron or between three garbs of the same, and for badge a lion guardant, wi' the ditton 'Thole feud.'"

"My motto is my answer. Would you have me shame my kin and run from a challenge?"

"But what kind o' challenge, my lamb? Ye'll be nae Black Agnes o' Dunbar--but a minister's wife, fechtin' against lees and clypes and fause tongues and ignorance--the cauld law o' the land and the caulder laws o' the Kirk. Ye'll hae to thole and thole wi' never a back-straik o' your ain, and keep a smilin' face and a high heid when your heart is sick. Ye maun bow to them ye scorn and bend the knee to them that your guidsire would have refused for horse-boys, and be servant to the silliest body that summons ye in the name o' Christ. Have ye made your market for that, my doo? There never was Yester--or Hawkshaw neither--that feared feud, but can ye thole sic dreidfu' servitude, day in day out, in a wee house in a dreich parochine wi' nae company but hinds and wabsters?"

The girl looked at David, and there was that in her eyes which made him both exultant and very humble, so that he longed at once to sing and to weep. She turned to the Bible which lay on the great table, ran a finger over its pages and read, and the words were those which Ruth spoke to Naomi:

"Intreat me not to leave thee, or to return from following after thee: for whither thou goest, I will go; and where thou lodgest, I will lodge: thy people shall be my people, and thy God my God: where thou diest, will I die, and there will I be buried: the Lord do so to me, and more also, if ought but death part thee and me."

"So that's the way o't," said the old woman. "Weel, I've said my say. Ye're a pair o' fules, but there's maybe waur things than fules in God's sicht. . . . Davie, lad, get down on your hunkers and I'll gie ye my blessing--the blessing o' a warldly auld wife that yet has orra glints o' better things. . . . Man, I kenna where ye got it, but there's gentle bluid in ye. Your common body would have chosen the saft seat."

CHAPTER XVIII

THE PLAGUE

In the first week of the New Year the miraculous weather showed no sign of breaking. The sun from rising to setting shone temperately in a clear sky, the nights were little less warm than May, and even the old folk cast the blankets from them and opened the doors of their press-beds; the peat-stacks and the fuel-stacks were scarcely touched, and the fires smouldered only for cooking; the burns were shrunken to summer size, and the spawning fish could not pass the shallows of Rood. But a change had come over the mind of the parish. Men no longer called down blessings on the fine open winter, for such weather seemed in defiance of nature, and an uneasy anticipation of portents weighed on their spirits. The sun did not warm, the unclouded skies did not cheer, the hard roads did not invite to movement. A curious languor fell upon Woodilee.

It seemed as if the same apprehension were felt by the natural world. The cattle and sheep, in spite of the good pasture, grew thinner than in the rigours of winter. The packman's pony turned away from the rich bite by the roadside. Though the air was cool and tonic, beast and man sweated with the smallest exertion. David, tramping the high moors, found that he was more weary after five miles than after twenty in the summer heats. The deer from Melanudrigill had none of their winter boldness, and indeed all wild animals had become shyer of the presence of man than the oldest inhabitant remembered. But all were aware and restless; there were more worm-casts on the turf than in spring, and migrant birds, which usually tarried long in the sheltered glen, now passed high in air for the south. David saw many a drove as he opened his window in the morning. Even the fieldfares, which Amos Ritchie used to snare in the Mirehope fields, did not come within sight of his bird-lime. . . . A brooding strangeness had come into the air, and apathy silenced the very tykes in the village street. Neighbours rarely gathered at Lucky Weir's for a mutchkin, though it was thirsty weather; men seemed to be afraid lest what they saw in another's eye might give substance to their own fears.

Peter Pennecuik, sitting on the stone by the smithy door and mopping a wet forehead, watched Amos drop his tools heavily as he returned from a job at Reiverslaw.

"What mak' ye o' the weather?" he asked.

Amos straightened his back.

"I dinna like it. The gillyflowers in my yaird are ettlin' to bloom. My grannie had a verse o' auld Thomas the Rhymer--what was it?--

"A Yule wi'out snaws, A Januar' wi' haws, Bring the deid thraws."

"There's a judgment preparin'," said Peter, "but whatna kind o' judgment I daurna guess. Certes, it's no canny."

"I've heard o' nane ailin', but there's seeckness comin'. I can smell it in the air, and the brute beasts can smell it, for they're sweir to come near Woodilee. There's no a tod or a maukin on a' the Hill o' Deer. D'ye no find a queer savour in the countryside, Peter? There's wind enough to shake the saughs, but the warld smells like the inside o' a press-bed when the door's steekit. Oh for a snell, dirlin' blast! There's something rotten and stawsome and unearthly about the blue lift and the saft air. It's like withered floo'ers on a midden. . . . If there's nae seeckness yet, there's seeckness on the road. I maun awa' in and see to Ailie, for this morn she was complaining o' a sair heid."

Two days later the child of a cotter at Mirehope returned from school in the manse kitchen, and to his mother's amazement beat his head against the door. He fell asleep on the wedder's skin beside the fire, and when he was wakened for his supper his cheeks were flaming and he seemed to have difficulty with his speech. He was put with the rest into the box which was the children's bed, and all night filled it with his cries, so that the others sought peace on the floor. In the morning his face and throat were swollen, his eyes were sightless, and he struggled terribly for breath. Before noon he was dead.

In this way came the plague to Woodilee.

Its coming was realized in an instant, for the sinister weather had prepared the people for calamity. Before the dark the rumour of the breaking out of the pest was in the uttermost sheilings. With it went the word that Peter Pennecuik had sickened, and that another child at Mirehope and one of the Chasehope ewe-milkers were down with it. . . . Next day the place was a beleaguered city. Johnnie Dow, the packman, hearing the news at Cauldshaw, diverted his round to Kirk Aller, though thirty pounds Scots were owing to him in Woodilee. The roads were blocked as if Montrose's kerns commanded them. As it was winter-time there was little work on hand, and even that little was not done. A Sabbath hush fell on the glen, people shut their doors and sat within at their prayers, and that best seeding-ground for plague, a lively terror, was amply prepared.

Peter Pennecuik died in eight hours. There was no heart in the man, and in sickness his command of pious phrases fell away from him, and he passed out of life in a whimpering misery. It was not an edifying death-bed for one who had been a notable professor. But very soon Peter was forgotten--for he was an old man and ripe for his end--as the young and strong were, one by one, struck down. Amos Ritchie's wife, Ailie, followed--the less to be wondered at, for she had always been frail. But when Jess Morison at Chasehope- foot, dark-browed, high-coloured, and not yet twenty, swooned as she drew water at the well, and died in delirium before evening, fear in the parish became panic. The young herd at Windyways, the trimmest lad in the glen, and the miller's man, who looked as gnarled as an oak and as strong as a mill-wheel, followed. But the tragedy was the children. Two of them were struck down for each grown-up person, and perished with the speed of plucked flowers. . . . It was another kind of peril from that which old folk remembered in the year '10, for no pox attended it nor any of the usual sores. The ordinary first symptom was a blinding headache and a high fever; then came a swelling of the throat and glands and a quick delirium. But in many cases there was no outward swelling; the mischief seemed to descend straightway to the lungs and produce a severe haemorrhage. In such cases there was no final delirium; the patient died with clear mind and little bodily pain in an extreme languor. The first type commonly seized the young and full-bodied; children and old folk followed, as a rule, the second course. But both were fatal: in a week out of fifty-nine smitten, fifty-nine were dead.

There was no doctor to be had in all the countryside. The leech at Kirk Aller, sent for by David, refused to come within a mile of Woodilee, and the old women, the usual medical authorities of the village, had nothing but senseless concoctions and--in secret--more senseless charms. Presently even these were forgotten, and the place lay in a stupor of fear under a visitation from Heaven. Cottages which the pest had entered were, by popular consent, shut to the world, so that they became a hot-bed of infection for the other inmates. A man who had sickness in his dwelling dare not show his face in the street except under cover of night. There was no neighbourly assistance asked or given. The members of a stricken family had to conduct their life in a dreadful isolation, till they too sickened; there were shuttered dwellings where life was slowly blotted out, and the village only learned that the end had come for all by the fact that the chimney ceased to smoke. . . . At first an attempt was made to bury the dead decently, the remaining members of a household undertaking the task, but the spread of the pestilence soon made this impossible. The dead were laid in byre and stable beside the startled beasts, sometimes by the poorer households in the kailyard, and David more than once found a staring, unshrouded corpse in the nettles of the manse loan. There were cottages where all the inmates were dead and unburied, with a lean cat mewing round the barred doors. . . . And all the while the soft blue weather continued, and the wind came balmy from the hills over those silent fields of death.

At first the stupor of Woodilee was shot with an awful apprehension of divine wrath, and the people sought to propitiate their Maker by humbling themselves before Him, and--even the least devout--by constant prayer and the reading of Scripture. But this mood did not long survive. The fury of the blast which smote them drove all religion out of their minds, and left them stark and numb with mortal fear. To begin with, David was welcomed in the house of death, he was summoned in haste, his coming was watched for; even if his ministrations did no good to the unconscious sufferers, they seemed to comfort the others. But presently he found himself an unregarded intruder. Whenever he knew of a case he hastened to it, but the panic-stricken eyes of the living looked at him as blindly as the glazing eyes of the dying. His prayers even to himself seemed idle; at any rate they fell upon dulled ears. What contact could he establish with the sick in the delirium or languor of death, and with those who waited on the same fate with the wild despair of beasts in a trap? What use to point to God when God overshadowed them as a merciless tormentor? And all the while he was in a fever of anxiety. More than one of the dead were among those whom he had remarked in the Wood. Men and women were hastening to judgment with their sins heavy on them--sins unrepented and for ever unrepentable. He, their minister, had to stand feebly by and see souls descending into damnation.

The thought drove him frantic, but it alone gave him power to continue in his fruitless duties, for in this trial he found the flesh very weak. It was not that he feared death, even death by plague, but that a horror of Woodilee had fallen on his spirit. His shrinking from the Wood, his hatred of the sins of the Wood, his quarrel with the Session, the distrust in which he was held by many of his congregation, the episode of the pricker and Bessie Todd's death--all combined to make the place reek for him of ugliness and decay. The pest seemed merely to add rotting carcasses to rotting souls. . . . Then the pity of it would overcome him, when he thought of children whom he had taught and honest folk who had been kind to him, now cold in death. He was helpless to cure either body or spirit. He had no leechcraft--what would it have availed if he had, for he remembered the Edinburgh doctor by his father's bed?--and his spiritual ministrations were as idle as wind. . . . Above all, he felt himself a prisoner shut into a noisome cage from which there was no escape. None dare leave or enter Woodilee. One afternoon, in a mood of despair, he climbed the Hill of Deer for a glimpse of the outer world. There lay Calidon on its windy braes, but Calidon was now as distant for him as the moon. There lay the hills in whose spacious wildernesses no pest lurked, for there were no unclean mortals to harbour it, and beyond them was the world where men might live in daylight and honour. As he looked down on Woodilee a haze seemed to lie over it. Was it the effluvia of the plague, a miasma which walled it round more impenetrably than stone walls and iron shutters? . . . He struggled to conquer his shrinking. "Faithless servant," he told himself, "faithless even over a few things! David Sempill, you rebel against the Lord's will not because of the sufferings of your poor folk, but because of your own pitiable discomfort. Think shame, man, to be such a whingeing bairn. "For he had realized that the root of his trouble was that he was severed from Katrine.

But that evening Katrine came to him.

While he sat for a little in his study before starting on his melancholy visits, he heard Isobel's voice below high-pitched in excitement. Then he heard another voice which took him down the stairs three steps at a time.

The girl, booted as he had seen her in the mist on the eve of Hallowmass, stood in the light of Isobel's candle, one gloved hand raised in protest and with an embarrassed smile at her lips and eyes. To David it seemed the first smile that he had seen for an eternity.

"Awa' hame wi' ye, my leddy," Isobel cried. "Ye canna come here, for the pest's in ilka bite we eat and sowp we drink and breath we draw. Awa' wi' ye, an' keep your mouth tight steekit till ye're ower the Hill o' Deer. Oh, haste ye, or ye'll be smitten like the lave, and ye're ower young and bonny to dee."

"Katrine, Katrine," David exclaimed in agony. "What madness brought you here? Have you not heard that half the parish is sick or dead? There is poison in the very air. Oh, my dear, come not near me. Wrap a fold of your cloak over your mouth and never slacken rein till you are back in Calidon."

The girl drew off her gloves. Her eyes were on Isobel.

"I am his promised wife," she said. "Where should I be if not by his side?"

The news left Isobel staring. "His promised wife," she stammered. "Heard ye ever the like--the manse o' Woodilee to seek a mistress from Calidon! . . . But the mair reason why ye suld tak' tent. There's nae place for a bonny doo like yersel' in this stricken parish--ye canna help ithers and ye may get your ain death. Awa' hame, my braw leddy, for the minister has eneuch to trouble him without concern for his joe."

The girl walked to David's side and put her hand in his arm.

"You will not forbid me," she said, and her face was still smiling. "I do not fear the plague, and I do not think it will harm me, for it smites those who live in foul hovels, and I am always about the hills. But I do fear this loneliness. I have not seen you for two weeks, David, and I have been imagining terrible things. I have come to help you, for I have known the pest before--many times in France, and in Oxford too. I know what precautions to take, for I have heard wise men discuss them, but you in Woodilee, from all I hear, are no better than frightened bairns."

"But your aunt--Mistress Saintserf--"

"Aunt Grizel knows of my coming. She has given me this pomander of spices." She touched a trinket which hung from her neck by a gold chain.

David struggled to salve his conscience by energy in dissuasion, and though his heart cried for her presence, it was torn, too, by fear for her safety. He commanded, pled, expostulated, but she only turned a smiling face. She sat down before the peat fire and stretched out her feet to the hot ashes.

"You will not drive me away, David," she said. "Would you forbid me from a work of necessity and mercy--and you a minister?"

In the end he gave up the task, for here was a resolution stiffer than his own, and his strongest arguments faltered when he saw her smile, which was like sunlight in a world of darkness and grim faces. He found himself telling her how the plague had begun, and of the nature of its course--the lack of leeches and medicines, the dearth of helpers, the households perishing silently indoors. She listened calmly, and did not blanch even at the tale of the shuttered cottages and the unburied dead.

"A pretty mess your folk have made of it," she said. "You have turned Woodilee into a lazar-house, and given the pest a rare breeding-ground. Never mind your spiritual consolations, David. Let the miserable bodies come before the souls. You say you have no leech to cure the sick, and that maybe is as well, for I never yet heard of leech that could master the plague. But if you cannot cure, you may prevent its spread. Our first task is to safeguard those who are not yet smitten. If you shut up a cottage where there is one sick man, you condemn every member to death. That must be stopped without delay--and for God's sake let us bury the dead--bury or burn."

"Burn?" he cried out aghast.

"Burn," she nodded. "Fire is the best purifier."

"But we shall rouse the place to madness."

"Better that than death. But we want helpers--bold men who fear neither the pest nor an angry people."

He shook his head. "There are none such in Woodilee. The bones of all are turned to water."

"Then we must stiffen them. . . . There is the one whom we now call Mark Riddel. It was he who told me of your trouble, for he was at Calidon yesterday on his way back from Annandale. There is the black-avised man, too, at Reiverslaw. . . . Are there none more?"

The girl's briskness was rousing David's mind from its torpor.

"Amos Ritchie, maybe."

"That gives us three--four with yourself--and four resolved men can do wonders. Others will fall in once the drum is beaten. Rouse yourself, David, and be as eager to save bodies as you ever were to save souls. And do not forget to pray for a change in this lamentable weather. A ringing frost would do more to stay the pest than all the leeches in Scotland. . . ."

She departed as suddenly as she had come. "I dare not come by day," she told him, "for if Woodilee heard of a stranger its panic would be worse. We have to do with terrified bairns. But I will be here at the same hour to-morrow night, and by that time you must have gathered your helpers."

David did not return from his visitations till the small hours, but he brought back the first piece of good news. One of the hinds at the Mains, after lying for two days in delirium, was now quit of the fever and in a wholesome sweat--sleeping, too, a natural sleep. It was the first case of a possible recovery, and he was aware how much a single life saved would do to quiet the broken nerves of the parish. Also Katrine's advent had lifted him out of the slough of despond in which he had been sunk for weeks. She had spurred him to action, and shown him a duty which he had been too blind to see. He fiercely repressed the anxiety with which the mere thought of her presence in that tainted place filled him. He dare not forbid the exercise of courage in another--even in one who was dearer to him than life.

Next morning he went to Reiverslaw, but got no comfort. Andrew Shillinglaw met him out of doors, and made it very clear that he had no desire to come too near him. The conversation was conducted at a distance of a dozen yards.

"Na, na," he cried. "I'm off this verra day to Moffat, and I'll no set foot in Woodilee till the pest has gane. Ye ask ower muckle, Mr. Sempill. It's maybe YOUR duty to gang among them--though ye ken as weel as me that the haill parochine is no worth the life o' a tinkler's messan--but it's no duty o' Andra Shillinglaw's. I never could abide the reek o' the folk, and they have doubtless gotten what they deserved."

"Ay, I'm feared," he admitted in answer to David's appeals. "Ilka body has something that puts the grue on him, and with me it's aye been the pest. I'll face steel and pouther, angry men and angry beasts, but I'll no face what gars a man dee like a ratton in a hole. And what for should I face it for folk that are no a drap bluid's kin to me?"

The man spoke loudly and violently, as if a little ashamed of himself, and went into the house, where David could hear the bar falling.

From Amos Ritchie he had a different answer. Amos, since his wife's death, had gone about with bent shoulders and a grey face, and had sat for long hours in his smithy beside a dead fire. There David found him, and propounded his request.

"I'll do your will, sir," was the answer. "I've sae little left to live for that I've the less to fear. But there'll be need o' mair than you and me, for the parish is dementit, and daft folk are ill to guide. The first thing is to get the deid buried. For God's sake dinna speak of burnin', for though the body is but our earthly tenement, burnin' is ower like the Deil's wark."

That night Katrine came again, and with her Mark Riddel. The soldier had lost something of his bluff composure, and a troubled eye met David's.

"I have been listening to a sermon on courage," he said ruefully.

Katrine pointed a mocking finger at him.

"He would run away," she said, "he, the old soldier of a hundred battles."

"'Deed and I would. A hundred battles, nor a thousand battles, wouldna reconcile me to the pest. I could name you many a bold captain who at the rumour of pestilence shifted his leaguer, though he would have held his ground before all the Emperor's armies. But it seems I must take my orders from this child, when I hoped to slip off cannily to a cleaner countryside. . . . Ugh, Katrine, my dear, I wish you had set me an easier task than to sweep the midden of Woodilee and turn sexton."

"It's an armed and mailed sexton you must be," she said. "You may have to put reason into the folk with the flat of your sword. Comfort yourself, Mr. Mark, this task is not so much unlike that you were bred to."

The soldier grew visibly more cheerful when he heard that there were only three volunteers for the business. "There's trouble brewing, then," he said, "and it's God's mercy that I've won a certain respect in the parish, for it looks as if more persuasion would be needed than a good word and a clap on the back. When do we start our dowie job, for I confess I would sooner be at it than thinking of it?"

"A lean man like you, all bone and whipcord, need not fear," said David.

"Tut, man," said Mark impatiently, "fear is not in the question. My trouble is that I've a nice stomach and a fastidious nose. Death, whether it comes by pest or steel, is the same to me, and that's a thing worth less than a strae. . . . God's curse on this weather! . . . To work, Mr. David, or I'll be rueing my bargain."

For three days and nights the three men wrought at their repulsive task with niggardly intervals for food and sleep. They made a list of the stricken houses and forced their way into them, even when the doors were bolted. The dead were buried--some in the kirkyard, some in near-by fields, and this duty fell especially on Amos Ritchie, who performed it with dogged fidelity. Now and then there was trouble--a crazed wife or mother would refuse to part with the body of a husband or child, and in some cases the minister had to intervene with stern appeals. More difficult was the business of keeping houses, where the sick lay, open to the air and light. David and Mark had to drive cowering sons out of doors with threats of violence, and in some cases with violence itself. One obstinate household had their door smashed by Amos's axe; another was turned neck and crop into the byre that a sick woman might have peace and air. The three men constituted themselves a relieving force, and had often to do the fetching of food and water. Terrible were the sights revealed behind many of those bolted doors and windows, and though Amos seemed unaffected, the other two had often to rush to the air to check their nausea. Thanks they got none, rarely even curses; the miserable folk were too sunk in despair for either. Yet it is likely they would have failed, had not the news of recoveries got about. Besides the hind at the Mains, two children had now weathered the storm and were reported to be mending fast. The communal mind of Woodilee, which up to then had been blank fatalism and lethargy, was now shot with gleams of hope. The pest might have worked itself out and be on the decline: the corridor was still long and black, but there was a pinprick of light at the end of it. . . . Also Mark Riddel in himself was a cogent persuasion. The dark keen face and the reputation of mystery and command which he had won at the witch-pricking were arguments sufficiently potent, apart from the long sword which he wore at his side. For in this work the douce tacksman of Crossbasket had disappeared: it was the captain of Mackay's who gave orders and saw that they were obeyed.

By Candlemas it was clear that the tide had turned, for there were more on the way to recovery than dying. Well it was that the change had come, for the weather now broke--not, as David had prayed, in wholesome frost, but in perpetual drenching rains. The downpour had come in an instant; within half an hour during the night the wind had shifted, the sky had clouded, and the fall had begun. It was the night, the eve of Candlemas, which the three men had chosen for their work of burning. Now that people were beginning to move about the streets again, it was essential to get rid of centres of infection, and two of the worst were cottages in the clachan where all the inmates had died. Such houses could only be purified by burning, and about ten that night fire was put to them. Dry as tinder, they blazed furiously to heaven, and there were those in the parish, dabblers in witchcraft, who must have turned scared eyes to the glow which was fiercer than any that the altar in the Wood had known. . . . But in an hour came the rain, and the murky smoke-wreaths were turned to steaming embers.

It was a proof of the returning strength of the parish that the burning of the cots startled it out of apathy. Woodilee feebly and confusedly began to take stock of things, and tongues started to wag again. The numbness of loss, the languor of fear, gave place to recrimination. Who was responsible for the calamity of the pest? It must be a mark of the Lord's displeasure, but against whom? They remembered that their minister lay under the ban of the Kirk--had been forbidden to conduct ordinances--was convicted of malignancy and suspected of worse. In their search for a scapegoat many fastened upon David. Practical folk said that he had been in Edinburgh in the time of plague, and had maybe brought back the seeds of it. The devout averred that the uncanny weather had followed upon his public sins, and that the pest had come close on the heels of the Presbytery's condemnation. Was there not the hand of God in this, a manifest judgment? The ways of the Almighty were mysterious, and He might ordain that the people should die for the sins of one man. Even those who had been on David's side were shaken in their confidence.

To crown all, came the events of the past week. To his critics there was no reason in his doings: they believed the pestilence to be a visitation of Heaven, to be stayed not by the arm of flesh, but by fasting and prayer. He had been assiduous in his futile visiting, it was true, and he had buried the dead; but he had broken in on their suffering with violent hands, and had herded men and women like brute beasts. Doors and windows, open to the February rains, attested his methods; by his act two cottages, once snug and canty, were now grey ashes. . . . Amos Ritchie in such matters was but a tool; Mark Riddel was too much feared to be the mark of censorious tongues; but David, still their titular minister, was a predestined target.

And as the village crept back to life, and those who had escaped took heart to do a little work again, and the convalescent staggered to their doors and looked on the world, there arose stranger rumours. The minister was all day out and about--praying on occasion, but more often engaged in homely tasks like cleaning up a kitchen and boiling water for those who were too frail to help themselves. Dark looks and ugly mutterings often followed him, but he was too intent upon his work to take heed of them. The general sullenness he set down to the dregs of grief and terror. That was for the daylight hours, but--it was whispered--after nightfall he had a companion. There were stories of a woman, a creature beautiful and young, who sang in a honeyed voice, and appeared especially at the bedsides of the children. At first few credited the tale, but presently came ample confirmation. She had been seen at three houses in the clachan, at the Mirehope herd's, at the Mains; with her had been the minister; and the bairns to whom she had spoken cried for her return. . . . The old and wise shook their heads. There was no such woman in the parish or in all the countryside. And some remembered that the minister in the back-end had been observed to meet with a woman in the Wood, and that she had seemed to those who saw her to be no mortal, but the Queen of Elfhame.

The truth was that no commands of Mark, no protestations of David, could keep Katrine out of the village. She saw the reason for not appearing in the daylight, for a stranger in Woodilee--above all such a stranger as she--would have been too much for the brittle nerves of the parish. But after nightfall the case was different, and when with David she had once stood by the bed of a sick child, nothing could prevent her making a nightly duty of it. Into those sodden, woeful households she entered like a spring wind; the people may have marvelled, but they were still too apathetic to ask questions, and they felt dumbly her curative power.

Among unkempt pallid men and frowsy wild-eyed women the face bright with the weather, the curls dabbled with rain, the cool firm arm, the alert figure, worked a miracle, as if an angel had troubled the stagnant waters of their life. Her hand on a child's hot brow sent it into a peaceful sleep; her presence gave to the sick the will to live and to the fearful a gleam of courage. What they thought and said when she had gone will never be known, but for certain they longed for her coming again.

On the 18th day of February the pestilence took its last victim--an old woman, the mother of the Windyways herd, and the earth was still fresh on her grave when the rain ceased. The wind swung to the north, and the black frost for which David had longed settled on the land. It put an end to the pest, but it bore hard on the convalescent, and the older and feebler died under its rigour. In the pure cold air the taint seemed to pass from the land, and the problem of David and his helpers was now a straightforward fight with normal ailments and the normal winter poverty. Stock during the visitation had been scarcely tended, and the byres and infields were full of dead beasts; while in the general terror the customary frugality of the parish had been forgotten and many a meal-ark was empty. There was need of clothing and food, of fuel and cordials, and it did not appear where they were to come from.

There was no help to be looked for from outside, for to the neighbourhood Woodilee was like a leper settlement; none would have dared to enter the place, and had a Woodilee man shown his face in another parish he would have been driven back with stones. Mr. Fordyce managed to send to David more than one distressful letter, lamenting that for the sake of his own people he could not lend his brother a helping hand; but save for that, from the 8th day of January to the 15th day of March there was no communication with the outer world. In this crisis Mark Riddel wrought mightily. He had ways and means of getting supplies from distant places, and his pack-horses, guided by himself or Amos Ritchie, brought meal and homespun blankets from quarters which no man knew of. David exhausted the manse stores, and Isobel kilted her coats and, with a charity seasoned by maledictions, kept her pot or girdle continually on the fire. But it was the house of Calidon that provided the main necessaries. Its brew-house and its girnel, its stillroom and its cellars, not to speak of Mistress Grizel's private cordials, were plundered for the sake of a parish which Mistress Grizel could not refer to without a sour grimace. When Katrine rode to the manse of a night she would bring with her usually a laden shelty.

The end of the plague was for David a harder season even than its height. For with convalescence Woodilee seemed to lose its wits. Before it had sat dazed and broken under the rod; now it woke to an ardour of self-preservation. At the beginning the people seemed to be careless of infection; now the survivors were possessed with a craze to live, and fought like terrified animals to get out of danger. They could not leave the parish bounds, but those that were able fled from the village. The leaky sheilings on the hills, occupied by the ewe-milkers during the height of summer, gave lodging to many, and several died there of the violence of the frost. The outlying farms were believed to be the safer, so Mirehope and Nether Fennan had many undesired tenants in their outhouses. The result was that, in a season of convalescence, when nursing was especially needed, the bedridden were often left deserted. David tried to enlist men and women who had either escaped the plague or had been for some weeks recovered, but he got only fierce denials or an obstinate silence. The place had become brutish, and the selfishness of beasts seemed to have become the rule of life.

The one exception was Chasehope. During the worst weeks the clachan had had no news of him, but it was rumoured that he had made a fortress of his farm-town, and had assiduously tended his own people. At any rate at Chasehope there had been only one death. Now he appeared in the street, and to David's amazement it was clear that he came on an errand of mercy. His house seemed still to be well provided, and he brought with him a certain amount of provender. This he did not bestow indiscriminately but only on certain families, which David guessed to contain members of the coven. To these he spoke with authority, and he used his power to put reason into the distracted.

He alone in the place seemed to have no fear of infection--to be careless of the risk which had sent panic abroad among the others. He passed the minister with a grave salutation, and showed no wish to give or ask for help; he had some business afoot which was his private concern. But the fact stood out that this man, alone in Woodilee, had mastered fear.

Once in a cottage where a child was recovering he came upon David and Katrine. The girl was sitting on a stool by the bed making a toy out of reeds for the child's amusement, and singing a French nursery song about Cadet Roussel and his three houses. David lifted his eyes from admiring the grace and swiftness of her hands to see Chasehope's heavy white face in the glow of the firelight. The latter doffed his bonnet at the sight of Katrine, and murmured some civility. Clearly he knew her, for he picked up a reed from the floor. "Frae the Calidon mill-dam, belike," he said.

"You are the one man in Woodilee who has courage," David said. "You are no friend of mine, Ephraim Caird, but I give you the praise of a stout heart."

"Why should I be feared?" the other asked. "Why should I dread to walk even in the valley of death if His rod and staff are there to comfort me?"

"Why should you! But many professors are of a different mind."

"They are but poor professors, then. I fear no ill, for I am in the Lord's hand till His appointed time."

"But many who do not fear death fear to die by the pest."

"Ay, but I have my assurance. I have the Lord's own promise, Mr. Sempill. I ken as weel that no pest can touch me as that my name is Ephraim Caird and my habitation is Chasehope. It's the lack o' sound doctrine that gars folk turn cowards--they dinna lippen enough to the Lord--they havena a firm enough grip o' their calling and election. I have my compact sure, and I ken that the Lord will no gie me a back-cast. I can rejoice even in this sore affliction, for He hath demanded a sacrifice, and what is man to question His will? Dear in His sight is the death of His saints--ay, and of sinners, too, for His judgments are not exhausted. There's mair to come, Mr. Sempill--take tent o' that, sir--the conviction is heavy on me that the wind o' His displeasure has still a blast to blaw."

The pale eyes had almost the green of a cat's in the dim light, and the bald brows above gave the whole face the air of a mask, which at any moment might slip and reveal nightmare lineaments. The child in the bed looked up as he spoke, saw his face and screamed in terror, and Katrine, after one glance behind her, was busied in crooning consolations. . . . In that moment David had a revelation. This man, secure in his election to grace, secure against common fear, was likewise secure against common reason. He was no hypocrite. To him the foulest sin would be no sin--its indulgence would be part of his prerogative, its blotting out an incident in his compact with the Almighty. He could lead the coven in the Wood and wallow in the lusts of the flesh, and his crimes would be but the greater vindication of God's omnipotence. . . . In that illuminating instant madness had looked out of his eyes.

CHAPTER XIX

THE SACRIFICE

As March drew to its close the wheels of life began once again to run creakingly in Woodilee. The frost disappeared under a week of southwesterly gales, and then the wind moved to the east and blew dry and blighting, so that the lean beasts shivered in the infields. The gross unseasonable herbage of the winter had gone, and it promised to be a backward spring. The men went out feebly to the farm-work, and the ploughing began, though the draught-oxen were so poor in condition that the work moved slowly. The siege, too, was raised. Johnnie Dow once again showed his cautious face in the clachan and brought news of the outer world; the pack-horses again struggled through Carnwath Moss; and there came word from Kirk Aller that the meeting of the Presbytery to adjudicate on David's case was fixed for a day in April. Mr. James rode over from Cauldshaw and the kirk was opened, but David did not renew his preachings at the kirkyard gate.

The truth is that he was weary to the bone. Mark Riddel met him one morning on the road and drew rein sharply at the sight of his face.

"Man David, you're like a ghost. You've worked your body ower sore these last months, and if you dinna take care you'll be on your back. You and Katrine are two inconsiderate bairns. You've both of you done the work of ten men, and you'll no listen to wiser folk. Take my advice and get furth of this woeful parish till your body is rested and your mind quieter."

"I am summoned to my trial at Kirk Aller in a week's time."

"And that's the crown of it! That's what you get for wearing yourself to skin and bone for a thankless folk. There are times when I scunner at my native land. There's a rumour that Montrose has escaped abroad and is now at the Emperor's court, and if it werena for you and Katrine I could find it in me to join him. There's a blight on the country which affects even a brisk heart like mine, and I'm getting mortal sick of the eternal crack of nowt and wedders."

But though Mark came to the manse every evening and would have nursed him like a mother, David could not relax the tension of body and spirit. He slept badly, and in spite of Isobel's coaxing ate little; his nights were filled with wild dreams, and, worse, these dreams seemed to pursue him in his waking hours. He felt no special ailment of body to which he could attribute his distress, beyond an extreme fatigue. He would take long walks by day and night, but though he returned from them very stiff and weary, they did not bring him healthful sleep. He tried to master himself, to laugh at himself, but the malaise would not be expelled. . . . He was the prey of childish fears, looking nervously for something malign to come out of the dark or round the corner. And presently the barriers of the real seemed to crumble. He saw faces where there were none, he listened to voices in the deepest silence. Once, coming at night up the manse loan, he heard footsteps on the dry earth approaching him. They grew louder, passed and died away behind him, and he realized that the footsteps were his own.

A word of Chasehope's stuck evilly in his memory. The Lord had demanded a sacrifice, but the sacrifice was not yet complete, the man had said. The word tortured him and he could get no relief from thinking, for the thing was beyond thought. An oppression of coming disaster weighed on him. He told himself that his enemy had meant no more than the Presbytery trial, but he could not lay the ghost. Something darker, more terrible, hung on the skirts of his imagination. Chasehope was no doubt mad, but truth might lurk in madness; a maniac saw that which was hidden from others. It was for Katrine that he feared, and what he feared he could not give a shape to--there lay the agony of it.

Presently his old dread of the Wood returned--that dread which he thought he had exorcised for ever. He had defied it, but what if it should prove too strong for him? In his distraught thoughts the pestilence seemed to have come out of it--Chasehope had moved unscathed through the weeks of plague--Chasehope and the devils he served were the plague's masters. Was there some other terror still in its depths waiting to be loosed on him? He had moments of clear-sightedness, when he despised himself for his folly, and realized that to be thus faint of heart was to acknowledge defeat and to abase himself before his enemy. But the conviction returned, stronger than will or reason, and David would walk the hill with clenched hands and muttering lips, or in his closet struggle in blind prayer for a comfort that would not come.

After Katrine's nightly visits to Woodilee had ceased the minister had meant to go daily to Calidon. But with this new mood of terror upon him he was ashamed to face the girl; and he had sufficient manhood to put restraint upon his longings. The time came, however, when anxiety conquered scruples. He rode to Calidon with a fluttering heart, an excitement rather of fear than of joy.

Mistress Saintserf faced him grimly.

"What have ye done wi' my bairn?" she demanded. "She is fair broke wi' ridin' the roads and tendin' the riff-raff o' Woodilee--and the haill parochine no worth a hair o' her heid. Christian charity, says you--but there's bounds to Christian charity! Ye're a bonny lad to tak' so little care o' your joe."

Presently she condescended to details. "She has nae strength, the puir thing--clean worn out like an auld bauchle [shoe]. Yestreen I garred her tak' to her bed, and she's lyin' as biddable as a wean, and her for ordinar' sae sweir to bide still. . . . Na, ye canna see her. But dinna fash yoursel', my man. She's no sick--just weary wi' ower heavy a task. A long lie in her bed will put her richt, and a change in this dowie weather. Pray for a bit blink o' sun. . . . Ye're lookin' gey gash yoursel'. Ye'd be nane the waur o' a week on your back."

As David rode homeward he remembered the last words and laughed at the irony. A week in bed, when he could scarcely endure three hours in a night! Mistress Saintserf's news had put him into an agony of apprehension. He stabled his horse and set out to work off his anxiety by bodily fatigue, but it grew with every mile he walked. Weariness, he told himself, was only natural after such a winter's toil; was not he himself worn out, and did not even Mark Riddel confess to a great fatigue? But he could not console himself with such thoughts. At any moment she might fall into a fever, and then--he remembered with dreadful distinctness the stages of the malady. Was this the last lingering effort of the pest?--he had heard of such cases coming weeks after the thing seemed to have been stayed. And always there rose in his mind Chasehope's prophecy of a sacrifice still to come.

He would fain have gone back to Calidon and waited for news. Instead he sent Isobel with a message to Mistress Grizel. His housekeeper was noted as a skilful nurse and an amateur leech, and he begged that she should be allowed to help in waiting upon Katrine. The sending of her did something to ease his mind, for it was a direct piece of service to his beloved; moreover, if

Isobel was in Calidon, he could go there as often as he wished and have speech with her, for he was a little ashamed to reveal to Mistress Grizel his lack of fortitude. Meantime he could fend for himself, and cook what food he needed.

The time passed on leaden feet, and the hours of darkness were one long sleepless nightmare. Next day he was early at Calidon and found Isobel with a composed face. "Ye neednа tak' it sae sair, Mr. David," she assured him. "The leddy's no that bad. Nae doot she's sair weary, but the feck o' the time she sleeps like a bairn, and there's nae fever. There's strong bluid in her that will no be lang ere it conquers the weakness. But losh, sir, ye've the face o' a bogle. Awa' hame wi' ye and lie doun, or I'll no bide anither hour in Calidon. Are ye takin' your meat? Dinna look at me like a glum wean, but dae as I tell ye."

David returned to the manse, and under the influence of Isobel's cheerfulness fell asleep in his chair and slept till the late afternoon. He awoke freshened in body, but with a new alarm at his heart. Isobel had said there was no fever, but that meant that she dreaded fever. . . . By this time it might have come. Even now Katrine might be delirious. . . . He realized how swiftly during the pest fever had succeeded listlessness.

Nevertheless the hours of sleep had given him a greater power of self-control, and he curbed his instinct to ride forthwith to Calidon. He wandered through the house and out into the glebe, striving to fix his mind on small and homely things. It was the third day of April, but there was no sign of spring. The dislocation of the seasons had given the earth an autumnal air, for the shoals of fallen leaves lay as if it were November, and the frosts had not bleached the herbage. He remembered how a year ago at this time he had wandered on the hills and felt with joy the stirrings of new life. To-day the world was still clamped in bonds, and death was in the bare trees and the leaden sky. What had become of his high hopes? All gone save one--and that the dearest. A year ago he had had no thought of Katrine and had been happy in other things. Now these had been turned into ashes, but he had got Katrine in their stead. If she were to go--? The thought so chilled his heart that he fled indoors, as if in the house he could barricade himself against it.

In his study he turned over his books. He tried to pray, but set prayer was idle, for every breath he drew had become an impassioned supplication. He had out his notes on Isaiah and the prolegomena which he had completed, but his eyes could scarcely read them. How small and remote these labours seemed! Every now and then a quotation from the prophet stood out in his manuscript, and these were as ominous as a raven's croaking. "Burning instead of beauty. . . . Their faces shall be as flames. . . . Through the wrath of the Lord of hosts is the land darkened, and the people shall be as the fuel of the fire. . . . This is the rest wherewith ye may cause the weary to rest."

He turned from his notes in awe and took up his secular books. One he opened at random and saw that it was the Æneid, and the words which caught his eyes were "manibus date lilia plenis." Small wonder that the book had opened there, for it was a well-thumbed passage; but he shuddered as if he had cast the sortes Virgilianæ and had got a doleful answer.

In the evening he found himself some food, and since the dark was full of ghosts for him, he lit many candles and banked up the peats on the fire. He was in a strange mood, rapt out of himself, suffering not so much pain in his thoughts as a fever of expectation. His fingers drummed ceaselessly on his knees; as he looked into the glowing peats he saw forms and figures that seemed to mock him; to his unquiet ears a wind was blowing round the house--a wind that talked--though the night was very still. And always there was in his head, like the refrain of a ballad, the words "Burning instead of beauty."

He did not see Mark Riddel till the man was beside him and had touched his shoulder. Then he started up with a cry and encountered a grave, perturbed face.

"You had better come to Calidon," Mark said. "Katrine . . . she has taken a turn for the worse. She has been in a fever since midday."

It was the news he had been expecting, and David rose obediently.

"I'll go on foot," he said. "I can run faster than any horse."

Mark looked at him anxiously. "You'll do no such thing. You'd faint or you were across the Hill o' Deer. Bide where you are and I'll saddle your beast."

The two set off at a gallop, but in the rough parts of the road Mark slackened and took David's bridle. "Hold up," he cried. "It'll no mend matters if you break your neck."

David asked only one question. "Have you got a leech?" he said.

"I'll have no leeches. Your country botcher would only bleed her, and she hasna the strength for that. Grizel and yon wife Isobel are all the leeches that are needed, and I'm not without skill myself. Keep up your heart, David. All is no tint yet, and it's a young life."

At Calidon gate David spoke again. "Is it the pest?"

"I canna tell, for the pest has many shapes to it. Weakness and fever--there's no other signs, though God kens that's bad enough."

He was taken straight to her chamber by Isobel, and found there Mistress Grizel, a silent, stern-faced guardian. Katrine lay tossing in high delirium, moaning a little, and moving her arms feebly on the coverlet. A bandage of wet cloths was on her brow, and, as David laid his hand on it, he felt the pulse of the fever beneath. Her long dark lashes lay on her flushed cheeks, but every now and then her eyes would open in a glassy stare. He took her hand and it was dry and burning.

"We maun let the fever rin its course," said Mistress Grizel. "She maun fecht her ain battle without the help o' man. God be kind to my bairn," and she kissed the hot lips.

"Ye'll be puttin' up a prayer?" she turned to David.

"I cannot pray . . . I can only watch. . . . I beg you to let me watch here beside her."

"Have your way. There's little need o' speech if there be prayer in the heart. Isobel will get ready your chamber, for ye canna leave this house."

Presently David was in the sick-room alone, and if he could not pray he spent the hours on his knees. Isobel and Mistress Grizel returned from time to time; once Mark came in and put his hand on the girl's brow. The night passed and the dawn came, but still David knelt at a chair by the bedside, his head sometimes in his hands and sometimes lifted to gaze at the face on the pillow. He was tortured with the sense of his frailty. A sacrifice, another sacrifice, was required, and for what sins but his own? He had been lacking--oh, he had been lacking in every Christian grace. In those black moments he saw himself as the chief of sinners, his struggles to rise foiled by a dragging weight of self, his ardours half-hearted, the fruits he brought forth but poor pithless stalks, his errors dark and monstrous like birds of night. He was not conscious of any special sin--only of a deep unworthiness which made him unfit to touch the hem of her garment. . . . Had ever any one so made music in the world by merely passing through it? And now--burning instead of beauty. . . .

Mr. Fordyce came over from Cauldshaw in the evening. He spoke to David but got no answer--it may be doubted if his words were understood. But an invitation to follow him in prayer was rejected, so Mr. James prayed alone--"for Thy handmaiden who is in the pangs of a great sickness--and for him Thy servant to whom her welfare is especially dear." The prayer seemed to David to make an enclosure for Katrine and himself apart from the world. . . .

Mark took him to his room and made him lie down on his bed. He gave him a bowl of spiced ale, which David drank greedily, for he was very thirsty. Maybe the posset contained some innocent drug, for he slipped into dreams. They were pleasant dreams, shapeless and aimless, but with a sense of well-being in them which soothed him, so that he woke to Mark's pressure on his arm with a vacant smile. But one glimpse of the real world--the corner of a four- post bed, torn arras, and the skirts of Mark's frieze coat--brought down on him the dark battalion of his cares. He had no need to wait for the spoken word; Mark's eyes were message enough.

"Come! The fever has abated," were the words.

David's brain was sluggish: the words seemed to be at variance with the speaker's face; for a moment he had a bewildered spasm of comfort.

"She is recovered?"

"She is dying," said Mark. "It is now the afternoon. She is going out with the daylight."

The small lozenged windows, though there were two of them, lit the room faintly, for the sky was lowering and grey. Mr. Fordyce had returned, and poured out his soul at the bed-foot, but presently he grew silent like the others, for there was a hush in the room which made even the words of prayer a sacrilege. . . . The flush had gone from the girl's face, and the waxen cheeks and the blanched lips told of a mortal weakness. Her hand was in David's, as passive as a plucked flower. The lashes were quiet on her cheeks, and her faint, difficult breathing scarcely stirred the coverlet.

In that final hour peace of a kind entered into David's soul. He was truly humble at last, for all the flickerings and unrest of human desires were stilled. The joy which he had scarcely dared to hope for, the possession of that bright and rare thing, was now confirmed to him. Katrine was securely his for ever. . . . At the very end her eyes opened, and if they looked a little blindly at the others they seemed to enfold him in a passion of love. There was even the glimmer of a smile. And then the gloaming crept round them, and, as Mark had foretold, she went out with the daylight.

The quiet was broken by the loud wailing of the two women, for the composure of even the iron-Lipped Mistress Grizel now failed her. Mr. Fordyce stilled it with an uplifted hand. "The lamb is safe folded," he said.

Mistress Grizel, after the fashion of her kind, must speak. "She was a kind lassie, and had nae thochts but guid thochts, and if she was maybe no that weel instructed in sound doctrine, it was nae faut in her . . . she was aye blithe to hearken to Mr. James--" She stopped short at the sight of David's face.

"She is now at the right hand of the Throne," he said, "and I say that in the face of every minister that ever perverted the Word. She was made in the image of her Lord, and she has gone to meet Him."

Later in the evening the mind of the practical Mistress Grizel turned to the dismal apparatus of death. "She'll better lie in Cauldshaw in the Hawkshaw buryin' ground. There's room in the auld vault, the mair as it's no likely Nicholas will lay his banes there."

"Nay, but she will not lie in Cauldshaw. "David's face had a strange calm in it and his voice was toneless and steady. "She will he in the part of the greenwood which was her own, in the place she called Paradise. I know her wishes as if she had told them to me. I will not have her laid in any kirkyard vault. . . . She is too young. . . . She is not dead but sleeping."

Mistress Grizel protested, but half-heartedly. Mr. Fordyce had little objection to raise. "It is not the way of our Kirk," he said, "to consecrate ground for the dead. All earth is hallowed which receives Christian dust. But lest the graves of the departed be forgotten, it has been the custom to gather them together in some spot under the kirk's shadow. In a wild wood, among bracken and stones, it will be ill to keep mind of a place of sepulchre."

"I will not forget it."

"But when you yourself are dead and gone . . . ?"

"What matters it then?" He could have laughed at the meaninglessness of human fashions. He felt that Katrine and he were in a sphere of their own, safe for ever from intrusion, a sphere independent of time and space, even of life and death. But Paradise had been the spot where their love had first been born; it had become in the mind a symbol and a mystery; let Paradise, therefore, receive the earthly covering of the blessed spirit, for even the blessed have their terrestrial shrines.

So it came about that by night--for Mistress Grizel would not permit a ceremony so unconventional in daylight--and by the light of the torches of Jock Dodds and Edie the falconer, the girl was buried near the spring in Paradise, with David and Mr. Fordyce at the grave's head and foot.

To the former it was all a waking dream. The solid earth had become for him bodiless; the sun's progress, human speech, rain, wind, the ritual of daily life, no more than a phantasmagoria: reality lay only in that inner world where Katrine still lived for him. He abode solitary in the manse, and refused to let Isobel return. Indeed he begged Mistress Saintserf to keep her and be kind to her.

"'Deed, I will do that, and be glad to do it, for she's a skilly auld body and a great stand-by in the house. But, Davie, my man, what is to come o' you? I was lookin' to get ye as a guidson, and the Lord kens Calidon needs a man about the place--what wi' the forty thousand merks to be paid for Nicholas's fine. . . ."

But she saw that her words fell on unheeding ears. David's eyes seemed to be looking beyond her to an infinite distance.

CHAPTER XX

THE JUDGMENT

David rode to Kirk Aller to face the Presbytery in a blustering day of April rains. The wind blew high from the south-west in the leafless branches, and tossed the rotting leaves which should long ago have been powdered by frosts and snows. Aller was red with spate, and in the haughs the flood-water lay in leaden shallows. The birds, who should have been riotous in the bent, were few and silent; scarcely a plover or a curlew piped; only from the gnarled firs of the Wood came the croak of a nesting raven. It was a day to deaden a man's spirits, but David regarded it not. He was still in his secluded world, a chamber barred to all memories but one. He had no clear vision of the home of the blessed dead, and what he had would have been held unorthodox by the Kirk. Now he thought of her in a Platonic mood as inhabiting all things lovely and pure, a spirit as rare as the lingering light of sunset. But more often he pictured her as an embodied saint admitted into the fellowship of Christ, wrapped round with a richer love than mortals knew, but reaching out warm hands to his loneliness. And the words that came to his tongue were the lines of Peter Abelard:

"O quanta qualia sunt illa sabbata Quæ semper celebrat superna Curia;"

but the sabbaths he dreamed of were not the sabbaths of the Kirk.

The world, the tangible world, was broken for him in fragments. His chamber was not only shut to its winds, but it seemed set in a high tower from which common realities showed infinitely small and distant. The Presbytery--the General Assembly--the Kirk--seemed tiny things vanishing down the perspective of an inverted spy- glass. He was armoured against censure, for it was idle to censure one who was overwhelmed by his own unworthiness and who at the same time saw all human authorities diminished to cockle-shells. He had no fears and no hates: God had smitten him, and, humble under that awful rod, he could view with indifference the little whips of his fellows. He did not blame them--why should dust accuse dust?

In his detachment only one thought affected him with any passion. He retained his horror of the Wood. If he were to fall he would fain have brought down with him that unholy temple. For Chasehope he felt no hatred except as its high-priest; the man himself, with his crazy twisted soul, was rather a mark for pity. But he would fain have rid Woodilee of that incubus. . . . He had failed, and Chasehope was the victor--Chasehope and the Wood. For a moment his mind returned to realities, and he questioned himself if he had left anything undone. This day his original libel would come before the Presbytery, and he had the right to call his witnesses. But where were they? Reiverslaw had been absent two months from the parish and had not yet returned, and without his testimony Richie Smail and Rab Prentice were meaningless voices. He could give his own witness, but that the Presbytery had already officially rejected. Let it go--the Almighty in His own time would be his vindication--he who was filthy let him be filthy still. . . .

"Ubi molestiis finitis omnibus Securi cantica Sion cantabimus."

But even in his secret world regret penetrated and irked him, for Melanudrigill was nigh to the greenwood and to Paradise.

The old kirk on the brae above the Aller bridge was crowded to its full. Never had been so large a meeting of Presbytery, both lay and clerical, for the case of the minister of Woodilee had made a great talk all winter in the glens. Woodilee itself, now purged of its taint, was strongly represented by four members of Session, and in a prominent place at the Moderator's elbow sat Ephraim Caird. As David entered heads were averted, but as he advanced to the seat prescribed for him he found that Mr. Fordyce was his neighbour--Mr. Fordyce heavily muffled in his ancient plaid, and with a face whose ordinary sick pallor seemed to be flushed with a timid excitement. He seized David's hand, and his own was hot and nervous, and his lips moved as if he were praying under his breath.

The forty-third Psalm was sung, there were two lengthy readings of Scripture, and then Mr. Muirhead, the Moderator, constituted the Court and prayed for guidance. David's attention wandered, though he tried to supplement the public supplication with his own. . . . His eyes seemed to have become distorted and the whole assembly have gone crooked. The fathers and brethren were no more than a gathering of death's heads, their voices were like the creaking of wheels and the scraping of boughs and the grinding of stones. The Moderator's massive visage was the mask behind which his brain ticked small and foolish like a clock. The minister of Bold was only a child, a petted, noisy child. The grave countenances around him seemed shot with fear and confusion: almost it seemed he could look into their hearts and see terrors and jealousies writhing like coils of worms. . . . He rubbed his eyes and forced himself to attention. The Moderator was speaking of the charge against Chasehope and others anent the Wood.

"We have your written libel, Mr. Sempill," he said. "It is your right to implement it by the calling of witnesses. Have you them here?"

"My principal witness, Andrew Shillinglaw in Reiverslaw, has left the parish because of the pest and is not yet returned. Without him I can do nothing." David's voice, to his own surprise, came out full and clear.

"Do you seek a postponement?"

David shook his head. "What boots it? The Lord will judge the wickedness in His own time and in His own way. But I would ask that the matter be put to him whom I have accused as principal, and that he deny or affirm it on his solemn oath."

"You hear that, Ephraim," said Mr. Muirhead. "I'm loth to put such a task on one of your noted godly walk, but it would maybe conduce to the satisfaction of the Court if you would formally and finally give these monstrous charges a solemn denial."

Chasehope rose and called his Maker to witness that there was no word of truth in the accusation. His voice was steady, his expression of a decent gravity. He looked towards David, and there was not a quiver in the large placidity of his face.

"The Court is content," said Mr. Muirhead. "Have you anything to add, Mr. Sempill?"

"The Lord will yet judge between us," said David.

"That matter can therefore be dismissed," said the Moderator, in a voice in which solemnity wrestled with satisfaction. "We proceed to the charges against our unhappy brother."

He set forth--not unfairly--the counts against David. The principal was that abetting of malignancy with which the Court was already familiar, and which David had admitted and justified. But he added new matter.

"It has come to my knowledge," he said, "through the praiseworthy vigilance of our friend Chasehope, that there is further incriminating evidence on this score. In the recent melancholy visitation at Woodilee, our brother was guilty of strange deeds and in strange company. It seems that he harled the poor folk out of their bits of dwellings, on the plea that when they crept together they fomented the pest. Thereby it is alleged he spread the taint of the malady, and sorely troubled many a death-bed. Further, he violently and wrongfully broke open doors that were barred to him and set fire to cot-houses where the sick had lain, thereby destroying gear which was not his and depriving the folk of their lawful habitations. I have here an attested statement setting forth the wrongs complained of. What answer do you make to that, Mr. Sempill?"

"I admit the acts, and reply that by their means and by God's mercy the pest was stayed."

There was a murmur of disapproval throughout the gathering, and Mr. Muirhead cast up his eyes to Heaven.

"More of this sinful pride! As if the hand of the Lord was stayed by breaking in the doors and burning the thack of honest folks' houses! But these are matters which are properly for the civil courts, and do not come within the cognizance of this Presbytery. What deeply concerns us is the company in which it is alleged that these acts were done. Mr. Sempill had as his helper one Amos Ritchie, a dweller in Woodilee, of whom I had hoped better things, and one Mark Riddel, a new-come tenant of the mailing of Crossbasket. We have had news of this Riddel before. He took a leading part in defending a woman accused of witchcraft in the back-end, and--though it seems that the witch-pricker was a poor creature with some irregularities in his conduct--yet it cannot be denied that the words and doings of the man Mark Riddel on that occasion gave great offence to godly folk in Woodilee, and led to the just suspicion that he himself had meddled with unlawful matters. . . . Who think you that this Riddel turns out to be? Who but that Mark Kerr that was a colonel with Montrose and a notorious malignant and has been sought all winter by the arm of the law. Chasehope has riddled out the whole black business, and has those that will swear to the man. Information has been dispatched to the Procurator-Fiscal, and it's like that by this time hands will have been laid on him."

"I fear that he has gotten clean away," said Chasehope. "The word this morn was that there was no reek in the Crossbasket lum."

"He'll no gang far," said the Moderator, "for the countryside will be up against him. Now, Mr. Sempill, what say you on this count? Did you ken the true nature of this man Mark Riddel?"

"I knew that he had been a soldier of Montrose. What mattered his past if he were willing to help in a work of Christian duty?"

"Christian duty!" The Moderator's face crimsoned with wrath. "The words should choke in your throat, sir. You dare to call it Christian duty to harry the living and perplex the dying for some whim of your own ignorant heart? You found a yoke-fellow worthy of you. It is borne in on me that you and your presumption and your slackness of walk and doctrine have been the cause of this sore dispensation in Woodilee. Upon your head, sir, lie the deaths and sufferings of your afflicted people."

He checked himself with an effort and proceeded in a calmer tone.

"No evidence need be called on the main counts, for they have been admitted by the panel. By his own confession David Sempill, lately ordained minister of the Gospel in Woodilee, is guilty of the grievous sin of consorting with and abetting the declared enemies of Christ's Kirk in Scotland. Under the specious plea of charity-- whilk is a favourite device of the Enemy to delude mankind--he has given shelter to one whose hands were red with the blood of the saints, and has endeavoured to cumber the work of purging the accursed thing from our midst. Moreover, he has lately shown what was in his heart by further and intimate converse with the ungodly. I do not speak of other errors, of harsh and un-Christian conduct towards his congregation, of lack of judgment, and of a weakness in doctrine, whilk, if not actual heresy, is its near neighbour. I deal with the gravamen of the matter, a sin openly committed and indeed acknowledged and gloried in."

Mr. Muirhead pursed his lips, and a sigh of approval rose from his hearers.

"But it is needful at all times," he went on, "to temper mercy with justice. Our brother is young and has no doubt been led astray by evil conversation and by over-much carnal learning. There is yet room for repentance, and the Kirk is merciful to the penitent. If he will make full confession of his sins and renounce and abhor them and humbly seek forgiveness from an offended Jehovah, this Court will doubtless be prepared to deal tenderly with him. It would not consist with decency that he continue in the charge of Woodilee, but the matter of excommunication might be dispensed with. For let him understand clearly that if he persists in his contumacy he will be outcast not only from the ministry of Woodilee but from membership of the Kirk of Christ."

His voice had become sensibly gentler. If his main object was to avoid too great a scandal in the Church, there may have been a spice of pity for the youth and the haggard face of the accused.

"I acknowledge myself most heartily to be the chief of sinners," said David.

"There must be more than a general confession," said the Moderator. "You must condescend upon the transgression. You must in this place confess the heinousness of your guilt on the precise counts I have expounded, admit your grievous errors and your abhorrence of them, and humbly submit yourself to judgment."

"Nay," said David. "I cannot admit that to be sin which I hold to have been my duty."

Again from the assembly came a sound like sighing, but now it seemed to have a note of wrath in it, as if the breath came through clenched teeth. The Moderator shut his eyes as if to ward off an unbearable spectacle. Then he looked down on David with his brows drawn so that they made a line bisecting his great face.

"Man, man," he said, "you are far from Christ. You confess your sin, but you hug to your bosom one darling iniquity which you proclaim a grace. You are blinded and self-deluded, and I see no hope for you in this world or the next. You are an outcast from the commonwealth of Israel."

He inclined his head to Chasehope, who had plucked at his arm and now said something in his ear.

"I am reminded," he went on. "Malignancy is not all the sum of the sins of this unhappy man. There was a charge which I had hoped there would be no need to press, but which in his condition of resolute impenitence I am bound to bring forward. He was seen in the back-end to frequent the Black Wood in the company of a woman, and it is alleged--nay, it can be proved by many witnesses--that in his doubtful work during the time of pestilence a woman was in his company. To public sins he would seem to have added private lusts. Answer me, sir, as you will answer some day to your Maker, who and what was the woman, and where is she to be found?"

The words scarcely penetrated to David's brain, for he had already slipped away from the crowd of moody faces to his secret world. But in the hush that followed the question another voice spoke, a voice high-pitched and tremulous but as startling as a trumpet.

"She is with the angels in Heaven." Mr. Fordyce had dropped his plaid from his shoulders, and stood up with raised arm, his eyes burning in his pale face. His repute as a saint was so well established that at any time he would have commanded silence, but now he spoke in a quiet so deep that his hearers seemed to be frozen in their seats. Even the Moderator stopped in the act of settling his bands, and his hand remained at his throat.

"I will speak and not be silent," said the voice. "The woman whom you would accuse with your foul tongues is this day with her Lord in Paradise. Well I kenned her--she was Katrine Yester and she abode at Calidon--there was none like her for gentleness and grace. She was the promised wife of David Sempill--and in the time of calamity she left her bien dwelling and her secure life and wrought among the poor folk of Woodilee--ay, as Christ left His Father's house to succour sinful men. . . . She is far ayont us for evermore, and in the New Jerusalem she will be so near the Throne that blessed will I be if I get a glimpse of her."

The words--which when remembered later were accounted a horrid blasphemy--cast at the moment a strange spell over his hearers. The hush was broken by many turning their heads, as if they could not endure the sight of that prophetic face. Even the Moderator dropped his eyes; Chasehope stared at the speaker with half a smile on his lips.

"Fools, fools!" the voice went on. "I have been ower long silent because of the infirmities of my flesh. One came among you preaching Christ and you have stoned him, as the Jews stoned Stephen outside the walls of Jerusalem. I pray that it may be given him, like Stephen, to see the heavens open and the Son of Man standing on the right hand of God. . . . I tell you that there's those among us now that will burn in Hell for this day's work. Blind, blind . . ."

He choked, his face coloured with a rush of blood, he swayed and would have fallen had not David caught him. The cessation of the haunting voice restored the assembly to its senses. Murmurings began, and the Moderator dropped his hand from his throat and found speech.

"This is most unseemly. Our brother is sick and has forgotten himself. Let the work of the Court proceed."

David lifted the half-fainting Mr. Fordyce in his arms. He bowed to the Moderator. "My presence is no longer needed," he said. "I have no more to say and am in the hands of the Court. Meantime I must look to my friend."

He left the kirk with his burden.

He took him to the little inn in the Northgate and put him to bed. The landlady was a kindly soul and promised to tend him well; there was no serious illness--excitement and emotion and an unaccustomed effort had drawn heavily upon Mr. Fordyce's small reserve of strength--he needed only rest to be himself again. David found a Cauldshaw man just setting off up the water, and sent by him a message to ease the mind of Mrs. Fordyce and tell her that her husband would return on the morrow. When he left him he was sleeping.

This business occupied his time till late afternoon, and gloaming had already set in before he rode out of Kirk Aller. The Presbytery business was long since concluded, and the kirk on the brae was vacant and locked. The members had departed, for the yard of the Cross Keys, which in the morning had been like a horse fair, was now empty. The wind, which had been growing in violence all day, had now reached the force of a gale, and as David turned the corner above the gorge where the Aller breaks from the hills into the haugh, it met him full in the face. He pulled his hat low on his head and looked back. The little town, very bleak and grey in the chill April evening, lay smoking with its hundred chimneys. The sight affected him with a painful regret. It seemed a last look upon the life from which he was now an outcast, a life which eighteen months ago he had so warmly embraced.

He was coming out of his abstraction now, and looking at cold realities. Mr. Fordyce's outburst in the Presbytery had shattered his secret world. Katrine was in bliss, and he was left alone on the bare roads of earth. Very solitary he felt; his father was dead, Mark Riddel was a fugitive, Reiverslaw had failed him, his Church had cast him out; there was no place for him, it seemed, in all the habitable globe, no work to his hand, no friend to lean on. He was looking at life now in a light as bleak as that April day which was now vanishing from the hills. . . . He seemed to have lost the power of feeling. He had no grudge against his enemies, no hatred even for Chasehope; his humility had become so deep that it was almost the abnegation of manhood. He was very tired and had lost the will to contend. "Katrine, Katrine!" his heart cried, "I'm not wanted on earth, and there's no comfort here for the comfortless. O my love, that I were with you!"

The night grew colder as it advanced, and the wind, which commonly he welcomed, now cut him to the bone. He drew his cloak round him, and tried to urge his horse to a better pace. But apathy seemed to have fallen on beast as well as on master, and it jogged funereally, as if in no hurry to leave the chilly out-of-doors for the manse stable. There was a moon behind the flying rack of the sky, and there was light enough to see the dark huddle of the hills. Only where the track dipped to the trees by the river-side was there any depth of shadow.

It was in one such patch of blackness that David heard the sound of a horse behind him. Presently the rider was abreast of him, and even in the dark it seemed that he recognized him. "Guid e'en to ye, Mr. Sempill," said a voice, but a gust of wind made it hard to recognize it. The new-comer fell into step beside him, and when in a minute they came out of the trees, David saw that it was Chasehope.

"You are late on the road, friend," he said.

"I had weighty business on hand," was the answer. The man was in a good humour, for he was humming a tune.

"This has been a waesome day for you, Mr. Sempill," he went on. "Ye have set yoursel' up against God's law and man's law, and ye have taken a mighty fall. I bear no malice--though weel I might if the Lord hadna gi'en me grace to forgive. What I have done in your case I have done painfully as my solemn duty. But there's pardon even for the chief of sinners, and it's not to be believed that one like yoursel', that had once a title in Christ, can be cast away. Seek mercy where it is to be found, Mr. Sempill."

Chasehope spoke fast like one under the influence of drink, but the man was temperate, so it must have been some excitement of the spirit. In the dim light David could not see his face, but he knew the kind of light that was in his eye, for he had witnessed it before.

"I speak in all loving-kindness," he went on. "If ye're of the Elect, you and me will meet before the Throne. I would hold out a hand to a stumbling brother."

David made no answer, but his silence did not check Chasehope's flow, for he seemed to be burdened with that which must have vent.

"What have ye made of it wi' your railing accusations? Bethink ye of that, Mr. Sempill. What has become o' your uncovenanted Reiverslaw, and your Glee'd Mark wi' his warlockry, and the bonny may ye trysted wi'? Ane is vanished like a landlouper, and ane will soon ken the wuddy [hangman's rope], and ane is under the mools."

David spoke at last, and had the other had ears to hear he might have detected a strange note in the minister's voice.

"You speak the truth. I am indeed friendless and forlorn."

"Friendless and forlorn! 'Deed that's the word. And wherefore, Mr. Sempill? Because ye have flung yoursel' against the rock o' the Elect who are secure in the Lord's hands. What said the worthy Moderator after ye had gone? He likened the Kirk to the stone spoken of in Matthew twenty-one and forty-four--'Whosoever shall fall on this stone shall be broken: but on whomsoever it shall fall, it will grind him to powder.'"

"There was another word spoken--that some for this day's work would burn in Hell."

Chasehope laughed his rare and ugly laugh. "Hoots, man, that was just puir Mr. Fordyce, and a'body kens him. No but what he has the root o' the matter in him--but he's a dwaibly body wi' nae mair fushion than a thresh [rush]."

"Nevertheless he spoke truly. Hell is waiting for some, and maybe this very night."

Again Chasehope laughed. "Is Saul also among the prophets?" he asked. "Who are you, a minister outed and excommunicat, that you suld take to the prophesyin'?"

"God makes use of the feeblest pipes to proclaim His will. I tell you, Ephraim Caird, that this very night judgment may overtake you."

This time Chasehope did not laugh, but moved his horse a little apart.

"Do ye daur to threaten me--?"

"I threaten no man, but God threatens you."

"Awa' wi' you! I have a firm assurance. And if ye daur lift hand on me--"

"Be comforted. My hand will not be lifted."

The man seemed to recover his composure, for he edged his horse nearer and thrust forward his face.

"Ye've aye hated me. I could see it in your een the first day at the manse."

"I have never hated you. There is no man living in whose company I would rather ride this night. I love you so dearly that I would save your soul."

"You to speak of savin' souls!" Chasehope began, and then stopped. For there was something in David which struck a chill even to his excited mind. The quiet masterful voice cut into his wild gabble like iron into peat. If there was madness in the man, there was a fiercer madness in the minister, for in the last minutes David's weakness had fallen from him like rags, and he had quickened to a flaming zeal. It was a flame of such heat that it burned calmly, but the glow of it, radiating from him, made the other's mere wildfire.

David spoke no further word, but a nervous restlessness came upon Chasehope. He blustered and bragged. See to what a pitch of esteem he had come from following the narrow way! And he whined. He had the frailty of all mortals, but it was atoned for by the imputed righteousness of his Redeemer. He seemed to long for a word of confirmation, and he pawed at the minister's sleeve. But no answer came, and the silence of the other began to unnerve him. His voice had a startled note, he quoted texts as if they were supplications to the stony impassiveness of his companion. When his horse stumbled and he almost collided with the minister, he cried out suddenly, as if in fear.

They had crossed Aller half a mile below Roodfoot, and had come to the turning of the ways. The clouds had thinned and the struggling moon showed Melanudrigill before them, rising and falling like an ocean of darkness. David kept his horse's head straight for it, and Chasehope, who had been riding on his left, edged his beast across the path.

"Ye'll be for the short road. I'll gang quicker by the back o' Windyways. . . . Losh, that's an awesome wind."

"It is the wind of the Lord's anger."

"Guid e'en to ye, and God send ye a contrite heart!" Chasehope seemed to have recovered courage at the prospect of parting company.

David laid a hand on his bridle.

"Nay, you and I do not twine here. Our road lies yonder."

"Are ye daft, man?" Chasehope cried, his voice strong again. "Who are you to order a man like me?" The voice was strong, but in its shrillness was disquiet.

"I do not order you. Look in your heart and you will find the compulsion. It was not for nothing, Ephrairn Caird, that we forgathered this night. The Lord ordained it, and in your marrow you know that you cannot leave me. This night we are in a closer bond than man and wife."

"Havers!" It was the last spasm of bluster, and the voice was weaker than the word. "I'll do no man's bidding. Tak' your hand from my bridle."

The hand was raised, and the other cowered to his saddle-bow, as if to avert a stroke. But the hand did not fall. Instead it gripped his arm, and the grip seemed to crush his bones.

"You fool," said the grave voice. "This night I have the strength of ten men, for the Lord is in me. I could strike you dead if I were minded, but the command is on me that we ride together."

Chasehope's arrogance had drained out of him, but it had left some dregs of courage. He struggled to compose his voice and recover his everyday demeanour.

"Weel, since ye're so pressin' I'll do your will. There's no half a mile differ in the roads." But the words did nothing to break the spell which choked him. They were like the wry-mouthed bravado of a criminal at the gallows' foot.

No word was spoken as they crossed the haugh and skirted the Fennan Moss, but had there been any one to see he would have noted that David rode erect like a trooper, while Chasehope hung like a sack in his saddle, and that David's knee was hard pressed against the other's, as if the two were shackled.

They came to the edge of the Wood, where the road bent to the right among the pine roots towards the glen of Woodilee burn.

"We dismount here," said David, "for we cannot ride among the trees. The beasts will find their way home."

Chasehope cried out, and his voice now was strangled with terror.

"The Wud! No the Wud! Ye daurna gang there. . . ." He raised his arm and would have struck, but David caught his wrist. He overbalanced himself and rolled to the ground, and in a second David was beside him. The horses, alarmed by the scuffle, dashed up the track.

Fear made the man violent. He flung himself on David, but for all his weight found himself tossed down like a feather. Was this stern figure with the sinews of iron the minister whom he had despised?

The quiet voice spoke.

"You are gross and elderly and I have the exercised strength of youth. At no time could you hope to strive with me. But this night the might of the Lord is in me, and I could break you like a straw. . . . You will come with me, though I have to ding you senseless and carry you."

The man scrambled to his feet and made the place echo with his cries for help. No answer came, except the flap of disturbed night birds.

"Where would ye have me gang?" he whimpered.

"Into the Wood--to the place you know of. Ephraim Caird, this night I give you the chance of salvation. I may have erred--my eyes may have deceived me--it may not have been you that capered and piped in a dog's mask to yon lost crew. If I have been wrong, it will be proven yonder. If I have been right, you will be given a chance of repentance. We go up to the Mount together that you may choose between Abiron and Jehovah."

Chasehope crouched like a dog. "I daurna--I daurna," he wailed. "I'm a believin' man, but I daurna enter the Wud. . . . It's no the season--there's fearsome things ryngin' in't. Oh, ye dinna ken. . . . Let me gang hame, and the morn I'll gang on my hunkers to Kirk Aller and sweir that a' I hae said against ye was a lee. I'll confess . . ."

David's grip was on his arm, but he did not struggle. His legs were loosened, and his whole body drooped like a creature stricken with the palsy.

"I'll make confession--I'll tell ye things that are no to be named-- I took the Wud wi' ithers, but I kenned I was a redeemed soul and that the Lord wouldna cast me away. . . . I aye ettled to repent, for I was sure o' the Mercy Seat. . . . It is written that Solomon went after the abominations of Moab, and was yet numbered among the Elect. . . . But I'll hae nae mair o't frae this day. . . . I'll tak' my aith on the Word. . . . I'll cast my idols ahint my back . . . I'll burn the books . . . I'll forswear the Deil . . ."

"You will do it yonder," said David.

He had never entered the Wood from this side, and in the darkness the road would have been at all times hard to find, but now he seemed to have a map in his brain and to steer by an instinct. In this backward spring there was no sprouting undergrowth, but the dead bracken stalks had not yet shrunk to earth, and he waded waist-deep among them. The man beside him had lost the power of resistance. He followed like an obedient hound, without the need of David's grasp on his arm. Often he stumbled, and once he fell into the dell of a burn and had to be lifted out, but he made no attempt at resistance or escape. He walked and sometimes ran, crouching almost double, and as he went he made little moaning noises which might have been prayers.

The wind was wild in the tree-tops, and rushing down the aisles and corries of the hillside made a sound which was now like a great organ and now like muffled drums. Higher they mounted till they reached a broad shelf of more level ground, where the covert was thick and the speed slow. . . . And then, almost before he was aware of it, David found himself looking at an open space with a dark stone in the midst of it.

The moonlight was faint, but the glade was clear in its outlines, a patch of grey turf in a ring of inky shadow. The altar was no longer white as in the summer midnight, but dark with the drenching winter rains. A bleak, sodden place it now appeared to David, a trivial place, no more than a common howe in a wood.

But the other seemed to look on it with different eyes. When he saw the stone he gave one shrill cry of terror and collapsed on the ground, burying his face in the moss as if to shut out the sight. David seized him and dragged him forward till he lay by the altar, and all the while his screams rose piercingly above the wind.

"There is no need for confession," the minister said. "You have betrayed yourself. . . . Now I know with the uttermost certainty that it was you I saw here at Beltane and at Lammas."

The man did not raise his head, but clasped David's legs and nozzled him like a fawning dog, while, like a dog, he gave short, terrified yelps.

"Your sin is proven and acknowledged," said David. "Here on the scene of your guilt you will choose your road. I say to you, as Elijah said to the people of Israel, 'If the Lord be God, follow Him; but if Baal, then follow him.' This night you renounce Abiron or renounce Christ."

The man was silent, as if the extremity of fear had frozen his speech. But as David raised him, a shuddering like an epilepsy shook his body. His legs were limp, and David placed him on his knees so that his brow rested on the stone.

"Renounce your master here in his temple . . . I will give you words if you have none of your own. . . . Say after me, 'I abhor and reject the Devil and all his works, and I fling myself upon the mercy of God.' Man, man, it is your immortal soul that trembles above the Pit."

The huddled figure was still silent. Then, after a violent shiver, his voice came back to him. He began to stutter words, words meaningless to David's ear. It may be that it was the renunciation of his gods; but, whatever it was, it was not completed.

For suddenly energy returned to his limbs, and he sprang violently to his feet. Madness glowed in his eyes; his head was held for a second in a listening posture.

"They come," he screamed. "The dogs!--the red dogs!"

David seized him, but at that moment the maniac's strength far exceeded his own. He tore himself free with a rending of his clothes. His face was a limp vacancy of terror in which the eyes glared unseeingly. He leaped into the air, spun round, fell, laid his ear to the earth, and then, with incredible swiftness, ran uphill from the glade. Once he halted to listen, and then, so bent that he appeared to run on all-fours, and yelping like a stricken beast, he vanished into the shades. . . . In a pause of the wind David heard his movements grow fainter, and he thought he heard, too, a murmur of voices as at Beltane and Lammas. It seemed to him that these voices were now like the distant baying of hounds.

Lethargy returned upon David's soul. He had done his duty, and at the last moment, like Samson, had brought down the false temple; but what signified it to one who had no further hope or purpose? He walked out of the Wood as steeled to its awesomeness as to the other common emotions of man. His heart had dried up within him, and his vitality had run down like an unwound clock. He had but the one thought--to visit Paradise again and Katrine's grave, and this not for comfort but as a step enjoined by duty to complete the heavy weight of his loneliness. After that nothing mattered. His youth was gone, and he was become very old.

He crossed the barrier glen, brushed through the catkin-laden hazels, and came to his sacred glade. There was the well bubbling darkly, and there beyond it was the fresh-made mound of turf. . . . The sight melted something within him. He flung himself on the grass and his dry heart was loosened in tears. As he wept he prayed, and as he prayed he seemed to live once again the bright days when Katrine had sung to him among the flowers. Fragments of her songs came back to him:

"There's comfort for the comfortless And honey for the bee--"

Was there any comfort for a stricken man on this side of eternity? He had a vision of her face with its proud laughing courage, he heard again her voice coming faint and sweet from behind the hills of death. She was smiling, she was saying something too rare for mortal ears to catch, but it seemed to thaw within him the springs of life.

He lay long on the turf, and when at last he raised his head the dawn was breaking. The wind had fallen, and into the air had come the softness of spring. A thrush sang in the covert--he thought he caught the scent of flowers. . . . Of a sudden the world righted itself and youth came back to him. He saw brightness again on the roads of life and a great brightness at the end of them, where Katrine was his for ever among the eternal fields.

Rab Prentice, limping out in the early morning to see to the lambing ewes in his hirsel, had occasion to take a short cut through the hazel shaws. He was surprised to see a man walking with great strides from the coppice, and more surprised to recognize him as the minister. What did Mr. Sempill there at that hour? He watched the figure till it disappeared over the ridge, and then went home much puzzled to his cog of brose.

In after days Rab Prentice searched his memory for every detail of that sight, and often he recounted it to breathless listeners. For his were the last eyes in Woodilee to see the minister on earth.

CHAPTER XXI

THE GOING OF THE MINISTER

Woodilee was early astir, for it was to be a day of portents in the parish. Word had come the night before of the judgment of the Presbytery--that their minister was deposed and excommunicated, and that Mr. Muirhead of Kirk Aller and Mr. Proudfoot of Bold had been deputed to preach the kirk vacant that very day. There was little work on the farms, for the lambing had scarcely begun, the ploughing was finished, and the ground was not yet dry enough for the seedbed; so the whole parish waited at the kirkyard gate.

Resentment was still deep against the minister as the cause--under Heaven--of the pestilence, and for his high-handed dealings during that time of trial. There were also the old grievances against him, so that those faithful to him were very few. Isobel was at Calidon, Reiverslaw had gone no man knew where, and only Amos Ritchie and one or two women were left to defend him. Strange news had come about the tenant of Crossbasket. There had been soldiers seeking him with a warrant for his apprehension; it seemed that the decent, quiet-spoken farmer-body was Mark Kerr, a kinsman of the Lord Roxburghe, whose name had appeared in many proclamations of the Kirk and the Estates, and who since Philiphaugh had been zealously sought for through the length of Scotland. Men remembered his masterful ways and declared that they had always known that he was gentrice; they remembered his handling of the pricker and were confident that they had detected his ungodliness. But that he should have lived among them gave them a feeling of distinction and adventure, and the younger people cast curious eyes towards the empty house of Crossbasket.

It was the first day that spring seemed to have come into the air, and the congregation, waiting in the kirkyard for the arrival of the ministers, were warmed by a mild and pleasant sun. The elders stood by the gate, each in his best attire, wearing--even the miller--an air of ceremonial gravity.

"This is a great day for Woodilee," said Nether Fennan, "and a great day for Christ's Kirk in Scotland. We cleanse the tabernacle of an unworthy vessel, and woe is me that some o' the bauldest and stenchest Christians have no lived to see it. Peter Pennecuik--honest Peter had nae broo o' Sempill--clouts o' cauld morality, was his word--Peter has gane ower soon to his reward."

"What's come o' Chasehope?" Mirehope asked. "He suld have been here langsyne. He'll surely no be late on this heart-searching day."

"I heard from the Chasehope herd," said the miller, "that Ephraim never cam' hame last night. The wife was sair concerned, but she jaloused it would be Presbytery business."

"But that was a' by and done wi' by three in the afternoon. He would be seein' Edom Trumbull about the new aits. Still and on, it's no like Chasehope to let warldly matters interfere wi' his Christian duty. . . . Eh, sirs, what a testimony Woodilee will bear the day! Mr. Mungo is to proclaim the outing, and Mr. Ebenezer is to preach the sermon, and on sic an occasion Bold is like a hungry gled and the voice o' him like a Januar' blast."

Among the women sitting on the flat gravestones there was less talk of the Kirk and more of the minister. Most were bitter against him.

"They may out him and excommunicate him," cried Jean of the Chasehope-foot, "but wha will restore me the braw bairn that dee'd in the pest whilk was sent to punish him? Answer me that, kimmers. I wad be the better pleased if I got my ten fingers at his thrapple."

"Weel for you, wumman," said another, "that Isobel Veitch is no here, or it's your ain thrapple would suffer."

"There's a queer tale come up the water wi' Johnnie Dow," said a third. "There was talk, ye mind, o' a lassie that he met wi' in the Wud, and we a' ken that there was a lassie wi' him in the hinder days o' the pest--the fairest face, some folk say, that they ever looked on."

"Tuts, gossip, yon was nae lassie. Yon face was never flesh and bluid. It was a bogle oot o' the Wud, and some says--" The speaker lowered her voice and spoke into her neighbour's ear.

"Bogle or no, Aggie Vicar, it cured my wee Benjie, and nae word will be spoke oot o' my mouth against it. The callant is still greeting for anither sicht o' the bonny leddy."

"Haud your tongues and let me speak. Johnnie Dow says the Presbytery had it a' riddled out, and it seems it was nae fairy but a leevin' lassie. And wha think ye she was? Nae less than the young mistress o' Calidon."

The women exclaimed, most of them incredulous.

"But that's no a'. It seems that she and the minister had made it up thegither and she was promised till him. Mr. Fordyce o' Cauldshaw telled that to the Presbytery."

"Heard ye ever the like? Will Sempill be hingin' up his bonnet at Calidon and turnin' frae minister to laird? The lassie will no doubt heir the place, and it's weel kenned that Sempill has walth o' gear o' his ain."

"He canna weel do that if he's excommunicat. He'll aiblins [perhaps] be for fleein' the country like the auld laird, and takin' the quean wi' him."

"Ye havena heard the end o' the tale," said the first speaker. "Dinna yatter like pyets, or I winna get it telled. . . . The lassie is deid--deid three days syne o' a backcast o' the pest, and the minister is no to haud nor bind wi' grief. Johnnie said he sat yestreen at Kirk Aller wi' a face like a corp and took his paiks as mild as a wean, and him for ordinar' sic an ettercap. Johnnie thriepit that he had maybe lost his reason."

There was silence among her hearers, and only Jean of the Chasehope-foot laughed. "She's weel oot o' it," she said, "and he's weel served."

"Wheesht, wumman," said one. "The lad has sinned, but he's but young, and his punishment is maybe ower sair."

There was a movement among the crowd, for the ministers were seen approaching. They were received by the elders and conducted to the minute session-house, which was a pendicle on the east wall of the kirk. The congregation, according to custom, now entered the building, whence could presently be heard the sound of slow psalmody. Robb the beadle waited at the single door till the ministers reappeared, Mr. Muirhead in Geneva gown and bands, Mr. Proudfoot in his country homespun, for he was a despiser even of sanctioned forms. They too entered, and Robb followed, closing the door behind him, but leaving the great key in the lock.

Amos Ritchie arrived, moodily sauntering through the gate. He had been unable to face the kirkyard crowd, knowing that he would hear words spoken which might crack his brittle temper. He reached the door and was about to enter, when the sound of furious hoofs on the road made him pause. The rider hitched his bridle to the gate-post and strode up the path, and Amos saw that it was Reiverslaw.

"Am I ower late?" the new-comer panted. "What's asteer in the kirk?"

"Ye're ower late," said Amos bitterly. "Yestreen the minister was condemned and excommunicat by the Presbytery at Kirk Aller, and Chasehope was affirmed a saunt for want o' you to testify against him. This day Muirhead and Proudfoot are preachin' the kirk empty."

"God be merciful to me," Reiverslaw groaned. "I only got the word last nicht, and I've left weary beasts on the road atween here and Langholm. . . . Where is the minister? Where is Mr. Sempill?"

"The Lord kens. He's no in the manse, for I was there at skreigh o' day, and he hasna been seen since he left Kirk Aller. . . . What does it matter? The puir lad has his name blastit, and Woodilee loses the best man that ever walked its roads. . . . Are ye for in?"

"I'm for in," said Reiverslaw grimly. "If I canna help the minister I can mishandle some that hae brocht him doun. I'm thinkin' Chasehope will hae sair bones or nicht."

The two slipped through the door and stood in the dusk at the extreme back of the crowded kirk. The first exercises having been concluded, Mr. Muirhead was reading from the pulpit the finding of the Presbytery. The misdeeds of the minister were set forth seriatim with the crooked verbosity of a legal document. Then came the pith:

"Wherefore the Presbytery of Aller, in the name of the Lord Jesus Christ, the sole King and Head of the Church, and by the power committed by Him to them, did, and hereby do, summarily excommunicate David Sempill, at present residing in the parish of Woodilee, delivering him over to Satan for the destruction of the flesh that the spirit may be saved in the day of the Lord, and the Presbytery did, and hereby do, enjoin all the faithful to shun all dealings with him, as they would not be found to harden him in his sins, and so to partake with him in his judgments."

The Moderator read the words with a full voice and with relish. He outlined briefly the civil consequences attaching to excommunication, and dwelt terrifyingly on the religious state of one cut off from communion with Christ and His Kirk. Then he proceeded to depose the minister in absentia from the charge and to declare it vacant till such time as a successor was appointed. The appointment would be in the free gift of the people, subject to confirmation by the Presbytery, since Nicholas Hawkshaw, the chief, indeed the sole, heritor, was an outlaw and a fugitive. He concluded with prayer, a copious outpouring in which the godly in Woodilee were lauded for their zeal, condoled with in their sufferings, and recommended for a special mark of the Lord's favour. Then he drew the skirts of his gown delicately around him, and gave place to the minister of Bold.

Mr. Proudfoot chose for his text second Kings the tenth chapter, the twenty-fourth verse, the second clause of the verse: "If any of the men whom I have brought into your hands escape, he that letteth him go, his life shall be for the life of him." It was a theme that suited his genius, and never had he spoken with more freedom and power. Scripture was heaped upon Scripture to show the guilt of half-heartedness in God's cause ("Curse ye Meroz, said the angel of the Lord"); the other charges against David he neglected, and concentrated on the awful guilt of unfaithfulness to the Kirk in her hour of trial. The bulk of the world lay prone under the foot of Satan, but in Scotland the Lord had set His poor people erect and committed His cause to their charge, and woe be to them if they faltered in that trust. At this point Mr. Proudfoot almost attained sublimity. There was a crusading zeal in his voice; his picture of the stand of the faithful remnant against the world was the vision of a stout heart.

He passed to David and his backslidings. He drew the minister as a weakling, beginning no doubt with an honest purpose, but soon seduced from the narrow path by the lusts of the eye and the pride of life. "Oh, is it not pitiful," he cried, "in this short and perishing world, with the Pit yawning by the roadside and the fires of Hell banked beneath us--is it not pitiful and lamentable that the soul of man should have other thoughts than its hard-won salvation? What signify profane learning and the delights of the eye and the comforts of the body, and even good intents toward your fellows, if at the hinder end the Judge of all will ask but the one question--Have you your title in Christ?"

In especial, he dealt scornfully with the plea of charity. There could be no charity towards sin. The accursed thing must be destroyed wherever found, and were it the wife of a man's bosom or the son of the same mother the sinner must be struck down.

The congregation listened as if under a spell. So intent were they that neither the people on their stools nor the Moderator in his chair nor the preacher in the pulpit noticed that in the dim back- end of the kirk the door had opened and some one had entered.

But it was in the close of his discourse that the gale came upon Mr. Proudfoot's spirit. Now he was at his application. The history of Israel was searched to show how Jehovah the merciful was yet merciless towards error. Agag was hewn in pieces--the priests and worshippers of Baal were slain to a man--the groves were cut down and ploughed up and sown with salt. . . . So rapt were preacher and people that they did not observe that a new-comer was among them moving quietly up the kirk. . . . The minister of Bold concluded in a whirl of eloquence with his favourite instance of Barak the son of Abinoam--how with ten thousand men of Naphtali and Zebulun he went down from the mount Tabor and fell upon Sisera, the captain of the hosts of Canaan, so that not a man was left. He likened himself in all humility to Deborah the prophetess; he called upon the people of the Lord, even as she had called upon Barak, to rise and destroy the Canaanites without questioning and without respite. "Let us smite the chariots and the host with the edge of the sword, for in this day hath the Lord delivered Sisera into our hand, and let us pursue after the remnant even to Harosheth of the Gentiles!"

"Harosheth of your grannie!"

The minister's voice had stopped, and, in the profound hush that followed, the four words fell with a startling clearness. The blasphemy of them was not decreased by the tone, which was of measureless contempt. The scared eyes of the people saw Mark Riddel, for whom soldiers were now beating the countryside, standing easy and arrogant before the pulpit, and those near him drew away their stools in panic. He had not the look of a hunted man, and though his presence had always won him respect in Woodilee he seemed now to have expanded into some one most formidable and unfamiliar. He wore the same clothes as he had worn in field and market, but he held himself very differently from the friendly crony who had sat in Lucky Weir's. At his side, too, swung a long sword.

Mr. Proudfoot looked boldly down on him.

"Who are you that dares to cast scorn upon the Word?" he asked in a firm voice.

"Not on the Word," was the answer, "but on the auld wives that pervert it. "He nodded over his shoulder. "They ken me fine in the parish. I was baptized after the Apostle, and for my surname ye can choose Kerr or Riddel as it pleases you."

The Moderator sat with a flaming face. "It is Mark Kerr the malignant. I summon all law-abiding and Christian men to lay hands on him and convey him to a place of bondage."

But no one stirred. The dark face with the laugh at the lips, the fierce contemptuous eyes, the figure compact and light with a strength which the toil-bent shoulders of Woodilee could never equal, the repute for magical skill--these were things terrible enough without the long sword.

Mr. Muirhead rose. "Then I and my brother will get us forth of this place. Come, Mr. Ebenezer," and he gathered the skirts of his gown.

"Nay, friends," said Mark, "ye'll bide where ye are. And the folk will keep their seats, till I give them leave to skail [disperse]." He swung the key of the kirk door in his hand as he spoke. "Sit ye doun, Mr. Muirhead. Sit ye doun, worthy Mr. Proudfoot. You billies have the chance ilka Sabbath o' sayin' your say and no man can controvert you. This day for a change ye will have to hearken."

In justice to the two ministers let it be said that it was not the sword that kept them in their places. Neither lacked courage. But this man who stood confronting them, the very sight of whom seemed to paralyse the folk of Woodilee, this shameless malignant had a compelling something in his air. He spoke as one having authority; though he used the broad country speech, he had that in his voice which, whether it spring from camp or court or college, means command. Very sensitive to this note in their disciplined Kirk, the two ministers listened.

What fell from Mark's lips was discussed secretly for many a day in the countryside. Publicly it was rarely mentioned, for a more awful blasphemy, it seemed, was never spoken in the house of God. He told two pillars of the Kirk and a congregation of the devout that they had all failed utterly to interpret God's Word; that they were Pharisees faithful to an ill-understood letter and heedless of the spirit; that they were fools bemused with Jewish rites which they did not comprehend and Jewish names which they could not properly pronounce. "It's nothing but a bairn's ploy," he cried, "but it's a cruel ploy, for it has spilt muckle good blood in Scotland. If ye take the blood-thirstiness, and the hewing in pieces, and thrawnness of the auld Jews, and ettle to shape yourselves on their pattern, what for do ye no gang further? Wherefore d'ye no set up an altar and burn a wedder on't? What kind o' kirk is this, when ye suld have a temple with gopher and shittim wood and shew-bread and an ark o' the covenant and branched candlesticks, and busk your minister in an ephod instead of a black gown? Ye canna pick and choose in the Word. If one thing is to be zealously copied, wherefore not all? . . . Ye fatted calves! . . . Ye muckle weans, that play at being ancient Israelites!"

This was too much for Mr. Proudfoot.

"Silence, blasphemer," he cried. "In the name of Him that snappeth the spear asunder I will outface you." He stumbled down the pulpit stairs, and would no doubt have flung himself on Mark had not old Nance Kello who sat at the foot impeded him and given Mirehope time to catch his coat-skirts. He stopped, breathing heavily, about three yards from Mark, and, as he stood, it was not the sword that a second time deterred him. He felt dimly that this outlaw had come to wear a fearful authority. It was not the tacksman of Crossbasket that spoke, but the captain of Mackay's--not the farmer of Jed Water, but the kinsman of Roxburghe and the brigadier of Montrose.

Mr. Proudfoot turned to his colleague and saw that the Moderator's eye was puzzled and uncertain. He bethought him of his chief ally in the parish. "Where is Chasehope?" he cried. "Where is Ephraim Caird?"

The answer came from an unlooked-for quarter. Daft Gibbie sat crouched in a corner of the kirk, and those near him had marked his unwonted silence. He did not gabble as usual, but sat with his great head in his hands, murmuring softly and rolling his wild eyes. But at the mention of Chasehope he suddenly found voice.

"He's up in the hills," he cried. "I seen him at skreigh o' day at the buchts o' the Drygrain, and he was rivin' a yowe and cryin' that it was a hound o' hell and that it suldna devour him. He was a' lappered wi' bluid, and when he seen me he ran on me, and his een were red and he slavered like a mad tyke, and his face was thrawed oot o' the shape o' man. Eh, sirs, puir Gibbie was near his end, for I couldna stir a foot, but afore he wan to me there cam' anither sound, and as sure as death it was like a hound's yawp. At that he gangs off like the wund, and the next I seen o' him he was skelpin' through the flowe moss, cryin' like ane in torment, and I stottered hame to get Amos Ritchie to tak' his flintlock and stop yon awfu' skellochs. I'll never sleep till I ken that the lost soul o' him is free o' the body."

"Another has told my tale." Mark spoke in a voice out of which all scorn had gone, a voice penetratingly quiet and solemn. "I, too, have seen him that once was

Ephraim Caird, and I shudder at the swiftness of the judgment. There is no man or woman in Woodilee that does not ken that he was the leader of the coven that practised the devil's arts in the Wood, but he had a name for godliness, and he had the measure of the blind fools that call themselves ministers of God.--Sit still, sir! I would be loth to draw on an unarmed man, but my sword ere this has punished vermin. . . . He has sworn falsely against the innocent, and yestreen at Kirk Aller he prevailed. But in the night the Lord sent forth His vengeance--ask me not how, for I do not know--and this day he is running demented on the hills, pursued by the dogs of his own terrors. Go and look for him. You will find him in a bog-hole or a pool in the burn. Bury his body decently, but bury it face downward, so that you speed him on his road."

There was such a silence that the rasp of a stool on the earthen floor struck the hearers like a thunderclap. One voice--it was Amos Ritchie's--came out of the back of the kirk.

"Where is the minister?" it asked.

"He is gone where you will never see him more," said Mark. "A prophet came among you and you knew him not. For the sake of that witless thing that is now going four-foot among the braes you have condemned the innocent blood. He spent his strength for you and you rejected him, he yearned for you and you repelled him, he would have laid down his life for you and you scorned him. He is now beyond the reach of your ingratitude."

"Unless he be dead," said Mr. Proudfoot, "he is not beyond the reach of the law, and if he be dead he has fallen into the hands of a living and offended God."

"Man, man," said Mark gently, "you and your like have most lamentably confounded God and Devil."

"And you yourself," cried the Moderator, struggling valiantly to assert himself against an atmosphere which he felt inimical, "are within a span of the gallows."

"We are all and at all times within a span of death. . . . To you, reverend sirs, I have no more to say. You will gang your own ways, and some day others will play the tyrant over you and give you your ain kail through the reek. In that day of humiliation you will repent of what you did in your pride. . . . To those who have been partakers of the iniquity of the Wood I wish no less than the fate that has overtaken their master. . . . To the poor folk of Woodilee I leave their minister's blessing, and may they have whiles a kindly thought of one that loved them."

He turned at the door. "You will bide here till you are released. The ministers can while away the time excommunicatin' me. Guid day to you a'."

Amos Ritchie and Reiverslaw slipped out after him, and the key was turned in the lock. Amos wept bitterly, and Reiverslaw's dark face was working with suppressed tears.

"You have to live on in this parish," Mark said. "I need not involve you in my own peril. Let the bodies out in half an hour. No one saw you enter, so you will get no discredit by this day's work. Say you found the key by the roadside."

Amos turned on him with a distraught eye.

"Where is Mr. David? What have ye done with him? . . . We ken nocht o' you--ye come and gang like bog-fire--there's some says ye're the Deil himsel'. If ye've wiled a saunt doun the road to Hell--"

"Be comforted," said Mark, laying a hand on Amos's arm. "I think I have helped to open for him the gates of Paradise."

EPILOGUE

The Reverend John Dennistoun, in his once-famous work, Satan's Artifices against the Elect (written in the year 1719, but not published till 1821, when the manuscript came into the hands of Sir Walter Scott), has a chapter on the disturbances in Woodilee. In his pages can be found the tradition which established itself during the next fifty years. He has heard of the doings in Melanudrigill, but he lays no blame for them on the parish. The power of the Kirk has been sufficient to sanctify Chasehope; in Mr. Dennistoun's pages he appears as an elder of noted piety, who was the chief mark for the enmity of the Adversary, and who was, as that Adversary's last resort, driven crazy by hellish assaults on his person till his life ended in a fall from the rocks in the Garple Linn. There is no mention of Reiverslaw, and Amos Ritchie is treated with respect, for Amos carried his grandfather's matchlock to Rullion Green, played a notable part in the Killing Time, was an ally of the Black Macmichael, and has a paragraph to himself in Naphtali. Mr. Dennistoun represents the trouble as a deliberate campaign of the Devil against a parish famed for its godliness, and David as an unwitting instrument. The minister of Woodilee he portrays as a young man of good heart but of small experience, unstable, puffed up in his own conceit. He records that there was a faction in the place that took his side, and that his misfortunes, justly deserved as they were, were not unlamented. He mentions as a foolish fable the belief of some that he had been carried off by the Fairies; he notes, too, without approval, the counter-legend that he had been removed bodily by the Devil.

On one matter Mr. Dennistoun has no doubts. Mark Kerr is the villain of his pages: the lieutenant of Satan, or, as many believed, Satan himself; one at any rate who was sold irrevocably to evil. Of the real Mark Kerr's antecedents he is aware, but he is inclined to the belief that the figure that appeared in Woodilee was not Montrose's captain but another in his semblance. He makes a sinister tale of Mark's doings--his uncanny power over the minds of the people, his necromancy in the case of the witch-pricker, his devilries during the pest (these are explained as mere purposeless cruelties), his crowning blasphemy in the kirk, when he outfaced two godly ministers and spoke words of which the very memory made honest folk tremble. He is inclined to attribute to him also the warlockries of the Wood. When he disappeared on that April day he returned to the place whence he had come.

On this point Mr. Dennistoun reflected faithfully the tradition in Woodilee. Old folks for generations, with sighs and a shaking of the head, would tell of the departure of him who had so sorely troubled the Elect. The tale no doubt grew in the telling, and the children would creep close to their mother's knee, and the goodman would stir the peats into a glow, when grandfather with awe in his voice recounted the stages in that journey of the lost. . . . Sandy Nicoll saw him in the gloaming moving with leaps which were beyond a mortal's power across Charlie's Moss. Later, at the little lonely ale-house of Kilwauk, he was observed by a drover to cross the peat-road, and the drover--his name was Grieve--swore to his dying day that beside the traveller moved a coal-black shadow. There was a moon that night, and Robbie Hogg, herd in Glenwhappen, saw the fearful twosome--man and shadow, man and devil--flitting across the braes of Caerdrochit. At one in the morning a packman, late on the road, saw the figure on the Edinburgh highway, and, though he had been drinking and was therefore a doubtful witness, remembered that he could not be clear whether it was one man or two, and had been sobered by the portent. . . .

At this point, when all that remained was an awful imagining, it was the custom of a household where the tale was told to sing with dry throats the twenty-third Psalm.

Three hours after the fuddled packman was left rubbing his eyes, two men entered the back room of a little hostelry in Leith within a stone's throw of the harbour. The dust of moorburn and the April roads was on them, and one of the two was limping and very weary.

The only occupant of the room was a man in a great seaman's coat who was eating a hasty meal. He rose to his feet with an exclamation.

"Mark!" he cried. "In the name of God, man . . ."

"When does the sloop sail?"

"In the next hour with the tide."

"The Lord be thanked! . . . You'll have this gentleman and me as fellow-passengers, Patie . . ."

"Wheesht, man. They ken me in this place as Jens Gunnersen, a skipper out of Denmark. . . . I'm for Bergen."

"Bergen be it. All roads are the same for us that lead forth of this waesome land. A bite and sup would be welcome, Patie, and two ship's cloaks to cover our landward clothes. . . . I'm for the wars again, old friend, and I've gotten a braw recruit, but the tale can bide till we're on shipboard."

But three hours later the telling had not begun. Two men with wistful eyes leaned over the stern bulwarks, and watched the hills of Lothian dwindle in the bleak April dawn.

THE END

Sir Quixote of the Moors

Being Some Account of an Episode in the Life of the Sieur de Rohaine

By

John Buchan

PREFACE

The narrative, now for the first time presented to the world, was written by the Sieur de Rohaine to while away the time during the long period and painful captivity, borne with heroic resolution, which preceded his death. He chose the English tongue, in which he was extraordinarily proficient, for two reasons: first, as an exercise in the language; second, because he desired to keep the passages here recorded from the knowledge of certain of his kinsfolk in France. Few changes have been made in his work. Now and then an English idiom has been substituted for a French; certain tortuous expressions have been emended; and in general the portions in the Scots dialect have been rewritten, since the author's knowledge of this manner of speech seems scarcely to have been so great as he himself thought.

I.—ON THE HIGH MOORS

Before me stretched a black heath, over which the mist blew in gusts, and through whose midst the road crept like an adder. Great storm-marked hills flanked me on either side, and since I set out I had seen their harsh outline against a thick sky, until I longed for flat ground to rest my sight upon. The way was damp, and the soft mountain gravel sank under my horse's feet; and ever and anon my legs were splashed by the water from some pool which the rain had left. Shrill mountain birds flew around, and sent their cries through the cold air. Sometimes the fog would lift for a moment from the face of the land and show me a hilltop or the leaden glimmer of a loch, but nothing more—no green field or homestead; only a barren and accursed desert.

Neither horse nor man was in any spirit. My back ached, and I shivered in my sodden garments, while my eyes were dim from gazing on flying clouds. The poor beast stumbled often, for he had traveled far on little fodder, and a hill-road was a new thing in his experience. Saladin I called him—for I had fancied that there was something Turkish about his black face, with the heavy turban-like band above his forehead—in my old fortunate days when I bought him. He was a fine horse of the Normandy breed, and had carried me on many a wild journey, though on none so forlorn as this.

But to speak of myself. I am Jean de Rohaine, at your service; Sieur de Rohaine in the province of

Touraine—a gentleman, I trust, though one in a sorry plight. And how I came to be in the wild highlands of the place called Galloway, in the bare kingdom of Scotland, I must haste to tell. In the old days, when I had lived as became my rank in my native land, I had met a Scot,—one Kennedy by name,—a great man in his own country, with whom I struck up an intimate friendship. He and I were as brothers, and he swore that if I came to visit him in his own home he would see to it that I should have the best. I thanked him at the time for his bidding, but thought little more of it.

Now, by ill fortune, the time came when, what with gaming and pleasuring, I was a beggared man, and I bethought me of the Scot's offer. I had liked the man well, and I considered how it would be no ill thing to abide in that country till I should find some means of bettering my affairs. So I took ship and came to the town of Ayr, from which 'twas but a day's ride to the house of my friend. 'Twas in midsummer when I landed, and the place looked not so bare as I had feared, as I rode along between green meadows to my destination. There I found Quentin Kennedy, somewhat grown old and more full in flesh than I remembered him in the past. He had been a tall, black-avised man when I first knew him; now he was grizzled,—whether from hard living or the harshness of northern weather I know not,—and heavier than a man of action is wont to be. He greeted me most hospitably, putting his house at my bidding, and swearing that I should abide and keep him company and go no more back to the South.

So for near a month I stayed there, and such a time of riot and hilarity I scarce remember. *Mon Dieu*, but the feasting and the sporting would have rejoiced the hearts of my comrades of the Rue Margot! I had already learned much of the Scots tongue at the college in Paris, where every second man hails from this land, and now I was soon perfect in it, speaking it all but as well as my host. 'Tis a gift I have, for I well remember how, when I consorted for some months in the low countries with an Italian of Milan, I picked up a fair knowledge of his speech. So now I found myself in the midst of men of spirit, and a rare life we led. The gentlemen of the place would come much about the house, and I promise you 'twas not seldom we saw the morning in as we sat at wine. There was, too, the greatest sport at coursing and hunting the deer in Kennedy's lands by the Water of Doon.

Yet there was that I liked not among the fellows who came thither, nay, even in my friend himself. We have a proverb in France that the devil when he spoils a German in the making turns him into a Scot, and for certain there was much boorishness among them, which to my mind sits ill on gentlemen. They would jest at one another till I thought that in a twinkling swords would be out, and lo! I soon found that 'twas but done for sport, and with no evil intent. They were clownish in their understanding, little recking of the feelings of a man of honor, but quick to grow fierce on some tittle of provocation which another would scarce notice. Indeed, 'tis my belief that one of this nation is best in his youth, for Kennedy, whom I well remembered as a man of courage and breeding, had grown grosser and more sottish with his years, till I was fain to ask where was my friend of the past.

And now I come to that which brought on my departure and my misfortunes. 'Twas one night as I returned weary from riding after a stag in the haugh by the river, that Quentin cried hastily, as I entered, that now he had found something worthy of my attention.

"To-morrow, Jock," says he, "you will see sport. There has been some cursed commotion among the folk of the hills, and I am out the morrow to redd the marches. You shall have a troop of horse and ride with me, and, God's death, we will have a taste of better work!"

I cried out that I could have asked for naught better, and, indeed, I was overjoyed that the hard drinking and idleness were at an end, and that the rigors of warfare lay before me. For I am a soldier by birth and by profession, and I love the jingle of steel and the rush of battle.

So, on the morrow, I rode to the mountains with a score of dragoons behind me, glad and hopeful. *Diable!* How shall I tell my disappointment? The first day I had seen all—and more than I wished. We fought, not with men like ourselves, but with women and children and unarmed yokels, and butchered like Cossacks more than Christians. I grew sick of the work, and would have none of it, but led my men to the rendezvous sullenly, and hot at heart. 'Twas well the night was late when we arrived, else I should have met with Kennedy there and then, and God knows what might have happened.

The next day, in a great fit of loathing, I followed my host again, hoping that the worst was over, and that henceforth I should have something more to my stomach. But little I knew of the men with whom I journeyed. There was a cottage there, a shepherd's house, and God! they burned it down, and the man they shot before his wife and children, speaking naught to him but foul-mouthed reproaches and jabber about some creed which was strange to me. I could not prevent it, though 'twas all that I could do to keep myself from a mad attack.

I rode up to Quentin Kennedy.

"Sir," I said, "I have had great kindness at your hands, but you and I must part. I see that we are made of different stuff. I can endure war, but not massacre."

He laughed at my scruples, incredulous of my purpose, until at last he saw that I was fixed in my determination. Then he spoke half kindly:

"This is a small matter to stand between me and thee. I am a servant of the king, and but do my duty. I little thought to have disloyalty preached from your lips;

but bide with me, and I promise that you shall see no more of it."

But my anger was too great, and I would have none of him. Then—and now I marvel at the man's forbearance—he offered me money to recompense me for my trouble. 'Twas honestly meant, and oft have I regretted my action, but to me in my fury it seemed but an added insult.

"Nay," said I angrily; "I take no payment from butchers. I am a gentleman, if a poor one."

At this he flushed wrathfully, and I thought for an instant that he would have drawn on me; but he refrained, and I rode off alone among the moors. I knew naught of the land, and I must have taken the wrong way, for noon found me hopelessly mazed among a tangle of rocks and hills and peat-mosses. Verily, Quentin Kennedy had taken the best revenge by suffering me to follow my own leading.

In the early hours of my journey my head was in such a whirl of wrath and dismay, that I had little power to think settled thoughts. I was in a desperate confusion, half angry at my own haste, and half bitter at the coldness of a friend who would permit a stranger to ride off alone with scarce a word of regret. When I have thought the matter out in after days, I have been as perplexed as ever; yet it still seems to me, though I know not how, that I acted as any man of honor and heart would approve. Still this thought was little present to me in my discomfort, as I plashed through the sodden turf.

I had breakfasted at Kennedy's house of Dunpeel in the early morning, and since I had no provision of any sort with me, 'twas not long ere the biting of hunger began to set in. My race is a hardy stock, used to much hardships and rough fare, but in this inclement land my heart failed me wholly, and I grew sick and giddy, what with the famishing and the cold rain. For, though 'twas late August, the month of harvest and fruit-time in my own fair land, it seemed more like winter. The gusts of sharp wind came driving out of the mist and pierced me to the very marrow. So chill were they that my garments were of no avail to avert them; being, indeed, of the thinnest, and cut according to the fashion of fine cloth for summer wear at the shows and gallantries of the town. A pretty change, thought I, from the gardens of Versailles and the trim streets of Paris to this surly land; and sad it was to see my cloak, meant for no rougher breeze than the gentle south, tossed and scattered by a grim wind.

I have marked it often, and here I proved its truth, that man's thoughts turn always to the opposites of his present state. Here was I, set in the most uncharitable land on earth; and yet ever before my eyes would come brief visions of the gay country which I had forsaken. In a gap of hill I fancied that I descried a level distance with sunny vineyards and rich orchards, to which I must surely come if I but hastened. When I stooped to drink at a stream, I fancied ere I drank it that the water would taste like the Bordeaux I was wont to drink at the little hostelry in the Rue Margot; and when the tasteless liquid once entered my mouth, the disenchantment was severe. I met one peasant, an old man bent with toil, coarse-featured, yet not without some gleams of kindness, and I could not refrain from addressing him in my native tongue. For though I could make some shape at his barbarous patois, in my present distress it came but uneasily from my lips. He stared at me stupidly, and when I repeated the question in the English, he made some unintelligible reply, and stumbled onward in his way. I watched his poor figure as he walked. Such, thought I, are the *canaille* of the land, and 'tis little wonder if their bodies be misshapen, and their minds dull, for an archangel would become a boor if he dwelt here for any space of time.

But enough of such dreams, and God knows no man had ever less cause for dreaming. Where was I to go, and what might my purpose be in this wilderness which men call the world? An empty belly and a wet skin do not tend to sedate thinking, so small wonder if I saw little ahead. I was making for the end of the earth, caring little in what direction, weary and sick of heart, with sharp anger at the past, and never a hope for the morrow.

Yet, even in my direst days, I have ever found some grain of expectation to console me. I had five crowns in my purse; little enough, but sufficient to win me a dinner and a bed at some cheap hostelry. So all through the gray afternoon I looked sharply for a house, mistaking every monstrous bowlder for a gable-end. I cheered my heart with thinking of dainties to be looked for; a dish of boiled fish, or a piece of mutton from one of the wild-faced sheep which bounded ever and anon across my path. Nay, I was in no mood to be fastidious. I would e'en be content with a poor fare, provided always I could succeed in swallowing it, for my desire soon became less for the attainment of a pleasure than for the alleviation of a discomfort. For I was ravenous as a hawk, and had it in my heart more than once to dismount, and seek for the sparse hill-berries.

And, indeed, this was like to have been my predicament, for the day grew late and I came no nearer a human dwelling. The valley in which I rode grew wider, about to open, as I thought, into the dale of a river. The hills, from rising steeply by the wayside, were withdrawn to the distance of maybe a mile, where they lifted their faces through the network of the mist. All the land between them, save a strip where the road lay, was filled with a black marsh, where moor birds made a most dreary wailing. It minded me of the cries of the innocents whom King Herod slew, as I had seen the dead represented outside the village church of Rohaine in my far-away homeland. My heart grew sore with longing. I had bartered my native country for the most dismal on earth, and all for nothing. Madman that I was, were it not better to be a beggar in France than a horse-captain in any other place? I cursed my folly sorely, as each fresh blast sent a shiver through my body. Nor was my horse in any better state—Saladin, whom I had seen gayly decked at a procession with ribbons and pretty favors, who had carried me so often and so far, who had always fared on the best. The poor beast was in a woeful plight, with his pasterns bleeding from the rough stones and his head bent with weariness. Verily, I pitied him more than myself, and if I had had a crust we should have shared it.

The night came in, black as a draw-well and stormy as the Day of Doom. I had now no little trouble in picking out the way from among the treacherous morasses. Of a sudden my horse would have a forefoot in a pool of black peat-water, from which I would scarce, by much pulling, recover him. A sharp jag of stone in the way would all but bring him to his knees. So we dragged wearifully along, scarce fearing, caring, hoping for anything in this world or another.

It was, I judge, an hour after nightfall, about nine of the clock, when I fancied that some glimmer shot through the thick darkness. I could have clapped my hands for joy had I been able; but alas! these were so stiff, that clapping was as far from me as from a man with the palsy.

"Courage!" said I, "courage, Saladin! There is yet hope for us!"

The poor animal seemed to share in my expectations. He carried me quicker forward, so that soon the feeble gleam had grown to a broad light. Inn or dwelling, thought I, there I stay, for I will go not a foot further for man or devil. My sword must e'en be my *fourrier* to get me a night's lodging. Then I saw the house, a low, dark place, unillumined save for that front window which shone as an invitation to travelers. In a minute I was at the threshold. There, in truth, was the sign flapping above the lintel. 'Twas an inn at length, and my heart leaped out in gratitude.

II.—I FARE BADLY INDOORS

I dropped wearily from my horse and stumbled forward to the door. 'Twas close shut, but rays of light came through the chinks at the foot, and the great light in the further window lit up the ground for some yards. I knocked loudly with my sword-hilt. Stillness seemed to reign within, save that from some distant room a faint sound of men's voices was brought. A most savory smell stole out to the raw air and revived my hunger with hopes of supper.

Again I knocked, this time rudely, and the door rattled on its hinges. This brought some signs of life from within. I could hear a foot on the stone floor of a passage, a bustling as of many folk running hither and thither, and a great barking of a sheep-dog. Of a sudden the door was flung open, a warm blaze of light rushed forth, and I stood blinking before the master of the house.

He was a tall, grizzled man of maybe fifty years, thin, with a stoop in his back that all hill-folk have, and a face brown with sun and wind. I judged him fifty, but he may have been younger by ten years, for in that desert men age the speedier. His dress was dirty and ragged in many places, and in one hand he carried a pistol, which he held before him as if for protection. He stared at me for a second.

"Wha are ye that comes dirlin' here on sic a nicht?" said he, and I give his speech as I remember it. As he uttered the words, he looked me keenly in the face, and I felt his thin, cold glance piercing to the roots of my thoughts. I liked the man ill, for, what with his lean figure and sour countenance, he was far different from the jovial, well-groomed fellows who will give you greeting at any wayside inn from Calais to Bordeaux.

"You ask a strange question, and one little needing answer. If a man has wandered for hours in bog-holes, he will be in no mind to stand chaffering at inn doors. I seek a night's lodging for my horse and myself."

"It's little we can give you, for it's a bare, sinfu' land," said he, "but such as I ha'e ye're welcome to. Bide a minute, and I'll bring a licht to tak' ye to the stable."

He was gone down the passage for a few seconds, and returned with a rushlight encased against the wind in a wicker covering. The storm made it flicker and flare till it sent dancing shadows over the dark walls of the house. The stable lay round by the back end, and thither poor Saladin and his master stumbled over a most villainous rough ground. The place, when found, was no great thing to boast of—a cold shed, damp with rain, with blaffs of wind wheezing through it; and I was grieved to think of my horse's nightly comfort. The host snatched from a rack a truss of hay, which by its smell was old enough, and tossed it into the manger. "There ye are, and it's mair than mony a Christian gets in thae weary days."

Then he led the way back into the house. We entered a draughty passage with a window at one end, broken in part, through which streamed the cold air. A turn brought me into a little square room, where a fire flickered and a low lamp burned on the table. 'Twas so home-like and peaceful that my heart went out to it, and I thanked my fate for the comfortable lodging I had chanced on. Mine host stirred the blaze and bade me strip off my wet garments. He fetched me an armful of rough homespuns, but I cared little to put them on, so I e'en sat in my shirt and waited on the drying of my coat. My mother's portrait, the one by Grizot, which I have had set in gold and wear always near my heart, dangled to my lap, and I took this for an evil omen. I returned it quick to its place, the more so because I saw the landlord's lantern-jaw close at the sight, and his cold eyes twinkle. Had I been wise, too, I would have stripped my rings from my fingers ere I began this ill-boding travel, for it does not behoove a gentleman to be sojourning among beggars with gold about him.

"Have ye come far the day?" the man asked, in his harsh voice. "Ye're gey-like splashed wi' dirt, so I jalouse ye cam ower the *Angel's Ladder*."

"Angel's ladder!" quoth I, "devil's ladder I call it! for a more blackguardly place I have not clapped eyes on since I first mounted horse."

"*Angel's Ladder* they call it," said the man, to all appearance never heeding my words, "for there, mony a year syne, an holy man of God, one Ebenezer Clavershaws, preached to a goodly gathering on the shining ladder seen by the patriarch Jacob at Bethel, which extended from earth to heaven. 'Twas a rich discourse, and I have it still in my mind."

"'Twas more likely to have been a way to the Evil One for me. Had I but gone a further step many a time, I should have been giving my account ere this to my Maker. But a truce to this talk. 'Twas not to listen to such that I came here; let me have supper, the best you have, and a bottle of whatever wine you keep in this accursed place. Burgundy is my choice."

"Young man," the fellow said gravely, looking at me with his unpleasing eyes, "you are one who loves the meat that perisheth rather than the unsearchable riches of God's grace. Oh, be warned while yet there is time. You know not the delights of gladsome communion wi' Him, which makes the moss-hags and heather-busses more fair than the roses of Sharon or the balmy plains of Gilead. Oh, be wise and turn, for now is the accepted time, now is the day of salvation!"

SacrÃ©! what madman have I fallen in with, thought I, who talks in this fashion. I had heard of the wild deeds of those in our own land who call themselves Huguenots, and I was not altogether without fear. But my appetite was keen, and my blood was never of the coolest.

"Peace with your nonsense, sirrah," I said sternly; "what man are you who come and prate before your guests, instead of fetching their supper? Let me have mine at once, and no more of your Scripture."

As I spoke, I looked him angrily in the face, and my bearing must have had some effect upon him, for he turned suddenly and passed out.

A wench appeared, a comely slip of a girl, with eyes somewhat dazed and timorous, and set the table with viands. There was a moor-fowl, well-roasted and tasty to the palate, a cut of salted beef, and for wine, a bottle of French claret of excellent quality. 'Twas so much in excess of my expectation, that I straightway fell into a good humor, and the black cloud of dismay lifted in some degree from my wits. I filled my glass and looked at it against the fire-glow, and dreamed that 'twas an emblem of the after course of my life. Who knew what fine things I might come to yet, though now I was solitary in a strange land?

The landlord came in and took away the remnants himself. He looked at me fixedly more than once, and in his glance I read madness, greed, and hatred. I feared his look, and was glad to see him leave, for he made me feel angry and a little awed. However, thought I, 'tis not the first time I have met a churlish host, and I filled my glass again.

The fire bickered cheerily, lighting up the room and comforting my cold skin. I drew my chair close and stretched out my legs to the blaze, till in a little, betwixt heat and weariness, I was pleasantly drowsy. I fell to thinking of the events of the day and the weary road I had traveled; then to an earlier time, when I first came to Scotland, and my hopes were still unbroken. After all this I began to mind me of the pleasant days in France; for, though I had often fared ill enough there, all was forgotten but the good fortune; and I had soon built out of my brain a France which was liker Paradise than anywhere on earth. Every now and then a log would crackle or fall, and so wake me with a start, for the fire was of that sort which is common in hilly places—a great bank of peat with wood laid athwart. Blue, pungent smoke came out in rings and clouds, which smelt gratefully in my nostrils after the black out-of-doors.

By and by, what with thinking of the past, what with my present comfort, and what with an ever hopeful imagination, my prospects came to look less dismal. 'Twas true that I was here in a most unfriendly land with little money and no skill of the country. But Scotland was but a little place, after all. I must come to Leith in time, where I could surely meet a French skipper who would take me over, money or no. You will ask, whoever may chance to read this narrative, why, in Heaven's name, I did not turn and go back to Ayr, the port from which I had come? The reason is not far to seek. The whole land behind me stank in my nostrils, for there dwelt Quentin Kennedy, and there lay the scene of my discomfiture and my sufferings. Faugh! the smell of that wretched moor-road is with me yet. So, with thinking one way and another, I came to a decision to go forward in any case, and trust to God and my own good fortune. After this I must have ceased to have any thoughts, and dropped off snugly to sleep.

I wakened, at what time I know not, shivering, with a black fire before my knees. The room was black with darkness, save where through a chink in the window-shutter there came a gleam of pale moonlight. I sprang up in haste and called for a servant to show me to my sleeping room, but the next second I could have wished the word back, for I feared that no servant would be awake and at hand. To my mind there seemed something passing strange in thus leaving a guest to slumber by the fire.

To my amazement, the landlord himself came to my call, bearing a light in his hand. I was reasonably surprised, for though I knew not the hour of the night, I judged from the state of the fire that it must have been far advanced.

"I had fallen asleep," I said, in apology, "and now would finish what I have begun. Show me my bed."

"It'll be a dark nicht and a coorse, out-bye," said the man, as he led the way solemnly from the room, up a rickety stair, down a mirk passage to a chamber which, from the turnings of the house, I guessed to be facing the east. 'Twas a comfortless place, and ere I could add a word I found the man leaving the room with the light. "You'll find your way to bed in the dark," quoth he, and I was left in blackness.

I sat down on the edge of the bed, half-stupid with sleep, my teeth chattering with the cold, listening to the gusts of wind battering against the little window. 'Faith! thought I, this is the worst entertainment I ever had, and I have made trial of many. Yet I need not complain, for I have had a good fire and a royal supper, and my present discomfort is due in great part to my own ill habit of drowsiness. I rose to undress, for my bones were sore after the long day's riding, when, by some chance, I moved forward to the window and opened it to look on the night.

'Twas wintry weather outside, though but the month of August. The face of the hills fronting me were swathed in white mist, which hung low even to the banks of the stream. There was a great muttering in the air of swollen water, for the rain had ceased, and the red waves were left to roll down the channel to the lowlands and make havoc of meadow and steading. The sky was cumbered with clouds, and no clear light of the moon came through; but since 'twas nigh the time of the full moon the night was not utterly dark.

I lingered for maybe five minutes in this posture, and then I heard that which made me draw in my head and listen the more intently. A thud of horses' hoofs on the wet ground came to my ear. A second, and it was plainer, the noise of some half-dozen riders clearly approaching the inn. 'Twas a lonesome place, and I judged it strange that company should come so late.

I flung myself on the bed in my clothes, and could almost have fallen asleep as I was, so weary was my body. But there was that in my mind which forbade slumber, a vague uneasiness as of some ill approaching, which it behooved me to combat. Again and again I tried to drive it from me as mere cowardice, but again it returned to vex me. There was nothing for it but that I should lie on my back and bide what might come.

Then again I heard a sound, this time from a room beneath. 'Twas as if men were talking softly, and moving to and fro. My curiosity was completely aroused, and I thought it no shame to my soldierly honor to slip from my room and gather what was the purport of their talk. At such a time, and in such a place, it boded no good for me, and the evil face of the landlord was ever in my memory. The staircase creaked a little as it felt my weight, but it had been built for heavier men, and I passed it in safety. Clearly the visitors were in the room where I had supped.

"Will we ha'e muckle wark wi' him, think ye?" I heard one man ask.

"Na, na," said another, whom I knew for mine host, "he's a foreigner, a man frae a fremt land, and a' folk ken they're little use. Forbye, I had stock o' him mysel', and I think I could mak' his bit ribs crack thegither. He'll no' be an ill customer to deal wi'."

"But will he no' be a guid hand at the swird? There's no yin o' us here muckle at that."

"Toots," said another, "we'll e'en get him intil a corner, where he'll no git leave to stir an airm."

I had no stomach for more. With a dull sense of fear I crept back to my room, scarce heeding in my anger whether I made noise or not. Good God! thought I, I have traveled by land and sea to die in a moorland alehouse by the hand of common robbers! My heart grew hot at the thought of the landlord, for I made no doubt but it was my jewels that had first set his teeth. I loosened my sword in its scabbard; and now I come to think of it, 'twas a great wonder that it had not been taken away from me while I slept. I could only guess that the man had been afraid to approach me before the arrival of his confederates. I gripped my sword-hilt; ah, how often had I felt its touch under kindlier circumstances—when I slew the boar in the woods at Belmont, when I made the Sieur de Biran crave pardon before my feet, when I—— But peace with such memories! At all events, if Jean de Rohaine must die among ruffians, unknown and forgotten, he would finish his days like a gentleman of courage. I prayed to God that I might only have the life of the leader.

But this world is sweet to all men, and as I awaited death in that dark room, it seemed especially fair to live. I was but in the prime of my age, on the near side of forty, hale in body, a master of the arts and graces. Were it not passing hard that I should perish in this wise? I looked every way for a means of escape. There was but one—the little window which looked upon the ground east of the inn. 'Twas just conceivable that a man might leap it and make his way to the hills, and so baffle his pursuers. Two thoughts deterred me; first, that I had no horse and could not continue my journey; second, that in all likelihood there would be a watch set below. My heart sank within me, and I ceased to think.

For, just at that moment, I heard a noise below as of men leaving the room. I shut my lips and waited. Here, I concluded, is death coming to meet me. But the next moment the noise had stopped, and 'twas evident that the conclave was not yet closed. 'Tis a strange thing, the mind of man, for I, who had looked with despair at my chances a minute agone, now, at the passing of this immediate danger, plucked up heart, clapped my hat on my head, and opened the window.

The night air blew chill, but all seemed silent below. So, very carefully I hung over the ledge, gripped the sill with my hands, swung my legs into the air, and dropped. I lighted on a tussock of grass and rolled over on my side, only to recover myself in an instant and rise to my feet, and, behold, at my side, a tall man keeping sentinel on horseback.

At this the last flicker of hope died in my bosom. The man never moved or spake, but only stared fixedly at me. Yet there was that in his face and bearing which led me to act as I did.

"If you are a man of honor," I burst out, "though you are engaged in an accursed trade, dismount and meet me in combat. Your spawn will not be out for a little time, and the night is none so dark. If I must die, I would die at least in the open air, with my foe before me."

My words must have found some answering chord in the man's breast, for he presently spoke, and asked me my name and errand in the countryside. I told him in a dozen words, and at my tale he shrugged his shoulders.

"I am in a great mind," says he, "to let you go. I am all but sick of this butcher work, and would fling it to the winds at a word. 'Tis well enough for the others, who are mongrel bred, but it ill becomes a man of birth like me, who am own cousin to the Maxwells o' Drurie."

He fell for a very little time into a sort of musing, tugging at his beard like a man in perplexity. Then he spoke out suddenly:

"See you yon tuft of willows by the water? There's a space behind it where a horse and man might stand well concealed. There is your horse," and he pointed to a group of horses standing tethered by the roadside; "lead him to the place I speak of, and trust to God for the rest. I will raise a scare that you're off the other airt, and, mind, that whenever you see the tails o' us, you mount and ride for life in the way I tell you. You should win to Drumlanrig by morning, where there are quieter folk. Now, mind my bidding, and dae't before my good will changes."

"May God do so to you in your extremity! If ever I meet you on earth I will repay you for your mercy. But a word with you. Who is that man?" and I pointed to the house.

The fellow laughed dryly. "It's easy seen you're no acquaint here, or you would ha'e heard o' Long Jock o' the Hirsel. There's mony a man would face the devil wi' a regiment o' dragoons at his back, that would flee at a glint from Jock's een. You're weel quit o' him. But be aff afore the folk are stirring."

I needed no second bidding, but led Saladin with all speed to the willows, where I made him stand knee-keep in the water within cover of the trees, while I crouched by his side. 'Twas none too soon, for I was scarce in hiding when I heard a great racket in the house, and the sound of men swearing and mounting horse. There was a loud clattering of hoofs, which shortly died away, and left the world quiet, save for the broil of the stream and the loud screaming of moorbirds.

III.—I FARE BADLY ABROAD

All this has taken a long time to set down, but there was little time in the acting. Scarce half an hour had passed from my waking by the black fire till I found myself up to the waist in the stream. I made no further delay, but, as soon as the air was quiet, led Saladin out as stilly as I could on the far side of the willows, clambered on his back (for I was too sore in body to mount in any other fashion), and was riding for dear life along the moor road in the contrary direction to that from which I had come on the night before. The horse had plainly been well fed, since, doubtless, the ruffians had marked him for their own plunder. He covered the ground in gallant fashion, driving up jets and splashes of rain water from the pools in the way. Mile after mile was passed with no sound of pursuers; one hill gave place to another; the stream grew wider and more orderly; but still I kept up the breakneck pace, fearing to slacken rein. Fifteen miles were covered, as I judged, before I saw the first light of dawn in the sky, a red streak in a gray desert; and brought my horse down to a trot, thanking God that at last I was beyond danger.

I was sore in body, with clammy garments sticking to my skin, aching in back and neck, unslept, well-nigh as miserable as a man could be. But great as was my bodily discomfort, 'twas not one tittle to compare with the sickness of my heart. I had been driven to escape from a hostel by a window like a common thief; compelled to ride,—nay, there was no use in disguising it,—to flee, before a pack of ill-bred villains; I, a gentleman of France, who had ruffled it with the best of them in my fit of prosperity. Again and again I questioned with myself whether I had not done better to die in that place, fighting as long as the breath was in my body. Of this I am sure, at any rate, that it would have been the way more soothing to my pride. I argued the matter with myself, according to the most approved logic, but could come no nearer to the solution. For while I thought the picture of myself dying with my back to the wall the more heroical and gentleman-like, it yet went sore against me to think of myself, with all my skill of the sword and the polite arts, perishing in a desert place at the hand of common cut-throats. 'Twas no fear of death, I give my word of honor; that was a weakness never found in our race. Courage is a virtue I take no credit for; 'tis but a matter of upbringing. But a man loves to make some noise in the earth ere he leaves it, or at least to pass with blowings of the trumpet and some manner of show. To this day I cannot think of any way by which I could have mended my conduct. I can but set it down as a mischance of Providence, which meets all men in their career, but of which no man of spirit cares to think.

The sun rose clear, but had scarce shone for an hour, when, as is the way in this land, a fresh deluge of rain came on, and the dawn, which had begun in crimson, ended in a dull level of gray. I had never been used with much foul weather of this sort, so I bore it ill. 'Twas about nine of the morning when I rode into the village of Drumlanrig, a jumble of houses in the lee of a great wood, which runs up to meet the descending moorlands. Some ragged brats, heedless of the weather, played in the street, if one may call it by so fine a name; but for the most part the houses seemed quite deserted. A woman looked incuriously at me; a man who was carrying sacks scarce raised his head to view me; the whole place was like a dwelling of the dead. I have since learned the reason, which was no other than the accursed butchery on which I had quarreled with Quentin Kennedy, and so fallen upon misfortune. The young and manly were all gone; some to the hills for hiding, some to the town prisons, some across the seas to work in the plantations, and some on that long journey from which no man returns. My heart boils within me to this day to think of it—but there! it is long since past, and I have little need to be groaning over it now.

There was no inn in the place, but I bought bread from the folk of a little farm-steading at one end of the village street. They would scarce give it to me at first, and 'twas not till they beheld my woebegone plight that their hearts relented. Doubtless they took me for one of the soldiers who had harried them and theirs, little guessing that 'twas all for their sake that I was in such evil case. I did not tarry to ask the road, for Leith was too far distant for the people in that place to know it. Of this much I was sure, that it lay to the northeast, so I took my way in that direction, shaping my course by the sun. There was a little patch of green fields, a clump of trees, and a quiet stream beside the village; but I had scarce ridden half a mile beyond it when once more the moor swallowed me up in its desert of moss and wet heather.

I was now doubly dispirited. My short exhilaration of escape had gone, and all the pangs of wounded pride and despair seized upon me, mingled with a sort of horror of the place I had come through. Whenever I saw a turn of hill which brought the *Angel's Ladder* to my mind, I shivered in spite of myself, and could have found it in my heart to turn and flee. In addition, I would have you remember, I was soaked to the very skin, my eyes weary with lack of sleep, and my legs cramped with much riding.

The place in the main was moorland, with steep, desolate hills on my left. On the right to the south I had glimpses of a fairer country, woods and distant fields, seen for an instant through the driving mist. In a trice France was back in my mind, for I could not see an acre of green land without coming nigh to tears. Yet, and perhaps 'twas fortunate for me, such glimpses were all too rare. For the most part, the way was a long succession of sloughs and mires, with here a piece of dry, heathy ground, and there an impetuous water coming down from the highlands. Saladin soon fell tired, and, indeed, small wonder, since he had come many miles, and his fare had been of the scantiest. He would put his foot in a bog-hole and stumble so sharply that I would all but lose my seat. Then, poor beast, he would take shame to himself, and pick his way as well as his weary legs would suffer him. 'Twas an evil plight for man and steed, and I knew not which to pity the more.

At noon, I came to the skirts of a long hill, whose top was hidden with fog, but which I judged to be high and lonesome. I met a man—the first I had seen since Drumlanrig—and asked him my whereabouts. I learned that the hill was called Queen's Berry, and that in some dozen miles I would strike the high road to Edinburgh. I could get not another word out of him, but must needs content myself with this crumb of knowledge. The road in front was no road, nothing but a heathery moor, with walls of broken stones seaming it like the lines of sewing in an old coat. Gray broken hills came up for a minute, as a stray wind blew the mist aside, only to disappear the next instant in a ruin of cloud.

From this place I mark the beginning of the most wretched journey in my memory. Till now I had had some measure of bodily strength to support me. Now it failed, and a cold shivering fit seized on my vitals, and more than once I was like to have fallen from my horse. A great stupidity came over my brain; I could call up no remembrance to cheer me, but must plod on in a horror of darkness. The cause was not far distant—cold, wet, and despair. I tried to swallow some of the rain-soaked bread in my pouch, but my mouth was as dry as a skin. I dismounted to drink at a stream, but the water could hardly trickle down my throat so much did it ache. 'Twas as if I were on the eve of an ague, and in such a place it were like to be the end of me.

Had there been a house, I should have craved shelter. But one effect of my sickness was, that I soon strayed woefully from my path, such as it was, and found myself in an evil case with bogs and steep hillsides. I had much to do in keeping Saladin from danger; and had I not felt the obligation to behave like a man, I should have flung the reins on his neck and let him bear himself and his master to destruction. Again and again I drove the wish from my mind—"As well die in a bog-hole or break your neck over a crag as dwine away with ague in the cold heather, as you are like to do," said the tempter. But I steeled my heart, and made a great resolve to keep one thing, though I should lose all else—some shreds of my manhood.

Toward evening I grew so ill that I was fain, when we came to a level place, to lay my head on Saladin's neck, and let him stumble forward. My head swam, and my back ached so terribly that I guessed feverishly that someone had stabbed me unawares. The weather cleared just about even, and the light of day flickered out in a watery sunset. 'Twas like the close of my life, I thought, a gray ill day and a poor ending. The notion depressed me miserably. I felt a kinship with that feeble evening light, a kinship begotten of equality in weakness. However, all would soon end; my day must presently have its evening; and then, if all tales were true, and my prayers had any efficacy, I should be in a better place.

But when once the night in its blackness had set in, I longed for the light again, however dismal it might be. A ghoulish song, one which I had heard long before, was ever coming to my memory:

La pluye nous a débuez et lavez, Et le soleil desséchez et noirciz: Pies, corbeaulx—.

With a sort of horror I tried to drive it from my mind. A dreadful heaviness oppressed me. Fears which I am ashamed to set down thronged my brain. The way had grown easier, or I make no doubt my horse had fallen. 'Twas a track we were on, I could tell by the greater freedom with which Saladin stepped. God send, I prayed, that we be near to folk, and that they be kindly; this prayer I said many times to the accompaniment of the whistling of the doleful wind. Every gust pained me. I was the sport of the weather, a broken puppet tossed about by circumstance.

Now an answer was sent to me, and that a speedy one. I came of a sudden to a clump of shrubbery beside a wall. Then at a turn of the way a light shone through, as from a broad window among trees. A few steps more and I stumbled on a gate, and turned Saladin's head up a pathway. The rain dripped heavily from the bushes, a branch slashed me in the face, and my weariness grew tenfold with every second. I dropped like a log before the door, scarce looking to see whether the house was great or little; and, ere I could knock or make any call, swooned away dead on the threshold.

IV.—OF MY COMING TO LINDEAN

When I came to myself I was lying in a pleasant room with a great flood of sunlight drifting through the window. My brain was so confused that it was many minutes ere I could guess in which part of the earth I was laid. My first thought was that I was back in France, and I rejoiced with a great gladness; but as my wits cleared the past came back by degrees, till I had it plain before me, from my setting-out to my fainting at the door. Clearly I was in the house where I had arrived on the even of yesterday.

I stirred, and found my weakness gone, and my health, save for some giddiness in the head, quite recovered. This was ever the way of our family, who may be in the last desperation one day and all alive and active the next. Our frames are like the old grape tendrils, slim, but tough as whipcord.

At my first movement someone arose from another part of the room and came forward. I looked with curiosity, and found that it was a girl, who brought me some strengthening food-stuff in a bowl. The sunlight smote her full in the face and set her hair all aglow, as if she were the Madonna. I could not see her well, but, as she bent over me, she seemed tall and lithe and pretty to look upon.

"How feel you?" she asked, in a strange, soft accent, speaking the pure English, but with a curious turn in her voice. "I trust you are better of your ailment."

"Yes, that I am," I said briskly, for I was ashamed to be lying there in good health, "and I would thank you, mademoiselle, for your courtesy to a stranger."

"Nay, nay," she cried, "'twas but common humanity. You were sore spent last night, both man and horse. Had you traveled far? But no," she added hastily, seeing me about to plunge into a narrative; "your tale will keep. I cannot have you making yourself ill again. You had better bide still a little longer." And with a deft hand she arranged the pillows and was gone.

For some time I lay in a pleasing inaction. 'Twas plain I had fallen among gentlefolk, and I blessed the good fortune which had led me to the place. Here I might find one to hear my tale and help me in my ill-luck. At any rate for the present I was in a good place, and when one has been living in a nightmare, the present has the major part in his thoughts. With this I fell asleep again, for I was still somewhat wearied in body.

When I awoke 'twas late afternoon. The evil weather seemed to have gone, for the sun was bright and the sky clear with the mellowness of approaching even. The girl came again and asked me how I fared. "For," said she, "perhaps you wish to rise, if you are stronger. Your clothes were sadly wet and torn when we got you to bed last night, so my father has bade me ask you to accept of another suit till your own may be in better order. See, I have laid them out for you, if you will put them on." And again, ere I could thank her, she was gone.

I was surprised and somewhat affected by this crowning kindness, and at the sight of so much care for a stranger whose very name was unknown. I longed to meet at once with the men of the house, so I sprung up and drew the clothes toward me. They were of rough gray cloth, very strong and warm, and fitting a man a little above the ordinary height, of such stature as mine is. It did not take me many minutes to dress, and when once more I found myself arrayed in wholesome garments I felt my spirit returning, and with it came hope, and a kindlier outlook on the world.

No one appeared, so I opened my chamber door and found myself at the head of a staircase, which turned steeply down almost from the threshold. A great window illumined it, and many black-framed pictures hung on the walls adown it. At the foot there was a hall, broad and low in the roof, whence some two or three doors opened. Sounds of men in conversation came from one, so I judged it wise to turn there. With much curiosity I lifted the latch and entered unbidden.

'Twas a little room, well furnished, and stocked to the very ceiling with books. A fire burned on the hearth, by which sat two men talking. They rose to their feet as I entered, and I marked them well. One was an elderly man of maybe sixty years, with a bend in his back as if from study. His face was narrow and kindly; blue eyes, like a Northman, a thin, twitching lip, and hair well turned to silver. His companion was scarce less notable—a big, comely man, dressed half in the fashion of a soldier, yet with the air of one little versed in cities. I love to be guessing a man's station from his looks, and ere I had glanced him over, I had set him down in my mind as a country *laird*, as these folk call it. Both greeted me courteously, and then, as I advanced, were silent, as if waiting for me to give some account of myself.

"I have come to thank you for your kindness," said I awkwardly, "and to let you know something of myself, for 'tis ill to be harboring folk without names or dwelling."

"Tush!" said the younger; "'twere a barbarity to leave anyone without, so travel-worn as you. The Levite in the Scriptures did no worse. But how feel you now? I trust your fatigue is gone."

"I thank you a thousand times for your kindness. Would I knew how to repay it!"

"Nay, young man," said the elder, "give thanks not to us, but to the Lord who led you to this place. The moors are hard bedding, and right glad I am that you fell in with us here. 'Tis seldom we have a stranger with us, since my brother at Drumlanrig died in the spring o' last year. But I trust you are better, and that Anne has looked after you well. A maid is a blessing to sick folk, if a weariness to the hale."

"You speak truly," I said, "a maid is a blessing to the sick. 'Tis sweet to be well tended when you have fared hardly for days. Your kindness has set me at peace with the world again. Yesterday all was black before me, and now, I bethink me, I see a little ray of light."

"'Twas a good work," said the old man, "to give you hope and set you right with yourself, if so chance we have done it. What saith the wise man, 'He that hath no rule over his own spirit is like a city that is broken down and without walls'? But whence have you come? We would hear your story."

So I told them the whole tale of my wanderings, from my coming to Kennedy to my fainting fit at their own threshold. At the story of my quarrel they listened eagerly, and I could mark their eyes flashing, and as I spake of my sufferings in the desert I could see sympathy in their faces. When I concluded, neither spake for a little, till the elder man broke silence with:

"May God bless and protect you in all your goings! Well I see that you are of the upright in heart. It makes me blithe to have you in my house."

The younger said nothing but rose and came to me.

"M. de Rohaine," he said, speaking my name badly, "give me your hand. I honor you for a gentleman and a man of feeling."

"And I am glad to give it you," said I, and we clasped hands and looked into each other's eyes. Then we stepped back well satisfied. For myself I love to meet a man, and in the great-limbed young fellow before me I found one to my liking.

"And now I must tell you of ourselves," said the old man, "for 'tis fitting that a guest should know his entertainers. This is the manse of Lindean, and I am the unworthy man, Ephraim Lambert, whom God hath appointed to watch over his flock in this place. Sore, sore are we troubled by evil men, such as you have known; and my folk, from dwelling in decent cots, have to hide in peat-hags and the caves of the hills. The Lord's hand is heavy upon this country; 'tis a time of trial, a passing through the furnace. God grant we be not found faithless! This home is still left to us, and thankful we should be for it; and I demand that you dwell with us till you have settled on your course. This man," he went on, laying his hand on the shoulder of the younger, "is Master Henry Semple of Clachlands, a fine inheritance, all ridden and rieved by these devils on earth, Captain Keith's dragoons. Henry is of our belief, and a man of such mettle that the Privy Council was fain to send down a quartering of soldiers to bide in his house and devour his substance. 'Twas a thing no decent man could thole, so off he comes here to keep us company till the wind blows by. If you look out of the window over by the side of yon rig of hill, ye'll get a glimmer of Clachlands chimneys, reeking with the smoke of their evil preparations. Ay, ay, lads, burn you your peats and fill up the fire with logs till the vent's choked, but you'll burn brawly yourselves some fine day, when your master gives you your wages."

He looked out as he spoke, and into his kindly eyes came a gleam of such anger and decision as quite transfigured his face and made it seem more like that of a troop captain than a peaceful minister.

And now Master Semple spoke up: "God send, sir, they suffer for no worse a crime than burning my peats and fire-wood. I should count myself a sorry fellow if I made any complaint about a little visitation, when the hand of the Lord is smiting so sorely among my fellows. I could take shame to myself every time I eat good food or sleep in a decent bed, to think of better men creeping aneath the lang heather like etherts, or shivering on the cauld hill-side. There'll be no such doings in your land, M. de Rohaine? I've heard tell of folk there like us, dwelling in the hills to escape the abominations of Rome. But perhaps," and he hesitated, "you are not of them?"

"No," said I, "I am of your enemies by upbringing; but I dearly love a brave man, whereever I meet him. 'Tis poor religion, say I, which would lead one to see no virtue in those of another belief. There is one God above all."

"Ay, you speak truly," said the old man. "He has made of one blood all the nations of the earth. But I yearn to see you of a better way of thinking. Mayhap I may yet show you your errors?"

"I thank you, but I hold by 'every man to his upbringing.' Each man to the creed of his birth. 'Tis a poor thing to be changing on any pretext. For, look you, God, who appointed a man his place of birth, set him his religion with it, and I hold if he but stick to it he is not far in error."

I spoke warmly, but in truth I had thought all too little about such things. One who has to fight his way among men and live hardly, has, of necessity, little time for his devotions, and if he but live cleanly, his part is well done. *Mon Dieu!* Who will gainsay me?

"I fear your logic is faulty," said Master Semple, "but it is mighty inhospitable to be arguing with a guest. See, here Anne comes with the lamp, and supper will soon be ready."

The girl came in as he spake, bearing a great lamp, which she placed on a high shelf, and set about laying the table for supper. I had noticed her little at first sight, for I was never given to staring at maids; but now, as she moved about, I found myself ever watching her. The ruddy firelight striving with the serene glow of the lamp met and flickered about her face and hair. She was somewhat brown in skin, like a country maiden; but there was no semblance of rusticity in her fair features and deep brown eyes. Her hair hung over her neck as brown as the soft fur of a squirrel, and the fire filled it with fantastic shadows. She was singularly graceful in figure, moving through the room and bending over the table with a grace which 'twas pretty to contemplate. 'Twas strange to note that when her face was averted one might have guessed her to be some village girl or burgher's daughter; but as soon as she had turned her imperial eyes on you she looked like a queen in a play. Her face was a curious one, serious and dignified beyond her years and sex, yet with odd sparkles of gayety dancing in her eyes and the corners of her rosy mouth.

Master Semple had set about helping her, and a pretty sight it was to see her reproving and circumventing his clumsiness. 'Twas not hard to see the relation between the two. The love-light shone in his eye whenever he looked toward her; and she, for her part, seemed to thrill at his chance touch. One strange thing I noted, that, whereas in France two young folks could not have gone about the business of setting a supper-table without much laughter and frolic, all was done here as if 'twere some solemn ceremonial.

To one who was still sick with the thought of the black uplands he had traversed, of the cold, driving rain and the deadly bogs, the fare in the manse was like the apple to Eve in the garden. 'Twas fine to be eating crisp oaten cakes, and butter fresh from the churn, to be drinking sweet, warm milk—for we lived on the plainest; and, above all, to watch kindly faces around you in place of marauders and low ruffians. The minister said a lengthy grace before and after the meal; and when the table was cleared the servants were called in to evening prayer. Again the sight pleased me—the two maids with their brown country faces seated decently by the door; Anne, half in shadow, sitting demurely with Master Semple not far off, and at the table-head the white hairs of the old man bowed over the Bible. He read I know not what, for I am not so familiar with the Scriptures as I should be, and, moreover, Anne's grave face was a more entrancing study. Then we knelt, and he prayed to God to watch over us in all our ways and bring us at last to his prepared kingdom. Truly, when I arose from my knees, I felt more tempted to be devout than I have any remembrance of before.

Then we sat and talked of this and that, and I must tell over all my misfortunes again for mademoiselle's entertainment. She listened with open wonder, and thanked me with her marvelous eyes. Then to bed with a vile-smelling lamp, in a wide, low-ceilinged sleeping room, where the sheets were odorous of bog-myrtle and fresh as snow. Sleep is a goddess easy of conquest when wooed in such a fashion.

V.—I PLEDGE MY WORD

Of my life at Lindean for the next three days I have no clear remembrance. The weather was dry and languid, as often follows a spell of rain, and the long hills which huddled around the house looked near and imminent. The place was so still that if one shouted it seemed almost a profanation. 'Twas so Sabbath-like that I almost came to dislike it. Indeed, I doubt I should have found it irksome had there not been a brawling stream in the glen, which kept up a continuous dashing and chattering. It seemed the one link between me and that far-away world in which not long agone I had been a dweller.

The life, too, was as regular as in the king's court. Sharp at six I was awakened, and ere seven we were assembled for breakfast. Then to prayers, and then to the occupations of the day. The minister would be at his books or down among his people on some errand of mercy. The church had been long closed, for the Privy Council, seeing that Master Lambert was opposed to them, had commanded him to be silent; and yet, mark you, so well was he loved in the place that they durst set no successor in his stead. They tried it once and a second time, but the unhappy man was so taken with fear of the people that he shook the dust of Lindean off his feet, and departed in search of a more hospitable dwelling. But the minister's mouth was shut, save when covertly, and with the greatest peril to himself, he would preach at a meeting of the hill-folk in the recesses of the surrounding uplands.

The library I found no bad one—I who in my day have been considered to have something of a taste in books. To be sure there was much wearisome stuff, the work of old divines, and huge commentaries on the Scriptures, written in Latin and plentifully interspersed with Greek and Hebrew. But there was good store of the Classics, both prose and poetry,—*Horace*, who has ever been my favorite, and *Homer*, who, to my thinking, is the finest of the ancients. Here, too, I found a *Plato*, and I swear I read more of him in the manse than I have done since I went through him with M. Clerselier, when we were students together in Paris.

The acquaintance which I had formed with Master Semple speedily ripened into a fast friendship. I found it in my heart to like this great serious man—a bumpkin if you will, but a man of courage and kindliness. We were wont to take long walks, always in some lonely part of the country, and we grew more intimate in our conversation than I should ever have dreamed of. He would call me John, and this much I suffered him, to save my name from the barbarity of his pronunciation; while in turn I fell to calling him Henry, as if we had been born and bred together. I found that he loved to hear of my own land and my past life, which, now that I think of it, must have had no little interest to one dwelling in such solitudes. From him I heard of his father, of his brief term at the College of Edinburgh, which he left when the strife in the country grew high, and of his sorrow and anger at the sufferings of those who withstood the mandate of the king. Though I am of the true faith, I think it no shame that my sympathy was all with these rebels, for had I not seen something of their misery myself? But above all, he would speak of *la belle Anne* as one gentleman will tell another of his love, when he found that I was a willing listener. I could scarce have imagined such warmth of passion to exist in the man as he showed at the very mention of her name.

"Oh!" he would cry out, "I would die for her; I would gang to the world's end to pleasure her! I whiles think that I break the first commandment every day of my life, for I canna keep her a moment out of my thoughts, and I fear she's more to me than any earthly thing should be. I think of her at nicht. I see her name in every page of the Book. I thought I was bad when I was over at Clachlands, and had to ride five miles to see her; but now I'm tenfold worse when I'm biding aside her. God grant it be not counted to me for sin!"

"Amen to that," said I. 'Tis a fine thing to see the love of a maid; but I hold 'tis a finer to witness the passion of a strong man.

Yet, withal, there was something sinister about the house and its folk which to me was the fly in the ointment. They were kindness and charity incarnate, but they were cold and gloomy to boot, lacking any grace or sprightliness in their lives. I find it hard to write this, for their goodness to me was beyond recompense; yet I must set it down, since in some measure it has to do with my story. The old man would look at me at times and sigh, nor did I think it otherwise than fitting, till I found from his words that the sighs were on account of my own spiritual darkness. I have no quarrel with any man for wishing to convert me, but to sigh at one's approach seems a doleful way of setting about it. Then he would break out from his wonted quietness at times to rail at his foes, calling down the wrath of Heaven to blight them. Such a fit was always followed by a painful exhaustion, which left him as weak as a child, and shivering like a leaf. I bitterly cursed the state of a country which could ruin the peace of mind of a man so sweet-tempered by nature, and make him the sport of needless rage. 'Twas pitiful to see him creep off to his devotions after any such outbreak, penitent and ashamed. Even to his daughter he was often cruelly sharp, and would call her to account for the merest trifle.

As for Master Henry, what shall I say of him? I grew to love him like my own brother, yet I no more understood him than the Sultan of Turkey. He had strange fits of gloom, begotten, I must suppose, of the harsh country and his many anxieties, in which he was more surly than a bear, speaking little, and that mainly from the Scriptures. I have one case in my memory, when, had I not been in a sense his guest, I had scarce refrained from quarreling. 'Twas in the afternoon of the second day, when we returned weary from one of our long wanderings. Anne tripped forth into the autumn sunlight singing a catch, a simple glee of the village folk.

"Peace, Anne," says Master Henry savagely; "it little becomes you to be singing in these days, unless it be a godly psalm. Keep your songs for better times."

"What ails you?" I ventured to say. "You praised her this very morning for singing the self-same verses."

"And peace, you," he says roughly, as he entered the house; "if the lass hearkened to your accursed creed, I should have stronger words for her."

My breath was fairly taken from me at this incredible rudeness. I had my hand on my sword, and had I been in my own land we should soon have settled it. As it was, I shut my lips firmly and choked down my choler.

Yet I cannot leave with this ill word of the man. That very night he talked with me so pleasingly, and with so friendly a purport, that I conceived he must have been scarce himself when he so insulted me. Indeed, I discerned two natures in the man—one, hard, saturnine, fanatically religious; the other, genial and kindly, like that of any other gentleman of family. The former I attributed to the accident of his fortune; the second I held to be the truer, and in my thoughts of him still think of it as the only one.

But I must pass to the events which befell on the even of the third day, and wrought so momentous a change in the life at Lindean. 'Twas just at the lighting of the lamp, when Anne and the minister and myself sat talking in the little sitting room, that Master Henry entered with a look of great concern on his face, and beckoned the elder man out.

"Andrew Gibb is here," said he.

"And what may Andrew Gibb be wanting?" asked the old man, glancing up sharply.

"He brings nae guid news, I fear, but he'll tell them to none but you; so hasten out, sir, to the back, for he's come far, and he's ill at the waiting."

The twain were gone for some time, and in their absence I could hear high voices in the back end of the house, conversing as on some matter of deep import. Anne fetched the lamp from the kitchen and trimmed it with elaborate care, lighting it and setting it in its place. Then, at last, the minister returned alone.

I was shocked at the sight of him as he re-entered the room. His face was ashen pale and tightly drawn about the lips. He crept to a chair and leaned his head on the table, speaking no word. Then he burst out of a sudden into a storm of pleading.

"O Lord God," he cried, "thou hast aye been good to us, thou has kept us weel, and bielded us frae the wolves who have sought to devour us. Oh, dinna leave us now. It's no' for mysel' or Henry that I care. We're men, and can warstle through ills; but oh, what am I to dae wi' the bit helpless lassie? It's awfu' to have to gang oot among hills and bogs to bide, but it's ten times waur when ye dinna ken what's gaun to come to your bairn. Hear me, O Lord, and grant me my request. I've no' been a' that I micht have been, but oh, if I ha'e tried to serve thee at a', dinna let this danger overwhelm us!"

He had scarcely finished, and was still sitting with bowed head, when Master Henry also entered the room. His eyes were filled with an austere frenzy, such as I had learned to look for.

"Ay, sir," said he, "'tis a time for us a' to be on our knees. But ha'e courage, and dinna let us spoil the guid cause by our weak mortal complaining. Is't no' better to be hunkering in a moss-hole and communing with the Lord than waxing fat like Jeshurun in carnal corruption? Call on God's name, but no' wi' sighing, but wi' exaltation, for He hath bidden us to a mighty heritage."

"Ye speak brave and true, Henry, and I'm wi' your every word. But tell me what's to become o' my bairn? What will Anne dae? I once thought there was something atween you——" He stopped abruptly and searched the face of the young man.

At his words Master Semple had started as under a lash. “Oh, my God,” he cried, “I had forgotten! Anne, Anne, my dearie, we canna leave ye, and you to be my wife. This is a sore trial of faith, sir, and I misdoubt I canna stand it. To leave ye to the tender mercies o’ a’ the hell-hounds o’ dragoons—oh, I canna dae’t!”

He clapped his hand to his forehead and walked about the room like a man distraught.

And now I put in my word. “What ails you, Henry? Tell me, for I am sore grieved to see you in such perplexity.”

“Ails me?” he repeated. “Aye, I will tell ye what ails me”; and he drew his chair before me. “Andrew Gibb’s come ower frae the Ruthen wi’ shure news that a warrant’s oot against us baith, for being at the preaching on Callowa’ Muir. ’Twas an enemy did it, and now the soldiers are coming at ony moment to lay hands on us and take us off to Embro’. Then there’ll be but a short lease of life for us; and unless we take to the hills this very nicht we may be ower late in the morning. I’m wae to tak’ sae auld a man as Master Lambert to wet mosses, but there’s nothing else to be dune. But what’s to become o’ Anne? Whae’s to see to her, when the dragoons come riding and cursing about the toon? Oh, it’s a terrible time, John. Pray to God, if ye never prayed before, to let it pass.”

Mademoiselle had meantime spoken never a word, but had risen and gone to her father's chair and put her arms around his neck. Her presence seemed to cheer the old man, for he ceased mourning and looked up, while she sat, still as a statue, with her grave, lovely face against his. But Master Semple's grief was pitiful to witness. He rocked himself to and fro in his chair, with his arms folded and a set, white face. Every now and then he would break into a cry like a stricken animal. The elder man was the first to counsel patience.

"Stop, Henry," says he; "it's ill-befitting Christian folk to set sic an example. We've a' got our troubles, and if ours are heavier than some, it's no' for us to complain. Think o' the many years o' grace we've had. There's nae doubt the Lord will look after the bairn, for he's a guid Shepherd for the feckless."

But now of a sudden a thought seemed to strike Henry, and he was on his feet in a twinkling and by my side.

"John," he almost screamed in my ear, "John, I'm going to ask ye for the greatest service that ever man asked. Ye'll no' say me nay?"

"Let me hear it," said I.

"Will *you* bide wi' the lass? You're a man o' birth, and I'll swear to it, a man o' honor. I can trust you as I would trust my ain brither. Oh, man, dinna deny me! It's the last hope I ha'e, for if ye refuse, we maun e'en gang to the hills and leave the puir thing alane. Oh, ye canna say me nae! Tell me that ye'll do my asking."

I was so thunderstruck at the request that I scarce could think for some minutes. Consider, was it not a strange thing to be asked to stay alone in a wild moorland house with another man's betrothed, for Heaven knew how many weary days? My life and prospects were none so cheerful for me to despise anything, nor so varied that I might pick and choose; but yet 'twas dreary, if no worse, to look forward to any length of time in this desolate place. I was grateful for the house as a shelter by the way, yet I hoped to push on and get rid, as soon as might be, of this accursed land.

But was I not bound by all the ties of gratitude to grant my host's request? They had found me fainting at their door, they had taken me in, and treated me to their best; I was bound in common honor to do something to requite their kindness. And let me add, though not often a man subject to any feelings of compassion, whatever natural bent I had this way having been spoiled in the wars, I nevertheless could not refrain from pitying the distress of that strong man before me. I felt tenderly toward him, more so than I had felt to anyone for many a day.

All these thoughts raced through my head in the short time while Master Henry stood before me. The look in his eyes, the pained face of the old man, and the sight of Anne, so fair and helpless, fixed my determination.

"I am bound to you in gratitude," said I, "and I would seek to repay you. I will bide in the house, if so you will, and be the maid's protector. God grant I may be faithful to my trust, and may he send a speedy end to your exile?"

So 'twas all finished in a few minutes, and I was fairly embarked upon the queerest enterprise of my life. For myself I sat dazed and meditative; as for the minister and Master Semple, one-half of the burden seemed to be lifted from their minds. I was amazed at the trusting natures of these men, who had habited all their days with honest folk till they conceived all to be as worthy as themselves. I felt, I will own, a certain shrinking from the responsibility of the task; but the Rubicon had been crossed and there was no retreat.

* * * * *

Of the rest of that night how shall I tell? There was such a bustling and pother as I had never seen in any house since the day that my brother Denis left Rohaine for the Dutch wars. There was a running and scurrying about, a packing of food, a seeking of clothes, for the fugitives must be off before the first light. Anne went about with a pale, tearful face; and 'twas a matter of no surprise, for to see a father, a man frail and fallen in years, going out to the chill moorlands in the early autumn till no man knew when, is a grievous thing for a young maid. Her lover was scarce in so dire a case, for he was young and strong, and well used to the life of the hills. For him there was hope; for the old man but a shadow. My heart grew as bitter as gall at the thought of the villains who brought it about.

How shall I tell of the morning, when the faint light was flushing the limits of the sky, and the first call of a heath-bird broke the silence! 'Twas sad to see these twain with their bundles (the younger carrying the elder's share) creep through the heather toward the hills. They affected a cheerful resolution, assumed to comfort Anne's fears and sorrow; but I could mark beneath it a settled despair. The old man prayed at the threshold, and clasped his daughter many times, kissing her and giving her his blessing. The younger, shaken with great sobs, bade a still more tender farewell, and then started off abruptly to hide his grief. Anne and I, from the door, watched their figures disappear over the crest of the ridge, and then went in, sober and full of angry counsels.

* * * * *

The soldiers came about an hour before mid-day—a band from Clachlands, disorderly ruffians, commanded by a mealy-faced captain. They were a scurrilous set, their faces bloated with debauchery and their clothes in no very decent order. As one might have expected, they were mightily incensed at finding their bird flown, and fell to cursing each other with great good-will. They poked their low-bred faces into every nook in the house and outbuildings; and when at length they had satisfied themselves that there was no hope from that quarter, they had all the folk of the dwelling out on the green and questioned them one by one. The two serving-lasses were stanch, and stoutly denied all knowledge of their master's whereabouts—which was indeed no more than the truth. One of the two, Jean Crichope by name, when threatened with ill-treatment if she did not speak, replied valiantly that she would twist the neck of the first scoundrelly soldier who dared to lay finger on her. This I doubt not she could have performed, for she was a very daughter of Anak.

As for Anne and myself, we answered according to our agreement. They were very curious to know my errand there and my name and birth; and when I bade them keep their scurvy tongues from defiling a gentleman's house, they were none so well pleased. I am not a vain man, and I do not set down the thing I am going to relate as at all redounding to my credit; I merely tell it as an incident in my tale.

The captain at last grew angry. He saw that the law was powerless to touch us, and that nought remained for him but to ride to the hills in pursuit of the fugitives. This he seemed to look upon as a hardship, being a man to all appearance more fond of the bottle and pasty than a hill gallop. At any rate he grew wroth, and addressed to Anne a speech so full of gross rudeness that I felt it my duty to interfere.

"Look you here, sir," said I, "I am here, in the first place, to see that no scoundrel maltreats this lady. I would ask you, therefore, to be more civil in your talk or to get down and meet me in fair fight. These gentlemen," and I made a mocking bow to his company, "will, I am assured, see an honest encounter."

The man flushed under his coarse skin. His reputation was at stake. There was no other course open but to take up my challenge.

"You, you bastard Frenchman," he cried, "would you dare to insult a captain of the king's dragoons? I' faith, I will teach you better manners;" and he came at me with his sword in a great heat. The soldiers crowded round like children to see a cock-fight.

He came at me with his sword in a great heat.

In an instant we crossed swords and fell to; I with the sun in my eyes and on the lower ground. The combat was not of long duration. In a trice I found that he was a mere child in my hands, a barbarian who used his sword like a quarter-staff, not even putting strength into his thrusts.

"Enough!" I cried; "this is mere fooling;" and with a movement which any babe in arms might have checked, twirled his blade from his hands and sent it spinning over the grass. "Follow your sword, and learn two things before you come back—civility to maids and the rudiments of sword-play. Bah! Begone with you!"

Some one of his men laughed, and I think they were secretly glad at their tyrant's discomfiture. No more need be said. He picked up his weapon and rode away, vowing vengeance upon me and swearing at every trooper behind him. I cared not a straw for him, for despite his bravado I knew that the fear of death was in his cowardly heart, and that we should be troubled no more by his visitations.

VI.—IDLE DAYS

I have heard it said by wise folk in France that the autumn is of all seasons of the year the most trying to the health of a soldier; since, for one accustomed to the heat of action and the fire and fury of swift encounter, the decay of summer, the moist, rotting air, and the first chill preludes of winter are hard to stand. This may be true of our own autumn days, but in the north country 'twas otherwise. For there the weather was as sharp and clear as spring, and the only signs of the season were the red leaves and the brown desolate moors. Lindean was built on the slope of the hills, with the steeps behind it, and a vista of level land to the front: so one could watch from the window the red woods of the low country, and see the stream, turgid with past rains, tearing through the meadows. The sun rose in the morning in a blaze of gold and crimson; the days were temperately warm, the afternoons bright, and the evening another procession of colors. 'Twas all so beautiful that I found it hard to keep my thoughts at all on the wanderers in the hills and to think of the house as under a dark shadow.

And if 'twas hard to do this, 'twas still harder to look upon Anne as a mourning daughter. For the first few days she had been pale and silent, going about her household duties as was her wont, speaking rarely, and then but to call me to meals. But now the pain of the departure seemed to have gone, and though still quiet as ever, there was no melancholy in her air; but with a certain cheerful gravity she passed in and out in my sight. At first I had had many plans to console her; judge then of my delight to find them needless. She was a brave maid, I thought, and little like the common, who could see the folly of sighing, and set herself to hope and work as best she could.

The days passed easily enough for me, for I could take Saladin and ride through the countryside, keeping always far from Clachlands; or the books in the house would stand me in good stead for entertainment. With the evenings 'twas different. When the lamp was lit, and the fire burned, 'twas hard to find some method to make the hours go by. I am not a man easily moved, as I have said; and yet I took shame to myself to think of the minister and Master Henry in the cold bogs, and Anne and myself before a great blaze. Again and again I could have kicked the logs off to ease my conscience, and was only held back by respect for the girl. But, of a surety, if she had but given me the word, I would have been content to sit in the fireless room and enjoy the approval of my heart.

She played no chess; indeed, I do not believe there was a board in the house; nor was there any other sport wherewith to beguile the long evenings. Reading she cared little for, and but for her embroidery work I know not what she would have set her hand to. So, as she worked with her threads I tried to enliven the time with some account of my adventures in past days, and some of the old gallant tales with which I was familiar. She heard me gladly, listening as no comrade by the tavern-board ever listened; and though, for the sake of decency, I was obliged to leave out many of the more diverting, yet I flatter myself I won her interest and made the time less dreary. I ranged over all my own experience and the memory of those tales which I had heard from others—and those who know anything of me know that that is not small. I told her of exploits in the Indies and Spain, in Germany and the Low Countries, and in far Muscovy, and 'twas no little pleasure to see her eager eyes dance and sparkle at a jest, or grow sad at a sorrowful episode. *Ma vie!* She had wonderful eyes—the most wonderful I have ever seen. They were gray in the morning and brown at noonday; now sparkling, but for the most part fixedly grave and serene. 'Twas for such eyes, I fancy, that men have done all the temerarious deeds concerning womankind which history records.

It must not be supposed that our life was a lively one, or aught approaching gayety. The talking fell mostly to my lot, for she had a great habit of silence, acquired from her lonely dwelling-place. Yet I moved her more than once to talk about herself.

I heard of her mother, a distant cousin of Master Semple's father; of her death when Anne was but a child of seven; and of the solitary years since, spent in study under her father's direction, in household work, or in acts of mercy to the poor. She spoke of her father often, and always in such a way that I could judge of a great affection between them. Of her lover I never heard, and, now that I think the matter over, 'twas no more than fitting. Once, indeed, I stumbled upon his name by chance in the course of talk, but as she blushed and started, I vowed to fight shy of it ever after.

As we knew well before, no message from the hills could be sent, since the moors were watched as closely as the gateway of a prison. This added to the unpleasantness of the position of each of us. In Anne's case there was the harassing doubt about the safety of her kinsfolk, that sickening anxiety which saps the courage even of strong men. Also, it rendered my duties ten times harder. For, had there been any communication between the father or the lover and the maid, I should have felt less like a St. Anthony in the desert. As it was, I had to fight with a terrible sense of responsibility and unlimited power for evil, and God knows how hard that is for any Christian to strive with. 'Twould have been no very hard thing to shut myself in a room, or bide outside all day, and never utter a word to Anne save only the most necessary; but I was touched by the girl's loneliness and sorrows, and, moreover, I conceived it to be a strange way of executing a duty, to flee from it altogether. I was there to watch over her, and I swore by the Holy Mother to keep the very letter of my oath.

And so the days dragged by till September was all but gone. I have always loved the sky and the vicissitudes of weather, and to this hour the impression of these autumn evenings is clear fixed on my mind. Strangely enough for that north country, they were not cold, but mild, with a sort of acrid mildness; a late summer, with the rigors of winter underlying, like a silken glove over a steel gauntlet.

One such afternoon I remember, when Anne sat busy at some needlework on the low bench by the door, and I came and joined her. She had wonderful grace of body, and 'twas a pleasure to watch every movement of her arm as she stitched. I sat silently regarding the landscape, the woods streaking the bare fields, the thin outline of hills beyond, the smoke rising from Clachlands' chimneys, and above all, the sun firing the great pool in the river, and flaming among clouds in the west. Something of the spirit of the place seemed to have entered into the girl, for she laid aside her needlework after a while and gazed with brimming eyes on the scene. So we sat, feasting our eyes on the picture, each thinking strange thoughts, I doubt not. By and by she spoke.

"Is France, that you love so well, more beautiful than this, M. de Rohaine?" she asked timidly.

"Ay, more beautiful, but not like this; no, not like this."

"And what is it like? I have never seen any place other than this."

"Oh, how shall I tell of it?" I cried. "'Tis more fair than words. We have no rough hills like these, nor torrents like the Lin there; but there is a great broad stream by Rohaine, as smooth as a mill-pond, where you can row in the evenings, and hear the lads and lasses singing love songs. Then there are great quiet meadows, where the kine browse, where the air is so still that one can sleep at a thought. There are woods, too—ah! such woods—stretching up hill, and down dale, as green as spring can make them, with long avenues where men may ride; and, perhaps, at the heart of all, some old chateau, all hung with vines and creepers, where the peaches ripen on the walls and the fountain plashes all the summer's day. Bah! I can hardly bear to think on it, 'tis so dear and home-like;" and I turned away suddenly, for I felt my voice catch in my throat.

"What hills are yonder?" I asked abruptly, to hide my feelings.

Anne looked up.

"The hills beyond the little green ridge you mean?" she says. "That will be over by Eskdalemuir and the top of the Ettrick Water. I have heard my father speak often of them, for they say that many of the godly find shelter there."

"Many of the godly!"

I turned round sharply, though what there was in the phrase to cause wonder I cannot see. She spoke but as she had heard the men of her house speak; yet the words fell strangely on my ears, for by a curious process of thinking I had already begun to separate the girl from the rest of the folk in the place, and look on her as something nearer in sympathy to myself. Faugh? that is not the way to put it. I mean that she had listened so much to my tales that I had all but come to look upon her as a countrywoman of mine.

"Are you dull here, Anne?" I asked, for I had come to use the familiar name, and she in turn would sometimes call me Jean—and very prettily it sat on her tongue. "Do you never wish to go elsewhere and see the world?"

"Nay," she said. "I had scarce thought about the world at all. 'Tis a place I have little to do with, and I am content to dwell here forever, if it be God's will. But I should love to see your France, that you speak of."

This seemed truly a desire for gratifying which there was little chance; so I changed the subject of our converse, and asked her if she ever sang.

"Ay, I have learned to sing two or three songs, old ballads of the countryside, for though my father like it little, Henry takes a pleasure in hearing them. I will sing you one if you wish it." And when I bade her do so, she laid down her work, which she had taken up again, and broke into a curious plaintive melody. I cannot describe it. 'Twould be as easy to describe the singing of the wind in the tree-tops. It minded me, I cannot tell how, of a mountain burn, falling into pools and rippling over little shoals of gravel. Now 'twas full and strong, and now 'twas so eerie and wild that it was more like a curlew's note than any human thing. The story was about a knight who sailed to Norway on some king's errand and never returned, and of his lady who waited long days at home, weeping for him who should never come back to her. I did not understand it fully, for 'twas in an old patois of the country, but I could feel its beauty. When she had finished the tears stood in my eyes, and I thought of the friends I had left, whom I might see no more.

But when I looked at her, to my amazement, there was no sign of feeling in her face.

"'Tis a song I have sung often," she said, "but I do not like it. 'Tis no better than the ringing of a bell at a funeral."

"Then," said I, wishing to make her cheerful, "I will sing you a gay song of my own country. The folk dance to it on the Sunday nights at Rohaine, when blind RenÃ© plays the fiddle." So I broke into the "May song," with its lilting refrain.

Anne listened intently, her face full of pleasure, and at the second verse she began to beat the tune with her foot. She, poor thing, had never danced, had never felt the ecstasy of motion; but since all mankind is alike in nature, her blood stirred at the tune. So I sang her another chanson, this time an old love ballad, and then again a war song. But by this time the darkness was growing around us, so we must needs re-enter the house; and as I followed I could hear her humming the choruses with a curious delight.

"So ho, Mistress Anne," thought I, "you are not the little country mouse that I had thought you, but as full of spirit as a caged hawk. Faith, the town would make a brave lass of you, were you but there!"

From this hour I may date the beginning of the better understanding—I might almost call it friendship—between the two of us. She had been bred among moorland solitudes, and her sole companions had been solemn praying folk; yet, to my wonder, I found in her a nature loving gayety and mirth, songs and bright colors—a grace which her grave deportment did but the more set off. So she came soon to look at me with a kindly face, doing little acts of kindness every now and then in some way or other, which I took to be the return which she desired to make for my clumsy efforts to please her.

VII.—A DAUGHTER OF HERODIAS

The days at Lindean dragged past, and the last traces of summer began to disappear from the face of the hills. The bent grew browner, the trees more ragged, and the torrent below more turgid and boisterous. Yet no word came from the hills, and, sooth to tell, we almost ceased to look for it. 'Twas not that we had forgotten the minister and Master Semple in their hiding, for the thought of them was often at hand to sadden me, and Anne, I must suppose, had many anxious meditations; but our life at Lindean was so peaceful and removed from any hint of violence that danger did not come before our minds in terrible colors. When the rain beat at night on the window, and the wind howled round the house, then our hearts would smite us for living in comfort when our friends were suffering the furious weather. But when the glorious sun-lit morning had come, and we looked over the landscape, scarce free from the magic of dawn, then we counted it no hardship to be on the hills. And rain came so seldom during that time, and the sun so often, that the rigor of the hill-life did not appal us.

This may account for the way in which the exiles slipped from our memories for the greater part of the day. For myself I say nothing—'twas but natural; but from Anne I must confess that I expected a greater show of sorrow. To look at her you would say that she was burdened with an old grief, so serious was her face; but when she would talk, then you might see how little her heart was taken up with the troubles of her house and the care for her father and lover. The girl to me was a puzzle, which I gave up all attempting to solve. When I had first come to Lindean, lo! she was demure and full of filial affection, and tender to her lover. Now, when I expected to find her sorrowful and tearful at all times, I found her quiet indeed, but instinct with a passion for beauty and pleasure and all the joys of life. Yet ever and anon she would take a fit of solemnity, and muse with her chin poised on her hand; and I doubt not that at such times she was thinking of her father and her lover in their manifold perils.

One day the rain came again and made the turf plashy and sodden, and set the Lin roaring in his gorge. I had beguiled the morning by showing Anne the steps of dancing, and she had proved herself a ready pupil. To pleasure her I danced the sword-dance, which can only be done by those who have great dexterity of motion; and I think I may say that I acquitted myself well. The girl stood by in wonderment, looking at me with a pleasing mixture of surprise and delight. She had begun to look strangely at me of late. Every now and then when I lifted my head I would find her great eyes resting on me, and at my first glance she would withdraw them. They were strange eyes—a mingling of the fawn and the tiger.

As I have said, in a little time she had acquired some considerable skill, and moved as gracefully as though she had learned it from her childhood, while I whistled bars of an old dancing tune. She had a little maid who attended her,—Eff she called her,—and the girl stood by to watch while Anne did my bidding. Then when we were all wearied of the sport, I fell to thinking of some other play, and could find none. 'Twas as dull as ditch-water, till the child Eff, by a good chance, spoke of fishing. She could get her father's rod and hooks, she said, for he never used them now; and I might try my luck in the Lin Water. There were good trout there, it seemed, and the choice time of taking them was in the autumn floods.

Now I have ever been something of a fisherman, for many an hour have I spent by the big fish pond at Rohaine. So I got the tackle of Eff's father—rude enough it was in all conscience—and in the early afternoon I set out to the sport. Below the house and beyond the wood the Lin foams in a deep gully, falling over horrid cascades into great churning pools, or diving beneath the narrow rocks. But above the ravine there is a sudden change. The stream flows equably through a flat moor in sedgy deeps and bright shimmering streams. Thither I purposed to go, for I am no lover of the awesome black caldrons, which call to a man's mind visions of drowned bodies and pits which have no ending. On the moor with the wind blowing about one 'twas a pleasure to be, but faugh! no multitude of fish was worth an hour in that dismal chasm.

I had not great success, and little wonder, for my leisurely ways were ill suited for the alert mountain fish.

My time was spent in meditating on many things, but most of all on the strange case in which I found myself. For in truth my position was an odd one as ever man was in.

Here was I bound by my word of honor to bide in the house and protect its inmates till that indefinite time when its master might return. There was no fear of money, for the minister had come of a good stock, and had more gear than is usual with one of his class. But 'twas an evil thing to look forward to—to spend my days in a lonely manse, and wait the end of a persecution which showed no signs of ending.

But the mere discomfort was nothing had it not been for two delicate scruples which came to torment me. *Imprimis*, 'twas more than any man of honor could do to dwell in warmth and plenty, while his entertainers were languishing for lack of food or shivering with cold in the hags and holes of the mountains. I am a man tolerably hardened by war and travel, yet I could never abide to lie in bed on a stormy night or to eat my food of a sharp morning when I thought of the old man dying, it might be, unsheltered and forlorn. *Item*, there was the matter of the girl; and I cannot tell how heavy the task had come to lie on my shoulders. I had taken the trust of one whom I thought to be a staid country lass, and lo! I had found her as full of human passion as any lady of the court. 'Twas like some groom who offers to break a horse, and finds it too stiff in temper. I had striven to do my duty toward her and make her life less wearisome, and I had succeeded all too well. For I marked that in the days just past she had come to regard me with eyes too kindly by half. When I caught her unawares, and saw the curious look on her face, I could have bitten my tongue out with regret, for I saw the chasm to whose brink I had led her. I will take my oath there was no thought of guile in the maid, for she was as innocent as a child; but 'tis such who are oftentimes the very devil, since their inexperience adds an edge to their folly.

Thinking such thoughts, I fished up the Lin Water till the afternoon was all but past, and the sunset began to glimmer in the bog-pools. My mind was a whirl of emotions, and no plan or order could I conceive. But—and this one thing I have often marked, that the weather curiously affected my temper—the soft evening light brought with it a calm which eased me in the conflict. 'Tis hard to wrangle in spirit when the west is a flare of crimson, and later when each blue hill stands out sharp against the yellow sky. My way led through the great pine wood above the Lin gorge, thence over a short spit of heath to the hill path and the ordered shrubbery of the manse. 'Twas fine to see the tree stems stand out red against the gathering darkness, while their thick evergreen heads were blazing like flambeaux. A startled owl drove past, wavering among the trunks. The air was so still that the light and color seemed all but audible, and indeed the distant rumble of the falling stream seemed the interpretation to the ears of the vision which the eyes beheld. I love such sights, and 'tis rarely enough that we see them in France, for it takes a stormy upland country to show to its full the sinking of the sun. The heath with its dead heather, when I came on it, seemed alight, as happens in March, so I have heard, when the shepherds burn the mountain grass. But in the manse garden was the choicest sight, for there the fading light seemed drawn to a point and blazing on the low bushes and coarse lawns. Each window in the house glowed like a jewel, but—mark the wonder—when I gazed over the country there was no view to be seen, but only a slowly creeping darkness.

'Twas an eerie sight, and beautiful beyond telling. It awed me, and yet filled me with a great desire to see it to the full. So I did not enter the house, but turned my steps round by the back to gain the higher ground, for the manse was built on a slope. I loitered past the side window, and gained the place I had chosen; but I did not bide long, for soon the show was gone, and only a chill autumn dusk left behind. So I made to enter the house, when I noticed a light as of firelight dancing in the back window. Now, I had never been in that room before, so what must I do in my idle curiosity but go peeping there.

The room was wide and unfurnished, with a fire blazing on the hearth. But what held me amazed were the figures on the floor. Anne, with her skirts kilted, stood erect and agile as if about to dance. The girl Eff sat by the fireplace, humming some light measure. The ruddy light bathed the floor and walls and made all distinct as noonday.

'Twas as I had guessed. In a trice her feet began to move, and soon she was in the middle of the first dance I had taught her, while *la petite* Eff sang the tune in her clear, low voice. I have seen many dancers, great ladies and country dames, village lasses and burgher wives, gypsies and wantons, but, by my honor, I never saw one dance like Anne. Her body moved as if by one impulse with her feet. Now she would bend like a willow, and now whirl like the leaves of the wood in an autumn gale. She was dressed, as was her wont, in sober brown, but sackcloth could not have concealed the grace of her form. The firelight danced and leaped in her hair, for her face was turned from me; and 'twas fine to see the snow of her neck islanded among the waves of brown tresses. With a sudden swift dart she turned her face to the window, and had I not been well screened by the shadows, I fear I should have been observed. But such a sight as her face I never hope to see again. The solemnity was gone, and 'twas all radiant with youth and life. Her eyes shone like twin stars, the even brown of her cheeks was flushed with firelight, and her throat and bosom heaved with the excitement of the dance. Then she stopped exhausted, smiled on Eff, who sat like a cinder-witch all the while, and smoothed the hair from her brow.

"Have I done it well?" she asked.

"As weel as he did it himsel'," the child answered. "Eh, but you twae would make a bonny pair."

I turned away abruptly and crept back to the garden path, my heart sinking within me, and a feeling of guilt in my soul. I was angry at myself for eavesdropping, angry and ashamed. But a great dread came on me as I thought of the girl, this firebrand, who had been trusted to my keeping. Lackaday for the peace of mind of a man who has to see to a maid who could dance in this fashion, with her father and lover in the cold hills! And always I called to mind that I had been her teacher, and that my lessons, begun as a harmless sport to pass the time, were like to breed an overmastering passion. *Mon Dieu!* I was like the man in the Eastern tale who had raised a spirit which he was powerless to control.

And just then, as if to point my meditations, I heard the cry of a plover from the moor behind, and a plaff of the chill night-wind blew in my face.

VIII.—HOW I SET THE SIGNAL

When I set out to write this history in the English tongue, that none of my own house might read it, I did not know the hard task that lay before me. For if I were writing it in my own language, I could tell the niceties of my feelings in a way which is impossible for me in any other. And, indeed, to make my conduct intelligible, I should forthwith fall to telling each shade of motive and impulse which came to harass my mind. But I am little skilled in this work, so I must needs recount only the landmarks of my life, or I should never reach the end.

I slept ill that night, and at earliest daylight was awake and dressing. The full gravity of the case was open to me now, and you may guess that my mind was no easy one. I went down to the sitting room, where the remains of the last night's supper still lay on the table. The white morning light made all things clear and obtrusive, and I remember wishing that the lamp was lit again and the shutters closed. But in a trice all meditations were cast to the winds, for I heard the door at the back of the house flung violently open and the sound of a man's feet on the kitchen floor.

I knew that I was the only one awake in the house, so with much haste I passed out of the room to ascertain who the visitor might be. In the center of the back room stood a great swart man, shaking the rain from his clothes and hair, and waiting like one about to give some message. When he saw me he took a step forward, scanned me closely, and then waited my question.

"Who in the devil's name are you?" I asked angrily, for I was half amazed and half startled by his sudden advent.

"In the Lord's name I am Andrew Gibb," he responded solemnly.

"And what's your errand?" I asked further.

"Bide a wee and you'll hear. You'll be the foreigner whae stops at the manse the noo?"

"Go on," I said shortly.

"Thae twae sants, Maister Lambert and Maister Semple, 'ill ha'e made some kind o' covenant wi' you? At ony rate, hear my news and dae your best. Their hidy-hole at the heid o' the Stark Water's been betrayed, and unless they get warning it'll be little you'll hear mair o' them. I've aye been their freend, so I cam' here to do my pairt by them."

"Are you one of the hill-men?"

"Na, na! God forbid! I'm a douce, quiet-leevin' man, and I'd see the Kirk rummle aboot their lugs ere I'd stir my shanks frae my ain fireside. But I'm behauden to the minister for the life o' my bairn, whilk is ower lang a story for ye to hear; and to help him I would rin frae Maidenkirk to Berwick. So I've aye made it my wark to pick up ony word o' scaith that was comin' to him, and that's why I'm here the day. Ye've heard my news richt, ye're shure?"

"I've heard your news. Will you take any food before you leave?"

"Na; I maun be off to be back in time for the kye."

"Well, good-day to you, Andrew Gibb," I said, and in a minute the man was gone.

Now, here I must tell what I omitted to tell in a former place—that when the exiles took to the hills they bade me, if I heard any word of danger to their hiding-place, to go by a certain path, which they pointed out, to a certain place, and there overturn a little cairn of stones. This was to be a signal to them for instant movement. I knew nothing of the place of their retreat, and for this reason could swear on my oath with an easy conscience; but this scrap of enlightenment I had, a scrap of momentous import for both life and death.

I turned back to the parlor in a fine confusion of mind. By some means or other the task which was now before me had come to seem singularly disagreeable. The thought of my entertainers—I am ashamed to write it—was a bitter thought. I had acquired a reasonless dislike to them. What cause had they, I asked, to be crouching in hill-caves and first getting honest gentlemen into delicate and difficult positions, and then troubling them with dangerous errands. Then there was the constant vision of the maid to vex me. This was the sorest point of all. For, though I blush to own it, the sight of her was not altogether unpleasing to me; nay, to put it positively, I had come almost to feel an affection for her. She was so white and red and golden, all light and gravity, with the shape of a princess, the mien of a goddess, and, for all I knew the heart of a dancing-girl. She carried with her the air of comfort and gayety, and the very thought of her made me shrink from the dark moors and ill-boding errand as from the leprosy.

There is in every man a latent will, apart altogether from that which he uses in common life, which is apt at times to assert itself when he least expects it. Such was my honor, for lo! I found myself compelled by an inexorable force to set about the performance of my duty. I take no credit for it, since I was only half willing, my grosser inclination being all against it. But something bade me do it, calling me poltroon, coward, traitor, if I refused; so ere I left the kitchen I had come to a fixed decision.

To my wonder, at the staircase foot I met Anne, dressed, but with her hair all in disorder. I stood booted and cloaked and equipped for the journey, and at the sight of me her face filled with surprise.

"Where away so early, John?" says she.

"Where away so early, Mistress Anne?" said I.

"Ah, I slept ill, and came down to get the morning air." I noted that her eyes were dull and restless, and I do believe that the poor maid had had a sorry night of it. A sharp fear at my heart told me the cause.

"Anne," I said sullenly, "I am going on a hard errand, and I entreat you to keep out of harm's way till I return."

"And what is your errand, pray?" she asked.

"Nothing less than to save the lives of your father and your lover. I have had word from a secret source of a great danger which overhangs them, and by God's help I would remove it."

At my word a light, half angry and half pathetic, came to her eyes. It passed like a sungleam, and in its place was left an expression of cold distaste.

"Then God prosper you," she said, in a formal tone, and with a whisk of her skirts she was gone.

I strode out into the open with my heart the battlefield of a myriad contending passions.

I reached the hill, overturned the cairn, and set out on my homeward way, hardly giving but one thought to the purport of my errand or the two fugitives whom it was my mission to save, so filled was my mind with my own trouble. The road home was long and arduous; and more, I had to creep often like an adder lest I should be spied and traced by some chance dragoon. The weather was dull and cold, and a slight snow, the first token of winter, sprinkled the moor. The heather was wet, the long rushes dripped and shivered, and in the little trenches the peat-water lay black as ink. A smell of damp hung over all things, an odor of rotten-leaves and soaked earth. The heavy mist rolled in volumes close to the ground and choked me as I bent low. Every little while I stumbled into a bog, and foully bedaubed my clothes. I think that I must have strayed a little from the straight path, for I took near twice as long to return as to go. A swollen stream delayed me, for I had to traverse its bank for a mile ere I could cross.

In truth, I cannot put down on paper my full loathing of the place. I had hated the moors on my first day's journey, but now I hated them with a tenfold hatred. For each whiff of sodden air, each spit of chill rain brought back to my mind all the difficulty of my present state. Then I had always the vision of Anne sitting at home by the fire, warm, clean, and dainty, the very counter of the foul morasses in which I labored, and where the men I had striven to rescue were thought to lie hidden. My loathing was so great that I could scarce find it in my heart to travel the weary miles to the manse, every step being taken solely on the fear of remaining behind. To make it worse, there would come to vex me old airs of France, airs of childhood and my adventurous youth, fraught for me with memories of gay nights and brave friends. I own that I could have wept to think of them and find myself all the while in this inhospitable desert.

'Twould be near mid-day, I think, when I came to the manse door, glad that my journey was ended. Anne let me in, and in a moment all was changed. The fire crackled in the room, and the light danced on the great volumes on the shelves. The gray winter was shut out and a tranquil summer reigned within. Anne, like a Lent lily, so fair was she, sat sewing by the hearth.

"You are returned," she said coldly.

"I am returned," I said severely, for her callousness to the danger of her father was awful to witness, though in my heart of hearts I could not have wished it otherwise. As she sat there, with her white arms moving athwart her lap, and her hair tossed over her shoulders, I could have clasped her to my heart. Nay, I had almost done so, had I not gripped my chair, and sat with pale face and dazed eyes till the fit had passed. I have told you ere now how my feelings toward Anne had changed from interest to something not unlike a passionate love. It had been a thing of secret growth, and I scarcely knew it till I found myself in the midst of it. I tried to smother it hourly, when my better nature was in the ascendant, and hourly I was overthrown in the contest I fought against terrible odds. 'Twas not hard to see from her longing eyes and timorous conduct that to her I was the greater half of the world. I had but to call to her and she would come. And yet—God knows how I stifled that cry.

At length I rose and strode out into the garden to cool my burning head. The sleet was even grateful to me, and I bared my brow till hair and skin were wet with the rain. Down by the rows of birch trees I walked, past the rough ground where the pot-herbs were grown, till I came to the shady green lawn. Up and down it I passed, striving hard with my honor and my love, fighting that battle which all must fight some time or other in their lives and be victorious or vanquished forever.

Suddenly, to my wonder, I saw a face looking at me from beneath a tuft of elderberry.

I drew back, looked again, and at the second glance I recognized it. 'Twas the face of Master Henry Semple of Clachlands—and the hills.

'Twas liker the face of a wild goat than a man. The thin features stood out so strongly that all the rest seemed to fall back from them. The long, ragged growth of hair on lip and chin, and the dirt on his cheeks, made him unlike my friend of the past. But the memorable change was in his eyes, which glowed large and lustrous, with the whites greatly extended, and all tinged with a yellow hue. Fear and privation had done their work, and before me stood their finished product.

"Good Heavens, Henry! What brings you here, and how have you fared?"

He stared at me without replying, which I noted as curious.

"Where is Anne?" he asked huskily.

"She is in the house, well and unscathed. Shall I call her to you?"

"Nay, for God's sake, nay! I am no pretty sight for a young maid. You say she is well?"

"Ay, very well. But how is the minister?"

"Alas, he is all but gone. The chill has entered his bones, and even now he may be passing. The child will soon be an orphan."

"And you?"

"Oh, I am no worse than the others on whom the Lord's hand is laid. There is a ringing in my head and a pain at my heart, but I am still hale and fit to testify to the truth. Oh, man, 'twill ill befa' those in the day of judgment who eat the bread of idleness and dwell in peace in thae weary times."

"Come into the house; or nay, I will fetch you food and clothing."

"Nay, bring nought for me. I would rather live in rags and sup on a crust than be habited in purple and fare sumptuously. I ask ye but one thing: let the maid walk in the garden that I may see her. And, oh, man! I thank ye for your kindness to me and mine. I pray the Lord ilka night to think on ye here."

I could not trust myself to speak.

"I will do as you wish," I said, and without another word set off sharply for the house.

I entered the sitting room wearily, and flung myself on a chair. Anne sat sewing as before. She started as I entered, and I saw the color rise to her cheeks and brow.

"You are pale, my dear," I said; "the day is none so bad, and 'twould do you no ill to walk round the garden to the gate. I have just been there, and, would you believe it, the grass is still wondrous green."

She rose demurely and obediently as if my word were the law of her life.

"Pray bring me a sprig of ivy from the gate-side," I cried after her, laughing, "to show me that you have been there."

I sat and kicked my heels till her return in a miserable state of impatience. I could not have refused to let the man see his own betrothed, but God only knew what desperate act he might do. He might spring out and clasp her in his arms; she, I knew, had not a shred of affection left for him; she would be cold and resentful; he would suspect, and then—what an end there might be to it all! I longed to hear the sound of her returning footsteps.

She came in soon, and sat down in her wonted chair by the fire.

"There's your ivy, John," said she; "'tis raw and chilly in the garden, and I love the fireside better."

"'Tis well," I thought, "she has not seen Master Semple." Now I could not suffer him to depart without meeting him again, partly out of pity for the man, partly to assure my own mind that no harm would come of it. So I feigned an errand and went out.

I found him, as I guessed, still in the elder-bush, a tenfold stranger sight than before. His eyes burned uncannily. His thin cheeks seemed almost transparent with the tension of the bones, and he chewed his lips unceasingly. At the sight of me he came out and stood before me, as wild a figure as I ever hope to see—clothes in tatters, hair unkempt, and skin all foul with the dirt of the moors. His back was bowed, and his knees seemed to have lost all strength, for they tottered against one another. I prayed that his sufferings might not have turned him mad.

At the first word he spake I was convinced of it.

"I have seen her, I have seen her!" he cried. "She is more fair than a fountain of gardens, a well of living waters, and streams from Lebanon. Oh, I have dreamed of her by night among the hills, and seen her face close to me and tried to catch it, but 'twas gone. Oh, man, John, get down on your knees, and pray to God to make you worthy to have the charge of such a treasure. Had the Lord not foreordained that she should me mine, I should ne'er have lifted up my eyes to her, for who am I?"

"For God's sake, man," I broke in, "tell me where you are going, and be about it quick, for you may be in instant danger."

"Ay," says he, "you are right. I must be gone. I have seen enough. I maun away to the deserts and caves of the rocks, and it may be lang, lang ere I come back. But my love winna forget me. Na, na; the Lord hath appointed unto me that I shall sit at his right hand on the last, the great day, and she shall be by my side. For oh, she is the only one of her mother; she is the choice one of her that bare her; the daughters saw her and blessed her; yea, the queens and concubines, and they praised her." And with some like gibberish from the Scriptures he disappeared through the bushes, and next minute I saw him running along the moor toward the hills.

These were no love-sick ravings, but the wild cries of a madman, one whose reason had gone forever. I walked back slowly to the house. It seemed almost profane to think of Anne, so wholesome and sane, in the same thought as this foul idiot; and yet this man had been once as whole in mind and body as myself; he had suffered in a valiant cause; and I was bound to him by the strongest of all bonds—my plighted word. I groaned inwardly as I shut the house-door behind me and entered into the arena of my struggles.

IX.—I COMMUNE WITH MYSELF

Twas late afternoon when I re-entered, and ere supper was past 'twas time to retire for the night. The tension of these hours I still look back on as something altogether dreadful. Anne was quiet and gentle, unconscious of what had happened, yet with the fire of passion, I knew too well, burning in her heart. I was ill, restless, and abrupt, scarce able to speak lest I should betray my thoughts and show the war that raged in my breast.

I made some excuse for retiring early, bidding her good-night with as nonchalant an air as I could muster. The door of my bedroom I locked behind me, and I was alone in the darkened room to fight out my battles with myself.

I ask you if you can conceive any gentleman and man of honor in a more hazardous case. Whenever I tried to think on it, a mist came over my brain, and I could get little but unmeaning fantasies. I must either go or stay. So much was clear.

If I stayed—well, 'twas the Devil's own work that was cut for me. There was no sign of the violence of the persecution abating. It might be many months, nay years, before the minister and Master Semple might return. If they came back no more, and I had sure tidings of their death, then indeed I might marry Anne. But 'twas so hazardous an uncertainty that I rejected it at once. No man could dwell with one whom he loved heart and soul so long a time on such uncertain chances and yet keep his honor. Had the maid been dull and passive, or had I been sluggish in blood, then there might have been hope. But we were both quick as the summer's lightning.

If they came back, was not the fate of the girl more hard than words could tell? The minister in all likelihood would already have gone the way of all the earth; and she, poor lass, would be left to the care of a madman for whom she had no spark of liking. I pictured her melancholy future. Her pure body subject to the embraces of a loathsome fanatic, her delicate love of the joys of life all subdued to his harsh creed. Oh, God! I swore that I could not endure it. Her face, so rounded and lovely, would grow pinched and white, her eyes would lose all their luster, her hair would not cluster lovingly about her neck, her lithe grace would be gone, her footsteps would be heavy and sad. He would rave his unmeaning gibberish in her ears, would ill-treat her, it might be; in any case would be a perpetual sorrow to her heart. "Oh, Anne," I cried, "though I be damned for it, I will save you from this!"

If I left the place at once and forever, then indeed my honor would be kept, but yet not all; for my plighted word—where would it be? I had sworn that come what may I should stand by the maid and protect her against what evil might come to the house. Now I was thinking of fleeing from my post like a coward, and all because the girl's eyes were too bright for my weak resolution. When her lover returned, if he ever came, what story would she have to tell? This, without a doubt: "The man whom you left has gone, fled like a thief in the night, for what reason I know not." For though I knew well that she would divine the real cause of my action, I could not suppose that she would tell it, for thereby she would cast grave suspicion upon herself. So there would I be, a perjured traitor, a false friend in the eyes of those who had trusted me.

But more, the times were violent, Clachlands and its soldiery were not far off, and once they learned that the girl was unprotected no man knew what evil might follow. You may imagine how bitter this thought was to me, the thought of leaving my love in the midst of terrible dangers. Nay, more; a selfish consideration weighed not a little with me. The winter had all but come; the storms of this black land I dreaded like one born and bred in the South; I knew nothing of my future course; I was poor, bare, and friendless. The manse was a haven of shelter. Without it I should be even as the two exiles in the hills. The cold was hard to endure; I dearly loved warmth and comfort; the moors were as fearful to me as the deserts of Muscovy.

One course remained. Anne had money; this much I knew. She loved me, and would obey my will in all things; of this I was certain. What hindered me to take her to France, the land of mirth and all pleasant things, and leave the North and its wild folk behind forever?

With money we could travel expeditiously. Once in my own land perchance I might find some way to repair my fortunes, for a fair wife is a wonderous incentive. There beneath soft skies, in the mellow sunshine, among a cheerful people, she would find the life which she loved best. What deterred me? Nothing but a meaningless vow and some antiquated scruples. But I would be really keeping my word, I reasoned casuistically with myself, for I had sworn to take care of Anne, and what way so good as to take her to my own land where she would be far from the reach of fanatic or dragoon? And this was my serious thought, *comprenez bien*! I set it down as a sign of the state to which I had come, that I was convinced by my own quibbling. I pictured to myself what I should do. I would find her at breakfast in the morning. "Anne," I would say, "I love you dearly; may I think that you love me likewise?" I could fancy her eager, passionate reply, and then—— I almost felt the breath of her kisses on my cheek and the touch of her soft arms on my neck.

Some impulse led me to open the casement and look forth into the windy, inscrutable night. A thin rain distilled on the earth, and the coolness was refreshing to my hot face. The garden was black, and the bushes were marked by an increased depth of darkness. But on the grass to the left I saw a long shaft of light, the reflection from some lit window of the house. I passed rapidly in thought over the various rooms there, and with a start came to an end. Without a doubt 'twas Anne's sleeping room. What did the lass with a light, for 'twas near midnight? I did not hesitate about the cause, and 'twas one which inflamed my love an hundredfold. She was sleepless, love-sick maybe (such is the vanity of man). Maybe even now my name was the one on her lips, and my image the foremost in her mind. My finger-tips tingled, as the blood surged into them; and I am not ashamed to say that my eyes were not tearless. Could I ever leave my love for some tawdry honor? *Mille tonneres!* the thing was not to be dreamed of. I blamed myself for having once admitted the thought.

My decision was taken, and, as was always my way, I felt somewhat easier. I was weary, so I cast myself down upon the bed without undressing, and fell into a profound sleep.

How long I slept I cannot tell, but in that brief period of unconsciousness I seemed to be living ages. I saw my past life all inverted as 'twere; for my first sight was the horror of the moors. Quentin Kennedy, and the quarrel and the black desolation which I had undergone. I went through it all again, vividly, acutely. Then it passed, and I had my manhood in France before my eyes. And curiously enough, 'twas not alone, but confused with my childhood and youth. I was an experienced man of the world, versed in warfare and love, taverns and brawls, and yet not one whit jaded, but fresh and hopeful and boylike. 'Twas a very pleasing feeling. I was master of myself. I had all my self-respect. I was a man of unblemished honor, undoubted valor. Then by an odd trick of memory all kinds of associations became linked with it. The old sights and sounds of Rohaine: cocks crowing in the morning; the smell of hay and almond-blossom, roses and summer lilies; the sight of green leaves, of the fish leaping in the river; the plash of the boat's oars among the water-weeds—all the sensations of childhood came back with extraordinary clarity. I heard my mother's grave, tender speech bidding us children back from play, or soothing one when he hurt himself. I could almost believe that my father's strong voice was ringing in my ear, when he would tell stories of the chase and battle, or sing ballads of long ago, or bid us go to the devil if we pleased, but go like gentlemen. 'Twas a piece of sound philosophy, and often had it been before me in Paris, when I shrank from nothing save where my honor as a gentleman was threatened. In that dream the old saying came on me with curious force. I felt it to be a fine motto for life, and I was exulting in my heart that 'twas mine, and that I had never stained the fair fame of my house.

Suddenly, with a start I seemed to wake to the consciousness that 'twas mine no more. Still dreaming, I was aware that I had deceived a lover, and stolen his mistress and made her my bride. I have never felt such acute anguish as I did in that sleep when the thought came upon me. I felt nothing more of pride. All things had left me. My self-respect was gone like a ragged cloak. All the old, dear life was shut out from me by a huge barrier. Comfortable, rich, loving, and beloved, I was yet in the very jaws of Hell. I felt myself biting out my tongue in my despair. My brain was on fire with sheer and awful regret. I cursed the day when I had been tempted and fallen.

And then, even while I dreamed, another sight came to my eyes—the face of a lady, young, noble, with eyes like the Blessed Mother. In my youth I had laid my life at the feet of a girl, and I was in hopes of making her my wife. But Cecilia was too fair for this earth, and I scarcely dared to look upon her she seemed so saint-like. When she died in the Forest of Arnay, killed by a fall from her horse, 'twas I who carried her to her home, and since that day her face was never far distant from my memory. I cherished the image as my dearest possession, and oftentimes when I would have embarked upon some madness I refrained, fearing the reproof of those grave eyes. But now this was all gone. My earthy passion had driven out my old love; all memories were rapt from me save that of the sordid present.

The very violence of my feeling awoke me, and I found myself sitting up in bed with a mouthful of blood. Sure enough, I had gnawed my tongue till a red froth was over my lips. My heart was beating like a windmill in a high gale, and a deadly sickness of mind oppressed me. 'Twas some minutes before I could think; and then—oh, joy! the relief! I had not yet taken the step irremediable. The revulsion, the sudden ecstasy drove in a trice my former resolution into thinnest air.

I looked out of the window. 'Twas dawn, misty and wet. Thank God, I was still in the land of the living, still free to make my life. The tangible room, half lit by morning, gave me a promise of reality after the pageant of the dream. My path was clear before me, clear and straight as an arrow; and yet even now I felt a dread of my passion overcoming my resolve, and was in a great haste to have done with it all. My scruples about my course were all gone. I would be breaking my oath, 'twas true, in leaving the maid, but keeping it in the better way. The thought of the dangers to which she would be exposed stabbed me like a dart. It had almost overcome me. "But honor is more than life or love," I said, as I set my teeth with stern purpose.

Yet, though all my soul was steeled into resolution, there was no ray of hope in my heart—nothing but a dead, bleak outlook, a land of moors and rain, an empty purse and an aimless journey.

I had come to the house a beggar scarce two months before. I must now go as I had come, not free and careless as then, but bursting shackles of triple brass. My old ragged garments, which I had discarded on the day after my arrival, lay on a chair, neatly folded by Anne's deft hand. It behooved me to take no more away than that which I had brought, so I must needs clothe myself in these poor remnants of finery, thin and mud-stained, and filled with many rents.

X.—OF MY DEPARTURE

I passed through the kitchen out to the stable, marking as I went that the breakfast was ready laid in the sitting room. There I saddled Saladin, grown sleek by fat living, and rolling his great eyes at me wonderingly. I tested the joinings, buckled the girth tight, and led him round to the front of the house, where I tethered him to a tree and entered the door.

A savory smell of hot meats came from the room and a bright wood fire drove away the grayness of the morning. Anne stood by the table, slicing a loaf and looking ever and anon to the entrance. Her face was pale as if with sleeplessness and weeping. Her hair was not so daintily arranged as was her wont. It seemed almost as if she had augured the future. A strange catch—coming as such songs do from nowhere and meaning nothing—ran constantly in my head. 'Twas one of Philippe Desportes', that very song which the Duke de Guise sang just before his death. So, as I entered, I found myself humming half unwittingly:

'"Nous verrons, bergère Rosette, Qui premier s'en repentira."

Anne looked up as if startled at my coming, and when she saw my dress glanced fearfully at my face. It must have told her some tale, for a red flush mounted to her brow and abode there.

I picked up a loaf from the table. 'Twas my one sacrifice to the gods of hospitality. 'Twould serve, I thought, for the first stage in my journey.

Anne looked up at me with a kind of confused wonder. She laughed, but there was little mirth in her laughter.

"Why, what would you do with the loaf?" said she. "Do you seek to visit the widows and fatherless in their affliction?"

"Nay," said I gravely. "I would but keep myself unspotted from the world."

All merriment died out of her face.

"And what would you do?" she stammered.

"The time has come for me to leave, Mistress Anne. My horse is saddled at the door. I have been here long enough; ay, and too long. I thank you with all my heart for your kindness, and I would seek to repay it by ridding you of my company."

I fear I spoke harshly, but 'twas to hide my emotion, which bade fair to overpower me and ruin all.

"Oh, and why will you go?" she cried.

"Farewell, Anne," I said, looking at her fixedly, and I saw that she divined the reason.

I turned on my heel, and went out from the room.

"Oh, my love," she cried passionately, "stay with me; stay, oh, stay!"

Her voice rang in my ear with honeyed sweetness, like that of the Sirens to Ulysses of old.

"Stay!" she cried, as I flung open the house-door.

I turned me round for one last look at her whom I loved better than life. She stood at the entrance to the room, with her arms outstretched and her white bosom heaving. Her eyes were filled with an utterable longing, which a man may see but once in his life—and well for him if he never sees it. Her lips were parted as if to call me back once more. But no word came; her presence was more powerful than any cry.

I turned to the weather. A gray sky, a driving mist, and a chill piercing blast. The contrast was almost more than my resolution. An irresistible impulse seized me to fly to her arms, to enter the bright room again with her, and sell myself, body and soul, to the lady of my heart.

My foot trembled to the step backward, my arms all but felt her weight, when that blind Fate which orders the ways of men intervened. Against my inclination and desire, bitterly, unwilling, I strode to my horse and flung myself on his back. I dared not look behind, but struck spurs into Saladin and rode out among the trees.

A fierce north wind met me in the teeth, and piercing through my tatters, sent a shiver to my very heart.

I cannot recall my thoughts during that ride: I seem not to have thought at all. All I know is that in about an hour there came into my mind, as from a voice, the words: “Recreant! Fool!” and I turned back.

THE END

www.ingramcontent.com/pod-product-compliance
Lightning Source LLC
Chambersburg PA
CBHW031041110726
47900CB00003B/768

* 9 7 8 1 4 7 3 3 1 7 7 1 0 *